Church of Scotland

The Confession of Faith

the larger and shorter catechisms, with the scripture-proofs at large - together with

The sum of saving knowledge - contained in the Holy Scriptures, and held forth in

the said Confessions and Catechisms

Church of Scotland

The Confession of Faith
the larger and shorter catechisms, with the scripture-proofs at large - together with The sum of saving knowledge - contained in the Holy Scriptures, and held forth in the said Confessions and Catechisms

ISBN/EAN: 9783337291549

Printed in Europe, USA, Canada, Australia, Japan

Cover: Foto ©Lupo / pixelio.de

More available books at **www.hansebooks.com**

THE CONFESSION OF FAITH;

THE LARGER AND SHORTER CATECHISMS,

WITH THE

Scripture-Proofs at Large:

TOGETHER WITH

THE SUM OF SAVING KNOWLEDGE,

(CONTAINED IN THE HOLY SCRIPTURES, AND HELD FORTH IN THE SAID CONFESSION AND CATECHISMS,) AND PRACTICAL USE THEREOF;

COVENANTS, NATIONAL AND SOLEMN LEAGUE; ACKNOWLEDGMENT OF SINS, AND ENGAGEMENT TO DUTIES; DIRECTORIES FOR PUBLICK AND FAMILY WORSHIP;

FORM OF CHURCH GOVERNMENT, &C. OF PUBLICK AUTHORITY IN THE CHURCH OF SCOTLAND; WITH ACTS OF ASSEMBLY AND PARLIAMENT, RELATIVE TO, AND APPROBATIVE OF, THE SAME

Deut. vi. 6, 7.—And these words which I command thee this day shall be in thine heart; and thou shalt teach them diligently unto thy children, and shalt talk of them when thou sittest in thine house, and when thou walkest by the way, and when thou liest down, and when thou risest up.

EDINBURGH:
JOHNSTONE, HUNTER, & CO.

MDCCCXCIV.

TO THE
CHRISTIAN READER,
ESPECIALLY
HEADS OF FAMILIES.

AS we cannot but with grief of soul lament those multitudes of errors, blasphemies, and all kinds of profaneness, which have in this last age, like a mighty deluge, overflown this nation; so, among several other sins which have helped to open the flood-gates of all these impieties, we cannot but esteem the disuse of family instruction one of the greatest. The two great pillars upon which the kingdom of Satan is erected, and by which it is upheld, are ignorance and error; the first step of our manumission from this spiritual thraldom consists in having our *eyes opened, and being turned from darkness to light,* Acts xxvi. 18. How much the serious endeavours of godly parents and masters might contribute to an early seasoning the tender years of such as are under their inspection, is abundantly evident, not only from their special influence upon them, in respect of their authority over them, interest in them, continual presence with them, and frequent opportunities of being helpful to them; but also from the sad effects which, by woeful experience, we find to be the fruit of the omission of this duty. It were easy to set before you a cloud of witnesses, the language of whose practice hath been not only an eminent commendation of this duty, but also a serious exhortation to it. As *Abel, though dead, yet speaks* by his example to us for imitation of his faith, &c., Heb. xi. 4; so do the examples of Abraham, of Joshua, of the parents of Solomon, of the grandmother and mother of Timothy, the mother of Augustine, whose care was as well to nurse up the souls as the bodies of their little ones; and as their pains herein was great, so was their success no way unanswerable.

We should scarce imagine it any better than an impertinency, in this noon-day of the gospel, either to inform or persuade in a duty so expressly commanded, so frequently urged, so highly encouraged, and so eminently owned by the Lord in all ages with his blessing, but that our sad experience tells us, this duty is not more needful, than it is of late neglected. For the restoring of this duty to its due observance, give us leave to suggest this double advice.

The *first* concerns heads of families in respect of themselves; That as the Lord hath set them in place above the rest of their family, they would labour in all wisdom and spiritual understanding to be above them also. It is an uncomely sight to behold men in years babes in knowledge; and how unmeet are they to instruct others, who need themselves to be taught *which be the first principles of the oracles of God,* Heb. v. 12. Knowledge is an accomplishment so desirable, that the devils themselves knew not a more taking bait by which to tempt our first parents, than by the fruit of the tree of knowledge; *So shall you be as gods, knowing good and evil.* When Solomon had that favour shewed him of the Lord, that he was made his own chuser what to ask, he knew no greater mercy to beg than wisdom, 1 Kings iii. 5, 9. The understanding is the guide and pilot of the whole man, that faculty which sits at the stern of the soul : but as the most expert guide may mistake in the dark, so may the understanding, when it wants the light of knowledge: *Without knowledge the mind cannot be good*, Prov. xix. 2; nor the life good, nor the eternal condition safe, Eph. iv. 18. *My people are destroyed for lack of knowledge*, Hos. iv. 6. It is ordinary in scripture to set profaneness, and all kind of miscarriages, upon the score of ignorance. Diseases in the body have many times their rise from distempers in the head, and exorbitancies in practice from errors in judgment: and indeed in every sin there is something both of ignorance and error at the bottom : for, did sinners truly know what they do in sinning, we might say of every sin what the Apostle speaks concerning that great sin, *Had they known him, they would not have crucified the Lord of glory;* did they truly know that every sin is a provoking the Lord to jealousy, a proclaiming war against Heaven, *a crucifying the Lord Jesus afresh, a treasuring up wrath unto themselves against the day of wrath ;* and that, if ever they be pardoned, it must be at no lower a rate than the price of his blood ; it were scarce possible but sin, instead of alluring, should affright, and instead of tempting, scare. It is one of the arch devices and principal methods of Satan to deceive men into sin : thus he prevailed against our first parents, not as a lion, but as a serpent, acting his enmity under a pretence of friendship, and tempting them to evil under an appearance of good; and thus hath he all along carried on his designs of darkness, by transforming himself into an angel of light, making poor deceived men in love with their miseries, and hug their own destruction. A most sovereign antidote against all kind of errors, is to be grounded and settled in the faith : persons unfixed in the true religion, are very receptive of a false ; and they who are nothing in spiritual knowledge, are easily made any thing. *Clouds without water are driven to and fro with every wind*, and ships without ballast liable to the violence of every tempest. But yet the knowledge we especially commend, is not a brain-knowledge, a mere speculation ; this may be in the worst of men, nay, in the worst of creatures, the devils themselves, and that in such an eminency, as the best of saints cannot attain to in this life of imperfection ; but an inward, a savoury, an heart-knowledge, such as was in that martyr, who, though she could not dispute for Christ, could die for him. This is that spiritual sense and feeling of divine truths the Apostle speaks of, Heb. v. 14, *Having your senses exercised*, &c.

But, alas, we may say of most men's religion what learned Rivet* speaks concerning the errors of the fathers, "They were not so much their own errors, as the errors of the times wherein they lived." Thus do most men take up their religion upon no better an account than Turks and Papists take up theirs, because it is the religion of the times and places wherein they live; and what they take up thus slightly, they lay down as easily. Whereas an inward taste and relish of the things of God, is an excellent preservative to keep us settled in the most unsettled times. Corrupt and unsavoury principles have

* Rivet. Crit. Sacr.

great advantage upon us, above those that are spiritual and sound; the former being suitable to corrupt nature, the latter contrary; the former springing up of themselves, the latter brought forth not without a painful industry. The ground needs no other midwifery in bringing forth weeds than only the neglect of the husbandman's hand to pluck them up; the air needs no other cause of darkness than the absence of the sun; nor water of coldness than its distance from the fire; because these are the genuine products of nature. Were it so with the soul, (as some of the philosophers have vainly imagined,) to come into the world as an *abrasa tabula*, a mere blank or piece of white paper, on which neither any thing is written, nor any blots, it would then be equally receptive of good and evil, and no more averse to the one than to the other: but how much worse its condition indeed is, were scripture silent, every man's experience does evidently manifest. For who is there that knows any thing of his own heart, and knows not thus much, that the suggestions of Satan have so easy and free admittance into our hearts, that our utmost watchfulness is too little to guard us from them? whereas the motions of God's Spirit are so unacceptable to us, that our utmost diligence is too little to get our hearts open to entertain them. Let therefore the excellency, necessity, difficulty of true wisdom stir up endeavours in you somewhat proportionable to such an accomplishment; *Above all getting, get understanding*, Prov. iv. 7; and *search for wisdom as for hidden treasures*, Prov. ii. 4. It much concerns you in respect of yourselves.

Our *second* advice concerns heads of families, in respect of their families. Whatever hath been said already, though it concerns every private Christian that hath a soul to look after; yet, upon a double account, it concerns parents and masters, as having themselves and others to look after: some there are, who, because of their ignorance, cannot; others, because of their sluggishness, will not mind this duty. To the former we propound the method of Joshua, who first began with himself, and then is careful of his family. To the latter we shall only hint, what a dreadful meeting those parents and masters must have at that great day, with their children and servants, when all that were under their inspection shall not only accuse them, but charge their eternal miscarrying upon their score.

Never did any age of the Church enjoy such choice helps as this of ours. Every age of the gospel hath had its Creeds, Confessions, Catechisms, and such breviaries and models of divinity as have been singularly useful. Such forms of sound words (however in these days decried) have been in use in the Church ever since God himself wrote the Decalogue, as a summary of things to be done; and Christ taught us that prayer of his, as a directory what to ask. Concerning the usefulness of such compendiary systems, so much hath been said already by a learned divine* of this age, as is sufficient to satisfy all who are not resolved to remain unsatisfied.

Concerning the particular excellency of these ensuing treatises, we judge it unneedful to mention those eminent testimonies which have been given them from persons of known worth, in respect of their judgment, learning, and integrity, both at home and abroad, because themselves spake so much their own praise; gold stands not in need of

---

* Dr Tuckney in his Sermon on 2 Tim. i. 13.

varnish, nor diamonds of painting: give us leave only to tell you, that we cannot but account it an eminent mercy to enjoy such helps as these are. It is ordinary in these days for men to speak evil of things they know not; but if any are possessed with mean thoughts of these treatises, we shall only give the same counsel to them that Philip gives Nathanael, *Come and see,* John i. 46. It is no small advantage the reader now hath, by the addition of scriptures at large, whereby with little pains he may more profit, because with every truth he may behold its scripture foundation. And, indeed, considering what a Babel of opinions, what a strange confusion of tongues, there is this day among them who profess they speak the language of Canaan, there is no intelligent person but will conclude that advice of the prophet especially suited to such an age as this, Isa. viii. 20, *To the law, and to the testimony; if they speak not according to this word, it is because there is no light in them.* If the reverend and learned composers of these ensuing treatises were willing to take the pains of annexing scripture proofs to every truth, that the faith of people might not be built upon the dictates of men, but the authority of God, so some considerable pains hath now been further taken in transcribing those scriptures; partly to prevent that grand inconvenience, (which all former impressions, except the Latin, have abounded with, to the great perplexing and disheartening of the reader,) the misquotation of scripture, the meanest reader being able, by having the words at large, to rectify whatever mistake may be in the printer in citing the particular place; partly, to prevent the trouble of turning to every proof, which could not but be very great; partly, to help the memories of such who are willing to take the pains of turning to every proof, but are unable to retain what they read; and partly, that this may serve as a Bible common-place, the several passages of scripture, which are scattered up and down in the word, being in this book reduced to their proper head, and thereby giving light each to other. The advantages, you see, in this design, are many and great; the way to spiritual knowledge is hereby made more easy, and the ignorance of this age more inexcusable.

If, therefore, there be any spark in you of love to God, be not content that any of yours should be ignorant of him whom you so much admire, or any haters of him whom you so much love. If there be any compassion to the souls of them who are under your care, if any regard of your being found faithful in the day of Christ, if any respect to future generations, labour to sow these seeds of knowledge, which may grow up in after-times. That you may be faithful herein, is the earnest prayer of,

Henry Wilkinson, D.D. *A.M.P.*
Roger Drake.
William Taylor.
Samuel Annesley.
Thomas Gouge.
Charles Offspring.
Arthur Jackson.
John Cross.
Samuel Clerk.
Samuel Slater.
William Whitaker.

John Fuller.
James Nalton.
Thomas Goodwin.
Matthew Pool.
William Bates.
John Loder.
Francis Raworth.
William Cooper.
William Jenkin.
Thomas Manton.
Thomas Jacomb.
George Griffiths.

Edward Perkins.
Ralph Venning.
Jeremiah Burwell.
Joseph Church.
Has. Bridges.
Samuel Smith.
Samuel Rowles.
John Glascock.
Leo. Cooke.
John Sheffield.
Matthew Haviland.
William Blackmore.

Richard Kentish.
Alexander Pringle.
William Wickins.
Thomas Watson.
John Jackson.
John Seabrooke.
John Peachie.
James Jollife.
Obadiah Lee.

MR THOMAS MANTON'S EPISTLE TO THE READER.

CHRISTIAN READER,

I CANNOT suppose thee to be such a stranger in England as to be ignorant of the general complaint concerning the decay of the power of godliness, and more especially of the great corruption of youth. Wherever thou goest, thou wilt hear men crying out of bad children and bad servants; whereas indeed the source of the mischief must be sought a little higher: it is bad parents and bad masters that make bad children and bad servants; and we cannot blame so much their untowardness, as our own negligence in their education.

The devil hath a great spite at the kingdom of Christ, and he knoweth no such compendious way to crush it in the egg, as by the perversion of youth, and supplanting family-duties. He striketh at all those duties which are publick in the assemblies of the saints; but these are too well guarded by the solemn injunctions and dying charge of Jesus Christ, as that he should ever hope totally to subvert and undermine them; but at family-duties he striketh with the more success, because the institution is not so solemn, and the practice not so seriously and conscientiously regarded as it should be, and the omission is not so liable to notice and publick censure. Religion was first hatched in families, and there the devil seeketh to crush it; the families of the Patriarchs were all the Churches God had in the world for the time; and therefore, (I suppose,) when Cain went out from Adam's family, he is said to go out from the face of the Lord, Gen. iv. 16. Now, the devil knoweth that this is a blow at the root, and a ready way to prevent the succession of Churches: if he can subvert families, other societies and communities will not long flourish and subsist with any power and vigour; for there is the stock from whence they are supplied both for the present and future.

For the present: A family is the seminary of Church and State; and if children be not well principled there, all miscarrieth: a fault in the first concoction is not mended in the second; if youth be bred ill in the family, they prove ill in Church and Commonwealth; *there* is the first making or marring, and the presage of their future lives to be thence taken, Prov. xx. 11. By family discipline, officers are trained up for the Church, 1 Tim. iii. 4, *One that ruleth well his own house,* &c.; and *there* are men bred up in subjection and obedience. It is noted, Acts xxi. 5, that the disciples brought Paul on his way with their wives and children; their children probably are mentioned, to intimate, that their parents would, by their own example and affectionate farewell to Paul, breed them up in a way of reverence and respect to the pastors of the Church.

For the future: It is comfortable, certainly, to see a thriving nursery of young plants, and to have hopes that God shall have a people to serve him when we are dead and gone: the people of God comforted themselves in that, Ps. cii. 28, *The children of thy servants shall continue,* &c.

Upon all these considerations, how careful should ministers and parents be to train up young ones whilst they are yet pliable, and, like wax, capable of any form and impression, in the knowledge and fear of God; and betimes to instil the principles of our most holy faith, as they are drawn into a short sum in Catechisms, and so altogether laid in the view of conscience! Surely these seeds of truth planted in the field of memory, if they work nothing else, will at least be a great check and bridle to them, and, as the casting in of cold water doth stay the boiling of the pot, somewhat allay the fervours of youthful lusts and passions.

I had, upon entreaty, resolved to recommend to thee with the greatest earnestness the work of catechising, and, as a meet help, the usefulness of this book, as thus printed with the Scriptures at large: but meeting with a private letter of a very learned and godly divine, wherein that work is excellently done to my hand, I shall make bold to transcribe a part of it, and offer it to publick view.

The author having bewailed the great distractions, corruptions, and divisions that are in the Church, he thus represents the cause and cure: "Among others, a principal cause of these mischiefs is the great and common neglect of the governors of families, in the discharge of that duty which they owe to God for the souls that are under their charge, especially in teaching them the doctrine of Christianity. Families are societies that must be sanctified to God as well as Churches; and the governors of them have as truly a charge of the souls that are therein, as pastors have of the Churches. But, alas, how little is this considered or regarded! But while negligent ministers are (deservedly) cast out of their places, the negligent masters of families take themselves to be almost blameless. They offer their children to God in baptism, and there they promise to teach them the doctrine of the gospel, and bring them up in the nurture of the Lord; but they easily promise, and easily break it; and educate their children for the world and the flesh, although they have renounced these, and dedicated them to God. This covenant-breaking with God, and betraying the souls of their children to the devil, must lie heavy on them here or hereafter. They beget children, and keep families, merely for the world and the flesh; but little consider what a charge is committed to them, and what it is to bring up a child for God, and govern a family as a sanctified society.

"O how sweetly and successfully would the work of God go on, if we would but all join together in our several places to promote it! Men need not then run without sending to be preachers; but they might find that part of the work that belongeth to them to be enough for them, and to be the best that they can be employed in. Especially women should be careful of this duty; because as they are most about their children, and have early and frequent opportunities to instruct them, so this is the principal service they can do to God in this world, being restrained from more publick work. And doubtless many an excellent magistrate hath been sent into the Commonwealth, and many an excellent pastor into the Church, and many a precious saint to heaven, through the happy preparations of a holy education, perhaps by a woman that thought herself useless and unserviceable to the Church. Would parents but begin betimes, and labour to affect the hearts of their children with the great matters of everlasting life, and to acquaint them with the substance of the doctrine of Christ, and, when they find in them the knowledge and love of Christ, would bring them then to the pastors of the Church to be tried, confirmed, and admitted to the further privileges of the Church, what happy, well-ordered Churches might we have! Then one pastor need not be put to do the work of two or three hundred or thousand governors of families, even to teach their children those principles which they should have taught them long before; nor should we be put to preach to so many miserable ignorant souls, that be not prepared by education to understand us; nor should we have need to shut out so many from holy communion upon the account of ignorance, that yet have not the grace to feel it and lament it, nor the wit and patience to wait in a learning state, till they are ready to be fellow-citizens with the saints, and of the household of God. But now they come to us with aged self-conceitedness, being past children, and yet worse than children still; having the ignorance of children, but being overgrown the teachableness of children; and think themselves wise, yea, wise enough to quarrel with the wisest of their teachers, because they have lived long enough to have been wise, and the evidence of their knowledge is their aged ignorance; and they are readier to flee in our faces for Church-privileges, than to learn of us, and obey our instructions, till they are prepared for them, that they may do them good; like snappish curs, that will snap us by the fingers for their meat, and snatch it out of our hands; and not like children, that stay till we give it them. Parents have so used them to be unruly, that ministers have to deal but with too few but the unruly. And it is for want of this laying the foundation well at first, that professors themselves are so ignorant as most are, and that so many, especially of the younger sort, do swallow down almost any error that is offered them, and follow any sect of dividers that will entice them, so it be but done with earnestness and plausibility. For, alas! though by the grace of God their hearts may be changed in an hour, (whenever they understand but the essentials of the faith,) yet their understandings must have time and diligence to furnish them with such knowledge as must establish them, and fortify them against deceits. Upon these, and many the like considerations, we should entreat all Christian families to take more pains in this necessary work, and to get better acquainted with the substance of Christianity. And, to that end, (taking along some moving treatises to awake the heart,) I know not what work should be fitter for their use, than that compiled by the Assembly at Westminster; a Synod of as godly, judicious divines, (notwithstanding all the bitter words which they have received from discontented and self-conceited men,) I verily think, as ever England saw. Though they had the unhappiness to be employed in calamitous times, when the noise of wars did stop men's ears, and the licentiousness of wars did set every wanton tongue and pen at liberty to reproach them, and the prosecution and event of those wars did exasperate partial discontented men to dishonour themselves by seeking to dishonour them; I dare say, if in the days of old, when councils were in power and account, they had had but such a council of bishops, as this of presbyters was, the fame of it for learning and holiness, and all ministerial abilities, would, with very great honour, have been transmitted to posterity.

"I do therefore desire, that all masters of families would first study well this work themselves, and then teach it their children and servants, according to their several capacities. And, if they once understand these grounds of religion, they will be able to read other books more understandingly, and hear sermons more profitably, and confer more judiciously, and hold fast the doctrine of Christ more firmly, than ever you are like to do by any other course. First, let them read and learn the Shorter Catechism, and next the Larger, and lastly, read the Confession of Faith."

Thus far he, whose name I shall conceal, (though the excellency of the matter, and present style, will easily discover him,) because I have published it without his privity and consent, though, I hope, not against his liking and approbation I shall add no more, but that I am,

Thy servant,
in the Lord's work,
THOMAS MANTON.

An Ordinance of the Lords and Commons assembled in Parliament, for the calling of an Assembly of learned and godly Divines, and others, to be consulted with by the Parliament, for the settling of the government and liturgy of the Church of England; and for vindicating and clearing of the doctrine of the said Church from false aspersions and interpretations. June 12, 1643.

WHEREAS, amongst the infinite blessings of Almighty God upon this nation, none is nor can be more dear unto us than the purity of our religion; and for that, as yet, many things remain in the liturgy, discipline, and government of the Church, which do necessarily require a further and more perfect reformation than as yet hath been attained; and whereas it hath been declared and resolved by the Lords and Commons assembled in Parliament, that the present Church-government by archbishops, their chancellors, commissars, deans, deans and chapters, archdeacons, and other ecclesiastical officers depending upon the hierarchy, is evil, and justly offensive and burdensome to the kingdom, a great impediment to reformation and growth of religion, and very prejudicial to the state and government of this kingdom; and therefore they are resolved that the same shall be taken away, and that such a government shall be settled in the Church as may be most agreeable to God's holy word, and most apt to procure and preserve the peace of the Church at home, and nearer agreement with the Church of Scotland, and other Reformed Churches abroad; and, for the better effecting hereof, and for the vindicating and clearing of the doctrine of the Church of England from all false calumnies and aspersions, it is thought fit and necessary to call an Assembly of learned, godly, and judicious Divines, who, together with some members of both the Houses of Parliament, are to consult and advise of such matters and things, touching the premises, as shall be proposed unto them by both or either of the Houses of Parliament, and to give their advice and counsel therein to both or either of the said Houses, when, and as often as they shall be thereunto required: Be it therefore ordained, by the Lords and Commons in this present Parliament assembled, That all and every the persons hereafter in this present ordinance named, that is to say,—

And such other person or persons as shall be nominated and appointed by both Houses of Parliament, or so many of them as shall not be letted by sickness, or other necessary impediment, shall meet and assemble, and are hereby required and enjoined, upon summons signed by the clerks of both Houses of Parliament, left at their respective dwellings, to meet and assemble themselves at Westminster, in the Chapel called King Henry the VII.'s Chapel, on the first day of July, in the year of our Lord one thousand six hundred and forty-three; and after the first meeting, being at least the number of forty, shall from time to time sit, and be removed from place to place; and also that the said Assembly shall be dissolved in such manner as by both Houses of Parliament shall be directed: and the said persons, or so many of them as shall be so assembled, or sit, shall have power and authority, and are hereby likewise enjoined from time to time, during this present Parliament, or until further order be taken by both the said Houses, to confer and treat among themselves of such matters and things, touching and concerning the liturgy, discipline, and government of the Church of England, for the vindicating and clearing of the doctrine of the same from all false aspersions and misconstructions, as shall be proposed unto them by both or either of the said Houses of Parliament, and no other; and deliver their opinion, advices of, or touching the matters aforesaid, as shall be most agreeable to the word of God, to both or either of the Houses, from time to time, in such manner and sort as by both or either of the said Houses of Parliament shall be required; and the same not to divulge, by printing, writing, or otherwise, without the consent of both or either Houses of Parliament. And be it further ordained by the authority aforesaid, That William Twisse, doctor in divinity, shall sit in the chair, as prolocutor of the said Assembly; and if he happen to die, or be letted by sickness, or other necessary impediment, then such other person to be appointed in his place as shall be agreed on by the said Houses of Parliament: And in case any difference in opinion shall happen amongst the said persons so assembled, touching any the matters that shall be proposed to them as aforesaid, that then they shall represent the same, together with the reasons thereof, to both or either the said Houses respectively, to the end such further direction may be given therein as shall be requisite to that behalf. And be it further ordained by the authority aforesaid, That, for the charges and expences of the said Divines, and every one of them, in attending the said service, there shall be allowed every one of them that shall so attend, during the time of their said attendance, and for ten days before and ten days after, the sum of four shillings for every day, at the charges of the Commonwealth, at such time, and in such manner as by both Houses of Parliament shall be appointed. And be it further ordained, That all and every the said Divines, so, as aforesaid, required and enjoined to meet and assemble, shall be freed and acquitted of and from every offence, forfeiture, penalty, loss, or damage, which shall or may ensue or grow by reason of any non-residence or absence of them, or any of them, from his or their, or any of their church, churches, or cures, for or in respect of their said attendance upon the said service; any law or statute of non-residence, or other law or statute enjoining their attendance upon their respective ministries or charges, to the contrary thereof notwithstanding. And if any of the persons above named shall happen to die before the said Assembly shall be dissolved by order of both Houses of Parliament, then such other person or persons shall be nominated and placed in the room and stead of such person or persons so dying, as by both the said Houses shall be thought fit and agreed upon; and every such person or persons, so to be named, shall have the like power and authority, freedom and acquittal, to all intents and purposes, and also all such wages and allowances for the said service, during the time of his or their attendance, as to any other of the said persons in this ordinance is by this ordinance limited and appointed. Provided always, That this ordinance, or any thing therein contained, shall not give unto the persons aforesaid, or any of them, nor shall they in this Assembly assume to exercise any jurisdiction, power, or authority ecclesiastical whatsoever, or any other power than is herein particularly expressed.

Assembly at EDINBURGH, August 19, 1643. Sess. 14.

Commission of the General Assembly to some Ministers and Ruling Elders, for repairing to the Kingdom of England.

THE General Assembly of the Church of Scotland finding it necessary to send some godly and learned of this Kirk to the kingdom of England, to the effect under written; therefore gives full power and commission to Mr Alexander Henderson, Mr Robert Douglas, Mr Samuel Rutherford, Mr Robert Baillie, and Mr George Gillespie, Ministers, John Earl of Cassilis, John Lord Maitland, and Sir Archibald Johnstoun of Warristoun, Elders, or any three of them, whereof two shall be Ministers, to repair to the kingdom of England, and there to deliver the declaration sent unto the Parliament of England, and the letter sent unto the Assembly of Divines now sitting in that kingdom; and to propone, consult, treat, and conclude with that Assembly, or any Commissioners deputed by them, or any Committees or Commissioners deputed by the Houses of Parliament, in all matters which may further the union of this Island in one Form of Kirk-government, one Confession of Faith, one Catechism, one Directory for the worship of God, according to the instructions which they have received from the Assembly, or shall receive from time to time hereafter from the Commissioners of the Assembly deputed for that effect: with power also to them to convey to His Majesty the humble answer sent from this Assembly to His Majesty's letter, by such occasion as they shall think convenient; and sicklike, to deliver the Assembly's answer to the letter sent from some well-affected brethren of the ministry there; and generally authorises them to do all things which may further the so much desired union.

and nearest conjunction of the two Churches of Scotland and England, conform to their instructions aforesaid.

Many of the persons who were called by the foresaid Ordinance of the Lords and Commons (in that broken state of the Church) to attend the Assembly appeared not; whereupon the whole work lay on the hands of the persons hereafter mentioned.

The Promise and Vow taken by every Member admitted to sit in the Assembly.

I A. B. do seriously promise and vow, in the presence of Almighty GOD, That in this Assembly, whereof I am a member, I will maintain nothing in point of doctrine, but what I believe to be most agreeable to the word of GOD; nor in point of discipline, but what may make most for GOD's glory, and the peace and good of this Church.

A List of the Divines who met in the Assembly at Westminster.

Dr WILLIAM TWISSE of Newbury, Prolocutor,
Dr Cornelius Burges of Waterford, John White of Dorchester, *Assessors*,
Dr William Gouge of Blackfriars, London,
Robert Harris of Hanwell, B.D.
Thomas Gattaker of Rotherhithe,
Oliver Bowles of Sutton, B.D.
Edward Reynolds of Bramston,
Jeremiah Whitaker of Streton,
Dr Anthony Tuckney of Boston,
John Arrowsmith of Lynne,
Simeon Ashe of St Brides,
Philip Nye of Kimbolton,
Jeremiah Burroughs of Stepney,
John Lightfoot of Ashley,
Stanley Gower of Brampton Bryan,
Richard Heyrick of Manchester,
Thomas Case of London,
Dr Thomas Temple of Battery,
George Gipps of Ayleston,
Thomas Carter,
Dr Humphrey Chambers of Claverstoun,
Thomas Micklethwait of Cherryburton,
John Guibon of Waltham,
Christopher Tesdale of Uphusborne,
Henry Philps,
George Walker, B.D.
Edmund Calamy, B.D. of Aldermanbury,
Dr Lazarus Seaman of London,
Joseph Caryl of Lincoln's Inn,
Dr Henry Wilkinson senior of Waderston,
Richard Vines of Calcot,
Nicholas Profit of Marlborough,
Stephen Marshall, B.D. of Finchingfield,
Dr Joshua Hoyle late of Dublin,
Thomas Wilson of Otham,
Thomas Hodges of Kensington,
Thomas Baillie of Mildenhall, B.D.
Francis Taylor of Yalding,
Thomas Young of Stownmarket,
Thomas Valentine, B.D. of Chalfont, St Giles,
William Greenhill of Stepney,
Edward Pele of Compton,
John Green of Pencomb,
Andrew Pern of Wilby,
Samuel de la Place,
John de la March,
John Dury,
Philip Deline,
Sidrach Simpson of London,
John Langley of Westuderly,
Richard Clayton of Showers,
Arthur Sallaway of Seavernestock,
John Ley of Budworth,
Charles Herle of Winwick, prolocutor after Dr Twisse,
Herbert Palmer, B.D. of Ashwel, assessor after Mr White,
Daniel Cawdrey of Great Billing,
Henry Painter, B.D. of Exeter,
Henry Scudder of Colinborn,
Thomas Hill, B.D. of Tichmarsh,
William Reynor, B.D. of Egham,
Dr Thomas Goodwin of London,
Dr William Spurstow of Hampden,
Matthew Newcomb of Dedham,
Dr Edmond Staunton of Kingston,
John Conant of Lymmington, B.D.
Anthony Burges of Sutton Coldfield,
William Rathband,
Dr Francis Cheynel of Oxen,
Dr Henry Wilkinson younger of Oxford,
Obadiah Sedgwick, B.D. of Cogshal,
Edward Corbist of Marton College, Oxford,
Samuel Gibson of Burley,
Thomas Coleman of Bliton,
Theodore Backhurst,
William Carter of London,
Peter Smith,
John Maynard of Mayfield,
William Price of Paul's Church in Covent Garden,
John Whincop of St Martins in the Fields,
William Bridge of Yarmouth,
Peter Sterry of London,
William Mew, B.D. of Eslington,
Benjamin Pickering of East Hoatly,
John Strickland of St Edmonds in Sarum,
Humphrey Hardwick,
Jasper Hicks of Lawrick or Lanrake,
John Bond,
Henry Hall, B.D. of Norwich,
Thomas Ford of London, afterwards of Exeter,
Thomas Thorogood of Massingham,
Peter Clerk of Kerby Underhill,
William Good,
John Foxcroft of Cotham,
John Ward,
Richard Byfield of Long-Ditton,
Francis Woodcock,
John Jackson of Marske.

Commissioners from the General Assembly of the Church of Scotland.

ALEXANDER HENDERSON of Edinburgh,
Robert Douglas of Edinburgh,
Samuel Rutherford of St Andrews,
Robert Baillie of Glasgow,
George Gillespie of Edinburgh, *Ministers,*
John Earl of Cassilis,

John Lord Maitland, afterwards Duke of Lauderdale,
Sir Archibald Johnstoun of Waristoun,
Henry Robrough, [*Ruling Elders,*
Adoniram Byfield,
John Wallis, *Scribes.*

Assembly at EDINBURGH, August 27, 1647. Sess. 23.

Act approving the CONFESSION *of* FAITH.

A CONFESSION of Faith for the Kirks of God in the three kingdoms, being the chiefest part of that uniformity in religion which, by the Solemn League and Covenant, we are bound to endeavour: And there being accordingly a Confession of Faith agreed upon by the Assembly of Divines sitting at Westminster, with the assistance of Commissioners from the Kirk of Scotland; which Confession was sent from our Commissioners at London to the Commissioners of the Kirk met at Edinburgh in January last, and hath been in this Assembly twice publickly read over, examined, and considered; copies thereof being also printed, that it might be particularly perused by all the members of this Assembly, unto whom frequent intimation was publickly made, to put in their doubts and objections, if they had any: And the said Confession being, upon due examination thereof, found by the Assembly to be most agreeable to the word of God, and in nothing contrary to the received doctrine, worship, discipline, and government of this Kirk. And, lastly, It being so necessary, and so much longed for, that the said Confession be, with all possible diligence and expedition, approved and established in both kingdoms, as a principal part of the intended uniformity in religion, and as a special means for the more effectual suppressing of the many dangerous errors and heresies of these times; the General Assembly doth therefore, after mature deliberation, agree unto, and approve the said Confession, as to the truth of the matter; (judging it to be most orthodox, and grounded upon the word of God;) and also, as to the point of uniformity, agreeing for our part, that it be a common Confession of Faith for the three Kingdoms. The Assembly doth also bless the Lord, and thankfully acknowledge his great mercy, in that so excellent a Confession of Faith is prepared, and thus far agreed upon in both kingdoms; which we look upon as a great strengthening of the true reformed religion against the common enemies thereof. But, lest our intention and meaning be in some particulars misunderstood, it is hereby expressly declared and provided, That the not mentioning in this Confession the several sorts of ecclesiastical officers and assemblies, shall be no prejudice to the truth of Christ in these particulars, to be expressed fully in the Directory of Government. It is further declared, That the Assembly understandeth some parts of the second article of the thirty-one chapter only of kirks not settled, or constituted in point of government: And that although, in such kirks, a synod of Ministers, and other fit persons, may be called by the Magistrate's authority and nomination, without any other call, to consult and advise with about matters of religion; and although, likewise, the Ministers of Christ, without delegation from their churches, may of themselves, and by virtue of their office, meet together synodically in such kirks not yet constituted, yet neither of these ought to be done in kirks constituted and settled; it being always free to the Magistrate to advise with synods of Ministers and Ruling Elders, meeting upon delegation from their churches, either ordinarily, or, being indicted by his authority, occasionally, and *pro re nata*; it being also free to assemble together synodically, as well *pro re nata* as at the ordinary times, upon delegation from the churches, by the intrinsical power received from Christ, as often as it is necessary for the good of the Church so to assemble, in case the Magistrate, to the detriment of the Church, withhold or deny his consent; the necessity of occasional assemblies being first remonstrate unto him by humble supplication. A. KER.

CHARLES I. Parl. 2. Sess. 2. Act 16.

Act anent the Catechisms, Confession of Faith, and Ratification thereof.

At EDINBURGH, February 7, 1649.

THE Estates of Parliament, now presently convened in this second Session of the second triennial Parliament, by virtue of an Act of the Committee of Estates, who had power and authority from the last Parliament for convening the Parliament, having seriously considered the Catechisms, *viz.* the Larger and Shorter ones, with the Confession of Faith, with three Acts of Approbation thereof by the Commissioners of the General Assembly, presented unto them by the Commissioners of the said General Assembly; do ratify and approve the said Catechisms, Confession of Faith, and Acts of Approbation of the same, produced as it is: and ordains them to be recorded, published, and practised.

ACT 7th June 1690.

Ratifying the Confession of Faith, and settling Presbyterian Church Government.

OUR Sovereign Lord and Lady, the King and Queen's Majesties, and three Estates of Parliament, conceiving it to be their bounden duty, after the great deliverance that God hath lately wrought for this Church and Kingdom, in the first place to settle and secure therein the true Protestant religion, according to the truth of God's word, as it hath of a long time been professed within this land; as also the government of Christ's Church within this Nation, agreeable to the word of God, and most conducive to the advancement of true piety and godliness, and the establishing of peace and tranquillity within this realm,—they, by these presents, ratify and establish the *Confession of Faith* now read in their presence, and voted and approven by them, as the public and avowed Confession of this Church, containing the sum and substance of the Doctrine of the Reformed Churches, (which Confession of Faith is subjoined to this present Act,) as also they do establish, ratify, and confirm the Presbyterian Church Government and Discipline; that is to say, the Government of the Church by Kirk Sessions, Presbyteries, Provincial Synods, and General Assemblies, ratified and established by the 114 Act James VI., Parl. 12, Anno 1592, entitled Ratification of the Liberty of the Kirk, &c., and thereafter received by the general consent of this nation, to be the only Government of Christ's Church within this kingdom; reviving, renewing, and confirming the same in the whole heads thereof, except that part of it relating to Patronages, which is hereafter to be taken into consideration.

THE

CONFESSION OF FAITH;

AGREED UPON BY

THE ASSEMBLY OF DIVINES AT WESTMINSTER,

WITH THE ASSISTANCE OF

COMMISSIONERS FROM THE CHURCH OF SCOTLAND,

AS

A PART OF THE COVENANTED UNIFORMITY IN RELIGION BETWIXT THE CHURCHES OF CHRIST IN THE KINGDOMS OF SCOTLAND, ENGLAND, AND IRELAND.

Approved by the General Assembly 1647, and ratified and established by Acts of Parliament 1649 and 1690, as the publick and avowed Confession of the Church of Scotland, with the Proofs from the Scripture.

THE CONTENTS.

CHAP.
- I. Of the Holy Scripture.
- II. Of God, and of the Holy Trinity.
- III. Of God's Eternal Decree.
- IV. Of Creation.
- V. Of Providence.
- VI. Of the Fall of Man, of Sin, and of the Punishment thereof.
- VII. Of God's Covenant with Man.
- VIII. Of Christ the Mediator.
- IX. Of Free Will.
- X. Of Effectual Calling.
- XI. Of Justification.
- XII. Of Adoption.
- XIII. Of Sanctification.
- XIV. Of Saving Faith.
- XV. Of Repentance unto Life.
- XVI. Of Good Works.
- XVII. Of the Perseverance of the Saints.

CHAP.
- XVIII. Of Assurance of Grace and Salvation.
- XIX. Of the Law of God.
- XX. Of Christian Liberty, and Liberty of Conscience.
- XXI. Of Religious Worship, and the Sabbath-day.
- XXII. Of lawful Oaths and Vows
- XXIII. Of the Civil Magistrate.
- XXIV. Of Marriage and Divorce.
- XXV. Of the Church.
- XXVI. Of Communion of Saints.
- XXVII. Of the Sacraments.
- XXVIII. Of Baptism.
- XXIX. Of the Lord's Supper.
- XXX. Of Church Censures.
- XXXI. Of Synods and Councils.
- XXXII. Of the State of Men after Death, and of the Resurrection of the Dead.
- XXXIII. Of the last Judgment.

THE
CONFESSION OF FAITH,

Agreed upon by the ASSEMBLY OF DIVINES at Westminster: Examined and approved, *Anno* 1647, by the GENERAL ASSEMBLY of the CHURCH OF SCOTLAND; and ratified by ACTS OF PARLIAMENT 1649 and 1690.

CHAP. 1.—*Of the Holy Scripture.*

I. ALTHOUGH the light of nature, and the works of creation and providence, do so far manifest the goodness, wisdom, and power of God, as to leave men inexcusable;[a] yet they are not sufficient to give that knowledge of God, and of his will, which is necessary unto salvation:[b] therefore it pleased the Lord, at sundry times, and in divers manners, to reveal himself, and to declare that his will unto his Church;[c] and afterwards, for the better preserving and propagating of the truth, and for the more sure establishment and comfort of the Church against the corruption of the flesh, and the malice of Satan and of the world, to commit the same wholly unto writing;[d] which maketh

I. a Rom. ii. 14. *For when the Gentiles, which have not the law, do by nature the things contained in the law, these, having not the law, are a law unto themselves:* Ver. 15. *Which shew the work of the law written in their hearts, their conscience also bearing witness,* and their *thoughts the mean while accusing or else excusing one another.* Rom. i. 19. *Because that which may be known of God is manifest in them:* for God hath *shewed* it unto them. Ver. 20. *For the invisible things of him from the creation of the world are clearly seen,* being understood by the things that are made, even his eternal power and God head; *so that they are without excuse.* Ps. xix. 1. *The heavens declare the glory of God;* and the firmament *sheweth* his *handy-work.* Ver. 2. *Day unto day uttereth speech,* and night unto night *sheweth knowledge.* Ver. 3. *There is no speech nor language* where *their voice is not heard.* Rom. i. 32. *Who, knowing* the judgment of God, that they which commit such things are *worthy of death,* not only *do the same,* but have *pleasure* in them that do them. With Rom. ii. 1. Therefore thou art *inexcusable,* O man, whosoever thou art that judgest: for wherein thou judgest another, thou condemnest thyself; for thou that judgest doest the same things.

b 1 Cor. i. 21. *For after that, in the wisdom of God, the world by wisdom knew not God,* it pleased God by the foolishness of preaching to save them that believe. 1 Cor. ii. 13. Which things also we speak, not in the words which *man's wisdom teacheth,* but which the Holy Ghost teacheth; comparing spiritual things with spiritual. Ver. 14. But the *natural man* receiveth not the things of the Spirit of God: for they are *foolishness unto him;* neither can he know them, because they are *spiritually discerned.*

c Heb. i. 1. God, who at *sundry times,* and in *divers manners,* spake in time past unto the fathers by the prophets.

d Prov. xxii. 19. That thy trust may be in the Lord, I have *made known* to thee this day, even to thee. Ver. 20. Have not I *written* to thee excellent things in counsels and knowledge; Ver. 21. That I might make thee *know the certainty* of the words of truth; that thou mightest answer the words of truth to them that send unto thee? Luke i. 3. It seemed good to me also, having had perfect understanding of all things from the very first, to write unto thee in order, most excellent Theophilus, Ver. 4. That thou *mightest know the certainty* of those things wherein thou hast been instructed. Rom. xv. 4. For whatsoever things were written aforetime *were written* for our learning; that we, through patience and comfort of *the scriptures,* might have hope. Matt. iv. 4. But he answered and said, *It is written,* Man shall not live by bread alone, but by every word that proceedeth out of the mouth of God. Ver. 7. Jesus said unto him, *It is written* again, Thou shalt not tempt the Lord thy God. Ver. 10. Then saith Jesus unto him, Get thee hence, Satan: *for it is written,* Thou shalt worship the Lord thy God, and him only shalt thou serve. Isa. viii. 19. And when they shall say unto you, Seek unto them that have familiar spirits, and unto wizards that peep and that mutter: should not a people seek unto their *God?* for the living to the dead? Ver. 20. To the *law and to the testimony:* if they speak not according to *this word,* it is because there is no light in them.

B

the holy scripture to be most necessary;[e] those former ways of God's revealing his will unto his people being now ceased.[f]

II. Under the name of Holy Scripture, or the Word of God written, are now contained all the Books of the Old and New Testaments, which are these:—

OF THE OLD TESTAMENT.

Genesis.	I. Kings.	Ecclesiastes.	Amos.
Exodus.	II. Kings.	The Song of Songs.	Obadiah.
Leviticus.	I. Chronicles.		Jonah.
Numbers.	II. Chronicles.	Isaiah.	Micah.
Deuteronomy.	Ezra.	Jeremiah.	Nahum.
Joshua.	Nehemiah.	Lamentations.	Habakkuk.
Judges.	Esther.	Ezekiel.	Zephaniah.
Ruth.	Job.	Daniel.	Haggai.
I. Samuel.	Psalms.	Hosea.	Zechariah.
II. Samuel.	Proverbs.	Joel.	Malachi.

OF THE NEW TESTAMENT.

The Gospels according to Matthew.	Paul's Epistles to the Romans.	Thessalonians II. To Timothy I.	The first and second Epistles of Peter.
Mark.	Corinthians I.	To Timothy II.	The first, second, and third Epistles of John.
Luke.	Corinthians II.	To Titus.	
John.	Galatians.	To Philemon.	
The Acts of the Apostles.	Ephesians.	The Epistle to the Hebrews.	The Epistle of Jude.
	Philippians.	The Epistle of James.	
	Colossians.		The Revelation.
	Thessalonians I.		

All which are given by inspiration of God, to be the rule of faith and life.[g]

III. The Books commonly called Apocrypha, not being of divine inspiration, are no part of the canon of the scripture; and therefore are of no authority in the Church of God, nor to be any otherwise approved, or made use of, than other human writings.[h]

---

[e] 2 Tim. iii. 15. *And that from a child thou hast known the holy scriptures*, which are able to make thee *wise unto salvation* through faith which is in Christ Jesus. 2 Pet. i. 19. We have also a *more sure word of prophecy*; whereunto ye do *well* that ye *take heed*, as unto a light that shineth in a dark place, until the day dawn, and the day-star arise in your hearts.

[f] Heb. i. 1. God, who at *sundry times*, and in *divers manners*, spake *in time past unto the fathers* by the *prophets*, Ver. 2. Hath in these *last days spoken* unto us *by his Son*, whom he hath appointed heir of all things, by whom also he made the worlds.

II. [g] Luke xvi. 29. *Abraham* saith unto him, They have *Moses and the prophets;* let them *hear* them. Ver. 31. And he said unto him, If they hear not *Moses and the prophets*, neither will they be persuaded though one rose from the dead. Eph. ii. 20. And are built upon the foundation of the *apostles and prophets*, Jesus Christ himself being the chief *corner-stone*. Rev. xxii. 18. For I testify unto every man that heareth the words of the *prophecy* of this book, If any man *shall add* unto these things, God shall add unto him the plagues that are written in this book: Ver. 19. And if any man shall take away from the words of the book of *this prophecy*, God shall take away his part out of the book of life, and out of the holy city, and from the things which are written in this book. 2 Tim. iii. 16. All scripture is *given by inspiration* of God, and is profitable for *doctrine*, for *reproof*, for *correction*, for *instruction in righteousness*.

III. [h] Luke xxiv. 27. And *beginning at Moses and the prophets*, he *expounded unto them in all the scriptures* the things concerning himself. Ver. 44. And he said unto them, These are the words which I spake unto you, while I was yet with you, that all things must be fulfilled which *were written in the law of Moses*, and in *the Prophets*, and in *the Psalms*, concerning *me*. Rom. iii. 2. Much every way: chiefly, because that unto them were committed the *oracles* of God. 2 Pet. i. 21. For the prophecy *came not* in old time by the *will of*

IV. The authority of the holy scripture, for which it ought to be believed and obeyed, dependeth not upon the testimony of any man or church, but wholly upon God, (who is truth itself,) the author thereof; and therefore it is to be received, because it is the word of God.[1]

V. We may be moved and induced by the testimony of the Church to an high and reverend esteem of the holy scripture,[k] and the heavenliness of the matter, the efficacy of the doctrine, the majesty of the style, the consent of all the parts, the scope of the whole, (which is to give all glory to God,) the full discovery it makes of the only way of man's salvation, the many other incomparable excellencies, and the entire perfection thereof, are arguments whereby it doth abundantly evidence itself to be the word of God; yet, notwithstanding, our full persuasion and assurance of the infallible truth, and divine authority thereof, is from the inward work of the Holy Spirit, bearing witness by and with the word in our hearts.[l]

VI. The whole counsel of God, concerning all things necessary for his own glory, man's salvation, faith, and life, is either expressly set down in scripture, or by good and necessary consequence may be deduced from scripture: unto which nothing at any time is to be added, whether by new revelations of the Spirit, or traditions of men.[m] Ne-

man; but *holy men of God* spake as they were moved *by the Holy Ghost.*
IV. [1] 2 Pet. i. 19. We have also *a more sure word of prophecy;* whereunto ye do well that ye take heed, as unto a light that shineth in a dark place, until the day dawn, and the day-star arise in your hearts. Ver. 21. For the prophecy came not in old time by the will of man; but *holy men of God spake* as they were *moved by the Holy Ghost.* 2 Tim. iii. 16. All scripture *is given by inspiration of God*, and is profitable for doctrine, for reproof, for correction, for instruction in righteousness. 1 John v. 9. If we receive the witness of men, *the witness of God is greater :* for this is the witness of God which he hath testified of his Son. 1 Thess. ii. 13. For this cause also thank we God without ceasing, because, when ye received the *word of God* which ye heard of us, ye received it *not as the word of men*, but (as it is in truth) *the word of God*, which effectually worketh also in you that believe.
V. [k] 1 Tim. iii. 15. But if I tarry long, that thou mayest know how thou oughtest to behave thyself in the house of God, which is the church of the living God, the *pillar and ground of the truth.*
[l] 1 John ii. 20. But ye have an *unction from the Holy One*, and ye know all things. Ver. 27. But the *anointing* which ye have received of him *abideth in you;* and ye need not that any man teach you: but as the same anointing teacheth you of all things, and is truth, and is no lie, and even as it hath taught you, ye shall abide in him. John xvi. 13. Howbeit when he, *the Spirit of truth*, is come, he will guide you into all truth: for he shall *not speak of himself;* but whatsoever he *shall hear, that shall he speak;* and he will shew you things to come. Ver. 14. He shall glorify me; for he *shall receive of mine*, and shall shew it unto you. 1 Cor. ii. 10. But God hath *revealed them* unto us *by his Spirit :* for *the Spirit searcheth all things*, yea, the deep things of God. Ver. 11. For what man knoweth the things of a man, save the spirit of man which is in him? even so *the things of God* knoweth no man, but *the Spirit of God.* Ver. 12. Now we have received, not the spirit of the world, but *the Spirit which is of God ;* that we might *know* the things that are freely given to us of God. Isa lix. 21. As for me, this is my covenant with them, saith the Lord; *My Spirit that is upon thee, and my words* which I have put in thy mouth, shall not depart out of thy mouth, nor out of the mouth of thy seed, nor out of the mouth of thy seed's seed, saith the Lord, from henceforth and for ever.
VI. [m] 2 Tim. iii. 15. And that from a child thou hast known the *holy scriptures*, which are *able* to make thee *wise unto salvation* through faith which is in Christ Jesus. Ver. 16. All scripture is given by inspiration of God, and is *profitable* for doctrine, for reproof, for correction, for instruction in righteousness; Ver. 17. That the man of God may be *perfect, thoroughly furnished unto all good works.* Gal. i. 8. But though we, or an angel from heaven, *preach any other gospel* unto you than that which we have preached unto you, let him be accursed. Ver. 9. As we said before, so say I now again, If any man *preach any other gospel* unto you than that ye have received, let him be accursed. 2 Thess. ii. 2. That ye be not soon shaken in mind, or be troubled, neither by *spirit, nor by word, nor by letter* as from us, as that the day of Christ is at hand.

vertheless, we acknowledge the inward illumination of the Spirit of God to be necessary for the saving understanding of such things as are revealed in the word ;ⁿ and that there are some circumstances concerning the worship of God, and government of the Church, common to human actions and societies, which are to be ordered by the light of nature and Christian prudence, according to the general rules of the word, which are always to be observed.°

VII. All things in scripture are not alike plain in themselves, nor alike clear unto all ;^p yet those things which are necessary to be known, believed, and observed, for salvation, are so clearly propounded and opened in some place of scripture or other, that not only the learned, but the unlearned, in a due use of the ordinary means, may attain unto a sufficient understanding of them.^q

VIII. The Old Testament in Hebrew, (which was the native language of the people of God of old,) and the New Testament in Greek, (which at the time of the writing of it was most generally known to the nations,) being immediately inspired by God, and by his singular care and providence kept pure in all ages, are therefore authentical ;^r so as in all controversies of religion, the Church is finally to appeal unto them.^s But because these original tongues are not known to all the people of God, who have right unto and interest in the scriptures, and are commanded, in the fear of God, to read and search them,^t therefore they are to be translated into the vulgar language of every nation unto which they come,^u that the word of God dwelling plenti-

---

n John vi. 45. It is written in the prophets, And they shall be all *taught of God*. Every man therefore that hath heard, and hath *learned of the Father*, cometh unto me. 1 Cor. ii. 9. But, as it is written, Eye *hath not seen, nor ear heard*, neither have *entered into the heart of man*, the things which God hath prepared for them that love him. Ver. 10. But God hath *revealed* them unto us by *his Spirit :* for the Spirit searcheth all things, yea, the deep things of God. Ver. 11. For what man knoweth the things of a man, save the spirit of man which is in him? even so *the things of God* knoweth no man, but *the Spirit of God*. Ver. 12. Now we have received, not the spirit of the world, but the *Spirit which is of God ;* that *we might know the things* that are freely given to us of God.

o 1 Cor. xi. 13. Judge in yourselves : *is it comely* that a woman pray unto God uncovered? Ver. 14. Doth not even *nature itself teach you*, that, if a man have long hair, it is a shame unto him? 1 Cor. xiv. 26. How is it then, brethren? when ye come together, every one of you hath a psalm, hath a doctrine, hath a tongue, hath a revelation, hath an interpretation. Let *all things be done unto edifying*. Ver. 40. Let *all things be done decently and in order*.

VII. p 2 Pet. iii. 16. As also in all his epistles, speaking in them of these things : in which are some things *hard to be understood*, which they that are *unlearned* and *unstable wrest*, as they do also the other scriptures, *unto their own destruction*.

q Ps. cxix. 105. Thy *word* is a *lamp* unto my feet, and *a light* unto my path. Ver. 130. The entrance of thy words giveth *light ;* it giveth *understanding unto the simple*.

VIII. r Matt. v. 18. For verily I say unto you, Till heaven and earth pass, *one jot or one tittle shall in no wise pass* from the law, *till all be fulfilled*.

s Isa. viii. 20. *To the law and to the testimony :* if they speak not according to *this word*, it is because there is no light in them. Acts xv. 15. And to this *agree the words of the prophets;* as it is written. John v. 39. *Search the scriptures;* for in them ye think ye have eternal life : and they are they which testify of me. Ver. 46. For had ye *believed Moses,* ye would have believed *me : for he wrote of me*.

t John v. 39. *Search the scriptures;* for in them ye think ye have eternal life : and they are they which testify of me.

u 1 Cor. xiv. 6. Now, brethren, if I come unto you *speaking with tongues*, what shall I profit you, except I shall speak to you either by revelation, or by knowledge, or by prophesying, or by doctrine? Ver. 9. So likewise ye, except ye utter by the tongue words *easy to be understood*, how shall it be known what is spoken? for ye shall speak into the air. Ver. 11. Therefore if I *know not the meaning of the voice*, I shall be unto him that speaketh a *barbarian*, and he that speaketh shall be a *barbarian* unto me. Ver. 12. Even so ye, forasmuch as ye are zealous of spiritual gifts, seek that ye may excel to the *edifying of the church*. Ver. 24. But if all *prophesy*, and there come in one that believeth not, or one *unlearned*, he is convinced of all, he is judged of all ;

fully in all, they may worship him in an acceptable manner,ʷ and, through patience and comfort of the scriptures, may have hope.ˣ

IX. The infallible rule of interpretation of scripture is the scripture itself; and therefore, when there is a question about the true and full sense of any scripture, (which is not manifold, but one,) it must be searched and known by other places that speak more clearly.ʸ

X. The supreme Judge, by which all controversies of religion are to be determined, and all decrees of councils, opinions of ancient writers, doctrines of men, and private spirits, are to be examined, and in whose sentence we are to rest, can be no other but the Holy Spirit speaking in the scripture.ᶻ

CHAP. II.—*Of God, and of the Holy Trinity.*

I. THERE is but one onlyᵃ living and true God,ᵇ who is infinite in being and perfection,ᶜ a most pure spirit,ᵈ invisible,ᵉ without body, parts,ᶠ

Ver. 27. If any man speak in an unknown tongue, let it be by two, or at the most by three, and that by course; and *let one interpret.* Ver. 28. But if there *be no interpreter*, let him keep *silence in the church;* and let him speak to himself, and to God.

ʷ Col. iii. 16. Let the word of Christ dwell in you *richly in all wisdom;* teaching and admonishing one another in psalms, and hymns, and spiritual songs, singing with *grace in your hearts* to the Lord.

ˣ Rom. xv. 4. For whatsoever things were written aforetime, were written for our learning; that we, *through patience and comfort of the scriptures, might have hope.*

IX. ʸ 2 Pet. i. 20. Knowing this first, that no prophecy of the scripture is of *any private interpretation.* Ver. 21. For the prophecy came not in old time by *the will of man;* but holy men of God spake as they were *moved by the Holy Ghost.* Acts xv. 15. And *to this agree the words of the prophets;* as it is written, Ver. 16. After this I will return, and will build again the tabernacle of *David,* which is fallen down; and I will build again the ruins thereof, and I will set it up.

X. ᶻ Matt. xxii. 29. Jesus answered and said unto them, Ye do *err, not knowing the scriptures,* nor the power of God. Ver. 31. But as touching the resurrection of the dead, *have ye not read* that which was spoken unto you by God, saying. Eph. ii. 20. And are built upon the *foundation of the apostles and prophets,* Jesus Christ himself being the chief corner-stone. With Acts xxviii. 25. And when they agreed not among themselves, they departed, after that Paul had spoken one word, Well *spake the Holy Ghost by Esaias* the prophet unto our fathers.

I. ᵃ Deut. vi. 4. Hear, O *Israel;* The Lord *our God is one Lord.* 1 Cor. viii. 4. As concerning therefore the eating of those things that are offered in sacrifice unto idols, we know that an idol is nothing in the world, and that there is *none other God but one.* Ver. 6. But to *us there is but one God,* the Father, of whom are all things, and we in him; and one Lord Jesus Christ, by whom are all things, and we by him.

ᵇ 1 Thess. i. 9. For they themselves shew of us what manner of entering in we had unto you, and how ye turned to God from idols, to serve *the living and true God.* Jer. x. 10. But the Lord is the *true God, he is the living God,* and an everlasting King.

ᶜ Job xi. 7. Canst thou by searching find out God? *canst thou find out the Almighty unto perfection?* Ver. 8. It is as *high as heaven;* what canst thou do? *deeper than hell;* what canst thou know? Ver. 9. The measure thereof is *longer than the earth, and broader than the sea.* Job xxvi. 14. Lo, these are parts of his ways; but *how little a portion is heard of* him? but the *thunder of his power who can understand?*

ᵈ John iv. 24. *God is a Spirit;* and they that worship him must worship him in spirit and in truth.

ᵉ 1 Tim. i. 17. Now, unto the King eternal, immortal, *invisible,* the only wise God, be honour and glory for ever and ever. *Amen.*

ᶠ Deut. iv. 15. Take ye therefore good heed unto yourselves, (for ye saw *no manner of similitude* on the day that the Lord spake unto you in *Horeb* out of the midst of the fire,) Ver. 16. Lest ye corrupt yourselves, and make you a *graven image, the similitude of any figure, the likeness of male or female.* John iv. 24. *God is a Spirit;* and they that worship him must worship him in spirit and in truth. With Luke xxiv. 39. Behold my hands and my feet, that it is I myself: handle me, and see; for a *spirit hath not flesh and bones, as ye see me have*

or passions,g immutable,h immense,i eternal,k incomprehensible,l almighty,m most wise,n most holy,o most free,p most absolute,q working all things according to the counsel of his own immutable and most righteous will,r for his own glory;s most loving,t gracious, merciful, long-suffering, abundant in goodness and truth, forgiving iniquity, transgression, and sin;u the rewarder of them that diligently seek him;w and withal most just and terrible in his judgments;x hating all sin,y and who will by no means clear the guilty.z

g Acts xiv. 11. And when the people saw what Paul had done, they lifted up their voices, saying in the speech of *Lycaonia*, *The gods are come down to us* in the likeness of men. Ver. 15. And saying, Sirs, why do ye these things? *We also are men of like passions* with you, and preach unto you, that ye should turn from these vanities unto the living God, which made heaven, and earth, and the sea, and all things that are therein.

h James i. 17. Every good gift and every perfect gift is from above, and cometh down from the Father of lights, *with whom is no variableness, neither shadow of turning*. Mal. iii. 6. For I am the Lord, *I change not;* therefore ye sons of *Jacob* are not consumed.

i 1 Kings viii. 27. But will God indeed dwell on the earth? *Behold, the heaven, and heaven of heavens, cannot contain thee;* how much less this house that I have builded! Jer. xxiii. 23. Am I *a God at hand*, saith the Lord, and *not a God afar off?* Ver. 24. Can any hide himself in secret places that I shall not see him? saith the Lord: *do not I fill heaven and earth?* saith the Lord.

k Ps. xc. 2. Before the mountains were brought forth, or ever thou hadst formed the earth and the world, even *from everlasting to everlasting, thou art God*. 1 Tim. i. 17. Now, unto the *King eternal*, immortal, invisible, the only wise God, be honour and glory for ever and ever. *Amen*.

l Ps. cxlv. 3. Great is the Lord, and greatly to be praised; and *his greatness is unsearchable*.

m Gen. xvii. 1. And when *Abram* was ninety years old and nine, the Lord appeared to *Abram*, and said unto him, *I am the Almighty God:* walk before me, and be thou perfect. Rev. iv. 8. And the four beasts had each of them six wings about him; and they were full of eyes within: and they rest not day and night, saying, Holy, holy, holy, *Lord God Almighty*, which was, and is, and is to come.

n Rom. xvi. 27. To *God only wise*, be glory through Jesus Christ for ever. *Amen*.

o Isa. vi. 3. And one cried unto another, and said, *Holy, holy, holy, is the Lord of hosts:* the whole earth is full of his glory. Rev. iv. 8. [See letter m immediately foregoing.]

p Ps. cxv. 3. But our God is in the heavens; he *hath done whatsoever he hath pleased*.

q Exod. iii. 14. And God said unto *Moses*, I AM THAT I AM: and he said, Thus shalt thou say unto the children of Israel, I AM hath sent me unto you.

r Eph. i. 11. In whom also we have obtained an inheritance, being predestinated according to the purpose of him *who worketh all things after the counsel of his own will*.

s Prov. xvi. 4. The Lord hath *made all things for himself;* yea, even the *wicked for the day of evil*. Rom. xi. 36. For of him, and through him, *and to him, are all things:* to whom be glory for ever. Amen.

t 1 John iv. 8. He that loveth not, knoweth not God; for *God is love*. Ver. 16. And we have known and believed the love that God hath to us. *God is love;* and he that dwelleth in love, dwelleth in God, and God in him.

u Exod. xxxiv. 6. And the Lord passed by before him, and proclaimed, The Lord, The Lord God, *merciful and gracious, long-suffering, and abundant in goodness and truth*. Ver. 7. *Keeping mercy for thousands, forgiving iniquity, and transgression, and sin*, and that will by no means clear the guilty; visiting the iniquity of the fathers upon the children, and upon the children's children, unto the third and to the fourth generation.

w Heb. xi. 6. But without faith it is impossible to please him: for he that cometh to God must believe that he is, and that he is *a rewarder of them that diligently seek him*.

x Neh. ix. 32. Now therefore, our God, the great, the mighty, and *the terrible God*, who keepest covenant and mercy, let not all the trouble seem little before thee that hath come upon us, on our kings, on our princes, and on our priests, and on our prophets, and on our fathers, and on all thy people, since the time of the kings of *Assyria* unto this day. Ver. 33. Howbeit *thou art just in all that is brought upon us;* for *thou hast done right*, but *we have done wickedly*.

y Ps. v. 5. The foolish shall not stand in thy sight: *thou hatest all workers of iniquity*. Ver. 6. Thou shalt destroy them that speak leasing: the *Lord will abhor the bloody and deceitful man*.

z Nah. i. 2. God is jealous, and the Lord revengeth; the Lord revengeth, and is furious; the Lord *will take vengeance on his adversaries*, and he reserveth wrath for his enemies. Ver. 3. The Lord is slow to anger, and great in power, *and will not at all acquit the wicked:* the Lord hath his way in the whirlwind and in the storm, and the clouds are the dust of his feet. Exod.

II. God hath all life,^a glory,^b goodness,^c blessedness,^d in and of himself; and is alone in and unto himself all-sufficient, not standing in need of any creatures which he hath made,^e not deriving any glory from them,^f but only manifesting his own glory, in, by, unto, and upon them: he is the alone fountain of all being, of whom, through whom, and to whom, are all things;^g and hath most sovereign dominion over them, to do by them, for them, or upon them, whatsoever himself pleaseth.^h In his sight all things are open and manifest;ⁱ his knowledge is infinite, infallible, and independent upon the creature,^k so as nothing is to him contingent or uncertain.^l He is most holy in all his counsels, in all his works, and in all his commands.^m To him is due from angels and men, and every other creature, whatsoever worship, service, or obedience, he is pleased to require of them.ⁿ

III. In the unity of the Godhead there be three persons, of one substance, power, and eternity; God the Father, God the Son, and God the Holy Ghost.^o The Father is of none, neither begotten nor pro-

---

xxxiv. 7. Keeping mercy for thousands, forgiving iniquity, and transgression, and sin, and that *will by no means clear the guilty ;* visiting the iniquity of the fathers upon the children, and upon the children's children, unto the third and to the fourth generation.

II. ^a John v. 26. For as the *Father hath life in himself,* so hath he given to the Son to have life in himself.

^b Acts vii. 2. And he said, Men, brethren, and fathers, hearken ; the *God of glory* appeared unto our father *Abraham,* when he was in *Mesopotamia,* before he dwelt in *Charran.*

^c Ps. cxix. 68. *Thou art good, and doest good :* teach me thy statutes.

^d 1 Tim. vi. 15. Which in his times he shall shew, *who is the blessed* and only Potentate, the King of kings, and Lord of lords. Rom. ix. 5. Whose are the fathers, and of whom, as concerning the flesh, Christ came, who is *over all, God blessed for ever.* Amen.

^e Acts xvii. 24. God, that made the world, and all things therein, seeing that he is Lord of heaven and earth, dwelleth not in temples made with hands ; Ver. 25. Neither is worshipped with men's hands, *as though he needed any thing,* seeing he giveth to all life, and breath, and all things.

^f Job xxii. 2. *Can a man be profitable unto God,* as he that is wise may be profitable unto himself? Ver. 3. Is it any pleasure to the Almighty, that thou art righteous? or *is it gain to him,* that thou makest thy ways perfect?

^g Rom. xi. 36. For *of him, and through him, and to him, are all things:* to whom be glory for ever. *Amen.*

^h Rev. iv. 11. Thou art worthy, O Lord, to receive glory, and honour, and power : for *thou hast created all things, and for thy pleasure they are and were created.* 1 Tim. vi. 15. [See letter ^d immediately foregoing.] Dan. iv. 25. That they shall drive thee from men, and thy dwelling shall be with the beasts of the field, and they shall make thee to eat grass as oxen, and they shall wet thee with the dew of heaven, and seven times shall pass over thee, till thou know that *the Most High ruleth in the kingdom of men, and giveth it to whomsoever he will.* Ver. 35. And all the inhabitants of the earth are reputed as nothing : and *he doeth according to his will in the army of heaven, and among the inhabitants of the earth ; and none can stay his hand, or say unto him, What doest thou?*

ⁱ Heb. iv. 13. Neither is there any creature that is not manifest in his sight : but *all things are naked and opened unto the eyes of him with whom we have to do.*

^k Rom. xi. 33. O *the depth of the riches both of the wisdom and knowledge of God !* how unsearchable are his judgments, and his ways past finding out ! Ver. 34. For *who hath known the mind of the* Lord? or *who hath been his counsellor?* Ps. cxlvii. 5. Great is our Lord, and of great power : *his understanding is infinite.*

^l Acts xv. 18. *Known unto God are all his works* from the beginning of the world. Ezek. xi. 5. And the Spirit of the Lord fell upon me, and said unto me, Speak ; Thus saith the Lord, Thus have ye said, O house of *Israel* : for *I know the things that come into your mind,* every one *of them.*

^m Ps. cxlv. 17. The *Lord is righteous in all his ways, and holy in all his works.* Rom. vii. 12. Wherefore *the law is holy, and the commandment holy, and just, and good.*

ⁿ Rev. v. 12. Saying with a loud voice, *Worthy is the Lamb* that was slain *to receive power, and riches, and wisdom, and strength, and honour, and glory,* and blessing. Ver. 13. And every creature which is in heaven, and on the earth, and under the earth, and such as are in the sea, and all that are in them, heard I saying, *Blessing, and honour, and glory, and power, be unto* him that sitteth upon the throne, and unto the Lamb, for ever and ever. Ver. 14. And the four beasts said, *Amen.* And the four and twenty elders *fell down and worshipped him* that liveth for ever and ever.

III. ^o 1 John v. 7. For *there are three that bear record in* heaven, the Father, the Word, and the Holy Ghost : and *these three are one.* Matt. iii. 16. And Jesus, when he

ceeding; the Son is eternally begotten of the Father;p the Holy Ghost eternally proceeding from the Father and the Son.q

CHAP. III.—*Of God's Eternal Decree.*

I. GOD from all eternity did, by the most wise and holy counsel of his own will, freely and unchangeably ordain whatsoever comes to pass:a yet so, as thereby neither is God the author of sin,b nor is violence offered to the will of the creatures, nor is the liberty or contingency of second causes taken away, but rather established.c

II. Although God knows whatsoever may or can come to pass upon all supposed conditions;d yet hath he not decreed any thing because he foresaw it as future, or as that which would come to pass upon such conditions.e

was baptized, went up straightway out of the water: and, lo, the heavens were opened unto him, and he saw the Spirit of God descending like a dove, and lighting upon him: Ver. 17. And lo a voice from heaven, saying, *This is my beloved Son,* in whom I am well pleased. Matt. xxviii. 19. Go ye therefore, and teach all nations, baptizing them *in the name of the Father, and of the Son, and of the Holy Ghost.* 2 Cor. xiii. 14. *The grace of the Lord Jesus Christ,* and *the love of God,* and *the communion of the Holy Ghost,* be with you all. *Amen.*
p John i. 14. And the Word was made flesh, and dwelt among us, (and we beheld his glory, the glory as of *the only begotten of the Father,*) full of grace and truth. Ver. 18. No man hath seen God at any time; the *only begotten Son,* which is in the bosom of the Father, he hath declared him.
q John xv. 26. But when the Comforter is come, whom I will send unto you from the Father, even *the Spirit of truth, which proceedeth from the Father,* he shall testify of me. Gal. iv. 6. And because ye are sons, God hath sent forth the *Spirit of his Son* into your hearts, crying, *Abba, Father.*
I. a Eph. i. 11. In whom also we have obtained an inheritance, being predestinated according to the *purpose* of him who *worketh all things after the counsel of his own will.* Rom. xi. 33. O the *depth of the riches both of the wisdom and knowledge* of God! how unsearchable are his judgments, and his ways past finding out! Heb. vi. 17 Wherein God, willing more abundantly to shew unto the heirs of promise the *immutability of his counsel,* confirmed it by an oath. Rom. ix. 15. For he saith to *Moses,* I will have mercy *on whom I will* have mercy, and I will have compassion *on whom I will have* compassion. Ver. 18. Therefore hath he mercy *on whom he will have mercy,* and *whom he will* he hardeneth.
b James i. 13. Let no man say, when he is tempted, *I am tempted of God:* for God cannot be tempted with evil, *neither tempteth he any man.* Ver. 17. *Every good gift* and every *perfect gift is from above,* and cometh down from the Father of lights, with whom is no variableness, neither shadow of turning. 1 John i. 5. This then is the message which we have heard of him, and declare unto you, that God is light, and *in him is no darkness at all.*
c Acts ii. 23. Him, being delivered by *the determinate counsel and foreknowledge of God, ye have taken, and by wicked hands have* crucified and slain. Matt. xvii. 12. But I say unto you, That *Elias is* come already, and they knew him not, but have done *unto him whatsoever they listed:* likewise shall also the Son of man suffer of them. Acts iv. 27. For of a truth, against thy holy child Jesus, whom thou hast anointed, both *Herod* and *Pontius Pilate,* with the Gentiles, and the people of *Israel,* were gathered together, Ver. 28. For to do whatsoever thy *hand* and thy *counsel determined* before to be done. John xix. 11. Jesus answered, Thou couldest have no power at all against me, except it *were given thee from above:* therefore he that delivered me unto thee hath the greater sin. Prov. xvi. 33. The lot is cast into the lap; but the *whole disposing thereof is of the Lord.*
II. d Acts xv. 18. *Known* unto God are *all his works* from the beginning of the world. 1 Sam. xxiii. 11. *Will the men of* Keilah deliver me up into his hand? *will* Saul *come down,* as thy servant hath heard? O Lord God of *Israel,* I beseech thee, tell thy servant. *And the Lord said, He will come down.* Ver. 12. Then said *David, Will* the men of Keilah deliver me and my men into the hand of *Saul?* And the Lord said, *They will* deliver thee up. Matt. xi. 21. Woe unto thee, *Chorazin!* woe unto thee, *Bethsaida!* for if the mighty works, which were done in you, had been done in *Tyre and Sidon, they would have repented long ago* in sackcloth and ashes. Ver. 23. And thou, *Capernaum,* which art exalted unto heaven, shalt be brought down to hell: for if the mighty works, which have been done in thee, had been done in *Sodom,* it would have remained until this day.
e Rom. ix. 11. For *the children being not yet born, neither having done any good or evil,* that the purpose of God according to election might stand, not of works, but of him that calleth. Ver. 13. As it is written, *Jacob have I loved,* but *Esau have I hated.* Ver. 16. So then it is not of him that willeth, nor of him that runneth, *but of God that sheweth mercy.* Ver. 18. Therefore hath he

III. By the decree of God, for the manifestation of his glory, some men and angels[f] are predestinated unto everlasting life, and others foreordained to everlasting death.[g]

IV. These angels and men, thus predestinated and foreordained, are particularly and unchangeably designed; and their number is so certain and definite, that it cannot be either increased or diminished.[h]

V. Those of mankind that are predestinated unto life, God, before the foundation of the world was laid, according to his eternal and immutable purpose, and the secret counsel and good pleasure of his will, hath chosen in Christ unto everlasting glory,[i] out of his mere free grace and love, without any foresight of faith or good works, or perseverance in either of them, or any other thing in the creature, as conditions, or causes moving him thereunto;[k] and all to the praise of his glorious grace.[l]

VI. As God hath appointed the elect unto glory, so hath he, by the eternal and most free purpose of his will, foreordained all the means thereunto.[m] Wherefore they who are elected being fallen in Adam, are redeemed by Christ;[n] are effectually called unto faith in Christ

---

mercy *on whom he* will have mercy, and *whom he will* he hardeneth.
III. f 1 Tim. v. 21. I charge thee before God, and the Lord Jesus Christ, and the *elect angels*, that thou observe these things, without preferring one before another, doing nothing by partiality. Matt. xxv. 41. Then shall he say also unto them on the left hand, Depart from me, ye cursed, into everlasting fire, prepared for *the devil and his angels*.
g Rom. ix. 22. What if God, willing to shew his wrath, and to make his power known, endured with much long-suffering the *vessels of wrath fitted to destruction;* Ver. 23. And that he might make known the riches of his glory on the *vessels of mercy*, which he had *afore prepared unto glory*. Eph. i. 5. Having *predestinated* us unto the *adoption of children* by Jesus Christ to himself, according to the good pleasure of his will, Ver. 6. To the praise of the glory of his grace, wherein he hath made *us accepted* in the Beloved. Prov. xvi. 4. The Lord hath made all things for himself; yea, even the *wicked for the day of evil*.
IV. h 2 Tim. ii. 19. Nevertheless the foundation of God standeth sure, having this seal, The Lord *knoweth them that are his*. And, Let every one that nameth the name of Christ depart from iniquity. John xiii. 18. I speak not of you all; *I know whom I have chosen :* but, that the scripture may be fulfilled, He that eateth bread with me hath lifted up his heel against me.
V. i Eph. i. 4. According as he hath *chosen us* in him *before the foundation of the world*, that we should be holy, and without blame before him in love : Ver. 9. Having made known unto us the mystery of his will, according to *his good pleasure*, which he *hath purposed* in himself: Ver. 11. In whom also we have obtained an inheritance, being *predestinated according to the purpose* of him who worketh all things after the counsel of his own will. Rom. viii. 30. Moreover, whom he did *predestinate*, them he also called ; and whom he called, them he also justified ; and whom he justified, them he also glorified. 2 Tim. i. 9. Who hath saved us, and called us with an holy calling, not according to our works, but *according to his own purpose and grace*, which was given us in Christ Jesus *before the world began*. 1 Thess. v. 9. For God hath not *appointed* us to wrath, but to obtain *salvation* by our Lord Jesus Christ.
k Rom. ix. 11, 13, 16. [See letter e immediately foregoing.] Eph. i. 4, 9. [See letter i immediately foregoing.]
l Eph. i. 6. To *the praise of the glory of his grace*, wherein he hath made us accepted in the Beloved : Ver. 12. That we should be to *the praise of his glory*, who first trusted in Christ.
VI. m 1 Pet. i. 2. *Elect* according to the foreknowledge of God the Father, *through sanctification* of the Spirit, unto *obedience* and *sprinkling* of the blood of Jesus Christ. Eph. i. 4. According as he hath chosen us in him before the foundation of the world, that we should *be holy and without blame* before him in love : Ver. 5. Having *predestinated us* unto the *adoption of children* by Jesus Christ to himself, according to the good pleasure of his will. Eph. ii. 10. For we are his workmanship, *created* in Christ Jesus *unto good works*, which God hath *before ordained* that we *should walk in them*. 2 Thess. ii. 13. But we are bound to give thanks alway to God for you, brethren beloved of the Lord, because God hath from the beginning *chosen you to salvation through sanctification of the Spirit, and belief of the truth*.
n 1 Thess. v. 9. For God hath not appointed us to wrath, but to obtain *salvation by our Lord Jesus Christ*, Ver. 10. Who died for us, that, whether we wake or sleep, we should *live together with him*. Tit. ii. 14. Who gave himself for us, that he might *redeem us from all iniquity*, and purify unto himself a peculiar people, zealous of good works.

by his Spirit working in due season; are justified, adopted, sanctified,[c] and kept by his power through faith unto salvation.[p] Neither are any other redeemed by Christ, effectually called, justified, adopted, sanctified, and saved, but the elect only.[q]

VII. The rest of mankind, God was pleased, according to the unsearchable counsel of his own will, whereby he extendeth or withholdeth mercy as he pleaseth, for the glory of his sovereign power over his creatures, to pass by, and to ordain them to dishonour and wrath for their sin, to the praise of his glorious justice.[r]

VIII. The doctrine of this high mystery of predestination is to be handled with special prudence and care,[s] that men attending the will of God revealed in his word, and yielding obedience thereunto, may, from the certainty of their effectual vocation, be assured of their eternal election.[t] So shall this doctrine afford matter of praise, reverence, and admiration of God,[u] and of humility, diligence, and abundant consolation, to all that sincerely obey the Gospel.[w]

[o] Rom. viii. 30. Moreover, whom he did *predestinate*, them he also *called;* and whom he *called*, them he also *justified;* and whom he *justified*, them he also *glorified*. Eph. i. 5. Having predestinated us unto the *adoption of children by Jesus Christ* to himself, according to the good pleasure of his will. 2 Thess. ii. 13. But we are bound to give thanks alway to God for you, brethren beloved of the Lord, because God hath from the beginning chosen you to salvation *through sanctification of the Spirit*, and belief of the truth.

[p] 1 Pet. i. 5. Who are *kept by the power of God through faith unto salvation*, ready to be revealed in the last time.

[q] John xvii. 9. *I pray for them:* I pray not *for the world*, but for *them which thou hast given* me; for they are thine. Rom. viii. 28. And we know that all things work together for good to them that love God, to them who are the *called according to his purpose*, etc. [to the end of the chapter.] John vi. 64. But there are some of you that believe not. For Jesus *knew from the beginning who they were that believed not*, and who should betray him. Ver. 65. And he said, Therefore said I unto you, that *no man can come unto me, except it were given unto him of my Father*. John x. 26. But ye believe not ; *because ye are not of my sheep*, as I said unto you. John viii. 47. He that is of God heareth God's words: ye therefore *hear them not, because ye are not of God*. 1 John ii. 19. They went out from us, but they *were not of us;* for if they had been of us, they would no doubt have continued with us: but they went out, that they might be made *manifest that they were not all of us*.

VII. [r] Matt. xi. 25. At that time Jesus answered and said, I thank thee, O Father, Lord of heaven and earth, because thou hast *hid these things from the wise and prudent*, and hast *revealed them unto babes*. Ver. 26. Even so, Father: for so it seemed good in thy sight. Rom. ix. 17. For the scripture saith unto *Pharaoh*, Even for this same purpose have I raised thee up, that I might shew my power in thee, and that *my name might be declared throughout all the earth*. Ver. 18. Therefore hath he mercy on *whom he will* have mercy, and *whom he will* he hardeneth. Ver. 21. Hath not the *potter* power over the clay, of the same lump to make one vessel unto honour and another unto dishonour? Ver. 22. What if God, willing to *shew his wrath*, and to *make his power* known, *endured* with much longsuffering *the vessels of wrath fitted* to destruction? 2 Tim. ii. 19. Nevertheless the foundation of God standeth sure, having this seal, The Lord knoweth them that are his. And, Let every one that nameth the name of Christ depart from iniquity. Ver. 20. But in a great house there are not only vessels of gold and of silver, but also of wood and of earth; and *some to honour and some to dishonour*. Jude, ver. 4. For there are certain men crept in unawares, who were before *of old ordained to this condemnation*, *ungodly men*, turning the grace of our God into lasciviousness, and denying the only Lord God, and our Lord Jesus Christ. 1 Pet. ii. 8. And a stone of stumbling, and a rock of offence, even to them which stumble at the word, being disobedient; whereunto also they *were appointed*.

VIII. [s] Rom. ix. 20. Nay but, O man, who art thou that repliest against God? Shall the thing *formed say to him that formed it, Why hast thou made me thus?* Rom. xi. 33. O *the depth* of the riches both of the wisdom and knowledge of God! how *unsearchable* are his judgments, and his ways *past finding out!* Deut. xxix. 29. The *secret things belong unto the Lord* our God; but those things which are *revealed belong unto us* and to our children for ever, that we may do all the words of this law.

[t] 2 Pet. i. 10. Wherefore the rather, brethren, give diligence to *make* your calling *and election sure:* for if ye do these things, ye shall never fall.

[u] Eph. i. 6. To the *praise of the glory of his grace*, wherein he hath made us accepted in the Beloved. Rom. xi. 33. [See letter s immediately foregoing.]

[w] Rom. xi. 5. Even so then at this present time also there is a *remnant* according

CHAP. IV.—*Of Creation.*

I. IT pleased God the Father, Son, and Holy Ghost,[a] for the manifestation of the glory of his eternal power, wisdom, and goodness,[b] in the beginning, to create, or make of nothing, the world, and all things therein, whether visible or invisible, in the space of six days, and all very good.[c]

II. After God had made all other creatures, he created man, male and female,[d] with reasonable and immortal souls,[e] endued with knowledge, righteousness, and true holiness, after his own image,[f] having the law of God written in their hearts,[g] and power to fulfil it;[h] and yet under a possibility of transgressing, being left to the liberty of their own will, which was subject unto change.[i] Beside this law written

to the *election of grace.* Ver. 6. And if *by grace, then is it no more of works;* otherwise grace is no more grace. But if it be of works, then is it no more grace; otherwise work is no more work. Ver. 20. Well; because of unbelief they were broken off, and thou standest by faith. *Be not highminded, but fear.* 2 Pet. i. 10. [See letter t immediately foregoing.] Rom. viii. 33. Who shall lay any thing to the *charge of God's elect?* It is God that justifieth. Luke x. 20. Notwithstanding, in this rejoice not, that the spirits are subject unto you; but rather rejoice, *because your names are written in heaven.*

I. a Heb. i. 2. Hath in these last days spoken unto us *by his Son,* whom he hath appointed heir of all things, by *whom* also *he made the worlds.* John i. 2. The same was in the *beginning with God.* Ver. 3. All things were *made by him;* and *without him was not any thing made that was made.* Gen. i. 2. And the earth was without form, and void ; and darkness was upon the face of the deep : and *the Spirit of God moved upon the face of the waters.* Job xxvi. 13. By *his Spirit* he has garnished the heavens ; his hand hath formed the crooked serpent. Job xxxiii. 4. The *Spirit of God* hath made me, and the breath of the Almighty hath given me life.

b Rom. i. 20. For the *invisible things* of him from the creation of the world are *clearly seen, being understood by the things that are made, even his eternal power* and Godhead ; so that they are without excuse. Jer. x. 12. He hath made the earth *by his power,* he hath established the world by his *wisdom,* and hath stretched out the heavens by his *discretion.* Ps. civ. 24. O Lord, how manifold are thy works ! *in wisdom hast thou made them all :* the earth is full of thy riches. Ps. xxxiii. 5. He loveth righteousness and judgment: the earth is full of *the goodness of the Lord.* Ver. 6. By the *word of* the Lord were the heavens made ; and all the host of them by the *breath* of his mouth.

c [The whole first Chapter of Gen.] Heb. xi. 3. Through faith we understand that *the worlds were framed by the word of God;* so that things which are seen were not made of things which do appear. Col. i.

16. For by *him were all things created* that are in heaven, and that are in earth, *visible and invisible,* whether they be thrones, or dominions, or principalities, or powers ; all things were *created* by him, and for him. Acts xvii. 24. God, that *made the world, and all things therein,* seeing that he is Lord of heaven and earth, dwelleth not in temples made with hands.

II. d Gen. i. 27. So God created man in his own image : in the image of *God created he him; male and female created he them.*

e Gen. ii. 7. And the Lord God formed man of the dust of the ground, and *breathed into his nostrils* the *breath of life; and* man became *a living soul.* With Eccl. xii. 7. Then shall the dust return to the earth as it was ; and *the spirit shall return unto God who gave it.* And Luke xxiii. 43. And Jesus said unto him, Verily I say unto thee, *To-day shalt thou be with me in paradise.* And Matt. x. 28. And fear not them which kill the body, but are *not able to kill the soul :* but rather fear him which is able to destroy both soul and body in hell.

f Gen. i. 26. And God said, Let us make *man in our image, after our likeness ;* and let them have dominion over the fish of the sea, and over the fowl of the air, and over the cattle, and over all the earth, and over every creeping thing that creepeth upon the earth. Col. iii. 10. And have put on the new man, which is renewed *in knowledge after the image of him that created him.* Eph. iv. 24. And that ye put on the new man, which after God is created in *righteousness and true holiness.*

g Rom. ii. 14. For when the Gentiles, which have not the law, do by nature the things contained in the law, these, having not the law, *are a law unto themselves :* Ver. 15. Which shew the work of the *law written in their hearts,* their conscience also bearing witness, and their thoughts the mean while accusing or else excusing one another.

h Eccl. vii. 29. Lo, this only have I found, *that God hath made man upright;* but they have sought out many inventions.

i Gen. iii. 6. And when the woman saw that the tree was good for food, and that it was pleasant to the eyes, and a tree to be desired to make one wise, *she took of the*

in their hearts, they received a command not to eat of the tree of the knowledge of good and evil;[k] which while they kept, they were happy in their communion with God, and had dominion over the creatures.[l]

CHAP. V.—*Of Providence.*

I. GOD, the great Creator of all things, doth uphold,[a] direct, dispose, and govern all creatures, actions, and things,[b] from the greatest even to the least,[c] by his most wise and holy providence,[d] according to his infallible foreknowledge,[e] and the free and immutable counsel of his own will,[f] to the praise of the glory of his wisdom, power, justice, goodness, and mercy.[g]

fruit thereof, and did eat; and gave also unto her husband with her, and he did eat. Eccl. vii. 29. [See letter h immediately foregoing.]

[k] Gen. ii. 17. But of the *tree of the knowledge of good and* evil, *thou shalt not eat of it:* for in the day that thou eatest thereof *thou shalt surely die.* Gen. iii. 8. And they heard the voice of the Lord God walking in the garden in the cool of the day: and *Adam* and his wife *hid themselves from the presence of the Lord God* amongst the trees of the garden. Ver. 9. And the Lord God called unto *Adam,* and said unto him, *Where art thou?* Ver. 10. And he said, I heard thy voice in the garden, and I was afraid, because I was naked; *and I hid myself.* Ver. 11. And he said, Who told thee that thou wast naked? Hast thou *eaten of the tree,* whereof I commanded thee that thou shouldest not eat? Ver. 23. Therefore the *Lord God sent him forth* from the garden *of Eden,* to till the ground from whence he was taken.

[l] Gen. i. 26. And God said, Let us make man in our image, after our likeness; and let them have *dominion over the fish of the sea, and over the fowl of the air, and over the cattle, and over all the earth,* and over *every creeping thing that creepeth upon the earth.* Ver. 28. And God blessed them: and God said unto them, Be fruitful, and multiply, and replenish the earth, and subdue it; and have *dominion* over the fish of the sea, and over the fowl of the air, and over every living thing that moveth upon the earth.

I. [a] Heb. i. 3. Who, being the brightness of his glory, and the express image of his person, and *upholding all things* by the word of his power, when he had by himself purged our sins, sat down on the right hand of the Majesty on high.

[b] Dan. iv. 34. And at the *end of the days* I *Nebuchadnezzar* lifted up mine eyes unto heaven, and mine understanding returned unto me, and I blessed the Most High, and I praised and honoured him that liveth for ever, whose dominion is an everlasting dominion, and his kingdom is from generation to generation. Ver. 35. And all the inhabitants of the earth are reputed as nothing: and *he doeth according to his will* in the army of heaven, and among the inhabitants of the earth; and *none can stay his hand,* or say unto him, What doest thou? Ps. cxxxv. 6. *Whatsoever the Lord pleased, that did he* in heaven, and in earth, in the seas, and all deep places. Acts xvii. 25. Neither is worshipped with men's hands, as though he needed any thing, seeing he *giveth to all life, and breath, and all things;* Ver. 26. And hath made of one blood all nations of men for to dwell on all the face of the earth, and hath *determined* the times *before appointed,* and *the bounds of their habitation:* Ver. 28. For *in him we live, and move, and have our being;* as certain also of your own poets have said, For we are also his offspring. Job, Chapters xxxviii., xxxix., xl., xli.

[c] Matt. x. 29. Are not *two sparrows* sold for a farthing? and *one* of them *shall not fall on the ground without your Father.* Ver. 30. But the *very hairs of your head are all numbered.* Ver. 31. Fear ye not therefore, ye are of more value than *many sparrows.*

[d] Prov. xv. 3. The *eyes of the Lord* are in every place, beholding the evil and the good. Ps. civ. 24. O Lord, how manifold are thy works! *in wisdom hast thou made them all:* the earth is full of thy riches. Ps. cxlv. 17. The Lord is *righteous* in all his ways, and *holy* in all his works.

[e] Acts xv. 18. *Known unto God are all his works* from the beginning of the world. Ps. xciv. 8. Understand, ye brutish among the people: and ye fools, when will ye be wise? Ver. 9. He that *planted the ear,* shall he not hear? he that formed the eye, shall he not see? Ver. 10. He that chastiseth the heathen, shall not he correct? he that *teacheth man knowledge, shall not he know?* Ver. 11. The Lord *knoweth the thoughts of man,* that they are vanity.

[f] Eph. i. 11. In whom also we have obtained an inheritance, being predestinated according to the *purpose of him who worketh all things after the counsel of his own will.* Ps. xxxiii. 10. The Lord *bringeth the counsel of the heathen to nought:* he maketh the devices of the people of none effect. Ver. 11. The *counsel of the Lord standeth for ever, the thoughts of his heart to all generations.*

[g] Isa. lxiii. 14. As a beast goeth down into the valley, the Spirit of the Lord caused

CHAP. V.   THE CONFESSION OF FAITH.

II. Although, in relation to the foreknowledge and decree of God, the first cause, all things come to pass immutably and infallibly;[h] yet, by the same providence, he ordereth them to fall out according to the nature of second causes, either necessarily, freely, or contingently.[i]

III. God in his ordinary providence maketh use of means,[k] yet is free to work without,[l] above,[m] and against them,[n] at his pleasure.

IV. The almighty power, unsearchable wisdom, and infinite goodness of God, so far manifest themselves in his providence, that it extendeth itself even to the first fall, and all other sins of angels and men,[o]

---

him to rest ; so didst thou lead thy people, to make thyself a glorious name. Eph. iii. 10. To the intent that now, unto the principalities and powers in heavenly places, might be known by the church the manifold wisdom of God. Rom. ix. 17. For the Scripture saith unto Pharaoh, Even for this same purpose have I raised thee up, that I might shew my power in thee, and that my name might be declared throughout all the earth. Gen. xlv. 7. And God sent me before you to preserve you a posterity in the earth, and to save your lives by a great deliverance. Ps. cxlv. 7. They shall abundantly utter the memory of thy great goodness, and shall sing of thy righteousness.

II. h Acts ii. 23. Him, being delivered by the determinate counsel and foreknowledge of God, ye have taken, and by wicked hands have crucified and slain.

i Gen. viii. 22. While the earth remaineth, seed time and harvest, and cold and heat, and summer and winter, and day and night, shall not cease. Jer. xxxi. 35. Thus saith the Lord, which giveth the sun for a light by day, and the ordinances of the moon and of the stars for a light by night, which divideth the sea when the waves thereof roar ; The Lord of hosts is his name. Exod. xxi. 13. And if a man lie not in wait, but God deliver him into his hand ; then I will appoint thee a place whither he shall flee. With Deut. xix. 5. As when a man goeth into the wood with his neighbour to hew wood, and his hand fetcheth a stroke with the axe to cut down the tree, and the head slippeth from the helve, and lighteth upon his neighbour, that he die; he shall flee unto one of those cities, and live. 1 Kings xxii. 28. And Micaiah said, If thou return at all in peace, the Lord hath not spoken by me. And he said, Hearken, O people, every one of you. Ver. 34. And a certain man drew a bow at a venture, and smote the king of Israel between the joints of the harness : wherefore he said unto the driver of his chariot, Turn thine hand, and carry me out of the host ; for I am wounded. Isa. x. 6. I will send him against an hypocritical nation, and against the people of my wrath will I give him a charge, to take the spoil, and to take the prey, and to tread them down like the mire of the streets. Ver. 7. Howbeit he meaneth not so, neither doth his heart think so ; but it is in his heart to destroy and cut off nations not a few.

III. k Acts xxvii. 31. Paul said to the centurion and to the soldiers, Except these abide in the ship, ye cannot be saved. Ver. 44. And the rest, some on boards, and some on broken pieces of the ship. And so it came to pass that they escaped all safe to land. Isa. lv. 10. For as the rain cometh down, and the snow from heaven, and returneth not thither, but watereth the earth, and maketh it bring forth and bud, that it may give seed to the sower, and bread to the eater ; Ver. 11. So shall my word be that goeth forth out of my mouth : it shall not return unto me void ; but it shall accomplish that which I please, and it shall prosper in the thing whereto I sent it. Hos. ii. 21. And it shall come to pass in that day, I will hear, saith the Lord : I will hear the heavens, and they shall hear the earth ; Ver. 22. And the earth shall hear the corn, and the wine, and the oil ; and they shall hear Jezreel.

l Hos. i. 7. But I will have mercy upon the house of Judah, and will save them by the Lord their God, and will not save them by bow, nor by sword, nor by battle, by horses, nor by horsemen. Matt. iv. 4. But he answered and said, It is written, Man shall not live by bread alone, but by every word that proceedeth out of the mouth of God. Job xxxiv. 10. Therefore hearken unto me, ye men of understanding : Far be it from God, that he should do wickedness ; and from the Almighty, that he should commit iniquity.

m Rom. iv. 19. And being not weak in faith, he considered not his own body now dead, when he was about an hundred years old, neither yet the deadness of Sarah's womb : Ver. 20. He staggered not at the promise of God through unbelief ; but was strong in faith, giving glory to God ; Ver. 21. And being fully persuaded, that what he had promised, he was able also to perform.

n 2 Kings vi. 6. And the man of God said, Where fell it ? And he shewed him the place. And he cut down a stick, and cast it in thither ; and the iron did swim. Dan. iii. 27. And the princes, governors, and captains, and the king's counsellors, being gathered together, saw these men, upon whose bodies the fire had no power, nor was an hair of their head singed, neither were their coats changed, nor the smell of fire had passed on them.

IV. o Rom. xi. 32. For God hath concluded them all in unbelief, that he might have mercy upon all. Ver. 33. O the depth of the riches both of the wisdom and knowledge of God ! how unsearchable are his judgments, and his ways past finding out ! Ver. 34. For who hath known the mind of the Lord ? or who hath been his counsellor ?

and that not by a bare permission,P but such as hath joined with it a most wise and powerful bounding,q and otherwise ordering and governing of them, in a manifold dispensation, to his own holy ends;r yet so as the sinfulness thereof proceedeth only from the creature, and not from God; who, being most holy and righteous, neither is nor can be the author or approver of sin.s

V. The most wise, righteous, and gracious God, doth oftentimes leave for a season his own children to manifold temptations, and the corruption of their own hearts, to chastise them for their former sins, or to discover unto them the hidden strength of corruption, and deceitfulness of their hearts, that they may be humbled;t and to raise them to a more close and constant dependence for their support upon

---

2 Sam. xxiv. 1. And again the anger of the Lord was kindled against Israel, and *he moved David against them to say*, Go, *number Israel and Judah*. With 1 Chron. xxi. 1. And Satan stood up against Israel, and *provoked David* to number Israel. 1 Kings xxii. 22. And the Lord said unto him, Wherewith? And he said, I will go forth, and I will be a lying spirit in the mouth of all his prophets. And he said, *Thou shalt persuade him*, and *prevail* also: go forth, and do so. Ver. 23. Now, therefore, behold, *the Lord hath put a lying spirit in the mouth of all these thy prophets*, and *the Lord hath spoken evil* concerning thee. 1 Chron. x. 4. Then said *Saul* to his armour-bearer, Draw thy sword, and thrust me through therewith, lest these uncircumcised come and abuse me. But his armour-bearer would not; for he was sore afraid. So *Saul* took a sword, and fell upon it. Ver. 13. So *Saul* died for his transgression which he committed against the Lord, even against the word of the Lord, which he kept not, and also for asking counsel of one that had a familiar spirit, to enquire of it; Ver. 14. And enquired not of the Lord: *therefore he slew him, and turned the kingdom unto David the son of Jesse*. 2 Sam. xvi. 10. And the king said, What have I to do with you, ye sons of *Zeruiah?* so let him curse, because *the Lord hath said unto him, Curse David*. Who shall then say, Wherefore hast thou done so? Acts ii. 23. Him, being delivered by *the determinate counsel and foreknowledge of God*, ye have taken, and by wicked hands have crucified and slain. Acts iv. 27. For of a truth against thy holy child Jesus, whom thou hast anointed, both Herod and Pontius Pilate, with the Gentiles, and the people of Israel, were gathered together, Ver. 28. For to do whatsoever thy hand and *thy counsel determined before* to be done.

p Acts xiv. 16. Who in times past *suffered* all nations to *walk in their own ways*.

q Ps. lxxvi. 10. Surely the wrath of man shall praise thee; the *remainder of wrath shalt thou restrain*. 2 Kings xix. 28. Because thy rage against me and thy tumult is come up into mine ears, therefore I will put *my hook in thy nose, and my bridle in thy lips*, and I will turn thee back by the way by which thou camest.

r Gen. l. 20. But as for you, *ye thought evil against me; but God meant it unto good*, to bring to pass, as it is this day, to save much people alive. Isa. x. 6. *I will send him* against an hypocritical nation, and against the people of my wrath *will I give* him a charge, to take the spoil, and to take the prey, and to tread them down like the mire of the streets. Ver. 7. Howbeit *he meaneth not so, neither doth his heart think so;* but it is in his heart to destroy and cut off nations not a few. Ver. 12. Wherefore it shall come to pass, that, when the Lord hath performed his whole work upon mount Zion and on Jerusalem, *I will punish the fruit of the stout heart* of the king of Assyria, and the glory of his high looks.

s James i. 13. Let no man say, when he is tempted, I am tempted of God: for God cannot be tempted with evil, *neither tempteth he any man:* Ver. 14. But every man is tempted, when he is drawn away of his *own lust,* and enticed. Ver. 17. *Every good gift and every perfect gift is from above*, and cometh down from the Father of lights, with whom is no variableness, neither shadow of turning. 1 John ii. 16. For all that is in the world, the lust of the flesh, and the lust of the eyes, and the pride of life, is *not of the Father*, but is of the world. Ps. l. 21. These things *hast thou done*, and I kept silence; thou thoughtest that I was altogether such an one as thyself: but *I will reprove thee, and set them in order before thine eyes*.

V. t 2 Chron. xxxii. 25. But *Hezekiah* rendered not again according to the benefit done unto him; for his heart was lifted up: therefore there was wrath upon him, and upon *Judah and Jerusalem*. Ver. 26. Notwithstanding *Hezekiah humbled himself for the pride of his heart*, (both he and the inhabitants of Jerusalem,) so that the wrath of the Lord came not upon them in the days of *Hezekiah*. Ver. 31. Howbeit in the business of the ambassadors of the princes of Babylon, who sent unto him to enquire of the wonder that was done in the land, *God left him, to try him, that he might know all that was in his heart*. 2 Sam. xxiv. 1. And again the anger of the Lord was kindled against Israel, and *he moved David against them to say, Go, number Israel and Judah*

himself, and to make them more watchful against all future occasions of sin, and for sundry other just and holy ends.u

VI. As for those wicked and ungodly men, whom God as a righteous judge, for former sins, doth blind and harden,x from them he not only withholdeth his grace, whereby they might have been enlightened in their understandings, and wrought upon in their hearts;y but sometimes also withdraweth the gifts which they had,z and exposeth them to such objects as their corruption makes occasion of sin;a and withal, gives them over to their own lusts, the temptations of the world, and the power of Satan:b whereby it comes to pass, that they harden themselves, even under those means which God useth for the softening of others.c

---

u 2 Cor. xii. 7. And *lest I should be exalted above measure* through the abundance of the revelations, *there was given to me a thorn in the flesh*, the messenger of Satan to buffet me, *lest I should be exalted above measure*. Ver. 8. For this thing I besought the Lord thrice, that it might depart from me. Ver. 9. And he said unto me, *My grace is sufficient for thee;* for my strength is made perfect in weakness. Most gladly therefore will I rather glory in my infirmities, that the power of Christ may rest upon me. Ps. lxxiii. *throughout*. *Ps. lxxvii. 1. *I cried unto God* with my voice, even unto God with my voice; and he gave ear unto me. Ver. 10. And I said, This is my infirmity: but I will remember the years of the *right hand of the Most High.* Ver. 12. *I will meditate also of all thy work*, and talk of thy doings. [*Read the intermediate verses in the Bible.*] Mark xiv. *from the 66th verse to the end*, with John xxi. 15. So, when they had dined, Jesus saith to *Simon Peter, Simon, son of Jonas,* lovest thou me more than these? He saith unto him, Yea, Lord; thou knowest that I love thee. He saith unto him, *Feed my lambs.* Ver. 16. He saith to him again the second time, *Simon, son of Jonas,* lovest thou me? He saith unto him, Yea, Lord; thou knowest that I love thee. He saith unto him, *Feed my sheep.* Ver. 17. He saith unto him the third time, *Simon, son of Jonas,* lovest thou me? *Peter* was grieved because he said unto him the third time, Lovest thou me? And he said unto him, Lord, thou knowest all things; thou knowest that I love thee. Jesus saith unto him, *Feed my sheep.*

VI. x Rom. i. 24. Wherefore *God also gave them up* to uncleanness, through the lusts of their own hearts, to dishonour their own bodies between themselves. Ver. 26. For this cause *God gave them up* unto vile affections: for even their women did change the natural use into that which is against nature. Ver. 28. And even as they did not like to retain God in their knowledge, *God gave them over* to a reprobate mind, to do those things which are not convenient. Rom. xi. 7. What then? *Israel* hath not obtained that which he seeketh for; but the election hath obtained it, and the rest *were blinded*, Ver. 8. (According as it is written, God *hath given them the spirit of* slumber, eyes that they should not see, and ears that they should not hear) unto this day.

y Deut. xxix. 4. Yet the *Lord hath not given you* an heart to perceive, and eyes to see, and ears to hear, unto this day.

z Matt. xiii. 12. For whosoever hath, to him shall be given, and he shall have more abundance: but whosoever hath not, *from him shall be taken away even that he hath.* Matt. xxv. 29. For unto every one that hath shall be given, and he shall have abundance: but from him that hath not, shall *be taken away even that which he hath.*

a Deut. ii. 30. But Sihon king of Heshbon would not let us pass by him: *for the Lord thy God hardened his spirit*, and made his heart obstinate, that he might deliver him into thy hand, as appeareth this day. 2 Kings viii. 12. And *Hazael* said, Why weepeth my lord? And he answered, Because I know the evil that thou wilt do unto the children of Israel: their strong holds wilt thou set on fire, and their young men wilt thou slay with the sword, and wilt dash their children, and rip up their women with child. Ver. 13. And *Hazael* said, But what! is thy servant a dog, that he should do this great thing? And *Elisha* answered, *The Lord hath shewed me that thou shalt be king over Syria.*

b Ps. lxxxi. 11. But my people would not hearken to my voice; and *Israel* would none of me. Ver. 12. So *I gave them up unto their own hearts' lusts:* and they walked in their own counsels. 2 Thess. ii. 10. And with all deceivableness of unrighteousness in them that perish; because they received not the love of the truth, that they might be saved. Ver. 11. And for this cause God shall send them strong delusion, that they should believe a lie; Ver. 12. That they all might be damned who believed not the truth, but had pleasure in unrighteousness.

c Exod. vii. 3. And *I will harden Pharaoh's heart*, and multiply my signs and my wonders in the land of Egypt. With Exod. viii. 15. But when *Pharaoh* saw that there was respite, *he hardened his heart*, and hearkened not unto them; *as the Lord had said.* Ver. 32. *And Pharaoh hardened his heart* at this time also, neither would he let the people go. 2 Cor. ii. 15. For we are unto God a *sweet savour* of Christ, *in them that are saved*, and *in them that perish*

VII. As the providence of God doth, in general, reach to all creatures; so, after a most special manner, it taketh care of his church, and disposeth all things to the good thereof.d

CHAP. VI.—*Of the Fall of Man, of Sin, and of the Punishment thereof.*

I. OUR first parents being seduced by the subtilty and temptation of Satan, sinned in eating the forbidden fruit.a This their sin God was pleased, according to his wise and holy counsel, to permit, having purposed to order it to his own glory.b

II. By this sin they fell from their original righteousness, and communion with God,c and so became dead in sin,d and wholly defiled in all the faculties and parts of soul and body.e

Ver. 16. To the *one* we are the *savour of death* unto *death; and to the other the savour of life* unto *life:* and who is sufficient for these things? Isa. viii. 14. And he shall be for a *sanctuary;* but for a *stone of stumbling,* and *for a rock of offence,* to both the houses of Israel; *for a gin* and *for a snare to the inhabitants of Jerusalem.* 1 Pet. ii. 7. *Unto you* therefore which believe he is *precious;* but *unto them* which be disobedient, the *stone* which the builders *disallowed,* the same is made the head of the corner, Ver. 8. And a *stone of stumbling,* and a rock of offence, even to them which stumble at the word, being disobedient; *whereunto also they were appointed.* Isa. vi. 9. And he said, Go, and tell this people, *Hear ye indeed, but understand not; and see ye indeed, but perceive not.* Ver. 10. *Make the heart of this people fat,* and make their ears heavy, and shut their eyes; lest they see with their eyes, and hear with their ears, and understand with their heart, and convert, and be healed. With Acts xxviii. 26. Saying, *Go unto this people, and say, Hearing ye shall hear, and shall not understand;* and seeing ye shall see, and not perceive: Ver. 27. For *the heart* of this people is *waxed gross,* and *their ears* are *dull* of hearing, and their eyes have they closed; lest they should see with their eyes, and hear with their ears, and understand with their heart, and should be converted, and I should heal them.
VII. d 1 Tim. iv. 10. For therefore we both labour and suffer reproach, because we trust in the living God, who is the *Saviour of all men, specially of those that believe.* Amos ix. 8. Behold, the eyes of the Lord God are upon the sinful kingdom, and I will destroy it from off the face of the earth; saving that *I will not utterly destroy the house of Jacob,* saith the Lord. Ver. 9. For, lo, I will command, and *I will sift the house of Israel* among all nations, like as corn is sifted in a sieve, *yet shall not the least grain fall upon the earth.* Rom. viii. 28. And we know that *all things work together for good to them that love God,* to them who are the called according to his purpose. Isa. xliii. 3. For I am the Lord thy God, the Holy One of Israel, *thy Saviour:* I gave Egypt *for thy ransom,* Ethiopia and Seba *for thee.* Ver. 4. Since *thou wast precious in my sight,* thou hast been honourable, and I have loved thee: therefore will *I give men for thee, and people for thy life.* Ver. 5. Fear not; for *I am with thee:* I will bring thy seed from the east, and gather thee from the west. Ver. 14. Thus saith the Lord, your Redeemer, the Holy One of Israel, *For your sake* I have sent to *Babylon,* and *have brought down all their nobles, and the Chaldeans,* whose cry is in the ships.
I. a Gen. iii. 13. And the Lord God said unto the woman, What is this that thou hast done? And the woman said, The *serpent beguiled me, and I did eat.* 2 Cor. xi. 3. But I fear, lest by any means, as *the serpent beguiled* Eve *through his subtilty,* so your minds should be corrupted from the simplicity that is in Christ.
b Rom. xi. 32. For *God hath concluded them all in unbelief,* that *he might have mercy* upon all.
II. c Gen. iii. 6. And when the woman saw that the tree was good for food, and that it was pleasant to the eyes, and a tree to be desired to make one wise, she took of the fruit thereof, and did eat; and gave also unto her husband with her, and he did eat. Ver. 7. And the eyes of them both were opened, and they knew that *they were naked;* and they sewed fig-leaves together, and made themselves aprons. Ver. 8. And they heard the voice of the Lord God walking in the garden in the cool of the day: and *Adam and his wife hid themselves from the presence of the Lord God* amongst the trees of the garden. Eccl. vii. 29. Lo, this only have I found, that *God hath made man upright; but they have sought out many inventions.* Rom. iii. 23. *For all have sinned, and come short of the glory of God.*
d Gen. ii. 17. But of the tree of the knowledge of good and evil, thou shalt not eat of it: for in the day that thou eatest thereof *thou shalt surely die.* Eph. ii. 1. And you hath he quickened, who were *dead in trespasses and sins.*
e Tit. i. 15. Unto the pure all things are

III. They being the root of all mankind, the guilt of this sin was imputed,[f] and the same death in sin and corrupted nature conveyed to all their posterity, descending from them by ordinary generation.[g]

IV. From this original corruption, whereby we are utterly indisposed, disabled, and made opposite to all good,[h] and wholly inclined to all evil,[i] do proceed all actual transgressions.[k]

pure: but unto them that are defiled and unbelieving is nothing pure; but even *their mind and conscience is defiled.* Gen. vi. 5. And God saw that the wickedness of man was great in the earth, and that *every imagination of the thoughts of his heart was only evil continually.* Jer. xvii. 9. The *heart is deceitful* above all things, and *desperately wicked;* who can know it? Rom. iii. 10. As it is written, There is *none righteous,* no, not one: Ver. 11. There is *none that understandeth,* there is *none that seeketh after God.* Ver. 12. They are *all gone out of the way,* they are together become *unprofitable;* there is *none that doeth good, no, not one.* Ver. 13. Their *throat is an open sepulchre;* with their *tongues* they have used deceit: the *poison of asps* is under *their lips;* Ver. 14. Whose *mouth is full of cursing and bitterness;* Ver. 15. Their *feet are swift to shed blood;* Ver. 16. *Destruction and misery are in their ways;* Ver. 17. And the *way of peace have they not known;* Ver. 18. *There is no fear of God before their eyes.*

III. f Gen. i. 27. So God created man in his own image: in the image of God created he him; *male and female* created he them. Ver. 28. And God blessed *them;* and God said unto *them,* Be fruitful, and multiply, and replenish the earth, and subdue it; and have dominion over the fish of the sea, and over the fowl of the air, and over every living thing that moveth upon the earth. And Gen. ii. 16. And the Lord God commanded *the man,* saying, Of every tree of the garden thou mayest freely eat; Ver. 17. But of the tree of the knowledge of good and evil, thou shalt not eat of it: for in the day that thou eatest thereof *thou shalt surely die.* And Acts xvii. 26. And hath *made of one blood all nations of men* for to dwell on all the face of the earth, and hath determined the times before appointed, and the bounds of their habitation. With Rom. v. 12. Wherefore, as by *one man sin entered into the world,* and death by sin; and so *death passed upon all men, for that all have sinned.* Ver. 15. But not as the offence, so also is the free gift. For if through the *offence of one many be dead;* much more the grace of God, and the gift by grace, which is by one *man,* Jesus Christ, hath abounded unto many Ver. 16. And not as it was by *one that sinned,* so is the gift: for *the judgment was by one to condemnation,* but the free gift is of many offences unto justification. Ver. 17. For if by *one man's offence death reigned by one;* much more they which receive abundance of grace, and of the gift of righteousness, shall reign in life by one, Jesus Christ. Ver. 18. Therefore, as *by the offence of one judgment came upon all men* to condemnation; even so by the righteousness of one the free gift came upon all men unto justification of life. Ver. 19. For as by *one man's disobedience many were made sinners;* so by the obedience of one shall many be made righteous. And 1 Cor. xv. 21. For since *by man came death,* by man came also the resurrection of the dead. Ver. 22. For as *in Adam all die,* even so in Christ shall all be made alive. *Ver. 45. And so it is written, The first man *Adam was made a living soul,* the last *Adam* was made a quickening spirit. *Ver. 49. And as we have borne the *image* of the earthy, we shall also bear the image of the heavenly.

g Ps. li. 5. Behold, I was *shapen in iniquity;* and *in sin did my mother conceive me.* Gen. v. 3. And *Adam* lived an hundred and thirty years, and *begat a son in his own likeness,* after his *image;* and called his name Seth. Job xiv. 4. *Who can bring a clean thing out of an unclean? not one.* Job xv. 14. What is man, that *he should be clean?* and he which is *born of a woman,* that *he should be righteous?*

IV. h Rom. v. 6. For when we were yet *without strength,* in due time Christ died for the ungodly. Rom. viii. 7. Because the carnal mind is *enmity against God;* for it is not *subject* to the law of God, neither indeed can be. Rom. vii. 18. For I know that in me (that is, *in my flesh*) *dwelleth no good thing;* for to will is present with me; but how to *perform that which is good I find not.* Col. i. 21. And you, that were sometime *alienated, and enemies in your mind* by wicked works, yet now hath he reconciled.

i Gen. vi. 5. And God saw that the wickedness of man was great in the earth, and that every *imagination of the thoughts of his heart was only evil continually.* Gen. viii. 21. And the Lord smelled a sweet savour; and the Lord said in his heart, I will not again curse the ground any more for man's sake; for *the imagination of man's heart is evil from his youth;* neither will I again smite any more every thing living, as I have done. Rom. iii. 10. As it is written, There is *none righteous,* no, not one: Ver. 11. There is none that understandeth, there is *none that seeketh after* God. Ver. 12. They are all *gone out of the way,* they are together become *unprofitable; there is none that doeth good, no, not one.*

k James i. 14. But every man is tempted, when he is *drawn away of his own lust, and enticed.* Ver. 15. Then, when *lust hath conceived,* it bringeth forth sin; and sin, when it is finished, bringeth forth death. Eph. ii. 2. Wherein in time past, ye *walked according to the course of this world,* according to the prince of the power of the air, the spirit that now worketh in the

V. This corruption of nature, during this life, doth remain in those that are regenerated:[1] and although it be through Christ pardoned and mortified, yet both itself, and all the motions thereof, are truly and properly sin.[m]

VI. Every sin, both original and actual, being a transgression of the righteous law of God, and contrary thereunto,[n] doth, in its own nature, bring guilt upon the sinner,[o] whereby he is bound over to the wrath of God,[p] and curse of the law,[q] and so made subject to death,[r] with all miseries spiritual,[s] temporal,[t] and eternal.[u]

CHAP. VII.—*Of God's Covenant with Man.*

I. THE distance between God and the creature is so great, that although reasonable creatures do owe obedience unto him as their Creator, yet they could never have any fruition of him as their blessed-

children of disobedience: Ver. 3. Among whom also we all had our conversation in times past *in the lusts of our flesh, fulfilling the desires of the flesh* and of the mind; and were by nature the children of wrath, even as others. Matt. xv. 19. For *out of the heart proceed evil thoughts, murders, adulteries, fornications, thefts, false witness, blasphemies.*

V. l 1 John i. 8. *If we say that we have no sin, we deceive ourselves,* and the truth is not *in us.* Ver. 10. *If we say that we have not sinned,* we make him a liar, and his word is not *in us.* Rom. vii. 14. For we know that the law is spiritual; but *I am carnal, sold under sin.* Ver. 17. Now then, it is no more I that do it, but *sin that dwelleth in me.* Ver. 18. For I know that in me (that is, in *my flesh*) *dwelleth no good thing:* for to will is present with me; but how *to perform that which is good I find not.* Ver. 23. But I see *another law in my members warring* against the law of my mind, and *bringing me into captivity to the law of sin which is in my members.* James iii. 2. For in many things *we offend all.* If any man offend not in word, the same is a perfect man, and able also to bridle the whole body. Prov. xx. 9. *Who can say, I have made my heart clean, I am pure from my sin?* Eccl. vii. 20. For there is *not a just man* upon earth, that doeth good, and *sinneth not.*

m Rom. vii. 5. For when we were in the flesh, the motions of sins, which were by the law, did work in our members to *bring forth fruit unto death.* Ver. 7. What shall we say then? Is the law sin? God forbid. Nay, I had not known sin but *by the law:* for I had not known lust, *except the law had said,* Thou shalt not covet. Ver. 8. But sin, taking occasion by the *commandment,* wrought in me all manner of concupiscence. For *without the law sin was dead.* Ver. 25. I thank God, through Jesus Christ our Lord. So then with the *mind I myself serve* the law of God, but *with the flesh the law of sin.* Gal. v. 17. For *the flesh lusteth against the Spirit,* and the Spirit against the flesh: and *these are contrary* the one to the other; so that ye cannot do the things that ye would.

VI. n 1 John iii. 4. Whosoever committeth sin transgresseth also the law: for *sin is the transgression of the law.*

o Rom. ii. 15. Which shew the work of the law written in their hearts, *their conscience also bearing witness,* and their thoughts the mean while *accusing* or else *excusing* one another. Rom. iii. 9. What then? are we better than they? No, in no wise: for we have before proved both Jews and Gentiles, that *they are all under sin.* Ver. 19. Now we know, that what things soever the law saith, it saith to them who are under the law; that every mouth may be stopped, and all *the world may become guilty* before God.

p Eph. ii. 3. Among whom also we all had our conversation in times past in the lusts of our flesh, fulfilling the desires of the flesh and of the mind; and were by nature *the children of wrath,* even as others.

q Gal. iii. 10. For as many as are of the works of the law are *under the curse:* for it is written, *Cursed is every one that continueth not in all things* which are written in the book of the law to do them.

r Rom. vi. 23. For the *wages of sin is death;* but the gift of God is eternal life through Jesus Christ our Lord.

s Eph. iv. 18. Having the *understanding darkened,* being *alienated from the life of God* through the ignorance that is in them, because of the blindness of their heart.

t Rom. viii. 20. For the creature was made *subject to vanity,* not willingly, but by reason of him who hath subjected the same in hope. Lam. iii. 39. Wherefore doth a living man complain, a man for the *punishment of his sins?*

u Matt. xxv. 41. Then shall he say also unto them on the left hand, Depart from me, ye cursed, into *everlasting fire,* prepared for the devil and his angels. 2 Thess. i. 9. Who shall be punished with *everlasting destruction* from the presence of the Lord, and from the glory of his power.

ness and reward, but by some voluntary condescension on God's part, which he hath been pleased to express by way of covenant.[a]

II. The first covenant made with man was a covenant of works,[b] wherein life was promised to Adam, and in him to his posterity,[c] upon condition of perfect and personal obedience.[d]

III. Man by his fall having made himself incapable of life by that covenant, the Lord was pleased to make a second,[e] commonly called the Covenant of Grace: whereby he freely offereth unto sinners life and salvation by Jesus Christ, requiring of them faith in him, that they may be saved;[f] and promising to give unto all those that are or-

---

I. [a] Isa. xl. 13. Who hath directed the Spirit of the Lord, or, being his counsellor, hath taught him? Ver. 14. With whom took he counsel, and who instructed him, and taught him in the path of judgment, and taught him knowledge, and shewed to him the way of understanding? Ver. 15. Behold, *the nations are as a drop of a bucket*, and are *counted as the small dust of the balance:* behold, he taketh up the isles as a very little thing. Ver. 16. And *Lebanon is not sufficient to burn*, nor the *beasts* thereof *sufficient for a burnt-offering*. Ver. 17. *All nations before him are as nothing;* and they are counted to him *less than nothing, and vanity*. Job ix. 32. For *he is not a man, as I am*, that I should answer him, and we *should come together* in judgment. Ver. 33. Neither is there any daysman betwixt us, that might lay his hand *upon us both*. 1 Sam. ii. 25. If one man sin against another, the judge shall judge him ; but *if a man sin against the Lord, who shall entreat for him?* Ps. cxiii. 5. Who is like unto the Lord our God, who *dwelleth on high*, Ver. 6. Who *humbleth himself to behold the things that are in heaven*, and in the earth ! Ps. c. 2. Serve the Lord with gladness ; come before his presence with singing. Ver. 3. Know ye that the Lord *he is God;* it is he *that hath made us*, and not we ourselves : we *are his people*, and the sheep of his pasture. Job xxii. 2. Can a man be *profitable unto God*, as he that is wise may be profitable unto himself? Ver. 3. Is it *any pleasure to the Almighty*, that thou art righteous? or is it *gain* to him, that thou makest thy ways perfect? Job xxxv. 7. If thou be righteous, what *givest* thou him? or what *receiveth he of thine hand?* Ver. 8. Thy wickedness may hurt a *man* as thou art, and thy righteousness may profit the *son of man*. Luke xvii. 10. So likewise ye, when ye shall have *done all those things* which are commanded you, say, We are *unprofitable servants:* we have done that which was *our duty to do*. Acts xvii. 24. God, that made the world, and all things therein, seeing that he is Lord of heaven and earth, *dwelleth not in temples made with hands;* Ver 25. Neither is worshipped with men's hands, as though *he needed any thing*, seeing he giveth to all life, and breath, and all things.

II. [b] Gal. iii. 12. And the *law is not of faith :* but, The *man that doeth them shall live in them.*

[c] Rom. x. 5. For Moses describeth the righteousness which is of the law, That the man which *doeth those things shall live by them*. Rom. v. 12 to 20. [*See Chap.* vi. *Sect.* 3. *letter* f.]

[d] Gen. ii. 17. But of the tree of the knowledge of good and evil, thou shalt not eat of it : for in the day that thou eatest thereof *thou shalt surely die*. Gal. iii. 10. For *as many as are of the works of the law* are under the curse: For it is written, Cursed is every one that continueth not in all things which are written in the book of the law to do them.

III. [e] Gal. iii. 21. Is the law then against the promises of God? God forbid : for if there had been a *law given* which could have given *life*, verily righteousness should have *been by the law*. Rom. viii. 3. For what the *law could not do*, in that it was *weak through the flesh, God* sending his own Son in the likeness of sinful flesh, and for sin condemned sin in the flesh. Rom. iii. 20. Therefore by the *deeds of the law* there shall *no flesh be justified* in his sight: for by the law is the knowledge of sin. Ver. 21. But now the *righteousness* of God *without the law* is manifested, being witnessed by the law and the prophets. Gen. iii. 15. And I will put enmity between thee and the woman, and between thy seed and her seed : it shall *bruise thy head*, and thou shalt bruise his heel. Isa. xlii. 6. I the Lord have called thee in righteousness, and will hold thine hand, and will keep thee, and give *thee for a covenant* of the people, for a light of the Gentiles.

[f] Mark xvi. 15. And he said unto them, Go ye into all the world, and preach the *gospel* to every creature. Ver. 16. He that *believeth*, and is baptized, *shall be saved ;* but he that believeth not shall be damned. John iii. 16. For God so loved the world that he gave his only begotten Son, that whosoever *believeth in* him, should not *perish*, but *have everlasting life*. Rom. x. 6. But the *righteousness which is of faith* speaketh on this wise, Say not in thine heart, Who shall ascend into heaven ? (that is, to bring Christ down from above.) Ver. 9. That if thou shalt confess with thy mouth the Lord Jesus, and shalt *believe in thine heart* that God hath raised him from the dead, thou shalt be saved. Gal. iii. 11. But that no man is *justified by the law* in the sight of God, it is evident: for, The *just shall live by faith*.

dained unto life his Holy Spirit, to make them willing and able to believe.g

IV. This covenant of grace is frequently set forth in the scripture by the name of a Testament, in reference to the death of Jesus Christ the testator, and to the everlasting inheritance, with all things belonging to it, therein bequeathed.h

V. This covenant was differently administered in the time of the law, and in the time of the gospel;[i] under the law it was administered by promises, prophecies, sacrifices, circumcision, the paschal lamb, and other types and ordinances delivered to the people of the Jews, all foresignifying Christ to come,[k] which were for that time sufficient and efficacious through the operation of the Spirit, to instruct and build up the elect in faith in the promised Messiah,[l] by whom they had full remission of sins, and eternal salvation; and is called the Old Testament.[m]

VI. Under the gospel, when Christ the substance[n] was exhibited,

g Ezek. xxxvi. 26. A *new heart also will I give you*, and *a new spirit will I put* within you; and I will take away the stony heart out of your flesh, and I *will give you an heart of flesh*. Ver. 27. And I will *put my Spirit within you, and cause you to walk in my statutes, and ye shall keep my judgments, and do them.* John vi. 44. No man can come to me, except the *Father*, which hath sent me, *draw him;* and I will raise him up at the last day. Ver. 45. It is written in the prophets, And they shall be all *taught of God.* Every man therefore that hath heard, and hath learned of the Father, cometh unto me.

IV. h Heb. ix. 15. And for this cause he is the mediator of the *new testament,* that by means of death, for the redemption of the transgressions that were under the first testament, they which are called might receive the *promise of eternal inheritance.* Ver. 16. For where a testament is, there must also of necessity be *the death of the testator.* Ver. 17. For a testament is of *force* after *men are dead;* otherwise it is of *no strength* at all while *the testator liveth.* Heb. vii. 22. By so much was Jesus made a surety of a *better testament.* Luke xxii. 20. Likewise also the cup after supper, saying, This cup is the *new testament* in my blood, which is shed for you. 1 Cor. xi. 25. After the same manner also he took the cup, when he had supped, saying, This cup is the *new testament in my blood;* this do ye, as oft as ye drink it, in remembrance of me.

V. i 2 Cor. iii. 6. Who also hath made us *able ministers* of the new testament; *not of the letter, but of the spirit;* for the letter killeth, but the spirit giveth life. Ver. 7. But if the *ministration of death,* written and engraven in stones, was *glorious,* so that the children of Israel could not steadfastly behold the face of Moses for the glory of his countenance; which glory was to be done away; Ver. 8. How shall not the *ministration of the Spirit* be *rather glorious?* Ver. 9. For if the ministration of condemnation be glory, much more doth the *ministration of righteousness exceed in glory.*

k (Heb. *Chapters* viii., ix., x.) Rom. iv. 11. And he received the sign of *circumcision, a seal of the righteousness of the faith* which he had yet being uncircumcised: that he might be the father of all them that believe, though they be not circumcised; that righteousness might be imputed unto them also. Col. ii. 11. In whom also ye are circumcised with the *circumcision* made *without hands,* in *putting off the body of the sins* of the flesh by the circumcision of Christ; Ver. 12. Buried with him in *baptism,* wherein also ye are risen with him through the faith of the operation of God, who hath raised him from the dead. 1 Cor. v. 7. Purge out therefore the old leaven, that ye may be a new lump, as ye are unleavened. For even *Christ our passover* is sacrificed for us.

l 1 Cor. x. 1. Moreover, brethren, I would not that ye should be ignorant, how that all our fathers were *under the cloud,* and all passed through the sea; Ver. 2. And *were all baptized* unto Moses in the cloud and in the sea; Ver. 3. And *did all eat the same spiritual meat;* Ver. 4. And did all drink the *same spiritual drink;* (for they drank of that spiritual Rock that followed them; and that *Rock was Christ.*) Heb. xi. 13. These all died in faith, not having received the promises, but having seen them afar off, and were *persuaded of them,* and embraced them, and *confessed* that they were strangers and pilgrims on the earth. John viii. 56. Your father Abraham rejoiced to see my day; and he *saw it,* and was glad.

m Gal. iii. 7. Know ye therefore, that *they which are of faith,* the same are the *children of Abraham.* Ver. 8. And the scripture, foreseeing that God would *justify the heathen through faith,* preached before the gospel unto *Abraham,* saying, In thee shall *all nations be blessed.* Ver. 9. So then they which be of faith are *blessed* with *faithful Abraham.* Ver. 14. That the *blessing of Abraham* might come on the Gentiles through Jesus Christ; that we might receive the promise of the Spirit through faith.

VI. n Col. ii. 17. Which are a shadow of things to come; *but the body is of Christ.*

the ordinances in which this covenant is dispensed are the preaching of the word, and the administration of the sacraments of Baptism and the Lord's Supper,⁰ which, though fewer in number, and administered with more simplicity and less outward glory, yet in them it is held forth in more fulness, evidence, and spiritual efficacy,ᵖ to all nations, both Jews and Gentiles;ᑫ and is called the New Testament.ʳ There are not therefore two covenants of grace differing in substance, but one and the same under various dispensations.ˢ

o Matt. xxviii. 19. Go ye therefore, and *teach all nations, baptizing them* in the name of the Father, and of the Son, and of the Holy Ghost. Ver. 20. *Teaching them* to observe all things whatsoever I have commanded you: and, lo, I am with you alway, even unto the end of the world. Amen. 1 Cor. xi. 23. For I have received of the Lord that which also I delivered unto you, That the Lord JESUS, the same night in which he was betrayed, *took bread:* Ver. 24. And, when he had given thanks, he brake it, and said, *Take, eat: this is my body*, which is broken for you: *this do* in remembrance of me. Ver. 25. After the same manner also he took *the cup*, when he had supped, saying, This cup is the new testament in my blood: *this do ye*, as oft as ye drink it, in remembrance of me.

p Heb. xii. 22. But ye are come unto mount Sion, and unto the city of the living God, the heavenly Jerusalem, and to an innumerable company of angels. Ver. 23. To the general assembly and church of the first-born, which are written in heaven, and to God the judge of all, and to the spirits of just men made perfect, Ver. 24. And to Jesus the mediator of the new covenant, and to the blood of sprinkling, that speaketh better things than that of *Abel*. Ver. 25. See that ye refuse not him that *speaketh:* for if they escaped not who refused him that *spake on earth*, much more shall not we escape, if we turn away from him that *speaketh from heaven;* Ver. 26. Whose voice then shook the earth: but now he hath promised, saying, Yet once more I shake not the earth only, but also *heaven*. Ver. 27. And this word, Yet once more, signifieth the *removing* of those *things that are shaken*, as of things that are made, that those things which cannot be shaken may remain. Jer. xxxi. 33. But this shall be the covenant that I will make with the house of Israel; After those days, saith the Lord, *I will put my law in their inward parts*, and *write* it in their *hearts;* and will be their God, and they shall be my people. Ver. 34. And they shall teach no more every man his neighbour, and every man his brother, saying, Know the Lord: for they *shall all know me*, from the least of them unto the greatest of them, saith the Lord: for I will forgive their iniquity, and I will remember their sin no more.

q Matt. xxviii. 19. [*See letter* o *immediately foregoing.*] Eph. ii. 15. Having *abolished* in his flesh the *enmity*, even the law of commandments contained in ordinances; for to make in himself of *twain* one new man, so making peace; Ver. 16. And that he might reconcile *both* unto God in *one body* by the cross, having slain the enmity thereby; Ver. 17. And came and preached peace to you which were *afar off*, and to them that were *nigh*. Ver. 18. For through him we both have *an access by one Spirit* unto the Father. Ver. 19. Now therefore ye are no more strangers and foreigners, but *fellow-citizens with the saints*, and of the *household of God*.

r Luke xxii. 20. Likewise also the cup after supper, saying, This cup is the *new testament* in my blood, which is shed for you.

s Gal. iii. 14. That the *blessing of Abraham* might come on *the Gentiles* through Jesus Christ; that we might receive the promise of the Spirit through faith. Ver. 16. Now to Abraham and his seed were the promises made. He saith not, And *to seeds*, as *of many;* but *as of one*, And *to thy* seed, *which is Christ.* Acts xv. 11. But we believe that, through the *grace* of the Lord *Jesus Christ*, we *shall be saved*, even *as they*. Rom. iii. 21. But now the *righteousness* of God *without the law is manifested*, being witnessed by the law and the prophets; Ver. 22. Even the *righteousness* of God which is by faith of Jesus Christ *unto all* and *upon all* them *that believe;* for there is *no difference:* Ver. 23. For all have sinned, and come short of the glory of God. Ver. 30. Seeing it is *one God* which shall *justify* the *circumcision by faith*, and *uncircumcision through faith.* Ps. xxxii. 1. Blessed is he whose *transgression is forgiven*, whose *sin is covered.* With Rom. iv. 3. For what saith the scripture? Abraham *believed* God, and it was *counted unto him for righteousness*. Ver. 6. Even as David also describeth the blessedness of the man, unto whom God *imputeth righteousness without works*. Ver. 16. Therefore it is of faith, that it might be by grace; to the end the *promise* might be *sure* to all the seed: not to *that only which is of the law*, but to *that also* which is of the *faith of Abraham*, who is the father of us all, Ver. 17. (As it is written, I have made thee *a father of many nations*,) before him whom he *believed*, even God, who quickeneth the dead, and calleth those things which be not as though they were. Ver. 23. Now, it was not written for his sake alone, that it was *imputed* to him; Ver. 24. But *for us also*, to whom it shall be imputed, if we believe on him that raised up Jesus our Lord from the dead. Heb. xiii. 8. Jesus Christ *the same yesterday, and to-day, and for ever.*

CHAP. VIII.—*Of Christ the Mediator.*

I. IT pleased God, in his eternal purpose, to choose and ordain the Lord Jesus, his only begotten Son, to be the Mediator between God and man;[a] the Prophet,[b] Priest,[c] and King;[d] the Head and Saviour of his Church;[e] the Heir of all things;[f] and Judge of the world;[g] unto whom he did from all eternity give a people to be his seed,[h] and to be by him in time redeemed, called, justified, sanctified, and glorified.[i]

II. The Son of God, the second person in the Trinity, being very and eternal God, of one substance, and equal with the Father, did, when the fulness of time was come, take upon him man's nature,[k] with all the essential properties and common infirmities thereof, yet without sin;[l] being conceived by the power of the Holy Ghost, in the womb of the Virgin Mary, of her substance.[m] So that two whole, perfect,

---

I. a Isa. xlii. 1. Behold my servant, whom I uphold; *mine elect*, in whom my soul delighteth: *I have put my Spirit upon him;* he shall bring forth *judgment to the Gentiles.* 1 Pet. i. 19. But with the *precious blood of Christ,* as of a lamb without blemish and without spot: Ver. 20. *Who* verily was *foreordained* before the foundation of the world, but was manifest in these last times *for you.* John iii. 16. For God so loved the world, that he *gave his only begotten Son,* that *whosoever believeth* in him should not perish, but have *everlasting life.* 1 Tim. ii. 5. For there is one God, and *one mediator* between God and men, the man *Christ Jesus.*

b Acts iii. 22. For Moses truly said unto the fathers, *A prophet shall the Lord your God raise up unto you of your brethren, like unto me;* him shall ye hear in all things whatsoever he shall say unto you.

c Heb. v. 5. So also Christ *glorified not himself to be made an high-priest;* but he that said unto him, Thou art my Son, to-day have I begotten thee, Ver. 6. As he saith also in another place, *Thou art a priest for ever, after the order of Melchisedec.*

d Ps. ii. 6. Yet *have I set my King* upon my holy hill of Zion. Luke i. 33. And *he shall reign over the house of Jacob* for ever; and of his kingdom there shall be no end.

e Eph. v. 23. For the husband is the head of the wife, even as *Christ is the head of the church;* and *he is the saviour of the body.*

f Heb. i. 2. Hath in these last days spoken unto us by his Son, *whom* he hath appointed *heir of all things,* by whom also he made the worlds.

g Acts xvii. 31. Because he hath appointed a day, in the which he will *judge the world* in righteousness *by that man whom he hath ordained;* whereof he hath given assurance unto all men, in that he hath raised him from the dead.

h John xvii. 6. I have manifested thy name unto the men *which thou gavest me out of the world:* thine they were, and thou *gavest them me;* and they have kept thy word. Ps. xxii. 30. *A seed shall serve him;* it shall be accounted to the Lord for a generation. Isa. liii. 10. Yet it pleased the Lord to bruise him; he hath put him to grief: when thou shalt make his soul an offering for sin, *he shall see his seed,* he shall prolong his days, and the pleasure of the Lord shall prosper in his hand.

i 1 Tim. ii. 6. Who gave himself a *ransom for all,* to be testified *in due time.* Isa. lv. 4. Behold, I have given him for a witness to the people, a leader and commander to the people. Ver. 5. Behold, *thou shalt call a nation that thou knowest not;* and nations that knew not thee *shall run unto thee,* because of the Lord thy God, and for the Holy One of Israel; for *he hath glorified thee.* 1 Cor. i. 30. But of him are ye in Christ Jesus, who *of God is made unto us wisdom, and righteousness, and sanctification, and redemption.*

II. k John i. 1. In the beginning was the Word, and the Word was with God, and *the Word was God.* Ver. 14. And the Word *was made flesh, and dwelt among us,* (and we beheld his glory, the glory as of the only begotten of the Father,) full of grace and truth. 1 John v. 20. And we know that the *Son of God is come,* and hath given us an understanding, that we may know him that is true; and we are in him that is true, even in his Son Jesus Christ. *This is the true God,* and eternal life. Phil. ii. 6. Who, being in the *form of God,* thought it not robbery to be *equal with God.* Gal. iv. 4. But when *the fulness of the time was come, God sent forth his Son, made of a woman,* made under the law.

l Heb. ii. 14. Forasmuch then as the children are partakers of flesh and blood, *he also* himself *likewise* took part *of the same; that through death* he might destroy him that had the power of death, that is, the devil. Ver. 16. For verily he took not on him the nature of angels; but *he took on him the seed of Abraham.* Ver. 17. Wherefore *in all things it behoved him to be made like unto his brethren,* that he might be a merciful and faithful high-priest in things pertaining to God, to make reconciliation for the sins of the people. Heb. iv. 15. For we have not an high-priest which *cannot be touched* with the feeling of our infirmities; but *was in all points tempted like as we are, yet without sin.*

m Luke i. 27. *To a virgin* espoused to a man, whose name was Joseph, of the house

CHAP. VIII.   THE CONFESSION OF FAITH.   39

and distinct natures, the Godhead and the manhood, were inseparably joined together in one person, without conversion, composition, or confusion.ⁿ Which person is very God and very man, yet one Christ, the only Mediator between God and man.°

III. The Lord Jesus, in his human nature thus united to the divine, was sanctified and anointed with the Holy Spirit above measure;ᵖ having in him all the treasures of wisdom and knowledge;ᑫ in whom it pleased the Father that all fulness should dwell:ʳ to the end, that being holy, harmless, undefiled, and full of grace and truth,ˢ he might be thoroughly furnished to execute the office of a Mediator and Surety.ᵗ Which office he took not unto himself, but was thereunto called by his Father;ᵘ who put all power and judgment into his hand, and gave him commandment to execute the same.ˣ

IV. This office the Lord Jesus did most willingly undertake;ʸ which

---

of David ; and the virgin's name was Mary. Ver. 31. And, behold, thou shalt *conceive in thy womb*, and bring forth a son, and shalt call his name JESUS. Ver. 35. And the angel answered and said unto her, The *Holy Ghost* shall come upon thee, and the *power of the Highest shall overshadow thee:* therefore also that holy thing, which shall be born of thee, shall be called the Son of God. Gal. iv. 4. [*See letter* ᵏ *immediately foregoing.*]

ⁿ Luke i. 35. [*See the foregoing verse.*] Col. ii. 9. For in him dwelleth all the fulness of the *Godhead bodily*. Rom. ix. 5. Whose are the fathers, and of whom, as concerning *the flesh, Christ came*, who is over all, *God blessed for ever.* Amen. 1 Pet. iii. 18. For Christ also hath once suffered for sins, the just for the unjust, that he might bring us to God, being put to death in *the flesh,* but *quickened by the Spirit.* 1 Tim. iii. 16. And, without controversy, great is the mystery of godliness : *God was manifest in the flesh,* justified in the Spirit, seen of angels, preached unto the Gentiles, believed on in the world, received up into glory.

° Rom. i. 3. Concerning his Son, Jesus Christ our Lord, which was *made of the seed of David according to the flesh,* Ver. 4. And declared *to be the Son of God* with power, according to the Spirit of holiness, by the resurrection from the dead. 1 Tim. ii. 5. For there is one God, and *one mediator between God and men, the man Christ Jesus.*

III. ᵖ Ps. xlv. 7. Thou lovest righteousness, and hatest wickedness : therefore God, thy God, hath *anointed* thee with *the oil of gladness above thy fellows*. John iii. 34. For he whom God hath sent speaketh the words of God : for God *giveth not the Spirit by measure unto him.*

ᑫ Col. ii. 3. *In whom are hid all the treasures of wisdom and knowledge.*

ʳ Col. i. 19. For *it pleased the Father,* that in *him* should *all fulness dwell.*

ˢ Heb. vii. 26. For such an high priest became us, *who is holy, harmless, undefiled, separate from sinners,* and made higher than the heavens. John i. 14. And the Word was made flesh, and dwelt among us,

(and we beheld his glory, the glory as of the only begotten of the Father,) *full of grace and truth.*

ᵗ Acts x. 38. How God *anointed Jesus* of Nazareth with *the Holy Ghost*, and with power ; *who went about* doing good, and healing all that were *oppressed of the devil:* for God was with him. Heb. xii. 24. And to Jesus the mediator of the new covenant, and to the *blood of sprinkling,* that speaketh better things than that of Abel. Heb. vii. 22. By so much was Jesus *made a surety* of a better testament.

ᵘ Heb. v. 4. And *no man taketh this honour* unto himself, but he that is called of God, as was Aaron. Ver. 5. So also *Christ glorified not himself to be made an high priest;* but he that said unto him, Thou art my Son, to-day have I begotten thee.

ˣ John v. 22. For the Father judgeth no man, but hath *committed all judgment unto the Son:* Ver. 27. And hath *given him authority to execute judgment also,* because he is the Son of man. Matt. xxviii. 18. And Jesus came and spake unto them, saying, All *power is given unto me* in heaven and in earth. Acts ii. 36. Therefore let all the house of Israel know assuredly, that God hath made that same Jesus, whom ye have crucified, *both Lord and Christ.*

IV. ʸ Ps. xl. 7. Then said I, *Lo, I come:* in the volume of the book it is written of me, Ver. 8. *I delight to do thy will, O my God;* yea, thy *law is within my heart.* With Heb. x. 5. Wherefore, when he cometh into the world, he saith, Sacrifice and offering thou wouldest not, but a body hast thou prepared me : Ver. 6. In burnt-offerings and sacrifices for sin thou hast had no pleasure : Ver. 7. Then said I, *Lo, I come* (in the volume of the book it is written of me) *to do thy will,* O God. Ver. 8. Above, when he said, Sacrifice, and offering, and burnt-offerings, and offering for sin, thou wouldest not, neither hadst pleasure therein ; (which are offered by the law ;) Ver. 9. Then said he, *Lo, I come to do thy will,* O God. He taketh away the first, that he may establish the second. Ver. 10. By the which *will* we are sanctified, through the offering of the body of Jesus Christ once for all. John x. 18. No man taketh it from me, but

that he may discharge, he was made under the law,ᶻ and did perfectly fulfil it;ᵃ endured most grievous torments immediately in his soul,ᵇ and most painful sufferings in his body;ᶜ was crucified, and died;ᵈ was buried, and remained under the power of death, yet saw no corruption.ᵉ On the third day he arose from the dead,ᶠ with the same body in which he suffered;ᵍ with which also he ascended into heaven, and there sitteth at the right hand of his Father,ʰ making intercession;ⁱ and shall return to judge men and angels at the end of the world.ᵏ

V. The Lord Jesus, by his perfect obedience and sacrifice of himself, which he through the eternal Spirit once offered up unto God, hath

I lay it down of myself: I have power to lay it down, and I have power to take it again. This commandment have I received of my Father. Phil. ii. 8. And being found in fashion as a man, *he humbled himself, and became obedient unto death, even the death of the cross.*
z Gal. iv. 4. But when the fulness of the time was come, God sent forth his Son, made of a woman, *made under the law.*
a Matt. iii. 15. And Jesus answering, said unto him, Suffer it to be so now; for thus it *becometh us to fulfil all righteousness.* Then he suffered him. Matt. v. 17. Think not that I am come to destroy the law or the prophets: I am not come to destroy, *but to fulfil.*
b Matt. xxvi. 37. And he took with him Peter and the two sons of Zebedee, and began to be *sorrowful and very heavy.* Ver. 38. Then saith he unto them, *My soul is exceeding sorrowful, even unto death:* tarry ye here, and watch with me. Luke xxii. 44. And, being *in an agony,* he prayed more earnestly: and his sweat was as it were great drops of blood falling down to the ground. Matt. xxvii. 46. And about the ninth hour, Jesus cried with a loud voice, saying, *Eli, Eli, lama sabachthani?* that is to say, *My God, my God, why hast thou forsaken me?*
c Matt. Chapters xxvi. and xxvii.
d Phil. ii. 8. [See the last scripture in y immediately foregoing.]
e Acts ii. 23. Him, being delivered by the determinate counsel and foreknowledge of God, ye have taken, and by wicked hands have *crucified and slain;* Ver. 24. Whom God hath raised up, having loosed *the pains of death:* because it was not possible that he should be *holden of it.* Ver. 27. Because thou wilt *not leave my soul in hell, neither* wilt thou *suffer thine Holy One to see corruption.* And Acts xiii. 37. But he, whom God raised again, *saw no corruption.* Rom. vi. 9. Knowing that Christ, being *raised from the dead,* dieth no more; death hath *no more dominion over him.*
f 1 Cor. xv. 3. For I delivered unto you first of all that which I also received, how that Christ died for our sins according to the scriptures; Ver. 4. And that he was buried, and that *he rose again the third day* according to the scriptures; *Ver. 5. And that he was seen of Cephas, then of the twelve.
g John xx. 25. The other disciples therefore said unto him, We have seen the Lord. But he said unto them, Except I shall see in his hands *the print of the nails,* and put my finger into the print of the nails, and thrust my hand into his side, I will not believe. Ver. 27. Then saith he to Thomas, Reach hither thy finger, and behold *my hands;* and reach hither thy hand, and *thrust it into my side;* and be not faithless, but believing.
h Mark xvi. 19. So then, after the *Lord had spoken unto them,* he was *received up into heaven, and sat on the right hand of God.*
i Rom. viii. 34. Who is he that condemneth? It is Christ that died, yea rather, that is risen again, who is even at the right hand of God, who also *maketh intercession for us.* Heb. ix. 24. For Christ is not entered into the holy places made with hands, which are the figures of the true; but into heaven itself, now to *appear in the presence of God for us.* Heb. vii. 25. Wherefore he is able also to save them to the uttermost that come unto God by him, seeing he ever liveth *to make intercession for them.*
k Rom. xiv. 9. For to this end Christ both died, and rose, and revived, that he *might be Lord both of the dead and living.* Ver. 10. But why dost thou judge thy brother? or why dost thou set at nought thy brother? for *we shall all stand before the judgment-seat of Christ.* Acts i. 11. Which also said, Ye men of Galilee, why stand ye gazing up into heaven? this same Jesus, which is taken up from you into heaven, *shall so come* in like manner as ye have seen him go into heaven. Acts x. 42. And he commanded us to preach unto the people, and to testify that it is he which was ordained of God *to be the Judge of quick and dead.* Matt. xiii. 40. As therefore the tares are gathered and burned in the fire; *so shall it be in the end* of this world. Ver. 41. The *Son of man shall send forth* his angels, and they shall gather out of his kingdom all things that offend, and them which do iniquity. Ver. 42. And shall *cast them* into a furnace of fire: there shall be wailing and gnashing of teeth. Jude, ver. 6. And the angels which kept not their first estate, but left their own habitation, *he hath reserved* in everlasting chains, under darkness, *unto the judgment* of the great day. 2 Pet. ii. 4. For if God spared not the angels that sinned, but cast them down to hell, and *de-*

fully satisfied the justice of his Father;[1] and purchased not only reconciliation, but an everlasting inheritance in the kingdom of heaven, for all those whom the Father hath given unto him.[m]

VI. Although the work of redemption was not actually wrought by Christ till after his incarnation, yet the virtue, efficacy, and benefits thereof, were communicated unto the elect in all ages successively from the beginning of the world, in and by those promises, types, and sacrifices, wherein he was revealed and signified to be the Seed of the woman, which should bruise the serpent's head, and the Lamb slain from the beginning of the world, being yesterday and to-day the same, and for ever.[n]

VII. Christ, in the work of mediation, acteth according to both natures; by each nature doing that which is proper to itself:[o] yet, by reason of the unity of the person, that which is proper to one nature is sometimes in scripture attributed to the person denominated by the other nature.[p]

VIII. To all those for whom Christ hath purchased redemption, he

---

livered them into chains of darkness, to be reserved unto judgment.

V. l Rom. v. 19. For as by one man's disobedience many were made sinners; so by *the obedience of one* shall *many be made righteous.* Heb. ix. 14. How much more shall the *blood of Christ,* who through the eternal Spirit offered himself without spot to God, *purge your conscience* from dead works, to serve the living God? Ver. 16. For where a testament is, there must also of necessity *be the death of the testator.* Heb. x. 14. For *by one offering* he hath *perfected for ever them that are sanctified.* Eph. v. 2. And walk in love, as Christ also hath loved us, and hath given himself *for us an offering* and a sacrifice to God for a *sweet-smelling savour.* Rom. iii. 25. Whom God hath set forth to be a *propitiation* through faith *in his blood,* to declare his righteousness for the remission of sins that are past, *through the forbearance of God;* Ver. 26. To declare, I say, at this time his righteousness; that he might be just, and the justifier of him which believeth in Jesus.

m Dan. ix. 24. Seventy weeks are determined upon thy people, and upon thy holy city, to *finish the transgression,* and to make an *end of sins,* and to make *reconciliation for iniquity,* and to bring in *everlasting righteousness,* and to seal up the vision and prophecy, and to anoint the most holy. Ver. 26. And after threescore and two weeks shall *Messiah* be *cut off,* but *not for himself:* and the people of the prince that shall come shall destroy the city and the sanctuary; and the end thereof shall be with a flood, and unto the end of the war desolations are determined. Col. i. 19. For it pleased the Father that in him should all fulness dwell: Ver. 20. And (having *made peace* through the *blood of his cross*), by him to *reconcile all things* unto himself; by him, I say, whether they be things in earth, or things in heaven. Eph. i. 11. In whom also we have *obtained an inheritance,* being predestinated according to the purpose of him who worketh all things after the counsel of his own will. Ver. 14. Which is the earnest *of our inheritance,* until the redemption of the *purchased possession,* unto the praise of his glory. John xvii. 2. As thou hast given him power over all flesh, that he should *give eternal life* to as many as *thou hast given him.* Heb. ix. 12. Neither by the blood of goats and calves, but by his own blood, he entered in once into the holy place, having *obtained eternal redemption for us.* Ver. 15. And for this cause he is the mediator of the new testament, that by means of death, for the redemption of the transgressions that were under the first testament, they which are called *might receive the promise of eternal inheritance.*

VI. n Gal. iv. 4. But when the *fulness of the time was come,* God *sent forth his Son,* made of a woman, made under the law, Ver. 5. To redeem them that *were under the law,* that we might receive the adoption of sons. Gen. iii. 15. And I will put enmity between thee and the woman, and between thy seed and *her seed;* it shall *bruise thy head,* and thou shalt bruise his heel. Rev. xiii. 8. And all that dwell upon the earth shall worship him, whose names are not written in the book of life of *the Lamb slain from the foundation of the world.* Heb. xiii. 8. *Jesus Christ the same yesterday, and to-day, and for ever.*

VII. o Heb. ix. 14. [*See letter* l, *scripture the second.*] 1 Pet. iii. 18. For Christ also hath once suffered for sins, the just for the unjust, that he might bring us to God, being *put to death in the flesh,* but *quickened by the Spirit.*

p Acts xx. 28. Take heed therefore unto yourselves, and to all the flock over the which the Holy Ghost hath made you overseers, to feed the church *of God, which he hath purchased with his own blood.* John iii. 13. And *no man* hath ascended up to heaven, but *he that came down* from heaven, even the *Son of man* which *is in heaven.* 1 John iii. 16. Hereby perceive we the love of God, because *he laid down his life* for

doth certainly and effectually apply and communicate the same;q making intercession for them;r and revealing unto them, in and by the word, the mysteries of salvation;s effectually persuading them by his Spirit to believe and obey; and governing their hearts by his word and Spirit;t overcoming all their enemies by his almighty power and wisdom, in such manner and ways as are most consonant to his wonderful and unsearchable dispensation.u

CHAP. IX.—*Of Free Will.*

I. GOD hath endued the will of man with that natural liberty, that it is neither forced, nor by any absolute necessity of nature determined, to good or evil.a

II. Man, in his state of innocency, had freedom and power to will

us: and we ought to lay down our lives for the brethren.
VIII. John vi. 37. All that the Father giveth me *shall come to me;* and him that cometh to me I will in no wise cast out. Ver. 39. And this is the Father's will which hath sent me, that of all which he hath given me *I should lose nothing,* but should raise *it up again* at the last day. John x. 15. As the Father knoweth me, even so know I the Father: and I lay down my life for the *sheep.* Ver. 16. And other *sheep* I have, which are not of this fold: them also I must bring, and *they shall hear my voice;* and there shall be one *fold,* and one shepherd.

r 1 John ii. 1. My little children, these things write I unto you, that ye sin not. And if any man sin, we *have an advocate with the Father, Jesus Christ* the righteous: Ver. 2. And he is the propitiation for our sins; and not for ours only, but also *for the sins* of the whole world. Rom. viii. 34. Who is he that condemneth? It is Christ that died, yea rather, that is risen again, who is even *at the right hand of God,* who also *maketh intercession for us.*

s John xv. 13. Greater love hath no man than this, that a man lay down his life for his *friends.* Ver. 15. Henceforth I call you not servants; for the servant knoweth not what his lord doeth: but I have called you friends; for *all things that I have heard of my Father I have made known unto you.* Eph. i. 7. In whom we have redemption through his blood, the forgiveness of sins, according to the riches of his grace; Ver. 8. Wherein he hath abounded toward us in all wisdom and prudence; Ver. 9. Having *made known unto us the mystery of his will,* according to his good pleasure which he hath purposed in himself. John xvii. 6. *I have manifested thy name unto the men* which thou gavest me out of the world; thine they were, and thou gavest them me; and they have kept thy word.

t John xiv. 16. And I will pray the Father, and he shall give you another *Comforter,* that he *may abide with you* for ever. Heb. xii. 2. Looking unto *Jesus, the author and finisher of our faith;* who, for the joy that was set before him, endured the cross, despising the shame, and is set down at the right hand of the throne of God. 2 Cor. iv. 13. We having the same *spirit of faith,* according as it is written, I believed, and therefore have I spoken; we also believe, and therefore speak. Rom. viii. 9. But ye are not in the flesh, but *in the Spirit,* if so be that the *Spirit of God dwell in you.* Now, if any man have not the Spirit of Christ, he is none of his. Ver. 14. For as many as are led by the *Spirit of God, they* are the sons of God. Rom. xv. 18. For I will not dare to speak of any of those things which Christ hath not wrought by me, to make the Gentiles obedient, by word and deed, Ver. 19. Through mighty signs and wonders, by the *power of the Spirit* of God; so that from Jerusalem, and round about unto Illyricum, I have fully preached the gospel of Christ. John xvii. 17. *Sanctify them through thy truth:* thy word is truth.

u Ps. cx. 1. The Lord said unto my Lord, Sit thou at my right hand, *until I make thine enemies thy footstool.* 1 Cor. xv. 25. For he must reign, till *he hath put all enemies under his feet.* Ver. 26. The last enemy that shall be *destroyed* is death. Mal. iv. 2. But unto you that fear my name shall the Sun of righteousness arise *with healing in his wings;* and ye shall go forth, and grow up as calves of the stall. Ver. 3. And ye *shall tread down the wicked;* for they shall be ashes under the soles of your feet, in the day that I shall do this, saith the Lord of hosts. Col. ii. 15. And, having *spoiled principalities and powers,* he made a shew of them openly, *triumphing over them in it.*

I. a Matt. xvii. 12. But I say unto you, That *Elias* is come already, and they knew him not, but have done unto him *whatsoever they listed:* likewise shall also the Son of man suffer of them. James i. 14. But every man is tempted, when he is *drawn away of his own lust,* and enticed. Deut. xxx. 19. I call heaven and earth to record this day against you, that I have set before you life and death, blessing and cursing: therefore *choose* life, that both thou and thy seed may live.

and to do that which is good and well-pleasing to God;[b] but yet mutably, so that he might fall from it.[c]

III. Man, by his fall into a state of sin, hath wholly lost all ability of will to any spiritual good accompanying salvation;[d] so as a natural man, being altogether averse from that good,[e] and dead in sin,[f] is not able, by his own strength, to convert himself, or to prepare himself thereunto.[g]

IV. When God converts a sinner, and translates him into the state of grace, he freeth him from his natural bondage under sin,[h] and by his grace alone enables him freely to will and to do that which is spiritually good;[i] yet so as that, by reason of his remaining corruption, he doth not perfectly nor only will that which is good, but doth also will that which is evil.[k]

II. b Eccl. vii. 29. Lo this only have I found, that *God hath made man upright;* but they have sought out many inventions. Gen. i. 26. And God said, Let us make *man in our image, after our likeness;* and let them have dominion over the fish of the sea, and over the fowl of the air, and over the cattle, and over all the earth, and over every creeping thing that creepeth upon the earth.

c Gen. ii. 16. And the Lord God commanded the man, saying, Of every tree of the garden thou mayest *freely* eat; Ver. 17. But of the tree of the knowledge of good and evil, *thou shalt not eat* of it: for in the day that thou eatest thereof thou shalt surely die. Gen. iii. 6. And when the woman saw that the tree was good for food, and that it was pleasant to the eyes, and a tree to be desired to make one wise, *she took of the fruit thereof, and did eat;* and gave also unto her husband with her, and *he did eat.*

III. d Rom. v. 6. For when we were *yet without strength,* in due time Christ died for the ungodly. Rom. viii. 7. Because the carnal mind is *enmity against God:* for it is *not subject to the law* of God, *neither indeed can be.* John xv. 5. I am the vine, ye are the branches: he that abideth in me, and I in him, the same bringeth forth much fruit; for *without me ye can do nothing.*

e Rom. iii. 10. As it is written, *There is none righteous,* no, not one. Ver. 12. They are *all gone out of the way,* they are together become unprofitable; there is *none that doeth good,* no, *not one.*

f Eph. ii. 1. And you hath he quickened, *who were dead in trespasses and sins.* Ver. 5. Even when *we were dead in sins,* hath quickened us together with Christ; (by grace ye are saved.) Col. ii. 13. And you, *being dead in your sins* and the uncircumcision of your flesh, hath he quickened together with him, having forgiven you all trespasses.

g John vi. 44. No man can come to me, except *the Father,* which hath sent me, *draw him:* and I will raise him up at the last day. Ver. 65. And he said, Therefore said I unto you, that no man can come unto me, except it were given unto him of my Father. Eph. ii. 2. Wherein in time past *ye walked according to the course of this world,* according to the prince of the power of the air, the spirit that now worketh in the children of disobedience: Ver. 3. Among whom also we *all had our conversation* in times past in the lusts of our flesh, fulfilling the desires of the flesh and of the mind; and were by nature the children of wrath, even as others. Ver. 4. But *God, who is* rich in mercy, for his great love wherewith he loved us, Ver. 5. Even when *we were dead* in sins, hath *quickened us* together with Christ; (by grace ye are saved.) 1 Cor. ii. 14. But the *natural man receiveth not the things of the Spirit of God:* for they are foolishness unto him; neither can he know them, because they are spiritually discerned. Tit. iii. 3. For *we* ourselves also were *sometimes foolish, disobedient,* deceived, *serving divers lusts* and pleasures, *living in malice and envy, hateful, and hating one another.* Ver. 4. But after that the kindness and love of God our Saviour toward man appeared, Ver. 5. Not *by works of righteousness which we have done,* but according to his mercy he saved us, by *the washing of regeneration,* and *renewing* of the Holy Ghost.

IV. h Col. i. 13. Who hath *delivered us from the power of darkness,* and hath translated us into the kingdom of his dear Son. John viii. 34. Jesus answered them, Verily, verily, I say unto you, Whosoever committeth sin *is the servant of sin.* Ver. 36. If the Son therefore shall *make you free,* ye shall be *free indeed.*

i Phil. ii. 13. For it is *God which worketh in you,* both *to will* and *to do* of his good pleasure. Rom. vi. 18. Being then made free from sin, ye became the *servants of righteousness.* Ver. 22. But now, being made free from sin, and become *servants to God,* ye have your fruit unto holiness, and the end everlasting life.

k Gal. v. 17. For the *flesh lusteth against the Spirit,* and the *Spirit against the flesh:* and these are contrary the one to the other; so that ye *cannot do the things that ye would.* Rom. vii. 15. For that *which I do I allow not;* for what I would, *that do I not;* but *what I hate, that do I.* Ver. 18. For I know that in me (that is, in *my flesh) dwelleth no good thing:* for *to will is present with* me; but how to *perform that which is good* I find not. Ver. 19. For the *good that I*

V. The will of man is made perfectly and immutably free to do good alone in the state of glory only.[1]

CHAP. X.—*Of Effectual Calling.*

I. ALL those whom God hath predestinated unto life, and those only, he is pleased, in his appointed and accepted time, effectually to call,[a] by his word and Spirit,[b] out of that state of sin and death in which they are by nature, to grace and salvation by Jesus Christ;[c] enlightening their minds spiritually and savingly to understand the things of God;[d] taking away their heart of stone, and giving unto them an heart of flesh;[e] renewing their wills, and by his almighty

would I do not: but the evil *which I would not, that I do.* Ver. 21. I find then a law, that, when I *would do good, evil is present with me.* Ver. 23. But I see another law in *my members warring against the law of my mind,* and bringing me into *captivity to the law of sin which is* in my members. V. I Eph. iv. 13. Till we all come in the unity of the faith, and of the knowledge of the Son of God, *unto a perfect man,* unto the *measure of the stature of the fulness of Christ.* Heb. xii. 23. To the general assembly and church of the first-born, which are written in heaven, and to God the Judge of all, and to the *spirits of just men made perfect.* 1 John iii. 2. Beloved, now are we the sons of God; and it doth not yet appear what we shall be: but we know that, when he shall appear, *we shall be like him;* for we shall see him as he is. Jude, ver. 24. Now unto him that is able to keep you from falling, and to present *you faultless before the presence of his glory* with exceeding joy.
I. a Rom. viii. 30. Moreover, whom he did predestinate, *them he also called;* and whom he called, them he also justified; and whom he justified, them he also glorified. Rom. xi. 7. What then? Israel hath not obtained that which he seeketh for; but *the election hath obtained it,* and the rest were blinded. Eph. i. 10. That in the dispensation of the fulness of times, *he might gather together in one all things in Christ,* both which are in heaven, and which are on earth, even in him; Ver. 11. In whom *also we have obtained an inheritance,* being predestinated according to the purpose of him who worketh all things after the counsel of his own will.
b 2 Thess. ii. 13. But we are bound to give thanks alway to God for you, brethren, beloved of the Lord, because God hath from the beginning *chosen you to salvation through sanctification of the Spirit, and belief of the truth:* Ver. 14. Whereunto he *called you by our gospel,* to the obtaining of the glory of our Lord Jesus Christ. 2 Cor. iii. 3. Forasmuch as ye are manifestly *declared to be the epistle of Christ ministered by us,* written not with ink, but with the Spirit of the living God; not in tables of stone, but in fleshly tables of the heart. Ver. 6. Who also hath made us *able ministers* of the new testament; *not of the letter, but of the spirit:* for the letter killeth, but the spirit giveth life.
c Rom. viii. 2. For the law of the *Spirit of life in Christ* Jesus hath made me free from *the law of sin and death.* Eph. ii. 1. And you hath he *quickened,* who *were dead* in trespasses and sins; Ver. 2. Wherein in time *past ye walked* according to the course of this world, *according to the prince* of the power of the air, the spirit that now worketh in the children of disobedience: Ver. 3. Among whom also *we all had our conversation* in times past *in the lusts of our flesh,* fulfilling the desires of the flesh and of the mind; and were by nature *the children of wrath,* even as others. Ver. 4. But *God, who is rich in mercy,* for his great love wherewith he loved us, Ver. 5. Even when we were dead in sins, hath *quickened us together* with Christ; (by grace ye are saved.) 2 Tim. i. 9. Who hath *saved us, and called us* with an holy calling, not according to our works, but according to his own purpose and grace, which was given us in Christ Jesus before the world began; Ver. 10. But is now made manifest by the appearing of our Saviour Jesus Christ, who hath *abolished death,* and hath *brought life* and immortality to light through the gospel.
d Acts xxvi. 18. *To open their eyes, and to turn them from darkness to light,* and from the power of Satan unto God, that they may receive forgiveness of sins, and inheritance among them which are sanctified by faith that is in me. 1 Cor. ii. 10. But God hath *revealed them unto us by his Spirit:* for the Spirit searcheth all things, yea, the deep things of God. Ver. 12. Now we have received, not the spirit of the world, but *the spirit which is of God; that we might know the things* that are freely given to us of God. Eph. i. 17. That the God of our Lord Jesus Christ, the Father of glory, may give unto *you the spirit of wisdom and revelation* in the knowledge of him: Ver. 18. *The eyes of your understanding being enlightened;* that ye *may know what is* the hope of his calling, and what the riches of the glory of his inheritance in the saints.
e Ezek. xxxvi. 26. A new heart also will I give you, and a new spirit will I put within you; and I will take *away the stony*

power determining them to that which is good;[f] and effectually drawing them to Jesus Christ;[g] yet so as they come most freely, being made willing by his grace.[h]

II. This effectual call is of God's free and special grace alone, not from any thing at all foreseen in man;[i] who is altogether passive therein, until, being quickened and renewed by the Holy Spirit,[k] he is thereby enabled to answer this call, and to embrace the grace offered and conveyed in it.[l]

III. Elect infants, dying in infancy, are regenerated and saved by Christ through the Spirit,[m] who worketh when, and where, and how

heart out of your flesh, and I *will give you an heart of flesh.*
f Ezek. xi. 19. And I will give them one heart, and I will put a new spirit within you; and I will take the stony heart out of their flesh, and will give them an heart of flesh. Phil. ii. 13. For it is *God which worketh in you, both to will* and to do of his good pleasure. Deut. xxx. 6. And the Lord thy *God will circumcise thine heart,* and the heart of thy seed, to *love the Lord thy God* with all thine heart, and with all thy soul, that thou mayest live. Ezek. xxxvi. 27. And I will *put my Spirit within you,* and *cause you to walk in my statutes,* and ye shall keep my judgments, and do them.
g Eph. i. 19. And what is the *exceeding greatness of his power* to usward *who believe,* according to *the working of his mighty power.* John vi. 44. No man *can come to me, except the Father, which hath sent me, draw him:* and I will raise him up at the last day. Ver. 45. It is written in the prophets, And they shall *be all taught* of God. Every man therefore that hath heard, and hath *learned of the Father, cometh unto me.*
h Cant. i. 4. Draw me, *we will run after thee.* Ps. cx. 3. Thy people *shall be willing* in the day of thy power, in the beauties of holiness from the womb of the morning: thou hast the dew of thy youth. John vi. 37. All that the Father giveth me shall come to me: and *him that cometh to me* I will in no wise cast out. Rom. vi. 16. Know ye not, that to whom ye *yield yourselves servants* to obey, his servants ye are to whom ye obey; whether of sin unto death, *or of obedience unto righteousness?* Ver. 17. But God be thanked, that ye were the servants of sin; but ye *have obeyed from the heart* that form of doctrine which was delivered you. Ver. 18. Being then made free from sin, *ye became the servants of righteousness.*
II. i 2 Tim. i. 9. Who hath saved us, and called us with an holy calling, *not according to our works,* but *according to his own purpose and grace, which was given* us in Christ Jesus before the world began. Tit. iii. 4. But after that the kindness and love of God our Saviour toward man appeared, Ver. 5. *Not by works of righteousness which we have done, but according* to his mercy he saved us, by the washing of regeneration, and renewing of the Holy Ghost. Eph. ii. 4. But God, who is rich in mercy, *for his great love wherewith he loved* us Ver. 5. Even when we were dead in sins, *hath quickened* us together with Christ; *(by grace ye are saved.)* Ver. 8. For by grace are ye saved through faith; and that *not of yourselves:* it is the gift of God: Ver. 9. Not *of works,* lest any man should boast. Rom. ix. 11. For the children being not yet born, neither having done any good or evil, that the purpose of God according to election *might stand, not of works,* but of him that calleth.
k 1 Cor. ii. 14. But the *natural man receiveth not the things of the Spirit of God,* for they are foolishness unto him; *neither can he know* them, because they are spiritually discerned. Rom. viii. 7. Because the carnal mind is enmity against God: for *it is not subject to the law* of God, neither *indeed can be.* Eph. ii. 5. Even when we *were dead in sins,* hath quickened us together with Christ; (by grace ye are saved.)
l John vi. 37. All that the Father giveth me *shall come to me:* and him that cometh to me I will in no wise cast out. Ezek. xxxvi. 27. And I will put my Spirit within you, and *cause you to walk in my statutes,* and *ye shall keep* my judgments, and do them. John v. 25. Verily, verily, I say unto you, The hour is coming, and now is, when *the dead shall hear the voice* of the Son of God; and they that hear shall live.
III. m Luke xviii. 15. And they brought unto him also *infants,* that he would touch them: but when his disciples saw it, they rebuked them. Ver. 16. But Jesus called them unto him, and said, Suffer *little children* to come unto me, and forbid them not: for *of such* is the kingdom of God. And Acts ii. 38. Then Peter said unto them, Repent, *and be baptized every one of* you in the name of Jesus Christ for the remission of sins, and ye shall receive the gift of the Holy Ghost. Ver. 39. For the promise is unto *you, and to your children,* and to all that are afar off, even as many as the Lord our God shall call. And John iii. 3. Jesus answered and said unto him, Verily, verily, I say unto thee, *Except a man be born again, he cannot see the kingdom of God.* Ver. 5. Jesus answered, Verily, verily, I say unto thee, *Except a man be born of water, and of the Spirit, he cannot enter* into the kingdom of God. And 1 John v. 12. *He that hath the Son hath life;* and he that hath not the Son of God hath not life. And Rom. viii. 9. But ye are not in the flesh, but in the Spirit, *if so be that the Spirit* of God dwell in you. Now, if any man have not the Spirit of Christ, he is none of his. [*Compared together.*]

he pleaseth.ⁿ So also are all other elect persons, who are incapable of being outwardly called by the ministry of the word.º

IV. Others not elected, although they may be called by the ministry of the word,ᵖ and may have some common operations of the Spirit,ᑫ yet they never truly come unto Christ, and therefore cannot be saved:ʳ much less can men not professing the Christian religion be saved in any other way whatsoever, be they ever so diligent to frame their lives according to the light of nature, and the law of that religion they do profess;ˢ and to assert and maintain that they may, is very pernicious, and to be detested.ᵗ

CHAP. XI.—*Of Justification.*

I. THOSE whom God effectually calleth he also freely justifieth;ᵃ not by infusing righteousness into them, but by pardoning their sins, and by accounting and accepting their persons as righteous: not for any thing wrought in them, or done by them, but for Christ's sake alone: not by imputing faith itself, the act of believing, or any other evangelical obedience, to them as their righteousness; but by imputing

---

n John iii. 8. The wind *bloweth where it listeth*, and thou hearest the sound thereof, but canst not tell whence it cometh, and whither it goeth : *so is every one that is born of the Spirit.*

o 1 John v. 12. He *that hath the Son hath life;* and he that hath not the Son of God hath not life. Acts iv. 12. Neither *is there salvation in any other:* for *there is none other name* under heaven given among men whereby we must be saved.

IV. p Matt. xxii. 14. For *many are called*, but few are chosen.

q Matt. vii. 22. Many will say to me in that day, Lord, Lord, have *we not prophesied in thy name?* and in thy name have *cast out devils?* and in thy name *done many wonderful works?* Matt. xiii. 20. But he that received the seed into stony places, the same is he that heareth the word, *and anon with joy receiveth it:* Ver. 21. Yet *hath he not root in himself,* but dureth for a while ; for when tribulation or persecution ariseth because of the word, by and by he is offended. Heb. vi. 4. For it is impossible for those *who were once enlightened*, and *have tasted of the heavenly gift*, and *were made partakers of the Holy Ghost*, Ver. 5. And *have tasted the good word of God*, and *the powers of the world to come.*

r John vi. 64. But *there are some of you that believe not.* For Jesus knew from the beginning who they were that *believed not*, and who *should betray* him. Ver. 65. And he said, Therefore said I unto you, that no man can come unto me, except it were given unto him of my Father. Ver. 66. From that time *many of his disciples went back,* and walked *no more with him.* John viii. 24. I said therefore unto you, that *ye shall die in your sins;* for *if ye believe not that I am he, ye shall die in your sins.*

s Acts iv. 12. *Neither is there salvation in any other : for there is none other name under heaven* given among men *whereby we must be saved.* John xiv. 6. Jesus saith unto him, I am the *way,* and the truth, and the life: no man *cometh unto the Father, but by me.* Eph. ii. 12. That at that time ye were *without Christ, being aliens from the commonwealth of Israel,* and *strangers* from the covenants of promise, *having no hope,* and *without God* in the world. *John iv. 22. We worship ye know not what ; we know what we worship : for *salvation is of the* Jews. John xvii. 3. And this *is life eternal, that they might know thee the only true God,* and *Jesus Christ,* whom thou hast sent.

t 2 John, ver. 9. Whosoever transgresseth, and *abideth not in the doctrine* of Christ, *hath not God: he* that *abideth* in the doctrine of Christ, he *hath both the Father and the Son.* Ver. 10. If there come any unto you, and *bring not this* doctrine, *receive him not into your house,* neither bid him God speed : Ver. 11. For he that *biddeth him God speed is partaker of his evil deeds.* 1 Cor. xvi. 22. If any man *love not the Lord Jesus Christ, let him be Anathema Maranatha.* Gal. i. 6. I marvel that ye are so soon *removed* from him that called you into the grace of Christ *unto another gospel:* Ver. 7. *Which is not another;* but there be some that trouble you, and would pervert the gospel of Christ. Ver. 8. But *though we, or an angel* from heaven, *preach any other gospel unto you than that* which we have preached unto you, *let him be accursed.*

I. a Rom. viii. 30. Moreover, whom he did predestinate, them he also called ; and *whom he called, them he also justified ;* and whom he justified, them he also glorified. Rom. iii. 24. Being *justified freely by his grace,* through the redemption that is in Christ Jesus.

the obedience and satisfaction of Christ unto them,[b] they receiving and resting on him and his righteousness by faith: which faith they have not of themselves; it is the gift of God.[c]

II. Faith, thus receiving and resting on Christ and his righteousness, is the alone instrument of justification;[d] yet is it not alone in the person justified, but is ever accompanied with all other saving graces, and is no dead faith, but worketh by love.[e]

III. Christ, by his obedience and death, did fully discharge the debt of all those that are thus justified, and did make a proper, real, and full satisfaction to his Father's justice in their behalf.[f] Yet, in as

---

[b] Rom. iv. 5. But to him that worketh not, but believeth on him that *justifieth the ungodly, his faith is counted for righteousness.* Ver. 6. Even as David also describeth the blessedness of the man, unto whom God *imputeth righteousness without works,* Ver. 7. Saying, Blessed are they whose *iniquities are forgiven, and whose sins are covered.* Ver. 8. Blessed is the man to whom the Lord *will not impute sin.* 2 Cor. v. 19. To wit, that God was in Christ, reconciling the world unto himself, *not imputing their trespasses* unto them: and hath committed unto us the word of reconciliation. Ver. 21. For he hath made him to be sin for us, who knew no sin ; that we might be *made the righteousness of God in him.* Rom. iii. 22. Even *the righteousness of* God, which *is by faith* of Jesus Christ unto all and *upon all them that believe;* for there is no difference. Ver. 24. Being *justified freely by* his grace, *through the redemption* that is in Christ Jesus ; Ver. 25. Whom God hath set forth to be *a propitiation through faith in his blood,* to declare *his righteousness for the remission* of sins that are past, through the forbearance of God ; Ver. 27. Where is boasting then? It is excluded. By what law? of works? Nay ; but *by the law of faith.* Ver. 28. Therefore we conclude, that a man is justified *by faith without the deeds of the law.* Tit. iii. 5. Not *by works of righteousness* which we have done, but according *to his mercy* he saved us, by the washing of regeneration, and renewing of the Holy Ghost ; Ver. 7. That, being *justified by his grace,* we should be made heirs according to the hope of eternal life. Eph. i. 7. In whom we have *redemption through his blood,* the forgiveness of sins, according to the riches of his grace. Jer. xxiii. 6. In his days Judah shall be saved, and Israel shall dwell safely ; and this is his name whereby he shall be called, *THE LORD OUR RIGHTEOUSNESS.* 1 Cor. i. 30. But of him are ye *in Christ Jesus,* who of God is *made unto us wisdom, and righteousness, and sanctification, and redemption;* Ver. 31. That, according as it is written, He that glorieth, *let him glory in the Lord.* Rom. v. 17. For if by one man's offence death reigned by one ; much more they which receive abundance of grace, and of the gift of righteousness, *shall reign* in life *by one, Jesus Christ;* Ver. 18. Therefore, as by the offence of one judgment came upon all men to condemnation ; even so *by the righteousness of one* the free gift came upon all men *unto justification of life.* Ver. 19. For as by one man's disobedience many were made sinners; so *by the obedience of one* shall many *be made righteous.*

[c] Acts x. 44. While Peter yet spake these words, the *Holy Ghost fell on all them* which heard the word. Gal. ii. 16. Knowing that a man is not justified by the works of the law, but *by the faith of Jesus Christ,* even we have believed in Jesus Christ, that we might *be justified by the faith of Christ,* and not by the works of the law : for by the works of the law shall no flesh be justified. Phil. iii. 9. And be found in him, not having mine own righteousness, which is of the law, but *that which is through the faith of Christ,* the righteousness *which is of God by faith.* Acts xiii. 38. Be it known unto you, therefore, men and brethren, that *through this man is preached* unto you *the forgiveness of sins;* Ver. 39. And by him *all that believe are justified* from all things, from which ye could not be justified by the law of Moses. Eph. ii. 7. That in the ages to come he might shew the *exceeding riches of his grace,* in his kindness toward us through *Christ Jesus.* Ver. 8. For by grace are ye saved *through faith;* and that not of yourselves : *it is the gift of God.*

II. [d] John i. 12. But as *many as received* him, to them *gave he power to become the sons of God,* even to them that *believe on his name.* Rom. iii. 28. Therefore we conclude, that a man is *justified by faith* without the deeds of the law. Rom. v. 1. Therefore, being *justified by faith,* we have peace with God through our Lord Jesus Christ.

[e] James ii. 17. Even so *faith,* if it *hath not works, is dead,* being alone. Ver. 22. Seest thou how *faith wrought with his works,* and *by works* was faith made *perfect?* Ver. 26. For as the body without the spirit is dead, so *faith without works is dead also.* Gal. v. 6. For in Jesus Christ neither circumcision availeth any thing, nor uncircumcision ; but *faith which worketh by love.*

III. [f] Rom. v. 8. But God commendeth his love toward us, in that, while we were yet sinners, Christ *died for us.* Ver. 9. Much more then, being now justified by his *blood, we shall be saved from wrath through him.* Ver. 10. For if, when we were enemies, we were reconciled to God by the death of his Son ; much more, *being reconciled,* we shall *be saved by his life.* Ver. 19. For as by one man's disobedience many were made sinners ; so by the *obedience of one shall many*

much as he was given by the Father for them,[g] and his obedience and satisfaction accepted in their stead,[h] and both freely, not for any thing in them, their justification is only of free grace;[i] that both the exact justice and rich grace of God might be glorified in the justification of sinners.[k]

IV. God did, from all eternity, decree to justify all the elect;[l] and Christ did, in the fulness of time, die for their sins, and rise again for their justification:[m] nevertheless they are not justified, until the Holy Spirit doth in due time actually apply Christ unto them.[n]

---

be made righteous. 1 Tim. ii. 5. For there is one God, and *one mediator between God and men,* the man *Christ Jesus;* Ver. 6. Who *gave himself a ransom for all,* to be testified in due time. Heb. x. 10. By the which will we are *sanctified, through the offering of the body of Jesus Christ* once for all. Ver. 14. For *by one offering he hath perfected for ever them that are sanctified.* Dan. ix. 24. Seventy weeks are determined upon thy people, and upon thy holy city, *to finish the transgression,* and *to make an end of sins,* and to make *reconciliation for iniquity,* and to *bring in everlasting righteousness,* and to seal up the vision and prophecy, and to anoint the most Holy. Ver. 26. And after threescore and two weeks shall Messiah be cut off, *but not for himself:* and the people of the prince that shall come shall destroy the city and the sanctuary; and the end thereof shall be with a flood, and unto the end of the war desolations are determined. Isa. liii. 4. Surely he hath *borne our griefs, and carried our sorrows:* yet we did esteem him stricken, smitten of God, and afflicted. Ver. 5. But he was *wounded for our transgressions,* he was bruised *for our iniquities:* the *chastisement of our peace was upon him;* and *with his stripes we are healed.* Ver. 6. All we, like sheep, have gone astray; we have turned every one to his own way; and the Lord *hath laid on him the iniquity of us all.* Ver. 10. Yet it *pleased the Lord to bruise him;* he hath *put him to grief:* when thou *shalt make his soul an offering for sin,* he shall see his seed, he shall prolong his days, and the pleasure of the Lord shall prosper in his hand. Ver. 11. He shall see of *the travail of his soul,* and shall be satisfied: by his knowledge shall my righteous servant justify many; for he *shall bear their iniquities.* Ver. 12. Therefore will I divide him a portion with the great, and he shall divide the spoil with the strong; because he hath *poured out his soul unto death:* and he was numbered with the transgressors; and he *bare the sin of many, and made intercession for the transgressors.*

[g] Rom. viii. 32. He that spared not his own Son, but *delivered him up for us all,* how shall he not with him also freely give us all things?

[h] 2 Cor. v. 21. For he hath *made him to be sin for us,* who knew no sin; that we might be made the righteousness of God in him. Matt. iii. 17. And lo a voice from heaven, saying, This is my beloved Son, *in whom I am well pleased.* Eph. v. 2. And walk in love, as Christ also hath loved us, and hath given himself for us an offering and a sacrifice to God *for a sweet-smelling savour.*

[i] Rom. iii. 24. Being *justified freely by his grace,* through the redemption that is in Christ Jesus. Eph. i. 7. In whom we have redemption through his blood, the forgiveness of sins, *according to the riches of his grace.*

[k] Rom. iii. 26. To declare, I say, at this time his righteousness; *that he might be just, and the justifier of him which believeth in Jesus.* Eph. ii. 7. That in the ages to come he might *shew the exceeding riches of his grace,* in his kindness toward us through Christ Jesus.

IV. [l] Gal. iii. 8. And the scripture, *foreseeing that God would justify the heathen through faith,* preached before the gospel unto Abraham, saying, In thee shall all nations be blessed. 1 Pet. i. 2. *Elect according to the foreknowledge of God* the Father, through sanctification of the Spirit, unto obedience and sprinkling of the blood of Jesus Christ. Ver. 19. But *with the precious blood of Christ,* as of a lamb without blemish and without spot: Ver. 20. Who verily *was foreordained before the foundation of the world,* but was manifest in these last times for you. Rom. viii. 30. Moreover, *whom he did predestinate,* them he also called; and whom he called, *them he also justified;* and whom he justified, them he also glorified.

[m] Gal. iv. 4. But *when the fulness of the time was come,* God sent forth his Son, made of a woman, made under the law. 1 Tim. ii. 6. Who gave himself a ransom for all, *to be testified in due time.* Rom. iv. 25. Who was delivered for our offences, and *was raised again for our justification.*

[n] Col. i. 21. And you, that were some time alienated, and enemies in your mind by wicked works, *yet now hath he reconciled* Ver. 22. In *the body of his flesh* through death, to present you holy, and unblameable, and unreproveable in his sight. Gal. ii. 16. [*See letter c immediately foregoing.*] Tit. iii. 4. But after that the kindness and love of God our Saviour toward man appeared, Ver. 5. Not by works of righteousness which we have done, but *according to his mercy he saved us, by the washing of regeneration, and renewing* of the Holy Ghost; Ver. 6. Which he shed on us abundantly through Jesus Christ our Saviour; Ver. 7. That, *being justified by his grace,* we should be made heirs according to the hope of eternal life.

V. God doth continue to forgive the sins of those that are justified:[o] and although they can never fall from the state of justification,[p] yet they may by their sins fall under God's fatherly displeasure, and not have the light of his countenance restored unto them, until they humble themselves, confess their sins, beg pardon, and renew their faith and repentance.[q]

VI. The justification of believers under the Old Testament was, in all these respects, one and the same with the justification of believers under the New Testament.[r]

CHAP. XII.—*Of Adoption.*

I. ALL those that are justified, God vouchsafeth, in and for his only Son Jesus Christ, to make partakers of the grace of adoption:[a] by which they are taken into the number, and enjoy the liberties and privileges of the children of God;[b] have his name put upon them,[c] re-

V. [o] Matt. vi. 12. And *forgive us our debts*, as we forgive our debtors. 1 John i. 7. But if we walk in the light, as he is in the light, we have fellowship one with another, and *the blood of Jesus Christ his Son cleanseth us from all sin.* Ver. 9. If we confess our sins, *he is faithful and just to forgive us our sins,* and to cleanse us from all unrighteousness. 1 John ii. 1. My little children, these things write I unto you, that ye sin not. And *if any man sin, we have an advocate with the Father,* Jesus Christ the righteous: Ver. 2. And he is the *propitiation for our sins;* and not for ours only, but also for the sins of the whole world.

[p] Luke xxii. 32. But I have prayed for thee, *that thy faith fail not:* and when thou art converted, strengthen thy brethren. John x. 28. And I give unto them eternal life; and *they shall never perish, neither shall any pluck them out of my hand.* Heb. x. 14. For by one offering he hath *perfected for ever* them that are sanctified.

[q] Ps. lxxxix. 31. If they break my statutes, and keep not my commandments; Ver. 32. Then will I visit their transgression *with the rod, and their iniquity with stripes.* Ver. 33. Nevertheless my lovingkindness will I *not utterly take from him,* nor suffer my faithfulness to fail. Ps. li. 7. *Purge me with hyssop,* and I shall be clean; *wash me, and I shall be whiter* than snow. Ver. 8. Make me to *hear joy and gladness, that the bones which thou hast broken* may rejoice. Ver. 9. *Hide thy face from my sins,* and blot out all mine iniquities. Ver. 10. Create in me a clean heart, O God; and renew a right spirit within me. Ver. 11. Cast me *not away from thy presence;* and take not thy Holy Spirit from me. Ver. 12. Restore *unto me the joy of thy salvation;* and uphold me with thy free Spirit. Ps. xxxii. 5. I *acknowledged my sin unto thee,* and mine iniquity have I not hid. I said, I will confess my transgressions unto the Lord; and thou *forgavest the iniquity of my sin.* Matt. xxvi. 75 And Peter remembered the word of Jesus, which said unto him, Before the cock crow, thou shalt deny me thrice. And he went out, *and wept bitterly.* 1 Cor. xi. 30. For *this cause* many *are weak and sickly* among you, and many sleep. Ver. 32. But when we are judged, *we are chastened* of the Lord, that we should not be condemned with the world. Luke i. 20. And, behold, *thou shalt be dumb,* and *not able to speak,* until the day that these things shall be performed, *because thou believest not my words,* which shall be fulfilled in their season.

VI. [r] Gal. iii. 9. So then they which be of faith are *blessed with faithful Abraham* Ver. 13. Christ hath *redeemed us from the curse of the law,* being made a curse for us: for it is written, Cursed is every one that hangeth on a tree: Ver. 14. That the *blessing of Abraham might come on the Gentiles* through Jesus Christ; that we might receive the promise of the Spirit through faith. Rom. iv. 22. And therefore it was imputed to him for righteousness. Ver. 23. Now, *it was not written for his sake alone,* that it was imputed to him; Ver. 24. But *for us also,* to whom it shall be imputed, if we believe on him that raised up Jesus our Lord from the dead. Heb. xiii. 8. *Jesus Christ the same yesterday, and to-day, and for ever.*

I. [a] Eph. i. 5. Having predestinated us *unto the adoption of children by Jesus Christ* to himself, according to the good pleasure of his will. Gal. iv. 4. But when the fulness of the time was come, *God sent forth his Son,* made of a woman, made under the law, Ver. 5. To redeem them that were under the law, *that we might receive the adoption of sons.*

[b] Rom. viii. 17. And if children, then heirs; *heirs of God,* and *joint-heirs with Christ;* if so be that we suffer with him, that we may be also *glorified together.* John i. 12. But as many as received him, to them *gave he power to become the sons of God,* even to them that believe on his name.

[c] Jer. xiv. 9. Yet thou, O Lord, art in the midst of us, and we are *called by thy name;*

ceive the Spirit of adoption;^d have access to the throne of grace with boldness;^e are enabled to cry, Abba, Father;^f are pitied,^g protected,^h provided for,ⁱ and chastened by him as by a father;^k yet never cast off,^l but sealed to the day of redemption,^m and inherit the promises,ⁿ as heirs of everlasting salvation.^o

CHAP. XIII.—*Of Sanctification.*

I. THEY who are effectually called and regenerated, having a new heart and a new spirit created in them, are farther sanctified really and personally, through the virtue of Christ's death and resurrection,^a by his word and Spirit dwelling in them;^b the dominion of the whole body of sin is destroyed,^c and the several lusts thereof are more and more weakened and mortified,^d and they more and more

leave us not. 2 Cor. vi. 18. And will *be a Father unto you, and ye shall be my sons and daughters*, saith the Lord Almighty. Rev. iii. 12. Him that overcometh will I make a pillar in the temple of my God, and he shall go no more out: and I will write upon him the *name of my God*, and the name of the city of my God, which is new Jerusalem, which cometh down out of heaven from my God; and I will write upon him *my new name.*

^d Rom. viii. 15. For ye have not received the spirit of bondage again to fear; but ye *have received the spirit of adoption*, whereby we cry, Abba, Father.

^e Eph. iii. 12. *In whom* we have *boldness and access with confidence* by the faith of him. Rom. v. 2. *By whom* also we *have access* by faith into this grace wherein we stand, and rejoice in hope of the glory of God.

^f Gal. iv. 6. And because ye are sons, God hath sent forth the *Spirit of his Son* into your hearts, *crying, Abba, Father.*

^g Ps. ciii. 13. Like as a father pitieth his children, *so the Lord pitieth them that fear him.*

^h Prov. xiv. 26. In the fear of the Lord is *strong confidence;* and *his children shall have a place of refuge.*

ⁱ Matt. vi. 30. Wherefore, if God so clothe the grass of the field, which to day is, and to morrow is cast into the oven, shall he not *much more clothe you, O ye of little faith?* Ver. 32. *For your heavenly Father knoweth that ye have need of all these things.* 1 Pet. v. 7. Casting all your care upon him; for *he careth for you.*

^k Heb. xii. 6. For whom the Lord loveth he *chasteneth, and scourgeth every son* whom he receiveth.

^l Lam. iii. 31. For the *Lord will not cast off for ever.*

^m Eph. iv. 30. And grieve not the Holy Spirit of God, *whereby ye are sealed unto the day of redemption.*

ⁿ Heb. vi. 12. That ye be not slothful, but followers of them *who through faith and patience inherit the promises.*

^o 1 Pet. i. 3. Blessed be the God and Father of our Lord Jesus Christ, which, according to his abundant mercy, hath begotten us again *unto a lively hope*, by the resurrection of Jesus Christ from the dead. Ver. 4. *To an inheritance incorruptible*, and undefiled, and that fadeth not away, reserved in heaven for you. Heb. i. 14. Are they not all ministering spirits, sent forth to minister for them *who shall be heirs of salvation?*

I. ^a 1 Cor. vi. 11. And such were some of you: but ye are washed, *but ye are sanctified*, but ye are justified *in the name of the Lord Jesus*, and by the Spirit of our God. Acts xx. 32. And now, brethren, I commend you to God, and to the word of his grace, *which is able to build you up*, and to give you an inheritance among all them which are sanctified. Phil. iii. 10. That I may know him, and *the power of his resurrection*, and the fellowship of his sufferings, *being made conformable unto his death.* Rom. vi. 5. For if we have been planted together *in the likeness of his death*, we shall be also *in the likeness of his resurrection:* Ver. 6. Knowing this, that our *old man is crucified* with him, *that the body of sin might be destroyed*, that henceforth we should not serve sin.

^b John xvii. 17. *Sanctify them through thy truth:* thy word is truth. Eph. v. 26. That he might *sanctify* and cleanse it with the washing of water *by the word.* 2 Thess. ii. 13. But we are bound to give thanks alway to God for you, brethren beloved of the Lord, because God hath from the beginning chosen you to salvation *through sanctification of the Spirit, and belief of the truth.*

^c Rom. vi. 6. Knowing this, that our *old man is crucified* with him, that *the body of sin might be destroyed*, that henceforth we should not serve sin. Ver. 14. For *sin shall not have dominion over you:* for ye are not under the law, but under grace.

^d Gal. v. 24. And they that are Christ's *have crucified the flesh*, with the affections and lusts. Rom. viii. 13. For if ye live after the flesh, ye shall die; but if ye through *the Spirit do mortify the deeds of the body*, ye shall live.

quickened and strengthened in all saving graces,c to the practice of true holiness, without which no man shall see the Lord.f

II. This sanctification is throughout in the whole man,g yet imperfect in this life; there abideth still some remnants of corruption in every part:h whence ariseth a continual and irreconcilable war; the flesh lusting against the Spirit, and the Spirit against the flesh.i

III. In which war, although the remaining corruption for a time may much prevail,k yet, through the continual supply of strength from the sanctifying Spirit of Christ, the regenerate part doth overcome:l and so the saints grow in grace,m perfecting holiness in the fear of God.n

---

CHAP. XIV.—*Of Saving Faith.*

I. THE grace of faith, whereby the elect are enabled to believe to the saving of their souls,a is the work of the Spirit of Christ in their hearts,b and is ordinarily wrought by the ministry of the

c Col. i. 11. *Strengthened with all might,* according to his glorious power, unto all patience and long-suffering with joyfulness. Eph. iii. 16. That he would grant you, according to the riches of his glory, *to be strengthened with might* by his Spirit *in the inner man;* Ver. 17. That Christ may dwell in your hearts by faith ; that ye, *being rooted and grounded in love,* Ver. 18. May be *able to comprehend* with all saints what is the breadth, and length, and depth, and height; Ver. 19. And to know the love of Christ, which passeth knowledge, that ye might *be filled with all the fulness of God.*

f 2 Cor. vii. 1. Having therefore these promises, dearly beloved, let us cleanse ourselves from all filthiness of the flesh and spirit, *perfecting holiness in the fear of God.* Heb. xii. 14. Follow peace with all men, and holiness, *without which no man shall see the Lord.*

II. g 1 Thess. v. 23. And the very God of peace *sanctify you wholly:* and I pray God *your whole spirit, and soul, and body, be preserved blameless* unto the coming of our Lord Jesus Christ.

h 1 John i. 10. If we say that *we have not sinned, we make him a liar,* and his word is not in us. Rom. vii. 18. For I know that in me (that is, *in my flesh) dwelleth no good thing:* for to will is present with me ; but *how to perform that which is good I find not.* Ver. 23. But I see *another law in my members warring against the law of my mind,* and bringing me into captivity to the law of sin which is in my members. Phil. iii. 12. Not *as though I had already attained, either were already perfect;* but I follow after, if that I may apprehend that for which also I am apprehended of Christ Jesus.

i Gal. v. 17. For the *flesh lusteth against the Spirit, and the Spirit against the flesh:* and these are contrary the one to the other ; so that ye cannot do the things that ye would. 1 Pet. ii. 11. Dearly beloved, I beseech you, as strangers and pilgrims, ab-

stain from fleshly lusts, *which war against the soul.*

III. k Rom. vii. 23. But I see another law in my members warring against the law of my mind, and *bringing me into captivity* to the law of sin which is in my members.

l Rom. vi. 14. For *sin shall not have dominion over you:* for ye are not under the law, *but under grace.* 1 John v. 4. For whatsoever is born of God *overcometh the world:* and this is the victory that over cometh the world, even our faith. Eph iv. 15. But, speaking the truth in love, *may grow up into him in all things,* which is the head, even Christ: Ver. 16. From whom the whole body fitly joined together and compacted by that which every joint supplieth, according to the effectual working in the measure of every part, *maketh increase of the body,* unto the edifying of itself in love.

m 2 Pet. iii. 18. *But grow in grace,* and in the knowledge of our Lord and Saviour Jesus Christ. To him be glory both now and for ever. Amen. 2 Cor. iii. 18. But we all, with open face beholding as in a glass the glory of the Lord, *are changed* into the same image, *from glory to glory,* even as by the Spirit of the Lord.

n 2 Cor. vii. 1. Having therefore these promises, dearly beloved, let us cleanse ourselves from all filthiness of the flesh and spirit, *perfecting holiness in the fear of God.*

I. a Heb. x. 39. But we are not of them who draw back unto perdition ; but of them *that believe to the saving of the soul.*

b 2 Cor. iv. 13. We having *the same spirit of faith,* according as it is written, I believed, and therefore have I spoken ; we also believe, and therefore speak. Eph. i. 17. That the God of our Lord Jesus Christ, the Father of glory, may give unto you *the spirit of wisdom* and revelation in the knowledge of him : Ver. 18. The eyes of your understanding being enlightened ; that ye may know what is the hope of his calling,

word:c by which also, and by the administration of the sacraments, and prayer, it is increased and strengthened.d

II. By this faith, a Christian believeth to be true whatsoever is revealed in the word, for the authority of God himself speaking therein;e and acteth differently upon that which each particular passage thereof containeth; yielding obedience to the commands,f trembling at the threatenings,g and embracing the promises of God for this life and that which is to come.h But the principal acts of saving faith are, accepting, receiving, and resting upon Christ alone for justification, sanctification, and eternal life, by virtue of the covenant of grace.i

III. This faith is different in degrees, weak or strong;k may be often and many ways assailed and weakened, but gets the victory;l growing

and what the riches of the glory of his inheritance in the saints, Ver. 19. And what is the exceeding greatness *of his power to us-ward who believe,* according to the working of his mighty power. Eph. ii. 8. For by grace are ye saved *through faith;* and that not of yourselves: it is the *gift of God.*
c Rom. x. 14. How then shall they call on him in whom they have not believed? and *how shall they believe in him of whom they have not heard?* and how shall they hear without a preacher? Ver. 17. So then *faith cometh by hearing,* and hearing by the word of God.
d 1 Pet. ii. 2. As new-born babes, desire the sincere *milk of the word, that ye may grow thereby.* Acts xx. 32. And now, brethren, I commend you to God, and to *the word of his grace, which is able to build you up,* and to give you an inheritance among all them which are sanctified. Rom. iv. 11. And he received the sign of *circumcision, a seal of the righteousness of the faith* which he had yet being uncircumcised: that he might be the father of all them that believe, though they be not circumcised; that righteousness might be imputed unto them also. Luke xvii. 5. And the apostles said unto the *Lord, Increase our faith.* Rom. i. 16. For I am not ashamed of the *gospel of Christ:* for it is *the power of God unto salvation* to every one that believeth; to the Jew first, and also to the Greek. Ver. 17. For therein is the righteousness of God *revealed from faith to faith:* as it is written, The just shall live by faith.
II. e John iv. 42. And said unto the woman, Now we believe, not because of thy saying: for *we have heard him ourselves, and know that this is indeed the Christ,* the Saviour of the world. 1 Thess. ii. 13. For this cause also thank we God without ceasing, because, when ye received the word of God which ye heard of us, *ye received it* not as the word of men, but *(as it is in truth) the word of God,* which effectually worketh also in you that believe. 1 John v. 10. He that *believeth on the Son of God hath the witness in himself:* he that believeth not God hath made him a liar; because he believed not the record that God gave of his Son. Acts xxiv. 14. But this I confess unto thee, that after the way which they call heresy, so worship I *the God of my fathers, believing all things which are written in the law and in the prophets.*

f Rom. xvi. 26. But now is made manifest, and by the Scriptures of the prophets, according to the *commandment* of the everlasting God, made known to all nations for the *obedience of faith.*
g Isa. lxvi. 2. For all those things hath mine hand made, and all these things have been, saith the Lord: but to this man will I look, even to him that is poor, and of a contrite spirit, *and trembleth at my word.*
h Heb. xi. 13. These all died in faith, not having received the promises, but having seen them afar off, and were persuaded of them, *and embraced them,* and confessed that they were strangers and pilgrims on the earth. 1 Tim. iv. 8. For bodily exercise profiteth little; but godliness is profitable unto all things, *having promise of the life that now is, and of that which is to come.*
i John i. 12. But as many *as received him,* to them gave he power to become the sons of God, even to them that believe on his name. Acts xvi. 31. And they said, *Believe on the Lord Jesus Christ, and thou shalt be saved,* and thy house. Gal. ii. 20. I am crucified with Christ: nevertheless I live; yet not I, but Christ liveth in me: *and the life which I now live in the flesh I live by the faith* of the Son of God, who loved me, and gave himself for me. Acts xv. 11. But *we believe* that through the grace of the Lord Jesus Christ *we shall be saved, even as they.*
III. k Heb. v. 13. For every one that useth milk is *unskilful in the word of righteousness; for he is a babe.* Ver. 14. But *strong meat belongeth to them that are of full age,* even those who by reason of use have their senses exercised to discern both good and evil. Rom. iv. 19. And being *not weak in faith,* he considered not his own body now dead, when he was about an hundred years old, neither yet the deadness of Sarah's womb: Ver. 20. He staggered not at the promise of God through unbelief; but *was strong in faith,* giving glory to God. Matt. vi. 30. Wherefore, if God so clothe the grass of the field, which to-day is, and to-morrow is cast into the oven, shall he not much more clothe you, *O ye of little faith?* Matt. viii. 10. When Jesus heard it, he marvelled, and said to them that followed, Verily I say unto you, *I have not found so great faith, no, not in Israel.*
l Luke xxii. 31. And the Lord said, Simon, Simon, behold, Satan hath desired to

up in many to the attainment of a full assurance through Christ,ᵐ who is both the author and finisher of our faith.ⁿ

CHAP. XV.—*Of Repentance unto Life.*

I. REPENTANCE unto life is an evangelical grace,ᵃ the doctrine whereof is to be preached by every minister of the gospel, as well as that of faith in Christ.ᵇ

II. By it a sinner, out of the sight and sense, not only of the danger, but also of the filthiness and odiousness of his sins, as contrary to the holy nature and righteous law of God, and upon the apprehension of his mercy in Christ to such as are penitent, so grieves for and hates his sins, as to turn from them all unto God,ᶜ purposing

---

have you, that he may sift you as wheat: Ver. 32. But I have prayed for thee, *that thy faith fail not;* and when thou art converted, strengthen thy brethren. Eph. vi. 16. Above all, taking the *shield of faith,* wherewith ye shall be *able to quench all the fiery darts* of the wicked. 1 John v. 4. For whatsoever is born of God overcometh the world: and this is *the victory that overcometh the world, even our faith.* Ver. 5. Who is he that *overcometh the world,* but *he that believeth* that Jesus is the Son of God?

ᵐ Heb. vi. 11. And we desire that every one of you do shew the same diligence, to the *full assurance of hope* unto the end: Ver. 12. That ye be not slothful, but followers of them *who through faith* and patience *inherit the promises.* Heb. x. 22. Let us draw near with a true heart, in *full assurance of faith,* having our hearts sprinkled from an evil conscience, and our bodies washed with pure water. Col. ii. 2. That their hearts might be comforted, being knit together in love, and unto all riches of the *full assurance of understanding,* to the *acknowledgment* of the mystery of God, and of the Father, and of Christ.

ⁿ Heb. xii. 2. Looking unto *Jesus, the author and finisher of our faith;* who, for the joy that was set before him, endured the cross, despising the shame, and is set down at the right hand of the throne of God.

I. ᵃ Zech. xii. 10. And I will pour upon the house of David, and upon the inhabitants of Jerusalem, the spirit of grace and of supplications; and they shall look upon me whom they have pierced, and *they shall mourn for him,* as one mourneth for his only son, and shall be in bitterness for him, as one that is in bitterness for his first-born. Acts xi. 18. When they heard these things, they held their peace, and glorified God, saying, Then hath God also to the Gentiles *granted repentance unto life.*

ᵇ Luke xxiv. 47. And that repentance and remission of sins *should be preached in his name among all nations,* beginning at Jerusalem. Mark i. 15. And *saying,* The time is fulfilled, and the kingdom of God is at hand: *repent ye, and believe the gospel.* Acts xx. 21. *Testifying* both to the Jews, and also to the Greeks, *repentance toward God, and faith toward our Lord Jesus Christ.*

II. ᶜ Ezek. xviii. 30. Therefore I will judge you, O house of Israel, every one according to his ways, saith the Lord God. Repent, and *turn yourselves from all your transgressions;* so iniquity shall not be your ruin. Ver. 31. *Cast away* from you *all your transgressions,* whereby ye have *transgressed;* and make you a new heart and a new spirit: for why will ye die, O house of Israel? Ezek. xxxvi. 31. Then shall ye remember you *own evil ways,* and *your doings that were not good,* and shall *loathe* yourselves in your own sight, *for your iniquities, and for your abominations.* Isa. xxx. 22. *Ye shall defile also the covering of thy graven images* of silver, and the ornament of thy molten images of gold: thou shalt cast them away as a *menstruous cloth;* thou shalt say unto it, *Get thee hence.* Ps. li. 4. Against thee, *thee only, have I sinned, and done this evil in thy sight;* that thou mightest be justified when thou speakest, and be clear when thou judgest. Jer. xxxi. 18. I have surely heard *Ephraim bemoaning himself thus;* Thou hast chastised me, and I was chastised, as a bullock unaccustomed to the yoke: turn thou me, and I shall be turned; for thou art the Lord my God. Ver. 19. Surely after that I was turned, I repented; and after that I was instructed, *I smote upon my thigh: I was ashamed, yea, even confounded,* because I did bear the reproach of my youth. Joel ii. 12. Therefore also now, saith the Lord, *Turn ye even to me with all your heart, and with fasting, and with weeping, and with mourning;* Ver. 13. And *rend your heart, and not your garments, and turn unto the Lord your God:* for he is gracious and merciful, slow to anger, and of great kindness, and repenteth him of the evil. Amos v. 15. *Hate the evil,* and love the good, and establish judgment in the gate: it may be that the Lord God of hosts will be gracious unto the remnant of Joseph. Ps. cxix. 128. Therefore I esteem all thy precepts concerning all things to be right; and *I hate every false way.* 2 Cor. vii. 11. For, behold, this self-same thing, that ye *sorrowed* after a godly sort, what *carefulness* it

and endeavouring to walk with him in all the ways of his commandments.[d]

III. Although repentance be not to be rested in, as any satisfaction for sin, or any cause of the pardon thereof,[e] which is the act of God's free grace in Christ;[f] yet is it of such necessity to all sinners, that none may expect pardon without it.[g]

IV. As there is no sin so small but it deserves damnation;[h] so there is no sin so great, that it can bring damnation upon those who truly repent.[i]

V. Men ought not to content themselves with a general repentance, but it is every man's duty to endeavour to repent of his particular sins particularly.[k]

VI. As every man is bound to make private confession of his sins

wrought in you, yea, what *clearing of yourselves,* yea, what *indignation,* yea, what *fear,* yea, what *vehement desire,* yea, what *zeal,* yea, what *revenge!* In all things ye have approved yourselves to be clear in this matter.

d Ps. cxix. 6. Then shall I not be ashamed, when I *have respect unto all thy commandments.* Ver. 59. I *thought on my ways, and turned my feet unto thy testimonies.* Ver. 106. *I have sworn,* and *I will perform it,* that I *will keep thy righteous judgments.* Luke i. 6. And they were both righteous before God, *walking in all the commandments and ordinances* of the Lord blameless. 2 Kings xxiii. 25. And like unto him was there no king before him, that *turned to* the Lord with all his heart, and with all his soul, and with all his might, *according to all the law of Moses;* neither after him arose there any like him.

III. e Ezek. xxxvi. 31. Then shall ye remember your own evil ways, and your doings that were not good, and shall *loathe yourselves in your own sight,* for your iniquities, and for your abominations. Ver. 32. *Not for your sakes* do I this, saith the Lord God, be it known unto you: *be ashamed and confounded for your own ways,* O house of Israel. Ezek. xvi. 61. Then thou shalt remember *thy ways, and be ashamed,* when thou sha..t receive thy sisters, thine elder and thy younger: and I will give them unto thee for daughters, but not by thy covenant. Ver. 62. And I will establish my covenant with thee; and thou shalt know that I am the Lord: Ver. 63. That thou mayest remember, *and be confounded, and never open thy mouth any more because of thy shame,* when I am pacified toward thee for all that thou hast done, saith the Lord God.

f Hos. xiv. 2. Take with you words, and turn to the Lord: say unto him, Take away all iniquity, and *receive us graciously:* so will we render the calves of our lips. Ver. 4. I will heal their backsliding, *I will love them freely:* for mine anger is turned away from him. Rom. iii. 24. Being *justified freely by his grace,* through the redemption that is in Christ Jesus. Eph. i. 7. In whom we have redemption through his blood, the forgiveness of sins *according to the riches of his grace.*

g Luke xiii. 3. I tell you, Nay: but, *except ye repent, ye shall all likewise perish.* Ver. 5. I tell you, Nay: but, *except ye repent, ye shall all likewise perish.* Acts xvii. 30. And the times of this ignorance God winked at; *but now commandeth all men every where to repent:* Ver. 31. Because he hath appointed a day, in the which he will judge the *world* in righteousness by that man whom he hath ordained; whereof he hath given assurance unto *all men,* in that he hath raised him from the dead.

IV. h Rom. vi. 23. For the *wages of sin is death;* but the gift of God is eternal life through Jesus Christ our Lord. Rom. v. 12. Wherefore, as by one man *sin entered into the world,* and *death by sin;* and so *death passed upon all men, for that all have sinned.* Matt. xii. 36. But I say unto you, That *every idle word* that men shall speak, they shall give *account thereof in the day of judgment.*

i Isa. lv. 7. Let the *wicked forsake his way,* and the *unrighteous man his thoughts:* and let him return unto the Lord, and *he will have mercy upon him;* and to our God, for he will *abundantly pardon.* Rom. viii. 1. There is therefore *now no condemnation* to them which are *in Christ Jesus,* who walk not after the flesh, but after the Spirit. Isa. i. 16. Wash you, make you clean; put away the evil of your doings from before mine eyes; cease to do evil. Ver. 18. Come now, and let us reason together, saith the Lord: Though *your sins be as scarlet, they shall be as white as snow;* though they be *red* like crimson, they shall be as *wool.*

V. k Ps. xix. 13. Keep back thy servant also *from presumptuous sins;* let them not have dominion over me: then shall I be upright, and I shall be *innocent from the great transgression.* Luke xix. 8. And Zaccheus stood, and said unto the Lord, Behold, Lord, the half of my goods I give to the poor; and if *I have taken any thing from* any man by false accusation, I restore him fourfold. 1 Tim. i. 13. Who was before a *blasphemer,* and a *persecutor,* and *injurious:* but I obtained mercy, because I did it *ignorantly in unbelief.* Ver. 15. This is a faithful saying, and worthy of all acceptation, that Christ Jesus came into the world to save *sinners; of whom I am chief.*

to God, praying for the pardon thereof;[1] upon which, and the forsaking of them, he shall find mercy;[m] so he that scandalizeth his brother, or the church of Christ, ought to be willing, by a private or publick confession and sorrow for his sin, to declare his repentance to those that are offended;[n] who are thereupon to be reconciled to him, and in love to receive him.[o]

CHAP. XVI.—*Of Good Works.*

I. GOOD works are only such as God hath commanded in his holy word,[a] and not such as, without the warrant thereof, are devised by men out of blind zeal, or upon any pretence of good intention.[b]

II. These good works, done in obedience to God's commandments, are the fruits and evidences of a true and lively faith:[c] and by them

---

VI. [1] Ps. li. 4. *Against thee, thee only, have I sinned, and done this evil in thy sight;* that thou mightest be justified when thou speakest, and be clear when thou judgest. Ver. 5. Behold, I was *shapen in iniquity; and in sin did my mother conceive me.* Ver. 7. Purge *me with hyssop,* and I shall be clean; *wash me,* and I shall be whiter than snow. Ver. 9. *Hide thy face from my sins,* and blot out all mine iniquities. Ver. 14. *Deliver me from bloodguiltiness,* O God, thou God of my salvation; and my tongue shall sing aloud of thy righteousness. Ps. xxxii. 5. *I acknowledged my sin* unto thee, and *mine iniquity have I not hid.* I said, I will *confess my transgressions unto the Lord;* and thou forgavest the iniquity of my sin. Selah. Ver. 6. For this shall every one that is *godly pray unto thee* in a time when thou mayest be found: surely in the floods of great waters they shall not come nigh unto him.

[m] Prov. xxviii. 13. He that covereth his sins shall not prosper; but *whoso confesseth and forsaketh them shall have mercy.* 1 John i. 9. If we *confess our sins,* he is *faithful and just to forgive us our sins,* and to cleanse us from all unrighteousness.

[n] James v. 16. *Confess your faults one to another,* and pray one for another, that ye may be healed. The effectual fervent prayer of a righteous man availeth much. Luke xvii. 3. Take heed to yourselves: If *thy brother trespass against thee, rebuke him;* and if he *repent, forgive him.* Ver. 4. And if he trespass against thee seven times in a day, and *seven times in a day turn again to thee,* saying, *I repent;* thou shalt *forgive him.* Josh. vii. 19. And Joshua said unto Achan, My son, give, I pray thee, glory to the Lord God of Israel, and make *confession* unto him; and *tell me now* what thou hast done; *hide it not* from me. [Ps. li. throughout.]

[o] 2 Cor. ii. 8. Wherefore I beseech you, that ye *would confirm your love toward him.*

I. [a] Micah vi. 8. *He hath shewed thee,* O man, *what is good;* and what doth the Lord require of thee, but to do justly, and to love mercy, and to walk humbly with thy God? Rom. xii. 2. And be not conformed to this world; but be ye transformed by the renewing of your mind, that ye may prove what is *that good, and acceptable, and perfect will of God.* Heb. xiii. 21. Make you perfect in every *good work* to do *his will, working in you that which is well-pleasing in his sight,* through Jesus Christ; to whom be glory for ever and ever. Amen.

[b] Matt. xv. 9. But *in vain they do worship me, teaching for doctrines the commandments of men.* Isa. xxix. 13. Wherefore the Lord said, Forasmuch as this people draw near me with their mouth, and with their lips do honour me, but have removed their heart far from me, and their *fear toward me is taught by the precept of men.* 1 Pet. i. 18. Forasmuch as ye know that ye were not redeemed with corruptible things, as silver and gold, from your vain conversation *received by tradition* from your fathers. Rom. x. 2. For I bear them record, that they have *a zeal of God,* but not *according to knowledge.* John xvi. 2. They shall put you out of the synagogues: yea, the time cometh, that whosoever killeth you will *think that he doeth God service.* 1 Sam. xv. 21. But the people took of the spoil, sheep and oxen, the chief of the things which should have been utterly destroyed, to sacrifice unto the Lord thy God in Gilgal. Ver. 22. And Samuel said, Hath the Lord as great delight in burnt-offerings and sacrifices, as *in obeying the voice of the Lord?* Behold, to *obey is better than sacrifice,* and to *hearken* than the *fat of rams.* Ver. 23. For rebellion is as the sin of witchcraft, and stubbornness is as iniquity and idolatry. Because thou hast *rejected the word of the Lord,* he hath also rejected thee from being king.

II. [c] James ii. 18. Yea, a man may say, Thou hast faith, and I have works; *shew me thy faith without thy works,* and I will *shew thee my faith by my works.* Ver. 22. Seest thou how faith wrought with his works, and by *works* was *faith made perfect?*

believers manifest their thankfulness,[d] strengthen their assurance,[e] edify their brethren,[f] adorn the profession of the gospel,[g] stop the mouths of the adversaries,[h] and glorify God,[i] whose workmanship they are, created in Christ Jesus thereunto;[k] that, having their fruit unto holiness, they may have the end eternal life.[l]

III. Their ability to do good works is not at all of themselves, but wholly from the Spirit of Christ.[m] And that they may be enabled thereunto, besides the graces they have already received, there is required an actual influence of the same Holy Spirit to work in them to will and to do of his good pleasure:[n] yet are they not hereupon to grow negligent, as if they were not bound to perform any duty unless upon a special motion of the Spirit; but they ought to be diligent in stirring up the grace of God that is in them.[o]

[d] Ps. cxvi. 12. What *shall I render unto the Lord* for all his benefits toward me? Ver. 13. I will take *the cup of salvation*, and call upon the name of the Lord. 1 Pet. ii. 9. But ye are a chosen generation, a royal priesthood, an holy nation, a peculiar people; that ye *should shew forth the praises of him* who hath called you out of darkness into his marvellous light.

[e] 1 John ii. 3. And hereby *we do know that we know him*, if we *keep his commandments*. Ver. 5. But whoso keepeth his word, in him verily is the love of God perfected : *hereby know we that we are in him*. 2 Pet. i. 5. And besides this, giving *all diligence*, add to your faith, virtue ; and to virtue, knowledge ; Ver. 6. And to knowledge, temperance ; and to temperance, patience ; and to patience, godliness ; Ver. 7. And to godliness, brotherly kindness ; and to brotherly kindness, charity. Ver. 8. For if these things be in you, and abound, they make you that ye shall neither be barren nor unfruitful in the knowledge of our Lord Jesus Christ. Ver. 9. But he that *lacketh these things is blind*, and cannot see afar off, and hath forgotten that he was purged from his old sins. Ver. 10. Wherefore the rather, brethren, give diligence *to make your calling and election sure;* for if ye do these things, ye shall never fall.

[f] 2 Cor. ix. 2. For I know the forwardness of your mind, for which I boast of you to them of Macedonia, that Achaia was ready a year ago ; and *your zeal hath provoked very many*. Matt. v. 16. Let your light so shine before *men, that they may see your good works*, and *glorify* your Father which is in heaven.

[g] Tit. ii. 5. To be discreet, chaste, keepers at home, good, obedient to their own husbands, *that the word of God be not blasphemed*. Ver. 9. Exhort servants to be obedient unto their own masters, and to please them well in all things ; not answering again ; Ver. 10. Not purloining, but shewing all good fidelity ; that they may *adorn the doctrine of God our Saviour in all things*. Ver. 11. For the grace of God that bringeth salvation hath appeared to all men, Ver. 12. Teaching us, that, denying ungodliness and worldly lusts, we should live soberly, righteously, and godly, *in this present world*. 1 Tim. vi. 1. Let as many servants as are under the yoke count their own masters worthy of all honour, *that the name of God and his doctrine be not blasphemed*.

[h] 1 Pet. ii. 15. For so is the will of God, that with well-doing *ye may put to silence the ignorance* of foolish men.

[i] 1 Pet. ii. 12. Having your conversation honest among the Gentiles : that, whereas *they speak against you as evil-doers*, they may, *by your good works*, which they shall behold, *glorify God* in the day of visitation. Phil. i. 11. Being filled with the fruits of righteousness, which are by Jesus Christ, *unto the glory and praise of God*. John xv. 8. Herein is *my Father glorified*, that ye bear much fruit ; so shall ye be my disciples.

[k] Eph. ii. 10. For we are his *workmanship*, created in Christ Jesus unto *good works*, which God hath before *ordained* that we *should walk in them*.

[l] Rom. vi. 22. But now, being made free from sin, and *become servants* to God, ye have your fruit unto holiness, *and the end everlasting life*.

III. [m] John xv. 4. Abide in me, and I in you. As the branch cannot bear fruit of itself, *except it abide in the vine;* no more can ye, except ye abide in me. Ver. 5. I am the vine, ye are the branches : he that *abideth* in me, and *I in him*, the same bringeth forth much *fruit ;* for *without me* ye can do nothing. Ver. 6. If a man abide not in me, he is *cast forth* as a branch, and *is withered;* and men gather them, and cast them into the fire, and they are burned. Ezek. xxxvi. 26. A new heart also will I give you, and a new spirit will I put within you ; and I will take away the stony heart out of your flesh, and I will give you an heart of flesh. Ver. 27. And *I will put my Spirit within you*, and *cause you to walk in my statutes*, and ye shall *keep* my judgments, and *do them*.

[n] Phil. ii. 13. For it *is God which worketh in you both to will and to do of his good pleasure*. Phil. iv. 13. *I can do all things* through *Christ which strengtheneth* me. 2 Cor. iii. 5. Not that we are sufficient *of ourselves* to *think* any thing as of ourselves , but *our sufficiency is of God*.

[o] Phil. ii. 12. Wherefore, my beloved, as ye have always obeyed, not as in my pre

IV. They who in their obedience attain to the greatest height which is possible in this life, are so far from being able to supererogate, and to do more than God requires, as that they fall short of much which in duty they are bound to do.p

V. We cannot, by our best works, merit pardon of sin, or eternal life, at the hand of God, by reason of the great disproportion that is between them and the glory to come, and the infinite distance that is between us and God, whom by them we can neither profit nor satisfy for the debt of our former sins;q but when we have done all we can, we have done but our duty, and are unprofitable servants;r and because, as they are good, they proceed from his Spirit;s and as they are wrought by us, they are defiled and mixed with so much weakness and imperfection, that they cannot endure the severity of God's judgment.t

sence only, but now much more in my absence, *work out your own salvation with fear and trembling.* Heb. vi. 11. And we desire that every one of you *do shew the same diligence,* to the full assurance of hope unto the end: Ver. 12. That ye *be not slothful,* but followers of them who through faith and patience inherit the promises. 2 Pet. i. 3. According as his divine power hath given unto us all things that pertain unto life and godliness, through the knowledge of him that hath called us to glory and virtue. Ver. 5. And besides this, giving *all diligence,* add to your faith, virtue; and to virtue, knowledge; Ver. 10. Wherefore the rather, brethren, *give diligence* to make your calling and election sure; for if ye do these things, ye shall never fall; Ver. 11. For so an entrance shall be ministered unto you abundantly into the everlasting kingdom of our Lord and Saviour Jesus Christ. Isa. lxiv. 7. And there is none that calleth upon thy name, that *stirreth up himself* to take hold of thee: for thou hast hid thy face from us, and hast consumed us, because of our iniquities. 2 Tim. i. 6. Wherefore I put thee in remembrance, that thou *stir up the gift of God,* which is in thee by the putting on of my hands. Acts xxvi. 6. And now I stand and am judged for the hope of the promise made of God unto our fathers: Ver. 7. Unto which promises our twelve tribes, *instantly serving God day and night,* hope to come: for which hope's sake, king Agrippa, I am accused of the Jews. Jude, ver. 20. But ye, beloved, *building up yourselves on your most holy faith,* praying in the Holy Ghost, Ver. 21. *Keep yourselves in the love of God,* looking for the mercy of our Lord Jesus Christ unto eternal life.

IV. p Luke xvii. 10. So likewise ye, when ye shall have done all those things which are commanded you, say, *We are unprofitable servants: we have done that which was our duty to do.* Neh. xiii. 22. And I commanded the Levites, that they should cleanse themselves, and that they should come and keep the gates, to sanctify the sabbath-day. Remember me, O my God, concerning this also, and *spare me according to the greatness* of thy mercy. Job ix. 2. I know it is so of a truth: but *how should man be just with God?* Ver. 3. If he will contend with him, *he cannot answer him one of a thousand* Gal. v. 17. For the flesh lusteth against the Spirit, and the Spirit against the flesh: and these are contrary the one to the other; so *that ye cannot do the things that ye would.*

V. q Rom. iii. 20. Therefore *by the deeds of the law there shall no flesh be justified* in his sight: for *by the law is the knowledge of sin.* Rom. iv. 2. For if Abraham were justified by works, he hath whereof to glory, but not before God. Ver. 4. Now to *him that worketh* is the *reward not reckoned of grace, but of debt.* Ver. 6. Even as David also describeth the blessedness of the man, unto whom God *imputeth righteousness without works.* Eph. ii. 8. For *by grace are ye saved* through faith: and that *not of yourselves: it is the gift of God;* Ver. 9. Not *of works,* lest *any man should boast.* Tit. iii. 5. Not *by works of righteousness* which *we have done,* but *according to his mercy* he saved us, by the washing of regeneration, and renewing of the Holy Ghost; Ver. 6. Which he shed on us abundantly through Jesus Christ our Saviour; Ver. 7. That, *being justified by his grace,* we should be made *heirs* according to the *hope* of eternal life. Rom. viii. 18. For I reckon, that the sufferings of this present time are *not worthy to be compared with the glory which shall be revealed in us.* Psal. xvi. 2. O my soul, thou hast said unto the Lord, Thou art my Lord: *my goodness extendeth not to thee.* Job xxii. 2. *Can a man be profitable unto God,* as he that is wise may be profitable unto himself? Ver. 3. *Is it any pleasure to the Almighty, that thou art righteous?* or is it *gain to him, that thou makest thy ways perfect?* Job xxxv. 7. If thou be *righteous, what givest thou him?* or *what receiveth he of thine hand?* Ver. 8. Thy wickedness may hurt a man as thou art, and thy righteousness may profit the *son of man.*

r Luke xvii. 10. [See letter p in this Chapter.]

s Gal. v. 22. But the *fruit of the Spirit is* love, joy, peace, long-suffering, gentleness, goodness, faith, Ver. 23. Meekness, temperance: *against such there is no law.*

t Isa. lxiv. 6. But we are all as *an unclean thing,* and *all our righteousnesses are as filthy rags;* and we all do fade as a leaf: and our iniquities, like the wind, have taken us away. Gal. v. 17. For the *flesh lusteth*

VI. Yet notwithstanding, the persons of believers being accepted through Christ, their good works also are accepted in him;[v] not as though they were in this life wholly unblameable and unreprovable in God's sight;[w] but that he, looking upon them in his Son, is pleased to accept and reward that which is sincere, although accompanied with many weaknesses and imperfections.[x]

VII. Works done by unregenerate men, although, for the matter of them, they may be things which God commands, and of good use both to themselves and others;[y] yet, because they proceed not from an heart purified by faith;[z] nor are done in a right manner, according to the word;[a] nor to a right end, the glory of God;[b] they are therefore sin-

against the Spirit; and the Spirit against the flesh: and these are contrary the one to the other; so that ye cannot do the things that ye would. Rom. vii. 15. For *that which I do I allow not: for what I would, that do I not; but what I hate, that do I.* Ver. 18. For I know that *in me* (that is, in my flesh) *dwelleth no good thing:* for to will is present with me; but how to perform that which is good *I find not.* Ps. cxliii. 2. And *enter not into judgment with thy servant:* for *in thy sight shall no man living be justified.* Ps. cxxx. 3. If thou, Lord, *shouldest mark iniquities, O Lord, who shall stand?*

VI. [v] Eph. i. 6. To the praise of the glory of his grace, wherein he *hath made us accepted in the Beloved.* 1 Pet. ii. 5. Ye also, as lively stones, are built up a spiritual house, an holy priesthood, to offer up *spiritual sacrifices, acceptable to God by Jesus Christ.* Exod. xxviii. 38. And it shall be upon *Aaron's* forehead, that *Aaron may bear the iniquity of the holy things,* which the children of Israel shall hallow in all their holy gifts; and it shall be always upon his forehead, *that they may be accepted before the Lord.* Gen. iv. 4. And Abel, he also brought of the firstlings of his flock, and of the fat thereof. And *the Lord had respect unto Abel,* and to *his offering.* With Heb. xi. 4. By *faith Abel offered unto God a more excellent sacrifice than Cain,* by which he obtained witness that he was righteous, God testifying of his gifts; and by it, being dead, yet speaketh.

[w] Job ix. 20. If *I justify myself, mine own mouth shall condemn me:* if *I say, I am perfect, it shall also prove me perverse.* Ps. cxliii. 2. And enter not into judgment with thy servant: for *in thy sight shall no man living be justified.*

[x] Heb. xiii. 20. Now the God of peace, that brought again from the dead our Lord Jesus, that great Shepherd of the sheep, through the blood of the everlasting covenant, Ver. 21. Make you perfect in every good work to do his will, *working in you that which is well-pleasing in his sight, through Jesus Christ;* to whom be glory for ever and ever. Amen. 2 Cor. viii. 12. For if there be *first a willing mind, it is accepted according to that a man hath,* and not according to that he hath not. Heb. vi. 10. For God is not unrighteous, *to forget your work and labour of love,* which ye have shewed toward his name, in that ye have ministered to the saints, and do mi-nister. Matt. xxv. 21. His lord said unto him, Well done, thou good and faithful servant; thou hast been *faithful over a few things,* I will make thee ruler over many things: enter thou into the joy of thy lord. Ver. 23. His lord said unto him, Well done, good and faithful servant; thou hast been faithful over *a few things,* I will make thee ruler over *many things:* enter thou into the joy of thy lord.

VII. [y] 2 Kings x. 30. And the Lord said unto Jehu, *Because thou hast done well in executing that which is right in mine eyes,* and hast done unto the house of Ahab *according to all that was in mine heart,* thy children of the fourth generation shall sit on the throne of Israel. Ver. 31. But Jehu took no heed to walk in the law of the Lord God of Israel with all his heart; for he departed not from the sins of Jeroboam, which made Israel to sin. 1 Kings xxi. 27. And it came to pass, when *Ahab* heard those words, that he *rent his clothes, and put sackcloth upon his flesh, and fasted,* and lay in sackcloth, and went softly. Ver. 29. Seest thou how Ahab humbleth himself before me? *Because he humbleth himself before me, I will not bring the evil in his days;* but in his son's days will I bring the evil upon his house. Phil. i. 15. Some indeed *preach Christ even of envy and strife;* and some also of good will. Ver. 16. The one preach Christ of contention, not sincerely, supposing to add affliction to my bonds. Ver. 18. What then? Notwithstanding, *every way, whether in pretence,* or in truth, *Christ is preached; and I therein do rejoice,* yea, and will rejoice.

[z] Gen. iv. 5. But unto *Cain* and to *his offering,* he had *not respect.* And Cain was very wroth, and his countenance fell. With Heb. xi. 4. *By faith Abel offered unto God a more excellent sacrifice than Cain, by which he obtained witness* that he was righteous, God testifying of his gifts; and by it he, being dead, yet speaketh. Ver. 6. But *without faith it is impossible to please him:* for he that *cometh to God must believe that he is, and that he is a rewarder of them that diligently seek him.*

[a] 1 Cor. xiii. 3. And though I *bestow all my goods to feed the poor,* and though I *give my body to be burned, and have not charity, it profiteth me nothing.* Isa. i. 12. When ye come to appear before me, *who hath required this at your hand, to tread my courts?*

[b] Matt. vi. 2. Therefore, when thou doest

ful, and cannot please God, or make a man meet to receive grace from God.c And yet their neglect of them is more sinful, and displeasing unto God.d

---

CHAP. XVII.—*Of the Perseverance of the Saints.*

I. THEY whom God hath accepted in his Beloved, effectually called and sanctified by his Spirit, can neither totally nor finally fall away from the state of grace; but shall certainly persevere therein to the end, and be eternally saved.a

II. This perseverance of the saints depends not upon their own free will, but upon the immutability of the decree of election, flowing from the free and unchangeable love of God the Father;b upon the efficacy

thine alms, *do not sound a trumpet before thee, as the hypocrites do* in the synagogues, and in the streets, that *they may have glory of men.* Verily I say unto you, They have their reward. Ver. 5. And when thou prayest, thou shalt not be as the *hypocrites* are: *for they love to pray standing in the synagogues,* and in the corners of the streets, that *they may be seen of men.* Verily I say unto you, They have their reward. Ver. 16. Moreover, when ye fast, be not, as the *hypocrites, of a sad countenance;* for they disfigure their faces *that they may appear unto men to fast.* Verily I say unto you, They have their reward.
c Hag. ii. 14. Then answered Haggai, and said, So is this people, and so is this nation before me, saith the Lord; and so is every work of their hands; and *that which they offer there is unclean.* Tit. i. 15. Unto the pure all things are pure: but *unto them that are defiled and unbelieving is nothing pure;* but even *their mind and conscience is defiled.* Amos v. 21. I hate, I *despise your feast-days,* and *I will not smell in your solemn assemblies.* Ver. 22. Though ye offer me burnt-offerings, and your *meat-offerings, I will not accept them; neither will I regard the peace-offerings of your fat beasts.* Hosea i. 4. And the Lord said unto him, Call his name Jezreel; for yet a little while, *and I will avenge the blood of Jezreel* upon the house of Jehu, and will cause to cease the kingdom of the house of Israel. Rom. ix. 16. So then *it is not of him that willeth,* nor *of him that runneth,* but *of God that sheweth mercy.* Tit. iii. 5. *Not by works of righteousness which we have done, but according to his mercy he saved us,* by the washing of regeneration, and renewing of the Holy Ghost.
d Ps. xiv. 4. *Have all the workers of iniquity no knowledge?* who eat up my people as they eat bread, and call not upon the Lord. Ps. xxxvi. 3. The words of his mouth are iniquity and deceit: *he hath left off to be wise, and to do good.* Job xxi. 14. Therefore they say unto God, *Depart from us; for we desire not the knowledge of thy ways.* Ver. 15. What is the Almighty, that *we should serve him?* and what profit should we have, if we pray unto him? Matt. xxv.

41. Then shall he say also unto them on the left hand, Depart from me, ye cursed, into everlasting fire, prepared for the devil and his angels: Ver. 42. For I was an hungered, and *ye gave me no meat:* I was thirsty, and *ye gave me no drink:* Ver. 43. I was a stranger, *and ye took me not in:* naked, and *ye clothed me not:* sick, and in prison, and *ye visited me not.* Ver. 45. Then shall he answer them, saying, Verily I say unto you, Inasmuch as ye did it not to one of the least of these, ye did it not to me. Matt. xxiii. 23. Woe unto you, scribes and Pharisees, hypocrites! for ye pay tithe of mint, and anise, and cummin, and *have omitted the weightier matters* of the law, *judgment, mercy, and faith: these ought ye to have done,* and not to leave the other undone.

I. a Phil. i. 6. Being confident of this very thing, that he which hath *begun a good work* in you, *will perform it until the day of Jesus Christ.* 2 Pet. i. 10. Wherefore the rather, brethren, give diligence to make your calling and election sure: for if ye do these things, *ye shall never fall.* John x. 28. And I give unto *them eternal life;* and they shall never perish, *neither shall any pluck them out of my hand.* Ver. 29. My Father, which gave them me, is greater than all; and *none is able to pluck them out of my Father's hand.* 1 John iii. 9. Whosoever is born of God *doth not commit sin; for his seed remaineth in him:* and *he cannot sin,* because he is born of God. 1 Pet. i. 5. Who are *kept by the power of God through faith unto salvation,* ready to be revealed in the last time. Ver. 9. Receiving the *end of your faith,* even the *salvation of your souls.*
II. b 2 Tim. ii. 18. Who concerning the truth have erred, saying that the resurrection is past already, and overthrow the faith of some. Ver. 19. Nevertheless *the foundation of God standeth sure, having this seal, The Lord knoweth them that are his.* And, Let every one that nameth the name of Christ depart from iniquity. Jer. xxxi. 3. The Lord hath appeared of old unto me, saying, Yea, *I have loved thee with an everlasting love;* therefore *with loving-kindness have I drawn thee.*

of the merit and intercession of Jesus Christ;^c the abiding of the Spirit, and of the seed of God within them;^d and the nature of the covenant of grace:^e from all which ariseth also the certainty and infallibility thereof.^f

III. Nevertheless they may, through the temptations of Satan and of the world, the prevalency of corruption remaining in them, and the neglect of the means of their preservation, fall into grievous sins;^g and for a time continue therein:^h whereby they incur God's displeasure,ⁱ

---

^c Heb. x. 10. By the which will we are sanctified, through the offering of the body of Jesus Christ once for all. Ver. 14. For by *one offering he hath perfected for ever them that are sanctified.* Heb. xiii. 20. Now the God of peace, that brought again from the dead our Lord Jesus, that great Shepherd of the sheep, *through the blood of the everlasting covenant,* Ver. 21. *Make you perfect in every good work* to do his will, working in you that which is well-pleasing in his sight, through Jesus Christ; to whom be glory for ever and ever. Amen. Heb. ix. 12. Neither by the blood of goats and calves, but by his *own blood,* he entered in once into the holy place, having *obtained eternal redemption* for us. Ver. 13. For if the blood of bulls and of goats, and the ashes of an heifer sprinkling the unclean, sanctifieth to the purifying of the flesh; Ver. 14. How much *more shall the blood of Christ,* who through the eternal Spirit offered himself without spot to God, *purge your conscience from dead works,* to serve the living God? Ver. 15. And for this cause he is the *mediator of the new testament,* that by means of death, for the redemption of the transgressions that were under the first testament, they which are *called might receive the promise of eternal inheritance.* Rom. viii. 33. Who shall lay any thing to the charge of God's elect? It is God that justifieth; Ver. 34. Who is he that condemneth? *It is Christ that died, yea rather, that is risen again,* who is even at the right hand of God, who *also maketh intercession for us.* Ver. 35. Who shall separate us from the love of Christ? shall tribulation, or distress, or persecution, or famine, or nakedness, or peril, or sword? Ver. 36. (As it is written, For thy sake we are killed all the day long; we are accounted as sheep for the slaughter.) Ver. 37. Nay, in all these things we are *more than conquerors, through him that loved us.* Ver. 38. For I am persuaded, that neither death, nor life, nor angels, nor principalities, nor powers, nor things present, nor things to come, Ver. 39. Nor height, nor depth, nor any other creature, shall be able to *separate us from the love of God, which is in Christ Jesus our Lord.* John xvii. 11. And now I am no more in the world, but these are in the world, and I come to thee. Holy Father, *keep through thine own name those whom thou hast given me,* that they may be one, as we are. Ver. 24. Father, I *will that they also whom thou hast given me be with me where I am;* that they may behold my glory, which thou hast given me : for thou lovedst me before the foundation of the world.

Luke xxii. 32. But *I have prayed for thee, that thy faith fail not:* and when thou art converted, strengthen thy brethren. Heb. vii. 25. Wherefore he is *able also to save them to the uttermost* that come unto God by him, *seeing he ever liveth to make intercession for them.*

^d John xiv. 16. And I will pray the Father, and he shall give you another *Comforter,* that he may *abide with you for ever;* Ver. 17. Even *the Spirit of truth;* whom the world cannot receive, because it seeth him not, neither knoweth him : but ye know him; for he *dwelleth with you,* and *shall be in you.* 1 John ii. 27. But the *anointing which ye have received of him abideth in you;* and ye need not that any man teach you : but as the same anointing teacheth you of all things, and is truth, and is no lie, and even as it hath taught you, ye shall abide in him. 1 John iii. 9. Whosoever is born of God doth not commit sin ; *for his seed remaineth in him:* and he cannot sin, because he is born of God.

^e Jer. xxxii. 40. And I will make an *everlasting covenant with them,* that I will not turn away from them, to do them good ; but *I will put my fear in their hearts, that they shall not depart from me.*

^f John x. 28. And I give unto them eternal life ; and they shall never perish, *neither shall any pluck them out of my hand.* 2 Thess. iii. 3. But *the Lord is faithful, who shall stablish you,* and keep you from evil. 1 John ii. 19. They went out from us, but they were not of us ; for *if they had been of us, they would no doubt have continued with us:* but they went out, that they might be made manifest that they were not all of us.

III. ^g Matt. xxvi. 70. But *he denied before them all,* saying, I know not what thou sayest. Ver. 72. *And* again *he denied with an oath, I do not* know the man. Ver. 74. *Then began he to curse and to swear,* saying, I know not the man. And immediately the cock crew.

^h Ps. li. [*the title.*] To the chief musician A Psalm of David, when Nathan the prophet came unto him, after he had gone in to Bath-sheba. Ver. 14. *Deliver me from blood-guiltiness,* O God, thou God of my salvation ; and my tongue shall sing aloud of thy righteousness.

ⁱ Isa. lxiv. 5. Thou meetest him that rejoiceth and worketh righteousness ; those that remember thee in thy ways : behold, *thou art wroth;* for we *have sinned:* in those is continuance, and we shall be saved. Ver. 7. And there is none that calleth upon thy name, that stirreth up himself to take hold of thee : for thou hast *hid thy face from us,*

and grieve his Holy Spirit;^k come to be deprived of some measure of their graces and comforts;^l have their hearts hardened,^m and their consciences wounded;^n hurt and scandalize others,^o and bring temporal judgments upon themselves.^p

---

CHAP. XVIII.—*Of Assurance of Grace and Salvation.*

1. ALTHOUGH hypocrites, and other unregenerate men, may vainly deceive themselves with false hopes and carnal presumptions of being in the favour of God and estate of salvation;^a which hope of theirs shall perish;^b yet such as truly believe in the Lord Jesus, and love him in sincerity, endeavouring to walk in all good conscience before him, may in this life be certainly assured that they are in the state of grace,^c

and hast consumed us, because of our iniquities. Ver. 9. *Be not wroth very sore,* O Lord, neither remember iniquity for ever : behold, see, we beseech thee, we are all thy people. 2 Sam. xi. 27. And when the mourning was past, David sent and fetched her to his house, and she became his wife, and bare him a son. But the *thing* that David had done *displeased the Lord.*
k Eph. iv. 30. And *grieve not the Holy Spirit of God,* whereby ye are sealed unto the day of redemption.
l Ps. li. 8. *Make me to hear joy and gladness;* that the bones which thou hast broken may rejoice. Ver. 10. *Create in me a clean heart,* O God; and *renew a right spirit within* me. Ver. 12. *Restore* unto me *the joy of thy salvation;* and uphold me with thy free Spirit. Rev. ii. 4. Nevertheless I have somewhat against thee, *because thou hast left thy first love.* Cant. v. 2. I sleep, but my heart waketh : it is the voice of my beloved that knocketh, saying, Open to me, my sister, my love, my dove, my undefiled : for my head is filled with dew, and my locks with the drops of the night. Ver. 3. I have put off my coat ; how shall I put it on? I have washed my feet; how shall I defile them? Ver. 4. My beloved put in his hand by the hole of the door, and my bowels were moved for him. Ver. 6. I opened to my beloved ; but my beloved *had withdrawn himself, and was gone:* my soul failed when he spake: I sought him, but I could not find him ; *I called him, but he gave me no answer.*
m Isa. lxiii. 17. O Lord, why hast thou made us to err from thy ways, and *hardened our heart from thy fear?* Return for thy servants' sake, the tribes of thine inheritance. Mark vi. 52. For they considered not the miracle of the loaves: for their *heart was hardened.* Mark xvi. 14. Afterward he appeared unto the eleven as they sat at meat, and upbraided them with their *unbelief and hardness of heart,* because they believed not them which had seen him after he was risen.
n Ps. xxxii. 3. When I *kept silence, my bones waxed old, through my roaring all the day long:* Ver. 4. For day and night *thy hand was heavy upon me:* my moisture is turned into the drought of summer. Ps. li. 8. Make me to hear joy and gladness ; that *the bones which thou hast broken* may rejoice.
o 2 Sam. xii. 14. Howbeit, because by this deed *thou hast given great occasion to the enemies of the Lord to blaspheme,* the child also that is born unto thee shall surely die.
p Ps. lxxxix. 31. If they break my statutes, and keep not my commandments ; Ver. 32. Then *will I visit their transgression with the rod, and their iniquity with stripes.* 1 Cor. xi. 32. But when we are judged, we *are chastened of the Lord,* that we should not be condemned with the world.

I. a Job viii. 13. So are the paths of all that forget God ; and *the hypocrite's hope shall perish:* Ver 14. *Whose hope shall be cut off, and whose trust shall be a spider's web.* Micah iii. 11. The heads thereof judge for reward, and the priests thereof teach for hire, and the prophets thereof divine for money : *yet will they lean upon the Lord,* and say, *Is not the Lord among us?* none evil can come upon us. Deut. xxix. 19. And it come to pass, when he heareth the words of this curse, that he *bless himself in his heart,* saying, *I shall have peace,* though I walk in the imagination of mine heart, to add drunkenness to thirst. John viii. 41. Ye do the deeds of your father. Then said they to him, We be not born of fornication ; *we have one Father, even God.*
b Matt. vii. 22. Many will say to me in that day, Lord, Lord, have we not prophesied in thy name? and in thy name have cast out devils? and in thy name done many wonderful works? Ver. 23. And then *will I profess unto them, I never knew you: depart from me, ye that work iniquity.*
c 1 John ii. 3. And hereby *we do know that we know him,* if we keep his commandments. 1 John iii. 14. *We know that we have passed from death unto life,* because we love the brethren : he that loveth not his brother abideth in death. Ver. 18. My little children, let us not love in word, neither in tongue ; but in deed, and in truth. Ver. 19. And *hereby we know that we are of the truth,* and shall assure our hearts before him. Ver 21. Beloved, *if*

and may rejoice in the hope of the glory of God; which hope shall never make them ashamed.^d

II. This certainty is not a bare conjectural and probable persuasion, grounded upon a fallible hope;^e but an infallible assurance of faith, founded upon the divine truth of the promises of salvation,^f the inward evidence of those graces unto which these promises are made,^g the testimony of the Spirit of adoption witnessing with our spirits that we are the children of God:^h which Spirit is the earnest of our inheritance, whereby we are sealed to the day of redemption.ⁱ

III. This infallible assurance doth not so belong to the essence of faith, but that a true believer may wait long, and conflict with many difficulties, before he be partaker of it:^k yet, being enabled by the Spirit to know the things which are freely given him of God, he may, without extraordinary revelation, in the right use of ordinary means, attain thereunto.^l And therefore it is the duty of every one to give

our heart condemn us not, then have we confidence toward God. Ver. 24. And he that keepeth his commandments dwelleth in him, and he in him: *and hereby we know that he abideth in us,* by the Spirit which he hath given us. 1 John v. 13. These things have I written unto you that believe on the name of the Son of God, *that ye may know that ye have eternal life,* and that ye may believe on the name of the Son of God. ^d Rom. v. 2. By whom also we have access by faith into this grace wherein we stand, and rejoice in hope of the glory of God. Ver. 5. And *hope maketh not ashamed; because the love of God is shed abroad in our hearts* by the Holy Ghost, which is given unto us.

II. ^e Heb. vi. 11. And we desire that every one of you do shew the same diligence, to the *full assurance of hope* unto the end. Ver. 19. Which *hope* we have as an *anchor of the soul, both sure and steadfast,* and which entereth into that within the vail. ^f Heb. vi. 17. Wherein God, willing more abundantly to shew unto the heirs of promise the *immutability of his counsel, confirmed it by an oath;* Ver. 18. That by *two immutable things,* in which it was impossible for God to lie, we *might have a strong consolation,* who have fled for refuge to lay hold upon the hope set before us. ^g 2 Pet. i. 4. Whereby are given unto us exceeding *great and precious promises;* that by these *ye might be partakers of the divine nature,* having escaped the corruption that is in the world through lust. Ver. 5. And besides this, *giving all diligence, add to your faith, virtue;* and to virtue, *knowledge.* Ver. 10. Wherefore the rather, brethren, give diligence to *make your calling and election sure:* for if ye do these things, ye shall never fall: Ver. 11. For so *an entrance shall be ministered unto you abundantly* into the everlasting kingdom of our Lord and Saviour Jesus Christ. 1 John ii. 3. And hereby *we do know* that we know him, *if we keep his commandments.* 1 John iii. 14. We know that we have passed from death unto life, *because we love the brethren:* he that loveth not his brother abideth in death. 2 Cor. i. 12. For our rejoicing is this, *the testimony of our conscience,* that in simplicity and godly sincerity, not with fleshly wisdom, but *by the grace of God, we have had our conversation in the world,* and more abundantly to you-ward.

^h Rom. viii. 15. For ye have not received the spirit of bondage again to fear; but ye have *received the Spirit of adoption,* whereby we cry, Abba, Father. Ver. 16. The *Spirit itself beareth witness with our spirit,* that we are the children of God. ⁱ Eph. i. 13. In whom ye also trusted, after that ye heard the word of truth, the gospel of your salvation: in whom also, after that ye believed, ye *were sealed with that Holy Spirit of promise,* Ver. 14. *Which is the earnest of our inheritance, until* the *redemption* of the purchased possession, unto the praise of his glory. Eph. iv. 30. And grieve not the Holy Spirit of God, whereby ye are *sealed unto the day of redemption.* 2 Cor. i. 21. Now he which stablisheth us with you in Christ, and hath anointed us, is God; Ver. 22. Who hath *also sealed us, and given the earnest of the Spirit in our hearts.*

III. ^k 1 John v. 13. These things have I written unto you that believe on the name of the Son of God, *that ye may know* that ye have eternal life, and that ye may believe on the name of the Son of God. Isa. l. 10. Who is among you that feareth the Lord, that obeyeth the voice of his servant, that *walketh in darkness, and hath no light?* let him trust in the name of the Lord, and stay upon his God. Mark ix. 24. And straightway the father of the child cried out, and said with tears, Lord, *I believe; help thou mine unbelief.* [See Ps. lxxxviii. throughout. Ps. lxxvii. to the 12th verse.]

^l 1 Cor. ii. 12. Now we have received, not the spirit of the world, but the Spirit which is of God; *that we might know the things that are freely given to us of God.* 1 John iv. 13. Hereby *know* we that we dwell in him, and he in us, *because he hath given us of his Spirit.* Heb. vi. 11. And we desire that every one of you *do shew the same diligence,* to the full assurance of hope unto the end: Ver. 12. That *ye be not slothful,* but

all diligence to make his calling and election sure;[m] that thereby his heart may be enlarged in peace and joy in the Holy Ghost, in love and thankfulness to God, and in strength and cheerfulness in the duties of obedience,[n] the proper fruits of this assurance: so far is it from inclining men to looseness.[o]

IV. True believers may have the assurance of their salvation divers ways shaken, diminished, and intermitted; as, by negligence in preserving of it; by falling into some special sin, which woundeth the conscience, and grieveth the Spirit; by some sudden or vehement temptation; by God's withdrawing the light of his countenance, and suffering even such as fear him to walk in darkness, and to have no light:[p] yet are they never utterly destitute of that seed of God, and life of faith, that love of Christ and the brethren, that sincerity of heart and conscience of duty, out of which, by the operation of the Spirit,

followers of them who through faith and patience inherit the promises. Eph. iii. 17. That *Christ may dwell in your hearts by faith; that ye, being rooted and grounded in love,* Ver. 18. *May be able to comprehend* with all saints what is the breadth, and length, and depth, and height; Ver. 19. And to know the love of Christ, which passeth knowledge, that ye might be filled with all the fulness of God.

m 2 Pet. i. 10. Wherefore the rather, brethren, *give diligence to make your calling and election sure:* for if ye do these things, ye shall never fall.

n Rom. v. 1. Therefore, *being justified by faith,* we *have peace with God,* through our Lord Jesus Christ: Ver. 2. By whom also we have access by faith into this grace wherein we stand, and *rejoice in hope of the glory of God.* Ver. 5. And *hope maketh not ashamed;* because the love of God is shed abroad in our hearts by the Holy Ghost, which is given unto us. Rom. xiv. 17. For the kingdom of God is not meat and drink; but *righteousness,* and *peace,* and *joy in the Holy Ghost.* Rom. xv. 13. Now the God of hope *fill you with all joy and peace in believing,* that ye *may abound in hope,* through the power of the Holy Ghost. Eph. i. 3. Blessed be the God and Father of our Lord Jesus Christ, who hath *blessed us with all spiritual blessings* in heavenly places in Christ: Ver. 4. According as he hath chosen us in him before the foundation of the world, that *we should be holy* and without blame before him in love. Ps. iv. 6. There be many that say, Who will shew us any good? *Lord, lift thou up the light of thy countenance upon us.* Ver. 7. Thou *hast put gladness in my heart,* more than in the time that their corn and their wine increased. Ps. cxix. 32. I will run the way of thy commandments, when *thou shalt enlarge my heart.*

o 1 John ii. 1. My little children, these things write I unto you, that *ye sin not.* And if any man sin, we have an advocate with the Father, Jesus Christ the righteous: Ver. 2. And he is the propitiation for our sins; and not for ours only, but also for the sins of the whole world. Rom. vi. 1. What shall we say then? *Shall we continue in sin, that grace may abound?* Ver. 2 God forbid. *How shall we, that are dead to sin, live any longer therein?* Tit. ii. 11. For *the grace of God* that bringeth salvation hath appeared to all men, Ver. 12. *Teaching us,* that, *denying ungodliness and worldly lusts, we should live soberly, righteously,* and *godly,* in this present world. Ver. 14. Who *gave himself for us, that he might redeem us from all iniquity,* and *purify unto himself a peculiar people, zealous of good works.* 2 Cor. vii. 1. *Having* therefore *these promises,* dearly beloved, *let us cleanse ourselves from all filthiness of the flesh and spirit, perfecting holiness in the fear of God.* Rom. viii. 1. There is therefore now no condemnation to them which are in Christ Jesus, *who walk not after the flesh,* but after the Spirit. Ver. 12. Therefore, brethren, we are *debtors, not to the flesh,* to live after the flesh. 1 John iii. 2. Beloved, now are we the sons of God; and it doth not yet appear what we shall be: but we *know* that, when he shall appear, we shall be *like him;* for we shall see him as he is. Ver. 3. And every man that hath *this hope in him, purifieth himself, even as he is pure.* Ps. cxxx. 4. But there is forgiveness with thee, *that thou mayest be feared.* 1 John i. 6. If we say that we have *fellowship with him,* and *walk in darkness, we lie,* and do not the truth: Ver. 7. But if we walk in the light, as he is in the light, we have fellowship one with another, and the *blood of Jesus Christ his Son cleanseth us from all sin.*

IV. p Cant. v. 2. *I sleep,* but my heart waketh: it is the voice of my beloved that knocketh, saying, Open to me, my sister, my love, my dove, my undefiled: for my head is filled with dew, and my locks with the drops of the night. Ver. 3. *I have put off my coat; how shall I put it on? I have washed my feet; how shall I defile them?* Ver. 6. I opened to my beloved; but *my beloved had withdrawn himself,* and was gone: my soul failed when he spake: *I sought him, but I could not find him; I called him, but he gave no answer.* Ps. li. 8. Make me to hear joy and gladness; *that the bones which thou hast broken may rejoice.* Ver. 12. *Restore unto me the joy of thy salvation;* and uphold me with thy free Spirit. Ver. 14. *Deliver me from blood*

this assurance may in due time be revived,q and by the which, in the mean time, they are supported from utter despair.r

CHAP. XIX.—*Of the Law of God.*

I. GOD gave to Adam a law, as a covenant of works, by which he bound him, and all his posterity, to personal, entire, exact, and perpetual obedience; promised life upon the fulfilling, and threatened death upon the breach of it; and endued him with power and ability to keep it.a

guiltiness, O God, thou God of my salvation; and my tongue shall sing aloud of thy righteousness. Eph. iv. 30. And *grieve not the Holy Spirit of God*, whereby ye are sealed unto the day of redemption. Ver. 31. Let all *bitterness*, and *wrath*, and *anger*, and *clamour*, and *evil-speaking*, be put away from you, with *all malice*. Ps. lxxvii. 1. I cried unto God with my voice, even unto God with my voice; and he gave ear unto me. Ver. 2. In the *day of my trouble I sought the Lord:* my *sore ran* in the night, and *ceased not: my soul refused to be comforted.* Ver. 3. *I remembered God, and was troubled:* I complained, and *my spirit was overwhelmed.* Selah. Ver. 4. *Thou holdest mine eyes waking:* I am *so troubled that I cannot speak.* Ver. 5. I have considered the days of old, the years of ancient times. Ver. 6. I call to remembrance my song in the night : I commune with mine own heart ; and my spirit made diligent search. Ver. 7. Will the Lord *cast off for ever?* and will he be *favourable no more?* Ver. 8. Is *his mercy clean gone for ever? doth his promise fail for evermore?* Ver. 9. Hath God *forgotten to be gracious?* hath he in *anger shut up his tender mercies?* Selah. *Ver. 10. And I said, This is my infirmity: but I will remember the years of the right hand of the most High. Matt. xxvi. 69. Now Peter sat without in the palace : and *a damsel came unto him, saying,* Thou also wast with Jesus of Galilee. Ver. 70. But *he denied before them all*, saying, I know not what thou sayest. Ver. 71. And when he was gone out into the porch, *another maid saw him, and said unto them* that were there, *This fellow was also with Jesus of Nazareth.* Ver. 72. And *again he denied with an oath*, I do not know the man. Ps. xxxi. 22. For *I said in my haste*, I am cut off from before thine eyes: nevertheless thou heardest the voice of my supplications when I cried unto thee. [Ps. lxxxviii. throughout.] Isa. l. 10. Who is among you that feareth the Lord, that obeyeth the voice of his servant, that *walketh in darkness, and hath no light?* let him trust in the name of the Lord, and stay upon his God.

q 1 John iii. 9. Whosoever is born of God doth not commit sin ; for *his seed remaineth in him;* and he cannot sin, because he is born of God. Luke xxii. 32. But I have prayed for thee, that *thy faith fail not:* and when thou art converted, strengthen thy brethren. Job xiii. 15. Though he slay me, yet will *I trust in him:* but I will maintain mine own ways before him. Ps. lxxiii. 15. *If I say, I will speak thus; behold I should offend* against the generation of thy children. Ps. li. 8, 12. [See letter p immediately before.] Isa. l. 10. [See letter p immediately foregoing.]

r Micah vii. 7. Therefore *I will look unto the Lord; I will wait for the God of my salvation:* my God will hear me. Ver. 8. Rejoice not against me, O mine enemy : when I fall, *I shall arise;* when I sit in darkness, *the Lord shall be a light unto me.* Ver. 9. I will bear the indignation of the Lord, because I have sinned against him, until he plead my cause, and execute judgment for me : *he will bring me forth to the light, and I shall behold his righteousness.* Jer. xxxii. 40. And I will *make an everlasting covenant* with them, that I will not turn away from them, to do them good ; but I will put my fear in their hearts, *that they shall not depart from me.* Isa. liv. 7 For a *small moment have I forsaken thee;* but with great mercies will I gather thee. Ver. 8. In a little wrath *I hid my face from thee for a moment;* but with everlasting *kindness will I have mercy on thee,* saith the Lord thy Redeemer. Ver. 9. For this is as the waters of Noah unto me : for as I have sworn that the waters of Noah should no more go over the earth ; so *have I sworn that I would not be wroth with thee*, nor rebuke thee. Ver. 10. For the mountains shall depart, and the hills be removed ; but *my kindness shall not depart from thee*, neither *shall the covenant of my peace be removed*, saith the Lord that hath mercy on thee. Ps. xxii. 1. My God, my God, why hast thou forsaken me? why art *thou so far from helping me*, and from the words of my roaring? [Ps. lxxxviii. throughout.]

I. a Gen. i. 26. And God said, Let us make man in our image, after our likeness ; and let them have dominion over the fish of the sea, and over the fowl of the air, and over the cattle, and over all the earth, and over every creeping thing that creepeth upon the earth. Ver. 27. So God *created man in his own image: in the image of God created he him;* male and female created he them. With Gen. ii. 17. But of *the tree of the knowledge of good and evil, thou shalt not eat* of it : for *in the day that thou eatest thereof thou shalt surely die.* Rom. ii 14. For when the Gentiles, which have not

II. This law, after his fall, continued to be a perfect rule of righteousness; and, as such, was delivered by God upon mount Sinai in ten commandments, and written in two tables;^b the first four commandments containing our duty towards God, and the other six our duty to man.^c

III. Besides this law, commonly called moral, God was pleased to give to the people of Israel, as a church under age, ceremonial laws containing several typical ordinances; partly of worship, prefiguring Christ, his graces, actions, sufferings, and benefits;^d and partly holding forth divers instructions of moral duties.^e All which ceremonial laws are now abrogated under the New Testament.^f

the law, do *by nature the things contained in the law*, these, having not the law, *are a law unto themselves*: Ver. 15. Which shew *the work of the law written in their hearts*, their conscience also bearing witness, and their thoughts the mean while accusing or else excusing one another. Rom. x. 5. For Moses describeth *the righteousness which is of the law*, That the man which doeth those things shall live by them. Rom. v. 12. Wherefore, as by one man *sin entered into the world*, and *death by sin;* and *so death passed upon all men*, for that *all have sinned*. Ver. 19. For as *by one man's disobedience many were made sinners;* so by the obedience of one shall many be made righteous. Gal. iii. 10. For as many as are of the works of the law are under the curse: for it is written, *Cursed is every one that continueth not in all things* which are written in the book of the law to do them. Ver. 12. And the law is not of faith: but, The man that *doeth them shall live in them*. Eccl. vii. 29. Lo, this only have I found, that *God hath made man upright;* but they have sought out many inventions. Job xxviii. 28. And unto man he said, Behold, the fear of the Lord, that is wisdom ; and *to depart from evil is understanding*.

II. ^b James i. 25. But whoso looketh into the *perfect law* of liberty, and continueth therein, he being not a forgetful hearer, but a doer of the work, this man shall be blessed in his deed. James ii. 8. If ye fulfil the *royal law* according to the scripture, Thou shalt love thy neighbour as thyself, ye do well. Ver. 10. For whosoever shall *keep the whole law*, and yet *offend in one point*, he is *guilty of all*. Ver. 11. For *he that said*, Do not commit adultery, *said also*, Do not kill. Now, if thou commit no adultery, yet if thou kill, thou art become a transgressor of the law. Ver. 12. So speak ye, and so do, as they that shall be judged by the *law of liberty*. Rom. xiii. 8. Owe no man any thing, but to love one another ; for *he that loveth another* hath *fulfilled the law*. Ver. 9. For this, Thou shalt not commit adultery, Thou shalt not kill, Thou shalt not steal, Thou shalt not bear false witness, Thou shalt not covet ; and *if there be any other commandment, it is briefly comprehended in this saying*, namely, Thou shalt *love thy neighbour as thyself*. Deut. v. 32. *Ye shall observe to do* therefore *as the Lord your God hath commanded you;* ye shall not turn aside to the right hand or to the left. Deut.

x. 4. And he *wrote on the tables*, according to the first writing, *the ten commandments*, which the Lord spake unto you in the mount, out of the midst of the fire, in the day of the assembly : and the Lord gave them unto me. Exod. xxxiv. 1. And the Lord said unto Moses, Hew thee two tables of stone like unto the first ; and I will *write upon these tables the words that were in the first tables*, which thou brakest.

^c Matt. xxii. 37. Jesus said unto him, Thou shalt *love the Lord thy God, with all thy heart, and with all thy soul, and with all thy mind*. Ver. 38. *This is the first and great commandment*. Ver. 39. And *the second* is like unto it, *Thou shalt love thy neighbour as thyself*. Ver. 40. On these *two commandments hang all the law and the prophets*.

III. ^d [Heb. Chapter ix.] Heb. x. 1. For the law having a *shadow of good things to come*, and not the very image of the things, can never with those sacrifices, which they offered year by year continually, make the comers thereunto perfect. Gal. iv. 1. Now I say, That *the heir, as long as he is a child, differeth nothing from a servant*, though he be lord of all ; Ver. 2. But is under tutors and governors, until the time appointed of the father. Ver. 3. Even *so we, when we were children, were* in bondage *under the elements of the world*. Col. ii. 17. Which are *a shadow of things to come;* but *the body is of Christ*.

^e 1 Cor. v. 7. *Purge out* therefore *the old leaven*, that ye may be *a new lump*, as ye are unleavened. For even *Christ our passover is sacrificed* for us. 2 Cor. vi. 17. Wherefore, come out from among them, and *be ye separate*, saith the Lord, and *touch not the unclean thing;* and I will receive you. Jude, ver. 23. And others save with fear, pulling them out of the fire ; *hating* even the *garment spotted by the flesh*.

^f Col. ii. 14. *Blotting out the handwriting of ordinances* that was against us, which was contrary to us, and *took it out of the way, nailing it to his cross*. Ver. 16. *Let no man therefore judge you in meat*, or in *drink*, or in respect of an *holiday*, or of the new moon, or of the *sabbath-days;* Ver. 17. Which are a *shadow of things* to come ; but *the body is of Christ*. Dan. ix. 27. And he shall confirm the covenant with many for one week : and in the midst of the week *he shall cause the sacrifice and the oblation to cease*, and for the overspreading of abo-

IV. To them also, as a body politick, he gave sundry judicial laws, which expired together with the state of that people, not obliging any other now, further than the general equity thereof may require.[g]

V. The moral law doth for ever bind all, as well justified persons as others, to the obedience thereof;[h] and that not only in regard of the matter contained in it, but also in respect of the authority of God, the Creator, who gave it.[i] Neither doth Christ in the gospel any way dissolve, but much strengthen this obligation.[k]

VI. Although true believers be not under the law as a covenant of works, to be thereby justified or condemned;[l] yet is it of great use to them, as well as to others; in that, as a rule of life, informing them of the will of God and their duty, it directs and binds them to walk accordingly;[m] discovering also the sinful pollutions of their nature,

minations he shall make it desolate, even until the consummation, and that determined shall be poured upon the desolate. Eph. ii. 15. Having *abolished in his flesh* the enmity, even *the law of commandments contained in ordinances;* for to make in himself of twain one new man, so making peace; Ver. 16. And *that he might reconcile both unto God in one body* by the cross, *having slain the enmity* thereby.

IV. g [Exod. Chapter xxi. Exod. xxii. 1. to the 29th verse. See both in the Bible.] Gen. xlix. 10. *The sceptre shall not depart from Judah,* nor a *lawgiver* from between his feet, until Shiloh come; and unto him shall the gathering of the people be. With 1 Pet. ii. 13. *Submit yourselves to every ordinance of man for the Lord's sake:* whether it be to the king, as supreme; Ver. 14. Or unto governors, as unto them that are sent by him for the punishment of evildoers, and for the praise of them that do well. Matt. v. 17. Think not that I am come to *destroy the law* or the prophets: I am not come to destroy, *but to fulfil.* With ver. 38. Ye have heard that *it hath been said,* An eye for an eye, and a tooth for a tooth: Ver. 39. *But I say unto you,* That ye resist not evil; but whosoever shall smite thee on thy right cheek, turn to him the other also. 1 Cor. ix. 8. Say I these things as a man? or *saith not the law the same* also? Ver. 9. For *it is written in the law* of Moses, Thou shalt not muzzle the mouth of the ox that treadeth out the corn. Doth God take care for oxen? Ver. 10. Or *saith he it altogether for our sakes?* For our sakes, no doubt, *this is written:* that he that ploweth should plow in hope; and that he that thrasheth in hope should be partaker of his hope.

V. h Rom. xiii. 8, 9. [See above in letter b.] Ver. 10. Love worketh no ill to his neighbour: therefore *love is the fulfilling of the law.* Eph. vi. 2. Honour thy father and mother, (which is the first *commandment with promise.*) 1 John ii. 3. And hereby we do know that we know him, if we *keep his commandments.* Ver 4. He that saith, I know him, and keepeth not *his commandments,* is a liar, and the truth is not in him. Ver. 7. Brethren, I write no *new commandment* unto you, but *an old commandment,* which ye had *from the beginning:* the old commandment *is the word which ye have heard from the beginning.* Ver. 8. Again, a new commandment I write unto you, which thing *is true in him and in you;* because the darkness is past, and the true light now shineth.

i James ii. 10, 11. [See in letter b.]

k Matt. v. 17. [See in letter g.] Ver. 18. For verily I say unto you, Till *heaven and earth pass, one jot or one tittle shall in no wise pass from the law, till all be fulfilled.* Ver. 19. Whosoever therefore shall *break one of these least commandments,* and shall *teach* men so, *he shall be called the least in the kingdom of heaven:* but whosoever shall do and teach them, the same shall be called great in the kingdom of heaven. James ii. 8. [See in letter b before.] Rom. iii. 31. Do we then *make void the law* through faith? God forbid; yea, *we establish the law.*

VI. l Rom. vi. 14. For sin shall not have dominion over you: for *ye are not under the law,* but under grace. Gal. ii. 16. Knowing that *a man is not justified by the works of the law,* but by the faith of Jesus Christ, even we have believed in Jesus Christ, that we might be justified by the faith of Christ, and not by the works of the law: for *by the works of the law shall no flesh be justified.* Gal. iii. 13. *Christ hath redeemed us from the curse of the law,* being made a curse for us: for it is written, Cursed is every one that hangeth on a tree. Gal. iv. 4. But when the fulness of the time was come, God sent forth his Son, made of a woman, *made under the law,* Ver. 5. To *redeem them that were under the law,* that we might receive the adoption of sons. Acts xiii. 39. And by him all that believe are justified from all things, *from which ye could not be justified by the law of Moses.* Rom. viii. 1. There is therefore now *no condemnation to them which are in Christ Jesus,* who walk not after the flesh, but after the Spirit.

m Rom. vii. 12. Wherefore *the law is holy,* and the *commandment holy, and just, and good.* Ver. 22. For *I delight in the law of God after the inward man.* Ver. 25. I thank God, through Jesus Christ our Lord. So then *with the mind I myself serve the law of God,* but with the flesh the law of sin. Ps. cxix. 4. Thou hast commanded us *to keep thy precepts diligently.* Ver. 5. O that my ways were directed *to keep thy statutes!* Ver 6. Then shall I not be ashamed, when

hearts, and lives;ⁿ so as, examining themselves thereby, they may come to further conviction of, humiliation for, and hatred against sin;º together with a clearer sight of the need they have of Christ, and the perfection of his obedience.ᵖ It is likewise of use to the regenerate, to restrain their corruptions, in that it forbids sin;ᑫ and the threatenings of it serve to shew what even their sins deserve, and what afflictions in this life they may expect for them, although freed from the curse thereof threatened in the law.ʳ The promises of it, in like manner, shew them God's approbation of obedience, and what blessings they may expect upon the performance thereof,ˢ although not as due to them by the law as a covenant of works:ᵗ so as a man's doing good, and refraining from evil, because the law encourageth to the one, and deterreth from the other, is no evidence of his being under the law, and not under grace.ᵛ

I have *respect unto all thy commandments.* 1 Cor. vii. 19. Circumcision is nothing, and uncircumcision is nothing, *but the keeping of the commandments of God.* Gal. v. 14, 16, 18, 19, 20, 21, 22, 23. See in the Bible.
ⁿ Rom. vii. 7. What shall we say then? Is the law sin? God forbid. Nay, *I had not known sin but by the law:* for I had not known lust, except the law had said, Thou shalt not covet. Rom. iii. 20. Therefore by the deeds of the law there shall no flesh be justified in his sight: for *by the law is the knowledge of sin.*
º James i. 23. For if any be a hearer of the word, and not a doer, he is like unto a man beholding his natural face in a glass: Ver. 24. For he beholdeth himself, and goeth his way, and straightway forgetteth what manner of man he was. Ver. 25. But *whoso looketh into the perfect law of liberty,* and continueth therein, he being not a forgetful hearer, but a doer of the work, this man shall be blessed in his deed. Rom. vii. 9. For *I was alive without the law* once; but when the *commandment came, sin revived, and I died.* Ver. 14. For we know that the law is spiritual; *but I am carnal, sold under sin.* Ver. 24. O wretched man that I am! *who shall deliver me from the body of this death?*
ᵖ Gal. iii. 24. Wherefore the *law was our schoolmaster to bring us unto Christ,* that we might be justified by faith. Rom. vii. 24. [See before in letter º. Verse 25 in letter ᵐ.] Rom. viii. 3. For what the *law could not do, in that it was weak* through the flesh, *God sending his own Son* in the likeness of sinful flesh, and for sin, condemned sin in the flesh; Ver. 4. That the *righteousness of the law might be fulfilled in us,* who walk not after the flesh, but after the Spirit.
ᑫ James ii. 11. For he that said, *Do not commit adultery,* said also, *Do not kill.* Now, if thou commit no adultery, yet if thou kill, thou art become a transgressor of the law. Ps. cxix. 101. I have refrained my feet from every evil way, *that I might keep thy word.* Ver. 104. *Through thy precepts I get understanding:* therefore *I hate every false way.* Ver. 128. Therefore *I esteem all thy precepts concerning all things to be right;* and *I hate every false way.*

ʳ Ezra ix. 13. And after *all* that *is come upon us for our evil deeds,* and *for our great trespass, seeing* that thou our God hast *punished us less than our iniquities deserve,* and hast given us such deliverance as this; Ver. 14. Should we again *break thy commandments,* and join in affinity with the people of these abominations? *wouldest not thou be angry with us* till *thou hadst consumed us, so that there should be no remnant nor escaping?* Ps. lxxxix. 30. If his children *forsake my law,* and *walk not in my judgments;* Ver. 31 If they *break my statutes,* and *keep not my commandments;* Ver. 32. Then will I *visit their transgression with the rod,* and *their iniquity with stripes.* Ver. 33. Nevertheless *my loving-kindness will I not utterly take from him, nor suffer my faithfulness to fail.* Ver. 34. *My covenant will I not break, nor alter the thing that is gone out of my lips.*
ˢ [Lev. xxvi. to the 14th verse.] With 2 Cor. vi. 16. And what agreement hath the temple of God with idols? for ye are the temple of the living God; as God hath said, *I will dwell in them,* and *walk in them;* and *I will be their God,* and *they shall be my people.* Eph. vi. 2. Honour thy father and mother, (which is the *first commandment with promise,*) Ver. 3. That it may be *well with thee,* and thou mayest *live long on the earth.* Ps. xxxvii. 11. But the *meek shall inherit the earth;* and shall *delight themselves in the abundance of peace.* With Matt. v. 5. Blessed are the *meek;* for *they shall inherit the earth.* Ps. xix. 11. Moreover, by them is thy servant warned: and *in keeping of them there is great reward.*
ᵗ Gal. ii. 16. Knowing that a man is *not justified by the works of the law,* but by the faith of Jesus Christ, even we have believed in Jesus Christ, that we might be justified by the faith of Christ, and *not by the works of the law:* for *by the works of the law shall no flesh be justified.* Luke xvii. 10. So likewise ye, when ye shall have *done all those things* which are *commanded you,* say, We *are unprofitable servants:* we have done that which was *our duty to do.*
ᵛ Rom. vi. 12. Let not sin therefore reign in your mortal body, that ye should obey it in the lusts thereof. Ver. 14. For *sin shall not have dominion over you:* for *ye are not*

VII. Neither are the forementioned uses of the law contrary to the grace of the gospel, but do sweetly comply with it;[w] the Spirit of Christ subduing and enabling the will of man to do that freely and cheerfully which the will of God revealed in the law requireth to be done.[x]

CHAP. XX.—*Of Christian Liberty, and Liberty of Conscience.*

I. THE liberty which Christ hath purchased for believers under the gospel, consists in their freedom from the guilt of sin, the condemning wrath of God, the curse of the moral law;[a] and in their being delivered from this present evil world, bondage to Satan, and dominion of sin,[b] from the evil of afflictions, the sting of death, the victory of the grave, and everlasting damnation;[c] as also in their free access to God,[d] and their yielding obedience unto him, not out of slavish

---

under the law, but under grace. 1 Pet. iii. 8. Finally, be ye all of one mind, having compassion one of another; love as brethren, be pitiful, be courteous: Ver. 9. Not rendering evil for evil, or railing for railing: but contrariwise blessing; knowing that ye are thereunto called, that ye should inherit a blessing. Ver. 10. For he that will love life, and see good days, *let him refrain his tongue from evil, and his lips that they speak no guile;* Ver. 11. Let him *eschew evil, and do good;* let him seek peace, and ensue it. Ver. 12. For the eyes of the Lord are over the righteous, and his ears are open unto their prayers: but *the face of the Lord is against them that do evil.* With Ps. xxxiv. 12. What man is he that desireth life, and loveth many days, that he may see good? Ver. 13. *Keep thy tongue from evil, and thy lips from speaking guile.* Ver. 14. *Depart from evil, and do good;* seek peace, and pursue it. Ver. 15. The eyes of the Lord are upon the righteous, and his ears are open unto their cry. Ver. 16. *The face of the Lord is against them that do evil,* to cut off the remembrance of them from the earth. Heb. xii. 28. Wherefore, we receiving a kingdom which cannot be moved, let *us have grace, whereby we may serve God acceptably with reverence and godly fear;* Ver. 29. For *our God is a consuming fire.*

VII. w Gal. iii. 21. *Is the law then against the promises of God? God forbid;* for if there had been a law given which could have given life, verily righteousness should have been by the law.

x Ezek. xxxvi. 27. And I will put *my Spirit within you, and cause you to walk in my statutes,* and ye shall keep my judgments, and do them. Heb. viii. 10. For this is the covenant that I will make with the house of Israel, after those days, saith the Lord; *I will put my laws into their mind, and write them in their hearts;* and I will be to them a God, and they shall be to me a people. With Jer. xxxi. 33. But this shall be the covenant that I will make with the house of Israel; After those days, saith the Lord, *I will put my law in their inward parts,* and *write it in their hearts;*

and will be their God, and they shall be my people.

I. a Tit. ii. 14. Who gave himself for us, that he might *redeem us from all iniquity,* and purify unto himself a peculiar people, zealous of good works. 1 Thess. i. 10. And to wait for his Son from heaven, whom he raised from the dead, even Jesus, which *delivered us from the wrath to come.* Gal. iii. 13. Christ hath *redeemed us from the curse of the law,* being made a curse for us: for it is written, Cursed is every one that hangeth on a tree.

b Gal. i. 4. Who gave himself for our sins, that he might *deliver us from this present evil world,* according to the will of God and our Father. Col. i. 13. Who hath *delivered us from the power of darkness,* and hath translated us into the kingdom of his dear Son. Acts xxvi. 18. To open their eyes, and to *turn them from darkness to light,* and from *the power of Satan* unto God, that they may receive forgiveness of sins, and inheritance among them which are sanctified by faith that is in me. Rom. vi. 14. For *sin shall not have dominion over you;* for ye are not under the law, but under grace.

c Rom. viii. 28. We know that *all things work together for good to them that love God,* to them who are the called according to his purpose. Ps. cxix. 71. It is *good for me that I have been afflicted;* that I might learn thy statutes. 1 Cor. xv. 54. So when this corruptible shall have put on incorruption, and this mortal shall have put on immortality, then shall be brought to pass the saying that is written, *Death is swallowed up in victory.* Ver. 55. *O death! where is thy sting? O grave! where is thy victory?* Ver. 56. The sting of death is sin; and the strength of sin is the law. Ver. 57. But thanks be to God, which *giveth us the victory,* through our Lord Jesus Christ. Rom. viii. 1. There is therefore now *no condemnation* to them which are in Christ Jesus, who walk not after the flesh, but after the Spirit.

d Rom. v. 1. Therefore, being justified by faith, we have *peace with God,* through our Lord Jesus Christ: Ver. 2. By whom also

fear, but a child-like love, and willing mind.ᵉ All which were common also to believers under the law;ᶠ but under the new testament, the liberty of Christians is further enlarged in their freedom from the yoke of the ceremonial law, to which the Jewish Church was subjected,ᵍ and in greater boldness of access to the throne of grace,ʰ and in fuller communications of the free Spirit of God, than believers under the law did ordinarily partake of.ⁱ

II. God alone is lord of the conscience,ᵏ and hath left it free from the doctrines and commandments of men which are in any thing contrary to his word, or beside it, in matters of faith or worship.ˡ So that to believe such doctrines, or to obey such commandments out of conscience, is to betray true liberty of conscience:ᵐ and the requiring

we have *access by faith into this grace wherein we stand, and rejoice in hope of the glory of God.*
ᵉ Rom. viii. 14. For as many as are *led by the Spirit of God, they are the sons of God.* Ver. 15. For ye have not received the *spirit of bondage again to fear;* but ye have received the *spirit of adoption, whereby we cry, Abba, Father.* 1 John iv. 18. There is *no fear in love;* but perfect *love casteth out fear;* because fear hath torment. He that feareth is not made perfect in love.
ᶠ Gal. iii. 9. So then *they which be of faith* are *blessed with faithful Abraham.* Ver. 14. That *the blessing of Abraham* might come *on the Gentiles* through Jesus Christ, that we might receive the promise of the Spirit through faith.
ᵍ Gal. iv. 1. Now I say, That *the heir, as long as he is a child, differeth nothing from a servant,* though he be lord of all; Ver. 2. But *is under tutors and governors,* until the time appointed of the father. Ver. 3. Even so we, *when we were children, were in bondage under the elements of the world.* Ver. 6. And because ye are sons, *God hath sent forth the Spirit of his Son into your hearts,* crying, Abba, Father. Ver. 7. Wherefore thou art *no more a servant, but a son;* and if a son, then an heir of God through Christ. Gal. v. 1. *Stand fast therefore in the liberty wherewith Christ hath made us free,* and be not entangled again with *the yoke of bondage.* Acts xv. 10. Now therefore why tempt ye God, *to put a yoke upon the neck of the disciples,* which neither our fathers nor we were able to bear? Ver. 11. But we believe that, through the grace of the Lord Jesus Christ, *we shall be saved, even as they.*
ʰ Heb. iv. 14. Seeing then that *we have a great high priest, that is passed into the heavens,* Jesus the Son of God, let us hold fast our profession. Ver. 16. Let us therefore come *boldly unto the throne of grace,* that we may obtain mercy, and find grace to help in time of need. Heb. x. 19. Having therefore, brethren, *boldness to enter into the holiest* by the blood of Jesus, Ver. 20. By a *new and living way,* which he hath *consecrated* for us through the *vail, that is to say, his flesh;* Ver. 21. And having an high priest over the house of God; Ver. 22. Let us draw near with a true heart, *in full assurance of faith,* having our hearts sprinkled from an evil conscience, and our bodies washed with pure water.
ⁱ John vii. 38. He that believeth on me, as the scripture hath said, *out of his belly shall flow rivers of living water.* Ver. 39. (But *this spake he of the Spirit* which they that believe on him *should receive:* for the Holy Ghost was not yet given; because that Jesus was not yet glorified.) 2 Cor. iii. 13 And not as *Moses,* which *put a vail over his face,* that the children of Israel *could not steadfastly look to the end of that which is abolished.* Ver. 17. Now the *Lord is that Spirit:* and where the *Spirit of the Lord is, there is liberty.* Ver. 18. But we all, *with open face beholding* as in a glass the *glory of the Lord,* are changed into the same image, from glory to glory, even as by the Spirit of the Lord.
II. ᵏ James iv. 12. There is *one lawgiver,* who is able to save and to destroy: who art thou that judgest another? Rom. xiv. 4. Who art thou that judgest another man's servant? *to his own master he standeth or falleth;* yea, he shall be holden up: for God is able to make him stand.
ˡ Acts iv. 19. But Peter and John answered and said unto them, Whether it be right in the sight of God to hearken unto *you more than unto God,* judge ye. Acts v. 29. Then Peter and the other apostles answered and said, *We ought to obey God rather than men.* 1 Cor. vii. 23. Ye are bought with a price : *be not ye the servants of men.* Matt. xxiii. 8. But be not ye called Rabbi : for *one is your Master,* even Christ; and *all ye are brethren.* Ver. 9. And call no man your father upon the earth : for *one is your Father,* which is in heaven. Ver. 10. Neither be ye called masters : for *one is your Master, even Christ.* 2 Cor. i. 24. Not for that we have *dominion over your faith,* but are helpers of your joy : for by faith ye stand. Matt. xv. 9. But in vain they do worship me, *teaching for doctrines the commandments of men.*
ᵐ Col. ii. 20. Wherefore, if ye be dead with Christ from the rudiments of the world, *why, as though living in the world, are ye subject to ordinances,* Ver. 22. (Which all are to *perish* with the using,) *after the commandments and doctrines of men?* Ver. 23. Which things have indeed a *shew of wisdom in will-worship, and humility, and*

of an implicit faith, and an absolute and blind obedience, is to destroy liberty of conscience, and reason also.ⁿ

III. They who, upon pretence of Christian liberty, do practise any sin, or cherish any lust, do thereby destroy the end of Christian liberty; which is, that, being delivered out of the hands of our enemies, we might serve the Lord without fear, in holiness and righteousness before him, all the days of our life.º

IV. And because the powers which God hath ordained, and the liberty which Christ hath purchased, are not intended by God to destroy, but mutually to uphold and preserve one another; they who, upon pretence of Christian liberty, shall oppose any lawful power, or the lawful exercise of it, whether it be civil or ecclesiastical, resist the ordinance of God.ᵖ And for their publishing of such opinions, or maintaining of such practices, as are contrary to the light of nature, or to the known principles of Christianity, whether concerning faith, worship, or conversation; or to the power of godliness; or such erroneous opinions or practices, as either in their own nature, or in the manner of publishing or maintaining them, are destructive to the external peace and order which Christ hath established in the church; they may lawfully be called to account,ᑫ and proceeded

neglecting of the body; not in any honour to the satisfying of the flesh. Gal. i. 10. For do I now persuade men, or God? or do I seek to please men? *for if I yet pleased men, I should not be the servant of Christ.* Gal. ii. 4. And that because of *false brethren* unawares brought in, who came in privily to *spy out our liberty* which we have in Christ Jesus, *that they might bring us into bondage;* Ver. 5. To whom we gave place by subjection, *no, not for an hour,* that the truth of *the gospel might continue* with you. Gal. v. 1. *Stand fast* therefore *in the liberty wherewith Christ hath made us free,* and be *not entangled again with the yoke of bondage.*

ⁿ Rom. x. 17. So then *faith cometh by hearing,* and *hearing by the word of God.* Rom. xiv. 23. And he *that doubteth is damned if he eat,* because he eateth not of faith: for *whatsoever is not of faith is sin.* Isa. viii. 20. *To the law and to the testimony:* if they speak not according to this word, it is because there is no light in them. Acts xvii. 11. These were more noble than those in Thessalonica, in that they received the word with all readiness of mind, and searched the scriptures daily, whether those things were so. John iv. 22. *Ye worship ye know not what;* we know what we worship: for salvation is of the Jews. Hos. v. 11. Ephraim is oppressed and broken in judgment, because he *willingly walked after the commandment.* Rev. xiii. 12. And he exerciseth all the power of the first beast before him, and *causeth the earth, and them which dwell therein, to worship the first beast,* whose deadly wound was healed. Ver. 16. And he *caused all,* both small and great, rich and poor, free and bond, to *receive a mark* in their right hand, or in their foreheads: Ver. 17. And that *no man might buy or sell, save he that had the mark,* or the name of the beast, or the number of his name. Jer. viii. 9. The wise men are ashamed, they are dismayed and taken: lo, *they have rejected the word of the Lord; and what wisdom is in them?*

III. º Gal. v. 13. For, brethren, ye have been called unto liberty; only *use not liberty for an occasion to the flesh,* but by love serve one another. 1 Pet. ii. 16. As free, and not *using your liberty for a cloak of maliciousness,* but as the servants of God. 2 Pet. ii. 19. While they promise them liberty, they themselves are the *servants of corruption:* for *of whom a man is overcome, of the same* is he brought *in bondage.* John viii. 34. Jesus answered them, Verily, verily, I say unto you, Whosoever *committeth sin* is *the servant of sin.* Luke i. 74. That he would grant unto us, that we, *being delivered out of the hands of our enemies, might serve him without fear,* Ver. 75. In holiness and righteousness before him, all the days of our life.

IV. ᵖ Matt. xii. 25. And Jesus knew their thoughts, and said unto them, Every *kingdom divided against itself is brought to desolation;* and every *city or house divided against itself shall not stand.* 1 Pet. ii. 13. *Submit yourselves to every ordinance of man for the Lord's sake:* whether it be to the *king,* as supreme; Ver. 14. Or unto *governors, as unto them that are sent by him* for the punishment of evildoers, and for the praise of them that do well. Ver. 16. As free, and not using your liberty for a cloak of maliciousness, but *as the servants of God.* [Rom. xiii. 1. to the 8th verse.] Heb. xiii. 17. *Obey them that have the rule over you,* and *submit yourselves:* for they watch for your souls, *as they that must give account;* that they may do it with joy, and not with grief: for that is unprofitable for you.

ᑫ Rom. i. 32. Who, *knowing the judgment of God, that they which commit such things are worthy of death,* not only do the same,

against by the censures of the church, and by the power of the civil magistrate.ʳ

but have pleasure in them that do them. With 1 Cor v. 1. It is reported commonly that there is *fornication among you,* and *such fornication as is not so much as named among the Gentiles,* that one should have his father's wife. Ver. 5. To *deliver such an one unto Satan* for the destruction of the flesh, that the spirit may be saved in the day of the Lord Jesus. Ver. 11. But now I have written unto you not to keep company, if any man that is called a *brother* be a *fornicator,* or *covetous,* or an *idolater,* or a *railer,* or a *drunkard,* or an *extortioner; with such an one no not to eat.* Ver. 13. But them that are without God judgeth. Therefore *put away from among yourselves that wicked person.* 2 John, ver. 10. If there come any unto you, and *bring not this doctrine, receive him not* into your house, *neither bid him God speed:* Ver. 11. For he that biddeth him God speed *is partaker of his evil deeds.* And 2 Thess. iii. 14. And if any man *obey not our word by this epistle, note that man,* and have no company with him, that he may be ashamed. And 1 Tim. vi. 3. If any man *teach otherwise,* and *consent not to wholesome words, even the words of our Lord Jesus Christ,* and to the *doctrine which is according to godliness;* Ver. 4. He is proud, knowing nothing, but doting about questions and strifes of words, whereof cometh envy, strife, railings, evil surmisings, Ver. 5. Perverse disputings of men of corrupt minds, and destitute of the truth, supposing that gain is godliness : *from such withdraw thyself.* And Tit. i. 10. For there are many unruly and vain talkers and deceivers, specially they of the circumcision : Ver. 11. *Whose mouths must be stopped;* who subvert whole houses, teaching things which they ought not, for filthy lucre's sake. Ver. 13. This witness is true : wherefore *rebuke them sharply,* that they may be sound in the faith. And Tit. iii. 10. A man that is an heretick, *after the first and second admonition, reject.* With Matt. xviii. 15. Moreover, if thy brother shall trespass against thee, *go and tell him his fault between thee and him alone:* if he shall hear thee, thou hast gained thy brother. Ver. 16. But if he will not hear thee, *then take with thee one or two more,* that in the mouth of two or three witnesses every word may be established. Ver. 17. And if he shall neglect to hear them, *tell it unto the church:* but if he neglect to hear the church, *let him be unto thee as an heathen man and a publican.* 1 Tim. i. 19. Holding faith, and a good conscience ; which some having put away, concerning faith have made shipwreck : Ver. 20. Of whom is Hymeneus and Alexander ; whom I have *delivered unto Satan,* that they may learn not to blaspheme. Rev. ii. 2. I know thy works, and thy labour, and thy patience, and how thou *canst not bear them which are evil:* and thou *hast tried them* which say they are apostles, and are not, and *hast found them* liars. Ver. 14. But I have a few things against thee, because thou hast there them that *hold the doctrine of Balaam,* who taught Balac to cast a stumbling-block before the children of Israel, to eat things sacrificed unto idols, and to commit fornication. Ver. 15. So hast thou also them that *hold the doctrine of the Nicolaitanes,* which thing I hate. Ver. 20. Notwithstanding I have a few things against thee, because thou *sufferest* that woman *Jezebel,* which calleth herself a prophetess, *to teach and to seduce* my servants to commit fornication, and to eat things sacrificed unto idols. Rev. iii. 9. Behold, I will make them of *the synagogue of Satan,* which say they are Jews, and are not, but do lie ; behold, I will make them to come and worship before thy feet, and to know that I have loved thee.

ʳ [Deut. xiii. 6. to the 12th.] Rom. xiii. 3. For *rulers are not a terror to good works, but to the evil.* Wilt thou then not be afraid of the power ? Do that which is good, and thou shalt have praise of the same. Ver. 4. For he is the minister of God to thee for good. But *if thou do that which is evil, be afraid; for he beareth not the sword in vain:* for *he is the minister of God, a revenger to execute wrath upon him that doeth evil.* With 2 John, verses 10, 11. [See in letter q.] Ezra vii. 23. Whatsoever is commanded by the God of heaven, let it be diligently done for the house of the God of heaven : for *why should there be wrath against the realm of the king and his sons ?* Ver. 25. And thou, Ezra, after the wisdom of thy God that is in thine hand, *set magistrates and judges, which may judge all the people* that are beyond the river, all such as know the laws of thy God ; and teach ye them that know them not. Ver. 26. And *whosoever will not do the law of thy God,* and the *law of the king, let judgment be executed speedily upon him, whether it be unto death, or to banishment, or to confiscation of goods, or to imprisonment.* Ver. 27. Blessed be the Lord God of our fathers, which hath put such a thing as this in the king's heart, to beautify the house of the Lord which is in Jerusalem ; Ver. 28. And hath extended mercy unto me before the king and his counsellors, and before all the king's mighty princes : and I was strengthened as the hand of the Lord my God was upon me ; and I gathered together out of Israel chief men to go up with me. Rev. xvii. 12. And the ten horns which thou sawest are ten kings, which have received no kingdom as yet ; but receive power as kings one hour with the beast. Ver. 16. And the *ten horns* which thou sawest upon the beast, these *shall hate the whore,* and *shall make her desolate and naked, and shall eat her flesh, and burn her with fire.* Ver. 17. For God hath put in their hearts to fulfil his will, and to agree, and give their kingdom unto the beast, until the words of God shall be fulfilled. Neh. xiii. 15. In those days saw I in Judah some treading wine-presses on

CHAP. XXI.—*Of Religious Worship, and the Sabbath-day.*

I. THE light of nature sheweth that there is a God, who hath lordship and sovereignty over all; is good, and doeth good unto all; and is therefore to be feared, loved, praised, called upon, trusted in, and served, with all the heart, and with all the soul, and with all the might.[a] But the acceptable way of worshipping the true God is instituted by himself, and so limited by his own revealed will, that he may not be worshipped according to the imaginations and devices of

the Sabbath, and bringing in sheaves, and lading asses ; as also wine, grapes, and figs, and all manner of burdens, *which they brought into Jerusalem on the sabbath-day: and I testified against them* in the day wherein they sold victuals. Ver. 17. Then *I contended with the nobles of Judah*, and said unto them, What evil thing is this that ye do, and *profane the sabbath-day ?* Ver. 21. Then *I testified against them*, and said unto them, Why lodge ye about the wall? if ye do so again, *I will lay hands on you.* From that time forth came they no more on the sabbath. Ver. 22. And *I commanded the Levites*, that they should cleanse themselves, and that they *should come and keep the gates, to sanctify the sabbath-day.* Remember me, O my God, concerning *this also*, and spare me according to the greatness of thy mercy. Ver. 25. And I *contended* with them, and *cursed them*, and *smote certain of them*, and *plucked off their hair*, and made them *swear by God*, saying, *Ye shall not* give your daughters unto their sons, nor take their daughters unto your sons, or for yourselves. Ver. 30. Thus *cleansed I them from all strangers*, and appointed the wards of the priests and the Levites, every one in his business. 2 Kings xxiii. 5. And *he put down the idolatrous priests*, whom the kings of Judah had ordained to burn incense in the high places in the cities of Judah, and in the places round about Jerusalem ; *them also that burnt incense unto Baal*, to *the sun*, and to *the moon*, and to *the planets*, and to *all the host of heaven.* Ver. 6. And he *brought out the grove from the house of the Lord*, without Jerusalem, unto the brook Kidron, and *burnt it* at the brook Kidron, and *stamped it small to powder*, and *cast the powder thereof upon the graves of the children of the people.* Ver. 9. Nevertheless *the priests of the high places came not up to the altar of the Lord in Jerusalem*, but they did eat of the unleavened bread among their brethren. Ver. 20. And *he slew all the priests of the high places* that were there upon the altars, and burnt men's bones upon them, and returned to Jerusalem. Ver. 21. And the king commanded all the people, saying, Keep the passover unto the Lord your God, as it is written in the book of this covenant. 2 Chron. xxxiv. 33. And Josiah *took away all the abominations out of all the countries* that pertained to the children of Israel, and *made all* that were present in Israel *to serve, even to serve the Lord their God.* And all his days they departed not from following the Lord, the God of their fathers. 2 Chron. xv. 12. And they entered into a covenant to seek the Lord God of their fathers with all their heart, and with all their soul ; Ver. 13. That *whosoever would not seek the Lord God of Israel should be put to death*, whether small or great, whether man or woman. Ver. 16. And also concerning Maachah, the mother of Asa the king, *he removed her from being queen, because she had made an idol* in a grove : and Asa *cut down her idol*, and *stamped it*, and *burnt it* at the brook Kidron. Dan. iii. 29. Therefore I make a decree, That every people, nation, and language, which speak any thing amiss against the God of Shadrach, Meshach, and Abed-nego, *shall be cut in pieces*, and *their houses shall be made a dunghill;* because there is no other God that can deliver after this sort. 1 Tim. ii. 2. For kings, *and for all that are in authority; that we may lead a quiet and peaceable life* in *all* godliness and honesty. Isa. xlix. 23. And *kings shall be thy nursing-fathers*, and their *queens thy nursing-mothers:* they shall *bow down to thee* with their face toward the earth, and *lick up the dust of thy feet;* and thou shalt know that I am the Lord : for they shall not be ashamed that wait for me. Zech. xiii. 2. And it shall come to pass in that day, saith the Lord of hosts, that I will cut off the names of the idols out of the land, and they shall no more be remembered ; and also I will cause the prophets and the unclean spirit to pass out of the land. Ver. 3. And it shall come to pass, that when any shall yet prophesy, then *his father and his mother* that begat him *shall say unto him, Thou shalt not live;* for thou speakest lies in the name of the Lord : and *his father and his mother* that begat him shall *thrust him through* when he prophesieth.

I. a Rom. i. 20. For the *invisible things of him from the creation of the world* are *clearly seen*, being understood by the things that are made, even *his eternal power and Godhead;* so that they are without excuse. Acts xvii. 24. *God, that made the world, and all things therein*, seeing that *he is Lord of heaven and earth*, dwelleth not in temples made with hands. Ps. cxix. 68. Thou *art good, and doest good:* teach me thy statutes. Jer. x. 7. *Who would not*

CHAP. XXI.   THE CONFESSION OF FAITH.   73

men, or the suggestions of Satan, under any visible representation, or any other way not prescribed in the holy Scripture.[b]

II. Religious worship is to be given to God, the Father, Son, and Holy Ghost; and to him alone:[c] not to angels, saints, or any other creature:[d] and, since the fall, not without a Mediator; nor in the mediation of any other but of Christ alone.[e]

III. Prayer, with thanksgiving, being one special part of religious worship,[f] is by God required of all men;[g] and, that it may be accepted, it is to be made in the name of the Son,[h] by the help of his Spirit,[i] according to his will,[k] with understanding, reverence, humi-

fear thee, O King of nations? for to thee doth it appertain: forasmuch as among all the wise men of the nations, and in all their kingdoms, there is *none like unto thee*. Ps. xxxi. 23. *O love the Lord*, all ye his saints: for the Lord preserveth the faithful, and plentifully rewardeth the proud doer. Ps. xviii. 3. I will *call upon the Lord*, who is *worthy to be praised:* so shall I be saved from mine enemies. Rom. x. 12. For there is no difference between the Jew and the Greek; for the same Lord over all is rich unto all that *call upon him*. Ps. lxii. 8. *Trust in him at all times;* ye people, pour out your heart before him: God is a refuge for us. Josh. xxiv. 14. Now therefore *fear the Lord*, and *serve him* in sincerity and in truth: and put away the gods which your fathers served on the other side of the flood, and in Egypt; and serve ye the Lord. Mark xii. 33. And to *love him with all the heart, and with all the understanding*, and *with all the soul*, and *with all the strength*, and to love his neighbour as himself, is more than all whole burnt-offerings and sacrifices.

b Deut. xii. 32. What thing soever I *command you, observe to do it:* thou shalt *not add* thereto, *nor diminish* from it. Matt. xv. 9. But *in vain they do worship me, teaching for doctrines the commandments of men.* Acts xvii. 25. *Neither is worshipped with men's hands*, as though he needed any thing, seeing he giveth to all life, and breath, and all things. Matt. iv. 9. And saith unto him, All these things will I give thee, if thou wilt fall down and worship me. Ver. 10. Then saith Jesus unto him, *Get thee hence, Satan:* for it is written, Thou shalt worship the Lord thy God, and him only shalt thou serve. [Deut. xv. to the 20th verse.] Exod. xx. 4. Thou shalt *not make* unto thee *any graven image*, or *any likeness of any thing* that is *in heaven above*, or that is *in the earth beneath*, or that is *in the water under the earth:* Ver. 5. Thou shalt not *bow down* thyself to them, nor serve them: for I the Lord thy God am a jealous God, visiting the iniquity of the fathers upon the children unto the third and fourth generation of them that hate me; Ver. 6. And shewing mercy unto thousands of them that love me, and *keep my commandments*. Col. ii. 23. Which things have indeed a *shew of wisdom in will-worship*, and humility, and neglecting of the body; not in any honour to the satisfying of the flesh.

II. c Matt. iv. 10. [See before in letter b.] With John v. 23. That all men should *honour the Son, even as they honour the Father*. He that honoureth not the Son, honoureth not the Father which hath sent him. And 2 Cor. xiii. 14. The *grace of the Lord Jesus Christ*, and the *love of God*, and the *communion of the Holy Ghost*, be with you all. Amen.

d Col. ii. 18. Let no man beguile you of your reward in a voluntary humility, and *worshipping of angels*,'intruding into those things which he hath not seen, vainly puffed up by his fleshly mind. Rev. xix. 10. And I fell at his feet to worship him. And he said unto me, See thou *do it not;* I am *thy fellow-servant*, and *of thy brethren* that have the testimony of Jesus: worship God: for the testimony of Jesus is the spirit of prophecy. Rom. i. 25. Who changed the truth of God into a lie, and *worshipped* and served the *creature* more than the Creator, who is blessed for ever. Amen.

e John xiv. 6. Jesus saith unto him, I am *the way*, and the truth, and the life: *no man cometh unto the Father, but by me.* 1 Tim. ii. 5. For there is one God, and *one mediator* between God and men, *the man Christ Jesus*. Eph. ii. 18. For *through him* we both *have access by one Spirit unto the Father*. Col. iii. 17. And whatsoever ye do in word or deed, do all *in the name of the Lord Jesus, giving thanks to God and the Father by him.*

III. f Phil. iv. 6. Be careful for nothing: but in every thing by *prayer and supplication, with thanksgiving*, let your requests be made known unto God.

g Ps. lxv. 2. O thou that hearest prayer, *unto thee shall all flesh come.*

h John xiv. 13. And whatsoever ye shall ask *in my name*, that will I do, that the Father may be glorified in the Son. Ver. 14. If ye shall ask any thing *in my name*, I will do it. 1 Pet. ii. 5. Ye also, as lively stones, are built up a spiritual house, an holy priesthood, to offer up *spiritual sacrifices, acceptable to God by Jesus Christ.*

i Rom. viii. 26. Likewise the Spirit also helpeth our infirmities: for we know not what we should pray for as we ought; but the *Spirit itself maketh intercession for us* with groanings which cannot be uttered.

k 1 John v. 14. And this is the confidence that we have in him, that, if we *ask* any thing *according to his will* he heareth us.

lity, fervency, faith, love, and perseverance;[l] and, if vocal, in a known tongue.[m]

IV. Prayer is to be made for things lawful,[n] and for all sorts of men living, or that shall live hereafter;[o] but not for the dead,[p] nor for those of whom it may be known that they have sinned the sin unto death.[q]

V. The reading of the Scriptures with godly fear;[r] the sound preaching,[s] and conscionable hearing of the word, in obedience unto God, with understanding, faith, and reverence;[t] singing of psalms with

[l] Ps. xlvii. 7. For God is the King of all the earth : sing ye praises *with understanding*. Eccl. v. 1. *Keep thy foot when thou goest to the house of God*, and be more ready to hear than to give the sacrifice of fools : for they consider not that they do evil. Ver. 2. *Be not rash with thy mouth*, and *let not thine heart be hasty* to utter any thing before God : for God is in heaven, and thou upon earth ; therefore let thy words be few. Heb. xii. 28. Wherefore, we receiving a kingdom which cannot be moved, let us have grace, whereby we may *serve God* acceptably with *reverence and godly fear*. Gen. xviii. 27. And Abraham answered and said, Behold now, *I have taken upon me to speak unto the Lord, which am but dust and ashes*. James v. 16. Confess your faults one to another, and pray one for another, that ye may be healed. The effectual *fervent prayer* of a righteous man *availeth much*. James i. 6. But let him ask *in faith, nothing wavering*: for he that wavereth is like a wave of the sea driven with the wind and tossed. Ver. 7. For let *not* that man *think* that *he shall receive* any thing of the Lord. Mark xi. 24. Therefore I say unto you, What things soever ye desire, when ye pray, *believe that ye receive them*, and ye shall have them. Matt. vi. 12. And forgive us our debts, *as we forgive our debtors*. Ver. 14. For *if ye forgive* men their trespasses, *your heavenly Father will also forgive you*: Ver. 15. But *if ye forgive not* men their trespasses, *neither will your Father forgive* your trespasses. Col. iv. 2. *Continue in prayer*, and *watch in the same* with thanksgiving. Eph. vi. 18. *Praying always* with all prayer and supplication in the Spirit, and watching thereunto *with all perseverance* and supplication for all saints.
[m] 1 Cor. xiv. 14. For *if I pray in an unknown tongue*, my spirit prayeth, but *my understanding is unfruitful*.
IV. [n] [1 John v. 14. See letter k.]
[o] 1 Tim. ii. 1. I exhort therefore, that, first of all, supplications, prayers, intercessions, and giving of thanks, *be made for all men;* Ver. 2. For kings, and for all that are in authority ; that we may lead a quiet and peaceable life in all godliness and honesty. John xvii. 20. *Neither pray I for these alone, but for them also which shall believe* on me through their word. 2 Sam. vii. 29. Therefore now let it please thee to *bless the house of thy servant*, *that it may continue for ever* before thee : for thou, O Lord God, hast spoken it : and with thy blessing *let the house of thy servant be blessed for ever*. Ruth iv. 12. And let *thy house be like the house of Pharez*, whom Tamar bare unto Judah, of the seed which the Lord shall give thee of this young woman.
[p] 2 Sam. xii. 21. Then said his servants unto him, What thing is this that thou hast done? Thou didst *fast and weep for the child, while it was alive;* but when *the child was dead, thou didst rise and eat bread*. Ver. 22. And he said, While the child was yet alive, I fasted and wept : for I said, Who can tell whether God will be gracious to me, that the child may live? Ver. 23. *But now he is dead, wherefore should I fast?* can I bring him back again? I shall go to him, but he shall not return to me. With Luke xvi. 25. But Abraham said, Son, remember that thou *in thy lifetime receivedst* thy good things, and likewise Lazarus evil things ; *but now* he is comforted, and thou art tormented. Ver. 26. And besides all this, between us and you there is a great gulph fixed : so that they which would pass from hence to you cannot ; neither can they pass to us, that would come from thence. Rev. xiv. 13. And I heard a voice from heaven saying unto me, Write, *Blessed* are the dead which *die in the Lord* from henceforth : Yea, saith the Spirit, that they may rest from their labours ; and *their works do follow them*.
[q] 1 John v. 16. If any man see his brother sin a sin which is not unto death, he shall ask, and he shall give him life for them that sin not unto death. *There is a sin unto death:* I do not say that *he shall pray for it*.
V. [r] Acts xv. 21. For Moses of old time hath in every city them that preach him, *being read in the synagogues* every sabbathday. Rev. i. 3. Blessed is *he that readeth*, and they that hear the words of this prophecy, and keep those things which are written therein : for the time is at hand.
[s] 2 Tim. iv. 2. *Preach the word; be instant* in season, out of season ; *reprove, rebuke, exhort* with all long-suffering and doctrine.
[t] James i. 22. But be ye *doers of the word, and not hearers only*, deceiving your own selves. Acts x. 33. Immediately therefore I sent to thee ; and thou hast well done that thou art come. Now therefore are *we all here present* before God, to *hear all things that are commanded* thee of God. Matt. xiii. 19. When any one *heareth the word of* the kingdom, and understandeth it not, then cometh the wicked one, and catcheth away that which was sown in his heart. This is he which received seed by the wayside. Heb. iv. 2. For unto us was the gospel preached, as well as unto them : but the

grace in the heart;[v] as also the due administration and worthy receiving of the sacraments instituted by Christ; are all parts of the ordinary religious worship of God:[w] besides religious oaths[x] and vows,[y] solemn fastings,[z] and thanksgivings upon special occasions,[a] which are, in their several times and seasons, to be used in a holy and religious manner.[b]

VI. Neither prayer, nor any other part of religious worship, is, now under the gospel, either tied unto, or made more acceptable by, any place in which it is performed, or towards which it is directed;[c] but God is to be worshipped every where[d] in spirit and in truth;[e] as in private families[f]

word preached did not profit them, *not being mixed with faith* in them that heard it. Isa. lxvi. 2. For all those things hath mine hand made, and all those things have been, saith the Lord : but to this man will I look, even to him that is poor, and of a contrite spirit, and *trembleth at my word.*

[v] Col. iii. 16. Let the word of Christ dwell in you richly in all wisdom ; teaching and admonishing one another *in psalms, and hymns, and spiritual songs, singing with grace in your hearts* to the Lord. Eph. v. 19. Speaking to yourselves in psalms, and hymns, and spiritual songs, singing and *making melody in your heart* to the Lord. James v. 13. Is any among you afflicted ? let him pray. Is any merry? *let him sing psalms.*

[w] Matt. xxviii. 19. Go ye therefore, and teach all nations, *baptising them in the name of the Father, and of the Son, and of the Holy Ghost.* [1 Cor. xi. 23. to verse 29.] Acts ii. 42. And they continued steadfastly in the apostles' doctrine and fellowship, and *in breaking of bread, and in prayers.*

[x] Deut. vi. 13. Thou shalt fear the Lord thy God, and serve him, and *shalt swear by his name.* With Neh. x. 29. They clave to their brethren, their nobles, and entered into a curse, *and into an oath, to walk in God's law,* which was given by Moses the servant of God, and to observe and do all the commandments of the Lord our God, and his judgments and his statutes.

[y] Isa. xix. 21. And the Lord shall be known to Egypt, and the Egyptians shall know the Lord in that day, and shall do sacrifice and oblation ; yea, they *shall vow a vow unto the Lord, and perform it.* With Eccl. v. 4. When thou *vowest a vow unto God,* defer not to pay it ; for he hath no pleasure in fools : pay *that which thou hast vowed.* Ver. 5. Better is it that thou *shouldest not vow,* than that thou *shouldest vow and not pay.*

[z] Joel ii. 12. Therefore also now, saith the Lord, Turn ye even to me with all your heart, and *with fasting, and with weeping, and with mourning.* Esth. iv. 16. Go, gather together all the Jews that are present in Shushan, and *fast ye for me, and neither eat nor drink three days,* night or day : I also and *my maidens will fast likewise;* and so will I go in unto the king, which is not according to the law ; and if I perish, I perish. Matt. ix. 15. And Jesus said unto them, Can the children of the bride-chamber mourn, as long as the bridegroom is with them? but the days will come, when the bridegroom shall be taken from them, and *then shall they fast.* 1 Cor. vii. 5. Defraud ye not one the other, except it be with consent for a time, that ye may *give yourselves to fasting and prayer;* and come together again, that Satan tempt you not for your incontinency.

[a] [Ps. cvii. throughout.] Esth. ix. 22. As the days wherein the Jews rested from their enemies, and the month which was turned unto them from sorrow to joy, and from mourning into a good day ; that they should make them *days of feasting and joy,* and of sending portions one to another, and gifts to the poor.

[b] Heb. xii. 28. Wherefore, we receiving a kingdom which cannot be moved, let us have grace, whereby we *may serve God acceptably with reverence and godly fear.*

VI. [c] John iv. 21. Jesus saith unto her, Woman, believe me, the hour cometh, when ye shall *neither in this mountain, nor yet at Jerusalem, worship the Father.*

[d] Mal. i. 11. For from the rising of the sun, even unto the going down of the same, my name shall be great among the Gentiles ; and *in every place* incense shall be offered unto my name, and a pure offering : for my name shall be great among the heathen, saith the Lord of hosts. 1 Tim. ii. 8. I will therefore *that men pray every where,* lifting up holy hands, without wrath and doubting.

[e] John iv. 23. But the hour cometh, and now is, when the true worshippers *shall worship the Father in spirit and in truth:* for the Father seeketh such to worship him. Ver. 24. God is a Spirit; and they that worship him *must worship him in spirit and in truth.*

[f] Jer. x. 25. Pour out thy fury upon the heathen that know thee not, *and upon the families that call not on thy name:* for they have eaten up Jacob, and devoured him, and consumed him, and have made his habitation desolate. Deut. vi. 6. And these words, which I command thee this day, shall be in thine heart ; Ver. 7. And *thou shalt teach them diligently unto thy children,* and shalt talk of them when thou sittest in thine house, and when thou walkest by the way, and when thou liest down, and when thou risest up. Job i. 5. And it was so, when the days of their feasting were gone about, that *Job sent and sanctified them,* and rose up early in the morning, and offered burnt-offerings according to the number of them all : for Job said, It may be that my sons have sinned, and cursed

daily,ᵍ and in secret each one by himself;ʰ so more solemnly in the publick assemblies, which are not carelessly or wilfully to be neglected or forsaken, when God, by his word or providence, calleth thereunto.ⁱ

VII. As it is of the law of nature, that, in general, a due proportion of time be set apart for the worship of God; so, in his word, by a positive, moral, and perpetual commandment, binding all man in all ages, he hath particularly appointed one day in seven for a sabbath, to be kept holy unto him:ᵏ which, from the beginning of the world to the resurrection of Christ, was the last day of the week; and, from the resurrection of Christ, was changed into the first day of the week,ˡ which in Scripture is called the Lord's Day,ᵐ and is to be continued to the end of the world, as the Christian Sabbath.ⁿ

God in their hearts. *Thus did Job continually.* 2 Sam. vi. 18. And as soon as David had made an end of offering burnt-offerings and peace-offerings, he blessed the people in the name of the Lord of hosts. Ver. 20. *Then David returned to bless his household.* 1 Pet. iii. 7. Likewise, *ye husbands,* dwell with them according to knowledge, giving honour unto the wife, as unto the weaker vessel, and as *being heirs together of the grace of life; that your prayers be not hindered.* Acts x. 2. A devout man, and one that *feared God with all his house,* which gave much alms to the people, and prayed to God alway.

ᵍ Matt. vi. 11. *Give us this day our daily bread.*

ʰ Matt. vi. 6. But thou, when thou prayest, *enter into thy closet; and when thou hast shut thy door, pray* to thy Father which is in secret; and thy Father, which seeth in secret, shall reward thee openly. Eph. vi. 18. *Praying always with all prayer and supplication* in the Spirit, and watching thereunto with all perseverance and supplication for all saints.

ⁱ Isa. lvi. 6. Also the sons of the stranger, that *join themselves to the Lord, to serve him,* and to love the name of the Lord, to be his servants, every one that keepeth the sabbath from polluting it, and taketh hold of my covenant; Ver. 7. Even *them will I bring to my holy mountain, and make them joyful in my house of prayer:* their burnt-offerings and their sacrifices shall be accepted upon mine altar; for *mine house shall be called an house of prayer for all people.* Heb. x. 25. *Not forsaking the assembling* of ourselves together, as the manner of some is; but exhorting one another: and so much the more, as ye see the day approaching. Prov. i. 20. *Wisdom crieth without; she uttereth her voice in the streets:* Ver. 21. *She crieth in the chief place of concourse,* in the openings of the gates: in the city she uttereth her words, saying, Ver. 24. Because I have called, and ye refused; I have stretched out my hand, and no man regarded. Prov. viii. 34. Blessed is the man that heareth me, *watching daily at my gates, waiting at the posts of my doors.* Acts xiii. 42. And when the Jews were gone out of the synagogue, the Gentiles besought *that these words might be preached to them the next sabbath.* Luke iv. 16. And he came to Nazareth, where he had been brought up: and, as his custom was, he *went into the synagogue on the sabbath-day, and stood up for to read.* Acts ii. 42. *And they continued steadfastly* in the apostles' doctrine and fellowship, and in breaking of bread, and in prayers.

VII. ᵏ Exod. xx. 8. *Remember the Sabbath-day, to keep it holy.* Ver. 10. *But the seventh day is the sabbath of the Lord thy God: in it thou shalt not do any work,* thou, nor thy son, nor thy daughter, thy man-servant, nor thy maid-servant, nor thy cattle, nor thy stranger that is within thy gates: Ver. 11. For in six days the Lord made heaven and earth, the sea, and all that in them is, and *rested the seventh day: wherefore the Lord blessed the sabbath-day, and hallowed it.* Isa. lvi. 2. Blessed is the man that doeth this, and the son of man that layeth hold on it; *that keepeth the sabbath from polluting it,* and keepeth his hand from doing any evil. Ver. 4. For thus saith the Lord unto the eunuchs that *keep my sabbaths,* and choose the things that please me, and take hold of my covenant. Ver. 6, 7. [See in letter ⁱ.]

ˡ Gen. ii. 2. And on the seventh day God ended his work which he had made; and *he rested on the seventh day* from all his work which he had made. Ver. 3. And God *blessed the seventh day, and sanctified it;* because that in it he had rested from all his work which God created and made. 1 Cor. xvi. 1. Now concerning the collection for the saints, as I have given order to the churches of Galatia, even so do ye. Ver. 2. *Upon the first day of the week* let every one of you lay by him in store, as God hath prospered him, that there be no gatherings when I come. Acts xx. 7. And upon *the first day of the week,* when the disciples came together to break bread, Paul preached unto them, ready to depart on the morrow, and continued his speech until midnight.

ᵐ Rev. i. 10. I was in the Spirit *on the Lord's day,* and heard behind me a great voice, as of a trumpet.

ⁿ Exod. xx. 8, 10. [See letter ᵏ.] With Matt. v. 17. Think not that *I am come to destroy the law* or the prophets: *I am not come to destroy, but to fulfil.* Ver. 18. For verily I say unto you, Till heaven and earth pass, *one jot or one tittle shall in no wise pass from the law, till all be fulfilled.*

VIII. This sabbath is then kept holy unto the Lord, when men, after a due preparing of their hearts, and ordering of their common affairs before-hand, do not only observe an holy rest all the day from their own works, words, and thoughts about their worldly employments and recreations;[o] but also are taken up the whole time in the publick and private exercises of his worship, and in the duties of necessity and mercy.[p]

CHAP. XXII.—*Of lawful Oaths and Vows.*

I. A LAWFUL oath is a part of religious worship,[a] wherein, upon just occasion, the person swearing solemnly calleth God to witness what he asserteth or promiseth; and to judge him according to the truth or falsehood of what he sweareth.[b]

II. The name of God only is that by which men ought to swear,

---

VIII. o Exod. xx. 8. [See letter k.] Exod. xvi. 23. And he said unto them, This is that which the Lord hath said, Tomorrow is the rest of the holy sabbath unto the Lord: *bake that which ye will bake to-day, and seethe that ye will seethe;* and that which remaineth over lay up for you, to be kept until the morning. Ver. 25. And Moses said, *Eat that to-day; for to-day is a sabbath unto the Lord; to-day ye shall not find it in the field.* Ver. 26. Six days ye shall gather it; but on the seventh day, which is the sabbath, in it there shall be none. Ver. 29. See, for that the Lord hath given you the sabbath, therefore he giveth you on the sixth day the bread of two days: abide ye every man in his place; *Let no man go out of his place on the seventh day.* Ver. 30. So the people *rested on the seventh day.* Exod. xxxi. 15. Six days may work be done; but in the seventh is the sabbath of rest, holy to the Lord: *whosoever doeth any work in the sabbath-day, he shall surely be put to death.* Ver. 16. Wherefore the children of Israel shall *keep the sabbath, to observe the sabbath* throughout their generations, for a perpetual covenant. Ver. 17. It is a sign between me and the children of Israel for ever: for in six days the Lord made heaven and earth, and *on the seventh day he rested,* and was refreshed. Isa. lviii. 13. *If thou turn away thy foot from the sabbath, from doing thy pleasure on my holy day;* and call the sabbath a delight, the holy of the Lord, honourable; and shalt honour him, *not doing thine own ways, nor finding thine own pleasure, nor speaking thine own words.* Neh. xiii. 15. In those days saw I in Judah some treading winepresses on the sabbath, and bringing in sheaves, and lading asses; as also wine, grapes, and figs, and all manner of burdens, which they brought into Jerusalem on the sabbath-day: and *I testified against them in the day wherein they sold victuals.* Ver. 16. There dwelt men of Tyre also therein, which brought fish, and all manner of ware, and sold on the sabbath unto the children of Judah, and in Jerusalem. Ver. 17. Then *I contended with the nobles of Judah, and said unto them, What evil thing is this that ye do, and profane the sabbath-day?* Ver. 18. Did not your fathers thus, and did not our God bring all this evil upon us, and upon this city? *yet ye bring more wrath upon Israel, by profaning the sabbath.* Ver. 19. And it came to pass, that, when the gates of Jerusalem began to be dark before the sabbath, *I commanded that the gates should be shut, and charged that they should not be opened till after the sabbath;* and some of my servants set I at the gates, *that there should no burden be brought in on the sabbath-day.* Ver. 21. Then I testified against them, and said unto them, Why lodge ye about the wall? *if ye do so again, I will lay hands on you. From that time forth came they no more on the sabbath.* Ver. 22. And *I commanded the Levites, that they should cleanse themselves, and that they should come and keep the gates, to sanctify the sabbath-day.* Remember me, O my God, concerning *this* also, and spare me according to the greatness of thy mercy. p Isa. lviii. 13. [See in letter o. Matt. xii. 1. to the 13th verse.]

I. a Deut. x. 20. Thou shalt fear the Lord thy God; him shalt thou serve, and to him shalt thou cleave, and *swear by his name.*
b Exod. xx. 7. *Thou shalt not take the name of the Lord thy God in vain:* for the Lord will not hold him guiltless that taketh his name in vain. Lev. xix. 12. And *ye shall not swear by my name falsely, neither shalt thou profane the name of thy God:* I am the Lord. 2 Cor. i. 23. Moreover, *I call God for a record upon my soul,* that to spare you I came not as yet unto Corinth. 2 Chron. vi. 22. If a man sin against his neighbour, and *an oath be laid upon him to make him swear, and the oath come before thine altar in this house;* Ver. 23. Then hear thou from heaven, and do, and judge thy servants, by requiting the wicked, by recompensing his way upon his own head; and by justifying the righteous, by giving him according to his righteousness.

and therein it is to be used with all holy fear and reverence;c therefore to swear vainly or rashly by that glorious and dreadful name, or to swear at all by any other thing, is sinful, and to be abhorred.d Yet as, in matters of weight and moment, an oath is warranted by the word of God under the New Testament, as well as under the Old;e so a lawful oath, being imposed by lawful authority, in such matters, ought to be taken.f

III. Whosoever taketh on oath, ought duly to consider the weightiness of so solemn an act, and therein to avouch nothing but what he is fully persuaded is the truth.g Neither may any man bind himself by oath to any thing but what is good and just, and what he believeth so to be, and what he is able and resolved to perform.h Yet it is a sin to refuse an oath touching any thing that is good and just, being imposed by lawful authority.i

II. c Deut. vi. 13. Thou shalt fear the Lord thy God, and serve him, *and shalt swear by his name.*
d Exod. xx. 7. [See letter b.] Jer. v. 7. How shall I pardon thee for this? thy children have forsaken me, *and sworn by them that are no gods:* when I had fed them to the full, they then committed adultery, and assembled themselves by troops in the harlots' houses. Matt. v. 34. But I say unto you, *Swear not at all: neither by heaven;* for it is God's throne. Ver. 37. But let your communication be, Yea, yea; Nay, nay: for *whatsoever is more than these* cometh of evil. James v. 12. But above all things, my brethren, *swear not; neither by heaven, neither by the earth, neither by any other oath:* but let your yea be yea; and your nay, nay; lest ye fall into condemnation.
e Heb. vi. 16. For men verily swear by the greater: and *an oath for confirmation is to them an end of all strife.* 2 Cor. i. 23. [See letter b.] Isa. lxv. 16. That he who blesseth himself in the earth, shall bless himself in the God of truth; and he that *sweareth in the earth, shall swear by the God of truth;* because the former troubles are forgotten, and because they are hid from mine eyes.
f 1 Kings viii. 31. If any man trespass against his neighbour, and *an oath be laid upon him to cause him to swear,* and the oath come before thine altar in this house. Neh. xiii. 25. And I contended with them, and cursed them, and smote certain of them, and plucked off their hair, *and made them swear by God,* saying, Ye shall not give your daughters unto their sons, nor take their daughters unto your sons, or for yourselves. Ezra x. 5. Then arose Ezra, and *made the chief priests, the Levites, and all Israel, to swear* that they should do according to this word: and they sware.
III. g Exod. xx. 7. [See letter b.] Jer. iv. 2. *And thou shalt swear, The Lord liveth, in truth, in judgment, and in righteousness;* and the nations shall bless themselves in him, and in him shall they glory.
h Gen. xxiv. 2. And Abraham said unto his eldest servant of his house, that ruled over all that he had, Put, I pray thee, thy hand under my thigh; Ver. 3. And I will make thee swear by the Lord, the God of heaven, and the God of the earth, that thou shalt not take a wife unto my son of the daughters of the Canaanites, among whom I dwell. Ver. 5. And the servant said unto him, Peradventure the woman will not be willing to follow me unto this land: must I needs bring thy son again unto the land from whence thou camest? Ver. 6. And Abraham said unto him, Beware thou that thou bring not my son thither again. Ver. 8. And if the woman will not be willing to follow thee, then thou shalt be clear from this my oath: only bring not my son thither again. Ver. 9. *And the servant put his hand under the thigh of Abraham his master, and sware to him concerning that matter.*
i Numb. v. 19. And the priest shall *charge her by an oath,* and say unto the woman, If no man have lain with thee, and if thou hast not gone aside to uncleanness with another instead of thy husband, be thou free from this bitter water that causeth the curse. Ver. 21. Then the *priest shall charge the woman with an oath of cursing;* and the priest shall say unto the woman, The Lord make thee a curse and an oath among thy people, when the Lord doth make thy thigh to rot, and thy belly to swell. Neh. v. 12. Then said they, We will restore them, and will require nothing of them; so will we do as thou sayest. Then I called the priests, and *took an oath of them,* that they should do according to this promise. Exod. xxii. 7. If a man shall deliver unto his neighbour money or stuff to keep, and it be stolen out of the man's house; if the thief be found, let him pay double. Ver. 8. If the thief be not found, then the master of the house shall be brought unto the judges, to see whether he have put his hand unto his neighbour's goods. Ver. 9. For all manner of trespass, whether it be for ox, for ass, for sheep, for raiment, or for any manner of lost thing, which another challengeth to be his, the cause of both parties shall come before the judges; and whom the judges shall condemn, he shall pay double unto his neighbour. Ver. 10. If a man deliver unto his neighbour an ass, or an ox, or a sheep,

CHAP. XXII.   THE CONFESSION OF FAITH.   79

IV. An oath is to be taken in the plain and common sense of the words, without equivocation or mental reservation.ᵏ It cannot oblige to sin; but in any thing not sinful, being taken, it binds to performance, although to a man's own hurt;ˡ nor is it to be violated, although made to hereticks or infidels.ᵐ

V. A vow is of the like nature with a promissory oath, and ought to be made with the like religious care, and to be performed with the like faithfulness.ⁿ

VI. It is not to be made to any creature, but to God alone:ᵒ and that it may be accepted, it is to be made voluntarily, out of faith, and conscience of duty, in way of thankfulness for mercy received, or for the obtaining of what we want; whereby we more strictly bind ourselves to necessary duties, or to other things, so far and so long as they may fitly conduce thereunto.ᵖ

or any beast, to keep, and it die, or be hurt, or driven away, no man seeing it: Ver. 11. *Then shall an oath of the Lord be between them both,* that he hath not put his hand unto his neighbour's goods; and the owner of it shall accept thereof, and he shall not make it good.

IV. ᵏ Jer. iv. 2. [See letter g.] Ps. xxiv. 4. He that hath clean hands, and a pure heart; who hath not lifted up his soul unto vanity, *nor sworn deceitfully.*

ˡ 1 Sam. xxv. 22. So and more also do God unto the enemies of David, if I leave of all that pertain to him, by the morning-light, any that pisseth against the wall. Ver. 32. And David said to Abigail, Blessed be the Lord God of Israel, which sent thee this day to meet me: Ver. 33. And blessed be thy advice, and blessed be thou, which hast kept me this day from coming to shed blood, and from avenging myself with mine own hand. Ver. 34. For in very deed, as the Lord God of Israel liveth, which hath kept me back from hurting thee, except thou hadst hasted and come to meet me, surely there had not been left unto Nabal, by the morning-light, any that pisseth against the wall. Ps. xv. 4. In whose eyes a vile person is contemned; but he honoureth them that fear the Lord: *he that sweareth to his own hurt, and changeth not.*

ᵐ Ezek. xvii. 16. As I live, saith the Lord God, surely in the place where the king dwelleth that made him king, *whose oath he despised, and whose covenant he brake,* even with him in the midst of Babylon he shall die. Ver. 18. *Seeing he despised the oath by breaking the covenant, when, lo, he had given his hand,* and hath done all these things, he shall not escape. Ver. 19. Therefore thus saith the Lord God, As I live, *surely mine oath that he hath despised, and my covenant that he hath broken, even it will I recompense upon his own head.* Josh. ix. 18. And the children of Israel smote them not, because the princes of the congregation had sworn unto them by the Lord God of Israel. And all the congregation murmured against the princes. Ver. 19. But all the princes said unto all the congregation, *We have sworn unto them by the Lord God of Israel: now therefore we may not touch them.* With 2 Sam xxi. 1.

Then there was a famine in the days of David three years, year after year; and David enquired of the Lord. And the Lord answered, *It is for Saul, and for his bloody house, because he slew the Gibeonites.*

V. ⁿ Isa. xix. 21. And the Lord shall be known to Egypt, and the Egyptians shall know the Lord in that day, and shall do sacrifice and oblation; yea, *they shall vow a vow unto the Lord,* and perform it. Eccl. v. 4. When thou *vowest a vow unto God,* defer not to pay it; for he hath no pleasure in fools: pay that which *thou hast vowed.* Ver. 5. Better is it that thou shouldest *not vow, than that thou shouldest vow* and not pay. Ver. 6. Suffer not thy mouth to cause thy flesh to sin; neither say thou before the angel, that it was an error: wherefore should God be angry at thy voice, and destroy the work of thine hands? Ps. lxi. 8. So will I sing praise unto thy name for ever, that I may daily *perform my vows.* Ps. lxvi. 13. I will go into thy house with burnt-offerings; *I will pay thee my vows,* Ver. 14. Which my lips have uttered, and my mouth hath spoken, when I was in trouble.

VI. ᵒ Ps. lxxvi. 11. *Vow, and pay unto the Lord your God;* let all that be round about him bring presents unto him that ought to be feared. Jer. xliv. 25. Thus saith the Lord of hosts, the God of Israel, saying, Ye and your wives have both spoken with your mouths, and fulfilled with your hand, saying, We will surely perform our vows that *we have vowed, to burn incense to the queen of heaven,* and to pour out drink-offerings unto her: ye will surely accomplish your vows, and surely perform your vows. Ver. 26. Therefore hear ye the word of the Lord, all Judah that dwell in the land of Egypt; Behold, I have sworn by my great name, saith the Lord, that my name shall no more be named in the mouth of any man of Judah in all the land of Egypt, saying, The Lord God liveth.

ᵖ Deut. xxiii. 21. When *thou shalt vow a vow unto the Lord thy God,* thou shalt not slack to pay it: for the Lord thy God will surely require it of thee; and it would be sin in thee. Ver. 22. But if thou shalt forbear to vow, it shall be no sin in thee. Ver. 23. That which is gone out of thy lips thou shalt keep and perform; even a free-

VII. No man may vow to do any thing forbidden in the word of God, or what would hinder any duty therein commanded, or which is not in his power, and for the performance whereof he hath no promise of ability from God.q In which respects, Popish monastical vows of perpetual single life, professed poverty, and regular obedience, are so far from being degrees of higher perfection, that they are superstitious and sinful snares, in which no Christian may entangle himself.r

CHAP. XXIII.—*Of the Civil Magistrate.*

I. GOD, the supreme Lord and King of all the world, hath ordained civil magistrates to be under him over the people, for his own glory, and the publick good; and, to this end, hath armed them with the power of the sword, for the defence and encouragement of them that are good, and for the punishment of evil-doers.a

will-offering, according as thou hast vowed unto the Lord thy God, which thou hast promised with thy mouth. Ps l. 14. *Offer unto God thanksgiving; and pay thy vows unto the Most High.* Gen. xxviii. 20. And Jacob vowed a vow, saying, *If God will be with me,* and will keep me in this way that I go, and will give me bread to eat, and raiment to put on, Ver. 21. So that I come again to my father's house in peace, then shall the Lord be my God: Ver. 22. And this stone, which I have set for a pillar, shall be God's house: and of all that thou shalt give me, *I will surely give the tenth unto thee.* 1 Sam. i. 11. And *she vowed a vow,* and said, O Lord of hosts, if thou wilt indeed look on the affliction of thine handmaid, and remember me, and not forget thine handmaid, but wilt give unto thine handmaid a man child, *then I will give him unto the Lord all the days of his life,* and there shall no razor come upon his head. Ps. lxvi. 13, 14. [See letter n.] Ps. cxxxii. 2. How he sware unto the Lord, and *vowed unto the mighty God of Jacob;* Ver. 3. *Surely I will not come into the tabernacle of my house, nor go up into my bed;* Ver. 4. *I will not give sleep to mine eyes, or slumber to mine eyelids,* Ver. 5. *Until I find out a place for the Lord, an habitation for the mighty God of Jacob.*

VII. q Acts xxiii. 12. And when it was day, certain of the Jews banded together, and *bound themselves under a curse,* saying *that they would neither eat nor drink till they had killed Paul.* Ver. 14. And they came to the chief priests and elders, and said, *We have bound ourselves under a great curse, that we will eat nothing until we have slain Paul.* Mark vi. 26. And the king was exceeding sorry; *yet for his oath's sake, and for their sakes which sat with him,* he would not reject her. Numb. xxx. 5. But if her father disallow her in the day that he heareth; not any of her vows, or of her bonds wherewith she hath bound her soul, shall stand; and the Lord shall forgive her, because her father disallowed her. Ver. 8. But if her husband disallowed her on the day that he heard it; then he shall make her vow which she vowed, and that which she uttered with her lips, wherewith she bound her soul, of none effect; and the Lord shall forgive her. Ver. 12. *But if her husband hath utterly made them void on the day he heard them;* then whatsoever *proceeded out of her lips concerning her vows, or concerning the bond of her soul, shall not stand; her husband hath made them void;* and the Lord shall forgive her. Ver. 13. Every vow, and every binding oath to afflict the soul, her husband may establish it, or her husband may make it void.

r Matt. xix. 11. But he said unto them, *All men cannot receive this saying,* save they to whom it is given. Ver. 12. For there are some eunuchs, which were so born from their mother's womb; and there are some eunuchs, which were made eunuchs of men; and there be eunuchs, which have made themselves eunuchs for the kingdom of heaven's sake. *He that is able to receive it, let him receive it.* 1 Cor. vii. 2. Nevertheless, to avoid fornication, *let every man have his own wife, and let every woman have her own husband.* Ver. 9. But if they cannot contain, let them marry: for it is better to marry than to burn. Eph. iv. 28. Let him that stole steal no more: *but rather let him labour, working with his hands* the thing which is good, that he may have to give to him that needeth. 1 Pet. iv. 2. That he no longer should live the rest of his time in the flesh *to the lusts of men, but to the will of God.* 1 Cor. vii. 23. Ye are bought with a price: *be not ye the servants of men.*

I. a Rom. xiii. 1. *Let every soul be subject unto the higher powers. For there is no power but of God: the powers that be are ordained of God.* Ver. 2. Whosoever therefore resisteth the power, resisteth the ordinance of God; and they that resist shall receive to themselves damnation. Ver. 3. *For rulers are not a terror to good works, but to the evil.* Wilt thou then not be afraid of the power? Do that which is good, and thou shalt have praise of the same: Ver. 4. For

II. It is lawful for Christians to accept and execute the office of a magistrate, when called thereunto:[b] in the managing whereof, as they ought especially to maintain piety, justice, and peace, according to the wholesome laws of each commonwealth;[c] so, for that end, they may lawfully, now under the New Testament, wage war upon just and necessary occasions.[d]

III. The civil magistrate may not assume to himself the administration of the word and sacraments, or the power of the keys of the kingdom of heaven:[e] yet he hath authority, and it is his duty, to take order, that unity and peace be preserved in the church, that the truth of God be kept pure and entire, that all blasphemies and heresies be suppressed, all corruptions and abuses in worship and discipline prevented or reformed, and all the ordinances of God duly settled, administered, and observed.[f] For the better effecting whereof, he hath

he is *the minister of God to thee for good. But if thou do that which is evil, be afraid; for he beareth not the sword in vain: for he is the minister of God, a revenger to execute wrath upon him that doeth evil.* 1 Pet. ii. 13. Submit yourselves to every ordinance of man for the Lord's sake: whether it be to the king, as supreme; Ver. 14. Or unto governors, as unto them that are sent by him *for the punishment of evil-doers, and for the praise of them that do well.*

II. [b] Prov. viii. 15. *By me kings reign, and princes decree justice.* Ver. 16. *By me princes rule, and nobles, even all the judges of the earth.* Rom. xiii. 1, 2, 4. [See in letter a.]

[c] Ps. ii. 10. *Be wise now therefore, O ye kings; be instructed, ye judges of the earth.* Ver. 11. *Serve the Lord with fear,* and rejoice with trembling. Ver. 12. *Kiss the Son, lest he be angry, and ye perish from the way, when his wrath is kindled but a little.* Blessed are all they that put their trust in him. 1 Tim. ii. 2. For kings, and for all that are in authority; *that we may lead a quiet and peaceable life in all godliness and honesty.* Ps. lxxxii. 3. *Defend the poor and fatherless; do justice to the afflicted and needy.* Ver. 4. *Deliver the poor and needy; rid them out of the hand of the wicked.* 2 Sam. xxiii. 3. The God of Israel said, the Rock of Israel spake to me, *He that ruleth over men must be just, ruling in the fear of God.* 1 Pet. ii. 13. [See in letter a.]

[d] Luke iii. 14. *And the soldiers likewise demanded of him,* saying, And what shall we do? And *he said unto them, Do violence to no man,* neither accuse any falsely; and be content with your wages. Rom. xiii. 4. [See letter a.] Matt. viii. 9. For I am a man under authority, *having soldiers under me;* and I say to this man, Go, and he goeth; and to another, Come, and he cometh; and to my servant, Do this, and he doeth it. Ver. 10. When Jesus heard it, he marvelled, and said to them that followed, Verily I say unto you, I have not found so great faith, no, not in Israel. Acts x. 1. There was a certain man in Cesarea called *Cornelius, a centurion of the band* called the Italian band, Ver. 2. *A devout man, and one that feared God with all his house,* which gave much alms to the people, and prayed to God alway. Rev. xvii. 14. *These shall make war with the Lamb,* and the Lamb shall overcome them: for he is Lord of lords, and King of kings; and they that are with him are called, and chosen, and faithful. Ver. 16. And the ten horns which thou sawest upon the beast, these *shall hate the whore, and shall make her desolate and naked, and shall eat her flesh, and burn her with fire.*

III. [e] 2 Chron. xxvi. 18. And they withstood Uzziah the king, and said unto him, *It appertaineth not unto thee, Uzziah, to burn incense unto the Lord,* but to the priests, the sons of Aaron, that are consecrated to burn incense: *go out of the sanctuary; for thou hast trespassed;* neither shall it be for thine honour from the Lord God. With Matt. xviii. 17. And if he shall neglect to hear them, *tell it unto the church;* but if he *neglect to hear the church,* let him be unto thee as an heathen man and a publican. And Matt. xvi. 19. And I will *give unto thee the keys of the kingdom of heaven;* and whatsoever thou shalt bind on earth shall be bound in heaven; and whatsoever thou shalt loose on earth shall be loosed in heaven. 1 Cor. xii. 28. And God hath *set some in the church, first, apostles; secondarily, prophets;* thirdly, teachers; after that miracles; then gifts of healings, helps, governments, diversities of tongues. Ver. 29. Are all *apostles?* are all *prophets?* are all *teachers?* are all *workers of miracles?* Eph. iv. 11. And he gave some, apostles; and some, prophets; and some, evangelists; and some, pastors and teachers; Ver. 12. For the perfecting of the saints, for the work of the ministry, for the edifying of the body of Christ. 1 Cor. iv. 1. Let a man so *account of us as of the ministers of Christ, and stewards of the mysteries of God.* Ver. 2. Moreover, it is required in stewards, that a man be found faithful. Rom. x. 15. *And how shall they preach except they be sent?* as it is written, How beautiful are the feet of them that preach the gospel of peace, and bring glad tidings of good things! Heb. v. 4. And *no man taketh this honour unto himself, but he that is called of God,* as was Aaron.

[f] Isa. xlix. 23. And *kings shall be thy*

power to call synods, to be present at them, and to provide that whatsoever is transacted in them be according to the mind of God.g

IV. It is the duty of people to pray for magistrates,h to honour their persons,i to pay them tribute and other dues,k to obey their lawful commands, and to be subject to their authority for conscience' sake.l Infidelity, or difference in religion, doth not make void the magistrate's

nursing-fathers, and their queens thy nursing-mothers; they shall bow down to thee with their face toward the earth, and lick up the dust of thy feet ; and thou shalt know that I am the Lord: for they shall not be ashamed that wait for me. Ps. cxxii. 9. Because of the house of the Lord our God I will seek thy good. Ezra vii. 23. Whatsoever is commanded by the God of heaven, let it be diligently done for the house of the God of heaven : for why should there be wrath against the realm of the king and his sons? Ver. 25. And thou, Ezra, after the wisdom of thy God that is in thine hand, set *magistrates and judges, which may judge all the people* that are beyond the river, *all such as know the laws of thy God;* and teach ye them that know them not. Ver. 26. And *whosoever will not do the law of thy God,* and the law of the king, *let judgment be executed speedily upon him, whether it be unto death, or to banishment, or to confiscation of goods, or to imprisonment.* Ver. 27. Blessed be the Lord God of our fathers, which hath put such a thing *as this in the king's heart, to beautify the house of the Lord,* which is in Jerusalem ; Ver. 28. And hath extended mercy unto me before the king and his counsellors, and before all the king's mighty princes : and I was strengthened as the hand of the Lord my God was upon me ; and I gathered together out of Israel chief men to go up with me. Lev. xxiv. 16. And he *that blasphemeth the name of the Lord, he shall surely be put to death,* and all the congregation shall certainly stone him: as well the stranger, as he that is born in the land, when he blasphemeth the name of the Lord, shall be put to death. Deut. xiii. 5. And that prophet, or *that dreamer of dreams, shall be put to death;* because he hath spoken to turn you away from the Lord your God, which brought you out of the land of Egypt, and redeemed you out of the house of bondage, to thrust thee out of the way which the Lord thy God commanded thee to walk in : so shalt thou put the evil away from the midst of thee. Ver. 6. If thy brother, the son of thy mother, or thy son, or thy daughter, or the wife of thy bosom, or thy friend, which is as thine own soul, entice thee secretly, saying, Let us go and serve other gods, which thou hast not known, thou, nor thy fathers. Ver. 12. If thou shalt hear say in one of thy cities, which the Lord thy God hath given thee to dwell there, saying, &c. 2 Kings xviii. 4. *He removed the high places, and brake the images, and cut down the groves, and brake in pieces the brazen serpent that* Moses had made : for unto those days the children of Israel did burn incense to it; and he called it Nehushtan. [1 Chron. xiii. 1. to the 9th verse. 2 Kings xxiv. 1. to the 26th verse.] 2 Chron. xxxiv. 33. *And Josiah took away all the abominations* out of all the countries that pertained to the children of Israel, and *made all that were present in Israel to serve, even to serve the Lord their God.* And all his days they departed not from following the Lord, the God of their fathers. 2 Chron. xv. 12. And they entered into a covenant to seek the Lord God of their fathers with all their heart, and with all their soul ; Ver. 13. That whosoever would not seek the Lord God of Israel *should be put to death,* whether small or great, whether man or woman.

g 2 Chron. xix. 8. Moreover, in *Jerusalem* did *Jehoshaphat set of the Levites, and of the priests, and of the chief of the fathers of Israel, for the judgment of the Lord,* and for controversies, when they returned to Jerusalem. Ver. 9. And he charged them, saying, Thus shall ye do in the fear of the Lord, faithfully, and with a perfect heart. Ver. 10. And what cause soever shall come to you of your brethren that dwell in their cities, between blood and blood, between law and commandment, statutes and judgments, ye shall even warn them that they trespass not against the Lord, and so wrath come upon you, and upon your brethren : this do, and ye shall not trespass. Ver. 11. And, behold, Amariah the chief priest is over you in all matters of the Lord ; and Zebadiah the son of Ishmael, the ruler of the house of Judah, for all the king's matters : also the Levites shall be officers before you. Deal courageously, and the Lord shall be with the good. [2 Chron. chapters xxix. and xxx.] Matt. ii. 4. *And when he had gathered all the chief priests and scribes of the people together, he demanded of them* where Christ should be born. Ver. 5. And they said unto him, In Bethlehem of Judea : for thus it is written by the prophet.

IV. h 1 Tim. ii. 1. I exhort therefore, that, first of all, *supplications, prayers, intercessions, and giving of thanks, be made for all men;* Ver. 2. For kings, and *for all that are in authority;* that we may lead a quiet and peaceable life in all godliness and honesty.

i 1 Pet. ii. 17. Honour all men. Love the brotherhood. Fear God. *Honour the king.*

k Rom. xiii. 6. For, for this *cause pay ye tribute also: for they are God's ministers,* attending continually upon this very thing. Ver. 7. *Render therefore to all* their dues: *tribute to whom tribute is due; custom to whom custom; fear to whom fear; honour to whom honour.*

l Rom. xiii. 5. Wherefore ye must needs be subject, not only for wrath, *but also for conscience' sake.* Tit. iii. 1. Put *them in mind to be subject to principalities and*

just and legal authority, nor free the people from their due obedience to him:^m from which ecclesiastical persons are not exempted;^n much less hath the Pope any power or jurisdiction over them in their dominions, or over any of their people; and least of all to deprive them of their dominions or lives, if he shall judge them to be hereticks, or upon any other pretence whatsoever.^o

CHAP. XXIV.—*Of Marriage and Divorce.*

I. MARRIAGE is to be between one man and one woman: neither is it lawful for any man to have more than one wife, nor for any woman to have more than one husband, at the same time.[a]

II. Marriage was ordained for the mutual help of husband and wife;[b] for the increase of mankind with a legitimate issue, and of the church with an holy seed;[c] and for preventing of uncleanness.[d]

---

powers, to obey magistrates, to be ready to every good work.

m 1 Pet. ii. 13. *Submit yourselves to every ordinance of man for the Lord's sake:* whether it be to the king, as supreme; Ver. 14. Or unto governors, as unto them that are sent by him for the punishment of evil-doers, and for the praise of them that do well. Ver. 16. As free, and *not using your liberty for a cloak of maliciousness, but as the servants of God.*

n Rom. xiii. 1. *Let every soul be subject unto the higher powers.* For there is no power but of God: the powers that be are ordained of God. 1 Kings ii. 35. And the king put Benaiah the son of Jehoiada in his room over the host; and *Zadok the priest did the king put in the room of Abiathar.* Acts xxv. 9. But Festus, willing to do the Jews a pleasure, answered Paul, and said, Wilt thou go up to Jerusalem, and there be judged of these things before me? Ver. 10. Then said Paul, I stand at Cesar's judgment-seat, where I ought to be judged: to the Jews have I done no wrong, as thou very well knowest. Ver. 11. *For if I be an offender, or have committed any thing worthy of death, I refuse not to die:* but if there be none of these things whereof these accuse me, no man may deliver me unto them. *I appeal unto Cesar.* 2 Pet. ii. 1. But there were false prophets also among the people, even as there shall be false teachers among you, who privily shall bring in damnable heresies, even denying the Lord that bought them, and bring upon themselves swift destruction. Ver. 10. But chiefly them that walk after the flesh in the lust of uncleanness, and *despise government;* presumptuous are they, self-willed, *they are not afraid to speak evil of dignities:* Ver. 11. Whereas angels, which are greater in power and might, *bring not railing accusation against them before the Lord.* Jude, ver. 8. Likewise also these filthy dreamers defile the flesh, *despise dominion,* and *speak evil of dignities.* Ver. 9. Yet Michael the archangel, when contending with the devil, he disputed about the body of Moses, *durst not bring against him a railing accusation,* but said, The Lord rebuke thee. Ver. 10. But these speak evil of those things which they know not : but what they know naturally, as brute beasts, in those things they corrupt themselves. Ver. 11. Woe unto them! for they have gone in the way of Cain, and ran greedily after the error of Balaam for reward, and perished in the gainsaying of Core.

o 2 Thess. ii. 4. *Who opposeth and exalteth himself above all that is called God,* or that is worshipped; so that he, as God, sitteth in the temple of God, shewing himself that he is God. Rev. xiii. 15. And he had power to give life unto the image of the beast, that the image of the beast should both speak, and cause that as many *as would not worship the image of the beast should be killed.* Ver. 16. *And he caused all, both small and great, rich and poor, free and bond, to receive a mark in their right hand, or in their foreheads:* Ver. 17. *And that no man might buy or sell, save he that had the mark, or the name of the beast, or the number of his name.*

I. a Gen. ii. 24. Therefore shall a man leave his father and his mother, and shall cleave unto his wife; *and they shall be one flesh.* Matt. xix. 5. And said, For this cause shall a man leave father and mother, and shall cleave to his wife: and *they twain shall be one flesh.* Ver. 6. *Wherefore they are no more twain, but one flesh.* What therefore God hath joined together, let not man put asunder. Prov. ii. 17. Which forsaketh *the guide of her youth,* and forgetteth the covenant of her God.

II. b Gen. ii. 18. And the Lord God said, It is not good that the man should be alone; *I will make him an help meet for him.*

c Mal. ii. 15. And did not he make one? Yet had he the residue of the Spirit. And wherefore one? *That he might seek a godly seed.* Therefore take heed to your spirit, and let none deal treacherously against the wife of his youth.

d 1 Cor. vii. 2. *Nevertheless, to avoid fornication, let every man have his own wife*

III. It is lawful for all sorts of people to marry who are able with judgment to give their consent:[e] yet it is the duty of Christians to marry only in the Lord.[f] And therefore such as profess the true reformed religion should not marry with infidels, Papists, or other idolaters: neither should such as are godly be unequally yoked, by marrying with such as are notoriously wicked in their life, or maintain damnable heresies.[g]

IV. Marriage ought not to be within the degrees of consanguinity or affinity forbidden in the word;[h] nor can such incestuous marriages ever be made lawful by any law of man, or consent of parties, so as those persons may live together as man and wife.[i] The man may not marry any of his wife's kindred nearer in blood than he may of his

and let every woman have her own husband. Ver. 9. *But if they cannot contain, let them marry:* for it is better to marry than to burn.

III. [e] Heb. xiii. 4. *Marriage is honourable in all,* and the bed undefiled: but whoremongers and adulterers God will judge. 1 Tim. iv. 3. *Forbidding to marry,* and commanding to abstain from meats, which God hath created to be received with thanksgiving of them which believe and know the truth. 1 Cor. vii. 36. But if any man think that he behaveth himself uncomely toward his virgin, if she pass the flower of her age, and need so require, let him do what he will, he sinneth not ; *let them marry.* Ver. 37. Nevertheless he that standeth steadfast in his heart, having no necessity, but hath power over his own will, and hath so decreed in his heart that he will keep his virgin, doeth well. Ver. 38. *So then he that giveth her in marriage doeth well:* but he that giveth her not in marriage, doeth better. Gen. xxiv. 57. And they said, We will call the damsel, and enquire at her mouth. Ver. 58. And they called Rebekah, and said unto her, Wilt thou go with this *man ? And she said, I will go.*

[f] 1 Cor. vii. 39. The wife is bound by the law as long as her husband liveth ; but if her husband be dead, she is at liberty to be married to whom she will; *only in the Lord.*

[g] Gen. xxxiv. 14. And they said unto them, *We cannot do this thing, to give our sister to one that is uncircumcised; for that were* a reproach unto us. Exod. xxxiv. 16. And thou *take of their daughters unto thy sons,* and their daughters go a whoring after their gods, and make thy sons go a whoring after their gods. Deut. vii. 3. *Neither shalt thou make marriages with them; thy daughter thou shalt not give unto his son, nor his daughter shalt thou take unto thy son.* Ver. 4. *For they will turn away thy son from following me, that they may serve other gods;* so will the anger of the Lord be kindled against you, and destroy thee suddenly. 1 Kings xi. 4. For it came to pass, when *Solomon was old,* that *his wives turned away his heart after other gods:* and his heart was not perfect with the Lord his God, as was the heart of David his father. Neh. xiii. 25. And I contended with them, and cursed them, and smote certain of them, and plucked off their hair, and made them swear by God, saying, *Ye shall not give your daughters unto their sons, nor take their daughters unto your sons, or for yourselves.* Ver. 26. *Did not Solomon king of Israel sin by these things ?* yet among many nations was there no king like him, who was beloved of his God, and God made him king over all Israel : *nevertheless even him did outlandish women cause to sin.* Ver. 27. Shall we then hearken unto you to do all *this great evil, to transgress against our God in marrying strange wives ?* Mal. ii. 11. Judah hath dealt treacherously, and an abomination is committed in Israel and in Jerusalem : for Judah hath profaned the holiness of the Lord which he loved, *and hath married the daughter of a strange god.* Ver. 12. *The Lord will cut off the man that doeth this,* the master and the scholar, out of the tabernacles of Jacob, and him that offereth an offering unto the Lord of hosts. 2 Cor. vi. 14. *Be ye not unequally yoked together with* unbelievers : for what fellowship hath righteousness with unrighteousness ? and what communion hath light with darkness ?

IV. [h] [Ler. Chapter xviii.] 1 Cor. v. 1. It is reported commonly that there is fornication among you, and such fornication as is not so much as named among the Gentiles, *that one should have his father's wife.* Amos ii. 7. That pant after the dust of the earth on the head of the poor, and turn aside the way of the meek : and *a man and his father will go in unto the same maid,* to profane my holy name.

[i] Mark vi. 18. For John had said unto Herod, *It is not lawful for thee to have thy brother's wife.* Lev. xviii. 24. *Defile not ye yourselves in any of these things:* for in all these the nations are defiled which I cast out before you. Ver. 25. And the land is defiled : therefore I do visit the iniquity thereof upon it, and the land itself vomiteth out her inhabitants. Ver. 26. Ye shall therefore keep my statutes and my judgments, and shall not commit any of these abominations ; neither any of your own nation, nor any stranger that sojourneth among you ; Ver. 27. (For all these abominations have the men of the land done which were before you, and the land is defiled ;) Ver. 28. That the land spue not you out also, when ye defile it, as it spued out the nations that were before you.

own, nor the woman of her husband's kindred nearer in blood than of her own.[k]

V. Adultery or fornication committed after a contract being detected before marriage, giveth just occasion to the innocent party to dissolve that contract.[l] In the case of adultery after marriage, it is lawful for the innocent party to sue out a divorce,[m] and, after the divorce, to marry another, as if the offending party were dead.[n]

VI. Although the corruption of man be such as is apt to study arguments, unduly to put asunder those whom God hath joined together in marriage; yet nothing but adultery, or such wilful desertion as can no way be remedied by the church or civil magistrate, is cause sufficient of dissolving the bond of marriage:[o] wherein a publick and orderly course of proceeding is to be observed, and the persons concerned in it not left to their own wills and discretion in their own case.[p]

CHAP. XXV.—*Of the Church.*

I. THE catholick or universal church, which is invisible, consists of the whole number of the elect that have been, are, or shall be gathered into one, under Christ the head thereof; and is the spouse, the body, the fulness of him that filleth all in all.[a]

[k] Lev. xx. 19. And *thou shalt not uncover the nakedness of thy mother's sister, nor of thy father's sister;* for he uncovereth his near kin: they shall bear their iniquity. Ver. 20. And if a man *shall lie with his uncle's wife,* he hath uncovered his uncle's nakedness: they shall bear their sin; they shall die childless. Ver. 21. And if a *man shall take his brother's wife,* it is an unclean thing; he hath uncovered his brother's nakedness: they shall be childless.

[V.] [l] Matt. i. 18. Now the birth of Jesus Christ was on this wise: When as his mother Mary was espoused to Joseph, *before they came together, she was found with child of the Holy Ghost.* Ver. 19. Then *Joseph her husband,* being a just man, and not willing to make her a publick example, *was minded to put her away privily.* Ver. 20. But while he thought on these things, behold, the angel of the Lord appeared unto him in a dream, saying, Joseph, thou son of David, fear not to take unto thee Mary thy wife: for that which is conceived in her is of the Holy Ghost.

[m] Matt. v. 31. It hath been said, Whosoever shall put away his wife, let him give her a writing of divorcement: Ver. 32. But I say unto you, That whosoever shall *put away his wife, saving for the cause of fornication,* causeth her to commit adultery: and whosoever shall marry her that is divorced committeth adultery.

[n] Matt. xix. 9. And I say unto you, Whosoever shall *put away his wife, except it be for fornication,* and shall marry another, committeth adultery; and whoso marrieth her which is put away doth commit adultery. Rom. vii. 2. For the woman which hath an husband is bound by the law to her husband so long as he liveth: but *if the husband be dead, she is loosed from the law of her husband.* Ver. 3. So then if, while her husband liveth, she be married to another man, she shall be called an adulteress: but if *her husband be dead, she is free from that law;* so that she is no adulteress, though she be married to another man.

VI. [o] Matt. xix. 8. He saith unto them, Moses, because of the hardness of your hearts, suffered you to put away your wives: *but from the beginning it was not so.* Ver. 9. [See letter n.] 1 Cor. vii. 15. But if the *unbelieving depart, let him depart. A brother or a sister is not under bondage in such cases:* but God hath called us to peace. Matt. xix. 6. Wherefore they are no more twain, but one flesh. What therefore *God hath joined together, let not man put asunder.*

[p] Deut. xxiv. 1. When a man hath taken a wife, and married her, and it come to pass that she find no favour in his eyes, because he hath found some uncleanness in her; *then let him write her a bill of divorcement,* and give it in her hand, and send her out of his house. Ver. 2. And when she is departed out of his house, she may go and be another man's wife. Ver. 3. And if the latter husband hate her, and write her a bill of divorcement, and giveth it in her hand, and sendeth her out of his house; or if the latter husband die, which took her to be his wife; Ver. 4. Her former husband, which sent her away, may not take her again to be his wife, after that she is defiled; for that is abomination before the Lord: and thou shalt not cause the land to sin, which the Lord thy God giveth thee for an inheritance.

I. [a] Eph. i. 10. That, in the dispensation of the fulness of times, he might *gather together in one all things in Christ,* both

II. The visible church, which is also catholick or universal under the gospel, (not confined to one nation, as before under the law,) consists of all those throughout the world that profess the true religion,[b] together with their children;[c] and is the kingdom of the Lord Jesus Christ,[d] the house and family of God,[e] out of which there is no ordinary possibility of salvation.[f]

III. Unto this catholick visible church Christ hath given the ministry, oracles, and ordinances of God, for the gathering and perfecting of the saints in this life, to the end of the world; and doth by his own presence and Spirit, according to his promise, make them effectual thereunto.[g]

which are in heaven, and which are on earth, even in him. Ver. 22. And hath put all things under his feet, and *gave him to be the head over all things to the church,* Ver. 23. *Which is his body,* the fulness of him that filleth all in all. Eph. v. 23. For the husband is the head of the wife, even as *Christ is the head of the church;* and he is the saviour of the body. Ver. 27. That he might present it to himself a glorious church, not having spot, or wrinkle, or any such thing; but that it should be holy, and without blemish. Ver. 32. This is a great mystery: but I speak concerning Christ and the church. Col. i. 18. And *he is the head of the body,* the church; who is the beginning, the first-born from the dead; that in all things he might have the preeminence.

II. [b] 1 Cor. i. 2. Unto the church of God which is at Corinth, to them that are sanctified in Christ Jesus, called to be saints, *with all that in every place call* upon the name of Jesus Christ our Lord, both theirs and ours. 1 Cor. xii. 12. For as the body is one, and hath many members, and *all the members of that one body, being many, are one body; so also is Christ.* Ver. 13. For by one Spirit *are we all baptized into one body, whether we be Jews or Gentiles, whether we be bond or free;* and have been all made to drink into one Spirit. Ps. ii. 8. Ask of me, and I shall give thee *the heathen for thine inheritance, and the uttermost parts of the earth for thy possession.* Rev. vii. 9. After this I beheld, and, lo, a great multitude, which no man could number, *of all nations, and kindreds, and people, and tongues, stood before the throne, and before the Lamb,* clothed with white robes, and palms in their hands. Rom. xv. 9. *And that the Gentiles might glorify God for his mercy;* as it is written, For this cause I will *confess to thee among the Gentiles,* and sing unto thy name. Ver. 10. And again he saith, *Rejoice, ye Gentiles, with his people.* Ver. 11. And again, Praise the Lord, *all ye Gentiles; and laud him, all ye people.* Ver. 12. And again Esaias saith, There shall be a root of Jesse, and he that shall *rise to reign over the Gentiles;* in him *shall the Gentiles trust.*

[c] 1 Cor. vii. 14. For the unbelieving husband is sanctified by the wife, and the unbelieving wife is sanctified by the husband: else *were your children unclean; but now are they holy.* Acts ii. 39. For the *promise is unto you, and to your children, and to all that are afar off, even as many as the Lord our God shall call.* Ezek. xvi. 20. Moreover, *thou hast taken thy sons and thy daughters, whom thou hast born unto me,* and these hast thou sacrificed unto them to be devoured. Is this of thy whoredoms a small matter, Ver. 21. That thou *hast slain my children,* and delivered them to cause them to pass through the fire for them? Rom. xi. 16. For if the *first-fruit be holy, the lump is also holy;* and if the root be holy, so are the branches. Gen. iii. 15. And I will put enmity between thee and the woman, and between *thy seed and her seed;* it shall bruise thy head, and thou shalt bruise his heel. Gen. xvii. 7. And I will establish my covenant between me and thee, and *thy seed after thee, in their generations,* for an everlasting covenant, to be a God unto thee, *and to thy seed after thee.*

[d] Matt. xiii. 47. Again, the *kingdom of heaven* is like unto a net, that was cast into the sea, and *gathered of every kind.* Isa. ix. 7. Of the increase of his *government* and peace there shall be no end, upon the throne of David, and *upon his kingdom,* to order it, and to establish it with judgment and with justice from henceforth even for ever. The zeal of the Lord of hosts will perform this.

[e] Eph. ii. 19. Now therefore ye are no more strangers and foreigners, *but fellow-citizens with the saints, and of the household of God.* Eph. iii. 15. Of whom the whole *family in heaven and earth is* named.

[f] Acts ii. 47. Praising God, and having favour with all the people. And the Lord added to *the church daily such as should be saved.*

III. [g] 1 Cor. xii. 28. *And God hath set some in the church, first, apostles; secondarily, prophets; thirdly, teachers;* after that miracles; then gifts of healings, helps, governments, diversities of tongues. Eph. iv. 11. And he *gave some, apostles; and some, prophets; and some, evangelists; and some, pastors and teachers;* Ver. 12. For *the perfecting of the saints, for the work of the ministry, for the edifying of the body of Christ:* Ver. 13. *Till we all come in the unity of the faith, and of the knowledge of the Son of God, unto a perfect man, unto the measure of the stature of the fulness of Christ.* Matt. xxviii. 19. Go ye *therefore, and teach all nations, baptizing them* in the name of the Father, and of the Son, and of

IV. This catholick church hath been sometimes more, sometimes less visible.[h] And particular churches, which are members thereof, are more or less pure, according as the doctrine of the gospel is taught and embraced, ordinances administered, and publick worship performed more or less purely in them.[i]

V. The purest churches under heaven are subject both to mixture and error;[k] and some have so degenerated as to become no churches of Christ, but synagogues of Satan.[l] Nevertheless, there shall be always a church on earth to worship God according to his will.[m]

VI. There is no other head of the church but the Lord Jesus Christ:[n] nor can the Pope of Rome in any sense be head thereof; but is that antichrist, that man of sin, and son of perdition, that exalteth himself in the church against Christ, and all that is called God.[o]

---

the Holy Ghost; Ver. 20. *Teaching them to observe all things whatsoever I have commanded you: and, lo, I am with you alway, even unto the end of the world. Amen.* Isa. lix. 21. As for me, *this is my covenant with them,* saith the Lord; *My Spirit that is upon thee, and my words which I have put in thy mouth, shall not depart* out of thy mouth, nor out of the mouth of thy seed, nor out of the mouth of thy seed's seed, saith the Lord, from henceforth and for ever.

IV. h Rom. xi. 3. Lord, they have killed thy prophets, and digged down thine altars; and *I am left alone,* and they seek my life. Ver. 4. But what saith the answer of God unto him? *I have reserved to myself seven thousand men,* who have not bowed the knee to the image of Baal. Rev. xii. 6. And the woman *fled into the wilderness,* where she hath a place prepared of God, that they should feed her there a thousand two hundred and threescore days. Ver. 14. And to the woman were given two wings of a great eagle, that she might fly into the wilderness, into her place, where she is nourished for a time, and times, and half a time, from the face of the serpent.

i [Rev. Chapters ii. and iii. throughout.] 1 Cor. v. 6. Your glorying is not good. Know ye not *that a little leaven leaveneth the whole lump?* Ver. 7. Purge out therefore the *old leaven, that ye may be a new lump,* as ye are unleavened. For even Christ our passover is sacrificed for us.

V. k 1 Cor. xiii. 12. For now *we see through a glass, darkly;* but then face to face: now I know in part; but then shall I know even as also I am known. [Rev. Chapters ii. and iii.] Matt. xiii. 24-30. Another parable put he forth unto them, saying, The kingdom of heaven is likened unto a man which sowed good seed in his field; but while men slept, *his enemy came and sowed tares among the wheat,* and went his way. But when the blade was sprung up, and brought forth fruit, then appeared *the tares also,* &c. Ver. 47. Again, the kingdom of heaven is like unto a net, that was cast into the sea, and gathered of *every* kind.

l Rev. xviii. 2. And he cried mightily with a strong voice, saying, Babylon the great is fallen, is fallen, and *is become the habitation of devils, and the hold of every foul spirit, and a cage of every unclean and hateful bird.* Rom. xi. 18. Boast not against the *branches:* but if thou boast, thou bearest not the root, but the root thee. Ver. 19. Thou wilt say then, The *branches were broken off,* that I might be graffed in. Ver. 20. Well; *because of unbelief they were broken off,* and thou standest by faith. Be not high-minded, but fear; Ver. 21. For if God spared not the *natural branches, take heed lest he also spare not thee.* Ver. 22. Behold therefore the goodness and severity of God: on them *which fell,* severity; but toward thee, goodness, if thou continue in his goodness; otherwise thou also shalt be cut off.

m Matt. xvi. 18. And I say also unto thee, That thou art Peter, and upon this rock I will build my *church; and the gates of hell shall not prevail against it.* Ps. lxxii. 17. His *name shall endure for ever:* his name shall be *continued as long as the sun;* and men shall be blessed in him: all nations shall call him blessed. Ps. cii. 28. *The children of thy servants shall continue,* and *their seed shall be established before thee.* Matt. xxviii. 19, 20. [See in letter g.]

VI. n Col. i. 18. And *he is the head of the body, the church;* who is the beginning, the first-born from the dead; that in all things he might have the pre-eminence. Eph. i. 22. And hath put all things under his feet, and gave him to be *the head over all things to the church.*

o Matt. xxiii. 8. But be *not ye called Rabbi:* for *one is your Master,* even Christ; and *all ye are brethren.* Ver. 9. And call *no man your father upon the earth:* for *one is your Father, which is in heaven.* Ver. 10. Neither be ye called masters: for one is your Master, even Christ. 2 Thess. ii. 3. Let no man deceive you by any means: for that day shall not come, except there come a falling away first, and *that man of sin be revealed, the son of perdition;* Ver. 4. Who *opposeth and exalteth himself above all that is called God,* or that is worshipped; *so that he, as God, sitteth in the temple of God,* shewing himself that he is God. Ver. 8. And *then shall that Wicked be revealed,* whom the Lord shall consume with the spirit of his mouth, and shall destroy with the brightness of his coming: Ver. 9. Even him, whose coming is after the working of

CHAP. XXVI.—*Of Communion of Saints.*

I. ALL saints that are united to Jesus Christ their head by his Spirit, and by faith, have fellowship with him in his graces, sufferings, death, resurrection, and glory.[a] And being united to one another in love, they have communion in each other's gifts and graces;[b] and are obliged to the performance of such duties, publick and private, as do conduce to their mutual good, both in the inward and outward man.[c]

II. Saints, by profession, are bound to maintain an holy fellowship and communion in the worship of God, and in performing such other spiritual services as tend to their mutual edification;[d] as also in relieving each other in outward things, according to their several abili-

Satan, with all power, and signs, and lying wonders. Rev. xiii. 6. And *he opened his mouth in blasphemy against God, to blaspheme his name, and his tabernacle, and them that dwell in heaven.*
I. a 1 John i. 3. *That which we have seen and heard declare we unto you, that ye also may have fellowship with us: and truly our fellowship is with the Father, and with his Son Jesus Christ.* Eph. iii. 16. That he would grant you, according to the riches of his glory, to be strengthened with might *by his Spirit in the inner man;* Ver. 17. That *Christ may dwell in your hearts by faith;* that ye, being rooted and grounded in love, Ver. 18. May be *able to comprehend with all saints* what is the breadth, and length, and depth, and height; Ver. 19. And to know the love of Christ, which passeth knowledge, that ye might be filled with all the fulness of God. John i. 16. And *of his fulness have all we received, and grace for grace.* Eph. ii. 5. Even when we were dead in sins, *hath quickened us together with Christ;* (by grace ye are saved;) Ver. 6. And hath *raised us up together, and made us sit together in heavenly places* in Christ Jesus. Phil. iii. 10. That I may know him, and the power of his resurrection, *and the fellowship of his sufferings*, being made *conformable unto his death.* Rom. vi. 5. For *if we have been planted together in the likeness* of his death, *we shall be also in the likeness of his resurrection:* Ver. 6. Knowing this, that our old man *is crucified with him*, that the body of sin might be destroyed, that henceforth we should not serve sin. 2 Tim. ii. 12. *If we suffer, we shall also reign with him;* if we deny him, he also will deny us.
b Eph. iv. 15. But, speaking the truth in love, may grow up into him in all things, which is the head, even Christ: Ver. 16. From whom the *whole body fitly joined together and compacted by that* which every joint supplieth, according to the effectual working in the measure of every part, maketh increase of the body, *unto the edifying of itself in love.* 1 Cor. xii. 7. But the *manifestation of the Spirit is given to every man to profit withal.* 1 Cor. iii. 21. Therefore let no man glory in men: *for all things are yours;* Ver. 22. *Whether Paul,* or *Apollos,* or *Cephas,* or *the world, or life, or death, or things present, or things to come; all are yours;* Ver. 23. And ye are Christ's; and Christ is God's. Col. ii. 19. And not holding the head, from which *all the body by joints and bands having nourishment ministered, and knit together, increaseth with the increase of God.*
c 1 Thess. v. 11. *Wherefore comfort yourselves together, and edify one another,* even as also ye do. Ver. 14. Now we exhort you, brethren, *warn them that are unruly, comfort the feeble-minded, support the weak, be patient toward all men.* Rom. i. 11. For I long to see you, that I may *impart unto you some spiritual gift,* to the end ye may be established; Ver. 12. That is, that *I may be comforted together with you, by the mutual faith both of you and me.* Ver. 14. I am *debtor both to the Greeks and to the Barbarians, both to the wise and to the unwise.* 1 John iii. 16. Hereby perceive we the love of God, because he laid down his life for us: and we ought *to lay down our lives for the brethren.* Ver. 17. But whoso hath this world's good, and *seeth his brother have need, and shutteth up his bowels of compassion from him,* how dwelleth the love of God in him? Ver. 18. My little children, let us not love in word, neither in tongue; but in deed, and in truth. Gal. vi. 10. *As we have therefore opportunity, let us do good unto all men, especially unto them who are of the household of faith.*
II. d Heb. x. 24. And let us *consider one another, to provoke unto love, and to good works:* Ver. 25. *Not forsaking the assembling of ourselves together,* as the manner of some is; but *exhorting one another:* and so much the more, as ye see the day approaching. Acts ii. 42. And they *continued* steadfastly *in the apostles'* doctrine and *fellowship,* and in breaking of bread, and in prayers. Ver. 46. And they, *continuing daily with one accord in the temple,* and breaking bread from house to house, did eat their meat with gladness and singleness of heart. Isa. ii. 3. And *many people shall go and say, Come ye, and let us go up to the mountain of the Lord,* to the house of the God of Jacob; and he will teach us of his ways, and we will walk in his paths:

ties and necessities. Which communion, as God offereth opportunity, is to be extended unto all those who in every place call upon the name of the Lord Jesus.ᶜ

III. This communion which the saints have with Christ doth not make them in any wise partakers of the substance of his Godhead, or to be equal with Christ in any respect: either of which to affirm is impious and blasphemous.ᶠ Nor doth their communion one with another, as saints, take away or infringe the title or property which each man hath in his goods and possessions.ᵍ

CHAP. XXVII.—*Of the Sacraments.*

I. SACRAMENTS are holy signs and seals of the covenant of grace,ᵃ immediately instituted by God,ᵇ to represent Christ and his benefits, and to confirm our interest in him;ᶜ as also to put a visible

---

for out of Zion shall go forth the law, and the word of the Lord from Jerusalem. 1 Cor. xi. 20. *When ye come together therefore into one place,* this is not to eat the Lord's supper.

ᵉ Acts ii. 44. *And all that believed were together,* and had all things common ; Ver. 45. And sold their possessions and goods, and parted them *to all men, as every man had need.* 1 John iii. 17. [See in letter c. 2 Cor. Chapters viii. and ix.] Acts xi. 29. Then the disciples, every man according to his ability, *determined to send relief unto the brethren which dwelt in Judea:* Ver. 30. Which also they did, and sent it to the elders by the hands of Barnabas and Saul.

III. ᶠ Col. i. 18. And he is the head of the body, the church ; who is the beginning, the *first-born from the dead; that in all things he might have the pre-eminence:* Ver. 19. For it pleased the Father, that *in him should all fulness dwell.* 1 Cor. viii. 6. But to us there is but *one God,* the Father, of whom are all things, and we in him ; and *one Lord Jesus Christ,* by whom are all things, and we by him. Isa. xlii. 8. I am the Lord ; that is my name : *and my glory will I not give to another,* neither my praise to graven images. 1 Tim. vi. 15. Which in his times he shall shew, who *is the blessed and only Potentate,* the King of kings, and Lord of lords ; Ver. 16. Who *only hath immortality,* dwelling in the light *which no man can approach unto;* whom no man hath seen, nor can see : to whom be honour and power everlasting. Amen. Ps. xlv. 7. Thou lovest righteousness, and hatest wickedness : therefore God, thy God, *hath anointed thee with the oil of gladness above thy fellows.* With Heb. i. 8. *But unto the Son he saith, Thy throne, O God, is for ever and ever;* a sceptre of righteousness is the sceptre of thy kingdom. Ver. 9. Thou hast loved righteousness, and hated iniquity ; therefore God, even thy God, hath anointed thee *with the oil of gladness above thy fellows.*

ᵍ Exod. xx. 15. Thou shalt not steal.

Eph. iv. 28. Let him that stole steal no more : but rather let him labour, *working with his hands the thing which is good,* that he may have to give to him that needeth. Acts v. 4. Whiles it *remained, was it not thine own?* and after it was sold, *was it not in thine own power?* why hast thou conceived this thing in thine heart ? thou hast not lied unto men, but unto God.

I. ᵃ Rom. iv. 11. And he received the *sign of circumcision, a seal of the righteousness of the faith* which he had yet being uncircumcised : that he might be the father of all them that believe, though they be not circumcised ; that righteousness might be imputed unto them also. Gen. xvii. 7. And *I will establish my covenant between me and thee,* and thy seed after thee, in their generations, for an everlasting covenant, to be a God unto thee, and to thy seed after thee. Ver. 10. [See below in letter f.]

ᵇ Matt. xxviii. 19. Go ye therefore, and teach all nations, baptizing them *in the name of the Father, and of the Son, and of the Holy Ghost.* 1 Cor. xi. 23. For *I have received of the Lord that which also I delivered unto you, That the Lord Jesus,* the same night in which he was betrayed, took bread.

ᶜ 1 Cor. x. 16. *The cup of blessing which we bless, is it not the communion of the blood of Christ? the bread which we break, is it not the communion of the body of Christ?* 1 Cor. xi. 25. After the same manner *also he took the cup, when he had supped,* saying, This cup is the new testament in my blood : this do ye, as oft as ye drink it, in remembrance of me. Ver. 26. For as often as ye eat this bread, and drink this cup, ye do shew the Lord's death till he come. *Gal. iii. 27. For as many of you as have been *baptized into Christ* have put on Christ. Gal. iii. 17. And this I say, that the *covenant, that was confirmed before of God in Christ,* the law, which was four hundred and thirty years after, cannot disannul, that it should make the promise of none effect.

difference between those that belong unto the church and the rest of the world;[d] and solemnly to engage them to the service of God in Christ, according to his word.[e]

II. There is in every sacrament a spiritual relation, or sacramental union, between the sign and the thing signified; whence it comes to pass, that the names and effects of the one are attributed to the other.[f]

III. The grace which is exhibited in or by the sacraments, rightly used, is not conferred by any power in them; neither doth the efficacy of a sacrament depend upon the piety or intention of him that doth administer it,[g] but upon the work of the Spirit,[h] and the word of institution; which contains, together with a precept authorizing the use thereof, a promise of benefit to worthy receivers.[i]

IV. There be only two sacraments ordained by Christ our Lord in the gospel, that is to say, Baptism, and the Supper of the Lord; neither of which may be dispensed by any but by a minister of the word, lawfully ordained.[k]

V. The sacraments of the Old Testament, in regard of the spiritual things thereby signified and exhibited, were, for substance, the same with those of the New.[l]

[d] Rom. xv. 8. Now I say, that Jesus Christ was *a minister of the circumcision* for the truth of God, to confirm the promises made unto the fathers. Exod. xii. 48. And when a stranger shall sojourn with thee, and will keep the passover to the Lord, let all his males be circumcised, and then let him come near and keep it; *and he shall be as one that is born in the land: for no uncircumcised person shall eat thereof.* Gen. xxxiv. 14. And they said unto them, We cannot do this thing, *to give our sister to one that is uncircumcised;* for that were a reproach unto us.

[e] Rom. vi. 3. Know ye not, that *so many of us as were baptized into Jesus Christ were baptized into his death?* Ver. 4. Therefore we are buried with him by baptism into death; that *like as Christ was raised up from the dead by the glory of the Father, even so we also should walk in newness of life.* 1 Cor. x. 16. [See in letter e.] Ver. 21. *Ye cannot drink the cup of the Lord, and the cup of devils: ye cannot be partakers of the Lord's table, and of the table of devils.*

II. [f] Gen. xvii. 10. This *is my covenant,* which ye shall keep, between me and you, and thy seed after thee; Every man child among you *shall be circumcised.* Matt. xxvi. 27. And he took the cup, and gave thanks, and gave it to them, saying, Drink ye all of it: Ver. 28. *For this is my blood of the new testament,* which is shed for many for the remission of sins. Tit. iii. 5. Not by works of righteousness which we have done, but according to his mercy he saved us, *by the washing of regeneration, and renewing of* the Holy Ghost.

III. [g] Rom. ii. 28. For he is *not a Jew which is one outwardly; neither is that circumcision which is outward in the flesh:* Ver. 29. But he is a Jew which is one inwardly: and circumcision is that of the heart, in the spirit, and not in the letter; whose praise is not of men, but of God. 1 Pet. iii. 21. The like figure whereunto *even baptism doth also now save us,* (not the putting away of the filth of the flesh, but the *answer of a good conscience* toward God,) *by the resurrection of Jesus Christ.*

[h] Matt. iii. 11. I indeed baptize you with water unto repentance; but he that cometh after me is mightier than I, whose shoes I am not worthy to bear: *he shall baptize you with the Holy Ghost, and with fire.* 1 Cor. xii. 13. *For by one Spirit are we all baptized into* one body, whether we be Jews or Gentiles, whether we be bond or free; and *have been all made to drink into one Spirit.*

[i] Matt. xxvi. 27, 28. [See in letter f.] Matt. xxviii. 19. [See in letter b.] Ver. 20. Teaching them to *observe all things whatsoever I have commanded you: and, lo, I am with you alway, even unto the end of the world.* Amen.

IV. [k] Matt. xxviii. 19. *Go ye therefore, and teach all nations, baptizing them* in the name of the Father, and of the Son, and of the Holy Ghost. 1 Cor. xi. 20. When ye come together therefore into one place, this is not to eat the Lord's supper. Ver. 23. *For I have received* of the Lord that which also *I delivered unto you,* That the Lord Jesus, the same night in which he was betrayed, took bread. 1 Cor. iv. 1. Let a man *so account of us as of the ministers of Christ, and stewards of the mysteries of God.* Heb. v. 4. And *no man taketh this honour unto himself, but he that is called of God, as was Aaron.*

V. [l] 1 Cor. x. 1. Moreover, brethren, I would not that ye should be ignorant, how that *all our fathers* were under the cloud, and all passed through the sea; Ver. 2. And were all *baptized unto Moses in the cloud and in the sea;* Ver. 3. *And did all eat the same spiritual meat;* Ver. 4. *And did all drink the same spiritual drink; (for they drank of that spiritual Rock that followed them: and that Rock was Christ.)*

CHAP. XXVIII.—*Of Baptism.*

I. BAPTISM is a sacrament of the New Testament, ordained by Jesus Christ,a not only for the solemn admission of the party baptized into the visible church,b but also to be unto him a sign and seal of the covenant of grace,c of his ingrafting into Christ,d of regeneration,e of remission of sins,f and of his giving up unto God through Jesus Christ, to walk in newness of life:g which sacrament is, by Christ's own appointment, to be continued in his church until the end of the world.h

II. The outward element to be used in this sacrament is water, wherewith the party is to be baptized in the name of the Father, and of the Son, and of the Holy Ghost, by a minister of the gospel, lawfully called thereunto.i

III. Dipping of the person into the water is not necessary; but baptism is rightly administered by pouring or sprinkling water upon the person.k

IV. Not only those that do actually profess faith in and obedience unto Christ,l but also the infants of one or both believing parents are to be baptized.m

I. a Matt. xxviii. 19. [See letter k of the foregoing Chapter.]
b 1 Cor. xii. 13. For by one Spirit *are we all baptized into one body*, whether we be Jews or Gentiles, whether we be bond or free; and have been all made to drink into one Spirit.
c Rom. iv. 11. And he received the sign *of circumcision, a seal of the righteousness of the faith* which he had yet being uncircumcised : that he might be the father of all them that believe, though they be not circumcised ; that righteousness might be imputed unto them also. With Col. ii. 11. In whom also ye are circumcised with the circumcision made without hands, in putting off the body of the sins of the flesh by the circumcision of Christ; Ver. 12. *Buried with him in baptism, wherein also ye are risen with* him through the faith of the operation of God, who hath raised him from the dead.
d Gal. iii. 27. For as many of you as have been *baptized into Christ* have put on Christ. Rom. vi. 5. For if we have been *planted together in the likeness of his death*, we shall be also in the likeness of his resurrection.
e Tit. iii. 5. Not by works of righteousness which we have done, but according to his mercy he saved us, *by the washing of regeneration*, and renewing of the Holy Ghost.
f Mark i. 4. John did baptize in the wilderness, and *preach the baptism of repentance for the remission of sins.*
g Rom. vi. 3. Know ye not, that so many of us as *were baptized into Jesus Christ* were baptized into his death? Ver. 4. Therefore we are buried with *him by baptism into death;* that like as Christ was raised up from the dead by the glory of the Father, even *so we also should walk in newness of life.*
h Matt. xxviii. 19. [See in letter k foregoing Chapter.] Ver. 20. Teaching them to observe all things whatsoever I have commanded you : and, lo, I am with you alway, even *unto the end of the world.* Amen.
II. i Matt. iii. 11. I indeed *baptize you with water* unto repentance : but he that cometh after me is mightier than I, whose shoes I am not worthy to bear: he shall baptize you with the Holy Ghost, and with fire. John i. 33. And I knew him not, but he *that sent me to baptize with water*, the same said unto me, Upon whom thou shalt see the Spirit descending, and remaining on him, the same is he which baptizeth with the Holy Ghost. Matt. xxviii. 19. [See in letter k foregoing Chapter.] Ver. 20. [See in letter h.]
III. k Heb. ix. 10, 19, 20, 21, 22. Acts ii. 41. Then they that gladly received his word *were baptized;* and the same day there were added unto them about three thousand souls. Acts xvi. 33. And he took them the same hour of the night, and washed their stripes ; *and was baptized, he and all his, straightway.* Mark vii. 4. And when they come from the market, except they *wash*, they eat not. And many other things there be which they have received to hold, as the *washing* of cups, and pots, brazen vessels, and of tables.
IV. l Mark xvi. 15. And he said unto them, Go ye into all the world, and preach the gospel to every creature. Ver. 16. *He that believeth, and is baptized, shall be saved;* but he that believeth not shall be damned. Acts viii. 37. And Philip said, If thou believest with all thine heart, thou mayest. And he answered and said, *I believe that Jesus Christ is the Son of God.* Ver. 38. And he commanded the chariot to stand still : and they went down both into the water, both Philip and the eunuch ; and he *baptized him.*
m Gen. xvii. 7. And I will establish my

V. Although it be a great sin to contemn or neglect this ordinance,[n] yet grace and salvation are not so inseparably annexed unto it, as that no person can be regenerated or saved without it,[o] or that all that are baptized are undoubtedly regenerated.[p]

VI. The efficacy of baptism is not tied to that moment of time wherein it is administered;[q] yet notwithstanding, by the right use of this ordinance, the grace promised is not only offered, but really exhibited and conferred by the Holy Ghost, to such (whether of age or infants) as that grace belongeth unto, according to the counsel of God's own will, in his appointed time.[r]

VII. The sacrament of baptism is but once to be administered to any person.[s]

---

covenant between me and thee, *and thy seed after thee, in their generations,* for an everlasting covenant, *to be a God unto thee, and to thy seed after thee.* Ver. 9. And God said unto Abraham, Thou shalt keep my covenant therefore, *thou, and thy seed after thee,* in their generations. With Gal. iii. 9. So then *they which be of faith are blessed with faithful Abraham.* Ver. 14. *That the blessing of Abraham might come on the Gentiles* through Jesus Christ; that we might receive the promise of the Spirit through faith. And Col. ii. 11. In whom also ye are *circumcised with the circumcision made without hands,* in putting off the body of the sins of the flesh by the circumcision of Christ; Ver. 12. *Buried with him in baptism,* wherein also ye are risen with him through the faith of the operation of God, who hath raised him from the dead. And Acts ii. 38. Then Peter said unto them, Repent, and be *baptized every one of you* in the name of Jesus Christ for the remission of sins, and ye shall receive the gift of the Holy Ghost. Ver. 39. *For the promise is unto you, and to your children,* and to all that are afar off, even as many as the Lord our God shall call. And Rom. iv. 11. And he received the sign of circumcision, a seal of the *righteousness of the faith which he had yet being uncircumcised:* that he might be the father of all them that believe, though they be not circumcised ; that righteousness might be imputed unto them also: Ver. 12. And the father of circumcision to them who are not of the circumcision only, but who also walk in the steps of that faith of our father Abraham, which he had being yet uncircumcised. 1 Cor. vii. 14. For the unbelieving husband is sanctified by the wife, and the unbelieving wife is sanctified by the husband ; else *were your children unclean ; but now are they holy.* Matt. xxviii. 19. Go ye therefore, and *teach all nations, baptizing them in* the name of the Father, and of the Son, and of the Holy Ghost. Mark x. 13. *And they brought young children to him,* that he should touch them ; and his disciples rebuked those that brought them. Ver. 14. But when Jesus saw it, he was much displeased, and said unto them, *Suffer the little children to come unto me, and forbid them not: for of such is the kingdom of God.* Ver. 15. Verily I say unto you, Whosoever shall not *receive the king-* *dom of God as a little child, he shall not enter therein.* Ver. 16. And he took *them up in his arms,* put his *hands upon them,* and *blessed them.* Luke xviii. 15. And they *brought unto him also infants,* that he would touch them : but when his disciples saw it, they rebuked them.

V. n Luke vii. 30. But the Pharisees and lawyers *rejected the counsel of God against themselves, being not baptized of him.* With Exod. iv. 24. And it came to pass by the way in the inn, that the *Lord met him, and sought to kill him.* Ver. 25. Then Zipporah took a sharp stone, and cut off the foreskin of her son, and cast it at his feet, and said, Surely a bloody husband art thou to me. Ver. 26. So he let him go : then she said, *A bloody husband thou art, because of the circumcision.*

o Rom. iv. 11. [See in letter m.] Acts x. 2, 4, 22, 31, 45, 47.

p Acts viii. 13. Then Simon himself believed also : and when *he was baptized,* he continued with Philip, and wondered, beholding the miracles and signs which were done. Ver. 23. *For I perceive that thou art in the gall of bitterness, and in the bond of iniquity.*

VI. q John iii. 5. Jesus answered, Verily, verily, I say unto thee, Except *a man be born of water, and of the Spirit,* he cannot enter into the kingdom of God. Ver. 8. *The wind bloweth where it listeth,* and thou hearest the sound thereof, but canst not tell whence it cometh, and whither it goeth : *so is every one that is born of the Spirit.*

r Gal. iii. 27. For as many of you as have *been baptized into Christ have put on Christ.* Tit. iii. 5. Not by works of righteousness which we have done, but according to his mercy he saved us, *by the washing of regeneration, and renewing of the Holy Ghost.* Eph. v. 25. Husbands, love your wives, even *as Christ also loved the church,* and gave himself for it ; Ver. 26. That he *might sanctify and cleanse it with the washing of water* by the word. Acts ii. 38. Then Peter said unto them, Repent, and be *baptized every one of you in the name of Jesus Christ for the remission of sins, and ye shall receive the gift of the Holy Ghost.* Ver. 41. Then they that gladly received his word were *baptized:* and the same day there were *added unto them* about three thousand souls

VII. s Tit. iii. 5. [See in letter r.]

CHAP. XXIX.—*Of the Lord's Supper.*

I. OUR Lord Jesus, in the night wherein he was betrayed, instituted the sacrament of his body and blood, called the Lord's Supper, to be observed in his church unto the end of the world, for the perpetual remembrance of the sacrifice of himself in his death, the sealing all benefits thereof unto true believers, their spiritual nourishment and growth in him, their further engagement in and to all duties which they owe unto him, and to be a bond and pledge of their communion with him, and with each other, as members of his mystical body.ᵃ

II. In this sacrament Christ is not offered up to his Father, nor any real sacrifice made at all for remission of sins of the quick or dead;ᵇ but only a commemoration of that one offering up of himself, by himself, upon the cross, once for all, and a spiritual oblation of all possible praise unto God for the same;ᶜ so that the Popish sacrifice of the mass, as they call it, is most abominably injurious to Christ's one only sacrifice, the alone propitiation for all the sins of the elect.ᵈ

III. The Lord Jesus hath, in this ordinance, appointed his ministers to declare his word of institution to the people, to pray, and bless the elements of bread and wine, and thereby to set them apart from a common to a holy use; and to take and break the bread, to take the cup, and (they communicating also themselves) to give both to the communicants;ᵉ

I. ᵃ 1 Cor. xi. 23. For *I have received of the Lord* that which also I delivered unto you, That the *Lord Jesus, the same night in which he was betrayed,* took bread: Ver. 24. And, when he had given thanks, he *brake it, and said, Take, eat; this is my body, which is broken for you; this do in remembrance of me.* Ver. 25. After the same manner also he took the cup, when he had supped, saying, *This cup is the new testament in my blood: this do ye, as oft as ye drink it, in remembrance of me.* Ver. 26. *For as often as ye eat this bread, and drink this cup, ye do shew the Lord's death till he come.* 1 Cor. x. 16. *The cup of blessing which we bless, is it not the communion of the blood of Christ? the bread which we break, is it not the communion of the body of Christ?* Ver. 17. For we, being many, are one bread, and one body: for we are all *partakers of that one bread.* Ver. 21. Ye cannot drink *the cup of the Lord,* and the cup of devils: ye cannot be partakers *of the Lord's table,* and of the table of devils. 1 Cor. xii. 13. For by one Spirit are we all baptized into one body, whether we be Jews or Gentiles, whether we be bond or free; and have been all made to *drink into one Spirit.*

II. ᵇ Heb. ix. 22. And almost all things are by the law purged with blood; and *without shedding of blood is no remission.* Ver. 25. *Nor yet that he should offer himself often,* as the high priest entereth into the holy place every year with blood of others; Ver. 26. (For then must he *often have suffered* since the foundation of the world:) but *now once,* in the end of the world, hath he appeared, to put away sin *by the sacrifice of himself.* Ver. 28. So *Christ was once offered to bear the sins of many:* and unto them that look for him shall he appear the second time, without sin, unto salvation.

ᶜ 1 Cor. xi. 24, 25, 26. [See them in letter ᵃ.] Matt. xxvi. 26. And as they were eating, Jesus took bread, and *blessed* it, and brake it, and gave it to the disciples, and said, Take, eat; *this is my body.* Ver. 27. And he took the cup, and *gave thanks,* and gave it to them, saying, Drink ye all of it.

ᵈ Heb. vii. 23. And they truly were many priests, because they were not suffered to continue by reason of death: Ver. 24. But this man, because he continueth ever, hath an unchangeable priesthood. Ver. 27. *Who needeth not daily,* as those high priests, *to offer up sacrifice,* first for his own sins, and then for the people's: *for this he did once, when he offered up himself.* Heb. x. 11. And every priest standeth daily ministering, and *offering oftentimes* the same sacrifices, *which can never take away sins:* Ver. 12. But *this man, after he had offered one sacrifice for sins,* for ever sat down on the right hand of God. Ver. 14. For by *one offering he hath* perfected for ever them that are sanctified. Ver. 18. Now, where remission of these is, *there is no more offering for sin.*

III. ᵉ Matt. xxvi. 26, 27. [See in letter ᶜ.] Ver. 28. For *this is my blood of the new testament,* which is shed for many for the remission of sins. And Mark xiv. 22. And as they did eat, Jesus *took bread, and blessed, and brake it,* and gave to them, and said, *Take, eat: this is my body.* Ver. 23. And he took the cup, and when he had given thanks, he *gave it to them: and they all drank of it.* Ver. 24. And he said unto them, This is my blood of the new testament, which is shed for many. And Luke xxii. 19. And he *took bread, and gave thanks,*

but to none who are not then present in the congregation.ᶠ

IV. Private masses, or receiving this sacrament by a priest, or any other, alone;ᵍ as likewise the denial of the cup to the people;ʰ worshipping the elements, the lifting them up, or carrying them about for adoration, and the reserving them for any pretended religious use; are all contrary to the nature of this sacrament, and to the institution of Christ.ⁱ

V. The outward elements in this sacrament, duly set apart to the uses ordained by Christ, have such relation to him crucified, as that truly, yet sacramentally only, they are sometimes called by the name of the things they represent, to wit, the body and blood of Christ;ᵏ albeit, in substance and nature, they still remain truly and only bread and wine, as they were before.ˡ

VI. That doctrine which maintains a change of the substance of bread and wine into the substance of Christ's body and blood (commonly called Transubstantiation) by consecration of a priest, or by any other way, is repugnant not to Scripture alone, but even to common sense and reason; overthroweth the nature of the sacrament; and hath been and is the cause of manifold superstitions, yea, of gross idolatries.ᵐ

VII. Worthy receivers, outwardly partaking of the visible elements in this sacrament,ⁿ do then also inwardly by faith, really and indeed, yet not carnally and corporally, but spiritually, receive and feed upon Christ crucified, and all benefits of his death: the body and blood of Christ being then not corporally or carnally in, with, or under the

and brake it, and gave unto them, saying, This is my body, *which is given for you:* this do in remembrance of me. Ver. 20. Likewise *also the cup after supper*, saying, This cup is the new testament in my blood, *which is shed for you*. With 1 Cor. xi. 23-26. [See all in letter ᵃ.]

ᶠ Acts xx. 7. And upon the first day of the week, when the *disciples came together to break bread*, Paul preached unto them, ready to depart on the morrow; and continued his speech until midnight. 1 Cor. xi. 20. *When ye come together therefore into one place*, this is not to eat the Lord's supper.

IV. ᵍ 1 Cor. x. 6. Now these things were *our examples*, to the intent we should not lust after evil things, as they also lusted.

ʰ Mark xiv. 23. [See in letter ᵉ.] 1 Cor. xi. 25, 26. [See in letter ᵃ.] Ver 27. Wherefore, whosoever shall eat this bread, and *drink this cup* of the Lord, unworthily, shall be guilty of the *body and blood* of the Lord. Ver. 28. But let a man examine himself, and so let him eat of that bread, and *drink of that cup*. Ver. 29. For he that eateth and *drinketh unworthily*, eateth and *drinketh damnation* to himself, not discerning the Lord's body.

ⁱ Matt. xv. 9. But in vain they do worship me, *teaching for doctrines the commandments of men*.

V. ᵏ Matt. xxvi. 26. And as they were eating, Jesus *took bread*, and blessed it, and brake it, and gave it to the disciples, and said, Take, eat; *this is my body*. Ver. 27. And he took the *cup*, and gave thanks and gave it to them, saying, Drink ye all of it: Ver. 28. For *this is my blood of the new testament*, which is shed for many for the remission of sins.

ˡ 1 Cor. xi. 26. For as often as ye eat *this bread, and drink this cup, ye do shew the Lord's death till he come*. Ver. 27. Wherefore, whosoever *shall eat this bread, and drink this cup of the Lord, unworthily, shall be guilty of the body and blood of the Lord*. Ver. 28. But let a man examine himself, and so let *him eat of that bread, and drink of that cup*. Matt. xxvi. 29. But I say unto you, I will not drink henceforth of *this fruit of the vine*, until that day when I drink it new with you in my Father's kingdom.

VI. ᵐ Acts iii. 21. Whom *the heaven must receive until the times of restitution of all things*, which God hath spoken by the mouth of all his holy prophets since the world began. With 1 Cor. xi. 24. And, when he had given thanks, he brake it, and said, Take, eat; this is my body, which is broken for you: *this do in remembrance of me*. Ver. 25. After the same manner also he took the cup, when he had supped, saying, This cup is the new testament in my blood: this do ye, as oft as ye drink it, *in remembrance* of me. Ver. 26. [See in letter ˡ.] Luke xxiv. 6. *He is not here, but is risen:* remember how he spake unto you when he was yet in Galilee. Ver. 39. *Behold my hands and my feet, that it is I myself:* handle me, and see; for a spirit hath not flesh and bones, as ye see me have.

VII. ⁿ 1 Cor. xi. 28. [See in letter ˡ.]

bread and wine; yet as really, but spiritually, present to the faith of believers in that ordinance, as the elements themselves are to their outward senses.º

VIII. Although ignorant and wicked men receive the outward elements in this sacrament, yet they receive not the thing signified thereby; but by their unworthy coming thereunto are guilty of the body and blood of the Lord, to their own damnation. Wherefore all ignorant and ungodly persons, as they are unfit to enjoy communion with him, so are they unworthy of the Lord's table, and cannot, without great sin against Christ, while they remain such, partake of these holy mysteries,ᵖ or be admitted thereunto.ᑫ

CHAP. XXX.—*Of Church Censures.*

1. THE Lord Jesus, as king and head of his church, hath therein appointed a government in the hand of church-officers, distinct from the civil magistrate.ᵃ

II. To these officers the keys of the kingdom of heaven are committed, by virtue whereof they have power respectively to retain and remit sins, to shut that kingdom against the impenitent, both by the word and censures; and to open it unto penitent sinners, by the mi-

---

o 1 Cor. x. 16. The *cup of blessing* which we bless, *is it not the communion of the blood of Christ?* the *bread* which we break, *is it not the communion of the body of Christ?*

VIII. p 1 Cor. xi. 27, 28. [See in letter l.] Ver. 29. For he that *eateth and drinketh unworthily, eateth and drinketh damnation to himself,* not discerning the Lord's body. 2 Cor. vi. 14. Be ye not unequally yoked together with unbelievers : for *what fellowship hath righteousness with unrighteousness?* and what *communion hath light with darkness?* Ver. 15. And what *concord hath Christ with Belial?* or what part hath *he that believeth with an infidel?* Ver. 16. And what *agreement hath the temple of God with idols?* for ye are the temple of the living God; as God hath said, I will dwell in them, and walk in them ; and I will be their God, and they shall be my people.

q 1 Cor. v. 6. Your glorying is not good. Know ye not *that a little leaven leaveneth the whole lump?* Ver. 7. *Purge out therefore the old leaven,* that *ye may be a new lump, as ye are unleavened.* For even Christ our passover is sacrificed for us. Ver. 13. But them that are without God judgeth. Therefore put *away from among yourselves that wicked person.* 2 Thess. iii. 6. Now we command you, brethren, in the name of our Lord Jesus Christ, that ye *withdraw yourselves from every brother that walketh disorderly,* and not after the tradition which he received of us. Ver. 14. And if any man obey not our word by this epistle, *note that man, and have no company with him,* that he may be ashamed. Ver. 15. Yet count him not as an enemy, but admonish him as a brother. Matt. vii. 6. *Give not that which is holy unto the dogs, neither cast ye your pearls before swine, lest they trample them* under their feet, and turn again and rend you.

I. a Isa. ix. 6. For unto us a child is born, unto us a son is given ; *and the government shall be upon his shoulder:* and his name shall be called Wonderful, Counsellor, The mighty God, The everlasting Father, The Prince of Peace. Ver. 7. Of the increase *of his government and peace* there shall be no end, *upon the throne of David, and upon his kingdom, to order it, and to establish it with judgment* and with justice from henceforth even for ever. The zeal of the Lord of hosts will perform this. 1 Tim. v. 17. *Let the elders that rule* well be counted worthy of double honour, especially they who labour in the word and doctrine. 1 Thess. v. 12. And we beseech you, brethren, to know them which labour among you, *and are over you in the Lord,* and admonish you. Acts xx. 17. And from Miletus he sent to Ephesus, *and called the elders of the church.* Ver. 18. And when they were come to him, he said unto them, Ye know, from the first day that I came into Asia, after what manner I have been with you at all seasons. Heb. xiii. 7. Remember them which have *the rule over you,* who have spoken unto you the word of God ; whose faith follow, considering the end of their conversation. Ver. 17. *Obey them that have the rule over you, and submit yourselves;* for they watch for your souls, as they that must give account ; that they may do it with joy, and not with grief : for that is unprofitable for you. Ver. 24. Salute all them that *have the rule over you,* and all the saints. They of Italy salute you. 1 Cor. xii. 28. And *God hath set* some in the church, first, apostles ; secondarily, prophets ; thirdly, teachers ; after that miracles ; then gifts of healings.

nistry of the gospel, and by absolution from censures, as occasion shall require.b

III. Church censures are necessary for the reclaiming and gaining of offending brethren; for deterring of others from the like offences; for purging out of that leaven which might infect the whole lump; for vindicating the honour of Christ, and the holy profession of the gospel; and for preventing the wrath of God, which might justly fall upon the church, if they should suffer his covenant, and the seals thereof, to be profaned by notorious and obstinate offenders.c

IV. For the better attaining of these ends, the officers of the church are to proceed by admonition, suspension from the sacrament of the Lord's supper for a season, and by excommunication from the church, according to the nature of the crime, and demerit of the person.d

CHAP. XXXI.—*Of Synods and Councils.*

I. FOR the better government, and further edification of the church, there ought to be such assemblies as are commonly called Synods or Councils.a

helps, *governments*, diversities of tongues. Matt. xxviii. 18. And Jesus came and spake unto them, saying, *All power is given unto me in heaven and in earth.* Ver. 19. Go ye therefore, and teach all nations, baptizing them in the name of the Father, and of the Son, and of the Holy Ghost; Ver. 20. Teaching them *to observe all things whatsoever I have commanded you:* and, lo, I am with you alway, even unto the end of the world. Amen.

II. b Matt. xvi. 19. And I will give unto *thee the keys of the kingdom of heaven:* and whatsoever *thou shalt bind on earth shall be bound in heaven;* and whatsoever *thou shalt loose on earth shall be loosed in heaven.* Matt. xviii. 17. And if he shall neglect to hear them, tell it unto the church : but if he neglect to hear the church, let him be unto thee as an heathen man and a publican. Ver. 18. Verily I say unto you, *Whatsoever ye shall bind on earth shall be bound in heaven; and whatsoever ye shall loose on earth shall be loosed in heaven.* John xx. 21. Then said Jesus to them again, Peace be unto you: as my Father hath sent me, even so send I you. Ver. 22. And when he had said this, he breathed on them, and saith unto them, Receive ye the Holy Ghost. Ver. 23. *Whose soever sins ye remit, they are remitted unto them; and whose soever sins ye retain, they are retained.* 2 Cor. ii. 6. Sufficient to such a man is this *punishment,* which *was inflicted of many.* Ver. 7. So that contrariwise ye ought rather *to forgive him,* and comfort him, lest perhaps such an one should be swallowed up with over much sorrow. Ver. 8. Wherefore I beseech you, that ye *would confirm your love* toward him.

III. c [1 Cor. v. throughout.] 1 Tim. v. 20. Them that sin rebuke before all, *that others also may fear.* Matt. vii. 6. *Give not that which is holy unto the dogs,* neither cast ye your *pearls before swine, lest they trample them under their feet, and turn again and rend you.* 1 Tim. i. 20. Of whom is Hymeneus and Alexander; whom I have *delivered unto Satan, that they may learn not to blaspheme* [1 Cor. xi. 27 to the end.] With Jude, ver. 23. And others *save with fear, pulling them out* of the fire: hating even the garment spotted by the flesh.

IV. d 1 Thess. v. 12. And we beseech you, brethren, to know them which labour among you, and are over you in the Lord, and *admonish you.* 2 Thess. iii. 6. Now we command you, brethren, in the name of our Lord Jesus Christ, that ye *withdraw yourselves from every brother that walketh disorderly,* and not after the tradition which he received of us. Ver. 14. And if any man obey not our word by this epistle, *note that man, and have no company with him,* that he may be ashamed. Ver. 15. Yet count him *not as an enemy,* but *admonish him as a brother.* 1 Cor. v. 4. In the name of our Lord Jesus Christ, when ye are gathered together, and my spirit, with the power of our Lord Jesus Christ, Ver. 5. *To deliver such an one unto Satan* for the destruction of the flesh, that the spirit may be saved in the day of the Lord Jesus. Ver. 13. But them that are without God judgeth. Therefore *put away from among yourselves that wicked person.* Matt. xviii. 17. And if he shall neglect to hear them, tell *it unto the church:* but if he neglect to hear the church, *let him be unto thee as an heathen man and a publican.* Tit. iii. 10. A man that is an heretick, *after the first and second admonition, reject.*

I. a Acts xv. 2. When therefore Paul and Barnabas had no small dissension and disputation with them, they determined that Paul and Barnabas, and certain other of them, should go up to Jerusalem *unto the apostles and elders about this question.* Ver.

CHAP. XXXI. THE CONFESSION OF FAITH.

II. As magistrates may lawfully call a synod of ministers, and other fit persons, to consult and advise with about matters of religion;[b] so if magistrates be open enemies to the church, the ministers of Christ, of themselves, by virtue of their office, or they, with other fit persons upon delegation from their churches, may meet together in such assemblies.[c]

III. It belongeth to synods and councils ministerially to determine controversies of faith, and cases of conscience; to set down rules and directions for the better ordering of the publick worship of God, and government of his church; to receive complaints in cases of maladministration, and authoritatively to determine the same: which decrees and determinations, if consonant to the word of God, are to be received with reverence and submission, not only for their agreement with the word, but also for the power whereby they are made, as being an ordinance of God, appointed thereunto in his word.[d]

IV. All synods or councils since the apostles' times, whether general or particular, may err, and many have erred; therefore they are not to be made the rule of faith or practice, but to be used as an help in both.[e]

V. Synods and councils are to handle or conclude nothing but that which is ecclesiastical; and are not to intermeddle with civil affairs, which concern the commonwealth, unless by way of humble petition, in cases extraordinary; or by way of advice for satisfaction of conscience, if they be thereunto required by the civil magistrate.[f]

4. And when they were come to Jerusalem, they were received *of the church, and of the apostles and elders*, and they declared all things that God had done with them. Ver. 6. *And the apostles and elders came together for to consider of this matter.*

II. b Isa. xlix. 23. And *kings shall be thy nursing-fathers, and their queens thy nursing-mothers:* they shall bow down to thee with their face toward the earth, and lick up the dust of thy feet; and thou shalt know that I am the Lord: for they shall not be ashamed that wait for me. 1 Tim. ii. 1. I exhort therefore, that, first of all, supplications, prayers, intercessions, and giving of thanks, be made for all men: Ver. 2. *For kings, and for all that are in authority; that we may lead* a quiet and peaceable life in all godliness and honesty. [2 Chron. xix. 8 to the end. 2 Chron. Chapters xxix. and xxx. throughout.] Matt. ii. 4. And when *he had gathered all the chief priests and scribes* of the people together, *he demanded of them where Christ should be born.* Ver. 5. And they said unto him, In Bethlehem of Judea: for thus it is written by the prophet. Prov. xi. 14. Where *no counsel is, the people fall:* but in the *multitude of counsellors* there is safety.

c Acts xv. 2, 4. [See in letter a.] Ver. 22. *Then pleased it the apostles and elders, with the whole church*, to send chosen men of their own company to Antioch with Paul and Barnabas; namely, Judas surnamed Barsabas, and Silas, chief men among the brethren: Ver. 23. And they wrote letters by them after this manner; The *apostles, and elders, and brethren*, send greeting unto the brethren which are of the Gentiles in Antioch, and Syria, and Cilicia. Ver. 25. *It seemed good unto us, being assembled with one accord*, to send chosen men unto you with our beloved Barnabas and Paul.

III. d Acts xv. 15, 19, 24, 27, 28, 29, 30, 31. [See in the Bible.] Acts xvi. 4. And as they went through the cities, they delivered them the *decrees for to keep, that were ordained of the apostles and elders* which were at Jerusalem. Matt. xviii. 17. And if he shall neglect to hear them, *tell it unto the church:* but if he neglect to hear the church, let him be unto thee as an heathen man and a publican. Ver. 18. Verily I say unto you, *Whatsoever ye shall bind on earth shall be bound in heaven; and whatsoever ye shall loose on earth shall be loosed in heaven.* Ver. 19. Again I say unto you, That if *two of you shall agree on* earth as touching any thing that they shall ask, *it shall be done for them of my Father which is in heaven.* Ver. 20. For where two or three are gathered together in my name, there am I in the midst of them.

IV. e Eph. ii. 20. And are built upon *the foundation of the apostles and prophets,* Jesus Christ himself being the chief cornerstone. Acts xvii. 11. These were more noble than those in Thessalonica, in that they received the word with all readiness of mind, and *searched the scriptures daily, whether those things were so.* 1 Cor. ii. 5. *That your faith should not stand in the wisdom of men*, but in the power of God. 2 Cor. i. 24. *Not for that we have dominion over your faith, but are helpers of your joy:* for by faith ye stand.

V. f Luke xii. 13. And one of the company said unto him, Master, speak to my

CHAP. XXXII.—*Of the State of Men after Death, and of the Resurrection of the Dead.*

I. THE bodies of men after death return to dust, and see corruption;[a] but their souls, (which neither die nor sleep,) having an immortal subsistence, immediately return to God who gave them.[b] The souls of the righteous, being then made perfect in holiness, are received into the highest heavens, where they behold the face of God in light and glory, waiting for the full redemption of their bodies;[c] and the souls of the wicked are cast into hell, where they remain in torments and utter darkness, reserved to the judgment of the great day.[d] Besides these two places for souls separated from their bodies, the scripture acknowledgeth none.

II. At the last day, such as are found alive shall not die, but be changed:[e] and all the dead shall be raised up with the selfsame bodies, and none other, although with different qualities, which shall be united again to their souls for ever.[f]

brother, that he divide the inheritance with me. Ver. 14. And he said unto him, Man, *who made me a judge or a divider over you?* John xviii. 36. Jesus answered, *My kingdom is not of this world.* If my kingdom were of this world, then would my servants fight, that I should not be delivered to the Jews: but *now is my kingdom not from hence.*

I. a Gen. iii. 19. In the sweat of thy face shalt thou eat bread, *till thou return unto the ground;* for out of it wast thou taken: for dust thou art, and *unto dust shalt thou return.* Acts xiii. 36. For David, after he had served his own generation by the will of God, fell on sleep, and *was laid unto his fathers, and saw corruption.*

b Luke xxiii. 43. And Jesus said unto him, Verily I say unto thee, *To-day shalt thou be with me in paradise.* Eccl. xii. 7. Then shall the dust return to the earth as it was; and *the spirit shall return unto God who gave it.*

c Heb. xii. 23. To the general assembly and church of the first-born, which are written in heaven, and to *God the Judge* of all, and to the spirits of just men made perfect. 2 Cor. v. 1. For we know, that, if our earthly house of this tabernacle were dissolved, *we have a building of God,* an house not made with hands, eternal in the heavens. Ver. 6. Therefore we are always confident, knowing that, whilst we are at home in the body, we are absent from the Lord: Ver. 8. We are confident, I say, and willing rather to be *absent from the body, and to be present with the Lord.* Phil. i. 23. For I am in a strait betwixt two, having a desire *to depart, and to be with Christ;* which is far better. With Acts iii. 21. Whom the *heaven must receive until the times of restitution of all things,* which God hath spoken by the mouth of all his holy prophets since the world began. And Eph. iv. 10. He that descended is the same also that ascended up far above all heavens, that *he might fill all things.*

d Luke xvi. 23. And *in hell he lifted* up his eyes, *being in torments,* and seeth Abraham afar off, and Lazarus in his bosom. Ver. 24. And he cried, and said, Father Abraham, have mercy on me, and send Lazarus, that he may dip the tip of his finger in water, and cool my tongue; *for I am tormented in this flame* Acts i. 25. That he may take part of this ministry and apostleship, from which Judas by transgression fell, that *he might go to his own place.* Jude, ver. 6. And the angels which kept not their first estate, but left their own habitation, he *hath reserved in everlasting chains,* under darkness, unto *the judgment of the great day.* Ver. 7. Even as Sodom and Gomorrah, and the cities about them, in like manner, giving themselves over to fornication, and going after strange flesh, are set forth for an example, *suffering the vengeance of eternal fire.* 1 Pet. iii. 19. By which also he went and preached unto the *spirits in prison.*

II. e 1 Thess. iv. 17. *Then we which are alive and remain shall be caught up together with them in the clouds, to meet the Lord in the air:* and so shall we ever be with the Lord. 1 Cor. xv. 51. Behold, I shew you a mystery; *We shall not all sleep, but we shall all be changed,* Ver. 52. *In a moment, in the twinkling of an eye,* at the last trump, (for the trumpet shall sound;) and the dead shall be raised incorruptible, and *we shall be changed.*

f Job xix. 26. And though after my skin worms destroy this body, *yet in my flesh shall I see God:* Ver. 27. Whom I shall see for myself, and *mine eyes shall behold, and not another;* though my reins be consumed within me. 1 Cor. xv. 42. So also is the resurrection of the dead; it is sown in corruption, *it is raised in incorruption:* Ver. 43. It is sown in dishonour, *it is raised in glory;* it is sown in weakness, *it is raised in power;* Ver. 44. It is sown a natural body, *it is raised a spiritual body.* There is a natural body, and there is a spiritual body.

III The bodies of the unjust shall, by the power of Christ, be raised to dishonour; the bodies of the just, by his Spirit, unto honour, and be made conformable to his own glorious body.ᵍ

CHAP. XXXIII.—*Of the Last Judgment.*

I. GOD hath appointed a day wherein he will judge the world in righteousness by Jesus Christ,ᵃ to whom all power and judgment is given of the Father.ᵇ In which day, not only the apostate angels shall be judged,ᶜ but likewise all persons that have lived upon earth shall appear before the tribunal of Christ, to give an account of their thoughts, words, and deeds, and to receive according to what they have done in the body, whether good or evil.ᵈ

II. The end of God's appointing this day is for the manifestation of the glory of his mercy in the eternal salvation of the elect, and of his justice in the damnation of the reprobate, who are wicked and disobedient. For then shall the righteous go into everlasting life, and receive that fulness of joy and refreshing which shall come from the presence of the Lord; but the wicked, who know not God, and obey not the gospel of Jesus Christ, shall be cast into eternal torments, and be punished with everlasting destruction from the presence of the Lord, and from the glory of his power.ᵉ

III. As Christ would have us to be certainly persuaded that there

III. ᵍ Acts xxiv. 15. And have hope toward God, which they themselves also allow, that there shall be *a resurrection of the dead,* both of the *just* and *unjust.* John v. 28. Marvel not at this: for the hour is coming, in the which *all that are in the graves shall hear his voice,* Ver. 29. And shall come forth; they that *have done good, unto the resurrection of life; and they that have done evil, unto the resurrection of damnation.* 1 Cor. xv. 43. [See in letter f.] Philip. iii. 21. Who *shall change our vile body,* that it may be *fashioned like unto his glorious body,* according to the working whereby he is able even to subdue all things unto himself.

I. ᵃ Acts xvii. 31. Because he *hath appointed a day, in the which he will judge the world in righteousness by that man whom he hath ordained;* whereof he hath given assurance unto all men, in that he hath raised him from the dead.

ᵇ John v. 22. For the Father judgeth no man, *but hath committed all judgment unto the Son.* Ver. 27. And *hath given him authority to execute judgment* also, because he is the Son of man.

ᶜ 1 Cor. vi. 3. Know ye not that *we shall judge angels?* how much more things that pertain to this life? Jude, ver. 6. [See letter d Chapter foregoing.] 2 Pet. ii. 4. For if God *spared not the angels* that sinned, but cast them down to hell, and delivered them into chains of darkness, *to be reserved unto judgment.*

ᵈ 2 Cor. v. 10. For *we must all appear before the judgment-seat of Christ;* that every one may *receive the things done* in his body, according to that he hath done, *whether it be good or bad.* Eccl. xii. 14. For God shall *bring every work into judgment, with every secret thing, whether it be good, or whether it be evil.* Rom. ii. 16. In the day when *God shall judge the secrets of men* by Jesus Christ, according to my gospel. Rom. xiv. 10. But why dost thou judge thy brother? or why dost thou set at nought thy brother? for *we shall all stand before the judgment-seat of Christ.* Ver. 12. So then *every one of us shall give account of himself to God.* Matt. xii. 36. But I say unto you, That *every idle word that men shall speak, they shall give account thereof in the day of judgment.* Ver. 37. *For by thy words thou shalt be justified, and by thy words thou shalt be condemned.*

II. ᵉ [Matt. xxv. 31, to the end.] Rom. ii. 5. But, after thy hardness and impenitent heart, treasurest up unto thyself wrath *against the day of wrath and revelation of the righteous judgment of God;* Ver. 6. Who will render to every man according to his deeds. Rom. ix. 22. What if God, *willing to shew his wrath,* and to make his power known, endured with much long-suffering the *vessels of wrath fitted to destruction;* Ver. 23. And that he might make *known the riches of his glory on the vessels of mercy, which he had afore prepared unto glory?* Matt. xxv. 21. His lord said unto him, Well done, thou good and faithful servant; thou hast been faithful over a few things, I will make thee ruler over many things: *enter thou into the joy of thy Lord.* Acts iii. 19. Repent ye therefore, and be converted, that your *sins may be blotted out, when the times of refreshing shall come from the presence of the Lord.* 2 Thess. 1. 7-10. [See in the Bible.]

shall be a day of judgment, both to deter all men from sin, and for the greater consolation of the godly in their adversity;[f] so will he have that day unknown to men, that they may shake off all carnal security, and be always watchful, because they know not at what hour the Lord will come; and may be ever prepared to say, Come, Lord Jesus, come quickly. Amen.[g]

III. [f] 2 Pet. iii. 11. Seeing then that all these things shall be dissolved, *what manner of persons ought ye to be in all holy conversation* and godliness? Ver. 14. Wherefore, beloved, seeing that ye look for such things, be diligent, *that ye may be found of him in peace,* without spot, and blameless. 2 Cor. v. 10. [See letter d.] Ver. 11. Knowing therefore *the terror of the Lord,* we persuade men: but we are made manifest unto God; and I trust also are made manifest in your consciences. 2 Thess. i. 5. Which is a manifest token of the righteous judgment of God, *that ye may be counted worthy of the kingdom of God,* for which ye also suffer: Ver. 6 Seeing it is a *righteous thing with God to recompense tribulation* to them that trouble you; Ver. 7. And to you who are troubled *rest with us,* when the Lord Jesus shall be revealed from heaven with his mighty angels. Luke xxi. 27. And then shall they see the Son of man coming in a cloud, with power and great glory. Ver. 28. And when these things begin to come to pass, *then look up, and lift up your heads; for your redemption draweth nigh.* Rom. viii. 23. And not only they, but ourselves also, which have the first-fruits of the Spirit, even we ourselves groan within ourselves, *waiting for the adoption,* to wit, the *redemption of our body.* Ver. 24. For we are *saved by hope:* but *hope that is seen is not hope;* for what a man seeth, why doth he yet hope for? Ver. 25. But if we hope for that we see not, then do we with patience wait for it.

[g] Matt. xxiv. 36, 42, 43, 44. [See in the Bible.] Mark xiii. 35. Watch ye therefore: *for ye know not when the master of the house cometh,* at even, or at midnight, or at the cock-crowing, or in the morning; Ver. 36. *Lest, coming suddenly, he find you sleeping.* Ver. 37. And what I say unto you, *I say unto all, Watch.* Luke xii. 35. Let your loins be girded about, and your lights burning; Ver. 36. And ye yourselves like unto men *that wait for their lord,* when he will return from the wedding; that, when he cometh and knocketh, *they may open unto him immediately.* Rev. xxii 20. He which testifieth these things saith, Surely *I come quickly:* Amen. *Even so, come, Lord Jesus.*

THE LARGER CATECHISM;

AGREED UPON BY

THE ASSEMBLY OF DIVINES AT WESTMINSTER,

WITH THE ASSISTANCE OF

COMMISSIONERS FROM THE CHURCH OF SCOTLAND,

AS

A PART OF THE COVENANTED UNIFORMITY IN RELIGION BETWIXT THE
CHURCHES OF CHRIST IN THE KINGDOMS OF SCOTLAND,
ENGLAND, AND IRELAND.

*And Approved Anno 1648, by the General Assembly of the Church of Scotland,
to be a Directory for Catechising such as have made some proficiency in
the Knowledge of the Grounds of Religion, with the
Proofs from the Scripture.*

Assembly at EDINBURGH, July 2, 1648. Sess. 10.

Act approving the LARGER CATECHISM.

THE General Assembly having exactly examined and seriously considered the LARGER CATECHISM, agreed upon by the Assembly of Divines sitting at Westminster, with assistance of Commissioners from this Kirk, copies thereof being printed, and sent to Presbyteries, for the more exact trial thereof; and publick intimation being frequently made in this Assembly, that every one that had any doubts or objections upon it might put them in; do find, upon due examination thereof, That the said Catechism is agreeable to the word of God, and in nothing contrary to the received doctrine, worship, discipline, and government of this Kirk; a necessary part of the intended uniformity in religion, and a rich treasure for increasing knowledge among the people of God: and therefore the Assembly, as they bless the Lord that so excellent a Catechism is prepared, so they approve the same, as a part of uniformity; agreeing, for their part, that it be a common Catechism for the three kingdoms, and a Directory for catechising such as have made some proficiency in the knowledge of the grounds of religion.

THE LARGER CATECHISM.

QUEST. 1. **W**HAT *is the chief and highest end of man?*
 Ans. Man's chief and highest end is to glorify God,[a] and fully to enjoy him for ever.[b]

Q. 2. *How doth it appear that there is a God?*
A. The very light of nature in man, and the works of God, declare plainly that there is a God;[c] but his word and Spirit only do sufficiently and effectually reveal him unto men for their salvation.[d]

Q. 3. *What is the word of God?*
A. The holy scriptures of the Old and New Testament are the word of God,[e] the only rule of faith and obedience.[f]

---

1. [a] Rom. xi. 36. For of him, and through him, *and to him, are all things: to whom be glory for ever.* Amen. 1 Cor. x. 31. Whether therefore ye eat, or drink, or whatsoever ye do, *do all to the glory of God.* [b] Ps. lxxiii. 24. Thou shalt guide me with thy counsel, *and afterwards receive me to glory.* Ver. 25. *Whom have I in heaven but thee? and there is none upon earth that I desire besides thee.* Ver. 26. My flesh and my heart faileth: but God is the strength of my heart, and *my portion for ever.* Ver. 27. For, lo, they that are far from thee shall perish: thou hast destroyed all them that go a whoring from thee. Ver. 28. *But it is good for me to draw near to God:* I have put my trust in the Lord God, that I may declare all thy works. John xvii. 21. *That they all may be one; as thou, Father, art in me, and I in thee, that they also may be one in us;* that the world may believe that thou hast sent me. Ver. 22. And the glory which thou gavest me I have given them; that *they may be one, even as we are one.* Ver. 23. *I in them,* and *thou in me,* that they may be made perfect in one; and that the world may know that thou hast sent me, and hast loved them, as thou hast loved me.

2. [c] Rom. i. 19. Because *that which may be known of God is manifest in them:* for God hath *shewed* it unto them. Ver. 20. For the invisible things of him from the creation of the world are *clearly seen,* being *understood by the things that are made,* even his eternal power and Godhead; so that *they are without excuse.* Ps. xix. 1. The heavens *declare the glory of God;* and the firmament *sheweth* his *handy-work.* Ver. 2. Day unto day *uttereth speech,* and night unto night *sheweth knowledge.* Ver. 3. There is no *speech nor language* where their *voice is not heard.* Acts xvii. 28. For *in him we live,* and *move,* and have our *being.* [d] 1 Cor. ii. 9. But, as it is written, *Eye hath not seen,* nor ear *heard,* neither have entered *into the heart of man,* the things which God hath prepared for them that love him. Ver. 10. But God hath *revealed* them unto us *by his Spirit:* for the Spirit searcheth all things, yea, the deep things of God. 2 Tim. iii. 15. And that from a child thou hast known the *holy scriptures,* which are able to *make thee wise unto salvation* through *faith* which is in Christ Jesus. Ver. 16. All scripture is given by inspiration of God, and is profitable for doctrine, for reproof, for correction, for instruction in righteousness; Ver. 17. That the man of God may *be perfect, throughly furnished unto all good works.* Isa. lix. 21. As for me, this is my covenant with them, saith the Lord; *My Spirit* that is upon thee, and *my words which* I have put in thy mouth, shall not depart out of thy mouth, nor out of the mouth of thy seed, nor out of the mouth of thy seed's seed, saith the Lord, from henceforth and for ever.

3. [e] 2 Tim. iii. 16. All scripture is given *by inspiration* of God. 2 Pet. i. 19. We have also *a more sure word of prophecy;* whereunto ye do well that ye take heed, as unto a light that shineth in a dark place, until the day dawn, and the day-star arise in your hearts: Ver. 20. Knowing this first, that *no prophecy of the scripture is of any private interpretation.* Ver. 21. For the prophecy came not in old time by the will of man; but holy men of God spake *as they were moved by the Holy Ghost.*

[f] Eph. ii. 20. And are built upon the *foundation of the apostles and prophets, Jesus Christ* himself being the chief *corner-stone.* Rev. xxii. 18. For I testify unto every

Q. 4. *How doth it appear that the scriptures are the word of God?*

A. The scriptures manifest themselves to be the word of God, by their majesty[g] and purity;[h] by the consent of all the parts,[i] and the scope of the whole, which is to give all glory to God;[k] by their light and power to convince and convert sinners, to comfort and build up believers unto salvation:[l] but the Spirit of God bearing witness by and with the scriptures in the heart of man, is alone able fully to persuade it that they are the very word of God.[m]

Q. 5. *What do the scriptures principally teach?*

A. The scriptures principally teach, what man is to believe concerning God, and what duty God requires of man.[n]

---

man that heareth the words of the *prophecy of this book*. If any man *shall add* unto these things, God shall add unto him the plagues that are written in this book : Ver. 19. And if any man *shall take away* from the words of the book of this prophecy, God shall take away his part out of the book of life, and out of the holy city, and from the things which are written in this book. Isa. viii. 20. To the *law* and to the *testimony:* if they speak not according *to this word*, it is because there is no light in them. Luke xvi. 29. They have *Moses* and the *prophets;* let them hear them. Ver. 31. If they hear not *Moses* and the *prophets*, neither will they be persuaded though one rose from the dead. Gal. i. 8. But though we, or an angel from heaven, preach *any other gospel* unto you *than that* which we have preached unto you, let him be *accursed*. Ver. 9. As we said before, so say I now again, If any man preach *any other gospel* unto you than that ye have received, let him be *accursed*. 2 Tim. iii. 15, 16. [See in letter d.]

4. g Hos. viii. 12. I have written to him *the great things* of my law, but they were counted as a strange thing. 1 Cor. ii. 6. Howbeit *we speak wisdom* among them that are perfect ; yet not the wisdom of this world, nor of the princes of this world, that come to nought : Ver. 7. But we speak *the wisdom of God in a mystery*, even the *hidden wisdom*, which God ordained before the world unto our glory. Ver. 13. Which things also we speak, *not* in the words *which man's wisdom teacheth*, but which *the Holy Ghost teacheth;* comparing spiritual things with spiritual. Ps. cxix. 18. Open thou mine eyes, that I may behold *wondrous things out of thy law*. Ver. 129. Thy *testimonies are wonderful;* therefore doth my soul keep them.

h Ps. xii. 6. The words of the Lord *are pure words;* as silver tried in a furnace of earth, purified seven times. Ps. cxix. 140. Thy word *is very pure;* therefore thy servant loveth it.

i Acts x. 43. *To him give all the prophets witness*, that, through his name, whosoever believeth in him shall receive remission of sins. Acts xxvi. 22. Having therefore obtained help of God, I continue unto this day, witnessing both to small and great, *saying none other things than those which the prophets and Moses did say should come*.

k Rom. iii. 19. Now we know, that what things soever the law saith, it saith to them who are under the law ; *that every mouth may be stopped*, and *all the world may become guilty before God*. Ver. 27. Where is boasting then ? It is excluded. By what law ? of works ? Nay ; but by the law of faith.

l Acts xviii. 28. For *he mightily convinced* the Jews, and that publickly, *shewing by the scriptures* that Jesus was Christ. Heb. iv. 12. For the *word of God is quick, and powerful, and sharper* than any two-edged sword, *piercing* even to the dividing asunder of soul and spirit, and of the joints and marrow, and is *a discerner of the thoughts and intents of the heart*. James i. 18. Of his own will *begat he us with the word of truth*, *that* we should be a kind of first-fruits of his creatures. Ps. xix. 7. The law of the Lord is perfect, *converting the soul;* the testimony of the Lord is sure, *making wise* the simple : Ver. 8. The statutes of the Lord are right, *rejoicing the heart;* the commandment of the Lord is pure, *enlightening the eyes;* Ver. 9. The fear of the Lord is *clean*, enduring for ever : the judgments of the Lord are true and righteous altogether. Rom. xv. 4. For whatsoever things were written aforetime were written *for our learning;* that we, through *patience* and *comfort of the scriptures*, might *have hope*. Acts xx. 32. And now, brethren, I commend you to God, and to the *word of his grace*, which is *able to build you up*, and to give you an inheritance among all them which are sanctified.

m John xvi. 13. Howbeit when *he*, the *Spirit of truth*, is come, *he* will *guide you into all truth:* for *he* shall not speak of himself ; but whatsoever *he* shall hear, that shall he speak : and *he will shew you* things to come. Ver. 14. He shall glorify me ; for he shall receive of *mine*, and shall *shew it* unto you. 1 John ii. 20. But ye have an *unction from the Holy One*, and *ye know all things*. Ver. 27. But the *anointing* which ye have received of him abideth in you ; and ye need not that any man teach you : but as the *same anointing teacheth you* of all things, and is truth, and is no lie, and even as it hath taught you, ye shall abide in him. John xx. 31. But these are *written, that ye might believe* that Jesus is the Christ, the Son of God ; and that believing ye might have life through his name.

5. n 2 Tim. i. 13. Hold fast the *form of sound words*, which thou hast heard of me, *in faith and love* which is in Christ Jesus.

WHAT MAN OUGHT TO BELIEVE CONCERNING GOD.

Q. 6. *What do the scriptures make known of God?*

A. The scriptures make known what God is,[o] the persons in the Godhead,[p] his decrees,[q] and the execution of his decrees.[r]

Q. 7. *What is God?*

A. God is a spirit,[s] in and of himself infinite in being,[t] glory,[v] blessedness,[w] and perfection;[x] all-sufficient,[y] eternal,[z] unchangeable,[a] incomprehensible,[b] every where present,[c] almighty,[d] knowing all things,[e] most wise,[f] most holy,[g] most just,[h] most merciful and gracious, long-suffering, and abundant in goodness and truth.[i]

Q. 8. *Are there more Gods than one?*

A. There is but one only, the living and true God.[k]

---

6. o Heb. xi. 6. But without faith it is impossible to please him: for he that cometh to God must *believe that he is*, and that *he is a rewarder of them that diligently seek him.*

p 1 John v. 7. For there are *three* that bear record in heaven, the *Father*, the *Word*, and the *Holy Ghost*: and these *three are one.*

q Acts xv. 14. Simeon hath declared how God at the first did visit the Gentiles, to take out of them a people for his name. Ver. 15. And to this agree the *words of the prophets; as it is written.* Ver. 18. *Known unto God are all his works* from the beginning of the world.

r Acts iv. 27. For of a truth, against thy holy child Jesus, whom thou hast anointed, both Herod and Pontius Pilate, with the Gentiles, and the people of Israel, were gathered together. Ver 28. For *to do whatsoever thy hand and thy counsel determined before to be done.*

7. s John iv. 24. God *is a spirit:* and they that worship him must worship him in spirit and in truth.

t Exod. iii. 14. And God said unto Moses, *I AM THAT I AM;* and he said, Thus shalt thou say unto the children of Israel, *I AM* hath sent me unto you. Job xi. 7. Canst thou *by searching find out God?* canst thou find out the Almighty unto perfection? Ver. 8. It is as *high as heaven;* what canst thou do? *deeper than hell;* what canst thou know? Ver. 9. The measure thereof is *longer than the earth, and broader than the sea.*

v Acts vii. 2. The *God of glory* appeared unto our father Abraham, when he was in Mesopotamia, before he dwelt in Charran.

w 1 Tim. vi. 15. Which in his times he shall shew, who is *the blessed* and only Potentate, the King of kings, and Lord of lords.

x Matt. v. 48. Be ye therefore *perfect*, even as your *Father* which is in heaven is *perfect.*

y Gen. xvii. 1. And when Abram was ninety years old and nine, the Lord appeared to Abram and said unto him, I am *the Almighty God:* walk before me, and be thou perfect.

z Ps. xc. 2. Before the mountains were brought forth, or ever thou hadst formed the earth and the world, even *from everlasting to everlasting*, thou art God.

a Mal. iii. 6. For I am the Lord, I *change not;* therefore ye sons of Jacob are not consumed. James i. 17. Every good gift and every perfect gift is from above, and cometh down from the Father of lights, with whom is *no variableness, neither shadow of turning.*

b 1 Kings viii. 27. But will God indeed dwell on the earth? Behold, *the heaven, and heaven of heavens, cannot contain thee;* how much less this house that I have builded!

c Ps. cxxxix. 1-13. O Lord, thou hast searched me, and known me. Thou knowest my down-sitting and mine up-rising; thou understandest my thought afar off, &c. Whither shall I *go from thy spirit?* or *whither shall I flee from thy presence?* &c.

d Rev. iv. 8. And the four beasts had each of them six wings about him; and they were full of eyes within: and they rest not day and night, saying, Holy, holy, holy, Lord God *Almighty*, which was, and is, and is to come.

e Heb. iv. 13. Neither is there any creature that is not manifest in his sight; but *all things are naked* and *opened unto the eyes of him* with whom we have to do. Ps. cxlvii. 5. Great is our Lord, and of great power: *his understanding is infinite.*

f Rom. xvi. 27. To God *only wise*, be glory through Jesus Christ for ever. Amen.

g Isa. vi. 3. And one cried unto another, and said, *Holy, holy, holy* is the Lord of hosts: the whole earth is full of his glory. Rev. xv. 4. Who shall not fear thee, O Lord, and glorify thy name? for *thou only art holy:* for all nations shall come and worship before thee; for thy judgments are made manifest.

h Deut. xxxii. 4. He is the Rock, his work is perfect; for *all his ways are judgment:* a God of truth, and without iniquity; *just and right is he.*

i Exod. xxxiv. 6. And the Lord passed by before him, and proclaimed, The Lord, the Lord God, *merciful and gracious, long-suffering, and abundant in goodness and truth.*

8. k Deut. vi. 4. Hear, O Israel; *The Lord our God is one Lord.* 1 Cor. viii. 4. As concerning therefore the eating of those things that are offered in sacrifice unto idols, we know that an idol is nothing in the world, and that there is *none other God but one.* Ver. 6. But to us there is *but one God*, the Father, of whom are all things, and we in him; and *one Lord Jesus Christ*,

Q. 9. How many persons are there in the Godhead?

A. There be three persons in the Godhead, the Father, the Son, and the Holy Ghost; and these three are one true, eternal God, the same in substance, equal in power and glory; although distinguished by their personal properties.[l]

Q. 10. What are the personal properties of the three persons in the Godhead?

A. It is proper to the Father to beget the Son,[m] and to the Son to be begotten of the Father,[n] and to the Holy Ghost to proceed from the Father and the Son from all eternity.[o]

Q. 11. How doth it appear that the Son and the Holy Ghost are God equal with the Father?

A. The scriptures manifest that the Son and the Holy Ghost are God equal with the Father, ascribing unto them such names,[p] attributes,[q] works,[r] and worship,[s] as are proper to God only.

by whom are all things, and we by him. Jer. x. 10. But *the Lord is the true God, he is the living God,* and an everlasting King: at his wrath the earth shall tremble, and the nations shall not be able to abide his indignation.

9. l 1 John v. 7. For there are *three* that bear record in heaven, the *Father,* the *Word,* and the *Holy Ghost:* and *these three are one.* Matt. iii. 16. And Jesus, when he was baptized, went up straightway out of the water: and, lo, the heavens were opened unto him, and *he saw the Spirit of God* descending like a dove, and lighting upon him: Ver. 17. And lo a voice from heaven, saying, *This is my beloved Son,* in whom I am well pleased. Matt. xxviii. 19. Go ye therefore, and teach all nations, baptizing them in the name of the *Father,* and of *the Son,* and of *the Holy Ghost.* 2 Cor. xiii. 14. The grace of the *Lord Jesus Christ,* and the love of *God,* and the communion of the *Holy Ghost,* be with you all. Amen. John x. 30. *I and my Father are one.*

10. m Heb. i. 5. For unto which of the angels said he at any time, Thou art my Son, *this day have I begotten thee?* And again, I will be to him a Father, and he shall be to me a Son? Ver. 6. And again, when he bringeth in the *first-begotten* into the world, he saith, And let all the angels of God worship him. Ver. 8. But unto the *Son* he saith, Thy throne, *O God,* is for ever and ever; a sceptre of righteousness is the sceptre of thy kingdom.

n John i. 14. And the Word was made flesh, and dwelt among us, (and we beheld his glory, the glory as *of the only begotten of the Father,*) full of grace and truth. Ver. 18. No man hath seen God at any time; the *only begotten Son,* which is in the bosom of the Father, he hath declared him.

o John xv. 26. But when the Comforter is come, whom I will send unto you from the Father, even the *Spirit of truth,* which *proceedeth from the Father,* he shall testify of me. Gal. iv. 6. And because ye are sons, God hath *sent forth the Spirit of his Son* into your hearts, crying, Abba, Father.

11. p Isa. vi. 3. And one cried unto another, and said, Holy, holy, holy is the *Lord of hosts:* the *whole earth is full of his glory.* Ver. 5. Then said I, Woe is me! for I am undone; because I am a man of unclean lips, and I dwell in the midst of a people of unclean lips: for mine eyes have seen the *King, the Lord of hosts.* Ver. 8. Also I heard the voice *of the Lord,* saying, Whom shall I send, and who will go for us? Then said I, Here am I; send me. Compared with John xii. 41. These things said Esaias, when he *saw his glory,* and spake *of him.* And with Acts xxviii. 25. And when they agreed not among themselves, they departed, after that Paul had spoken one word, *Well spake the Holy Ghost by Esaias* the prophet unto our fathers. 1 John v. 20. And we know that the Son of God is come, and hath given us an understanding, that we may know him that is true; and we are in him that is true, even in his Son *Jesus Christ. This is the true God, and eternal life.* Acts v. 3. But Peter said, Ananias, why hath Satan filled thine heart to *lie to the Holy Ghost,* and to keep back part of the price of the land? Ver. 4. Whiles it remained, was it not thine own? and after it was sold, was it not in thine own power? why hast thou conceived this thing in thine heart? *thou hast not lied unto men, but unto God.*

q John i. 1 In the beginning was the Word, and the Word was with God, and *the Word was God.* Isa. ix. 6. For unto us a child is born, unto us a son is given; and the government shall be upon his shoulder: and his *name* shall be called *Wonderful, Counsellor,* The *Mighty God,* The *everlasting Father,* The *Prince of Peace.* John ii. 24. But Jesus did not commit himself unto them, because *he knew all men,* Ver. 25. And needed not that any should testify of man: for *he knew what was in man.* 1 Cor. ii. 10. But God hath revealed them unto us by his Spirit: for the *Spirit searcheth all things,* yea, *the deep things of God.* Ver. 11. For what man knoweth the things of a man, save the spirit of man which is in him? even so the things of God knoweth no man, *but the Spirit of God.*

r Col. i. 16. For *by him were all things created* that are in heaven, and that are in earth, visible and invisible, whether they

Q. 12. *What are the decrees of God?*

A. God's decrees are the wise, free, and holy acts of the counsel of his will,ᵗ whereby, from all eternity, he hath, for his own glory, unchangeably foreordained whatsoever comes to pass in time,ᵛ especially concerning angels and men.

Q. 13. *What hath God especially decreed concerning angels and men?*

A. God, by an eternal and immutable decree, out of his mere love for the praise of his glorious grace, to be manifested in due time, hath elected some angels to glory;ʷ and in Christ hath chosen some men to eternal life, and the means thereof:ˣ and also, according to his sovereign power, and the unsearchable counsel of his own will, (whereby he extendeth or withholdeth favour as he pleaseth,) hath passed by and foreordained the rest to dishonour and wrath, to be for their sin inflicted, to the praise of the glory of his justice.ʸ

Q. 14. *How doth God execute his decrees?*

---

be thrones, or dominions, or principalities, or powers; *all things* were *created by him*, and *for him.* Gen. i. 2. And the earth was without form, and void; and darkness was upon the face of the deep: and the *Spirit of God* moved upon the face of the waters.

ˢ Matt. xxviii. 19. Go ye therefore, and teach all nations, baptizing them in the name of *the Father*, and of *the Son*, and of *the Holy Ghost.* 2 Cor. xiii. 14. The *grace* of the *Lord Jesus Christ*, and the *love of God*, and the *communion of the Holy Ghost*, be with you all. Amen.

12. ᵗ Eph. i. 11. In whom also we have obtained an inheritance, being *predestinated according to the purpose of him* who worketh all things *after the counsel of his own will.* Rom. xi. 33. O the depth of the riches both of the *wisdom and knowledge* of God! how *unsearchable are his judgments*, and *his ways past finding out!* Rom. ix. 14. What shall we say then? Is there unrighteousness with God? God forbid. Ver. 15. For he saith to Moses, *I will have mercy* on whom *I will* have mercy, and *I will have compassion* on whom *I will* have compassion. Ver. 18. Therefore *hath he mercy on whom he will have mercy*, and whom *he will* be hardeneth.

ᵛ Eph. i. 4. According as he hath *chosen* us in him *before the foundation of the world*, that we should be holy and without blame before him in love. Ver. 11. In whom also we have obtained an inheritance, being *predestinated* according to *the purpose* of him who worketh all things after *the counsel of his own will.* Rom. ix. 22. What if God, willing to shew his wrath, and to *make his power known*, endured with much long-suffering the vessels of wrath fitted to destruction; Ver. 23. And that he might *make known the riches of his glory* on the vessels of mercy, which he had afore prepared unto glory? Ps. xxxiii. 11. The *counsel* of the Lord *standeth for ever*, the thoughts of his heart *to all generations.*

13. ʷ 1 Tim. v. 21. I charge thee before God, and the Lord Jesus Christ, and *the elect angels*, that thou observe these things, without preferring one before another, doing nothing by partiality.

ˣ Eph. i. 4. According as he hath *chosen us in him* before the foundation of the world, *that we should be holy* and without blame before him in love: Ver. 5. Having *predestinated us* unto the adoption of children *by Jesus Christ* to himself, according to the *good pleasure of his will*, Ver. 6. *To the praise of the glory of his grace*, wherein he hath made us accepted in the Beloved. 2 Thess. ii. 13. But we are bound to give thanks alway to God for you, brethren beloved of the Lord, because God hath *from the beginning chosen you to salvation through sanctification of the Spirit, and belief of the truth:* Ver. 14. Whereunto he called you by our gospel, to the obtaining of the glory of our Lord Jesus Christ.

ʸ Rom. ix. 17. For the scripture saith unto Pharaoh, Even for this same purpose have I raised thee up, that *I might shew my power in thee*, and that *my name might be declared* throughout all the earth. Ver. 18. Therefore hath he mercy on whom he will have mercy, and whom he will be hardeneth. Ver. 21. Hath not *the potter power over the clay*, of the same lump to make one vessel unto honour, and another unto dishonour? Ver. 22. What if God, willing to *shew his wrath*, and to *make his power known*, endured with much long-suffering the vessels of wrath *fitted to destruction?* Matt. xi. 25. At that time Jesus answered and said, I thank thee, O Father, Lord of heaven and earth, because thou *hast hid these things from the wise* and prudent, and hast revealed them unto babes. Ver. 26. Even so, Father: *for so it seemed good in thy sight.* 2 Tim. ii. 20. But in a great house there are not only vessels of gold and of silver, but also of wood and of earth; and some to honour, and *some to dishonour.* Jude, ver. 4. For there are certain men crept in unawares, who were *before of old ordained to this condemnation*, ungodly men, turning the grace of our God into lasciviousness, and denying the only Lord God, and our Lord Jesus Christ. 1 Pet. ii. 8. And a stone of stumbling, and a rock of offence, even to them which stumble at the word, being disobedient; *whereunto also they were appointed.*

A. God executeth his decrees in the works of dence, according to his infallible foreknowledge, a mutable counsel of his own will.ᶻ

Q. 15. What is the work of creation?

A. The work of creation is that wherein God d by the word of his power, make of nothing the v therein, for himself, within the space of six days,

Q. 16. How did God create angels?

A. God created all the angelsᵇ spirits,ᶜ immor in knowledge,ᶠ mighty in power,ᵍ to execute his (to praise his name,ʰ yet subject to change.ⁱ

Q. 17. How did God create man?

A. After God had made all other creatures, h and female;ᵏ formed the body of the man of the and the woman of the rib of the man,ᵐ endued th sonable, and immortal souls;ⁿ made them after knowledge,ᵖ righteousness, and holiness;ᵠ having ten in their hearts,ʳ and power to fulfil it,ˢ with creatures;ᵗ yet subject to fall.ᵛ

---

14. ᶻ Eph. i. 11. In whom also we have obtained an inheritance, being predestinated according to the purpose of him who *worketh all things after the counsel of his own will.*

15. ᵃ [Gen. Chapter i.] Heb. xi. 3. Through faith we understand that the worlds were *framed by the word* of God; so that things which are seen were not made of things which do appear. Prov. xvi. 4. The Lord hath *made all things for himself;* yea, even the wicked for the day of evil.

16. ᵇ Col. i. 16. For *by him* were *all things created* that are *in heaven,* and that are *in earth,* visible and invisible, whether they be thrones, or dominions, or principalities, or powers ; *all things were created by him,* and for him.

ᶜ Ps. civ. 4. Who maketh his *angels spirits;* his ministers a flaming fire.

ᵈ Matt. xxii. 30. For in the resurrection they neither marry, nor are given in marriage, but are *as the angels of God in heaven.*

ᵉ Matt. xxv. 31. When the Son of man shall come in his glory, and all the *holy angels* with him, then shall he sit upon the throne of his glory.

ᶠ 2 Sam. xiv. 17. Then thine handmaid said, The word of my lord the king shall now be comfortable : for *as an angel of God,* so is my lord the king, *to discern good and bad;* therefore the Lord thy God will be with thee. Matt. xxiv. 36. But of that day and hour knoweth no man, *no, not the angels of heaven,* but my Father only.

ᵍ 2 Thess. i. 7. And to you who are troubled rest with us, when the Lord Jesus shall be revealed from heaven with his *mighty angels.*

ʰ Ps. ciii. 20. Bless the Lord, ye *his angels, that excel in strength, that do his commandments,* hearkening unto the voice of his word. Ver. 21. Bless ye the Lord, all ye his hosts ; ye *ministers* of his, that *do his pleasure.*

ⁱ 2 Pet. ii. 4. P *angels that sinne hell,* and delivered ness, to be reserv

17. ᵏ Gen. i. 27 his own image : ir he him ; *male an*

l Gen. ii. 7. Ar *man of the dust o* into his nostrils t

ᵐ Gen. ii. 22. A *God had taken fro* and brought her t

ⁿ Gen. ii. 7. A man of the dust o *into his nostrils t* became a *living* xxxv. 11. Who te *beasts of the earth, the fowls* of heav 7. Then shall *the* as it was ; and th *God who gave it* And fear not ther *are not able to kil* him which is able body in hell. A And Jesus said ui thee, *To-day shal dise.*

ᵒ Gen. i. 27. So *own image: in th him;* male and fe

ᵖ Col. iii. 10. A man, which *is ren the image of him*

ᵠ Eph. iv. 24. A man, which after *ousness and true*

ʳ Rom. ii. 14. which have not t things contained not the law, are Ver. 15. Which s *written* in *their h* bearing witness,

Q. 18. *What are God's works of providence?*

A. God's works of providence are his most holy,^w wise,^x and powerful preserving^y and governing^z all his creatures; ordering them, and all their actions,^a to his own glory.^b

Q. 19. *What is God's providence towards the angels?*

A. God by his providence permitted some of the angels, wilfully and irrecoverably, to fall into sin and damnation,^c limiting and ordering that, and all their sins, to his own glory;^d and established the rest in holiness and happiness;^e employing them all,^f at his pleasure, in the administrations of his power, mercy, and justice.^g

Q. 20. *What was the providence of God toward man in the estate in which he was created?*

A. The providence of God toward man in the estate in which he was created, was the placing him in paradise, appointing him to dress

---

mean while *accusing* or else *excusing* one another. s Eccl. vii. 29. Lo, this only have I found, that *God hath made man upright;* but they have sought out many inventions. t Gen. i. 28. And God blessed them : and God said unto them, Be fruitful, and multiply, and replenish the earth, and subdue it ; and *have dominion* over the fish of the sea, and over the fowl of the air, and over every living thing that moveth upon the earth. v Gen. iii. 6. And when the woman saw that the tree was good for food, and that it was pleasant to the eyes, and a tree to be desired to make one wise, *she took of the fruit thereof, and did eat;* and gave also unto her husband with her, *and he did eat.* Eccl. vii. 29. Lo, this only have I found, that God hath made man upright ; *but they have sought out many inventions.* 18. w Ps. cxlv. 17. The Lord *is righteous in all his ways, and holy in all his works.* x Ps. civ. 24. O Lord, how manifold are thy works ! *in wisdom hast thou made them all:* the earth is full of thy riches. Isa. xxviii. 29. This also cometh forth from the Lord of hosts, which *is wonderful in counsel, and excellent in working.* y Heb. i. 3. Who, being the brightness of his glory, and the express image of his person, and *upholding all things by the word of his power,* when he had by himself purged our sins, sat down on the right hand of the Majesty on high. z Ps. ciii. 19. The Lord hath prepared his throne in the heavens ; and *his kingdom ruleth over all.* a Matt. x. 29. Are not two sparrows sold for a farthing? and *one of them shall not fall on the ground without your Father.* Ver. 30. But *the very hairs of your head are all numbered.* Ver. 31. Fear ye not, therefore, ye are of more value than many sparrows. Gen. xlv. 7. And *God sent me before you* to preserve you a posterity in the earth, and to save your lives by a great deliverance. b Rom. xi. 36. For of him, and *through him, and to him, are all things:* to whom be glory for ever. Amen. Isa. lxiii. 14. As a beast goeth down into the valley, the Spirit of the Lord caused him to rest ; so didst thou lead thy people, *to make thyself a glorious name.* 19. c Jude, ver. 6. And *the angels which kept not their first estate,* but left their own habitation, *he hath reserved in everlasting chains,* under darkness, unto the judgment of the great day. 2 Pet. ii. 4. For if God spared not the angels that sinned, but *cast them down to hell,* and delivered them into chains of darkness, to be reserved unto judgment. Heb. ii. 16. For verily *he took not on him the nature of angels;* but he took on him the seed of Abraham. John viii. 44. Ye are of your father the devil, and the lusts of your father ye will do : *he was a murderer from the beginning,* and *abode not in the truth,* because there is no truth in him. When he speaketh *a lie,* he speaketh *of his own:* for he is *a liar,* and *the father of it.* d Job i. 12. And the Lord said unto *Satan,* Behold, all that he hath is in thy power ; *only upon himself put not forth thine hand.* So Satan went forth from the presence of the Lord. Matt. viii. 31. So the devils besought him, saying, If thou cast us out, *suffer us to go away into the herd of swine.* e 1 Tim. v. 21. I charge thee before God, and the Lord Jesus Christ, and *the elect angels,* that thou observe these things, without preferring one before another, doing nothing by partiality. Mark viii. 38. Whosoever therefore shall be ashamed of me, and of my words, in this adulterous and sinful generation, of him also shall the Son of man be ashamed, when he cometh in the glory of his Father, with *the holy angels.* Heb. xii. 22. But ye are come unto mount Sion, and unto the city of the living God, the heavenly Jerusalem, and to *an innumerable company of angels.* f Ps. civ. 4. Who *maketh his angels spirits; his ministers a flaming fire.* g 2 Kings xix. 35. And it came to pass that night, that *the angel of the Lord went out, and smote in the camp of the Assyrians an hundred fourscore and five thousand:* and when they arose early in the morning, behold, they were all dead corpses. Heb. i. 14. Are they not *all ministering spirits, sent forth to minister for them who shall be heirs of salvation?*

it, giving him liberty to eat of the fruit of the earth;[h] putting the creatures under his dominion,[i] and ordaining marriage for his help:[k] affording him communion with himself;[l] instituting the Sabbath;[m] entering into a covenant of life with him, upon condition of personal, perfect, and perpetual obedience,[n] of which the tree of life was a pledge;[o] and forbidding to eat of the tree of the knowledge of good and evil, upon the pain of death.[p]

Q. 21. *Did man continue in that estate wherein God at first created him?*

A. Our first parents being left to the freedom of their own will, through the temptation of Satan, transgressed the commandment of God in eating the forbidden fruit; and thereby fell from the estate of innocency wherein they were created.[q]

Q. 22. *Did all mankind fall in that first transgression?*

A. The covenant being made with Adam as a publick person, not for himself only, but for his posterity, all mankind descending from him by ordinary generation,[r] sinned in him, and fell with him in that first transgression.[s]

---

20. h Gen. ii. 8. And the Lord God planted a garden eastward in Eden; and there he put the man whom he had formed. Ver. 15. And the Lord God took the man, and *put him into the garden of Eden, to dress it, and to keep it.* Ver. 16. And the Lord God commanded the man, saying, *Of every tree of the garden thou mayest freely eat.*

i Gen. i. 28. And God blessed them: and God said unto them, Be fruitful, and multiply, and replenish the earth, and subdue it; and *have dominion over* the fish of the sea, and over the fowl of the air, and over every living thing that moveth upon the earth.

k Gen. ii. 18. And the Lord God said, It is not good that the man should be alone; *I will make him an help meet for him.*

l Gen. i. 26. And God said, Let us *make man in our image, after our likeness;* and let them have dominion over the fish of the sea, and over the fowl of the air, and over the cattle, and over all the earth, and over every creeping thing that creepeth upon the earth. Ver. 27. So God created man in his own image: *in the image of God created he him;* male and female created he them. Ver. 28. And *God blessed them: and God said unto them, Be fruitful, and multiply, and replenish the earth,* and subdue it; and have dominion over the fish of the sea, and over the fowl of the air, and over every living thing that moveth upon the earth. Ver. 29. And *God said, Behold, I have given you* every herb bearing seed, which is upon the face of all the earth, and every tree, in the which is the fruit of a tree yielding seed; to you it shall be for meat. Gen. iii. 8. And they heard *the voice of the Lord God walking in the garden* in the cool of the day: and Adam and his wife hid themselves *from the presence of the Lord God* amongst the trees of the garden.

m Gen. ii. 3. And *God blessed the seventh day,* and sanctified it; because that in it he had rested from all his work which God had created and made.

n Gal. iii. 12. And *the law* is not of faith: but, *The man that doeth them shall live in them.* Rom. x. 5. For Moses describeth the righteousness which is of *the law,* That the man *which doeth those things shall live by them.*

o Gen. ii. 9. And out of the ground made the Lord God to grow every tree that is pleasant to the sight, and good for food; *the tree of life also* in the midst of the garden, and the tree of knowledge of good and evil.

p Gen. ii. 17. But of *the tree of the knowledge of good and evil, thou shalt not eat of it:* for in the day that thou eatest thereof *thou shalt surely die.*

21. q Gen. iii. 6. And when the woman saw that the tree was good for food, and that it was pleasant to the eyes, and a tree to be desired to make one wise, *she took of the fruit thereof,* and *did eat;* and gave also unto her husband with her, and *he did eat.* Ver. 7. And the eyes of them both were opened, and *they knew that they were naked;* and they sewed fig-leaves together, and made themselves aprons. Ver. 8. And they heard the voice of the Lord God walking in the garden in the cool of the day: and Adam and his wife *hid themselves from the presence of the Lord God* amongst the trees of the garden. Ver. 13. And the Lord God said unto the woman, What is this that thou hast done? And the woman said, *The serpent beguiled me,* and I did eat. Eccl. vii. 29. Lo, this only have I found, that God made man upright; but *they have sought out many inventions.* 2 Cor. xi. 3. But I fear, lest by any means, *as the serpent beguiled Eve through his subtilty,* so your minds should be corrupted from the simplicity that is in Christ.

22. r Acts xvii. 26. And hath *made of one blood all nations of men* for to dwell on all the face of the earth, and hath determined the times before appointed, and the bounds of their habitation.

s Gen. ii. 16. And the Lord God commanded the man, saying, Of every tree of

Q. 23. *Into what estate did the fall bring mankind?*
A. The fall brought mankind into an estate of sin and misery.ᵗ

Q. 24. *What is sin?*
A. Sin is any want of conformity unto, or transgression of, any law of God, given as a rule to the reasonable creature.ᵛ

Q. 25. *Wherein consisteth the sinfulness of that estate whereinto man fell?*
A. The sinfulness of that estate whereinto man fell, consisteth in the guilt of Adam's first sin,ʷ the want of that righteousness wherein he was created, and the corruption of his nature, whereby he is utterly indisposed, disabled, and made opposite unto all that is spiritually good, and wholly inclined to all evil, and that continually;ˣ which is commonly called Original Sin, and from which do proceed all actual transgressions.ʸ

Q. 26. *How is original sin conveyed from our first parents unto their posterity?*
A. Original sin is conveyed from our first parents unto their posterity by natural generation, so as all that proceed from them in that way are conceived and born in sin.ᶻ

the garden thou mayest freely eat; Ver. 17. But of the tree of the knowledge of good and evil, thou shalt not eat of it: for in the day that thou eatest thereof *thou shalt surely die.* Compared with Rom. v. 12-20. Wherefore, as *by one man sin entered into the world, and death by sin;* and so *death* passed upon *all men, for that all have sinned.* Ver. 15. For if through *the offence of one many be dead;* much more—Ver. 16. For the judgment was *by one* to condemnation —Ver. 17. For if *by one man's offence death reigned by one;* much more—Ver. 18. Therefore, as by the *offence of one judgment came upon all men* to condemnation; even so—Ver. 19. For as *by one man's disobedience many were made sinners;* so by the obedience—And with 1 Cor. xv. 21. For since *by man came death,* by man came also the resurrection of the dead. Ver. 22. For as *in Adam all die,* even so in Christ shall all be made alive.

23. t Rom. v. 12. Wherefore, as by one man *sin entered into the world, and death by sin: and so death passed upon all men,* for that all have sinned. Rom. iii. 23. For *all have sinned, and come short of the glory of God.*

24. v 1 John iii. 4. Whosoever committeth sin *transgresseth also the law: for sin is the transgression of the law.* Gal. iii. 10. For as many as are of the works of the law are under the curse: for it is written, Cursed is every one *that continueth not in all things which are written in the book of the law to do them.* Ver. 12. And the law is not of faith: but, The man that *doeth them* shall live in them.

25. w Rom. v. 12. Wherefore, as *by one man sin entered into the world,* and death by sin; and so death passed upon all men, *for that all have sinned.* Ver. 19. For as *by one man's disobedience many were made sinners;* so by the obedience of one shall many be made righteous.

x Rom. iii. 10. As it is written, There is *none righteous, no, not one:* Ver. 11. *There is none that understandeth,* there is *none that seeketh after God.* Ver. 12. They are *all gone out of the way,* they are *together become unprofitable;* there is *none that doeth good, no, not one.* Ver. 13. Their *throat* is an open sepulchre: with their *tongues* they have used *deceit:* the *poison of asps* is under their *lips.* Ver. 14. Whose *mouth* is full of *cursing and bitterness:* Ver. 15. Their *feet* are swift to *shed blood:* Ver. 16. *Destruction* and *misery* are in their ways; Ver. 17. And the way of peace *have they not known:* Ver. 18. There is *no fear of God before their eyes.* Ver. 19. Now we know, that what things soever the law saith, it saith to them who are under the law; that every mouth may be stopped, and *all the world may become guilty before God.* Eph. ii. 1. And you hath he quickened, who were *dead in trespasses and sins;* Ver. 2. Wherein in time past ye *walked according to the course of this world,* according to the prince of the power of the air, the spirit that now worketh in the children of disobedience: Ver. 3. Among whom also we all had *our conversation* in times past *in the lusts of our flesh, fulfilling the desires of the flesh and of the mind;* and were *by nature the children of wrath, even as others.* Rom. v. 6. For *when we were yet without strength,* in due time Christ died for the *ungodly.* Rom. viii. 7. Because the *carnal mind is enmity against God:* for it is *not subject to the law of God, neither indeed can be.* Ver. 8. So then *they that are in the flesh cannot please God.* Gen. vi. 5. And God saw that the wickedness of man was great in the earth, and that *every imagination of the thoughts of his heart was only evil continually.*

y James i. 14. But every man is tempted, when he is drawn away *of his own lust,* and enticed. Ver. 15. Then, when *lust hath conceived,* it *bringeth forth sin;* and sin, when it is finished, bringeth forth death. Matt. xv. 19. For *out of the heart proceed*

THE LARGER CATECHISM.

Q. 27. *What misery did the fall bring upon mankind?*

A. The fall brought upon mankind the loss of communion with God,[a] his displeasure and curse; so as we are by nature children of wrath,[b] bond slaves to Satan,[c] and justly liable to all punishments in this world, and that which is to come.[d]

Q. 28. *What are the punishments of sin in this world?*

A. The punishments of sin in this world are either inward, as blindness of mind,[e] a reprobate sense,[f] strong delusions,[g] hardness of heart,[h] horror of conscience,[i] and vile affections;[k] or outward, as the curse of God upon the creatures for our sakes,[l] and all other evils that befall us in our bodies, names, estates, relations, and employments;[m] together with death itself.[n]

Q. 29. *What are the punishments of sin in the world to come?*

A. The punishments of sin in the world to come, are everlasting evil thoughts, murders, adulteries, fornications, thefts, false witness, blasphemies.

26. [z] Ps. li. 5. Behold, *I was shapen in iniquity; and in sin did my mother conceive me.* Job xiv. 4. *Who can bring a clean thing out of an unclean?* not one. Job xv. 14. What is *man, that he should be clean? and he which is born of a woman, that he should be righteous?* John iii. 6. *That which is born of the flesh is flesh;* and that which is born of the Spirit is spirit.

27. [a] Gen. iii. 8. And they heard the voice of the Lord God walking in the garden in the cool of the day: and Adam and his wife *hid themselves from the presence of the Lord God* amongst the trees of the garden. Ver. 10. And he said, I heard thy voice in the garden, and *I was afraid because I was naked;* and *I hid myself.* Ver. 24. So he drove out *the man:* and he placed at the east of the garden of Eden cherubims, and a flaming sword which turned every way, to *keep the way of the tree of life.*

[b] Eph. ii. 2. Wherein in time past ye walked according to the course of this world, according to the prince of the power of the air, the spirit that now worketh in the children of disobedience: Ver. 3. Among whom also we all had our conversation in times past in the lusts of our flesh, fulfilling the desires of the flesh and of the mind; and were *by nature the children of wrath, even as others.*

[c] 2 Tim. ii. 26. And that they may recover themselves out of the *snare* of the *devil,* who are *taken captive by him at his will.*

[d] Gen. ii. 17. But of the tree of the knowledge of good and evil, thou shalt not eat of it: for in the day that thou eatest thereof *thou shalt surely die.* Lam. iii. 39. Wherefore doth a *living man complain,* a man *for the punishment of his sins?* Rom. vi. 23. For the *wages of sin is death;* but the gift of God is eternal life through Jesus Christ our Lord. Matt. xxv. 41. Then shall he say also unto them on the left hand, *Depart from me, ye cursed, into everlasting fire,* prepared for the devil and his angels. Ver. 46. And these shall go away *into everlasting punishment:* but the righteous into life eternal. Jude, ver. 7. Even as Sodom and Gomorrha, and the cities about them, in like manner, giving themselves over to fornication, and going after strange flesh, are set forth for an example, *suffering the vengeance of eternal fire.*

28. [e] Eph. iv. 18. Having the *understanding darkened,* being alienated from the life of God *through the ignorance that is in them, because of the blindness of their heart.*

[f] Rom. i. 28. Even as they did not like to retain God in their knowledge, God gave them over to a *reprobate mind,* to do those things which are not convenient.

[g] 2 Thess. ii. 11. And for this cause God shall send them *strong delusion,* that they should believe a lie.

[h] Rom. ii. 5. But, *after thy hardness and impenitent heart,* treasurest up unto thyself wrath against the day of wrath, and revelation of the righteous judgment of God.

[i] Isa. xxxiii. 14. The *sinners in Zion are afraid; fearfulness hath surprised the hypocrites:* who among us shall dwell with the devouring fire? who among us shall dwell with everlasting burnings? Gen. iv. 13. And *Cain* said unto the *Lord, My punishment is greater than I can bear.* Matt. xxvii. 4. *Saying, I have sinned,* in that *I have betrayed the innocent blood.* And they said, What is that to us? see thou to that.

[k] Rom. i. 26. For this cause God *gave them up unto vile affections:* for even their women did change the natural use into that which is against nature.

[l] Gen. iii. 17. And unto Adam he said, Because thou hast hearkened unto the voice of thy wife, and hast eaten of the tree, of which I commanded thee, saying, Thou shalt not eat of it: *cursed is the ground for thy sake; in sorrow shalt thou eat of it* all the days of thy life.

[m] Deut. xxviii. 15, to the end. But it shall come to pass, if thou wilt not hearken unto the voice of the Lord thy God, to observe to do all his commandments and his statutes, which I command thee this day, that *all these curses shall come upon thee, and overtake thee.* Ver. 16. *Cursed* shalt thou be in the *city,* and *cursed* shalt thou be in the *field.* Ver. 17. *Cursed* shall be thy *basket* and thy *store.* Ver. 18. Cursed shall be the *fruit of thy body,* and the *fruit of thy land,* etc.

[n] Rom. vi. 21. What fruit had ye then in those things whereof ye are now ashamed?

separation from the comfortable presence of God, and most grievous torments in soul and body, without intermission, in hell-fire for ever.º

Q. 30. *Doth God leave all mankind to perish in the estate of sin and misery?*

A. God doth not leave all men to perish in the estate of sin and misery,P into which they fell by the breach of the first covenant commonly called the Covenant of Works;q but of his mere love and mercy delivereth his elect out of it, and bringeth them into an estate of salvation by the second covenant, commonly called the Covenant of Grace.r

Q. 31. *With whom was the covenant of grace made?*

A. The covenant of grace was made with Christ as the second Adam, and in him with all the elect as his seed.s

Q. 32. *How is the grace of God manifested in the second covenant?*

A. The grace of God is manifested in the second covenant, in that he freely provideth and offereth to sinners a Mediator,t and life and salvation by him;v and requiring faith as the condition to interest them in him,w promiseth and giveth his Holy Spiritx to all his elect, to work

for *the end of those things is death.* Ver. 23. For the *wages of sin is death;* but the gift of God is eternal life through Jesus Christ our Lord.

29. o 2 Thess. i. 9. Who shall be punished with *everlasting destruction from the presence of the Lord,* and from the glory of his power. Mark ix. 43, 44, 46, 48.—*To go into hell,—Where their worm dieth not, and the fire is not quenched.* Luke xvi. 24. And he cried, and said, Father Abraham, have mercy on me, and send Lazarus, that he may dip the tip of his finger in water, and cool my tongue ; for *I am tormented in this flame.*

30. p 1 Thess. v. 9. For God hath *not appointed us to wrath,* but to obtain salvation by our Lord Jesus Christ.

q Gal. iii. 10. For as many as are of the *works of the law are under the curse:* for it is written, *Cursed is every one that continueth not in all things which are written in the book of the law to do them.* Ver. 12. And the law is not of faith : but, The man that doeth them shall live in them.

r Tit. iii. 4. But after that the kindness and love of God our Saviour toward man appeared, Ver. 5. *Not by works of righteousness* which we have done, but *according to his mercy he saved us,* by the washing of regeneration, and renewing of the Holy Ghost ; Ver. 6. Which he shed on us abundantly through Jesus Christ our Saviour; Ver. 7. That, being *justified by his grace,* we should be *made heirs according to the hope of eternal life.* Gal. iii. 21. Is the *law then against the promises* of God? God forbid : for if there had been a law given which could have given life, verily righteousness should have been by the law. Rom. iii. 20. Therefore by the *deeds of the law* there shall *no flesh be justified* in his sight : for by the law is the knowledge of sin. Ver. 21. But now *the righteousness of God without the law is manifested,* being witnessed by the law and the prophets ; Ver. 22.

Even *the righteousness of God, which is by faith of Jesus Christ unto all and upon all them that believe;* for there is no difference.

31. s Gal. iii. 16. Now to *Abraham and his seed were the promises made.* He saith not, And to seeds, as of many ; but as of one, And *to thy seed, which is Christ.* [Rom. v. 15. to the end.] Isa. liii. 10. Yet it pleased the Lord to bruise him ; he hath put him to grief : when thou shalt make his soul an offering for sin, *he shall see his seed,* he shall prolong his days, and the pleasure of the Lord shall prosper in his hand. Ver. 11. He shall *see of the travail of his soul,* and shall be satisfied : by his knowledge shall my righteous servant justify many ; for he shall bear their iniquities.

32. t Gen. iii. 15. And I will put enmity between thee and the woman, and *between thy seed and her seed: it shall bruise thy head,* and thou shalt bruise his heel. Isa. xlii. 6. I the Lord have *called thee* in righteousness, and will hold thine hand, and will keep thee, and *will give thee for a covenant of the people,* for a light of the Gentiles. John vi. 27. Labour not for the meat which perisheth, but for that meat which endureth unto everlasting life, which the Son *of man* shall give unto you : for *him hath God the Father sealed.*

v 1 John v. 11. And this is the record, that *God hath given to us eternal life;* and *this life is in his Son.* Ver. 12. He that hath the Son hath life ; and he that hath not the Son of God hath not life.

w John iii. 16. For God so loved the world, that *he gave his only begotten Son,* that whosoever believeth in him should not perish, *but have everlasting life.* John i. 12. But as many as received him, *to them gave he power to become the sons of God,* even to them that believe on his name.

x Prov. i. 23. Behold, *I will pour out my Spirit unto you,* I will make known my words unto you.

in them that faith,y with all other saving graces;z and to enable them unto all holy obedience,a as the evidence of the truth of their faithb and thankfulness to God,c and as the way which he hath appointed them to salvation.d

Q. 33. *Was the covenant of grace always administered after one and the same manner?*

A. The covenant of grace was not always administered after the same manner, but the administrations of it under the Old Testament were different from those under the New.e

Q. 34. *How was the covenant of grace administered under the Old Testament?*

A. The covenant of grace was administered under the Old Testament, by promises,f prophecies,g sacrifices,h circumcision,i the passover,k and other types and ordinances, which did all fore-signify Christ then to come, and were for that time sufficient to build up the elect in faith in the promised Messiah,l by whom they then had full remission of sin, and eternal salvation.m

Q. 35. *How is the covenant of grace administered under the New Testament?*

A. Under the New Testament, when Christ the substance was exhibited, the same covenant of grace was and still is to be administered

---

y 2 Cor. iv. 13. *We having the same spirit of faith,* according as it is written, I believed, and therefore have I spoken ; we also believe, and therefore speak.

z Gal. v. 22. But the *fruit of the Spirit is love, joy, peace, long-suffering, gentleness, goodness, faith,* Ver. 23. *Meekness, temperance:* against such there is no law.

a Ezek. xxxvi. 27. And I will put my Spirit within you, and *cause you to walk in my statutes,* and ye *shall keep my judgments, and do them.*

b James ii. 18. Yea, a man may say, Thou hast faith, and I have works ; shew me thy faith without thy works, and I will *shew thee my faith by my works.* Ver. 22. Seest thou how faith wrought with his works, and *by works was faith made perfect?*

c 2 Cor. v. 14. For *the love of Christ constraineth us; because we thus judge,* that if one died for all, then were all dead : Ver. 15. And that he died for all, *that they which live should not henceforth live unto themselves, but unto him which died for them,* and rose again.

d Eph. ii. 10. For we are his workmanship, *created in Christ Jesus unto good works,* which God hath *before ordained that we should walk in them.*

33. e 2 Cor. iii. 6. Who also hath made us able *ministers of the new testament; not of the letter, but of the Spirit:* for the letter killeth, but the spirit giveth life. Ver. 7. But if *the ministration of death,* written and engraven in stones, was glorious, so that the children of Israel could not stedfastly behold the face of *Moses* for the glory of his countenance ; which glory was to be done away : Ver. 8. How shall not *the ministration of the Spirit* be rather glorious ? Ver. 9. For if *the ministration of condemnation* be glory, much more doth *the ministration of righteousness* exceed in glory

34. f Rom. xv. 8. Now I say, that Jesus Christ was a minister of the circumcision for the truth of God, to confirm *the promises made unto the fathers.*

g Acts iii. 20. And he shall send *Jesus Christ,* which before was preached unto you. Ver. 24. Yea, and all the *prophets* from Samuel, and those that follow after, as many as have spoken, *have likewise foretold of these days.*

h Heb. x. 1. For the law having a *shadow of good things to come,* and not the very *image* of the things, can never with those *sacrifices, which they offered year by year continually,* make the comers thereunto perfect.

i Rom. iv. 11. And he received *the sign of circumcision,* a *seal of the righteousness of the faith* which he had yet being uncircumcised : that he might be the father of all them that believe, though they be not circumcised ; that righteousness might be imputed unto them also.

k 1 Cor. v. 7. Purge out therefore the old leaven, that ye may be a new lump, as ye are unleavened. For even *Christ our passover* is sacrificed for us.

l [Heb. Chapters viii. ix. and x.] Heb. xi. 13. These all died *in faith, not having received the promises,* but having *seen them afar off,* and were persuaded of them, and embraced them, and confessed that they were strangers and pilgrims on the earth.

m Gal. iii. 7. Know ye therefore, that *they which are of faith, the same are the children of Abraham.* Ver. 8. And the scripture, foreseeing that God would *justify the heathen through faith, preached before the gospel unto Abraham,* saying, In thee shall all nations be blessed. Ver. 9. So then *they which be of faith are blessed with faithful Abraham.* Ver. 14. That the *blessing of Abraham might come on the Gentiles* in the preaching of the word,ⁿ and the administration of the sacraments of baptism° and the Lord's supper;ᵖ in which grace and salvation are held forth in more fulness, evidence, and efficacy, to all nations.ᵠ

Q. 36. *Who is the Mediator of the covenant of grace?*

A. The only Mediator of the covenant of grace is the Lord Jesus Christ,ʳ who, being the eternal Son of God, of one substance and equal with the Father,ˢ in the fulness of time became man,ᵗ and so was and continues to be God and man, in two entire distinct natures, and one person, for ever.ᵛ

Q. 37. *How did Christ, being the Son of God, become man?*

A. Christ the Son of God became man, by taking to himself a true body, and a reasonable soul,ʷ being conceived by the power of the Holy Ghost in the womb of the Virgin Mary, of her substance, and born of her,ˣ yet without sin.ʸ

through Jesus Christ; that we might receive the promise of the Spirit *through faith.*
35. ⁿ Mark xvi. 15. And he said unto them, Go ye into all the world, and *preach the gospel* to every creature.
° Matt. xxviii. 19. Go ye therefore, and teach all nations, *baptizing them* in the name of the Father, and of the Son, and of the Holy Ghost; Ver. 20. Teaching them to observe all things whatsoever I have commanded you: and, lo, I am with you alway, even unto the end of the world. Amen.
ᵖ 1 Cor. xi. 23. For *I have received of the Lord that which also I delivered unto you, That the Lord Jesus, the same night in which he was betrayed, took bread:* Ver. 24. And, when he had given thanks, he brake it, and said, Take, eat; this is my body, which is broken for you: *this do in remembrance of me.* Ver. 25. After the same manner also he took the cup, when he had supped, saying, This cup is the new testament in my blood: *this do ye, as oft as ye drink it, in remembrance of me.*
ᵠ 2 Cor. iii. 6. to the end. Who also hath *made us able ministers of the new testament; not of the letter, but of the spirit: for the letter killeth,* but the *spirit giveth life.* Ver. 7. But if the *ministration of death,* written and engraven in stones was glorious,—Ver. 8. How shall not the *ministration of the Spirit be rather glorious.* Ver. 9. For if the ministration of condemnation be glory, much more doth the *ministration of righteousness exceed in glory,* etc. *Heb. viii. 6. But now hath he obtained a *more excellent ministry,* by how much also he is the mediator of a *better covenant,* which was established upon *better promises.* Ver. 10. For *this is the covenant* that I will make with the house of Israel, after those days, saith the Lord; I will *put my laws into their mind,* and *write them in their hearts; and I will be to them a God,* and *they shall be to me a people:* Ver. 11. And they shall not teach every man his neighbour, and every man his brother, saying, Know the Lord: for *all shall know me, from the least to the greatest.* Matt. xxviii. 19. Go ye therefore, and *teach all nations baptizing them in the name of,* etc.
36. ʳ 1 Tim. ii. 5. For there is one God, and *one mediator* between God and men, the man Christ Jesus.

ˢ John i. 1. In *the beginning was the Word,* and the Word was with God, and *the Word was God.* Ver. 14. And the Word was made flesh, and dwelt among us, (and we beheld his glory, the glory as of *the only begotten of the Father,*) full of grace and truth. John x. 30. *I and my Father are one.* Phil. ii. 6. Who, being *in the form of God, thought it not robbery to be equal with God.*
ᵗ Gal. iv. 4. But when the fulness of the time was come, *God sent forth his Son, made of a woman,* made under the law.
ᵛ Luke i. 35. And the angel answered and said unto her, The Holy Ghost shall come upon thee, and the power of the Highest shall overshadow thee: therefore also *that holy thing, which shall be born of thee, shall be called the Son of God.* Rom. ix. 5. Whose are the fathers, and of whom, as concerning the flesh, *Christ* came, who is over all, *God blessed for ever. Amen.* Col. ii. 9. For *in him dwelleth all the fulness of the Godhead bodily.* Heb. vii. 24. But this man, *because he continueth ever,* hath an unchangeable priesthood. Ver. 25. Wherefore he is able also to save them to the uttermost that come unto God by him, seeing *he ever liveth* to make intercession for them.
37. ʷ John i. 14. And the *Word was made flesh,* and dwelt among us, (and we beheld his glory, the glory as of the only begotten of the Father,) full of grace and truth. Matt. xxvi. 38. Then saith he unto them, *My soul is exceeding sorrowful, even unto* death: tarry ye here, and watch with me.
ˣ Luke i. 27. *To a virgin espoused to a man,* whose name was Joseph, of the house of David; and the *virgin's name* was Mary. Ver. 31. And, behold, *thou shalt conceive in thy womb, and bring forth a son,* and shalt call his name Jesus. Ver. 35. And the angel answered and said unto her, The *Holy Ghost shall come upon thee,* and the *power of the Highest shall overshadow thee:* therefore also that *holy thing,* which shall be born of thee, shall be called the *Son of God.* Ver. 42. And Elisabeth spake out with a loud voice, and said, Blessed art thou among women, and blessed is *the fruit of thy womb.* Gal. iv. 4. But when the fulness of the time was come, God sent forth *his Son, made of a woman,* made under the law.
ʸ Heb. iv. 15. For we have not an high

Q. 38. *Why was it requisite that the Mediator should be God?*

A. It was requisite that the Mediator should be God, that he might sustain and keep the human nature from sinking under the infinite wrath of God, and the power of death;[a] give worth and efficacy to his sufferings, obedience, and intercession;[a] and to satisfy God's justice,[b] procure his favour,[c] purchase a peculiar people,[d] give his Spirit to them,[e] conquer all their enemies,[f] and bring them to everlasting salvation.[g]

Q. 39. *Why was it requisite that the Mediator should be man?*

A. It was requisite that the Mediator should be man, that he might advance our nature,[h] perform obedience to the law,[i] suffer and make

priest which cannot be touched with the feeling of our infirmities; but was in all points tempted like as we are, *yet without sin*. Heb. vii. 26. For such an *high priest* became us, who is *holy, harmless, undefiled, separate from sinners*, and made higher than the heavens.

38. a Acts ii. 24. Whom God hath raised up, having loosed the pains of death: because it was *not possible that he should be holden* of it. Ver. 25. For David speaketh concerning him, I foresaw the Lord always before my face; for he is on my right hand, that I should not be moved. Rom. i. 4. And *declared to be the Son of God with power, according to the Spirit of holiness, by the resurrection from the dead*. Compared with Rom. iv. 25. Who was delivered for our offences, and was *raised again for our justification*. Heb. ix. 14. How much more shall the blood of *Christ, who through the eternal Spirit offered himself without spot to God*, purge your conscience from dead works, to serve the living God?

a Acts xx. 28. Take heed therefore unto yourselves, and to all the flock, over the which the Holy Ghost hath made you overseers, to feed the *church of God, which he hath purchased with his own blood*. Heb. ix. 14. How much more shall the *blood of Christ*, who through the eternal Spirit offered himself without spot to God, *purge your conscience from dead works*, to serve the living God? Heb. vii. 25. Wherefore he is *able also to save them to the uttermost* that come unto God by him, seeing *he ever liveth to make intercession for them*. Ver. 26. For *such an high priest* became us, who is *holy, harmless, undefiled, separate from sinners*, and made *higher than the heavens;* Ver. 27. *Who needeth not daily*, as those high priests, *to offer up sacrifice*, first for his own sins, and then for the people's: for *this he did once, when he offered up himself*. Ver. 28. For the law maketh men high priests which have infirmity; but the word of the oath, which was since the law, maketh *the Son, who is consecrated for evermore.*

b Rom. iii. 24. Being *justified freely by his grace, through the redemption that is in Christ Jesus;* Ver. 25. Whom God hath set forth to be a *propitiation* through *faith in his blood*, to declare his righteousness *for the remission of sins* that are past, through the forbearance of God; Ver. 26. To *declare*, I say, at this time his *righteousness;* that he might *be just*, and the *justifier of him which believeth in Jesus.*

c Eph. i. 6. To the praise of the glory of his grace, wherein he *hath made us accepted in the Beloved*. Matt. iii. 17. And lo a voice from heaven, saying, This is my *beloved Son, in whom I am well pleased.*

d Tit. ii. 13. Looking for that blessed hope, and the glorious appearing of the great God and our Saviour Jesus Christ; Ver. 14. Who gave himself for us, *that he might redeem us from all iniquity, and purify unto himself a peculiar people, zealous of good works.*

e Gal. iv. 6. And *because ye are sons*, God *hath sent forth the Spirit of his Son into your hearts*, crying, Abba, Father.

f Luke i. 68. Blessed be the Lord God of Israel; for he hath visited and redeemed his people, Ver. 69. And hath raised up an horn of salvation for us in the house of his servant David. Ver. 71. That we should *be saved from our enemies*, and *from the hand of all that hate us*. Ver. 74. That he would grant unto us, that we, being *delivered out of the hand* of our enemies, might serve him without fear.

g Heb. v. 8. Though he were a Son, yet learned he obedience by the things which he suffered; Ver. 9. And being made perfect, *he became the author of eternal salvation unto all them that obey him*. Heb. ix. 11. But *Christ* being come an high priest of good things to come, by a greater and more perfect tabernacle, not made with hands, that is to say, not of this building; Ver. 12. Neither by the blood of goats and calves, but by his own blood, he entered in once into the holy place, *having obtained eternal redemption for us*. Ver. 13. For if the blood of bulls and of goats, and the ashes of an heifer sprinkling the unclean, sanctifieth to the purifying of the flesh; Ver. 14. How much more shall the blood of Christ, who through the eternal Spirit offered himself without spot to God, purge your conscience from dead works, to serve the living God? Ver. 15. And for this cause he is the mediator of the new testament, that by means of death, for the redemption of the transgressions that were under the first testament, they which are called *might receive the promise of eternal inheritance.*

39. h Heb. ii. 16. For verily he took not on him the nature of angels; but *he took on him the seed of Abraham.*

i Gal. iv. 4. But when the fulness of the

intercession for us in our nature,^k have a fellow-feeling of our infirmities;^l that we might receive the adoption of sons,^m and have comfort and access with boldness unto the throne of grace.^n

Q. 40. *Why was it requisite that the Mediator should be God and man in one person?*

A. It was requisite that the Mediator, who was to reconcile God and man, should himself be both God and man, and this in one person, that the proper works of each nature might be accepted of God for us,^o and relied on by us, as the works of the whole person.^p

Q. 41. *Why was our Mediator called Jesus?*

A. Our Mediator was called Jesus, because he saveth his people from their sins.^q

Q. 42. *Why was our Mediator called Christ?*

A. Our Mediator was called Christ, because he was anointed with the Holy Ghost above measure;^r and so set apart, and fully furnished with all authority and ability,^s to execute the offices of prophet,^t priest,^v

---

time was come, God sent forth his Son, made of a woman, made under the law.

^k Heb. ii. 14. *Forasmuch then as the children are partakers of flesh and blood, he also himself likewise took part of the same; that through death* he might destroy him that had the power of death, that is, the devil. Heb. vii. 24. But this man, because he continueth ever, hath an unchangeable priesthood. Ver. 25. Wherefore he is able also to save them to the uttermost that come unto God by him, seeing he ever liveth *to make intercession for them.*

^l Heb. iv. 15. *For we have not an high priest which cannot be touched with the feeling of our infirmities;* but was in all points tempted like as we are, yet without sin.

^m Gal. iv. 5. To redeem them that were under the law, *that we might receive the adoption of sons.*

^n Heb. iv. 16. *Let us therefore come boldly unto the throne of grace, that we may obtain mercy,* and find *grace* to help in time of need.

40. ^o Matt. i. 21. And she shall bring forth a *son,* and thou shalt call his name JESUS; *for he shall save his people from their sins.* Ver. 23. Behold, a virgin shall be with child, and shall bring forth a *son,* and they shall call *his name Emmanuel,* which, being interpreted, is, *God with us.* Matt. iii. 17. And lo a voice from heaven saying, *This is my beloved Son, in whom I am well pleased.* Heb. ix. 14. How much more shall the *blood of Christ, who through the eternal Spirit offered himself without spot to God,* purge your conscience from dead works, to serve the living God?

^p 1 Pet. ii. 6. Wherefore also it is contained in the scripture, Behold, I lay in Sion a *chief corner-stone,* elect, precious: and *he that believeth on him shall not be confounded.*

41. ^q Matt. i. 21. And she shall bring forth a son, and thou *shalt call his name* JESUS; *for he shall save his people from their sins.*

42. ^r John iii. 34. For he whom God hath sent speaketh the words of God: for *God giveth not the Spirit by measure unto him.* Ps. xlv. 7. Thou lovest righteousness, and hatest wickedness: therefore God, *thy God, hath anointed thee with the oil of gladness above thy fellows.*

^s John vi. 27. Labour not for the meat which perisheth, but for that meat which endureth unto everlasting life, which the Son of man shall give unto you: for *him hath God the Father sealed.* Matt. xxviii. 18. And Jesus came and spake unto them, saying, *All power is given unto me in heaven and in earth.* Ver. 19. Go ye therefore, and teach all nations, baptizing them in the name of the Father, and of the Son, and of the Holy Ghost; Ver. 20. Teaching them to observe all things whatsoever I have commanded you: and, lo, I am with you alway, even unto the end of the world. Amen.

^t Acts iii. 21. Whom the heaven must receive until the times of restitution of all things, which God hath spoken by the mouth of all his holy prophets since the world began. Ver. 22. For Moses truly said unto the fathers, *A Prophet shall the Lord your God raise up unto you of your brethren, like unto me; him shall ye hear in all things* whatsoever he shall say unto you. Luke iv. 18. *The Spirit of the Lord* is upon me, because *he hath anointed me to preach the gospel* to the poor; he hath sent me to heal the broken-hearted, to preach deliverance to the captives, and recovering of sight to the blind, to set at liberty them that are bruised; Ver. 21. And he began to say unto them, *This day is this scripture fulfilled in your ears.*

^v Heb. v. 5. So also *Christ glorified not himself to be made an high priest;* but he that said unto him, Thou art my Son, to-day have I begotten thee. Ver. 6. As he saith also in another place, Thou *art a priest for ever, after the order of Melchisedec.* Ver. 7. Who in the days of his flesh, when he had offered up prayers and supplications, with strong crying and tears, unto him that

and king of his church,ʷ in the estate both of his humiliation and exaltation.

Q. 43. *How doth Christ execute the office of a prophet?*

A. Christ executeth the office of a prophet, in his revealing to the church,ˣ in all ages, by his Spirit and word,ʸ in divers ways of administration,ᶻ the whole will of God,ᵃ in all things concerning their edification and salvation.ᵇ

Q. 44. *How doth Christ execute the office of a priest?*

A. Christ executeth the office of a priest, in his once offering himself a sacrifice without spot to God,ᶜ to be a reconciliation for the sins of his people;ᵈ and in making continual intercession for them.ᵉ

Q. 45. *How doth Christ execute the office of a king?*

A. Christ executeth the office of a king, in calling out of the world

---

was able to save him from death, and was heard in that he feared. Heb. iv. 14. Seeing then that *we have a great high priest, that is passed into the heavens, Jesus the Son of God,* let us hold fast our profession. Ver. 15. For we have not an *high priest* which cannot be touched with the feeling of our infirmities; but was in all points tempted like as we are, yet without sin.

ʷ Ps. ii. 6. Yet *have I set my King upon my holy hill of Zion.* Matt. xxi. 5. Tell ye the daughter of Sion, *Behold, thy King cometh unto thee,* meek, and sitting upon an ass, and a colt the foal of an ass. Isa. ix. 6. For unto us a child is born, unto us a son is given; and *the government shall be upon his shoulder:* and his name shall be called Wonderful, Counsellor, The mighty God, The everlasting Father, *The Prince of Peace.* Ver. 7. *Of the increase of his government and peace there shall be no end, upon the throne of David, and upon his kingdom,* to order it, and to establish it with judgment and with justice from henceforth even for ever. The zeal of the Lord of hosts will perform this. Phil. ii. 8. And being found in fashion as a man, he humbled himself, and became obedient unto death, even the death of the cross. Ver. 9. Wherefore *God also hath highly exalted him,* and given him a name which is above every name: Ver. 10. That at the name of *Jesus* every knee should bow, of things in heaven, and things in earth, and things under the earth; Ver. 11. And that every tongue should confess that *Jesus Christ is Lord,* to the glory of God the Father.

43. ˣ John i. 18. No man hath seen God at any time; the only begotten Son, which is in the bosom of the Father, *he hath declared him.*

ʸ 1 Pet. i. 10. Of which salvation the prophets have enquired and searched diligently, who prophesied of the grace that should come unto you: Ver. 11. Searching what, or what manner of time, *the Spirit of Christ which was in them* did signify, when it *testified beforehand* the sufferings of Christ, and the glory that should follow. Ver. 12. *Unto whom it was revealed,* that not unto themselves, but unto us, they did minister the things which are now reported unto you by them that *have preached the gospel unto you with the Holy Ghost sent down from heaven;* which thing the angels desire to look into.

ᶻ Heb. i. 1. God, who *at sundry times, and in divers manners,* spake in time past unto the fathers by the prophets, Ver. 2. Hath in these last days spoken unto us by his Son, whom he hath appointed heir of all things, by whom also he made the worlds.

ᵃ John xv. 15. Henceforth I call you not servants; for the servant knoweth not what his lord doeth: but I have called you friends; for *all things that I have heard of my Father I have made known unto you.*

ᵇ Acts xx. 32. And now, brethren, I commend you to God, and to the *word of his grace, which is able to build you up, and to give you an inheritance among all them which are sanctified.* Eph. iv. 11. And he gave some, apostles; and some, prophets; and some, evangelists; and some, pastors and teachers; Ver. 12. *For the perfecting of the saints,* for the work of the ministry, *for the edifying of the body of Christ:* Ver. 13. *Till we all come* in the unity of the faith, and of the knowledge of the Son of God, *unto a perfect man,* unto the measure of the stature of the fulness of Christ. John xx. 31. But these are written, *that ye might believe that Jesus is the Christ,* the Son of God; and *that believing ye might have life through his name.*

44. ᶜ Heb. ix. 14. How much more shall the blood of Christ, who through the eternal Spirit *offered himself without spot to God,* purge your conscience from dead works, to serve the living God? Ver. 28. So *Christ was once offered* to bear the sins of many: and unto them that look for him shall he appear the second time, without sin unto salvation.

ᵈ Heb. ii. 17. Wherefore in all things it behoved him to be made like unto his brethren, that he might be a merciful and faithful high priest in things pertaining to God, *to make reconciliation for the sins of the people.*

ᵉ Heb. vii. 25. Wherefore he is able also to save them to the uttermost that come unto God by him, seeing *he ever liveth to make intercession for them.*

a people to himself,[f] and giving them officers,[g] laws,[h] and censures, by which he visibly governs them;[i] in bestowing saving grace upon his elect,[k] rewarding their obedience,[l] and correcting them for their sins,[m] preserving and supporting them under all their temptations and sufferings,[n] restraining and overcoming all their enemies,[o] and powerfully ordering all things for his own glory,[p] and their good;[q] and also in taking vengeance on the rest, who know not God, and obey not the gospel.[r]

Q. 46. *What was the estate of Christ's humiliation?*
A. The estate of Christ's humiliation was that low condition, wherein he for our sakes, emptying himself of his glory, took upon him the form of a servant, in his conception and birth, life, death, and after his death, until his resurrection.[s]

45. [f] Acts xv. 14. Simeon hath declared how God at the first *did visit the Gentiles, to take out of them a people for his name.* Ver. 15. And to this agree the words of the prophets; as it is written, Ver. 16. After this I will return, and will build again the tabernacle of David, which is fallen down; and I will build again the ruins thereof, and I will set it up. Isa. iv. 4. Behold, I have given him for a witness to the people, *a leader and commander to the people.* Ver. 5. Behold, *thou shalt call a nation that thou knowest not;* and *nations that knew not thee shall run unto thee*, because of the Lord thy God, and for the Holy One of Israel; for he hath glorified thee. Gen. xlix. 10. The *sceptre* shall not depart from Judah, nor *a lawgiver* from between his feet, until *Shiloh* come; and *unto him shall the gathering of the people be.* Ps. cx. 3. *Thy people shall be willing in the day of thy power,* in the beauties of holiness from the womb of the morning: thou hast the dew of thy youth.

[g] Eph. iv. 11. And he *gave some, apostles;* and some, *prophets;* and some, *evangelists;* and some, *pastors* and *teachers;* Ver. 12. For the perfecting of the saints, for the work of the ministry, for the edifying of the body of Christ. 1 Cor. xii. 28. And *God hath set some in the church,* first, *apostles;* secondarily, *prophets;* thirdly, *teachers;* after that *miracles;* then *gifts of healings, helps, governments,* diversities of tongues.

[h] Isa. xxxiii. 22. For *the Lord is our judge, the Lord is our lawgiver, the Lord is our king;* he will save us.

[i] Matt. xviii. 17. And if he shall neglect to hear them, *tell it unto the church;* but *if he neglect to hear the church, let him be unto thee as an heathen man and a publican.* Ver. 18. Verily I say unto you, *Whatsoever ye shall bind on earth shall be bound in heaven; and whatsoever ye shall loose on earth shall be loosed in heaven.* 1 Cor. v. 4. *In the name of our Lord Jesus Christ,* when ye are gathered together, and my spirit, *with the power of our Lord Jesus Christ,* Ver. 5. *To deliver such an one unto Satan* for the destruction of the flesh, that the spirit may be saved in the day of the Lord Jesus.

[k] Acts v. 31. Him hath God exalted with his right hand *to be a Prince and a Saviour, for to give repentance to Israel, and forgiveness of sins.*

[l] Rev. xxii. 12. And, behold, I come quickly; and *my reward is with me, to give every man according as his work shall be.* Rev. ii. 10. Fear none of those things which thou shalt suffer: behold, the devil shall cast some of you into prison, that ye may be tried; and ye shall have tribulation ten days: be thou faithful unto death, *and I will give thee a crown of life.*

[m] Rev. iii. 19. *As many as I love, I rebuke and chasten:* be zealous therefore, and repent.

[n] Isa. lxiii. 9. *In all their affliction* he was afflicted, and *the angel of his presence* saved them: in his love and in his pity *he redeemed them;* and he *bare them,* and *carried them* all the days of old.

[o] 1 Cor. xv. 25. For he *must reign,* till he *hath put all enemies under his feet.* Ps. cx. 1. The Lord said unto my Lord, Sit thou at my right hand, *until I make thine enemies thy footstool.* Ver. 2. The Lord shall send the rod of thy strength out of Sion: rule thou in the midst of thine enemies, etc. [See the Psalm throughout.]

[p] Rom. xiv. 10. But why dost thou judge thy brother? or why dost thou set at nought thy brother? for we shall all stand before the judgment-seat of Christ. Ver. 11. For it is written, As I live, saith the Lord, *every knee shall bow to me, and every tongue shall confess to God.*

[q] Rom. viii. 28. And we know that *all things work together for good* to them that love God, to them who are the called according to his purpose.

[r] 2 Thess. i. 8. In flaming fire, *taking vengeance on them that know not God, and that obey not the gospel of our Lord Jesus Christ:* Ver. 9. Who shall be *punished with everlasting destruction* from the presence of the Lord, and from the glory of his power. Ps. li. 8. Ask of me, and I shall give thee the heathen for thine inheritance, and the uttermost parts of the earth for thy possession. Ver. 9. *Thou shalt break them with a rod of iron; thou shalt dash them in pieces like a potter's vessel.*

46. [s] Phil. ii. 6. Who, being in the form of God, thought it not robbery to be equal with God; Ver. 7. But *made himself of no reputation, and took upon him the form of*

Q. 47. *How did Christ humble himself in his conception and birth?*

A. Christ humbled himself in his conception and birth, in that, being from all eternity the Son of God, in the bosom of the Father, he was pleased in the fulness of time to become the son of man, made of a woman of low estate, and to be born of her; with divers circumstances of more than ordinary abasement.[t]

Q. 48. *How did Christ humble himself in his life?*

A. Christ humbled himself in his life, by subjecting himself to the law,[v] which he perfectly fulfilled;[w] and by conflicting with the indignities of the world,[x] temptations of Satan,[y] and infirmities in his flesh, whether common to the nature of man, or particularly accompanying that his low condition.[z]

Q. 49. *How did Christ humble himself in his death?*

A. Christ humbled himself in his death, in that having been betrayed by Judas,[a] forsaken by his disciples,[b] scorned and rejected by the world,[c] condemned by Pilate, and tormented by his persecutors;[d] having also conflicted with the terrors of death, and the powers of

---

a servant, and was made *in the likeness of men:* Ver. 8. And being found in fashion as a man, *he humbled himself,* and became *obedient unto death, even the death of the cross.* Luke i. 31. And, behold, thou shalt *conceive* in thy womb, and *bring forth a son,* and shalt call his name JESUS. 2 Cor. viii. 9. For ye know the grace of our Lord Jesus Christ, that, though he was rich, yet *for your sakes he became poor,* that ye through his poverty might be rich. Acts ii. 24. Whom God hath raised up, *having loosed the pains of death:* because it was not possible that he should be holden of it.

47. t John i. 14. And the *Word was made flesh,* and dwelt among us, (and we beheld his glory, the glory *as of the only begotten of the Father,*) full of grace and truth. Ver. 18. No man hath seen God at any time; the only begotten Son, *which is in the bosom of the Father,* he hath declared him. Gal. iv. 4. But when the fulness of the time was come, *God sent forth his Son, made of a woman, made under the law.* Luke ii. 7. And *she brought forth her first-born son, and wrapped him in swaddling clothes, and laid him in a manger; because there was no room for them in the inn.*

48. v Gal. iv. 4. But when the fulness of the time was come, God sent forth *his Son, made of a woman, made under the law.*

w Matt. v. 17. Think not that *I am come to destroy the law* or the prophets : I am not come *to destroy, but to fulfil.* Rom. v. 19. For as by one man's disobedience many were made sinners ; so *by the obedience of one shall many be made righteous.*

x Ps. xxii. 6. But *I am a worm, and no man; a reproach of men, and despised of the people.* Heb. xii. 2. Looking unto Jesus, the author and finisher of our faith ; who, for the joy that was set before him, *endured the cross, despising the shame,* and is set down at the right hand of the throne of God. Ver. 3. For consider him *that endured such contradiction of sinners against himself,* lest ye be wearied and faint in your minds.

y Matt. iv. 1. to verse 12. Then was Jesus led up of the Spirit into the wilderness, to be *tempted of the devil,* etc. Luke iv. 13. And *when the devil had ended all the temptation,* he departed from him for a season.

z Heb. ii. 17. Wherefore *in all things it behoved him to be made like unto his brethren,* that he might be a merciful and faithful high priest in things pertaining to God, to make reconciliation for the sins of the people. Ver. 18. For in that he himself *hath suffered, being tempted,* he is able to succour them that are tempted. Heb. iv. 15. For *we have not an high priest which cannot be touched with the feeling of our infirmities; but was in all points tempted like as we are,* yet without sin. Isa. liii. 13. Behold, my servant shall deal prudently, he shall be exalted and extolled, and be very high. Ver. 14. As many were astonished at thee : (*his visage was so marred more than any man, and his form more than the sons of men.*)

49. a Matt. xxvii. 4. Saying, I have sinned, *in that I have betrayed the innocent blood.* And they said, What is that to us? see thou to that.

b Matt. xxvi. 56. But all this was done, that the scriptures of the prophets might be fulfilled. *Then all the disciples forsook him, and fled.*

c Isa. liii. 2. For he shall grow up before him as a tender plant, and as a root out of a dry ground : he *hath no form nor comeliness;* and when we shall see him, there is *no beauty that we should desire him.* Ver. 3. *He is despised and rejected of men;* a man of sorrows, and acquainted with grief; and we hid as it were our faces from him : *he was despised, and we esteemed him not.*

d Matt. xxvii. 26. to verse 50. Then released he Barabbas unto them : and *when he had scourged Jesus, he delivered him to be crucified,* etc. John xix. 34. but one of the soldiers *with a spear pierced his side,* and forthwith came thereout blood and water.

darkness, felt and borne the weight of God's wrath,ᵉ he laid down his life an offering for sin,ᶠ enduring the painful, shameful, and cursed death of the cross.ᵍ

Q. 50. *Wherein consisted Christ's humiliation after his death?*

A. Christ's humiliation after his death consisted in his being buried,ʰ and continuing in the state of the dead, and under the power of death till the third day;ⁱ which hath been otherwise expressed in these words, *He descended into hell.*

Q. 51. *What was the estate of Christ's exaltation?*

A. The estate of Christ's exaltation comprehendeth his resurrection,ᵏ ascension,ˡ sitting at the right hand of the Father,ᵐ and his coming again to judge the world.ⁿ

Q. 52. *How was Christ exalted in his resurrection?*

A. Christ was exalted in his resurrection, in that, not having seen corruption in death, (of which it was not possible for him to be held,ᵒ) and having the very same body in which he suffered, with the essential properties thereof,ᵖ (but without mortality, and other common infirmities belonging to this life,) really united to his soul,ᑫ he rose again from

---

ᵉ Luke xxii. 44. And, being in an *agony*, he prayed more earnestly: and *his sweat was as it were great drops of blood* falling down to the ground. Matt. xxvii. 46. And about the ninth hour Jesus cried with a loud voice, saying, *Eli, Eli, lama sabachthani?* that is to say, *My God, my God, why hast thou forsaken me?*
ᶠ Isa. liii. 10. Yet it pleased the Lord to bruise him; he hath put him to grief: *when thou shalt make his soul an offering for sin,* he shall see his seed, he shall prolong his days, and the pleasure of the Lord shall prosper in his hand.
ᵍ Phil. ii. 8. And being found in fashion as a man, he *humbled himself,* and *became obedient unto death, even the death of the cross.* Heb. xii. 2. Looking unto Jesus, the author and finisher of our faith; *who,* for the joy that was set before him, *endured the cross, despising the shame,* and is set down at the right hand of the throne of God. Gal. iii. 13. Christ hath redeemed us from the *curse* of the law, being *made a curse for us:* for it is written, *Cursed is every one that hangeth on a tree.*
50. ʰ 1 Cor. xv. 3. For I delivered unto you first of all that which I also received, how that Christ died for our sins according to the scriptures; Ver. 4. And *that he was buried,* and that he rose again the third day according to the scriptures.
ⁱ Ps. xvi. 10. For *thou wilt not leave my soul in hell;* neither wilt thou suffer thine Holy One *to see corruption.* Compared with Acts ii. 24. Whom God hath raised up, *having loosed the pains of death:* because it was not possible that he should be holden of it. Ver. 25. For David speaketh concerning him, I foresaw the Lord always before my face; for he is on my right hand, that I should not be moved: Ver. 26. Therefore did my heart rejoice, and my tongue was glad; moreover also, *my flesh shall rest in hope:* Ver. 27. Because thou wilt *not leave my soul in hell,* neither wilt thou suffer thine Holy One *to see corruption.*

Ver. 31. He, seeing this before, spake of the resurrection of Christ, *that his soul was not left in hell,* neither *his flesh did see corruption.* Rom. vi. 9. Knowing that *Christ, being raised from the dead, dieth no more;* death hath no more dominion over him. Matt. xii. 40. For as Jonas was three days and three nights in the whale's belly, *so shall the Son of man be three days and three nights in the heart of the earth.*
51. ᵏ 1 Cor. xv. 4. And that he was buried, and that he *rose again the third day* according to the scriptures.
ˡ Mark xvi. 19. So then, after the Lord had spoken unto them, *he was received up into heaven, and sat on the right hand of God.*
ᵐ Eph. i. 20. Which he wrought in Christ, when he raised him from the dead, and *set him at his own right hand in the heavenly places.*
ⁿ Acts i. 11. Which also said, Ye men of Galilee, why stand ye gazing up into heaven? this same Jesus, which is taken up from you into heaven, *shall so come in like manner as ye have seen him go into heaven.* Acts xvii. 31. Because he hath *appointed a day, in the which he will judge the world in righteousness by that man whom he hath ordained;* whereof he hath given assurance unto all men, in that he hath raised him from the dead.
52. ᵒ Acts ii. 24. Whom God hath raised up, having loosed the pains of death: because *it was not possible that he should be holden of it.* Ver. 27. Because thou wilt not leave my soul in hell, *neither wilt thou suffer thine Holy One to see corruption.*
ᵖ Luke xxiv. 39. *Behold my hands and my feet, that it is I myself: handle me, and see; for a spirit hath not flesh and bones, as ye see me have.*
ᑫ Rom. vi. 9. Knowing that Christ, being raised from the dead, *dieth no more; death hath no more dominion over him.* Rev. i. 18. I am *that liveth, and was dead;* and, behold, *I am alive for evermore,* Amen; and have the keys of hell and of death.

the dead the third day by his own power;[r] whereby he declared himself to be the Son of God,[s] to have satisfied divine justice,[t] to have vanquished death, and him that had the power of it,[v] and to be Lord of quick and dead:[w] all which he did as a publick person,[x] the head of his church,[y] for their justification,[z] quickening in grace,[a] support against enemies,[b] and to assure them of their resurrection from the dead at the last day.[c]

Q. 53. *How was Christ exalted in his ascension?*

A. Christ was exalted in his ascension, in that having after his resurrection often appeared unto and conversed with his apostles, speaking to them of the things pertaining to the kingdom of God,[d] and giving them commission to preach the gospel to all nations,[e] forty days after his resurrection, he, in our nature, and as our head,[f] triumphing over enemies,[g] visibly went up into the highest heavens, there to receive gifts for men,[h] to raise up our affections thither,[i] and to prepare a place

---

[r] John x. 18. No man taketh it from me, but I lay it down of myself. I have power to lay it down, and *I have power to take it again*. This commandment have I received of my Father.

[s] Rom. i. 4. And *declared to be the Son of God with power*, according to the Spirit of holiness, *by the resurrection from the dead.*

[t] Rom. viii. 34. *Who is he that condemneth? It is Christ that died, yea rather, that is risen again,* who is even at the right hand of God, who also maketh intercession for us.

[v] Heb. ii. 14. Forasmuch then as the children are partakers of flesh and blood, he also himself likewise took part of the same; that *through death he might destroy him that had the power of death, that is, the devil.*

[w] Rom. xiv. 9. For *to this end Christ both died, and rose, and revived, that he might be Lord both of the dead and living.*

[x] 1 Cor. xv. 21. For since *by man came death, by man came also the resurrection* of the dead. Ver. 22. For *as in Adam all die, even so in Christ* shall all be made alive.

[y] Eph. i. 20. Which he wrought in Christ, when he *raised him from the dead,* and set him at his own right hand in the heavenly places, Ver. 22. And hath put all things under his feet, and *gave him to be the head over all things to the church,* Ver. 23. Which is his body, the fulness of him that filleth all in all. Col. i. 18. And he is the *head of the body, the church;* who is the beginning, the *first-born from the dead;* that in all things he might have the pre-eminence.

[z] Rom. iv. 25. Who was delivered for our offences, and was *raised again for our justification.*

[a] Eph. ii. 1. And *you hath he quickened,* who were dead in trespasses and sins. Ver. 5. Even when we were dead in sins, *hath quickened us together with Christ;* (by grace ye are saved;) Ver. 6. And hath raised us up together, and made us sit together in heavenly places in Christ Jesus. Col. ii. 12. Buried with him in baptism, *wherein also ye are risen with him* through the faith of the operation of God, who hath raised him from the dead.

[b] 1 Cor. xv. 25. For he must reign, *till he hath put all enemies under his feet.* Ver. 26. The *last enemy* that shall be destroyed is *death.* Ver. 27. For he hath put *all things under his feet.* But when he saith, All things are put under him, it is manifest that he is excepted which did put all things under him.

[c] 1 Cor. xv. 20. But now is Christ risen from the dead, and become the *first-fruits of them that slept.*

53. [d] Acts i. 2. Until the day in which he was *taken up,* after that he through the Holy Ghost had given commandments unto the apostles whom he had chosen: Ver. 3. *To whom also he shewed himself alive* after his passion by many infallible proofs, *being seen of them forty days, and speaking of the things pertaining to the kingdom of God.*

[e] Matt. xxviii. 19. *Go ye therefore, and teach all nations, baptizing* them in the name of the Father, and of the Son, and of the Holy Ghost; Ver. 20. *Teaching them* to observe all things whatsoever I have commanded you: and, lo, I am with you alway, even unto the end of the world. Amen.

[f] Heb. vi. 20. *Whither the forerunner is for us entered,* even Jesus, made an high priest forever, after the order of Melchisedec.

[g] Eph. iv. 8. Wherefore he saith, *When he ascended up on high, he led captivity captive,* and gave gifts unto men.

[h] Acts i. 9. And when he had spoken these things, while they beheld, *he was taken up;* and a cloud received him out of their sight. Ver. 10. And, while they looked stedfastly toward heaven *as he went up,* behold, two men stood by them in white apparel; Ver. 11. Which also said, Ye men of Galilee, why stand ye gazing up into heaven? *this same Jesus, which is taken up from you into heaven,* shall so come in like manner as ye have seen him go into heaven. Eph. iv. 10. He that descended is the *same also that ascended up far above all heavens,* that he might fill all things. Ps. lxviii. 18. *Thou hast ascended on high,* thou hast led captivity captive; *thou hast received gifts for men;* yea, for the rebellious also, that the Lord God might dwell among them.

[i] Col. iii. 1. If *ye then be risen with*

for us,ᵏ where himself is, and shall continue till his second coming at the end of the world.¹

Q. 54 *How is Christ exalted in his sitting at the right hand of God?*

A. Christ is exalted in his sitting at the right hand of God, in that as God-man he is advanced to the highest favour with God the Father,ᵐ with all fulness of joy,ⁿ glory,ᵒ and power over all things in heaven and earth;ᵖ and doth gather and defend his church, and subdue their enemies; furnisheth his ministers and people with gifts and graces,ᑫ and maketh intercession for them.ʳ

Q. 55. *How doth Christ make intercession?*

A. Christ maketh intercession, by his appearing in our nature continually before the Father in heaven,ˢ in the merit of his obedience and sacrifice on earth,ᵗ declaring his will to have it applied to all believers;ᵛ answering all accusations against them,ʷ and procuring for them quiet of conscience, notwithstanding daily failings,ˣ access with

Christ, seek those things which are above, where Christ sitteth on the right hand of God. Ver. 2. Set your affection on *things above*, not on things on the earth.

k John xiv. 3. And *if I go and prepare a place for you*, I will come again, and receive you unto myself; *that where I am, there ye may be also*.

l Acts iii. 21. *Whom the heaven must receive until the times of restitution of all things*, which God hath spoken by the mouth of all his holy prophets since the world began.

54. m Phil. ii. 9. Wherefore God also hath *highly exalted him, and given him a name which is above every name*.

n Acts ii. 28. Thou hast made known to me the ways of life; *thou shalt make me full of joy with thy countenance*. Compared with Ps. xvi. 11. Thou wilt shew me the path of life: *in thy presence is fulness of joy*; at thy right hand there are *pleasures for evermore*.

o John xvii. 5. And now, O Father, glorify thou me with thine own self *with the glory which I had with thee before the world was*.

p Eph. i. 22. *And hath put all things under his feet*, and gave him to be *the head over all things* to the church. 1 Pet. iii. 22. Who is gone into heaven, and is on the right hand of God; *angels, and authorities, and powers, being made subject unto him*.

q Eph. iv. 10. He that *descended* is the same also that *ascended* up far above all heavens, that he might fill all things. Ver. 11. And he gave some, apostles; and some, prophets; and some, evangelists; and some, pastors and teachers; Ver. 12. For the *perfecting of the saints*, for the work of the ministry, *for the edifying of the body of Christ*. Ps. cx. 1. The LORD said unto my Lord, *Sit thou at my right hand*, until I make thine enemies thy footstool, etc. [See the Psalm throughout.]

r Rom. viii. 34. Who is he that condemneth? It is Christ that died, yea rather, that is risen again, who is even *at the right hand of God, who also maketh intercession for us*.

55. s Heb. ix. 12. Neither by the blood of goats and calves, but *by his own blood, he entered in once into the holy place*, having obtained eternal redemption for us. Ver. 24. For Christ is not entered into the holy places made with hands, which are the figures of the true; but into heaven itself, *now to appear in the presence of God for us*.

t Heb. i. 3. Who, being the brightness of his glory, and the express image of his person, and upholding all things by the word of his power, *when he had by himself purged our sins, sat down on the right hand of the Majesty on high*.

v John iii. 16. For God so loved the world, that he gave his only begotten Son, *that whosoever believeth in him should not perish, but have everlasting life*. John xvii. 9. *I pray for them:* I pray not for the world, but for them which thou hast given me; for they are thine. Ver. 20. Neither pray I *for these alone, but for them also which shall believe on me through their word*. Ver. 24. Father, *I will that they also whom thou hast given me be with me where I am; that they may behold my glory*, which thou hast given me: for thou lovedst me before the foundation of the world.

w Rom. viii. 33. *Who shall lay any thing to the charge of God's elect?* It is God that justifieth; Ver. 34. *Who is he that condemneth? It is Christ that died, yea rather, that is risen again*, who is even at the right hand of God, who also maketh intercession for us.

x Rom. v. 1. Therefore being justified by faith, *we have peace with God, through our Lord Jesus Christ:* Ver. 2. By whom also we have access by faith into this grace wherein we stand, and rejoice in hope of the glory of God. 1 John ii. 1. My little children, these things write I unto you, that ye sin not. And *if any man sin, we have an advocate with the Father, Jesus Christ the righteous*. Ver. 2. And he is the *propitiation for our sins;* and not for ours only, but also for the sins of the whole world.

boldness to the throne of grace,y and acceptance of their persons* and services.a

Q. 56. *How is Christ to be exalted in his coming again to judge the world?*

A. Christ is to be exalted in his coming again to judge the world, in that he, who was unjustly judged and condemned by wicked men,b shall come again at the last day in great power,c and in the full manifestation of his own glory, and of his Father's, with all his holy angels,d with a shout, with the voice of the archangel, and with the trumpet of God,e to judge the world in righteousness.f

Q. 57. *What benefits hath Christ procured by his mediation?*

A. Christ, by his mediation, hath procured redemption,g with all other benefits of the covenant of grace.h

Q. 58. *How do we come to be made partakers of the benefits which Christ hath procured?*

A. We are made partakers of the benefits which Christ hath procured, by the application of them unto us,i which is the work especially of God the Holy Ghost.k

Q. 59. *Who are made partakers of redemption through Christ?*

A. Redemption is certainly applied, and effectually communicated, to all those for whom Christ hath purchased it;l who are in time by the Holy Ghost enabled to believe in Christ according to the gospel.m

---

y Heb. iv. 16. Let us therefore come *boldly unto the throne of grace,* that we may obtain mercy, and find grace to help in time of need.

z Eph. i. 6. To the praise of the glory of his grace, wherein he hath *made us accepted in the Beloved.*

a 1 Pet. ii. 5. Ye also, as lively stones, are built up a spiritual house, an holy priesthood, *to offer up spiritual sacrifices, acceptable to God by Jesus Christ.*

56. b Acts iii. 14. But *ye denied the Holy One and the Just, and desired a murderer to be granted unto you;* Ver. 15. And *killed the Prince of life,* whom God hath raised from the dead ; whereof we are witnesses.

c Matt. xxiv. 30. And *then shall appear the sign of the Son of man in heaven;* and then shall all the tribes of the earth mourn, and *they shall see the Son of man coming in the clouds of heaven with power and great glory.*

d Luke ix. 26. For whosoever shall be ashamed of me, and of my words, of him shall the Son of man be ashamed, when *he shall come in his own glory, and in his Father's, and of the holy angels.* Matt. xxv. 31. When *the Son of man shall come in his glory, and all the holy angels with him,* then shall he sit upon the throne of his glory.

e 1 Thess. iv. 16. For *the Lord himself shall descend from heaven with a shout, with the voice of the archangel, and with the trump of God;* and the dead in Christ shall rise first.

f Acts xvii. 31. Because he hath appointed a day, in the which *he will judge the world in righteousness* by that man whom he hath ordained ; whereof he hath given assurance unto all men, in that he hath raised him from the dead.

57. g Heb. ix. 12. Neither by the blood of goats and calves, but by his own blood, he entered in once into the holy place, *having obtained eternal redemption for us.*

h 2 Cor. i. 20. For *all the promises of God in him are yea, and in him Amen,* unto the glory of God by us.

58. i John i. 11. He came unto his own, and his own received him not. Ver. 12. But *as many as received him, to them gave he power to become the sons of God,* even *to them that believe on his name.*

k Tit. iii. 5. Not by works of righteousness which we have done, but according to his mercy he saved us, *by the washing of regeneration, and renewing of the Holy Ghost;* Ver. 6. Which he shed on us abundantly through Jesus Christ our Saviour.

59. l Eph. i. 13. In whom ye also trusted, after that ye heard the word of truth, the gospel of your salvation : in whom also, after that ye believed, ye were sealed with that Holy Spirit of promise, Ver. 14. Which is the *earnest* of our inheritance, *until the redemption of the purchased possession,* unto the praise of his glory. John vi. 37. *All that the Father giveth me shall come to me:* and him that cometh to me *I will in no wise cast out.* Ver. 39. And this is the Father's will which hath sent me, that *of all which he hath given me I should lose nothing,* but should raise it up again at the last day. John x. 15. As the Father knoweth me, even so know I the Father : and *I lay down my life for the sheep.* Ver. 16. And other *sheep I have,* which are not of this fold : *them also I must bring, and they shall hear my voice;* and there shall be one fold, and one shepherd.

m Eph. ii. 8. For *by grace are ye saved,* through *faith;* and that *not of yourselves;* it is the *gift of God.* 2 Cor. iv. 13. We

Q. 60. *Can they who have never heard the gospel, and so know not Jesus Christ, nor believe in him, be saved by their living according to the light of nature?*

A. They who, having never heard the gospel,ⁿ know not Jesus Christ,^o and believe not in him, cannot be saved,^p be they never so diligent to frame their lives according to the light of nature,^q or the laws of that religion which they profess;^r neither is there salvation in any other, but in Christ alone,^s who is the Saviour only of his body the church.^t

Q. 61. *Are all they saved who hear the gospel, and live in the church?*

A. All that hear the gospel, and live in the visible church, are not saved; but they only who are true members of the church invisible.^v

Q. 62. *What is the visible church?*

A. The visible church is a society made up of all such as in all ages having the same spirit of faith, according as it is written, I believed, and therefore have I spoken ; *we also believe*, and therefore speak.

60. ⁿ Rom. x. 14. How then shall they call on him in whom they have not believed? and *how shall they believe in him of whom they have not heard?* and how shall they hear without a preacher?

^o 2 Thess. i. 8. *In flaming fire, taking vengeance on them that know not God*, and that obey not the gospel *of our Lord Jesus Christ:* Ver. 9. Who shall be punished with *everlasting destruction* from the presence of the Lord, and from the glory of his power. Eph. ii. 12. That at that time ye were *without Christ*, being *aliens from the commonwealth of Israel*, and *strangers from the covenants of promise*, having *no hope*, and without God in the world. John i. 10. He was in the world, and the world was made by him, and the *world knew him not*. Ver. 11. He came unto his own, and his own *received him not*. Ver. 12. But as many as received him, to them gave he power to become the sons of God, even to them that believe on his name.

^p John viii. 24. I said therefore unto you, that ye shall die in your sins : for *if ye believe not that I am he, ye shall die in your sins*. Mark xvi. 16. He that believeth, and is baptized, shall be saved ; but *he that believeth not shall be damned*.

^q 1 Cor. i. 20. Where is the *wise?* where is the *scribe?* where is the *disputer* of this world? hath not God made *foolish the wisdom of this world?* Ver. 21. For after that, in the wisdom of God, *the world by wisdom knew not God*, it pleased God by the foolishness of preaching to save them that believe. Ver. 22. For the *Jews* require a *sign*, and the *Greeks* seek after *wisdom:* Ver. 23. But we preach *Christ crucified*, unto the Jews a *stumblingblock*, and unto the Greeks *foolishness;* Ver. 24. But unto them which are called, both Jews and Greeks, *Christ* the *power* of God, and the *wisdom* of God.

^r John iv. 22. *Ye worship ye know not what;* we know what we worship : for *salvation is of the Jews.* Rom. ix. 31. But *Israel*, which *followed after the law of righteousness, hath not attained to the law of righteousness.* Ver. 32. Wherefore? Because they sought it not by faith, but as it were by the works of the law : for they stumbled at that stumbling-stone. Phil. iii. 4. Though I might also have confidence in the flesh. If any other man thinketh that he hath whereof he might trust in the flesh, I more : Ver. 5. Circumcised the eighth day, of the stock of Israel, of the tribe of Benjamin, an Hebrew of the Hebrews ; as touching the law, a Pharisee ; Ver. 6. Concerning zeal, persecuting the church ; *touching the righteousness which is in the law, blameless*. Ver. 7. But what things were *gain* to me, those *I counted loss for Christ*. Ver. 8. Yea doubtless, and I count *all things but loss* for the excellency of the *knowledge of Christ Jesus my Lord;* for whom I have suffered the loss of all things, and do count them but *dung*, that I may *win Christ*, Ver. 9. And be *found in him, not having mine own righteousness, which is of the law, but that which is through the faith of Christ*, the righteousness which is of God by faith.

^s Acts iv. 12. *Neither is there salvation in any other:* for there is *none other name under heaven given* among men *whereby we must be saved*.

^t Eph. v. 23. For the husband is the head of the wife, even as *Christ is the head of the church;* and he is *the saviour of the body*.

61. ^v John xii. 38. That the saying of Esaias the prophet might be fulfilled, which he spake, Lord, *who hath believed our report?* and to whom hath the arm of the Lord been revealed? Ver. 39. Therefore they *could not believe*, because that Esaias said again, Ver. 40. He hath *blinded their eyes*, and *hardened their heart; that they should not see with their eyes, nor understand with their heart, and be converted, and I should heal them*. Rom. ix. 6. Not as though the word of God hath taken none effect. For they are *not all Israel which are of Israel*. Matt. xxii. 14. For many are called, but few are chosen. Matt. vii. 21. *Not every one that saith unto me, Lord, Lord*, shall enter into the kingdom of heaven ; but he that doeth the will of my Father which is in heaven. Rom. xi. 7. What then? *Israel hath not obtained* that which he seeketh for ; *but the election hath obtained it,* and the rest were blinded.

and places of the world do profess the true religion,ʷ and of their children.ˣ

Q. 63. *What are the special privileges of the visible church?*

A. The visible church hath the privilege of being under God's special care and government;ʸ of being protected and preserved in all ages, notwithstanding the opposition of all enemies;ᶻ and of enjoying

---

62. ʷ 1 Cor. i. 2. Unto the *church of God which is at Corinth, to them that are sanctified in Christ Jesus, called to be saints,* with all that in every place *call upon the name of Jesus Christ our Lord,* both theirs and ours. 1 Cor. xii. 13. For by one Spirit *are we all baptized into one body,* whether we be Jews or Gentiles, whether we be bond or free; and have been *all made to drink into one Spirit.* Rom. xv. 9. And *that the Gentiles might glorify God for his mercy;* as it is written, For this cause *I will confess to thee among the Gentiles,* and sing unto thy name. Ver. 10. And again he saith, *Rejoice, ye Gentiles,* with his people. Ver. 11. And again, *Praise the Lord, all ye Gentiles;* and laud him, all ye people. Ver. 12. And again Esaias saith, There shall be a root of Jesse, and he that shall rise to reign over the Gentiles; *in him shall the Gentiles trust.* Rev. vii. 9. After this I beheld, and, lo, *a great multitude, which no man could number, of all nations,* and *kindreds,* and *people,* and *tongues,* stood before the throne, and before the Lamb, clothed with white robes, and palms in their hands. Ps. ii. 8. Ask of me, and I shall give thee *the heathen for thine inheritance,* and *the uttermost parts of the earth for thy possession.* Ps. xxii. 27. *All the ends of the world shall remember,* and *turn unto the Lord;* and *all the kindreds of the nations shall worship* before thee. Ver. 28. For the kingdom is the Lord's; and he is the *governor among the nations.* Ver. 29. All they that be *fat upon earth shall eat and worship:* all they that *go down to the dust shall bow before him;* and none can keep alive his own soul. Ver. 30. A seed shall serve him; it shall be *accounted to the Lord for a generation.* Ver. 31. They shall *come,* and shall *declare his righteousness* unto a people that shall be born, that he hath done this. Ps. xlv. 17. I will make thy name to be remembered *in all generations:* therefore *shall the people praise thee for ever and ever.* Matt. xxviii. 19. Go ye therefore, and *teach all nations, baptizing them* in the name of the Father, and of the Son, and of the Holy Ghost; Ver. 20. Teaching them to observe all things whatsoever I have commanded you: and, lo, *I am with you alway, even unto the end of the world.* Amen. Isa. lix. 21. As for me, this is my covenant with them, saith the Lord; My Spirit that is upon thee, and *my words* which I have put in thy mouth, shall *not depart out of thy mouth, nor out of the mouth of thy seed, nor out of the mouth of thy seed's seed,* saith the Lord, *from henceforth and for ever.*

ˣ 1 Cor. vii. 14. For the unbelieving husband is sanctified by the wife, and the unbelieving wife is sanctified by the husband: else were your children unclean; but *now are they holy.* Acts ii. 39. For the *promise* is unto you, *and to your children,* and to all that are afar off, even as many as the Lord our God shall call. Rom. xi. 16. For if the *first-fruit be holy, the lump is also holy;* and if the *root* be holy, so *are the branches.* Gen. xvii. 7. And I will establish my *covenant* between me and thee, and *thy seed after thee,* in their generations, for an everlasting covenant, to be a *God unto thee,* and to thy *seed after thee.*

63. ʸ Isa. iv. 5. And the Lord will create upon every dwelling-place of mount Zion, and upon her assemblies, a cloud and smoke by day, and the shining of a flaming fire by night: for *upon all the glory shall be a defence.* Ver. 6. And there shall be a *tabernacle for a shadow* in the day-time *from the heat,* and *for a place of refuge,* and *for a covert from storm* and *from rain.* 1 Tim. iv. 10. For therefore we both labour and suffer reproach, because we trust in the living God, *who is the Saviour of all men, specially of those that believe.*

ᶻ Ps. cxv. 1. Not unto us, O Lord, not unto us, but—Ver. 2. Wherefore should the heathen say, Where is now their God? &c. Ver. 9. O Israel, trust thou in the Lord; he is *their help and their shield,* &c. [See the Psalm throughout.] Isa. xxxi. 4. For thus hath the Lord spoken unto me, Like as the lion and the young lion roaring on his prey, when a multitude of shepherds is called forth against him, he will not be afraid of their voice, nor abase himself for the noise of them: so shall the Lord of hosts come down *to fight for mount Zion,* and *for the hill thereof.* Ver. 5. As birds flying, so will the Lord of hosts *defend Jerusalem;* defending also he *will deliver it;* and passing over he will *preserve it.* Zech. xii. 2. Behold, I will make *Jerusalem a cup of trembling unto all the people* round about, when they shall be in *the siege* both against Judah and against Jerusalem. Ver. 3. And in that day will I make *Jerusalem a burdensome stone* for all people: all that *burden themselves with it shall be cut in pieces, though all the people of the earth be gathered together against it.* Ver. 4. In that day, saith the Lord, I will *smite every horse* with astonishment, and his *rider with madness;* and I will open mine eyes upon the house of *Judah,* and will *smite every horse of the people with blindness.* Ver. 8. In that day shall the Lord *defend the inhabitants of Jerusalem;* and he that is *feeble* among them at that day shall be as *David;* and the house of *David* shall be *as God,* as *the angel* of the Lord before them. Ver. 9. And it shall come to pass in that day, that I will seek to *destroy all the nations that come against Jerusalem.*

the communion of saints, the ordinary means of salvation,[a] and offers of grace by Christ to all the members of it in the ministry of the gospel, testifying, that whosoever believes in him shall be saved,[b] and excluding none that will come unto him.[c]

Q. 64. *What is the invisible church?*

A. The invisible church is the whole number of the elect, that have been, are, or shall be gathered into one under Christ the head.[d]

Q. 65. *What special benefits do the members of the invisible church enjoy by Christ?*

A. The members of the invisible church by Christ enjoy union and communion with him in grace and glory.[e]

Q. 66. *What is that union which the elect have with Christ?*

A. The union which the elect have with Christ is the work of God's grace,[f] whereby they are spiritually and mystically, yet really and inseparably, joined to Christ as their head and husband;[g] which is done in their effectual calling.[h]

Q. 67. *What is effectual calling?*

A. Effectual calling is the work of God's almighty power and grace,[i] whereby (out of his free and special love to his elect, and from nothing

---

[a] Acts ii. 39. For the promise is unto you, and to your children, and to all that are afar off, even as many as the Lord our God shall call. Ver. 42. And they *continued* stedfastly in the apostles' *doctrine* and *fellowship*, and in *breaking of bread*, and in *prayers*.

[b] Ps. cxlvii. 19. He *sheweth* his *word* unto Jacob, his statutes and his *judgments* unto *Israel*. Ver. 20. He hath not dealt so with any nation : and as for his judgments, they have not known them. Praise ye the Lord. Rom. ix. 4. Who are Israelites ; *to whom pertaineth the adoption*, and the glory, and *the covenants*, and the giving of the law, and the service of God, and the *promises*. Eph. iv. 11. And *he gave* some, *apostles;* and some, *prophets;* and some, *evangelists;* and some, *pastors and teachers;* Ver. 12. For the *perfecting of the saints*, for the work of the ministry, for the *edifying of the body of Christ*. Mark xvi. 15. And he said unto them, *Go ye* unto all the world, and *preach the gospel* to every creature. Ver. 16. He that *believeth*, and *is baptized*, shall *be saved;* but he that believeth not shall be damned.

[c] John vi. 37. All that the Father giveth me shall come to me ; and *him that cometh to me I will in no wise cast out*.

[d] Eph. i. 10. That, in the dispensation of the fulness of times, he might *gather together in one all things in Christ*, both which are *in heaven*, and which are *on earth*, even in him. Ver. 22. And hath put all things under his feet, and gave *him* to be the *head over all things to the church*, Ver. 23. Which is his *body*, the fulness of him that filleth all in all. John x. 16. And *other sheep* I have, which are not of this fold : *them also I must bring*, and they shall *hear my voice;* and there shall be *one fold*, and *one shepherd*. John xi. 52. And not for that nation only, but that also he should *gather together in one the children of God that were scattered abroad*.

[e] John xvii. 21. That *they all may be one; as thou, Father, art in me, and I in thee, that they also may be one in us:* that the world may believe that thou hast sent me. Eph. ii. 5. Even when we were dead in sins, hath quickened us together with Christ ; (by grace ye are saved ;) Ver. 6. And hath *raised us up together*, and made *us sit together in heavenly places in Christ Jesus*. John xvii. 24. Father, I will that they also whom thou hast given me *be with me where* I am; *that they may behold my glory*, which thou hast given me : for thou lovedst me before the foundation of the world.

[f] Eph. i. 22. And hath put all things under his feet, and *gave him to be the head* over all things *to the church*. Eph. ii. 6. And hath raised us up together, and made us sit together in heavenly places in Christ Jesus ; Ver. 7. That in the ages to come he might shew the *exceeding riches of his grace*, in his kindness toward us through Christ Jesus. Ver. 8. For *by grace are ye saved*, through faith ; and that not of yourselves : *it is the gift of God*.

[g] 1 Cor. vi. 17. But *he that is joined unto the Lord* is one spirit. John x. 28. And I give unto them eternal life ; and *they shall never perish, neither shall any pluck them out of my hand*. Eph. v. 23. For *the husband is the head of the wife*, even as *Christ is the head of the church;* and he *is the saviour of the body*. Ver. 30. For *we are members of his body*, of *his flesh*, and of *his bones*.

[h] 1 Pet. v. 10. But the God of all grace, *who hath called us* unto his eternal glory by Christ Jesus, after that ye have suffered a while, make you perfect, stablish, strengthen, settle you. 1 Cor. i. 9. *God is* faithful, by *whom ye were called unto the fellowship of his Son Jesus Christ our Lord*.

[i] John v. 25. Verily, verily, I say unto you, The hour is coming, and now is,

in them moving him thereunto[k]) he doth, in his accepted time, invite and draw them to Jesus Christ, by his word and Spirit;[l] savingly enlightening their minds,[m] renewing and powerfully determining their wills,[n] so as they (although in themselves dead in sin) are hereby made willing and able freely to answer his call, and to accept and embrace the grace offered and conveyed therein.[o]

Q. 68. *Are the elect only effectually called?*

A. All the elect, and they only, are effectually called;[p] although others may be, and often are, outwardly called by the ministry of the word,[q] and have some common operations of the Spirit;[r] who, for their

when the dead shall hear the voice of the Son of God; and they that hear shall live. Eph. i. 18. The eyes of your understanding being enlightened; that ye may know what is the hope of his calling, and what the riches of the glory of his inheritance in the saints, Ver. 19. And what is *the exceeding greatness of his power* to us-ward who believe, *according to the working of his mighty power,* Ver. 20. Which he wrought in Christ, when he *raised* him from the *dead,* and set him at his own right hand in the heavenly places. 2 Tim. i. 8. Be not thou therefore ashamed of the testimony of our Lord, nor of me his prisoner: but be thou partaker of the afflictions of the gospel, *according to the power of God;* Ver. 9. Who hath saved us, and *called us* with an *holy calling,* not according to our works, *but according to his own purpose and grace,* which was *given us* in Christ Jesus before the world began.

[l] Tit. iii. 4. But after that the *kindness and love of God our Saviour* toward man appeared, Ver. 5. *Not by works of righteousness which we have done,* but *according to his mercy* he saved us, by the washing of regeneration, and renewing of the Holy Ghost. Eph. ii. 4. But God, who is rich in mercy, *for his great love wherewith he loved us,* Ver. 5. Even when we were dead in sins, hath quickened us together with Christ; *(by grace ye are saved.)* Ver. 7. That in the ages to come he might shew *the exceeding riches of his grace,* in his kindness toward us through Christ Jesus. Ver. 8. For *by grace are ye saved,* through faith; and that *not of yourselves:* it is the gift of God; Ver. 9. *Not of works,* lest any man should boast. Rom. ix. 11. For the children *being not yet born, neither having done any good or evil,* that the purpose of God according to election might stand, *not of works,* but of him that *calleth.*

[l] 2 Cor. v. 20. Now then we are *ambassadors for Christ,* as though God did beseech you by us: *we pray you in Christ's stead,* be ye reconciled to God. Compared with 2 Cor. vi. 1. *We then, as workers together with him, beseech you* also that ye receive not the grace of God in vain. Ver. 2. For he saith, *I have heard thee in a time accepted,* and in the day of salvation have I succoured thee: behold, *now is the accepted time;* behold, now is the day of salvation. John vi. 44. No man can come to me, *except the Father,* which hath sent me. *draw him:* nd I will raise him up at the last day. 2 Thess. ii. 13. But we are bound to give thanks alway to God for you, brethren, beloved of the Lord, because God hath from the beginning chosen you to salvation *through sanctification of the Spirit,* and *belief of the truth;* Ver. 14. *Whereunto he called you* by our *gospel,* to the obtaining of the glory of our Lord Jesus Christ.

[m] Acts xxvi. 18. To *open their eyes,* and to *turn them from darkness to light,* and from the power of Satan unto God, that they may receive forgiveness of sins, and inheritance among them which are sanctified by faith that is in me. 1 Cor. ii. 10. But God hath *revealed them unto us by his Spirit:* for the Spirit searcheth all things, yea, the deep things of God. Ver. 12. Now *we have received, not the spirit of the world,* but *the Spirit which is of God; that we might know* the things that are freely given to us of God.

[n] Ezek. xi. 19. I will give them one heart, and I will *put a new spirit within you;* and I will *take the stony heart* out of their flesh, and will give them an *heart of flesh.* Ezek. xxxvi. 26. *A new heart also will I give you,* and a *new spirit will I put within you;* and I will *take away the stony heart* out of your flesh, and I will *give you an heart of flesh.* Ver. 27. And I will *put my Spirit within you,* and *cause you to walk in my statutes,* and ye *shall keep my judgments,* and do them. John vi. 45. It is written in the prophets, And they shall be *all taught of God.* Every man therefore that hath *heard,* and hath *learned of the Father, cometh unto me.*

[o] Eph. ii. 5. Even *when we were dead in sins,* hath *quickened* us together with Christ; (by grace ye are saved.) Phil. ii. 13. For it is God which *worketh* in you, both *to will and to do* of his good pleasure. Deut. xxx. 6. And *the Lord thy God will circumcise thine heart,* and the heart of thy seed, *to love the Lord thy God with all thine heart,* and with all thy soul, that thou mayest live.

68. [p] Acts xiii. 48. And when the Gentiles heard this, they were glad, and glorified the word of the Lord: and *as many as were ordained to eternal life believed.*

[q] Matt. xxii. 14. For many are *called,* but *few are chosen.*

[r] Matt. vii. 22. Many will say to me in that day, Lord, have we not *prophesied in thy name?* and in thy name have *cast out devils?* and in thy name done *many wonderful works?* Matt. xiii. 20. But he that receiveth the seed into stony places, the same is he that *heareth the word.*

wilful neglect and contempt of the grace offered to them, being justly left in their unbelief, do never truly come to Jesus Christ.^s

Q. 69. *What is the communion in grace which the members of the invisible church have with Christ?*

A. The communion in grace which the members of the invisible church have with Christ, is their partaking of the virtue of his mediation, in their justification,^t adoption,^v sanctification, and whatever else, in this life, manifests their union with him.^w

Q. 70. *What is justification?*

A. Justification is an act of God's free grace unto sinners,^x in which he pardoneth all their sins, accepteth and accounteth their persons righteous in his sight;^y not for any thing wrought in them, or done by them,^z but only for the perfect obedience and full satis-

---

and anon *with joy receiveth* it: Ver. 21. Yet *hath he not root in himself,* but dureth for a while; for when tribulation or persecution ariseth because of the word, by and by he is offended. Heb. vi. 4. For it is impossible for those who were *once enlightened,* and have *tasted of the heavenly gift,* and were *made partakers of the Holy Ghost,* Ver. 5. And have *tasted the good word of God,* and *the powers of the world to come,* *Ver. 6. If they shall fall away, to renew them again unto repentance.

^s John xii. 38. That the saying of Esaias the prophet might be fulfilled, which he spake, Lord, *who hath believed our report?* and to whom hath the arm of the Lord been revealed? Ver. 39. Therefore they *could not believe,* because that Esaias said again, Ver. 40. He hath *blinded their eyes,* and *hardened their heart;* that they *should not see with their eyes, nor understand* with their *heart,* and be *converted,* and I should *heal* them. Acts xxviii. 25. And when they agreed not among themselves, they departed, after that Paul had spoken one word, Well spake the Holy Ghost by Esaias the prophet unto our fathers, Ver. 26. Saying, Go unto this people, and say, Hearing ye shall hear, and *shall not understand;* and seeing ye shall see, and *not perceive:* Ver. 27. For the *heart* of this people is *waxed gross,* and their *ears* are *dull of hearing,* and their eyes have they *closed: lest* they should *see* with their eyes, and *hear* with their *ears,* and *understand* with their *heart,* and should be *converted,* and I should *heal them.* John vi. 64. But there are some of you that *believe not.* For Jesus *knew* from the beginning *who they were that believed not,* and who should betray him. Ver. 65. And he said, Therefore said I unto you, that *no man can come* unto me, except it were *given unto him* of my Father. Ps. lxxxi. 11. But my people *would not hearken* to my voice; and Israel *would none of me.* Ver. 12. *So I gave them up unto their own hearts' lust:* and they walked in their own counsels.

69. ^t Rom. viii. 30. Moreover, whom he did predestinate, them he also called; and whom he called, *them he also justified;* and whom he justified, them he also glorified.

^v **Eph. i. 5.** Having predestinated us unto the adoption of children by Jesus Christ to himself, according to the good pleasure of his will.

^w 1 Cor. i. 30. But of him are ye in Christ Jesus, who of God is made unto us *wisdom,* and *righteousness,* and *sanctification,* and *redemption.*

70. ^x Rom. iii. 22. Even the righteousness of God which is by faith of Jesus Christ unto all and upon *all them that believe;* for there is no *difference:* Ver. 24. Being *justified freely by his grace,* through the redemption that is in Christ Jesus; Ver. 25. Whom God hath set forth to be a propitiation through faith in his blood, to declare his righteousness for the remission of sins that are past, through the forbearance of God. Rom. iv. 5. But to him that worketh not, but believeth on him that *justifieth the ungodly,* his faith is counted for righteousness.

^y 2 Cor. v. 19. To wit, that God was in Christ, reconciling the world unto himself, *not imputing their trespasses unto them:* and hath committed unto us the word of reconciliation. Ver. 21. For he hath made him to be sin for us, who knew no sin; *that we might be made the righteousness of God in him.* Rom. iii. 22. Even *the righteousness of God which is by faith of Jesus Christ unto all and upon all* them that believe; for there is no difference. Ver. 24. Being justified freely by his grace, through the redemption that is in Christ Jesus; Ver. 25. Whom God hath set forth to be a propitiation through faith in his blood, to declare his *righteousness for the remission of sins* that are past, through the forbearance of God. Ver. 27. Where is boasting then? It is excluded. By what law? of works? Nay; but by the law of faith. Ver. 28. Therefore we conclude, that a man is justified by faith *without* the deeds of the law.

^z Tit. iii. 5. *Not by works of righteousness which we have done,* but according to his mercy he saved us, by the washing of regeneration, and renewing of the Holy Ghost. *Ver. 7. That, being justified by his grace, we should be made heirs according to the hope of eternal life. Eph. i. 7. In whom we have redemption through his blood, the *forgiveness of sins, according to the riches of his grace.*

faction of Christ, by God imputed to them,[a] and received by faith alone.[b]

Q. 71. *How is justification an act of God's free grace?*

A. Although Christ, by his obedience and death, did make a proper, real, and full satisfaction to God's justice in the behalf of them that are justified;[c] yet in as much as God accepteth the satisfaction from a surety, which he might have demanded of them, and did provide this surety, his own only Son,[d] imputing his righteousness to them,[e] and requiring nothing of them for their justification but faith,[f] which also is his gift,[g] their justification is to them of free grace.[h]

---

[a] *Rom. v. 17. For if by one man's offence death reigned by one; much more they which receive *abundance of grace*, and *of the gift of righteousness*, shall reign in life by one, Jesus Christ. Ver. 18. Therefore, as by the offence of one judgment came upon all men to condemnation; even so *by the righteousness of one the free gift came upon all men unto justification of life*. Ver. 19. For *as by one man's disobedience many were made sinners; so by the obedience of one shall many be made righteous*. Rom. iv. 6. Even as David also describeth the blessedness of the man *unto whom God imputeth righteousness without works*, Ver. 7. Saying, Blessed are they whose iniquities are forgiven, and whose sins are covered. Ver. 8. Blessed is the man to whom the Lord will not impute sin.

[b] Acts x. 43. To him give all the prophets witness, that, through his name, *whosoever believeth in him shall receive remission of sins*. Gal. ii. 16. Knowing that a man is not justified by the works of the law, but *by the faith of Jesus Christ*, even we have believed in Jesus Christ, that we might be *justified by the faith of Christ*, and not by the works of the law: for by the works of the law shall no flesh be justified. Phil. iii. 9. And be found in him, not having mine own righteousness, which is of the law, but *that which is through the faith of Christ, the righteousness which is of God by faith.*

71. [c] Rom v. 8. But God commendeth his love toward us, in that, while we were yet sinners, *Christ died for us*. Ver. 9. Much more then, being now *justified by his blood*, we shall be saved from wrath through him. Ver. 10. For if, when we were enemies, we were *reconciled to God by the death of his Son;* much more, being reconciled, we shall be saved by his life. Ver. 19. For as by one man's disobedience many were made sinners; so *by the obedience of one shall many be made righteous.*

[d] 1 Tim. ii. 5. For there is one God, and one mediator between God and men, the man Christ Jesus; Ver. 6. Who *gave himself a ransom* for all, to be testified in due time. Heb. x. 10. By the which will we are sanctified, *through the offering of the body of Jesus Christ* once for all. Matt. xx. 28. Even as the Son of man came not to be ministered unto, but to minister, and *to give his life a ransom for many*. Dan. ix. 24. Seventy weeks are determined upon thy people, and upon thy holy city, to finish the transgression, and to make an end of sins, and *to make reconciliation for iniquity*, and *to bring in everlasting righteousness*, and to seal up the vision and prophecy, and to anoint the most Holy. Ver. 26. And after threescore and two weeks shall *Messiah be cut off, but not for himself:* and the people of the prince that shall come shall destroy the city and the sanctuary; and the end thereof shall be with a flood, and unto the end of the war desolations are determined. Isa liii. 4. Surely *he hath borne our griefs, and carried our sorrows:* yet we did esteem him stricken, smitten of God, and afflicted. Ver. 5. But he was *wounded for our transgressions*, he was *bruised for our iniquities:* the chastisement *of our peace was upon him; and with his stripes we are healed*. Ver. 6. All we, like sheep, have gone astray; we have turned every one to his own way; and the Lord hath *laid on him the iniquity of us all*. Ver. 10. Yet it pleased the Lord to bruise him; he hath put him to grief: when thou shalt make *his soul an offering for sin*, he shall see his seed, he shall prolong his days, and the pleasure of the Lord shall prosper in his hand. Ver. 11. He shall see of the *travail of his soul*, and shall be satisfied: by his knowledge shall my righteous servant justify many; *for he shall bear their iniquities*. Ver. 12. Therefore will I divide him a portion with the great, and he shall divide the spoil with the strong; because he hath *poured out his soul unto death:* and he was numbered with the transgressors; and *he bare the sin of many*, and made intercession for the transgressors. Heb. vii. 22. By so much was *Jesus made a surety* of a better testament. Rom. viii. 32. He *that spared not his own Son, but delivered him up for us all*, how shall he not with him also freely give us all things? 1 Pet. i. 18. Forasmuch as ye know that ye were not redeemed with corruptible things, as silver and gold, from your vain conversation received by tradition from your fathers; Ver. 19. *But with the precious blood of Christ*, as of a lamb without blemish and without spot.

[e] 2 Cor. v. 21. For *he hath made him to be sin for us*, who knew no sin; *that we might be made the righteousness of God in him.*

[f] Rom. iii. 24. Being *justified freely* by his grace, through the redemption that is in Christ Jesus; Ver. 25. Whom God hath set forth to be *a propitiation through faith*

Q. 72. *What is justifying faith?*

A. Justifying faith is a saving grace,[i] wrought in the heart of a sinner by the Spirit[k] and word of God,[l] whereby he, being convinced of his sin and misery, and of the disability in himself and all other creatures to recover him out of his lost condition,[m] not only assenteth to the truth of the promise of the gospel,[n] but receiveth and resteth upon Christ and his righteousness, therein held forth, for pardon of sin,[o] and for the accepting and accounting of his person righteous in the sight of God for salvation.[p]

Q. 73. *How doth faith justify a sinner in the sight of God?*

A. Faith justifies a sinner in the sight of God, not because of those other graces which do always accompany it, or of good works that are the fruits of it,[q] nor as if the grace of faith, or any act thereof, were imputed to him for his justification;[r] but only as it is an instrument by which he receiveth and applieth Christ and his righteousness.[s]

Q. 74. *What is adoption?*

in his blood, to declare his righteousness *for the remission of sins* that are past, through the forbearance of God.

g Eph. ii. 8. For by grace are ye saved, *through faith;* and that not of yourselves: it is the *gift of God.*

h Eph. i. 7. In whom we have *redemption* through his blood, *the forgiveness of sins, according to the riches of his grace.*

72. i Heb. x. 39. But we are not of them who draw back unto perdition; but of them *that believe to the saving of the soul.*

k 2 Cor. iv. 13. We *having the same spirit of faith,* according as it is written, I believed, and therefore have I spoken; we also believe, and therefore speak. Eph. i. 17. That the God of our Lord Jesus Christ, the Father of glory, may *give unto you the spirit of wisdom and revelation* in the knowledge of him: Ver. 18. The *eyes of your understanding being enlightened;* that ye may know what is the hope of his calling, and what the riches of the glory of his inheritance in the saints, Ver. 19. And what is the exceeding greatness of his power to us-ward *who believe, according to the working of his mighty power.*

l Rom. x. 14. How then shall they call on him in whom they have not believed? and *how shall they believe in him of whom they have not heard?* and how shall they hear without a preacher? *Ver. 17. So then faith cometh by *hearing,* and *hearing by the word of God.*

m Acts ii. 37. Now *when they heard this, they were pricked in their heart,* and said unto Peter, and to the rest of the apostles, *Men and brethren, what shall we do?* Acts xvi. 30. And brought them out, and said, Sirs, *what must I do to be saved?* John xvi. 8. And when he is come, he will *reprove the world of sin,* and of righteousness, and of judgment: Ver. 9. Of *sin,* because they believe not on me. Rom. v. 6. For *when we were yet without strength,* in due time Christ died for the ungodly. Eph. ii. 1. And you hath he quickened, *who were dead in trespasses and sins.* Acts iv. 12. *Neither is there salvation in any other:* for there is *none other name under heaven* given among men *whereby we must be saved.*

n Eph. i. 13. *In whom ye also trusted, after that ye heard the word of truth,* the gospel of your salvation: in whom also, after that ye believed, ye were sealed with that Holy Spirit of promise.

o John i. 12. But *as many as received him,* to them gave he power to become the sons of God, even to them that *believe on his name.* Acts xvi. 31. And they said, *Believe on the Lord Jesus Christ,* and thou shalt be saved, and thy house. Acts x. 43. To him give all the prophets witness, that, through his name, *whosoever believeth in him shall receive remission of sins.*

p Phil. iii. 9. And *be found in him, not having mine own righteousness,* which is of the law, but that which is through the faith of Christ, *the righteousness which is of God by faith.* Acts xv. 11. *But we believe* that, through the grace of the Lord Jesus Christ, *we shall be saved,* even as they.

73. q Gal. iii. 11. But that *no man is justified by the law in the sight of God,* it is evident: for, The just shall live by faith. Rom. iii. 28. Therefore we conclude, that a man *is justified* by faith *without the deeds of the law.*

r Rom. iv. 5. But to him that worketh not, but believeth on him that justifieth the ungodly, *his faith is counted for righteousness.* Compared with Rom. x. 10. For with the heart man *believeth unto righteousness;* and with the mouth *confession is made unto salvation.*

s John i. 12. But as many as *received him,* to them gave he power to become the sons of God, even *to them that believe on his name.* Phil. iii. 9. And be found in him, not having mine own righteousness, which is of the law, but *that* which is through the faith of Christ, *the righteousness which is of God by faith.* Gal. ii. 16. Knowing that a man is not justified by the works of the law, *but by the faith of Jesus Christ,* even we have believed in Jesus Christ, that *we might be justified by the faith of Christ,* and not by the works of the law: for by the works of the law shall no flesh be justified.

A. Adoption is an act of the free grace of God,[t] in and for his only Son Jesus Christ,[v] whereby all those that are justified are received into the number of his children,[w] have his name put upon them,[x] the Spirit of his Son given to them,[y] are under his fatherly care and dispensations,[z] admitted to all the liberties and privileges of the sons of God, made heirs of all the promises, and fellow-heirs with Christ in glory.[a]

Q. 75. *What is sanctification?*

A. Sanctification is a work of God's grace, whereby they whom God hath, before the foundation of the world, chosen to be holy, are in time, through the powerful operation of his Spirit[b] applying the death and resurrection of Christ unto them,[c] renewed in their whole man after the image of God;[d] having the seeds of repentance unto life, and all other saving graces, put into their hearts,[e] and those graces so stirred up, increased, and strengthened,[f] as that they more and more die unto sin, and rise unto newness of life.[g]

74. t 1 John iii. 1. Behold *what manner of love the Father hath bestowed upon us, that we should be called the sons of God!*
v Eph. i. 5. Having predestinated us *unto the adoption of children by Jesus Christ* to himself, according to the good pleasure of his will. Gal. iv. 4. But when the fulness of the time was come, *God sent forth his Son*, made of a woman, made under the law, Ver. 5. To redeem them that were under the law, *that we might receive the adoption of sons.*
w John i. 12. But as many as received him, *to them gave he power to become the sons of God*, even to them that believe on his name.
a 2 Cor. vi. 18. And will be a *Father* unto you, *and ye shall be my sons and daughters*, saith the Lord Almighty. Rev. iii. 12. Him that overcometh will I make a pillar in the temple of my God, and he shall go no more out: and *I will write upon him the name of my God*, and the name of the city of my God, which is new Jerusalem, which cometh down out of heaven from my God; and *I will write upon him my new name.*
y Gal. iv. 6. And because ye are sons, *God hath sent forth the Spirit of his Son into your hearts*, crying, Abba, Father.
z Ps. ciii. 13. Like *as a father pitieth his children, so the Lord pitieth them that fear him.* Prov. xiv. 26. In the fear of the Lord is strong confidence; and *his children shall have a place of refuge.* Matt. vi. 32. For your heavenly Father knoweth that ye have need *of all these things.*
a Heb. vi. 12. That ye be not slothful, but followers of them *who through faith and patience inherit the promises.* Rom. viii. 17. And *if children, then heirs; heirs of God, and joint heirs with Christ;* if so be that we suffer with him, that we may be also glorified together.
75. b Eph. i. 4. According as he hath *chosen us in him before the foundation of the world, that we should be holy* and without blame before him in love. 1 Cor. i. 11. And such were some of you; but ye are washed, but ye are *sanctified,* but ye are justified in the name of the Lord Jesus, and by the *Spirit of our God.* 2 Thess. ii. 13. But we are bound to give thanks alway to God for you, brethren, beloved of the Lord, because God hath from the beginning *chosen you* to salvation through *sanctification of the Spirit,* and belief of the truth.
c Rom. vi. 4. Therefore we are *buried with him by baptism into death;* that like *as Christ was raised up from the dead* by the glory of the Father, even *so we also* should walk in newness of life. Ver. 5. For if we have been *planted* together *in the likeness of his death,* we shall be also in the *likeness of his resurrection:* Ver. 6. Knowing this, that our *old man is crucified with him,* that the body of sin might be destroyed, that henceforth we should not serve sin.
d Eph. iv. 23. And be *renewed in the spirit of your mind;* Ver. 24. And that ye *put on the new man, which after God is created in righteousness and true holiness.*
e Acts xi. 18. When they heard these things, they held their peace, and glorified God, saying, Then hath *God also to the Gentiles granted repentance unto life.* 1 John iii. 9. Whosoever is born of God doth not commit sin; for *his seed remaineth in him;* and he cannot sin, because he is born of God.
f Jude, ver. 20. But ye, beloved, *building up yourselves on your most holy faith,* praying in the Holy Ghost. Heb. vi. 11. And we desire that every one of you do shew the *same diligence, to the full assurance of hope* unto the end: Ver. 12. That ye *be not slothful,* but *followers of them* who through faith and patience inherit the promises. Eph. iii. 16. That he would grant you, according to the riches of his glory, *to be strengthened with might by his Spirit in the inner man;* Ver. 17. That Christ may dwell in your hearts by faith; that ye, *being rooted and grounded in love,* Ver. 18. May be able to comprehend with all saints what is the breadth, and length, and depth, and height; Ver. 19. And to know the love of Christ, which passeth knowledge, that ye might be *filled with all the fulness of God.* Col. i. 10. That ye might walk worthy of the Lord unto all pleasing, *being fruitful in every good work, and increasing in the*

THE LARGER CATECHISM. 133

Q 76. *What is repentance unto life?*

A. Repentance unto life is a saving grace,[h] wrought in the heart of a sinner by the Spirit[i] and word of God,[k] whereby, out of the sight and sense, not only of the danger,[l] but also of the filthiness and odiousness of his sins,[m] and upon the apprehension of God's mercy in Christ to such as are penitent,[n] he so grieves for[o] and hates his sins,[p] as that he turns from them all to God,[q] purposing and endeavouring constantly to walk with him in all the ways of new obedience.[r]

knowledge of God; Ver. 11. *Strengthened with all might,* according to his glorious power, unto all patience and long-suffering with joyfulness.

g Rom. vi. 4. Therefore we are *buried with him by baptism into death;* that like as Christ was raised up from the dead by the glory of the Father, even *so we also should walk in newness of life.* Ver. 6. Knowing this, that our *old man is crucified with him,* that the *body of sin might be destroyed,* that *henceforth we should not serve sin.* Ver. 14. For *sin shall not have dominion over you:* for ye are not under the law, but under grace. Gal. v. 24. And they that are Christ's have *crucified the flesh, with the affections and lusts.*

76. h 2 Tim. ii. 25. In meekness instructing those that oppose themselves; if God peradventure will *give them repentance* to the acknowledging of the truth.

i Zech. xii. 10. And I will pour upon the house of David, and upon the inhabitants of Jerusalem, the *spirit of grace* and of supplications; and they shall look upon me whom they have pierced, and they shall *mourn for him, as one mourneth for his only son,* and shall *be in bitterness for him,* as one that is in bitterness for his first-born.

k Acts xi. 18. *When they heard these things,* they held their peace, and glorified God, saying, Then hath God also to the Gentiles *granted repentance unto life.* Ver. 20. And some of them were men of Cyprus and Cyrene, which, when they were come to Antioch, spake unto the Grecians, *preaching the Lord Jesus.* Ver. 21. And the hand of the Lord was with them: and a great number *believed, and turned unto the Lord.*

l Ezek. xviii. 28. Because he considereth, *and turneth away* from all his transgressions that he hath committed, he shall surely live, *he shall not die.* Ver. 30. Therefore I will judge you, O house of Israel, every one according to his ways, saith the Lord God. *Repent, and turn* yourselves from all your transgressions; *so iniquity shall not be your ruin.* Ver. 32. For I have no pleasure in the death of him that dieth, saith the Lord God: *wherefore turn yourselves, and live ye.* Luke xv. 17. *And when he came to himself, he said,* How many hired servants of my father's have bread enough, and to spare, and *I perish with hunger!* Ver. 18. I will arise, and go to my Father, and will say unto him, Father, I have sinned against heaven, and before thee. Hos. ii. 6. Therefore, behold, I will *hedge up thy way with thorns,* and make a wall, that she shall not find her paths. Ver. 7. And she shall follow after her lovers, but she shall not overtake them; and she shall seek them, but shall not find them: then shall she say, *I will go and return to my first husband; for then was it better with me than now.*

m Ezek. xxxvi. 31. Then shall ye remember your own *evil ways,* and your doings that were not good, and shall *loathe yourselves in your own sight, for your iniquities,* and for *your abominations.* Isa. xxx. 22. Ye shall *defile* also the covering of thy graven images of silver, and the ornament of thy molten images of gold: thou shalt *cast them away as a menstruous cloth;* thou shalt *say unto it, Get thee hence.*

n Joel ii. 12. Therefore also now, saith the Lord, *Turn ye even to me* with all your heart, and with fasting, and with weeping, and with mourning; Ver. 13. And rend your heart, and not your garments, and *turn unto the Lord your God: for he is gracious and merciful, slow to anger, and of great kindness,* and repenteth him of the evil.

o Jer. xxxi. 18. I have surely heard *Ephraim bemoaning himself thus;* Thou hast chastised me, and I was chastised, as a bullock unaccustomed to the yoke: turn thou me, and I shall be turned; for thou art the Lord my God. Ver. 19. Surely *after that I was turned, I repented;* and after that I was instructed, *I smote upon my thigh: I was ashamed, yea, even confounded,* because I did bear the reproach of my youth.

p 2 Cor. vii. 11. For, behold, this selfsame thing, *that ye sorrowed after a godly sort,* what carefulness it wrought in you, yea, what clearing of yourselves, yea, what indignation, yea, what fear, yea, what vehement desire, yea, what zeal, yea, what revenge! In all things ye have approved yourselves to be clear in this matter.

q Acts xxvi. 18. To open their eyes, and to *turn them from darkness to light, and from the power of Satan unto God,* that they may receive forgiveness of sins, and inheritance among them which are sanctified by faith that is in me. Ezek. xiv. 6. Therefore say unto the house of Israel, Thus saith the Lord God, *Repent, and turn yourselves from your idols; and turn away your faces from all your abominations.* 1 Kings viii. 47. Yet if they shall bethink themselves in the land whither they were carried captives, and *repent,* and make supplication unto thee in the land of them that carried them captives, saying, We have sinned, and have done perversely, we have committed wickedness; Ver. 48. And *so return unto thee with all their heart, and with all their soul.*

r Ps. cxix. 6. Then shall I not be ashamed, *when I have respect unto all thy com-*

Q. 77. *Wherein do justification and sanctification differ?*

A. Although sanctification be inseparably joined with justification,[s] yet they differ, in that God in justification imputeth the righteousness of Christ;[t] in sanctification his Spirit infuseth grace, and enableth to the exercise thereof;[v] in the former, sin is pardoned;[w] in the other, it is subdued;[x] the one doth equally free all believers from the revenging wrath of God, and that perfectly in this life, that they never fall into condemnation;[y] the other is neither equal in all,[z] nor in this life perfect in any,[a] but growing up to perfection.[b]

Q. 78. *Whence ariseth the imperfection of sanctification in believers?*

A. The imperfection of sanctification in believers ariseth from the remnants of sin abiding in every part of them, and the perpetual lustings of the flesh against the spirit; whereby they are often foiled with temptations, and fall into many sins,[c] are hindered in all their spiritual

mandments. Ver. 59. I thought on my ways, and *turned my feet unto thy testimonies.* Ver. 128. Therefore I esteem *all thy precepts* concerning all things to be right; and I hate *every false way.* Luke i. 6. And they were both righteous before God, walking *in all the commandments and ordinances of the Lord blameless.* 2 Kings xxiii. 25. And like unto him was there no king before him, that *turned to the Lord with all his heart, and with all his soul, and with all his might, according to all the law of Moses;* neither after him arose there any like him.

77. s 1 Cor. vi. 11. And such were some of you: but ye are washed, but *ye are sanctified,* but *ye are justified* in the name of the Lord Jesus, and by the Spirit of our God. 1 Cor. i. 30. But of him are ye in Christ Jesus, who of God is made unto us *wisdom,* and *righteousness,* and *sanctification,* and *redemption.*

t Rom. iv. 6. Even as David also describeth the blessedness of the man *unto whom God imputeth righteousness without works.* Ver. 8. Blessed is the man to whom the Lord *will not impute sin.*

v Ezek. xxxvi. 27. And I will *put my Spirit within you, and cause you to walk in my statutes, and ye shall keep my judgments, and do them.*

w Rom. iii. 24. Being *justified freely by his grace,* through the redemption that is in Christ Jesus; Ver. 25. Whom God hath set forth to be a propitiation through faith in his blood, to declare *his righteousness for the remission of sins that are past,* through the forbearance of God.

x Rom. vi. 6. Knowing this, that *our old man is crucified with him,* that the *body of sin might be destroyed,* that henceforth we *should not serve sin.* Ver. 14. For *sin shall not have dominion over you:* for ye are not under the law, but under grace.

y Rom. viii. 33. Who shall lay any thing to the charge of God's elect? *It is God that justifieth;* Ver. 34. *Who is he that condemneth?* It is Christ that died, yea rather, that is risen again, who is even at the right hand of God, who also maketh intercession for us.

z 1 John ii. 12. I write *unto you, little children,* because your sins are forgiven you for his name's sake. Ver. 13. I write *unto you, fathers,* because ye have known him that is from the beginning. I write *unto you, young men,* because ye have overcome the wicked one. I write *unto you, little children,* because ye have known the Father. Ver. 14. I have written *unto you, fathers,* because ye have known him that is from the beginning. I have written *unto you, young men, because ye are strong,* and the word of God abideth in you, and ye have overcome the wicked one. Heb. v. 12. For when for the time ye ought to be teachers, ye have need that one teach you again which be the first principles of the oracles of God; and are become such as *have need of milk, and not of strong meat.* Ver. 13. For every one that useth *milk is unskilful in the word of righteousness; for he is a babe.* Ver. 14. But *strong meat* belongeth to them *that are of full age,* even those who by reason of use have *their senses exercised to discern both good and evil.*

a 1 John i. 8. *If we say that we have no sin, we deceive ourselves,* and the truth is not in us. Ver. 10. If we say that *we have not sinned, we make him a liar,* and his word is not in us.

b 2 Cor. vii. 1. Having therefore these promises, dearly beloved, let us cleanse ourselves from all filthiness of the flesh and spirit, *perfecting holiness* in the fear of God. Phil. iii. 12. Not as though I had already attained, either were already perfect; but *I follow after, if that I may apprehend that for which also I am apprehended of Christ Jesus.* Ver. 13. Brethren, I count not myself to have apprehended: but this one thing I do, forgetting those things which are behind, and *reaching forth unto those things which are before,* Ver. 14. *I press toward the mark,* for the prize of the high calling of God in Christ Jesus.

78. c Rom. vii. 18. For I know that *in me (that is, in my flesh) dwelleth no good thing;* for to will is present with me; but how to perform that *which is good I find not.* Ver. 23. But I see *another law in my members warring against the law of my mind, and bringing me into captivity to the law of sin* which is in my members. Mark xiv. 66. to the end. And as Peter was beneath in the palace, there cometh one of the

services,d and their best works are imperfect and defiled in the sight of God.e

Q. 79. *May not true believers, by reason of their imperfections, and the many temptations and sins they are overtaken with, fall away from the state of grace?*

A. True believers, by reason of the unchangeable love of God,f and his decree and covenant to give them perseverance,g their inseparable union with Christ,h his continual intercession for them,i and the Spirit and seed of God abiding in them,k can neither totally nor finally fall away from the state of grace,l but are kept by the power of God through faith unto salvation.m

Q. 80. *Can true believers be infallibly assured that they are in the estate of grace, and that they shall persevere therein unto salvation?*

A. Such as truly believe in Christ, and endeavour to walk in all good conscience before him,n may, without extraordinary revelation, by faith grounded upon the truth of God's promises, and by the Spirit enabling them to discern in themselves those graces to which the promises of life are made,o and bearing witness with their spirits that

---

maids of the high priest, &c. Gal. ii. 11. But when Peter was come to Antioch, I withstood him to the face, because *he was to be blamed.* Ver. 12. For before that certain came from James, he did eat with the Gentiles : but when they were come, *he withdrew, and separated himself, fearing them which were of the circumcision.*

d Heb. xii. 1. Wherefore, seeing we also are compassed about with so great a cloud of witnesses, let us lay aside *every weight, and the sin which doth so easily beset us,* and let us run with patience the race that is set before us.

e Isa. lxiv. 6. But we are *all as an unclean thing,* and *all our righteousnesses are as filthy rags;* and we all do fade as a leaf; and our iniquities, like the wind, have taken us away. Exod. xxviii. 38. And it shall be upon Aaron's forehead, that Aaron may bear the *iniquity of the holy things,* which the children of Israel shall hallow *in all their holy gifts;* and it shall be *always* upon his forehead, *that they may be accepted before the Lord.*

79. f Jer. xxxi. 3. The Lord hath appeared of old unto me, saying, Yea, *I have loved thee with an everlasting love;* therefore with loving-kindness have I drawn thee.

g 2 Tim. ii. 19. Nevertheless the foundation of God standeth sure, having this *seal, The Lord knoweth them that are his.* And, Let every one that nameth the name of Christ depart from iniquity. Heb. xiii. 20. Now the God of peace, that brought again from the dead our Lord Jesus, that great Shepherd of the sheep, *through the blood of the everlasting covenant,* Ver. 21. *Make you perfect in every good work to do his will,* working in you that which is well-pleasing in his sight, through Jesus Christ ; to whom be glory for ever and ever. Amen. 2 Sam. xxiii. 5. Although my house be not so with God ; *yet he hath made with me an everlasting covenant, ordered in all things, and sure:* for this is all my salvation, and all my desire, although he make it not to grow.

h 1 Cor. i. 8. *Who shall also confirm you unto the end,* that ye may be blameless in the day of our Lord Jesus Christ. Ver. 9. *God is faithful,* by whom ye were *called unto the fellowship of his Son Jesus Christ* our Lord.

i Heb. vii. 25. Wherefore he is able also to save them *to the uttermost* that come unto God by him, *seeing he ever liveth to make intercession for them.* Luke xxii. 32. But *I have prayed for thee, that thy faith fail not:* and when thou art converted, strengthen thy brethren.

k 1 John iii. 9. Whosoever is born of God doth not commit sin ; *for his seed remaineth in him: and he cannot sin,* because he is born of God. 1 John ii. 27. But *the anointing which ye have received of him abideth in you;* and ye need not that any man teach you : but as the same anointing teacheth you of all things, and is truth, and is no lie, and even as it hath taught you, *ye shall abide in him.*

l Jer. xxxii. 40. And I will make an everlasting covenant with them, that *I will not turn away from them, to do them good;* but I will put my fear in their hearts, *that they shall not depart from me.* John x. 28. And I give unto them eternal life ; and *they shall never perish, neither shall any pluck them out of my hand.*

m 1 Pet. i. 5. Who are *kept by the power of God through faith unto salvation,* ready to be revealed in the last time.

80. n 1 John ii. 3. And *hereby we do know that we know him, if we keep his commandments.*

o 1 Cor. ii. 12. Now we have received, not the spirit of the world, but the *Spirit which is of God; that we might know the things that are freely given to us of God.* 1 John iii. 14. *We know that we have passed from death unto life, because we love the brethren:* he that loveth not his brother abideth in death. Ver. 18. My little children, let us not love in word, neither in tongue ; but in deed, and in truth. Ver. 19. And *hereby*

they are the children of God,p be infallibly assured that they are in the estate of grace, and shall persevere therein unto salvation.q

Q. 81. *Are all true believers at all times assured of their present being in the estate of grace, and that they shall be saved?*

A. Assurance of grace and salvation not being of the essence of faith,r true believers may wait long before they obtain it;s and, after the enjoyment thereof, may have it weakened and intermitted, through manifold distempers, sins, temptations, and desertions;t yet are they never left without such a presence and support of the Spirit of God as keeps them from sinking into utter despair.v

we know that we are of the truth, and shall assure our hearts before him. Ver. 21. *Beloved, if our heart condemn us not, then have we confidence toward God.* Ver. 24. *And he that keepeth his commandments dwelleth in him, and he in him: and hereby we know that he abideth in us, by the Spirit* which he hath given us. 1 John iv. 13. *Hereby know we that we dwell in him, and he in us, because he hath given us of his Spirit.* Ver. 16. *And we have known and believed* the love that God hath to us. *God is love;* and *he that dwelleth in love dwelleth in God, and God in him.* Heb. vi. 11. *And we desire that every one of you do shew the same diligence, to the full assurance of hope* unto the end: Ver. 12. *That ye be not slothful, but followers of them who through faith and patience inherit the promises.*

p Rom. viii. 16. The *Spirit itself beareth witness with our spirit,* that we are the children of God.

q 1 John v. 13. These things have I written unto you that believe on the name of the Son of God, *that ye may know that ye have eternal life,* and that ye may believe on the name of the Son of God.

81. r Eph. i. 13. In whom ye also trusted, after that ye heard the word of truth, the gospel of your salvation: in whom also, *after that ye believed, ye were sealed with that Holy Spirit of promise.*

s Isa. l. 10. Who is among you that feareth the Lord, that obeyeth the voice of his servant, that *walketh in darkness, and hath no light?* let him *trust in the name of the Lord, and stay upon his God.* Ps. lxxxviii. throughout. Ver. 1. O Lord God of my salvation, I have *cried day and night* before thee. Ver. 2. Let my prayer come before thee: incline thine ear unto my cry; Ver. 3. For my soul is full of troubles, and *my life draweth nigh unto the grave.* Ver. 6. Thou hast laid me in the lowest pit, in *darkness, in the deeps.* Ver. 7. Thy wrath lieth hard upon me, and thou hast afflicted me with all thy waves. Selah. Ver. 9. Mine eye mourneth by reason of affliction: Lord, I have called daily upon thee; I have stretched out my hands unto thee. Ver. 10. Wilt thou shew wonders to the dead? Ver. 13. But unto thee *have I cried,* O Lord; and in the morning shall my prayer prevent thee. Ver. 14. Lord, why *castest thou off my soul?* why *hidest thou thy face* from me? Ver. 15. I am afflicted and *ready to die* from my youth up: while I suffer thy terrors I am *distracted,* etc.

t [Ps. lxxvii. 1. to the 12th verse.] Ver. 1. I cried unto God with my voice, even unto God with my voice; and he gave ear unto me. Ver. 2. In the day of my trouble I sought the Lord: my sore ran in the night, and ceased not: *my soul refused to be comforted.* Ver. 3. I remembered God, and *was troubled;* I complained, and *my spirit was overwhelmed.* Ver. 7. Will the Lord cast *off for ever?* and will he be *favourable no more?* etc. Cant. v. 2. I sleep, but my heart waketh: it is the voice of my beloved that knocketh, saying, Open to me, my sister, my love, my dove, my undefiled: for my head is filled with dew, and my locks with the drops of the night. Ver. 3. I have put off my coat; how shall I put it on? I have washed my feet; how shall I defile them? Ver. 6. I opened to my beloved; but *my beloved had withdrawn himself, and was gone;* my soul failed when he spake: *I sought him, but I could not find him; I called him, but he gave me no answer.* Ps. li. 8. Make me to hear joy and gladness; that *the bones which thou hast broken* may rejoice. Ver. 12. *Restore unto me the joy of thy salvation;* and uphold me with thy free Spirit. Ps. xxxi. 22. For *I said in my haste, I am cut off from before thine eyes:* nevertheless thou heardest the voice of my supplications when I cried unto thee. Ps. xxii. 1. *My God, my God, why hast thou forsaken me? why art thou so far from helping me,* and from the words of my roaring?

v 1 John iii. 9. Whosoever is born of God doth not commit sin; for *his seed remaineth in him: and he cannot sin,* because he is born of God. Job xiii. 15. *Though he slay me, yet will I trust in him:* but I will maintain mine own ways before him. Ps. lxxiii. 15. *If I say, I will speak thus: behold, I should offend against the generation of thy children.* Ver. 23. Nevertheless I am *continually with thee; thou hast holden me by my right hand.* Isa. liv. 7. *For a small moment* have I forsaken thee; but *with great mercies will I gather thee.* Ver. 8. In a little wrath *I hid my face from thee for a moment;* but *with everlasting kindness will I have mercy* on thee, saith the Lord thy Redeemer. Ver. 9. For this is as the waters of Noah unto me: for as I have sworn that the waters of Noah should no more go over the earth; *so have I sworn that I would not be wroth with thee, nor rebuke thee.* Ver. 10. For the mountains shall depart, and the hills be removed; but *my kindness shall*

Q. 82. *What is the communion in glory which the members of the invisible church have with Christ?*

A. The communion in glory which the members of the invisible church have with Christ, is in this life,[w] immediately after death,[x] and at last perfected at the resurrection and day of judgment.[y]

Q. 83. *What is the communion in glory with Christ which the members of the invisible church enjoy in this life?*

A. The members of the invisible church have communicated to them in this life the first-fruits of glory with Christ, as they are members of him their head, and so in him are interested in that glory which he is fully possessed of;[z] and, as an earnest thereof, enjoy the sense of God's love,[a] peace of conscience, joy in the Holy Ghost, and hope of glory;[b] as, on the contrary, sense of God's revenging wrath, horror of conscience, and a fearful expectation of judgment, are to the wicked the beginning of their torments which they shall endure after death.[c]

Q. 84. *Shall all men die?*

A. Death being threatened as the wages of sin,[d] it is appointed unto all men once to die;[e] for that all have sinned.

Q. 85. *Death, being the wages of sin, why are not the righteous delivered from death, seeing all their sins are forgiven in Christ?*

A. The righteous shall be delivered from death itself at the last day, and even in death are delivered from the sting and curse of it;[g] so that, although they die, yet it is out of God's love,[h] to free them per-

---

not depart from thee, neither shall the covenant of my peace be removed, saith the Lord that hath mercy on thee.

82. [w] 2 Cor. iii. 18. But we all, *with open face beholding as in a glass the glory of the Lord,* are changed into the same image, from glory to glory, even as by the Spirit of the Lord.

[x] Luke xxiii. 43. And Jesus said unto him, Verily I say unto thee, *To-day shalt thou be with me in paradise.*

[y] 1 Thess. iv. 17. Then we which are alive and remain shall be caught up together with them in the clouds, to *meet the Lord in the air;* and so *shall we ever be with the Lord.*

83. [z] Eph. ii. 5. Even when we were dead in sins, hath *quickened us together with Christ;* (by grace ye are saved;) Ver. 6. *And hath raised us up together, and made us sit together in heavenly places in Christ Jesus.*

[a] Rom. v. 5. And hope maketh not ashamed; because *the love of God is shed abroad in our hearts by the Holy Ghost, which is given unto us.* Compared with 2 Cor. i. 22. Who hath also *sealed* us, and *given the earnest of the Spirit in our hearts.*

[b] Rom. v. 1. Therefore, being justified by faith, we have *peace with God,* through our Lord Jesus Christ: Ver. 2. By whom also we have access by faith into this grace wherein we stand, and *rejoice in hope of the glory of God.* Rom. xiv. 17. For the *kingdom of God* is not meat and drink; but righteousness, and *peace, and joy in the Holy Ghost.*

[c] Gen. iv. 13. And Cain said unto the Lord, *My punishment is greater than I can bear.* Matt. xxvii. 4. Saying, *I have sinned, in that I have betrayed the innocent blood.* And they said, What is that to us? see thou to that. Heb. x. 27. But a certain *fearful looking for of judgment and fiery indignation,* which shall devour the adversaries. Rom. ii. 9. *Tribulation and anguish, upon every soul of man that doeth evil,* of the Jew first, and also of the Gentile. Mark ix. 44. Where their *worm dieth not,* and the *fire is not quenched.*

84. [d] Rom. vi. 23. For *the wages of sin is death;* but the gift of God is eternal life through Jesus Christ our Lord.

[e] Heb. ix. 27. And as *it is appointed unto men once to die,* but after this the judgment.

[f] Rom. v. 12. Wherefore, as by one man sin entered into the world, and *death by sin;* and so *death passed upon all men, for that all have sinned.*

85. [g] 1 Cor. xv. 26. The *last enemy* that shall be destroyed *is death.* *Ver. 55. *O death, where is thy sting? O grave, where is thy victory?* Ver. 56. The sting of death is sin; and the strength of sin is the law. Ver. 57. But thanks be to God, which *giveth us the victory, through our Lord Jesus Christ.* Heb. ii. 15. And *deliver them who through fear of death were all their lifetime subject to bondage.*

[h] Isa. lvii. 1. The righteous perisheth, and no man layeth it to heart; and merciful men are taken away, none considering that the *righteous is taken away from the evil to come.* Ver. 2. *He shall enter into peace. they shall rest in their beds,* each one walking in his uprightness. 2 Kings xxii. 20. Behold, therefore, I will gather thee unto thy fathers, and *thou shalt be gathered into thy grave in peace;* and *thine eyes shall not see all the evil which I will bring upon this place.*

fectly from sin and misery,¹ and to make them capable of further communion with Christ in glory, which they then enter upon.ᵏ

Q. 86. *What is the communion in glory with Christ, which the members of the invisible church enjoy immediately after death?*

A. The communion in glory with Christ, which the members of the invisible church enjoy immediately after death, is, in that their souls are then made perfect in holiness,ˡ and received into the highest heavens,ᵐ where they behold the face of God in light and glory,ⁿ waiting for the full redemption of their bodies,ᵒ which even in death continue united to Christ,ᵖ and rest in their graves as in their beds,ᑫ till at the last day they be again united to their souls.ʳ Whereas the souls of the wicked are at their death cast into hell, where they remain in torments and utter darkness, and their bodies kept in their graves, as in their prisons, till the resurrection and judgment of the great day.ˢ

Q. 87. *What are we to believe concerning the resurrection?*

A. We are to believe, that at the last day there shall be a general resurrection of the dead, both of the just and unjust:ᵗ when they that are then found alive shall in a moment be changed; and the selfsame

---

l Rev. xiv. 13. And I heard a voice from heaven saying unto me, Write, Blessed are the dead which die in the Lord from henceforth: Yea, saith the Spirit, *that they may rest from their labours;* and their works do follow them. Eph. v. 27. That he might *present it to himself a glorious church, not having spot, or wrinkle, or any such thing;* but that it should be *holy, and without blemish.*

k Luke xxiii. 43. And Jesus said unto him, Verily I say unto thee, *To-day shalt thou be with me in paradise.* Phil. i. 23. For I am in a strait betwixt two, having a desire *to depart, and to be with Christ, which is far better.*

86. l Heb. xii. 23. To the general assembly and church of the first-born, which are written in heaven, and to God the Judge of all, and *to the spirits of just men made perfect.*

m 2 Cor. v. 1. For we know, that, if our earthly house of this tabernacle were dissolved, we have a *building of God, an house not made with hands, eternal in the heavens.* Ver. 6. Therefore we are always confident, knowing that, whilst we are at home in the body, we are absent from the Lord. Ver. 8. We are confident, I say, and willing rather to be *absent from the body,* and to be *present with the Lord.* Phil. i. 23. For I am in a strait betwixt two, having a desire *to depart, and to be with Christ, which is far better.* Compared with Acts iii. 21. *Whom the heaven must receive until the times of restitution of all things,* which God hath spoken by the mouth of all his holy prophets since the world began. And with Eph. iv. 10. He that descended is the same also that *ascended up far above all heavens,* that he might fill all things

n 1 John iii. 2. Beloved, now are we the sons of God; and it doth not yet appear what we shall be: but we know that, when he shall appear, we shall be like him; for *we shall see him as he is.* 1 Cor. xiii. 12. For now we see through a glass, darkly; but *then face to face:* now I know in part; but *then shall I know even as also I am known.*

o Rom. viii. 23. And not only they, but ourselves also, which have the first-fruits of the Spirit, even we ourselves groan within ourselves, *waiting for the adoption, to wit, the redemption of our body.* Ps. xvi. 9. Therefore my heart is glad, and my glory rejoiceth; *my flesh also shall rest in hope.*

p 1 Thess. iv. 14. For if we believe that Jesus died, and rose again, even so them also *which sleep in Jesus* will God bring with him.

q Isa. lvii. 2. He shall enter into peace: *they shall rest in their beds,* each one walking in his uprightness.

r Job xix. 26. And though after my skin worms destroy this body, *yet in my flesh shall I see God:* Ver. 27. Whom I shall see for myself, and *mine eyes shall behold,* and not another; though my reins be consumed within me.

s Luke xvi. 23. And *in hell he lifted up his eyes, being in torments,* and seeth Abraham afar off, and Lazarus in his bosom. Ver. 24. And he cried, and said, Father Abraham, have mercy on me, and send Lazarus, that he may dip the tip of his finger in water, and cool my tongue; for *I am tormented in this flame.* Acts i. 25. That he may take part of this ministry and apostleship, from which Judas by transgression fell, *that he might go to his own place.* Jude, ver. 6. And the angels which kept not their first estate, but left their own habitation, he hath *reserved in everlasting chains, under darkness, unto the judgment of the great day.* Ver. 7. Even as Sodom and Gomorrha, and the cities about them, in like manner, giving themselves over to fornication, and going after strange flesh, are set forth for an example, *suffering the vengeance of eternal fire.*

87. t Acts xxiv. 15. And have hope toward God, which they themselves also allow, that *there shall be a resurrection of the dead, both of the just and unjust.*

bodies of the dead which were laid in the grave, being then again united to their souls for ever, shall be raised up by the power of Christ.ᵛ The bodies of the just, by the Spirit of Christ, and by virtue of his resurrection as their head, shall be raised in power, spiritual, incorruptible, and made like to his glorious body;ʷ and the bodies of the wicked shall be raised up in dishonour by him, as an offended judge.ˣ

Q. 88. *What shall immediately follow after the resurrection?*

A. Immediately after the resurrection shall follow the general and final judgment of angels and men;ʸ the day and hour whereof no man knoweth, that all may watch and pray, and be ever ready for the coming of the Lord.ᶻ

Q. 89. *What shall be done to the wicked at the day of judgment?*

A. At the day of judgment, the wicked shall be set on Christ's left hand,ᵃ and, upon clear evidence, and full conviction of their own consciences,ᵇ shall have the fearful but just sentence of condemnation

---

ᵛ 1 Cor. xv. 51. Behold, I shew you a mystery; We shall not all sleep, but *we shall all be changed,* Ver. 52. *In a moment, in the twinkling of an eye,* at the last trump; (for the trumpet shall sound;) and *the dead shall be raised* incorruptible, and *we shall be changed.* Ver. 53. For this corruptible must put on incorruption, and this mortal must put on immortality. 1 Thess. iv. 15. For this we say unto you by the word of the Lord, that *we which are alive and remain unto the coming of the Lord* shall not prevent them which are asleep. Ver. 16. For the Lord himself shall descend from heaven with a shout, with the voice of the archangel, and with the trump of God: and *the dead in Christ shall rise first:* Ver. 17. Then *we which are alive and remain shall be caught up together with them* in the clouds, to meet the Lord in the air: and *so shall we ever be with the Lord.* John v. 28. Marvel not at this: for the hour is coming, in the which all that are in the *graves* shall hear his voice, Ver. 29. And *shall come forth;* they that have done good, unto the resurrection of life; and *they that have done evil, unto the resurrection of damnation.*

ʷ 1 Cor. xv. 21. For since by man came death, by man came also the resurrection of the dead. Ver. 22. For as in Adam all die, even so in Christ shall all be made alive. Ver. 23. But every man in his own order: *Christ the first-fruits; afterward they that are Christ's* at his coming. Ver. 42. So also is the resurrection of the dead: it is sown in corruption, *it is raised in incorruption:* Ver. 43. It is sown in dishonour, *it is raised in glory:* it is sown in weakness, *it is raised in power;* Ver. 44. It is sown a natural body, *it is raised a spiritual body.* Phil. iii. 21. Who shall *change our vile body,* that it may be fashioned *like unto his glorious body,* according to the working whereby he is able even to subdue all things unto himself.

ˣ John v. 27. And hath *given him authority to execute judgment* also, because he is the Son of man. Ver. 28. Marvel not at this: for the hour is coming, in the which all that are in the *graves* shall hear his voice,

Ver. 29. And *shall come forth;* they that have done good, unto the resurrection of life; and *they that have done evil, unto the resurrection of damnation.* Matt. xxv. 33. And he shall set the sheep on his right hand, *but the goats on the left.*

88. ʸ 2 Pet. ii. 4. For if God spared not the *angels* that sinned, but cast them down to hell, and delivered them into chains of darkness, *to be reserved unto judgment.* Jude, Ver. 6. And the angels which kept not their first estate, but left their own habitation, he hath *reserved in everlasting chains, under darkness, unto the judgment of the great day.* Ver. 7. Even as Sodom and Gomorrha, and the cities about them, in like manner, giving themselves over to fornication, and going after strange flesh, are set forth for an example, *suffering the vengeance of eternal fire.* Ver. 14. And Enoch also, the seventh from Adam, prophesied of these, saying, Behold, *the Lord cometh with ten thousands of his saints,* Ver. 15. *To execute judgment upon all,* and to convince all that are ungodly among them of all their ungodly deeds which they have ungodly committed, and of all their hard speeches which ungodly sinners have spoken against him. Matt. xxv. 46. And *these shall go away into everlasting punishment: but the righteous into life eternal.*

ᶻ Matt. xxiv. 36. *But of that day and hour knoweth no man,* no, not the angels of heaven, but my Father only. Ver. 42. *Watch therefore: for ye know not what hour your Lord doth come.* Ver. 44. *Therefore be ye also ready: for in such an hour as ye think not the Son of man cometh.* Luke xxi. 35. For *as a snare shall it come on all them that dwell on the face of the whole earth.* Ver. 36. *Watch ye therefore, and pray always,* that ye may be accounted worthy to escape all these things that shall come to pass, *and to stand before the Son of man.*

89. ᵃ Matt. xxv. 33. And he shall set the sheep on his right hand, *but the goats on the left.*

ᵇ Rom. ii. 15. Which shew the work of the law written in their hearts, *their conscience also bearing witness, and their*

pronounced against them;[c] and thereupon shall be cast out from the favourable presence of God, and the glorious fellowship with Christ, his saints, and all his holy angels, into hell, to be punished with unspeakable torments, both of body and soul, with the devil and his angels for ever.[d]

Q. 90. *What shall be done to the righteous at the day of judgment?*

A. At the day of judgment, the righteous, being caught up to Christ in the clouds,[e] shall be set on his right hand, and there openly acknowledged and acquitted,[f] shall join with him in the judging of reprobate angels and men,[g] and shall be received into heaven,[h] where they shall be fully and for ever freed from all sin and misery;[i] filled with inconceivable joys,[k] made perfectly holy and happy both in body and soul, in the company of innumerable saints and holy angels,[l] but especially in the immediate vision and fruition of God the Father, of our Lord Jesus Christ, and of the Holy Spirit, to all eternity.[m] And this is the perfect and full communion, which the members of the invisible church shall enjoy with Christ in glory, at the resurrection and day of judgment.

HAVING SEEN WHAT THE SCRIPTURES PRINCIPALLY TEACH US TO BELIEVE CONCERNING GOD, IT FOLLOWS TO CONSIDER WHAT THEY REQUIRE AS THE DUTY OF MAN.

Q. 91. *What is the duty which God requireth of man?*

thoughts the mean while accusing or else excusing one another, Ver. 16. In the day when God shall judge the secrets of men by Jesus Christ, according to my gospel.

[c] Matt. xxv. 41. Then shall he say also unto them on the left hand, *Depart from me, ye cursed*, into everlasting fire, prepared for the devil and his angels: Ver. 42. For I was an hungered, and ye gave me no meat: I was thirsty, and ye gave me no drink: Ver. 43. I was a stranger, and ye took me not in: naked, and ye clothed me not: sick, and in prison, and ye visited me not.

[d] Luke xvi. 26. And besides all this, between us and you there is *a great gulf fixed;* so that they which would pass from hence to you cannot; *neither can they pass to us, that would come from thence.* 2 Thess. i. 8. *In flaming fire, taking vengeance on them that know not God*, and that obey not the gospel of our Lord Jesus Christ: Ver. 9. *Who shall be punished with everlasting destruction from the presence of the Lord*, and from the glory of his power.

90. [e] 1 Thess. iv. 17. Then we which are alive and remain shall be *caught up together with them in the clouds*, to meet the Lord in the air: and so shall we ever be with the Lord.

[f] Matt. xxv. 33. And *he shall set the sheep on his right hand*, but the goats on the left. Matt. x. 32. Whosoever therefore shall confess me before men, *him will I confess also before my Father which is in heaven.*

[g] 1 Cor. vi. 2. *Do ye not know that the saints shall judge the world?* and if the world shall be judged by you, are ye unworthy to judge the smallest matters? Ver. 3. *Know ye not that we shall judge angels?* how much more things that pertain to this life?

[h] Matt. xxv. 34. Then shall the King say unto them on his right hand, *Come, ye blessed of my Father, inherit the kingdom* prepared for you from the foundation of the world. Ver. 46. And these shall go away into everlasting punishment: but *the righteous into life eternal.*

[i] Eph. v. 27. That he might *present it to himself a glorious church, not having spot, or wrinkle*, or any such thing; but *that it should be holy, and without blemish*. Rev. xiv. 13. And I heard a voice from heaven saying unto me, Write, Blessed are the dead which die in the Lord from henceforth: Yea, saith the Spirit, *that they may rest from their labours;* and their works do follow them.

[k] Ps. xvi. 11. Thou wilt shew me the path of life: *in thy presence is fulness of joy; at thy right hand there are pleasures for evermore.*

[l] Heb. xii. 22. But ye are come unto mount Sion, and unto the *city of the living God*, the heavenly Jerusalem, and *to an innumerable company of angels*, Ver. 23. *To the general assembly and church of the first-born, which are written in heaven*, and to God the Judge of all, and *to the spirits of just men made perfect.*

[m] 1 John iii. 2. Beloved, now are we the sons of God; and it doth not yet appear what we shall be: but we know that, when he shall appear, we shall be like him; for *we shall see him as he is.* 1 Cor. xiii. 12. For now *we see* through a glass, darkly; but *then face to face:* now I know in part; but *then shall I know even as also I am known.* 1 Thess. iv. 17. Then we which are alive and remain shall be caught up together with them in the clouds, to meet the Lord in the air: *and so shall we ever be with the Lord.*

A. The duty which God requireth of man, is obedience to his revealed will.ⁿ

Q. 92. *What did God at first reveal unto man as the rule of his obedience?*

A. The rule of obedience revealed to Adam in the estate of innocence, and to all mankind in him, besides a special command not to eat of the fruit of the tree of the knowledge of good and evil, was the moral law.°

Q. 93. *What is the moral law?*

A. The moral law is the declaration of the will of God to mankind, directing and binding every one to personal, perfect, and perpetual conformity and obedience thereunto, in the frame and disposition of the whole man, soul and body,ᵖ and in performance of all those duties of holiness and righteousness which he oweth to God and man:ᑫ promising life upon the fulfilling, and threatening death upon the breach of it.ʳ

Q. 94. *Is there any use of the moral law to man since the fall?*

A. Although no man, since the fall, can attain to righteousness and

---

Ver. 18. Wherefore comfort one another with these words.

91. ⁿ Rom. xii. 1. I beseech you, therefore, brethren, by the mercies of God, that ye *present your bodies a living sacrifice, holy, acceptable unto God, which is your reasonable service.* Ver. 2. And be not conformed to this world; but be ye transformed by the renewing of your mind, *that ye may prove what is that good, and acceptable, and perfect will of God.* Micah vi. 8. He hath shewed thee, O man, what is good; and *what doth the Lord require of thee, but to do justly, and to love mercy, and to walk humbly with thy God?* 1 Sam. xv. 22. And Samuel said, Hath the Lord as great delight in burnt offerings and sacrifices, *as in obeying the voice of the Lord?* Behold, *to obey is better than sacrifice, and to hearken than the fat of rams.*

92. ° Gen. i. 26. And God said, Let us make man *in our image, after our likeness;* and let them have dominion over the fish of the sea, and over the fowl of the air, and over the cattle, and over all the earth, and over every creeping thing that creepeth upon the earth. Ver. 27. So God created man *in his own image: in the image of God created he him;* male and female created he them. Rom. ii. 14. For when the Gentiles, which have not the law, do by nature the things contained in the law, these, having not the law, *are a law unto themselves;* Ver. 15. Which *shew the work of the law written in their hearts,* their *conscience also bearing witness,* and their thoughts the mean while *accusing* or else *excusing* one another. Rom. x. 5. For Moses describeth the *righteousness which is of the law,* That the man which doeth those things shall live by them. Gen. ii. 17. But *of the tree of the knowledge of good and evil, thou shalt not eat of it;* for in the day that thou eatest thereof thou shalt surely die.

93. ᵖ Deut. v. 1. And Moses called all Israel, and said unto them, Hear, O Israel, the *statutes* and *judgments* which I speak in your ears this day, that ye may *learn them, and keep and do them.* Ver. 2. The Lord our God made a covenant with us in Horeb. Ver. 3. The Lord made not this covenant with our fathers, but with us, even us, who are all of us here alive this day. Ver. 31. But as for thee, stand thou here by me, and I will speak unto thee all the commandments, and the statutes, and the judgments, which thou shalt teach them, *that they may do them* in the land which I give them to possess it. Ver. 33. Ye shall walk *in all the ways which the Lord your God hath commanded* you, that ye may live, and that it may be well with you, and that ye may prolong your days in the land which ye shall possess. Luke x. 26. He said unto him, What is written in the law? how readest thou? Ver. 27. And he answering, said, Thou shalt love the Lord thy God *with all thy heart,* and *with all thy soul,* and *with all thy strength,* and *with all thy mind;* and thy neighbour as thyself. Gal. iii. 10. For as many as are of the works of the law are under the curse: for it is written, *Cursed is every one that continueth not in all things which are written in the book of the law to do them.* 1 Thess. v. 23. And the very God of peace *sanctify you wholly;* and I pray God *your whole spirit, and soul, and body, be preserved blameless* unto the coming of our Lord Jesus Christ.

ᑫ Luke i. 75. *In holiness and righteousness before him, all the days of our life.* Acts xxiv. 16. And herein do I exercise myself, to have *always a conscience void of offence toward God, and toward men.*

ʳ Rom. x. 5. For Moses describeth the righteousness which is of the law, *the man which doeth those things shall live by them.* Gal. iii. 10. For as many as are of the works of the law are under the curse: for it is written, *Cursed is every one that continueth not in all things which are written in the book of the law to do them.* Ver. 12. And the law is not of faith: but, *The man that doeth them shall live in them.*

life by the moral law;ˢ yet there is great use thereof, as well common to all men, as peculiar either to the unregenerate, or the regenerate.ᵗ

Q. 95. *Of what use is the moral law to all men?*

A. The moral law is of use to all men, to inform them of the holy nature and will of God,ᵛ and of their duty, binding them to walk accordingly;ʷ to convince them of their disability to keep it, and of the sinful pollution of their nature, hearts, and lives:ˣ to humble them in the sense of their sin and misery,ʸ and thereby help them to a clearer sight of the need they have of Christ,ᶻ and of the perfection of his obedience.ᵃ

Q. 96. *What particular use is there of the moral law to unregenerate men?*

A. The moral law is of use to unregenerate men, to awaken their consciences to flee from wrath to come,ᵇ and to drive them to Christ;ᶜ or, upon their continuance in the estate and way of sin, to leave them inexcusable,ᵈ and under the curse thereof.ᵉ

Q. 97. *What special use is there of the moral law to the regenerate?*

94. ˢ Rom. viii. 3. For *what the law could not do, in that it was weak through the flesh,* God sending his own Son in the likeness of sinful flesh, and for sin, condemned sin in the flesh. Gal. ii. 16. Knowing that *a man is not justified by the works of the law,* but by the faith of Jesus Christ, even we have believed in Jesus Christ, that we might be justified by the faith of Christ, and not by the works of the law: for *by the works of the law shall no flesh be justified.*
ᵗ 1 Tim. i. 8. But we know that the *law is good,* if a man use it lawfully.
95. ᵛ Lev. xi. 44. *For I am the Lord* your God: ye shall therefore *sanctify* yourselves, and *ye shall be holy; for I am holy:* neither shall ye defile yourselves with any manner of creeping thing that creepeth upon the earth. Ver. 45. *For I am the Lord* that bringeth you up out of the land of Egypt, to be your God: *ye shall therefore be holy; for I am holy.* Lev. xx. 7. *Sanctify yourselves therefore, and be ye holy: for I am the Lord your God.* Ver. 8. And ye shall keep my statutes, and do them : *I am the Lord which sanctify you.* Rom. vii. 12. Wherefore *the law is holy,* and *the commandment holy,* and just, and good.
ʷ Micah vi. 8. He hath *shewed thee,* O man, what is good ; and *what doth the Lord require of thee, but to do justly, and to love mercy, and to walk humbly with thy God?* James ii. 10. For whosoever shall *keep the whole law, and yet offend in one point, he is guilty of all.* Ver. 11. For he that said, Do not commit adultery, said also, Do not kill. Now, if thou commit no adultery, yet if thou kill, thou art become a transgressor of the law.
ˣ Ps. xix. 11. Moreover, *by them is thy servant warned;* and in keeping of them there is great reward. Ver. 12. *Who can understand his errors?* cleanse thou me from secret faults. Rom. iii. 20. Therefore by the deeds of the law there shall no flesh be justified in his sight : for *by the law is the knowledge of sin.* Rom. vii. 7. What shall we say then? Is the law sin? God forbid. Nay, *I had not known sin but by the law:* for I had not known lust, except the law had said, Thou shalt not covet.
ʸ Rom. iii. 9. What then? are we better than they? No, in no wise: for we have before *proved* both Jews and Gentiles, *that they are all under sin.* Ver. 23. *For all have sinned, and come short of the glory of God.*
ᶻ Gal. iii. 21. Is the law then against the promises of God? God forbid : for if there had been a law given which could have given life, verily righteousness should have been by the law. Ver. 22. But *the scripture hath concluded all under sin, that the promise by faith of Jesus Christ might be given to them that believe.*
ᵃ Rom. x. 4. For *Christ is the end of the law for righteousness* to every one that believeth.
96. ᵇ 1 Tim. i. 9. Knowing this, that the *law is not made* for a righteous man, but for the *lawless and disobedient,* for the *ungodly* and for *sinners,* for *unholy* and *profane,* for *murderers of fathers* and *murderers of mothers,* for *man-slayers,* Ver. 10. For *whoremongers,* for them that *defile themselves with mankind,* for *men-stealers,* for *liars,* for *perjured persons,* and if there be any other thing that is contrary to sound doctrine.
ᶜ Gal. iii. 24. Wherefore the *law was our schoolmaster to bring us unto Christ,* that we might be justified by faith.
ᵈ Rom. i. 20. For the invisible things of him from the creation of the world are clearly seen, being understood by the things that are made, even his eternal power and Godhead ; *so that they are without excuse.* Compared with Rom. ii. 15. Which shew *the work of the law written in their hearts,* their *conscience* also *bearing witness,* and their *thoughts* the mean while *accusing* or else excusing one another.
ᵉ Gal. iii. 10. For as many as are of the works of the law *are under the curse:* for it is written, *Cursed is every one that continueth not* in all things which are written in the book of the law to do them.

A. Although they that are regenerate, and believe in Christ, be delivered from the moral law as a covenant of works,[f] so as thereby they are neither justified[g] nor condemned;[h] yet, besides the general uses thereof common to them with all men, it is of special use, to shew them how much they are bound to Christ for his fulfilling it, and enduring the curse thereof in their stead, and for their good;[i] and thereby to provoke them to more thankfulness,[k] and to express the same in their greater care to conform themselves thereunto as the rule of their obedience.[l]

Q. 98. *Where is the moral law summarily comprehended?*

A. The moral law is summarily comprehended in the ten commandments, which were delivered by the voice of God upon mount Sinai, and written by him in two tables of stone;[m] and are recorded in the twentieth chapter of Exodus. The four first commandments containing our duty to God, and the other six our duty to man.[n]

97. f Rom. vi. 14. For sin shall not have dominion over you: for *ye are not under the law,* but under grace. Rom. vii. 4. Wherefore, my brethren, ye also are *become dead to the law* by the body of Christ; that ye should be married to another, even to him who is raised from the dead, that we should bring forth fruit unto God. Ver. 6. But *now we are delivered from the law,* that being dead wherein we were held; that we should serve in newness of spirit, and not in the oldness of the letter. Gal. iv. 4. But when the fulness of the time was come, God sent forth his Son, made of a woman, made under the law, Ver. 5. *To redeem them that were under the law,* that we might receive the adoption of sons.

g Rom. iii. 20. Therefore *by the deeds of the law there shall no flesh be justified in his sight:* for by the law is the knowledge of sin.

h Gal. v. 23. Meekness, temperance: *against such there is no law.* Rom. viii. 1. There is therefore now *no condemnation to them which are in Christ Jesus,* who walk not after the flesh, but after the Spirit.

i Rom. vii. 24. O wretched man that I am! *who shall deliver me* from the body of this death? Ver. 25. *I thank God through Jesus Christ our Lord.* So then with the mind I myself serve the law of God, but with the flesh the law of sin. Gal. iii. 13. *Christ hath redeemed us from the curse of the law, being made a curse for us:* for it is written, Cursed is every one that hangeth on a tree: Ver. 14. *That the blessing of Abraham might come on the Gentiles through Jesus Christ;* that we might receive the promise of the Spirit through faith. Rom. viii. 3. For what the law could not do, in that it was weak through the flesh, God sending *his own Son in the likeness of sinful flesh, and for sin, condemned sin in the flesh;* Ver. 4. *That the righteousness of the law might be fulfilled in us,* who walk not after the flesh, but after the Spirit.

k Luke i. 68. *Blessed be the Lord God of Israel; for he hath visited and redeemed his people,* Ver. 69. And hath raised up an horn of salvation for us in the house of his servant David. Ver. 74. That he would grant unto us, *that we, being delivered out of the hand of our enemies, might serve him without fear,* Ver. 75. *In holiness and righteousness* before him, all the days of our life. Col. i. 12. *Giving thanks unto the Father, which hath made us meet* to be partakers of the inheritance of the saints in light: Ver. 13. *Who hath delivered us from the power of darkness,* and hath translated us into the kingdom of his dear Son; Ver. 14. *In whom we have redemption through his blood,* even the forgiveness of sins.

l Rom. vii. 22. For *I delight in the law of God after the inward man.* Rom. xii. 2. And be not conformed to this world; but *be ye transformed* by the renewing of your mind, *that ye may prove what is that good, and acceptable, and perfect will of God.* Tit. ii. 11. For the *grace of God* that bringeth salvation hath appeared to all men, Ver. 12. *Teaching us, that, denying ungodliness and worldly lusts,* we should live soberly, righteously, and godly, in this present world; Ver. 13. *Looking for that blessed hope,* and the glorious appearing of the great God and our *Saviour Jesus Christ;* Ver. 14. *Who gave himself for us,* that he might redeem us from all iniquity, and *purify unto himself a peculiar people, zealous of good works.*

98. m Deut. x. 4. *And he wrote on the tables, according to the first writing, the ten commandments, which the Lord spake unto you in the mount,* out of the midst of the fire, in the day of the assembly: and the Lord gave them unto me. Exod. xxxiv. 1. And the Lord said unto Moses, Hew thee two tables of stone like unto the first; and *I will write upon these tables* the words that were in the first tables, which thou brakest. Ver. 2. And be ready in the morning, and come up in the morning unto mount Sinai, and present thyself there to me in the top of the mount. Ver. 3. And no man shall come up with thee, etc. Ver. 4. And he hewed *two tables of stone,* like unto the first: and Moses rose up early in the morning, and went up unto mount Sinai, as the Lord had commanded him, *and took in his hand the two tables of stone.*

n Matt. xxii. 37. Jesus said unto him.

Q. 99. *What rules are to be observed for the right understanding of the ten commandments?*

A. For the right understanding of the ten commandments, these rules are to be observed:

1. That the law is perfect, and bindeth every one to full conformity in the whole man unto the righteousness thereof, and unto entire obedience for ever; so as to require the utmost perfection of every duty, and to forbid the least degree of every sin.º

2. That it is spiritual, and so reacheth the understanding, will, affections, and all other powers of the soul; as well as words, works, and gestures.p

3. That one and the same thing, in divers respects, is required or forbidden in several commandments.q

4. That as, where a duty is commanded, the contrary sin is forbidden;r and, where a sin is forbidden, the contrary duty is command-

---

Thou shalt love the Lord thy God with all thy heart, and with all thy soul, and with all thy mind. Ver. 38. This is the first and great commandment. Ver. 39. And the second is like unto it, *Thou shalt love thy neighbour as thyself.* Ver. 40. On these two commandments hang all the law and the prophets.

99. º Ps. xix. 7. *The law of the Lord is perfect*, converting the soul: the testimony of the Lord is sure, making wise the simple. James ii. 10. For *whosoever shall keep the whole law, and yet offend in one point, he is guilty of all.* Matt. v. 21. Ye have heard that it was said by them of old time, *Thou shalt not kill;* and whosoever shall kill shall be in danger of the judgment: Ver. 22. But *I say unto you,* That whosoever is *angry with his brother without a cause* shall be in danger of the *judgment;* and whosoever shall *say to his brother, Raca,* shall be in danger of the *council;* but whosoever shall say, *Thou fool,* shall be in danger of *hell-fire.*

p Rom. vii. 14. For we know that the law *is spiritual;* but I am carnal, sold under sin. Deut. vi. 5. And *thou shalt love the Lord thy God with all thine heart, and with all thy soul, and with all thy might.* Compared with Matt. xxii. 37. Jesus said unto him, Thou shalt *love the Lord thy God with all thy heart, and with all thy soul, and with all thy mind.* Ver. 38. *This is the first and great commandment.* Ver. 39. And the *second is like* unto it, Thou shalt *love thy neighbour as thyself.* Matt. v. 21, 22. [See letter o.] Ver. 27. Ye have heard that it was said by them of old time, *Thou shalt not commit adultery:* Ver. 28. But *I say unto you,* That whosoever *looketh on a woman to lust after her, hath committed adultery with her already in his heart.* Ver. 33. Again, ye have heard that it hath been said by them of old time, *Thou shalt not forswear thyself,* but shalt *perform unto the Lord thine oaths:* Ver. 34. But *I say unto you, Swear not at all;* neither by heaven; for it is God's throne: Ver. 37. But let your communication be, *Yea, yea; Nay, nay;* for *whatsoever is more than these cometh of evil.* Ver. 38. Ye have heard that it hath been said, *An eye for an eye, and a tooth for a tooth:* Ver. 39. But *I say unto you,* That ye *resist not evil.* Ver. 43. Ye have heard that it hath been said, Thou shalt love thy neighbour, and *hate thine enemy:* Ver. 44. But *I say unto you, Love your enemies, bless them that curse you, do good to them that hate you,* and *pray for them which despitefully use you, and persecute you,* &c.

q Col. iii. 5. Mortify therefore your members which are upon the earth; fornication, uncleanness, inordinate affection, evil concupiscence, and *covetousness, which is idolatry.* Amos viii. 5. Saying, *When* will the *new moon be gone,* that we may *sell corn?* and the *sabbath,* that we may *set forth wheat,* making the *ephah* small, and the *shekel* great, and *falsifying the balances by deceit?* Prov. i. 19. So are the ways of every one that is *greedy of gain; which taketh away the life of the owners thereof.* 1 Tim. vi. 10. For *the love of money* is the *root of all evil;* which while some *coveted after,* they have *erred from the faith, and pierced themselves through with many sorrows.*

r Isa. lviii. 13. If thou turn away thy foot from the *sabbath, from doing thy pleasure on my holy day;* and *call the sabbath a delight,* the holy of the Lord, honourable; and *shalt honour him, not doing thine own ways, nor finding thine own pleasure, nor speaking thine own words.* Deut. vi. 13. *Thou shalt fear the Lord thy God, and serve him,* and shalt swear by his name. Compared with Matt. iv. 9. And saith unto him, All these things will I give thee, if thou wilt fall down and worship me. Ver. 10. Then saith Jesus unto him, *Get thee hence, Satan: for it is written, Thou shalt worship the Lord thy God, and him only shalt thou serve.* Matt. xv. 4. For God commanded, saying, *Honour thy father and mother:* and, *He that curseth father or mother, let him die the death.* Ver. 5. *But ye say,* Whosoever shall say to his father, or his mother, It is a gift, by whatsoever thou mightest be profited by me, Ver. 6. *And honour not his father or his mother,* he shall be free. *Thus have ye made the commandment of God of none effect* by your tradition.

ed;⁵ so, where a promise is annexed, the contrary threatening is included;ᵗ and, where a threatening is annexed, the contrary promise is included.ᵛ

5. That what God forbids, is at no time to be done;ʷ what he commands, is always our duty;ˣ and yet every particular duty is not to be done at all times.ʸ

6. That under one sin or duty, all of the same kind are forbidden or commanded; together with all the causes, means, occasions, and appearances thereof, and provocations thereunto.ᶻ

7. That what is forbidden or commanded to ourselves, we are bound, according to our places, to endeavour that it may be avoided or performed by others, according to the duty of their places.ᵃ

ˢ Matt. v. 21, 22. [See letter o.] Ver. 23. Therefore, if thou bring thy gift to the altar, and there rememberest that thy brother hath ought against thee; Ver. 24. Leave there thy gift before the altar, and go thy way ; *first be reconciled to thy brother*, and then come and offer thy gift. Ver. 25. *Agree with thine adversary* quickly, whiles thou art in the way with him ; lest, &c. Eph. iv. 28. *Let him that stole steal no more: but rather let him labour, working with his hands the thing which is good*, that he may have to give to him that needeth.

ᵗ Exod. xx. 12. *Honour thy father and thy mother; that thy days may be long upon the land* which the Lord thy God giveth thee. Compared with Prov. xxx. 17. The *eye that mocketh at his father, and despiseth to obey his mother, the ravens of the valley shall pick it out, and the young eagles shall eat it.*

ᵛ Jer. xviii. 7. *At what instant I shall speak concerning a nation, and concerning a kingdom, to pluck up, and to pull down, and to destroy it;* Ver. 8. *If that nation, against whom I have pronounced, turn from their evil, I will repent of the evil* that I thought to do unto them. Exod. xx. 7. Thou shalt not take the name of the Lord thy God in vain : for the Lord will not hold him guiltless that taketh his name in vain. Compared with Ps. xv. 1. *Lord, who shall abide in thy tabernacle?* who shall dwell in thy holy hill? Ver. 4. In whose eyes a vile person is contemned ; but he honoureth them that fear the Lord : *he that sweareth to his own hurt, and changeth not.* Ver. 5. *He that putteth not out his money to usury, nor taketh reward against the innocent. He that doeth these things shall never be moved.* And with Ps. xxiv. 4. He that hath clean hands, and a pure heart; who hath not lifted up his soul unto vanity, *nor sworn deceitfully.* Ver. 5. *He shall receive the blessing from the Lord,* and righteousness from the God of his salvation.

ʷ Job xiii. 7. Will ye speak wickedly for God? and talk deceitfully for him? Ver. 8. Will ye accept his person? will ye contend for God? Rom. iii. 8. And not rather, (as we be slanderously reported, and as *some affirm that we say,*) *Let us do evil,that good may come?* whose damnation *is just.* Job xxxvi. 21. Take heed, *regard not iniquity:* for this hast thou chosen rather than affliction. Heb. xi. 25. *Choosing rather to suffer affliction* with the people of God, *than to enjoy the pleasures of sin for a season.*

ˣ Deut. iv. 8. And what nation is there so great, that hath statutes and judgments so righteous as all this law, which I set before you this day? Ver. 9. *Only take heed to thyself, and keep thy soul diligently, lest thou forget the things* which thine eyes have seen, and *lest they depart from thy heart all the days of thy life;* but teach them thy sons, and thy sons' sons.

ʸ Matt. xii. 7. But if ye had known what this meaneth, *I will have mercy, and not sacrifice,* ye would not have condemned the guiltless.

ᶻ Matt. v. 21, 22, 27, 28. [See in letter o before.] Matt. xv. 4. For God commanded, saying, *Honour thy father and mother:* and, He that curseth father and mother, let him die the death. Ver. 5. *But ye say, Whosoever shall say to his father, or his mother, It is a gift,* by whatsoever thou mightest be profited by me, Ver. 6. *And honour not his father, or his mother,* he shall be free. *Thus have ye made the commandment of God of none effect* by your tradition. Heb. x. 24. And *let us consider one another, to provoke unto love, and to good works:* Ver. 25. *Not forsaking the assembling of ourselves together,* as the manner of some is ; but *exhorting one another:* and so much the more, as ye see the day approaching. 1 Thess. v. 22. *Abstain from all appearance of evil.* Jude, ver. 23. And others *save with fear,* pulling them out of the fire ; *hating even the garment spotted by the flesh.* Gal. v. 26. *Let us not be desirous of vain-glory, provoking one another, envying one another.* Col. iii. 21. Fathers, *provoke not your children to anger,* lest they be discouraged.

ᵃ Exod. xx. 10. But the seventh day is the sabbath of the Lord thy God: in it thou shalt not do any work, *thou, nor thy son, nor thy daughter, thy man-servant, nor thy maid-servant, nor thy cattle, nor thy stranger that is within thy gates.* Lev. xix. 17. Thou shalt not hate thy brother in thine heart : *thou shalt in any wise rebuke thy neighbour, and not suffer sin upon him.* Gen. xviii. 19. For I know him, *that he will command his children and his household after him, and they shall keep the way of the Lord,* to do justice and judgment ; that the Lord may bring upon Abraham that which

8. That in what is commanded to others, we are bound, according to our places and callings, to be helpful to them;[b] and to take heed of partaking with others in what is forbidden them.[c]

Q. 100. *What special things are we to consider in the ten commandments?*

A. We are to consider, in the ten commandments, the preface, the substance of the commandments themselves, and several reasons annexed to some of them, the more to enforce them.

Q. 101. *What is the preface to the ten commandments?*

A. The preface to the ten commandments is contained in these words, *I am the Lord thy God, which have brought thee out of the land of Egypt, out of the house of bondage*.[d] Wherein God manifesteth his sovereignty, as being JEHOVAH, the eternal, immutable, and almighty God;[e] having his being in and of himself,[f] and giving being to all his words[g] and works:[h] and that he is a God in covenant, as with Israel of old, so with all his people;[i] who, as he brought them out of their bondage in Egypt, so he delivereth us from our spiritual thraldom;[k] and that therefore we are bound to take him for our God alone, and to keep all his commandments.[l]

Q. 102. *What is the sum of the four commandments which contain our duty to God?*

A. The sum of the four commandments containing our duty to God, is, to love the Lord our God with all our heart, and with all our soul, and with all our strength, and with all our mind.[m]

---

he hath spoken of him. Josh. xxiv. 15. And if it seem evil unto you to serve the Lord, choose you this day whom ye will serve; whether the gods which your fathers served, that were on the other side of the flood, or the gods of the Amorites, in whose land ye dwell: but *as for me and my house, we will serve the Lord.* Deut. vi. 6. And these words, which I command thee this day, shall be in thine heart; Ver. 7. And *thou shalt teach them diligently unto thy children*, and shalt *talk* of them when thou *sittest in thine house*, and when thou *walkest by the way*, and when thou *liest down*, and when thou *risest up.*

b 2 Cor. i. 24. Not for that we have dominion over your faith, *but are helpers of your joy:* for by faith ye stand.

c 1 Tim. v. 22. Lay hands suddenly on no man, *neither be partaker of other men's sins: keep thyself pure.* Eph. v. 11. And *have no fellowship with the unfruitful works of darkness*, but rather reprove them.

101. d Exod. xx. 2.

e Isa. xliv. 6. Thus saith *the Lord*, the King of Israel, and his Redeemer *the Lord of hosts; I am the first, and I am the last;* and besides me there is no God.

f Exod. iii. 14. And God said unto Moses, I AM THAT I AM: and he said, Thus shalt thou say unto the children of Israel, I AM hath sent me unto you.

g Exod. vi. 3. And I appeared unto Abraham, unto Isaac, and unto Jacob, by the name of God Almighty; *but by my name JEHOVAH was I not known to them.*

h Acts xvii. 24. *God, that made the world, and all things therein*, seeing that he is Lord of heaven and earth, dwelleth not in temples made with hands. Ver. 28. For *in him we live, and move, and have our being;* as certain also of your own poets have said, For we are also his offspring.

i Gen. xvii. 7. And *I will establish my covenant between me and thee, and thy seed after thee, in their generations, for an everlasting covenant, to be a God unto thee, and to thy seed after thee.* Compared with Rom. iii. 29. *Is he the God of the Jews only? is he not also of the Gentiles? Yes, of the Gentiles also.*

k Luke i. 74. That he would grant unto us, that we, *being delivered out of the hand of our enemies*, might serve him without fear, Ver. 75. In holiness and righteousness before him, all the days of our life.

l 1 Pet. i. 15. But *as he which hath called you is holy, so be ye holy* in all manner of conversation: Ver. 16. Because it is written, *Be ye holy; for I am holy.* Ver. 17. And if ye call on the Father, who without respect of persons judgeth according to every man's work, *pass the time of your sojourning here in fear:* Ver. 18. Forasmuch as ye know that ye were not *redeemed* with corruptible things, as silver and gold, *from your vain conversation* received by tradition from your fathers. Lev. xviii. 30. Therefore shall ye *keep mine ordinance*, that ye commit not any one of these abominable customs, which were committed before you, and that ye defile not yourselves therein: I am the Lord your God. Lev. xix. 37. *Therefore shall ye observe all my statutes, and all my judgments, and do them: I am the Lord.*

102. m Luke x. 27. And he answering, said, *Thou shalt love the Lord thy God with*

Q. 103. *Which is the first commandment?*
A. The first commandment is, *Thou shalt have no other gods before me.*[n]
Q. 104. *What are the duties required in the first commandment?*
A. The duties required in the first commandment are, the knowing and acknowledging of God to be the only true God, and our God;[o] and to worship and glorify him accordingly,[p] by thinking,[q] meditating,[r] remembering,[s] highly esteeming,[t] honouring,[v] adoring,[w] choosing,[x] loving,[y] desiring,[z] fearing of him;[a] believing him;[b] trusting,[c] hoping,[d] delighting,[e] rejoicing in him;[f] being zealous for him;[g] calling upon him, giving all praise and thanks,[h] and yielding all obedience and

all thy heart, and with all thy soul, and with all thy strength, and with all thy mind; and thy neighbour as thyself.
103. [n] Exod. xx. 3.
104. [o] 1 Chron. xxviii. 9. And thou, Solomon my son, *know thou the God of thy father*, and serve him with a perfect heart, and with a willing mind; for the Lord searcheth all hearts, and understandeth all the imaginations of the thoughts: if thou seek him, he will be found of thee; but if thou forsake him, he will cast thee off for ever. Deut. xxvi. 17. Thou hast *avouched the Lord this day to be thy God*, and to walk in his ways, and to keep his statutes, and his commandments, and his judgments, and to hearken unto his voice. Isa. xliii. 10. Ye are my witnesses, saith the Lord, and my servant whom I have chosen; that ye may *know and believe me, and understand that I am he: before me there was no God formed, neither shall there be after me.* Jer. xiv. 22. *Are there any among the vanities of the Gentiles that can cause rain?* or can the heavens give showers? *Art not thou he, O Lord our God?* therefore we will wait upon thee; for thou hast made all these things.
[p] Ps. xcv. 6. O come, *let us worship and bow down; let us kneel before the Lord our Maker.* Ver. 7. For he is our God; and we are the people of his pasture, and the sheep of his hand. Matt. iv. 10. Then saith Jesus unto him, Get thee hence, Satan: for it is written, *Thou shalt worship the Lord thy God*, and *him* only shalt thou *serve*. Ps. xxix. 2. *Give unto the Lord the glory* due unto his name; *worship the Lord* in the beauty of holiness.
[q] Mal. iii. 16. Then they that feared the Lord spake often one to another: and the Lord hearkened, and heard it; and a book of remembrance was written before him for them that *feared the Lord, and that thought upon his name*.
[r] Ps. lxiii. 6. When I remember thee upon my bed, and *meditate on thee* in the night-watches.
[s] Eccl. xii. 1 *Remember now thy Creator* in the days of thy youth, while the evil days come not, nor the years draw nigh, when thou shalt say, I have no pleasure in them.
[t] Ps. lxxi. 19. Thy righteousness also, O God, is very high, who hast done great things: *O God, who is like unto thee?*
[v] Mal. i. 6. A son *honoureth* his father, and a servant his master: *if then I be a father, where is mine honour?* and if I be a master, where is my fear? saith the Lord of hosts unto you, O priests, that despise my name.
[w] Isa. xlv. 23. I have sworn by myself, the word is gone out of my mouth in righteousness, and shall not return, *That unto me every knee shall bow*, every tongue shall swear.
[x] Josh. xxiv. 15. And if it seem evil unto you to serve the Lord, choose you this day whom ye will serve; whether the gods which your fathers served, that were on the other side of the flood, or the gods of the Amorites, in whose land ye dwell: but as for me and my house, we will serve the Lord. Ver. 22. And Joshua said unto the people, Ye are witnesses against yourselves *that ye have chosen you the Lord*, to serve him. And they said, We are witnesses.
[y] Deut. vi. 5. And *thou shalt love the Lord thy God* with all thine heart, and with all thy soul, and with all thy might.
[z] Ps. lxxiii. 25. Whom have I in heaven but thee? and there is *none upon earth that I desire besides thee*.
[a] Isa. viii. 13. Sanctify the Lord of hosts himself; and *let him be your fear*, and *let him be your dread*.
[b] Exod. xiv. 31. And Israel saw that great work which the Lord did upon the Egyptians; and the people feared the Lord, *and believed* the Lord, and his servant Moses.
[c] Isa. xxvi. 4. *Trust ye in the Lord for ever:* for in the Lord JEHOVAH is everlasting strength.
[d] Ps. cxxx. 7. *Let Israel hope in the Lord;* for with the Lord there is mercy, and with him is plenteous redemption.
[e] Ps. xxxvii. 4. *Delight thyself also in the Lord;* and he shall give thee the desires of thine heart.
[f] Ps. xxxii. 11. *Be glad in the Lord, and rejoice,* ye righteous: and *shout for joy,* all ye that are upright in heart.
[g] Rom. xii. 11. Not slothful in business; *fervent in spirit; serving the Lord.* Compared with Num. xxv. 11. *Phinehas,* the son of Eleazar, the son of Aaron the priest, hath turned my wrath away from the children of Israel, *while he was zealous* for my sake among them, that I consumed not the children of Israel in my jealousy.
[h] Phil. iv. 6. Be careful for nothing: but in every thing by *prayer and supplication, with thanksgiving, let your requests be made known unto God*.

submission to him with the whole man;^i being careful in all things to please him,^k and sorrowful when in any thing he is offended;^l and walking humbly with him.^m

Q. 105. *What are the sins forbidden in the first commandment?*

A. The sins forbidden in the first commandment, are, Atheism, in denying or not having a God;^n Idolatry, in having or worshipping more gods than one, or any with or instead of the true God;^o the not having and avouching him for God, and our God;^p the omission or neglect of any thing due to him, required in this commandment;^q ignorance,^r forgetfulness,^s misapprehensions,^t false opinions,^v unworthy and wicked thoughts of him;^w bold and curious searching into his secrets;^x all profaneness,^y hatred of God;^z self-love,^a self-seeking,^b and

---

^i Jer. vii. 23. But this thing commanded I them, saying, *Obey my voice, and I will be your God,* and ye shall be my people; and *walk ye in all the ways that I have commanded you,* that it may be well unto you. James iv. 7. *Submit yourselves therefore to God.* Resist the devil, and he will flee from you.

^k 1 John iii. 22. And whatsoever we ask, we receive of him, because we keep his commandments, *and do those things that are pleasing in his sight.*

^l Jer. xxxi. 18. I have surely heard *Ephraim bemoaning himself thus; Thou hast chastised me, and I was chastised, as a bullock unaccustomed to the yoke:* turn thou me, and I shall be turned; for thou art the Lord my God. Ps. cxix. 136. *Rivers of waters run down mine eyes, because they keep not thy law.*

^m Micah vi. 8. He hath shewed thee, O man, what is good; and what doth the Lord require of thee, but to do justly, and to love mercy, and *to walk humbly with thy God?*

105. ^n Ps. xiv. 1. The fool hath *said in his heart, There is no God.* They are corrupt; they have done abominable works; there is none that doeth good. Eph. ii. 12. That at that time ye were without Christ, being aliens from the commonwealth of Israel, and strangers from the covenants of promise, having no hope, and *without God in the world.*

^o Jer. ii. 27. *Saying to a stock, Thou art my father;* and *to a stone, Thou hast brought me forth;* for they have turned their back unto me, and not their face; but in the time of their trouble they will say, Arise, and save us. Ver. 28. But where are thy gods that thou hast made thee? let them arise, if they can save thee in the time of thy trouble: for *according to the number of thy cities are thy gods, O Judah.* Compared with 1 Thess. i. 9. For they themselves shew of us what manner of entering in we had unto you, and how ye *turned to God from idols, to serve the living and true God.*

^p Ps. lxxxi. 11. But my people would not hearken to my voice; and *Israel would none of me.*

^q Isa. xliii. 22. *But thou hast not called upon me,* O Jacob; but thou hast been weary of me, O Israel. Ver. 23. *Thou hast not brought me the small cattle of thy burnt-offerings, neither hast thou honoured me with thy sacrifices:* I have not caused thee to serve with an offering, nor wearied thee with incense. Ver. 24. *Thou hast bought me no sweet cane with money, neither hast thou filled me with the fat of thy sacrifices;* but thou hast made me to serve with thy sins, thou hast wearied me with thine iniquities.

^r Jer. iv. 22. For my people is foolish, *they have not known me;* they are sottish children, and *they have none understanding:* they are wise to do evil, but to do good they have no knowledge. Hos. iv. 1. Hear the word of the Lord, ye children of Israel: for *the Lord hath a controversy* with the inhabitants of the land, *because there is no truth,* nor *mercy,* nor *knowledge of God in the land.* Ver. 6. My people are *destroyed for lack of knowledge:* because thou hast rejected knowledge, I will also reject thee, that thou shalt be no priest to me: seeing thou hast forgotten the law of thy God, I will also forget thy children.

^s Jer. ii. 32. Can a maid forget her ornaments, or a bride her attire? yet *my people have forgotten me* days without number.

^t Acts xvii. 23. For as I passed by, and beheld your devotions, I found an altar with this inscription, TO THE UNKNOWN GOD. *Whom therefore ye ignorantly worship,* him declare I unto you. Ver. 29. Forasmuch then as we are the offspring of God, *we ought not to think that the Godhead is like unto gold,* or silver, or stone, graven by art and man's device.

^v Isa. xl. 18. *To whom then will ye liken God?* or what likeness will ye compare unto him?

^w Ps. l. 21. These things hast thou done, and I kept silence; *thou thoughtest that I was altogether such an one as thyself:* but I will reprove thee, and set them in order before thine eyes.

^x Deut. xxix. 29. The *secret things belong unto the Lord our God;* but those things which are revealed belong unto us and to our children for ever, that we may do all the words of this law.

^y Tit. i. 16. They profess that they know God; *but in works they deny him, being abominable, and disobedient, and unto every good work reprobate.* Heb. xii. 16. Lest there be any fornicator, or *profane person, as Esau,* who for one morsel of meat sold his birthright.

^z Rom. i. 30. Backbiters, *haters of God,* despiteful, proud, boasters.

all other inordinate and immoderate setting of our mind, will, or affections upon other things, and taking them off from him in whole or in part;[c] vain credulity,[d] unbelief,[e] heresy,[f] misbelief,[g] distrust,[h] despair,[i] incorrigibleness,[k] and insensibleness under judgments,[l] hardness of heart,[m] pride,[n] presumption,[o] carnal security,[p] tempting of God;[q] using unlawful means,[r] and trusting in unlawful means;[s] carnal delights and joys;[t] corrupt, blind, and indiscreet zeal;[v] lukewarmness,[w] and deadness in the things of God;[x] estranging ourselves, and apostatizing from God;[y] praying, or giving any religious worship, to

[a] 2 Tim. iii. 2. For men shall be *lovers of their own selves*, covetous, boasters, proud, blasphemers, disobedient to parents, unthankful, unholy.
[b] Phil. ii. 21. For *all seek their own*, not the things which are Jesus Christ's.
[c] 1 John ii. 15. *Love not the world, neither the things that are in the world. If any man love the world, the love of the Father is not in him.* Ver. 16. For all that is in the world, the lust of the flesh, and the lust of the eyes, and the pride of life, is not of the Father, but is of the world. 1 Sam. ii. 29. Wherefore kick ye at my sacrifice, and at mine offering, which I have commanded in my habitation; and *honourest thy sons above me*, to make yourselves fat with the chiefest of all the offerings of Israel my people? Col. iii. 2. *Set your affection* on things above, *not on things on the earth.* Ver. 5. Mortify therefore your members which are upon the earth; fornication, uncleanness, inordinate affection, evil concupiscence, and covetousness, which is idolatry.
[d] 1 John iv. 1. Beloved, *believe not every spirit*, but try the spirits whether they are of God; because many false prophets are gone out into the world.
[e] Heb. iii. 12. Take heed, brethren, lest there be in any of you *an evil heart of unbelief*, in departing from the living God.
[f] Gal. v. 20. Idolatry, witchcraft, hatred, variance, emulations, wrath, strife, seditions, *heresies*. Tit. iii. 10. *A man that is an heretic*, after the first and second admonition, reject.
[g] Acts xxvi. 9. *I verily thought with myself, that I ought to do many things contrary to the name of Jesus of Nazareth.*
[h] Ps. lxxviii. 22. Because they believed not in God, and *trusted not in his salvation.*
[i] Gen. iv. 13. And *Cain said* unto the Lord, *My punishment is greater than I can bear.*
[k] Jer. v. 3. O Lord, are not thine eyes upon the truth? *thou hast stricken them, but they have not grieved; thou hast consumed them, but they have refused to receive correction:* they have made their faces harder than a rock; *they have refused to return.*
[l] Isa. xlii. 25. Therefore he hath poured upon him the *fury of his anger*, and the *strength of battle:* and it hath *set him on fire* round about, *yet he knew not;* and it *burned him, yet he laid it not to heart.*
[m] Rom. ii. 5. But after *thy hardness and impenitent heart*, treasurest up unto thyself wrath against the day of wrath and revelation of the righteous judgment of God.

[n] Jer. xiii. 15. Hear ye, and give ear; *be not proud:* for the Lord hath spoken.
[o] Ps. xix. 13. *Keep back thy servant also from presumptuous sins;* let them not have dominion over me: then shall I be upright, and I shall be innocent from the great transgression.
[p] Zeph. i. 12. And it shall come to pass at that time, that I will search Jerusalem with candles, and *punish the men that are settled on their lees; that say in their heart, The Lord will not do good, neither will he do evil.*
[q] Matt. iv. 7. Jesus said unto him, It is written again, *Thou shalt not tempt the Lord thy God.*
[r] Rom. iii. 8. And not rather, (*as we be slanderously reported, and as some affirm that we say,*) *Let us do evil, that good may come?* *whose damnation is just.*
[s] Jer. xvii. 5. Thus saith the Lord, *Cursed be the man that trusteth in man, and maketh flesh his arm*, and whose heart departeth from the Lord.
[t] 2 Tim. iii. 4. Traitors, heady, highminded, *lovers of pleasures* more than lovers of God.
[v] Gal. iv. 17. They *zealously affect you, but not well;* yea, they would exclude you, that ye might affect them. John xvi. 2. They shall put you out of the synagogues: yea, the time cometh that *whosoever killeth you will think that he doeth God service.* Rom. x. 2. For I bear them record, that they have a *zeal of God, but not according to knowledge.* Luke ix. 54. And when his disciples James and John saw this, they said, Lord, wilt thou that we *command fire to come down from heaven,* and consume them, even as Elias did? Ver. 55. But he turned, and rebuked them, and said, *Ye know not what manner of spirit ye are of.*
[w] Rev. iii. 16. So then *because thou art lukewarm, and neither cold nor hot.* I will spue thee out of my mouth.
[x] Rev. iii. 1. And unto the angel of the *church in Sardis* write; These things saith he that hath the seven Spirits of God, and the seven stars; I know thy works, that *thou hast a name that thou livest, and art dead.*
[y] Ezek. xiv. 5. That I may take the house of Israel in their own heart, because *they are all estranged from me through their idols.* Isa. i. 4. Ah sinful nation, a people laden with iniquity, a seed of evil-doers, children that are corrupters! *They have forsaken the Lord,* they have provoked the Holy One of Israel unto anger, *they are gone away backward.* Ver. 5. Why should ye be stricken any more? *ye will revolt*

saints, angels, or any other creatures;ᶻ all compacts and consulting with the devil,ᵃ and hearkening to his suggestions;ᵇ making men the lords of our faith and conscience;ᶜ slighting and despising God and his commands;ᵈ resisting and grieving of his Spirit,ᵉ discontent and impatience at his dispensations, charging him foolishly for the evils he inflicts on us;ᶠ and ascribing the praise of any good we either are, have, or can do, to fortune,ᵍ idols,ʰ ourselves,ⁱ or any other creature.ᵏ

more and more. The whole head is sick, and the whole heart faint.
ᶻ Rom. x. 13. For whosoever shall call upon the name of the Lord shall be saved. Ver. 14. *How then shall they call on him in whom they have not believed?* and how shall they believe in whom they have not heard? and how shall they hear without a preacher? Hosea iv. 12. *My people ask counsel at their stocks,* and their staff declareth unto them: for the spirit of whoredoms hath caused them to err, and *they have gone a whoring from under their God.* Acts x. 25. And as Peter was coming in, *Cornelius met him, and fell down at his feet, and worshipped him.* Ver. 26. But *Peter took him up, saying, Stand up; I myself also am a man.* Rev. xix. 10. And *I fell at his feet to worship him. And he said unto me, See thou do it not:* I am thy fellow-servant, and of thy brethren that have the testimony of Jesus: worship God: for the testimony of Jesus is the spirit of prophecy. Matt. iv. 10. Then saith Jesus unto him, Get thee hence, Satan: for it is written, *Thou shalt worship the Lord thy God, and him only shalt thou serve.* Col. ii. 18. Let no man beguile you of your reward *in a voluntary humility, and worshipping of angels,* intruding into those things which he hath not seen, vainly puffed up by his fleshly mind. Rom. i. 25. Who changed the truth of God into a lie, and worshipped and *served the creature more than the Creator,* who is blessed for ever. Amen.
ᵃ Lev. xx. 6. And the soul *that turneth after such as have familiar spirits, and after wizards,* to go a whoring after them, I will even set my face against that soul, and will cut him off from among his people. 1 Sam. xxviii. 7. *Then said Saul unto his servants, Seek me a woman that hath a familiar spirit,* that I may go to her, and enquire of her. And his servants said to him, Behold, there is a woman that hath a familiar spirit at En-dor. Ver. 11. Then said the woman, Whom shall I bring up unto thee? And he said, Bring me up Samuel. Compared with 1 Chron. x. 13. *So Saul died for his transgression* which he committed against the Lord, even against the word of the Lord, which he kept not, and *also for asking counsel of one that had a familiar spirit, to enquire of it;* Ver. 14. And enquired not of the Lord: therefore he slew him, and turned the kingdom unto David the son of Jesse.
ᵇ Acts v. 3. But Peter said, Ananias, *why hath Satan filled thine heart to lie to the Holy Ghost,* and to keep back part of the price of the land?
ᶜ 2 Cor. i. 24. *Not for that we have dominion over your faith,* but are helpers of your joy: for by faith ye stand. Matt. xxiii. 9. And *call no man your father upon the earth:* for one is your Father, which is in heaven.
ᵈ Deut. xxxii. 15. But *Jeshurun waxed fat, and kicked:* thou art waxen fat, thou art grown thick, thou art covered with fatness: then *he forsook God which made him, and lightly esteemed the Rock of his salvation.* 2 Sam. xii. 9. Wherefore hast thou *despised the commandment of the Lord,* to do evil in his sight? Thou hast killed Uriah the Hittite with the sword, and hast taken his wife to be thy wife, and hast slain him with the sword of the children of Ammon. Prov. xiii. 13. *Whoso despiseth the word shall be destroyed:* but he that feareth the commandment shall be rewarded.
ᵉ Acts vii. 51. Ye stiff-necked and uncircumcised in heart and ears, *ye do always resist the Holy Ghost:* as your fathers did, so do ye. Eph. iv. 30. And *grieve not the Holy Spirit of God,* whereby ye are sealed unto the day of redemption.
ᶠ Ps. lxxiii. 2. But as for me, my feet were almost gone; my steps had well nigh slipped. Ver. 3. For *I was envious at the foolish, when I saw the prosperity of the wicked.* Ver. 13. *Verily I have cleansed my heart in vain,* and washed my hands in innocency. Ver. 14. *For all the day long have I been plagued,* and chastened every morning. Ver. 15. *If I say, I will speak thus; behold, I should offend against the generation of thy children.* Ver. 22. So *foolish* was I, *and ignorant:* I was as a beast before thee. Job i. 22. In all this Job sinned not, *nor charged God foolishly.*
ᵍ 1 Sam. vi. 7. Now therefore make a new cart, and take two milch kine, on which there hath come no yoke, and tie the kine to the cart, and bring their calves home from them: Ver. 8. And take the *ark of the Lord,* and lay it upon the cart; and put the jewels of gold, which ye return him for a trespass-offering, in a coffer by the side thereof; and send it away, that it may go. Ver. 9. And see *if it goeth up by the way of his own coast* to Beth-shemesh, *then he hath done us this great evil:* but *if not, then we shall know* that it is not his hand that smote us; *it was a chance that happened to us.*
ʰ Dan. v. 23. But hast lifted up thyself against the Lord of heaven; and they have brought the vessels of his house before thee, and thou and thy lords, thy wives and thy concubines, have drunk wine in them; *and thou hast praised the gods of silver, and gold, of brass, iron, wood, and stone, which see not, nor hear, nor know:* and the God in whose hand thy breath is, and whose are all thy ways, hast thou not glorified.

Q. 106. *What are we specially taught by these words* [before me *in the first commandment?*

A. These words [*before me*] or before my face, in the first commandment, teach us, that God, who seeth all things, taketh special notice of, and is much displeased with, the sin of having any other god: that so it may be an argument to dissuade from it, and to aggravate it as a most impudent provocation:[l] as also to persuade us to do as in his sight, whatever we do in his service.[m]

Q. 107. *Which is the second commandment?*

A. The second commandment is, *Thou shalt not make unto thee any graven image, or any likeness of any thing that is in heaven above, or that is in the earth beneath, or that is in the water under the earth. Thou shalt not bow down thyself to them, nor serve them: for I the Lord thy God am a jealous God, visiting the iniquity of the fathers upon the children unto the third and fourth generation of them that hate me; and shewing mercy unto thousands of them that love me, and keep my commandments.*[n]

Q. 108. *What are the duties required in the second commandment?*

A. The duties required in the second commandment are, the receiving, observing, and keeping pure and entire, all such religious worship and ordinances as God hath instituted in his word;[o] particularly prayer and thanksgiving in the name of Christ;[p] the reading, preaching, and hearing of the word;[q] the administration and receiving

---

l Deut. viii. 17. And thou say in thine heart, *My power, and the might of mine hand, hath gotten me this wealth.* Dan. iv. 30. *The king spake, and said, Is not this great Babylon, that I have built* for the house of the kingdom, *by the might of my power,* and for the honour of my majesty?

k Hab. i. 16. Therefore *they sacrifice unto their net, and burn incense unto their drag;* because by them their portion is fat, and their meat plenteous.

106. l Ezek. viii. 5. Then said he unto me, Son of man, *lift up thine eyes* now the way toward the north. So I lifted up mine eyes the way toward the north, and behold northward at the gate of the altar this *image of jealousy in the entry.* Ver. 6. He said furthermore unto me, Son of man, *seest thou what they do? even the great abominations that the house of Israel committeth here,* that I should go far off from my sanctuary? But turn thee yet again, and thou shalt *see greater abominations,* etc. [to the end of the chapter.] Ps. xliv. 20. If we have forgotten the name of our God, or stretched out our hands to a strange god; Ver. 21. *Shall not God search this out?* for he *knoweth the secrets of the heart.*

m 1 Chron. xxviii. 9. And thou, Solomon my son, *know thou the God of thy father,* and *serve him with a perfect heart,* and with a willing mind *for the Lord searcheth all hearts,* and understandeth all the imaginations of the thoughts: if thou seek him, he will be found of thee; but if thou forsake him, he will cast thee off for ever.

107. n Exod. xx. 4, 5, 6.

108. o Deut. xxxii. 46. And he said unto them, *Set your hearts unto all the words which I testify among you this day, which ye shall command your children to observe to do, all the words of this law.* Ver. 47. For *it is not a vain thing for you;* because *it is your life:* and through this thing ye shall prolong your days in the land whither ye go over Jordan to possess it. Matt. xxviii. 20. *Teaching them to observe all things whatsoever I have commanded you:* and, lo, I am with you alway, even unto the end of the world. Acts ii. 42. And *they continued stedfastly in the apostles' doctrine* and fellowship, and in breaking of bread, and in prayers. 1 Tim. vi. 13. I give thee charge in the sight of God, who quickeneth all things, and before Christ Jesus, who before Pontius Pilate witnessed a good confession, Ver. 14. *That thou keep this commandment without spot, unrebukeable,* until the appearing of our Lord Jesus Christ.

p Phil. iv. 6. Be careful for nothing: but in *every thing by prayer and supplication, with thanksgiving, let your requests be made known unto God.* Eph. v. 20. *Giving thanks always* for all things unto God and the Father in the name of our Lord Jesus Christ.

q Deut. xvii. 18. And it shall be, when he sitteth upon the throne of his kingdom, that he shall *write him a copy of this law in a book,* out of that which is before the priests the Levites: Ver. 19. And it shall be with him, *and he shall read therein all the days of his life;* that he may learn to fear the Lord his God, to keep all the words of this law, and these statutes, to do them. Acts xv. 21. For Moses of old time hath in every city them *that preach him, being read in the synagogues every sabbath-day.* 2 Tim. iv. 2. *Preach the word;* be instant *in season, out of season;* reprove, rebuke, exhort, with all long-suffering and doctrine. James l.

of the sacraments;[r] church government and discipline;[s] the ministry and maintainance thereof;[t] religious fasting;[v] swearing by the name of God,[w] and vowing unto him:[x] as also the disapproving, detesting, opposing, all false worship;[y] and, according to each one's place and calling, removing it, and all monuments of idolatry.[z]

Q. 109. *What are the sins forbidden in the second commandment?*

A. The sins forbidden in the second commandment are, all devising,[a] counselling,[b] commanding,[c] using,[d] and any wise approving, any

---

21. Wherefore, lay apart all filthiness, and superfluity of naughtiness, and *receive with meekness the ingrafted word,* which is able to save your souls: Ver. 22. But be ye doers of the word, and not *hearers only,* deceiving your own selves. Acts x. 33. Immediately therefore I sent to thee; and thou hast well done that thou art come. Now therefore *are we all here present before God, to hear all things that are commanded thee of God.*

[r] Matt. xxviii. 19. Go ye therefore, and *teach all nations, baptizing them* in the name of the Father, and of the Son, and of the Holy Ghost. 1 Cor. xi. from ver. 23. to ver. 30. For *I have received of the Lord that which also I delivered unto you,* That the Lord Jesus, the same night in which he was betrayed, *took bread,* etc.

[s] Matt. xviii. 15. Moreover, *if thy brother shall trespass against thee, go and tell him his fault between thee and him alone:* if he shall hear thee, thou hast gained thy brother. Ver. 16. But if he will not hear thee, *then take with thee one or two more,* that in the mouth of two or three witnesses every word may be established. Ver. 17. And if he shall neglect to hear them, *tell it unto the church:* but if he neglect to hear the church, *let him be unto thee as an heathen man and a publican.* Matt. xvi. 19. And I will give unto thee *the keys of the kingdom of heaven;* and whatsoever thou shalt bind on earth shall be bound in heaven; and whatsoever thou shalt loose on earth shall be loosed in heaven. 1 Cor. chapter v. 1 Cor. xii. 28. And *God hath set some in the church,* first,*apostles;* secondarily, *prophets;* thirdly, *teachers;* after that *miracles;* then *gifts of healings, helps, governments, diversities of tongues.*

[t] Eph. iv. 11. And *he gave some, apostles;* and some, *prophets;* and some, *evangelists;* and some, *pastors* and *teachers;* Ver. 12. For the perfecting of the saints, *for the work of the ministry,* for the edifying of the body of Christ. 1 Tim. v. 17. *Let the elders that rule well be counted worthy of double honour, especially they who labour in the word and doctrine.* Ver. 18. For the scripture saith, Thou shalt not muzzle the ox that treadeth out the corn. And, *The labourer is worthy of his reward.* 1 Cor. ix. 7-15. *Who goeth a warfare any time at his own charges?* who planteth a vineyard, and eateth not of the fruit thereof? or who feedeth a flock, and eateth not of the milk of the flock? etc.

[v] Joel ii. 12. Therefore also now, saith the Lord, *Turn ye even to me* with all your heart, and *with fasting,* and with *weeping,* and with *mourning;* Ver. 13. And rend your heart, and not your garments, and turn unto the Lord your God: for he is gracious and merciful. 1 Cor. vii. 5. Defraud ye not one the other, except it be with consent for a time, *that ye may give yourselves to fasting* and prayer.

[w] Deut. vi. 13. Thou shalt fear the Lord thy God, and serve him, and *shalt swear by his name.*

[x] Isa. xix. 21. And the Lord shall be known to Egypt, and the Egyptians shall know the Lord in that day, and shall do sacrifice and oblation; yea, *they shall vow a vow unto the Lord,* and perform it. Ps. lxxvi. 11. *Vow, and pay unto the Lord your God:* let all that be round about him bring presents unto him that ought to be feared.

[y] Acts xvii. 16. Now, while Paul waited for them at Athens, *his spirit was stirred in him, when he saw the city wholly given to idolatry.* Ver. 17. Therefore *disputed* he in the synagogue with the Jews, and with the devout persons, and in the market daily with them that met with him. Ps. xvi. 4. Their sorrows shall be multiplied *that hasten after another god: their drink-offerings of blood will I not offer, nor take up their names into my lips.*

[z] Deut. vii. 5. But thus shall ye deal with them; *ye shall destroy their altars, and break down their images, and cut down their groves, and burn their graven images with fire.* Isa. xxx. 22. *Ye shall defile also the covering of thy graven images of silver,* and the ornament of thy molten images of gold: *thou shalt cast them away* as a menstruous cloth; thou shalt say unto it, Get thee hence.

109. [a] Numb. xv. 39. And it shall be unto you for a fringe, that ye may look upon it, and remember all the commandments of the Lord, and do them; and *that ye seek not after your own heart, and your own eyes,* after which ye used to go a whoring.

[b] Deut. xiii. 6. *If thy brother,* the son of thy mother, or *thy son,* or *thy daughter,* or *the wife of thy bosom,* or *thy friend,* which is as thine own soul, *entice thee* secretly, *saying, Let us go and serve other gods,* which thou hast not known, thou, nor thy fathers; Ver. 7. Namely, of the gods of the people which are round about you, nigh unto thee, or far off from thee, from the one end of the earth even unto the other end of the earth; Ver. 8. *Thou shalt not consent unto him,* nor hearken unto him; *neither shall thine eye pity him,* neither shalt thou spare, *neither shalt thou conceal him.*

[c] Hosea v. 11. *Ephraim is oppressed* and broken in judgment, *because he willingly*

religious worship not instituted by God himself;ᶜ tolerating a false religion;ᶠ the making any representation of God, of all or of any of the three persons, either inwardly in our mind, or outwardly in any kind of image or likeness of any creature whatsoever;ᵍ all worshipping of it,ʰ or God in it or by it;ⁱ the making of any representation of feigned deities,ᵏ and all worship of them, or service belonging to

walked after the commandment. Micah vi. 16. For *the statutes of Omri are kept, and all the works of the house of Ahab, and ye walk in their counsels;* that I should make thee a desolation, and the inhabitants thereof an hissing: therefore ye shall bear the reproach of my people.
d * 1 Kings xi. 33. Because that they have forsaken me, and have *worshipped Ashtoreth the goddess of the Zidonians, Chemosh* the god of the *Moabites*, and *Milcom* the god of the children of *Ammon*, and have not walked in my ways, to do that which is right in mine eyes, and to keep my statutes and my judgments, as did David his father. 1 Kings xii. 33. So he offered upon the *altar which he had made in Beth-el* the fifteenth day of the eighth month, even in the month *which he had devised of his own heart;* and ordained a feast unto the children of Israel: and he offered upon the altar, and burnt incense.
e Deut. xii. 30. *Take heed to thyself that thou be not snared by following them,* after that they be destroyed from before thee; and *that thou enquire not after their gods, saying, How did these nations serve their gods? even so will I do likewise.* Ver. 31. Thou shalt not do so unto the Lord thy God : for every abomination to the Lord which he hateth have they done unto their gods ; for even their sons and their daughters they have burnt in the fire to their gods. Ver. 32. What thing soever I command you, observe to do it: thou shalt not *add* thereto, nor *diminish* from it.
f Deut. xiii. from verse 6. to 12. [See letter b.] Zech. xiii. 2. And it shall come to pass in that day, saith the Lord of hosts, that I will cut off the names of the idols out of the land, and they shall no more be remembered ; and also I will cause the prophets and the unclean spirit to pass out of the land. Ver. 3. And it shall come to pass, that *when any shall yet prophesy, then his father and his mother that begat him shall say unto him, Thou shalt not live; for thou speakest lies in the name of the Lord: and his father and his mother that begat him shall thrust him through when he prophesieth.* Rev. ii. 2. I know thy works, and thy labour, and thy patience, and *how thou canst not bear them which are evil:* and thou hast tried them which say they are apostles, and are not, and hast found them liars. Ver. 14. But I have a *few things against thee, because thou hast there them that hold the doctrine of Balaam,* who taught Balac to cast a stumbling-block before the children of Israel, to eat things sacrificed unto idols, and to commit fornication. Ver. 15. *So hast thou also them that hold the doctrine of the Nicolaitanes,* which thing I hate. Ver. 20. Notwithstanding I have a few things against thee, *because thou sufferest that woman Jezebel, which calleth herself a prophetess, to teach and to seduce my servants* to commit fornication, and to eat things sacrificed unto idols. Rev. xvii. 12. And the *ten horns* which thou sawest are *ten kings,* which have received no kingdom as yet; but *receive power as kings one hour with the beast.* Ver. 16. And the ten horns which thou sawest upon the beast, these shall hate the whore, and shall make her desolate and naked, and shall eat her flesh, and burn her with fire. Ver. 17. For God hath put in their hearts to fulfil his will, and to agree, *and give their kingdom unto the beast, until the words of God shall be fulfilled.*
g Deut. iv. 15. *Take ye therefore good heed unto yourselves, (for ye saw no manner of similitude on the day that the Lord spake unto you in Horeb* out of the midst of the fire,) Ver. 16. *Lest ye corrupt yourselves, and make you a graven image, the similitude of any figure, the likeness of male or female;* Ver. 17. The *likeness of any beast* that is on the earth, *the likeness of any winged fowl* that flieth in the air; Ver. 18. The *likeness of any thing that creepeth on the ground,* the *likeness of any fish* that is in the waters beneath the earth: Ver. 19. And *lest thou lift up thine eyes unto heaven,* and when thou seest the *sun,* and the *moon,* and the *stars,* even all the host of heaven, *shouldest be driven to worship them, and serve them,* which the Lord thy God hath divided unto all nations under the whole heaven. Acts xvii. 29. Forasmuch then as we are the offspring of God, *we ought not to think that the Godhead is like unto gold, or silver, or stone, graven by art and man's device.* Rom. i. 21. Because that, when they knew God, they glorified him not as God, neither were thankful; but *became vain in their imaginations,* and their foolish heart was darkened. Ver. 22. Professing themselves to be wise, *they became fools,* Ver. 23. And *changed the glory of the uncorruptible God into an image made like to corruptible man, and to birds, and four-footed beasts, and creeping things.* Ver. 25. *Who changed the truth of God into a lie,* and worshipped and served the creature more than the Creator, who is blessed for ever. Amen.
h Dan. iii. 18. But if not, be it known unto thee, O king, that *we will not serve thy gods, nor worship the golden image* which thou hast set up. Gal. iv. 8. Howbeit then, when ye knew not God, *ye did service unto them which by nature are no gods.*
i Exod. xxxii. 5. And when *Aaron saw it, he built an altar before it;* and Aaron made proclamation, and said, To-morrow is *a feast to the Lord.*
k Exod. xxxii. 8. They have turned aside

them;¹ all superstitious devices,ᵐ corrupting the worship of God,ⁿ adding to it, or taking from it,º whether invented and taken up of ourselves,ᵖ or received by tradition from others,ᑫ though with the title of antiquity,ʳ custom,ˢ devotion,ᵗ good intent, or any other pretence whatsoever;ᵛ simony;ʷ sacrilege;ˣ all neglect,ʸ contempt,ᶻ hinder-

quickly out of the way which I commanded them: *they have made them a molten calf, and have worshipped it, and have sacrificed thereunto, and said, These be thy gods, O Israel*, which have brought thee up out of the land of Egypt.
ˡ 1 Kings xviii. 26. And they took the *bullock* which was given them, and they dressed it, *and called on the name of Baal* from morning even until noon, saying, *O Baal, hear us!* But there was no voice, nor any that answered. And they leaped upon the altar which was made. Ver. 28. And they cried aloud, and cut themselves, after their manner, with knives and lancets, till the blood gushed out upon them. Isa. lxv. 11. But *ye are they that forsake the Lord*, that forget my holy mountain, that *prepare a table for that troop*, and that *furnish the drink-offering unto that number.*
ᵐ Acts xvii. 22. Then Paul stood in the midst of Mars-hill, and said, Ye men of Athens, I perceive *that in all things ye are too superstitious.* Col. ii. 21. (*Touch not, taste not, handle not;* Ver. 22. Which all are to perish with the using,) after the commandments and doctrines of men. Ver. 23. Which things have indeed *a shew of wisdom in will-worship*, and humility, and neglecting of the body; not in any honour to the satisfying of the flesh.
ⁿ Mal. i. 7. *Ye offer polluted bread upon mine altar;* and ye say, Wherein have we polluted thee? In that ye say, The table of the Lord is contemptible. Ver. 8. And *if ye offer the blind for sacrifice, is it not evil?* and if ye offer the *lame and sick, is it not evil?* offer it now unto thy governor; will he be pleased with thee, or accept thy person? saith the Lord of hosts. Ver. 14. But *cursed be the deceiver, which hath in his flock a male, and voweth, and sacrificeth unto the Lord a corrupt thing:* for *I am a great King,* saith the Lord of hosts, and my name is dreadful among the heathen.
º Deut. iv. 2. *Ye shall not add unto the word which I command you, neither shall ye diminish ought from it,* that ye may keep the commandments of the Lord your God which I command you.
ᵖ Ps. cvi. 39. Thus were they *defiled with their own works*, and *went a whoring with their own inventions.*
ᑫ Matt. xv. 9. But *in vain they do worship me,* teaching for doctrines the *commandments of men.*
ʳ 1 Pet. i. 18. Forasmuch as ye know that ye were not *redeemed* with corruptible things, as silver and gold, *from your vain conversation received by tradition from your fathers.*
ˢ Jer. xliv. 17. *But we will certainly do* whatsoever thing goeth forth out of our own mouth, to *burn incense unto the queen of heaven*, and to pour out drink-offerings unto her, *as we have done, we, and our fathers,* our kings, and our princes, in the cities of Judah, and in the streets of Jerusalem: for then had we plenty of victuals, and were well, and saw no evil.
ᵗ Isa. lxv. 3. A *people that provoketh me to anger* continually to my face; that *sacrificeth in gardens*, and *burneth incense upon altars of brick;* Ver. 4. Which remain *among the graves*, and *lodge in the monuments;* which eat *swine's flesh,* and broth of abominable things is in their vessels; Ver. 5. Which say, *Stand by thyself, come not near to me; for I am holier than thou* These are a *smoke in my nose*, a fire that burneth all the day. Gal. i. 13. For ye have heard of my conversation in time past in the Jews' religion, how that beyond measure I persecuted the church of God, and wasted it; Ver. 14. And profited in the Jews' religion above many my equals in mine own nation, *being more exceedingly zealous of the traditions of my fathers.*
ᵛ 1 Sam. xiii. 11. And Samuel said, What hast thou done? And Saul said, Because I saw that the people were scattered from me, and that thou camest not within the days appointed, and that the Philistines gathered themselves together at Michmash; Ver. 12. Therefore, said I, the Philistines will come down now upon me to Gilgal, and I have not made supplication unto the Lord: *I forced myself therefore, and offered a burnt-offering.* 1 Sam. xv. 21. But the people (said Saul) *took of the spoil*, sheep and oxen, the chief of the things which should have been utterly destroyed, *to sacrifice unto the Lord thy God in Gilgal.*
ʷ Acts viii. 18. And when *Simon* saw that through laying on of the apostles' hands the Holy Ghost was given, *he offered them money.*
ˣ Rom. ii. 22. Thou that abhorrest idols, *dost thou commit sacrilege?* Mal. iii. 8. Will a man rob God? *Yet ye have robbed me.* But ye say, Wherein have we robbed thee? *In tithes and offerings.*
ʸ Exod. iv. 24. And it came to pass by the way in the inn, that *the Lord met him, and sought to kill him.* Ver. 25. Then Zipporah took a sharp stone, *and cut off the foreskin of her son,* and cast it at his feet, and said, Surely a bloody husband art thou to me. Ver. 26. So he let him go: then she said, A bloody husband thou art, because of the circumcision.
ᶻ Matt. xxii. 5. But *they made light of it,* and went their ways, one to his farm, another to his merchandise. Mal. i. 7. *Ye offer polluted bread upon mine altar;* and ye say, Wherein have we polluted thee? *In that ye say, The table of the Lord is contemptible.* Ver. 13. Ye said also, Behold, what a weariness is it! and *ye have snuffed at it,* saith the Lord of hosts; and ye brought that *which was torn, and the lame,*

ing,[a] and opposing the worship and ordinances which God hath appointed.[b]

Q. 110. *What are the reasons annexed to the second commandment, the more to enforce it?*

A. The reasons annexed to the second commandment, the more to enforce it, contained in these words, *For I the Lord thy God am a jealous God, visiting the iniquity of the fathers upon the children unto the third and fourth generation of them that hate me; and shewing mercy unto thousands of them that love me, and keep my commandments;*[c] are, besides God's sovereignty over us, and propriety in us,[d] his fervent zeal for his own worship,[e] and his revengeful indignation against all false worship, as being a spiritual whoredom;[f] accounting the breakers of this commandment such as hate him, and threatening to punish them unto divers generations;[g] and esteeming the observers of it such as love him and keep his commandments, and promising mercy to them unto many generations.[h]

[a] Matt. xxiii. 13. But woe unto you, *scribes and Pharisees, hypocrites!* for ye shut up the kingdom of heaven against men : for ye neither go in yourselves, *neither suffer ye them that are entering to go in.*

[b] Acts xiii. 44. And the next sabbath-day came almost the whole city together to hear the word of God. Ver. 45. But when the *Jews* saw the multitudes, they were filled with envy, and *spake against those things which were spoken by Paul*, contradicting and blaspheming. 1 Thess. ii. 15. Who both killed the Lord Jesus and their own prophets, and have persecuted us ; and they please not God, and *are contrary to all men;* Ver. 16. *Forbidding us to speak to the Gentiles*, that they might be saved, to fill up their sins alway : for the wrath is come upon them to the uttermost.

110. [c] Exod. xx. 5, 6.

[d] Ps. xlv. 11. So shall the king greatly desire thy beauty : *for he is thy Lord,* and worship thou him. Rev. xv. 3. And they sing the song of *Moses the servant of God,* and the song of the Lamb, saying, *Great and marvellous are thy works, Lord God Almighty;* just and true are thy ways, thou *King of saints.* Ver. 4. Who shall not fear thee, O Lord, and glorify thy name? for *thou only art holy:* for all nations shall come and worship before thee ; for thy judgments are made manifest.

[e] Exod. xxxiv. 13. But ye shall destroy their altars, break their images, and cut down their groves. Ver. 14. For thou shalt worship no other god : *for the Lord, whose name is Jealous, is a jealous God.*

[f] 1 Cor. x. 20. But I say, that the things which the Gentiles sacrifice, *they sacrifice to devils, and not to God:* and I would not that ye should have fellowship with devils. Ver. 21. *Ye cannot drink the cup of the Lord, and the cup of devils:* ye cannot be partakers of the Lord's table, and of the table of devils. Ver. 22. *Do we provoke the Lord to jealousy?* are we stronger than he? Jer. vii. 18. The children gather wood, and the fathers kindle the fire, and the women knead their dough, *to make cakes to the queen of heaven,* and *to pour out drink-offerings unto other gods,* that *they may provoke me to anger.* Ver. 19. *Do they provoke me to anger? saith the Lord:* do they not provoke themselves to the confusion of their own faces? Ver. 20. Therefore *thus saith the Lord God, Behold, mine anger and my fury shall be poured out upon this place, upon man, and upon beast,* and upon the trees of the field, and upon the fruit of the ground ; and *it shall burn, and shall not be quenched.* Ezek. xvi. 26. *Thou hast also committed fornication with the Egyptians* thy neighbours, great of flesh ; and hast *increased thy whoredoms, to provoke me to anger.* Ver. 27. Behold, therefore I have stretched out my hand over thee, and have diminished thine ordinary food, and delivered thee unto the will of them that hate thee, the daughters of the Philistines, which are ashamed of thy lewd way. Deut. xxxii. 16. *They provoked him to jealousy with strange gods,* with abominations provoked they him to anger. Ver. 17. *They sacrificed unto devils,* not to God ; *to gods whom they knew not,* to new gods that came newly up, whom your fathers feared not. Ver. 18. Of the Rock that begat thee thou art unmindful, and hast forgotten God that formed thee. Ver. 19. And *when the Lord saw it, he abhorred them,* because of the provoking of his sons and of his daughters. Ver. 20. *And he said, I will hide my face from them,* I will see what their end shall be : for they are a very froward generation, children in whom is no faith.

[g] Hosea ii. 2. Plead with your mother, plead ; *for she is not my wife,* neither am I her husband : *let her therefore put away her whoredoms out of her sight,* and her adulteries from between her breasts ; Ver. 3. *Lest I strip her naked,* and set her as in the day that she was born, and make her as a wilderness, and set her like a dry land, and slay her with thirst. Ver. 4. *And I will not have mercy upon her children; for they be the children of whoredoms.*

[h] Deut. v. 29. Oh that there were such

Q. 111. *Which is the third commandment?*

A. The third commandment is, *Thou shalt not take the name of the Lord thy God in vain: for the Lord will not hold him guiltless that taketh his name in vain.*[i]

Q. 112. *What is required in the third commandment?*

A. The third commandment requires, That the name of God, his titles, attributes,[k] ordinances,[l] the word,[m] sacraments,[n] prayer,[o] oaths,[p] vows,[q] lots,[r] his works,[s] and whatsoever else there is whereby he makes himself known, be holily and reverently used in thought,[t] meditation,[v] word,[w] and writing;[x] by an holy profession,[y] and answer-

---

an heart in them, *that they would fear me, and keep all my commandments* always, *that it might be well with them, and with their children for ever!*

111. i Exod. xx. 7.

112. k Matt. vi. 9. After this manner therefore pray ye: Our Father, which art in heaven, *Hallowed be thy name.* Deut. xxviii. 58. If thou wilt not observe to do all the words of this law that are written in this book, *that thou mayest fear this glorious and fearful name,* THE LORD THY GOD. Ps. xxix. 2. *Give unto the Lord the glory due unto his name;* worship the Lord in the beauty of holiness. Ps. lxviii. 4. Sing unto God, *sing praises to his name: extol him* that rideth upon the heavens by *his name JAH,* and rejoice before him. Rev. xv. 3, 4. [See above in letter d.]

l Mal. i. 14. But *cursed be the deceiver,* which hath in his flock a male, and voweth, and *sacrificeth unto the Lord a corrupt thing: for I am a great King,* saith the Lord of hosts, and *my name is dreadful among the heathen.* Eccl. v. 1. *Keep thy foot when thou goest to the house of God, and be more ready to hear than to give the sacrifice of fools:* for they consider not that they do evil.

m Ps. cxxxviii. 2. I will worship toward thy holy temple, and praise thy name for thy loving-kindness, and for thy truth: *for thou hast magnified thy word above all thy name.*

n 1 Cor. xi. 24. And, when he had given thanks, he brake it, and said, *Take, eat; this is my body, which is broken for you;* this do in remembrance of me. Ver. 25. *After the same manner also he took the cup,* when he had supped, saying, *This cup is the new testament in my blood: this do ye, as oft as ye drink it, in remembrance of me.* Ver. 28. But *let a man examine himself, and so let him eat of that bread, and drink of that cup.* Ver. 29. For he that eateth and drinketh unworthily, eateth and drinketh *damnation* to himself, not discerning the Lord's body.

o 1 Tim. ii. 8. I will therefore that men pray every where, *lifting up holy hands,* without wrath and doubting.

p Jer. iv. 2. And *thou shalt swear, The Lord liveth, in truth, in judgment, and in righteousness;* and the nations shall bless themselves in him, and in him shall they glory.

q Eccl. v. 2. *Be not rash with thy mouth,* and let not thine heart be hasty to utter any thing before God: for God is in heaven, and thou upon earth; therefore let thy words be few. Ver. 4. *When thou vowest a vow unto God, defer not to pay it;* for he hath no pleasure in fools: *pay that which thou hast vowed.* Ver. 5. Better is it that thou shouldest not vow, than that thou shouldest vow and not pay. Ver. 6. *Suffer not thy mouth to cause thy flesh to sin;* neither say thou before the angel, that it was an error: wherefore should God be angry at thy voice, and destroy the work of thine hands?

r Acts i. 24. And they *prayed,* and said, Thou, Lord, which knowest the hearts of all men, shew whether of these two thou hast chosen. Ver. 26. *And they gave forth their lots:* and the lot fell upon Matthias; and he was numbered with the eleven apostles.

s Job xxxvi. 24. Remember *that thou magnify his work,* which men behold.

t Mal. iii. 16. Then they that feared the Lord spake often one to another: and the Lord hearkened, and heard it; and a book of remembrance was written before him for them that feared the Lord, and *that thought upon his name.*

v Ps. viii. 1. *O Lord our Lord, how excellent is thy name* in all the earth! who hast set thy glory above the heavens. Ver. 3. When I consider thy heavens, the work of thy fingers, the moon and the stars, which thou hast ordained; Ver. 4. What is man, that thou art mindful of him? Ver. 9. O Lord our Lord, *how excellent is thy name* in all the earth! [See the Psalm throughout.]

w Col. iii. 17. And *whatsoever ye do in word or deed, do all in the name of the Lord Jesus,* giving thanks to God and the Father by him. Ps. cv. 2. Sing unto him, sing psalms unto him: *talk ye of all his wondrous works.* Ver. 5. Remember his marvellous works that he hath done; his wonders, and the judgments of his mouth.

x Ps. cii. 18. *This shall be written for the generation to come:* and *the people* which shall be created *shall praise the Lord.*

y 1 Pet. iii. 15. But *sanctify the Lord God in your hearts:* and *be ready always to give an answer to every man that asketh you a reason of the hope that is in you* with meekness and fear. Micah iv. 5. For all people will walk every one in the name of his god, and *we will walk in the name of the Lord our God for ever and ever.*

able conversation,^{z} to the glory of God,^{a} and the good of ourselves,^{b} and others.^{c}

Q. 113. *What are the sins forbidden in the third commandment?*

A. The sins forbidden in the third commandment are, the not using of God's name as is required;^{d} and the abuse of it in an ignorant,^{e} vain,^{f} irreverent, profane,^{g} superstitious,^{h} or wicked mentioning or otherwise using his titles, attributes,^{i} ordinances,^{k} or works,^{l} by blasphemy,^{m}

---

z Phil. i. 27. Only let your *conversation be as it becometh the gospel of Christ.*

a 1 Cor. x. 31. Whether therefore ye eat, or drink, or whatsoever ye do, *do all to the glory of God.*

b Jer. xxxii. 39. And I will give them one heart, and one way, that they may fear me for ever, *for the good of them, and of their children after them.*

c 1 Pet. ii. 12. *Having your conversation honest among the Gentiles;* that, whereas they speak against you as evil-doers, *they may, by your good works, which they shall behold, glorify God* in the day of visitation.

113. d Mal. ii. 2. If ye will not hear, *and if ye will not lay it to heart, to give glory unto my name,* saith the Lord of hosts, I will even send a curse upon you, and I will curse your blessings; yea, I have cursed them already, because ye do not lay it to heart.

e Acts xvii. 23. For as I passed by, and beheld your devotions, I found an altar with this inscription, TO THE UNKNOWN GOD. *Whom therefore ye ignorantly worship, him declare I unto you.*

f Prov. xxx. 9. Lest I be full, and deny thee, and say, Who is the Lord? or lest I be poor, and steal, and *take the name of my God in vain.*

g Mal. i. 6. A son honoureth his father, and a servant his master: if then I be a father, *where is mine honour?* and if I be a master, *where is my fear?* saith the Lord of hosts unto you, O priests, *that despise my name.* And ye say, Wherein have we despised thy name? Ver. 7. *Ye offer polluted bread upon mine altar;* and ye say, Wherein have we polluted thee? *In that ye say, The table of the Lord is contemptible.* Ver. 12. But ye have *profaned it,* in that ye say, The table of the Lord is *polluted;* and the fruit thereof, even his meat, is *contemptible.* Mal. iii. 14. Ye have said, *It is vain to serve* God; and what profit is it that we have kept his ordinance, and that we have walked mournfully before the Lord of hosts?

h 1 Sam. iv. 3. And when the people were come into the camp, the elders of Israel said, Wherefore hath the Lord smitten us to-day before the Philistines? *Let us fetch the ark of the covenant of the Lord out of Shiloh unto us, that, when it cometh among us, it may save us out of the hand of our enemies.* Ver. 4. So the people sent to Shiloh, that they might bring from thence the ark of the covenant of the Lord of hosts, which dwelleth between the cherubims: and the two sons of Eli, Hophni and Phinehas, were there with the ark of the covenant of God. Ver. 5. And *when the ark of the covenant of the Lord came into the camp, all Israel* shouted with a great shout, so that the earth rang again. Jer. vii. 4. *Trust ye not in lying words, saying, The temple of the Lord, The temple of the Lord, The temple of the Lord,* are these. Ver. 9. Will ye steal, murder, and commit adultery, and swear falsely, and burn incense unto Baal, and walk after other gods whom ye know not: Ver. 10. And come and stand before me in this house, which is called by my name, and say, We are delivered to do all these abominations? Ver. 14. Therefore will I do *unto this house, which is called by my name, wherein ye trust,* and unto the place which I gave to you and to your fathers, as I have done to Shiloh. Ver. 31. And they have built the high places of Tophet, which is in the valley of the son of Hinnom, to burn their sons and their daughters in the fire; which I commanded them not, neither came it into my heart. Col. ii. 20. Wherefore, if ye be dead with Christ from the rudiments of the world, *why, as though living in the world, are ye subject to ordinances,* Ver. 21. (*Touch not, taste not, handle not;* Ver. 22. Which all are to perish with the using,) after the commandments and doctrines of men?

i 2 Kings xviii. 30. *Neither let Hezekiah make you trust in the Lord, saying, The Lord will surely deliver us,* and this city shall not be delivered into the hand of the king of Assyria. Ver. 35. Who are they among all the gods of the countries, that have delivered their country out of mine hand, *that the Lord should deliver Jerusalem out of mine hand?* Exod. v. 2. And Pharaoh said, *Who is the Lord, that I should obey his voice* to let Israel go? I know not the Lord, neither will I let Israel go. Ps. cxxxix. 20. For they speak against thee wickedly, and thine enemies *take thy name in vain.*

k Ps. l. 16. But unto the wicked God saith, *What hast thou to do to declare my statutes, or that thou shouldest take my covenant in thy mouth?* Ver. 17. Seeing thou hatest instruction, and castest my words behind thee.

l Isa. v. 12. And the harp and the viol, the tabret and pipe, and wine, are in their feasts: *but they regard not the work of the Lord, neither consider the operation of his hands.*

m 2 Kings xix. 22. *Whom hast thou reproached and blasphemed?* and against whom hast thou exalted thy voice, and lifted up thine eyes on high? even against the Holy One of Israel. Lev. xxiv. 11. And the Israelitish woman's son *blasphemed the name of the Lord, and cursed.* And they brought him unto Moses.

perjury;[n] all sinful cursings,[o] oaths,[p] vows,[q] and lots;[r] violating of our oaths and vows, if lawful;[s] and fulfilling them, if of things unlawful;[t] murmuring and quarrelling at,[v] curious prying into,[w] and misapplying of God's decrees[x] and providences;[y] misinterpreting,[z] misapplying,[a] or any way perverting the word, or any part of

[n] Zech. v. 4. I will bring it forth, saith the Lord of hosts, and it shall enter into the house of the thief, *and into the house of him that sweareth falsely by my name:* and it shall remain in the midst of his house, and shall consume it, with the timber thereof, and the stones thereof. Zech. viii. 17. And let none of you imagine evil in your hearts against his neighbour: *and love no false oath; for all these are things that I hate, saith the Lord.*

[o] 1 Sam. xvii. 43. And the Philistine said unto David, Am I a dog, that thou comest to me with staves? And *the Philistine cursed David by his gods.* 2 Sam. xvi. 5. And when king David came to Bahurim, behold, thence came out a man of the family of the house of Saul, whose name was *Shimei,* the son of Gera: he came forth, *and cursed still as he came.*

[p] Jer. v. 7. How shall I pardon thee for this? thy children have forsaken me, and *sworn by them that are no gods:* when I had fed them to the full, they then committed adultery, and assembled themselves by troops in the harlots' houses. Jer. xxiii. 10. For the land is full of adulterers; *for because of swearing the land mourneth;* the pleasant places of the wilderness are dried up, and their course is evil, and their force is not right.

[q] Deut. xxiii. 18. *Thou shalt not bring the hire of a whore, or the price of a dog, into the house of the Lord thy God for any vow;* for even both these are abomination unto the Lord thy God. Acts xxiii. 12. And when it was day, certain of the Jews banded together, and *bound themselves under a curse, saying that they would neither eat nor drink till they had killed Paul.* Ver. 14. And they came to the chief priests and elders, and said, We have bound ourselves under a great curse, that we will eat nothing until we have slain Paul.

[r] Esth. iii. 7. In the first month, (that is, the month Nisan,) in the twelfth year of king Ahasuerus, *they cast Pur, that is, the lot, before Haman, from day to day,* and from month to month, to the twelfth month, that is, the month Adar. Esth. ix. 24. Because Haman the son of Hammedatha the Agagite, the enemy of all the Jews, had devised against the Jews to destroy them, *and had cast Pur (that is, the lot) to consume them, and to destroy them.* Ps. xxii. 18. They part my garments among them, and *cast lots upon my vesture.*

[s] Ps. xxiv. 4. He that hath clean hands, and a pure heart; who hath not lifted up his soul unto vanity, *nor sworn deceitfully.* Ezek. xvii. 16. As I live, saith the Lord God, surely in the place where the king dwelleth that made him king, *whose oath he despised, and whose covenant he brake,* even with him in the midst of Babylon he shall die. Ver.

18. *Seeing he despised the oath by breaking the covenant,* when, lo, *he had given his hand,* and hath done all these things, *he shall not escape.* Ver. 19. Therefore thus saith the Lord God, As I live, *surely mine oath that he hath despised, and my covenant that he hath broken, even it will I recompense upon his own head.*

[t] Mark vi. 26. And the king was exceeding sorry; *yet for his oath's sake, and for their sakes which sat with him, he would not reject her.* 1 Sam. xxv. 22. So and more also do God unto the enemies of David, *if I leave of all that pertain to him, by the morning light,* any that pisseth against the wall. Ver. 32. *And David said to Abigail, Blessed be the Lord God of Israel,* which sent thee this day to meet me: Ver. 33. And *blessed be thy advice, and blessed be thou, which hast kept me this day from coming to shed blood, and from avenging myself with mine own hand,* Ver. 34. For in very deed, as the Lord God of Israel liveth, which hath kept me back from hurting thee, except thou hadst hasted and come to meet me, surely there had not been left unto Nabal, by the morning light, any that pisseth against the wall.

[v] Rom. ix. 14. What shall we say then? Is there unrighteousness with God? God forbid. Ver. 19. Thou wilt say then unto me, *Why doth he yet find fault?* For who hath resisted his will? Ver. 20. *Nay but, O man, who art thou that repliest against God?* Shall the thing formed say to him that formed it, Why hast thou made me thus?

[w] Deut. xxix. 29. *The secret things belong unto the Lord our God;* but those things which are revealed belong unto us and to our children for ever, that we may do all the words of this law.

[x] Rom. iii. 5. *But if our unrighteousness commend the righteousness of God, what shall we say? Is God unrighteous* who taketh vengeance? (I speak as a man.) Ver. 7. *For if the truth of God hath more abounded through my lie unto his glory; why yet am I also judged as a sinner?* Rom. vi. 1. What shall we say then? *Shall we continue in sin, that grace may abound?* Ver. 2. *God forbid.*

[y] Eccl. viii. 11. *Because sentence against an evil work is not executed speedily,* therefore *the heart of the sons of men is fully set in them to do evil.* Eccl. ix. 3. This is an evil among all things that are done under the sun, *that there is one event unto all; yea, also the heart of the sons of men is full of evil,* and madness is in their heart while they live, and after that they go to the dead. Ps. xxxix. throughout. I said, I will take heed to my ways, that I sin not with my tongue, etc.

[z] Matt. v. 21 to the end. [See Quest. 99, letter o.]

[a] Ezek. xlii. 22. *Because with lies ye have*

it,[b] to profane jests,[c] curious or unprofitable questions, vain janglings, or the maintaining of false doctrines;[d] abusing it, the creatures, or any thing contained under the name of God, to charms,[e] or sinful lusts and practices;[f] the maligning,[g] scorning,[h] reviling,[i] or any wise opposing of God's truth, grace, and ways;[k] making profession of re-

made the heart of the righteous sad, whom I have not made sad; and strengthened the hands of the wicked, that he should not return from his wicked way, by promising him life.

[b] 2 Pet. iii. 16. As also in all his epistles, speaking in them of these things: in which are some things hard to be understood, *which they that are unlearned and unstable wrest, as they do also the other scriptures, unto their own destruction.* Matt. xxii. 24. to verse 31. Saying, Master, Moses said, If a man die, having no children, his brother shall marry his wife, and raise up seed unto his brother. Ver. 25. Now there were with us seven brethren: and the first—Ver. 28 Therefore, in the resurrection, whose wife shall she be of the seven? for they all had her. Ver. 29. Jesus answered and said unto them, *Ye do err, not knowing the scriptures, nor the power of God.* Ver. 30. For in the resurrection, &c.

[c] Isa. xxii. 13. And behold joy and gladness, slaying oxen and killing sheep, eating flesh and drinking wine: *let us eat and drink, for to-morrow we shall die.* Jer. xxiii. 34. And as for the prophet, and the priest, and the people, *that shall say, The burden of the Lord,* I will even punish that man and his house. Ver. 36. *And the burden of the Lord shall ye mention no more;* for every man's word shall be his burden; *for ye have perverted the words of the living God,* of the Lord of hosts our God. Ver. 38. But *since ye say, The burden of the Lord;* therefore thus saith the Lord, Because ye say this word, The burden of the Lord, and I have sent unto you, saying, *Ye shall not say,* The burden of the Lord, &c.

[d] 1 Tim. i. 4. *Neither give heed to fables, and endless genealogies, which minister questions, rather than godly edifying* which is in faith; so do. Ver. 6. From which (faith) some having swerved, *have turned aside unto vain jangling;* Ver. 7. Desiring to be teachers of the law; understanding neither what they say, nor whereof they affirm. 1 Tim. vi. 4. He is proud, knowing nothing, but *doting about questions and strifes of words, whereof cometh envy, strife, railings, evil surmisings,* Ver. 5. *Perverse disputings of men of corrupt minds,* and destitute of the truth, supposing that gain is godliness: *from such withdraw thyself.* Ver. 20. O Timothy, keep that which is committed to thy trust, *avoiding profane and vain babblings, and oppositions of science falsely so called.* 2 Tim. ii. 14. Of these things put them in remembrance, *charging them before the Lord that they strive not about words to no profit,* but to the subverting of the hearers. Tit. iii. 9. But *avoid foolish questions,* and *genealogies,* and *contentions,* and *strivings about the law;* for they are *unprofitable* and *vain.*

[e] Deut. xviii. 10–14. There shall not be found among you any one that maketh his son or his daughter to pass through the fire, *or that useth divination, or an observer of times, or an enchanter, or a witch,* Ver. 11. Or a *charmer,* or a *consulter with familiar spirits,* or a *wizard,* or a *necromancer.* Ver. 12. For *all that do these things are an abomination unto the Lord,* &c. Acts xix. 13. Then certain of the *vagabond Jews, exorcists,* took upon them *to call over them which had evil spirits the name of the Lord Jesus,* saying, We adjure you by Jesus, whom Paul preacheth.

[f] 2 Tim. iv. 3. For the time will come when they will not endure sound doctrine; but *after their own lusts shall they heap to themselves teachers, having itching ears;* Ver. 4. And they shall turn away their ears from the truth, and shall be turned unto fables. Rom. xiii. 13. Let us walk honestly, as in the day; *not in rioting and drunkenness, not in chambering and wantonness, not in strife and envying;* Ver. 14. But put ye on the Lord Jesus Christ, and *make not provision for the flesh, to fulfil the lusts thereof.* 1 Kings xxi. 9. And she wrote in the letters, saying, *Proclaim a fast, and set Naboth on high* among the people; Ver. 10. And *set two men, sons of Belial, before him, to bear witness against him,* saying, Thou didst blaspheme God and the king: and *then carry him out,* and *stone him, that he may die.* Jude, ver. 4. For there are certain men crept in unawares, who were before of old ordained to this condemnation, *ungodly men, turning the grace of our God into lasciviousness,* and denying the only Lord God, and our Lord Jesus Christ.

[g] Acts xiii. 45. But when the Jews saw the multitudes, *they were filled with envy,* and spake against those things which were spoken by Paul, *contradicting and blaspheming.* 1 John iii. 12. Not *as Cain,* who was of that wicked one, and slew his brother. And *wherefore slew he him? Because his own works were evil, and his brother's righteous.*

[h] Ps. i. 1. Blessed is the man that walketh not in the counsel of the ungodly, nor standeth in the way of sinners, nor *sitteth in the seat of the scornful.* 2 Pet. iii. 3. Knowing this first, that *there shall come in the last days scoffers,* walking after their own lusts.

[i] 1 Pet. iv. 4. Wherein they think it strange that ye run not with them to the same excess of riot, *speaking evil of you.*

[k] Acts xiii. 45. But when the Jews saw the multitudes, they were filled with envy, *and spake against those things which were spoken by Paul, contradicting and blaspheming.* Ver. 46. Then Paul and Barnabas waxed bold, and said, It was necessary that the word of God should first have been spoken to you: but seeing ye put it from you, and judge yourselves unworthy of

ligion in hypocrisy, or for sinister ends;¹ being ashamed of it,ᵐ or a shame to it, by unconformable,ⁿ unwise,º unfruitful,ᵖ and offensive walking,ᵠ or backsliding from it.ʳ

Q. 114. *What reasons are annexed to the third commandment?*

A. The reasons annexed to the third commandment, in these words, [*The Lord thy God,*] and, [*For the Lord will not hold him guiltless that taketh his name in vain,* ˢ] are, because he is the Lord and our God, therefore his name is not to be profaned, or any way abused by us;ᵗ especially because he will be so far from acquitting and sparing the transgressors of this commandment, as that he will not suffer them to escape his righteous judgment,ᵛ albeit many such escape the censures and punishments of men.ʷ

everlasting life, lo, we turn to the Gentiles. Ver. 50. But the Jews stirred up the devout and honourable women, and the chief men of the city, and *raised persecution against Paul and Barnabas,* and expelled them out of their coasts. Acts iv. 18. And they called them, and *commanded them not to speak at all, nor teach, in the name of Jesus.* Acts xix. 9. But when divers were hardened, and believed not, but *spake evil of that way before the multitude,* he departed from them, and separated the disciples, disputing daily in the school of one Tyrannus. 1 Thess. ii. 16. *Forbidding us to speak to the Gentiles,* that they might be saved, to fill up their sins alway : for the wrath is come upon them to the uttermost. Heb. x. 29. Of how much sorer punishment, suppose ye, shall he be thought worthy, *who hath trodden under foot the Son of God,* and hath counted the blood of the covenant, wherewith he was sanctified, an unholy thing, and *hath done despite unto the Spirit of grace?*

ˡ 2 Tim. iii. 5. *Having a form of godliness, but denying the power thereof:* from such turn away. Matt. xxiii. 14. *Wce unto you, scribes and Pharisees, hypocrites!* for ye devour widows' houses, and for a pretence make long prayer : therefore ye shall receive the greater damnation. Matt. vi. 1. *Take heed that ye do not your alms before men, to be seen of them;* otherwise ye have no reward of your Father which is in heaven. Ver. 2. Therefore, when thou doest thine alms, *do not sound a trumpet before thee, as the hypocrites do* in the synagogues, and in the streets, *that they may have glory of men.* Verily I say unto you, *They have their reward.* Ver. 5. And when thou prayest, *thou shalt not be as the hypocrites are:* for they love to pray standing in the synagogues, and in the corners of the streets, that they may be seen of men. Verily I say unto you, They have their reward. Ver. 16. Moreover, when ye fast, *be not, as the hypocrites, of a sad countenance:* for they disfigure their faces, *that they may appear unto men to fast.* Verily I say unto you, *They have their reward.*

ᵐ Mark viii. 38. *Whosoever therefore shall be ashamed of me and of my words, in this adulterous and sinful generation,* of him also shall the Son of man be ashamed, when he cometh in the glory of his Father with the holy angels.

ⁿ Ps. lxxiii. 14. *For all the day long have I been plagued,* and chastened every morning. Ver. 15. *If I say, I will speak thus; behold, I should offend against the generation of thy children.*

º 1 Cor. vi. 5. *I speak to your shame. Is it so, that there is not a wise man among you?* no, not one that shall be able to judge between his brethren? Ver. 6. But brother goeth to law with brother, and that before the unbelievers. Eph. v. 15. See then *that ye walk circumspectly, not as fools, but as wise,* Ver. 16. Redeeming the time, because the days are evil. Ver. 17. Wherefore *be ye not unwise,* but understanding what the will of the Lord is.

ᵖ Isa. v. 4. What could have been done more to my vineyard, that I have not done in it? *wherefore, when I looked that it should bring forth grapes, brought it forth wild grapes?* 2 Pet. i. 8. For if these things be in you, and abound, they make you *that ye shall neither be barren nor unfruitful in the knowledge of our Lord Jesus Christ.* Ver. 9. But he that lacketh these things is blind, and cannot see afar off, and hath forgotten that he was purged from his old sins.

ᵠ Rom. ii. 23. Thou that makest thy boast of the law, *through breaking the law dishonourest thou God?* Ver. 24. For *the name of God is blasphemed among the Gentiles through you,* as it is written.

ʳ Gal. iii. 1. O foolish Galatians, who hath bewitched you, that ye should not obey the truth, before whose eyes Jesus Christ hath been evidently set forth, crucified among you? Ver. 3. Are ye so foolish? *having begun in the Spirit, are ye now made perfect by the flesh?* Heb. vi. 6. *If they shall fall away,* to renew them again unto repentance ; seeing they crucify to themselves the Son of God afresh, and put him to an open shame.

114. ˢ Exod. xx. 7.

ᵗ Lev. xix. 12. *And ye shall not swear by my name falsely, neither shalt thou profane the name of thy God: I am the Lord.*

ᵛ Ezek. xxxvi. 21. But I had pity *for mine holy name, which the house of Israel had profaned among the heathen,* whither they went. Ver. 22. Therefore say unto the house of Israel, Thus saith the Lord God, I do not this for your sakes, O house of Israel, *but for mine holy name's sake, which ye have profaned among the heathen,* whither

Q. 115. *Which is the fourth commandment?*

A. The fourth commandment is, *Remember the sabbath-day, to keep it holy. Six days shalt thou labour, and do all thy work; but the seventh day is the sabbath of the Lord thy God: in it thou shalt not do any work, thou, nor thy son, nor thy daughter, thy man-servant, nor thy maid-servant, nor thy cattle, nor thy stranger that is within thy gates. For in six days the Lord made heaven and earth, the sea, and all that in them is, and rested the seventh day: wherefore the Lord blessed the sabbath-day, and hallowed it.*[x]

Q. 116. *What is required in the fourth commandment?*

A. The fourth commandment requireth of all men the sanctifying or keeping holy to God such set times as he hath appointed in his word, expressly one whole day in seven; which was the seventh from the beginning of the world to the resurrection of Christ, and the first day of the week ever since, and so to continue to the end of the world; which is the Christian sabbath,[y] and in the New Testament called *The Lord's day.*[z]

---

ye went. Ver. 23. And *I will sanctify my great name,* which was *profaned among the heathen,* which ye have *profaned in the midst of them;* and the heathen shall know that I am the Lord, saith the Lord God, *when I shall be sanctified in you before their eyes.* Deut. xxviii. 58. *If thou wilt not observe to do all the words of this law* that are written in this book, *that thou mayest fear this glorious and fearful name,* THE LORD THY GOD ; Ver. 59. *Then the Lord will make thy plagues wonderful, and the plagues of thy seed,* even great plagues, and of long continuance, and sore sicknesses, and of long continuance. Zech. v. 2. And he said unto me, What seest thou? And I answered, I see *a flying roll;* the length thereof is twenty cubits, and the breadth thereof ten cubits. Ver. 3. Then said he unto me, *This is the curse that goeth forth over the face of the whole earth:* for every one that stealeth shall be cut off as on this side, according to it; *and every one that sweareth shall be cut off as on that side,* according to it. Ver. 4. I will bring it forth, saith the Lord of hosts, and *it shall enter into the house of the thief, and into the house of him that sweareth falsely by my name,* &c.

w 1 Sam. ii. 12. Now *the sons of Eli were sons of Belial;* they knew not the Lord. Ver. 17. Wherefore *the sin of the young men was very great before the Lord; for men abhorred the offering of the Lord.* Ver. 22. Now Eli was very old, and heard all that his sons did unto all Israel; and how they lay with the women that assembled at the door of the tabernacle of the congregation. Ver. 24. Nay, my sons ; for it is no good report that I hear : *ye make the Lord's people to transgress.* Compared with 1 Sam. iii. 13. For I have told him, *that I will judge his house for ever,* for the iniquity which he knoweth ; *because his sons made themselves vile, and he restrained them not.*

115. x Exod. xx. 8-11.
116. y Deut. v. 12. *Keep the sabbath-day to sanctify it,* as the Lord thy God hath commanded thee. Ver. 13. Six days thou shalt labour, and do all thy work : Ver.

14. But *the seventh day is the sabbath of the Lord thy God;* in it thou shalt not do any work, thou, nor thy son, nor thy daughter, nor thy man-servant, nor thy maid-servant, nor thine ox, nor thine ass, nor any of thy cattle, nor thy stranger that is within thy gates ; that thy man-servant and thy maid-servant may rest as well as thou. Gen. ii. 2. And *on the seventh day God ended his work which he had made; and he rested on the seventh day from all his work which he had made.* Ver. 3. And *God blessed the seventh day, and sanctified it;* because that in it he had rested from all his work which God created and made. 1 Cor. xvi. 1. Now concerning the collection for the saints, as I have given order to the churches of Galatia, even so do ye. Ver. 2. Upon *the first day of the week* let every one of you lay by him in store, as God hath prospered him, that there be no gatherings when I come. Acts xx. 7. And upon *the first day of the week, when the disciples came together to break bread,* Paul preached unto them, ready to depart on the morrow ; and continued his speech until midnight. Matt. v. 17. *Think not that I am come to destroy the law* or the prophets : I am not come to destroy, *but to fulfil.* Ver. 18. For verily I say unto you, Till heaven and earth pass, *one jot or one tittle shall in no wise pass from the law, till all be fulfilled.* Isa. lvi. 2. Blessed is the man that doeth this, and the son of man that layeth hold on it ; that *keepeth the sabbath from polluting it,* and keepeth his hand from doing any evil. Ver. 4. For thus saith the Lord unto *the eunuchs that keep my sabbaths,* and choose the things that please me, and take hold of my covenant ;—Ver. 6. Also the sons of the stranger, that join themselves to the Lord, to serve him, and to love the name of the Lord, to be his servants, *every one that keepeth the sabbath from polluting it,* and taketh hold of my covenant ; Ver. 7. *Even them will I bring to my holy mountain,* and make them joyful in my house of prayer : their burnt-offerings and their sacrifices shall be accepted upon mine altar ; for mine house

Q. 117. *How is the sabbath or the Lord's day to be sanctified?*

A. The sabbath or Lord's day is to be sanctified by an holy resting all the day,[a] not only from such works as are at all times sinful, but even from such worldly employments and recreations as are on other days lawful;[b] and making it our delight to spend the whole time (except so much of it as is to be taken up in works of necessity and mercy[c]) in the public and private exercises of God's worship:[d] and, to that end, we are to prepare our hearts, and with such foresight, diligence, and moderation, to dispose and seasonably dispatch our worldly business, that we may be the more free and fit for the duties of that day.[e]

shall be called an house of prayer for all people.

a Rev. i. 10. *I was in the Spirit on the Lord's day,* and heard behind me a great voice, as of a trumpet.

117. a Exod. xx. 8. Remember the *sabbath-day,* to keep it holy. Ver. 10. But the seventh day is the *sabbath* of the Lord thy God : *in it thou shalt not do any work, thou, nor thy son,* &c.

b Exod. xvi. 25. And Moses said, Eat that to-day ; for to-day is a sabbath unto the Lord : to-day ye shall not find it in the field. Ver. 26. Six days ye shall gather it ; *but on the seventh day, which is the sabbath, in it there shall be none.* Ver. 27. And it came to pass, that there went out some of the people on the seventh day for to gather, and they found none. Ver. 28. And the Lord said unto Moses, *How long refuse ye to keep my commandments and my laws ?* Neh. xiii. 15. In those days saw I in Judah *some treading wine-presses on the sabbath, and bringing in sheaves, and lading asses; as also wine, grapes, and figs, and all manner of burdens,* which they brought into Jerusalem *on the sabbath-day:* and *I testified against them in the day wherein they sold victuals.* Ver. 16. There dwelt men of Tyre also therein, which *brought fish, and all manner of ware, and sold on the sabbath unto the children of Judah, and in Jerusalem.* Ver. 17. Then *I contended with the nobles of Judah,* and said unto them, *What evil thing is this that ye do, and profane the sabbath-day ?* Ver. 18. *Did not your fathers thus, and did not our God bring all this evil upon us, and upon this city ? yet ye bring more wrath upon Israel, by profaning the sabbath.* Ver. 19. And it came to pass, that when the gates of Jerusalem began to be dark *before the sabbath,* I commanded *that the gates should be shut,* and charged that they should not be opened till after the sabbath : and some of my servants set I at the gates, *that there should no burden be brought in on the sabbath-day.* Ver. 20. So the merchants, and sellers of all kind of ware, lodged without Jerusalem once or twice. Ver. 21. Then I testified against them, and said unto them, Why lodge ye about the wall? if ye do so again, I will lay hands on you. *From that time forth came they no more on the sabbath.* Ver. 22. And I commanded the Levites, that they should cleanse themselves, and that they should come and keep the gates, *to sanctify the sabbath-day.* Remember me, O my God, concerning this also, and spare me according to the greatness of thy mercy. Jer. xvii. 21. Thus saith the Lord, Take heed to yourselves, and *bear no burden on the sabbath-day,* nor bring it in by the gates of Jerusalem ; Ver. 22. *Neither carry forth a burden out of your houses on the sabbath-day, neither do ye any work;* but hallow ye the sabbath-day, as I commanded your fathers.

c Matt. xii. from verse 1. to 13. At that time Jesus went *on the sabbath-day* through the corn ; and his disciples were an hungered, and *began to pluck the ears of corn, and to eat.* Ver. 2. But when the Pharisees saw it, &c.

d Isa. lviii. 13. If thou turn away thy foot from the sabbath, from doing thy pleasure on my holy day ; and *call the sabbath a delight, the holy of the Lord, honourable; and shalt honour him,* not doing thine own ways, nor finding thine own pleasure, nor speaking thine own words. Luke iv. 16. And he came to Nazareth, where he had been brought up : and, as his custom was, *he went into the synagogue on the sabbath-day,* and stood up to read. Acts xx. 7. And *upon the first day of the week, when the disciples came together to break bread, Paul preached unto them,* ready to depart on the morrow. 1 Cor. xvi. 1. Now *concerning the collection for the saints,* as I have given order to the churches of Galatia, even so do ye. Ver. 2. *Upon the first day of the week let every one of you lay by him in store,* as God hath prospered him, that there be no gatherings when I come. Ps. xcii. [title, A psalm or song for *the sabbath-day.*] Isa. lxvi. 23. And it shall come to pass, that from one new-moon to another, and *from one sabbath to another, shall all flesh come to worship before me, saith the Lord.* Lev. xxiii. 3. Six days shall work be done : but the *seventh day is the sabbath of rest, an holy convocation;* ye shall do no work therein : it is the sabbath of the Lord in all your dwellings.

e Exod. xx. 8. *Remember the sabbath-day, to keep it holy.* Luke xxiii. 54. And *that day was the preparation,* and the sabbath drew on. Ver. 56. And they returned, *and prepared spices and ointments; and rested the sabbath-day,* according to the commandment. Exod. xvi. 22. And it came to pass, that *on the sixth day they gathered twice as much bread,* two omers for one man : and

Q. 118. *Why is the charge of keeping the sabbath more specially directed to governors of families, and other superiors?*

A. The charge of keeping the sabbath is more specially directed to governors of families, and other superiors, because they are bound not only to keep it themselves, but to see that it be observed by all those that are under their charge; and because they are prone ofttimes to hinder them by employments of their own.f

Q. 119. *What are the sins forbidden in the fourth commandment?*

A. The sins forbidden in the fourth commandment are, all omissions of the duties required,g all careless, negligent, and unprofitable performing of them, and being weary of them;h all profaning the day by idleness, and doing that which is in itself sinful;i and by all needless works, words, and thoughts, about our worldly employments and recreations.k

Q. 120. *What are the reasons annexed to the fourth commandment, the more to enforce it?*

all the rulers of the congregation came and told Moses. Ver. 25. And Moses said, Eat that to-day; for to-day is a sabbath unto the Lord: to-day ye shall not find it in the field. Ver. 26. Six days ye shall gather it; but on the seventh day, which is the sabbath, in it there shall be none. Ver. 29. See, *for that the Lord hath given you the sabbath, therefore he giveth you on the sixth day the bread of two days:* abide ye every man in his place; let no man go out of his place on the seventh day. Neh. xiii. 19. [See letter b.]

118. f Exod. xx. 10. But the seventh day is the sabbath of the Lord thy God: in it thou shalt not do any work, *thou, nor thy son, nor thy daughter, thy man-servant, nor thy maid-servant, nor thy cattle, nor thy stranger that is within thy gates.* Josh. xxiv. 15. And if it seem evil unto you to serve the Lord, choose you this day whom ye will serve; whether the gods which your fathers served, that were on the other side of the flood, or the gods of the Amorites, in whose land ye dwell: *but as for me and my house, we will serve the Lord.* Neh. xiii. 15, 17. [See above in b.] Jer. xvii. 20. *And say unto them, Hear ye the word of the Lord, ye kings of Judah, and all Judah, and all the inhabitants of Jerusalem, that enter in by these gates.* Ver. 21, 22. [See above in b.] Exod. xxiii. 12. Six days thou shalt do thy work, and on the seventh day thou shalt rest; *that thine ox and thine ass may rest, and the son of thy hand-maid and the stranger may be refreshed.*

119. g Ezek. xxii. 26. Her priests have violated my law, and have profaned mine holy things: they have put no difference between the holy and profane, neither have they shewed difference between the unclean and the clean; and *have hid their eyes from my sabbaths,* and I am profaned among them.

h Acts xx. 7. And upon the first day of the week, when the disciples came together to break bread, Paul preached unto them, ready to depart on the morrow; and continued his speech until midnight. Ver. 9. And there sat in a window a certain young man named *Eutychus, being fallen into a* deep sleep: and as Paul was long preaching, he sunk down with sleep, and fell down from the third loft, and was taken up dead. Ezek. xxxiii. 30. Also, thou son of man, the children of thy people still are talking against thee by the walls, and in the doors of the houses, and speak one to another, every one to his brother, saying, Come, I pray you, and hear what is the word that cometh forth from the Lord. Ver. 31. And they come unto thee as the people cometh, and they sit before thee as my people, *and they hear thy words, but they will not do them;* for *with their mouth they shew much love, but their heart goeth after their covetousness.* Ver. 32. And, lo, thou art unto them as a very lovely song of one that hath a pleasant voice, and can play well on an instrument: *for they hear thy words, but they do them not.* Amos viii. 5. Saying, When will the new-moon be gone, that we may sell corn? *and the sabbath, that we may set forth wheat,* making the ephah small, and the shekel great, and falsifying the balances by deceit? Mal. i. 13. Ye said also, *Behold, what a weariness is it!* and ye have snuffed at it, saith the Lord of hosts: and ye brought that which was torn, and the lame, and the sick; thus ye brought an offering: should I accept this of your hand? saith the Lord.

i Ezek. xxiii. 38. Moreover, this they have done unto me: they have *defiled my sanctuary in the same day, and have profaned my sabbaths.*

k Jer. xvii. 24. And it shall come to pass, if ye diligently hearken unto me, saith the Lord, *to bring in no burden through the gates of this city on the sabbath-day,* but hallow the sabbath-day, *to do no work therein.* Ver. 27. But if ye will not hearken unto me to hallow the sabbath-day, *and not to bear a burden,* even entering in at the gates of Jerusalem on the sabbath-day; then will I kindle a fire in the gates thereof, and it shall devour the palaces of Jerusalem, and it shall not be quenched. Isa. lviii. 13. *If thou turn away thy foot from the sabbath, from doing thy pleasure on my holy day;* and call the sabbath a delight, the holy of

A. The reasons annexed to the fourth commandment, the more to enforce it, are taken from the equity of it, God allowing us six days of seven for our own affairs, and reserving but one for himself, in these words, *Six days shalt thou labour, and do all thy work:*[l] from God's challenging a special propriety in that day, *The seventh day is the sabbath of the Lord thy God:*[m] from the example of God, who *in six days made heaven and earth, the sea, and all that in them is, and rested the seventh day:* and from that blessing which God put upon that day, not only in sanctifying it to be a day for his service, but in ordaining it to be a means of blessing to us in our sanctifying it; *Wherefore the Lord blessed the sabbath-day, and hallowed it.*[n]

Q. 121. *Why is the word* Remember *set in the beginning of the fourth commandment?*

A. The word *Remember* is set in the beginning of the fourth commandment,[o] partly, because of the great benefit of remembering it, we being thereby helped in our preparation to keep it,[p] and, in keeping it, better to keep all the rest of the commandments,[q] and to continue a thankful remembrance of the two great benefits of creation and redemption, which contain a short abridgment of religion;[r] and partly, because we are very ready to forget it,[s] for that there is less light of nature for it,[t] and yet it restraineth our natural liberty in things at other times lawful;[v] that it cometh but once in seven days, and many

the Lord, honourable; and shalt honour him, *not doing thine own ways, nor finding thine own pleasure, nor speaking thine own words.*

120. [l] Exod. xx. 9.
[m] Exod. xx. 10.
[n] Exod. xx. 11.
121. [o] Exod. xx. 8.
[p] Exod. xvi. 23. And he said unto them, This is that which the Lord hath said, *To-morrow is the rest of the holy sabbath unto the Lord: bake that which ye will bake to-day,* and seethe that ye will seethe; and that which remaineth over lay up for you, to be kept until the morning. Luke xxiii. 54. And *that day was the preparation,* and the sabbath drew on. Ver. 56. And they returned, *and prepared spices and ointments; and rested the sabbath-day, according to the commandment.* Compared with Mark xv. 42. And now, when the even was come (*because it was the preparation,* that is, *the day before the sabbath.*) Neh. xiii. 19. And it came to pass, that when the gates of Jerusalem began to be dark *before the sabbath, I commanded that the gates should be shut,* and charged that they *should not be opened till after the sabbath:* and some of my servants set I at the gates, that there *should no burden be brought in on the sabbath-day.*

[q] Ps. xcii. [title, A psalm or song for *the sabbath-day.*] Compared with ver. 13. Those that be planted in the house of the Lord *shall flourish in the courts of our God.* And ver. 14. *They shall still bring forth fruit in old age;* they shall be *fat* and *flourishing.* Ezek. xx. 12. Moreover also, *I gave them my sabbaths, to be a sign between me and them, that they might know that I am the Lord that sanctify them.* Ver. 19. I am the Lord your God; walk in my statutes, and keep my judgments, and do them; Ver. 20. And *hallow my sabbaths;* and they shall be *a sign* between me and you, that ye may know that I am the Lord your God.

[r] Gen. ii. 2. And *on the seventh day God ended his work* which he had made; and *he rested on the seventh day* from all his work which he had made. Ver. 3. And God *blessed the seventh day, and sanctified it;* because *that in it he had rested from all his work* which God created and made. Ps. cxviii. 22. *The stone which the builders refused is become the head stone of the corner.* Ver. 24. *This is the day which the Lord hath made;* we will rejoice and be glad in it. Compared with Acts iv. 10. Be it known unto you all, and to all the people of Israel, that by the name of Jesus Christ of Nazareth, whom ye crucified, whom God raised from the dead, even by him doth this man stand here before you whole. Ver. 11. *This is the stone which was set at nought of you builders, which is become the head of the corner.* Rev. i. 10. *I was in the Spirit on the Lord's day,* and heard behind me a great voice, as of a trumpet.

[s] Ezek. xxii. 26. Her priests have violated my law, and have profaned mine holy things: they have put no difference between the holy and profane, neither have they shewed difference between the unclean and the clean, and *have hid their eyes from my sabbaths,* and I am profaned among them.

[t] Neh. ix. 14. And *madest known unto them thy holy sabbath,* and commandedst them precepts, statutes, and laws, by the hand of Moses thy servant.

[v] Exod. xxxiv. 21. Six days thou shalt work; but on *the seventh day thou shalt rest: in earing-time and in harvest thou shalt rest.*

worldly businesses come between, and too often take off our minds from thinking of it, either to prepare for it, or to sanctify it;w and that Satan with his instruments much labour to blot out the glory, and even the memory of it, to bring in all irreligion and impiety.x

Q. 122. *What is the sum of the six commandments which contain our duty to man?*

A. The sum of the six commandments which contain our duty to man, is, to love our neighbour as ourselves,y and to do to others what we would have them to do to us.z

Q. 123. *Which is the fifth commandment?*

A. The fifth commandment is, *Honour thy father and thy mother: that thy days may be long upon the land which the Lord thy God giveth thee.*a

Q. 124. *Who are meant by father and mother in the fifth commandment?*

A. By *father* and *mother*, in the fifth commandment, are meant, not only natural parents,b but all superiors in agec and gifts;d and especially such as, by God's ordinance, are over us in place of authority, whether in family,e church,f or commonwealth.g

w Deut. v. 14. But *the seventh day is the sabbath of the Lord thy God:* in it thou shalt not do any work, thou, nor thy son, nor thy daughter, nor thy man-servant, nor thy maid-servant, nor thine ox, nor thine ass, nor any of thy cattle, nor thy stranger that is within thy gates ; that thy man-servant and thy maid-servant may rest as well as thou. Ver. 15. And *remember that thou wast a servant in the land of Egypt,* and that the Lord thy God brought thee out thence through a mighty hand, and by a stretched-out arm : *therefore the Lord thy God commanded thee to keep the sabbath-day.* Amos viii. 5. Saying, when will the new-moon *be gone,* that we may sell corn ? *and the sabbath, that we may set forth wheat,* making the ephah small, and the shekel great, and falsifying the balances by deceit ?

x Lam. i. 7. Jerusalem remembered in the days of her affliction, and of her miseries, all her pleasant things that she had in the days of old, when her people fell into the hand of the enemy, and none did help her : *the adversaries saw her, and did mock at her sabbaths.* Jer. xvii. 21. Thus saith the Lord, *Take heed to yourselves, and bear no burden on the sabbath-day,* nor bring it in by the gates of Jerusalem ; Ver. 22. Neither carry forth a burden out of your houses on the sabbath-day, neither do ye any work ; but *hallow ye the sabbath-day,* as I commanded your fathers. Ver. 23. But *they obeyed not, neither inclined their ear, but made their neck stiff, that they might not hear, nor receive instruction.* Neh. xiii. from verse 15. to 23. In those days saw I in Judah some *treading wine-presses on the sabbath-day.*—[See in letter b.]

122. y Matt. xxii. 39. And the *second* is like unto it, *Thou shalt love thy neighbour as thyself.*

z Matt. vii. 12. Therefore *all things whatsoever ye would that men should do to you, do ye even so to them: for this is the law and the prophets.*

123. a Exod. xx. 12.

124. b Prov. xxiii. 22. *Hearken unto thy father that begat thee,* and despise not thy mother when she is old. Ver. 25. *Thy father and thy mother* shall be glad, and *she that bare thee shall rejoice.* Eph. vi. 1. *Children, obey your parents in the Lord:* for this is right. Ver. 2. *Honour thy father and mother,* (which is the first commandment with promise.)

c 1 Tim. v. 1. *Rebuke not an elder, but entreat him as a father;* and the younger men as brethren ; Ver. 2. The *elder women as mothers;* the younger as sisters, with all purity.

d Gen. iv. 20. And Adah bare Jabal : he was the father of such as dwell in tents, and of such as have cattle. Ver. 21. And his brother's name was Jubal : *he was the father of all such as handle the harp and organ.* Ver. 22. And Zillah, she also bare Tubal-cain, an instructor of every artificer in brass and iron. Gen. xlv. 8. So now, it was not you that sent me hither, but God : and *he hath made me a father to Pharaoh,* and lord of all his house, and a ruler throughout all the land of Egypt.

e 2 Kings v. 13. And his servants came near, and spake unto him, and said, *My father,* if the prophet had bid thee do some great thing, wouldest thou not have done it? how much rather then, when he saith to thee, Wash, and be clean?

f 2 Kings ii. 12. And Elisha saw it, and he cried, *My father, my father!* the chariot of Israel, and the horsemen thereof.—2 Kings xiii. 14. Now Elisha was fallen sick of his sickness whereof he died. And Joash the king of Israel came down unto him, and wept over his face, and said, *O my father, my father!* the chariot of Israel, and the horsemen thereof! Gal. iv. 19. *My little children, of whom I travail in birth again* until Christ be formed in you.

g Isa. xlix. 23. And *kings* shall be thy *nursing fathers,* and their *queens* thy nurs-

Q. 125. *Why are superiors styled* Father *and* Mother?

A. Superiors are styled *Father* and *Mother*, both to teach them in all duties toward their inferiors, like natural parents; to express love and tenderness to them, according to their several relations;[h] and to work inferiors to a greater willingness and cheerfulness in performing their duties to their superiors, as to their parents.[i]

Q. 126. *What is the general scope of the fifth commandment?*

A. The general scope of the fifth commandment is, the performance of those duties which we mutually owe in our several relations, as inferiors, superiors, or equals.[k]

Q. 127. *What is the honour that inferiors owe to their superiors?*

A. The honour which inferiors owe to their superiors is, all due reverence in heart,[l] word,[m] and behaviour;[n] prayer and thanksgiving for them;[o] imitation of their virtues and graces;[p] willing obedience to their lawful commands and counsels;[q] due submission to their correc-

---

ing-mothers: they shall bow down to thee with their face toward the earth, and lick up the dust of thy feet ; and thou shalt know that I am the Lord : for they shall not be ashamed that wait for me.

125. h Eph. vi. 4. And, *ye fathers, provoke not your children to wrath ; but bring them up in the nurture and admonition of the Lord.* 2 Cor. xii. 14. For the *children ought not to lay up for the parents, but the parents for the children.* 1 Thess. ii. 7. But we were *gentle* among you, *even as a nurse cherisheth her children:* Ver. 8. *So, being affectionately desirous of you,* we were willing to have imparted unto you, not the gospel of God only, but also our own souls, *because ye were dear unto us.* Ver. 11. As ye know how *we exhorted and comforted, and charged every one of you, (as a father doth his children.)* Numb. xi. 11. And Moses said unto the Lord, Wherefore hast thou afflicted thy servant? and wherefore have I not found favour in thy sight, that thou layest the burden of all this people upon me? Ver. 12. Have I conceived all this people? have *I begotten them, that thou shouldest say unto me,* Carry them *in thy bosom (as a nursing-father beareth the sucking child)* unto the land which thou swarest unto their fathers?

i 1 Cor. iv. 14. I write not these things to shame you, but, *as my beloved sons, I warn you.* Ver. 15. For though ye have ten thousand instructers in Christ, *yet have ye not many fathers:* for in Christ Jesus *I have begotten you through the gospel.* Ver. 16. *Wherefore, I beseech you, be ye followers of me.* 2 Kings v. 13. [See letter e.]

126. k Eph. v. 21. *Submitting yourselves one to another in the fear of God.* 1 Pet. ii. 17. *Honour all men. Love the brotherhood. Fear God. Honour the king.* Rom. xii. 10. *Be kindly affectioned one to another with brotherly love; in honour preferring one another.*

127. l Mal. i. 6. *A son honoureth his father,* and a servant his master : *if then I be a father, where is mine honour?* and if I be a master, where is my fear? saith the Lord of hosts unto you, O priests, that despise my name. And ye say, Wherein have we despised thy name? Lev. xix. 3. *Ye shall fear every man his mother and his father,* and keep my sabbaths : I am the Lord your God.

m Prov. xxxi. 28. *Her children arise up, and call her blessed;* her husband also, and he praiseth her. 1 Pet. iii. 6. Even *as Sarah obeyed Abraham, calling him lord:* whose daughters ye are as long as ye do well, and are not afraid with any amazement.

n Lev. xix. 32. *Thou shalt rise up before the hoary head, and honour the face of the old man,* and fear thy God : I am the Lord. 1 Kings ii. 19. *Bath-sheba* therefore went unto king *Solomon,* to speak unto him for Adonijah. *And the king rose up to meet her, and bowed himself unto her,* and sat down on his throne, and caused a seat to be set for the king's mother ; and she sat on his right hand.

o 1 Tim. ii. 1. I exhort therefore, that, first of all, *supplications, prayers, intercessions, and giving of thanks, be made for all men;* Ver. 2. *For kings, and for all that are in authority;* that we may lead a quiet and peaceable life in all godliness and honesty.

p Heb. xiii. 7. Remember them *which have the rule over you,* who have spoken unto you the word of God ; *whose faith follow,* considering the end of their conversation. Phil. iii. 17. Brethren, *be followers together of me,* and mark them which walk so, as ye have us for an ensample.

q Eph. vi. 1. *Children, obey your parents in the Lord:* for this is right. Ver. 2. *Honour thy father and mother,* (which is the first commandment with promise.) Ver. 5. *Servants, be obedient to them that are your masters according to the flesh,* with fear and trembling, *in singleness of your heart,* as unto Christ ; Ver. 6. *Not with eye service, as men-pleasers;* but as the servants of Christ, *doing the will of God from the heart;* Ver. 7. *With good will doing service, as to the Lord,* and not to men. 1 Pet. ii. 13. *Submit yourselves to every ordinance of man for the Lord's sake:* whether it be to the king, as supreme ; Ver. 14. Or unto governors, as unto them that are sent by him for the punishment of

tions;[r] fidelity to,[s] defence,[t] and maintenance of their persons and authority, according to their several ranks, and the nature of their places;[v] bearing with their infirmities, and covering them in love,[w] that so they may be an honour to them and to their government.[x]

Q. 128. *What are the sins of inferiors against their superiors?*

A. The sins of inferiors against their superiors are, all neglect of evil-doers, and for the praise of them that do well. Rom. xiii. 1. *Let every soul be subject unto the higher powers.* For there is no power but of God: the powers that be are ordained of God. Ver. 2. Whosoever therefore resisteth the power, resisteth the ordinance of God; and they that resist shall receive to themselves damnation. Ver. 3. For rulers are not a terror to good works, but to the evil. Wilt thou then not be afraid of the power? Do that which is good, and thou shalt have praise of the same: Ver. 4. For he is the minister of God to thee for good. But if thou do that which is evil, be afraid; for he beareth not the sword in vain: for he is the minister of God, a revenger to execute wrath upon him that doeth evil. Ver. 5. Wherefore *ye must needs be subject, not only for wrath, but also for conscience' sake.* Heb. xiii. 17. *Obey them that have the rule over you, and submit yourselves:* for they watch for your souls, as they that must give account; that they may do it with joy, and not with grief: for that is unprofitable for you. Prov. iv. 3. For I was my father's son, tender and only beloved in the sight of my mother. Ver. 4. He taught me also, *and said unto me, Let thine heart retain my words: keep my commandments, and live.* Prov. xiii. 22. *Hearken unto thy father that begat thee,* and *despise not thy mother* when she is old. Exod. xviii. 19. Hearken now unto my voice, I will give thee counsel, and God shall be with thee. Ver. 24. *So Moses hearkened to the voice of his father-in-law, and did all that he had said.*

[r] Heb. xii. 9. Furthermore, *we have had fathers of our flesh which corrected us, and we gave them reverence:* shall we not much rather be in subjection unto the Father of spirits, and live? 1 Pet. ii. 18. *Servants, be subject to your masters with all fear;* not only to the good and gentle, but *also to the froward.* Ver. 19. For *this is thankworthy, if a man for conscience toward God endure grief, suffering wrongfully.* Ver. 20. For what glory is it, *if, when ye be buffeted for your faults, ye shall take it patiently?* but if, when ye do well, and suffer for it, ye take it patiently, this is acceptable with God.

[s] Tit. ii. 9. Exhort servants to be obedient unto their own masters, and to please them well in all things; not answering again; Ver. 10. *Not purloining, but shewing all good fidelity;* that they may adorn the doctrine of God our Saviour in all things.

[t] 1 Sam. xxvi. 15. And David said to Abner, Art not thou a valiant man? and who is like to thee in Israel? *wherefore then hast thou not kept thy lord the king?* for there came one of the people in to destroy the king thy lord. Ver. 16. This thing is not good that thou hast done. As the Lord liveth, *ye are worthy to die, because ye have not kept your master, the Lord's anointed.* 2 Sam. xviii. 3. *But the people answered,* Thou shalt not go forth: for if we flee away, they will not care for us; neither if half of us die, will they care for us: but now *thou art worth ten thousand of us;* therefore now it is better that thou succour us out of the city. Esther vi. 2. And it was found written, that *Mordecai had told of Bigthana and Teresh,* two of the king's chamberlains, the keepers of the door, *who sought to lay hand on the king Ahasuerus.*

[v] Matt. xxii. 21. They say unto him, Cesar's. Then he saith unto them, *Render therefore unto Cesar the things which are Cesar's;* and unto God the things that are God's. Rom. xiii. 6. For, *for this cause pay ye tribute also:* for they are God's ministers, attending continually upon this very thing. Ver. 7. *Render therefore to all their dues: tribute to whom tribute is due; custom to whom custom; fear to whom fear; honour to whom honour.* 1 Tim. v. 17. *Let the elders that rule well be counted worthy of double honour, especially they who labour in the word and doctrine.* Ver. 18. For the scripture saith, Thou shalt not muzzle the ox that treadeth out the corn. And, *The labourer is worthy of his reward.* Gal. vi. 6. *Let him that is taught in the word communicate unto him that teacheth in all good things.* Gen. xlv. 11. And there will I nourish thee, (for yet there are five years of famine,) lest thou, and thy household, and all that thou hast, come to poverty. Gen. xlvii. 12. And *Joseph nourished his father, and his brethren, and all his father's household, with bread, according to their families.*

[w] 1 Pet. ii. 18. *Servants, be subject to your masters with all fear; not only to the good and gentle, but also to the froward.* Prov. xxiii. 22. Hearken unto thy father that begat thee, and *despise not thy mother when she is old.* Gen. ix. 23. And Shem and Japheth took a garment, and laid it upon both their shoulders, and went backward, and covered the nakedness of their father: and their faces were backward, *and they saw not their father's nakedness.*

[x] Ps. cxxvii. 3. Lo, *children are an heritage of the Lord:* and *the fruit of the womb is his reward.* Ver. 4. As arrows are in the hand of a mighty man; *so are children of the youth.* Ver. 5. *Happy is the man that hath his quiver full of them:* they shall not be ashamed, but they shall speak with the enemies in the gate. Prov. xxxi. 23. *Her husband is known in the gates, when he sitteth among the elders of the land.*

the duties required toward them;ʸ envying at,ᶻ contempt of,ᵃ and rebellionᵇ against, their personsᶜ and places,ᵈ in their lawful counsels,ᵉ commands, and corrections;ᶠ cursing, mocking,ᵍ and all such refractory and scandalous carriage, as proves a shame and dishonour to them and their government.ʰ

Q. 129. *What is required of superiors towards their inferiors?*

A. It is required of superiors, according to that power they receive from God, and that relation wherein they stand, to love,ⁱ pray for,ᵏ and bless their inferiors;ˡ to instruct,ᵐ counsel, and admonish them;ⁿ countenancing,ᵒ commending,ᵖ and rewarding such as do

---

128. ʸ Matt. xv. 4. For God commanded, saying, Honour thy father and mother: and, *He that curseth father or mother, let him die the death.* Ver. 5. *But ye say,* Whosoever shall say to his *father* or his *mother,* It is a gift, by whatsoever thou mightest be profited by me, Ver. 6. *And honour not his father or his mother,* he shall be free. *Thus have ye made the commandment of God of none effect by your tradition.*

ᶻ Numb. xi. 28. And Joshua the son of Nun, the servant of Moses, one of his young men, answered and said, *My lord Moses, forbid them.* Ver. 29. And Moses said unto him, *Enviest thou for my sake?* Would God that all the Lord's people were prophets, and that the Lord would put his Spirit upon them!

ᵃ 1 Sam. viii. 7. And the Lord said unto Samuel, Hearken unto the voice of the people in all that they say unto thee: *for they have not rejected thee, but they have rejected me,* that I should not reign over them. Isa. iii. 5. And the people shall be oppressed, every one by another, and every one by his neighbour: *the child shall behave himself proudly against the ancient, and the base against the honourable.*

ᵇ 2 Sam. xv. from ver. 1. to 12. And it came to pass after this, that *Absalom prepared him chariots and horses,* &c.

ᶜ Exod. xxi. 15. And *he that smiteth his father or his mother shall be surely put to death.*

ᵈ 1 Sam. x. 27. But the children of Belial said, *How shall this man save us? And they despised him,* and brought him no presents; but he held his peace.

ᵉ 1 Sam. ii. 25. Notwithstanding, *they* (viz. the sons of Eli) *hearkened not unto the voice of their father,* because the Lord would slay them.

ᶠ Deut. xxi. 18. If a man have *a stubborn and rebellious son,* which will not obey the voice of *his father,* or the voice of *his mother,* and that, *when they have chastened him, will not hearken unto them;* Ver. 19. Then shall his father and his mother lay hold on him, and bring him out unto the elders of his city, and unto the gate of his place: Ver. 20. And they shall say unto the elders of his city, This our son is stubborn and rebellious, he will not obey our voice; he is a glutton and a drunkard. Ver. 21. And all the men of his city *shall stone him with stones, that he die:* so shalt thou put evil away from among you; and all Israel shall hear, and fear.

ᵍ Prov. xxx. 11. There is a generation that *curseth their father,* and *doth not bless their mother.* Ver. 17. *The eye that mocketh at his father,* and despiseth to obey his mother, the *ravens of the valley shall pick it out,* and the *young eagles shall eat it.*

ʰ Prov. xix. 26. He that *wasteth his father,* and *chaseth away his mother, is a son that causeth shame, and bringeth reproach.*

129. ⁱ Col. iii. 19. *Husbands, love your wives,* and be not bitter against them. Tit. ii. 4. That they may teach the *young women* to be sober, *to love their husbands, to love their children.*

ᵏ 1 Sam. xii. 23. Moreover, as for me, *God forbid that I should sin against the Lord in ceasing to pray for you;* but I will teach you the good and the right way. Job i. 5. And it was so, when the days of their feasting were gone about, that *Job sent and sanctified them,* and rose up early in the morning, and *offered burnt-offerings according to the number of them all:* for Job said, It may be that my sons have sinned, and cursed God in their hearts. *Thus did Job continually.*

ˡ 1 Kings viii. 55. And he stood, and *blessed all the congregation of Israel* with a loud voice, saying, Ver. 56. Blessed be the Lord, that hath given rest unto his people Israel, according to all that he promised: there hath not failed—Heb. vii. 7. And, without all contradiction, *the less is blessed of the better.* Gen. xlix. 28. All these are the twelve tribes of Israel: and this is it that *their father spake unto them, and blessed them; every one according to his blessing he blessed them.*

ᵐ Deut. vi. 6. And these words, which I command thee this day, shall be in thine heart; Ver. 7. And *thou shalt teach them diligently unto thy children,* and *shalt talk of them* when thou *sittest in thine house,* and when thou *walkest by the way,* and when thou *liest down,* and when thou *risest up.*

ⁿ Eph. vi. 4. And, *ye fathers,* provoke not your *children* to wrath; but *bring them up in the nurture and admonition of the Lord.*

ᵒ 1 Pet. iii. 7. Likewise, *ye husbands,* dwell with them according to knowledge, *giving honour unto the wife, as unto the weaker vessel,* and as being heirs together of the grace of life; that your prayers be not hindered.

ᵖ 1 Pet. ii. 14. Or unto *governors,* as unto them that are sent by him for the punishment of evil-doers, *and for the praise of* well;^q and discountenancing,^r reproving, and chastising such as do ill;^s protecting,^t and providing for them all things necessary for soul^v and body:^w and by grave, wise, holy, and exemplary carriage, to procure glory to God,^x honour to themselves,^y and so to preserve that authority which God hath put upon them.^z

Q. 130. *What are the sins of superiors?*

A. The sins of superiors are, besides the neglect of the duties required of them,^a an inordinate seeking of themselves,^b their own glory,^c ease, profit, or pleasure;^d commanding things unlawful,^e or

them that do well. Rom. xiii. 3. For *rulers* are not a terror to good works, but to the evil. Wilt thou then not be afraid of the power? Do that which is good, and thou shalt have praise of the same.

q Esth. vi. 3. And *the king said, What honour and dignity hath been done to Mordecai for this?* Then said the king's servants that ministered unto him, There is nothing done for him.

r Rom. xiii. 3. For *rulers* are not a *terror* to good works, *but to the evil.* Wilt thou then not be afraid of the power? Do that which is good, and thou shalt have praise of the same: Ver. 4. For he is the minister of God to thee for good. But *if thou do that which is evil,* be afraid; for he beareth not the sword in vain; for *he is the minister of God, a revenger to execute wrath upon him that doeth evil.*

s Prov. xxix. 15. *The rod and reproof give wisdom; but a child left to himself bringeth his mother to shame.* 1 Pet. ii. 14. [See above in letter p.]

t Job xxix. 12. Because *I delivered the poor that cried, and the fatherless, and him that had none to help him.* Ver. 13. The *blessing of him that was ready to perish came upon me:* and *I caused the widow's heart to sing* for joy. Ver. 14. I put on righteousness, and it clothed me: my judgment was as a robe and a diadem. Ver. 15. I was *eyes to the blind,* and *feet was I to the lame.* Ver. 16. I was *a father to the poor;* and the cause which I knew not I searched out. Ver. 17. And *I brake the jaws of the wicked, and plucked the spoil out of his teeth.* Isa. i. 10. Hear the word of the Lord, ye rulers of Sodom; give ear unto the law of our God, ye people of Gomorrah. Ver. 17. Learn to do well; seek judgment; *relieve the oppressed; judge the fatherless; plead for the widow.*

v Eph. vi. 4. And, ye fathers, provoke not your *children* to wrath; but *bring them up in the nurture and admonition of the Lord.*

w 1 Tim. v. 8. But *if any provide not for his own,* and specially *for those of his own house, he hath denied the faith,* and is worse than an infidel.

x 1 Tim. iv. 12. Let no man despise thy youth; but *be thou an example of the believers, in word, in conversation, in charity, in spirit, in faith, in purity.* Tit. ii. 3. The *aged women* likewise, that they be *in behaviour as becometh holiness,* not false accusers, not given to much wine, teachers of good things; Ver. 4. That they may teach the young women to be sober to love their husbands, to love their children, Ver. 5. To be discreet, *chaste,* keepers at home, good, obedient to their own husbands, *that the word of God be not blasphemed.*

y 1 Kings iii. 28. And all Israel heard of the judgment which the king had judged; *and they feared the king: for they saw that the wisdom of God was in him to do judgment.*

z Tit. ii. 15. These things speak, and exhort, and *rebuke with all authority. Let no man despise thee.*

130. a Ezek. xxxiv. 2. Son of man, prophesy against the shepherds of Israel, prophesy, and say unto them, Thus saith the Lord God unto the shepherds, *Woe be to the shepherds of Israel* that do feed themselves! *should not the shepherds feed the flocks?* Ver. 3. Ye eat the fat, and ye clothe you with the wool, ye kill them that are fed: *but ye feed not the flock.* Ver. 4. *The diseased have ye not strengthened, neither have ye healed that which was sick, neither have ye bound up that which was broken, neither have ye brought again that which was driven away, neither have ye sought that which was lost;* but with force and with cruelty have ye ruled them.

b Phil. ii. 21. *For all seek their own,* not the things which are Jesus Christ's.

c John v. 44. How can ye believe, *which receive honour one of another,* and seek not the honour that cometh from God only? John vii. 18. *He that speaketh of himself seeketh his own glory;* but he that seeketh his glory that sent him, the same is true, and no unrighteousness is in him.

d Isa. lvi. 10. *His watchmen* are blind: they are all ignorant, they are all *dumb dogs,* they cannot bark; *sleeping, lying down, loving to slumber.* Ver. 11. Yea, *they are greedy dogs* which can never have enough, and they are shepherds that cannot understand: they *all look to their own way, every one for his gain, from his quarter.* Deut. xvii. 17. *Neither shall he multiply wives to himself,* that his heart turn not away; *neither shall he greatly multiply to himself silver and gold.*

e Dan. iii. 4. Then an herald cried aloud, *To you it is commanded, O people, nations, and languages,* Ver. 5. That at what time ye hear the sound of the cornet, flute, harp, sackbut, psaltery, dulcimer, and all kinds of musick, *ye fall down and worship the golden image* that Nebuchadnezzar the king hath set up: Ver. 6. And whoso falleth not down and worshippeth, shall the same hour be cast into the midst of a burning fiery furnace. Acts iv. 17. But, that it spread

not in the power of inferiors to perform;[f] counselling,[g] encouraging,[h] or favouring them in that which is evil;[i] dissuading, discouraging, or discountenancing them in that which is good;[k] correcting them unduly;[l] careless exposing, or leaving them to wrong, temptation, and danger;[m] provoking them to wrath;[n] or any way dishonouring themselves, or lessening their authority, by an unjust, indiscreet, rigorous, or remiss behaviour.[o]

Q. 131. *What are the duties of equals?*

A. The duties of equals are, to regard the dignity and worth of each

---

no further among the people, let us straitly threaten them, that they speak henceforth to no man in this name. Ver. 18. And they called them, and *commanded them not to speak at all, nor teach, in the name of Jesus.*

[f] Exod. v. from ver. 10. to 18. And the *taskmasters* of the people went out, and their officers, and they spake to the people, saying, *Thus saith Pharaoh, I will not give you straw,* &c. Matt. xxiii. 2. Saying, The scribes and the Pharisees sit in Moses' seat. Ver. 4. For they *bind heavy burdens, and grievous to be borne.*

[g] Matt. xiv. 8. And *she, being before instructed of her mother, said, Give me here John Baptist's head in a charger.* Compared with Mark vi. 24. And she went forth, and *said unto her mother, What shall I ask? And she said, The head of John the Baptist.*

[h] 2 Sam. xiii. 28. Now Absalom had commanded his servants, saying, Mark ye now when Amnon's heart is merry with wine, and when I say unto you, *Smite Amnon;* then kill him, *fear not: have not I commanded you? be courageous, and be valiant.*

[i] 1 Sam. iii. 13. For I have told him, that I will judge his house for ever, for the iniquity which he knoweth ; *because his sons made themselves vile, and he restrained them not.*

[k] John vii. 46. The officers answered, Never man spake like this man. Ver. 47. *Then answered them the Pharisees, Are ye also deceived?* Ver. 48. Have any of the rulers, or of the Pharisees, believed on him? Ver. 49. But this people, who knoweth not the law, are cursed. Col. iii. 21. *Fathers, provoke not your children to anger, lest they be discouraged.* Exod. v 17. *But he said, Ye are idle, ye are idle; therefore ye say, Let us go and do sacrifice to the Lord.*

[l] 1 Pet. ii. 18. *Servants,* be subject to your *masters* with all fear ; not only to the good and gentle, but also *to the froward.* Ver. 19. For this is thank-worthy, if a man for conscience toward God endure grief, *suffering wrongfully.* Ver. 20. For what glory is it, if, when ye be buffeted for your faults, ye shall take it patiently? *but if, when ye do well, and suffer for it, ye take it patiently,* this is acceptable with God. Heb. xii. 10. For *they* verily for a few days *chastened us after their own pleasure;* but he for our profit, that we might be partakers of his holiness. Deut. xxv. 3. *Forty stripes he may give him, and not exceed;* lest, if he should exceed, and beat him above these with many stripes, then thy brother should seem vile unto thee.

[m] Gen. xxxviii. 11. Then said Judah to Tamar his daughter-in-law, *Remain a widow at thy father's house, till Shelah my son be grown;* (for he said, Lest peradventure he die also, as his brethren did.) And Tamar went and dwelt in her father's house. Ver. 26. And Judah acknowledged them, and said, *She hath been more righteous than I; because that I gave her not to Shelah my son:* and he knew her again no more. Acts xviii. 17. Then all the Greeks took Sosthenes, the chief ruler of the synagogue, and beat him before the judgment-seat : *and Gallio cared for none of those things.*

[n] Eph. vi. 4. And, *ye fathers, provoke not your children to wrath;* but bring them up in the nurture and admonition of the Lord.

[o] Gen. ix. 21. And he drank of the wine, *and was drunken;* and *he was uncovered within his tent.* 1 Kings xii. 13. And *the king* (Rehoboam) *answered the people roughly,* and forsook the old men's counsel that they gave him; Ver. 14. And spake to them after the counsel of the young men, saying, *My father made your yoke heavy, and I will add to your yoke: my father also chastised you with whips,* but *I will chastise you with scorpions.* Ver. 15. Wherefore the king hearkened not unto the people ; for the cause was from the Lord.—Ver. 16. So when all Israel saw that the king hearkened not unto them, the people answered the king, saying, *What portion have we in David?* neither have we inheritance in the son of Jesse : to your tents, O Israel : now see to thine own house, David. *So Israel departed unto their tents.* 1 Kings i. 6. And *his father had not displeased him* (viz. Adonijah) at any time in saying, *Why hast thou done so?* 1 Sam. ii. 29. Wherefore kick ye at my sacrifice, and at mine offering, which I have commanded in my habitation ; and *honourest thy sons above me, to make yourselves fat with the chiefest of all the offerings of Israel my people?* Ver. 30. Wherefore the Lord God of Israel saith, I said indeed, that thy house, and the house of thy father, should walk before me for ever : but now the Lord saith, Be it far from me ; for them that honour me I will honour, and *they that despise me shall be lightly esteemed.* Ver. 31. Behold, the days come, that I will cut off thine arm, and the arm of thy father's house, that there shall not be an old man in thine house.

other,p in giving honour to go one before another;q and to rejoice in each others gifts and advancement, as their own.r

Q. 132. *What are the sins of equals?*

A. The sins of equals are, besides the neglect of the duties required,s the undervaluing of the worth,t envying the gifts,v grieving at the advancement or prosperity one of another;w and usurping preeminence one over another.x

Q. 133. *What is the reason annexed to the fifth commandment, the more to enforce it?*

A. The reason annexed to the fifth commandment, in these words, *That thy days may be long upon the land which the Lord thy God giveth thee,*y is an express promise of long life and prosperity, as far as it shall serve for God's glory and their own good, to all such as keep this commandment.z

Q. 134. *Which is the sixth commandment?*

A. The sixth commandment is, *Thou shalt not kill.*a

Q. 135. *What are the duties required in the sixth commandment?*

A. The duties required in the sixth commandment are, all careful studies, and lawful endeavours, to preserve the life of ourselvesb and othersc by resisting all thoughts and purposes,d subduing all pas-

---

131. p 1 Pet. ii. 17. *Honour all men. Love the brotherhood. Fear God. Honour the king.*
q Rom. xii. 10. *Be kindly affectioned one to another with brotherly love; in honour preferring one another.*
r Rom. xii. 15. *Rejoice with them that do rejoice,* and weep with them that weep. Ver. 16. *Be of the same mind one toward another.* Mind not high things, but condescend to men of low estate. Be not wise in your own conceits. Phil. ii. 3. Let nothing be done through strife or vain-glory; but in lowliness of mind *let each esteem other better than themselves.* Ver. 4. *Look* not every man on his own things, *but every man also on the things of others.*
132. s Rom. xiii. 8. *Owe no man any thing, but to love one another; for he that loveth another hath fulfilled the law.*
t 2 Tim. iii. 3. *Without natural affection,* truce-breakers, false accusers, incontinent, fierce, despisers of those that are good.
v Acts vii. 9. And *the patriarchs, moved with envy, sold Joseph into Egypt:* but God was with him. Gal. v. 26. Let us not be desirous of vain-glory, provoking one another, *envying one another.*
w Numb. xii. 2. And they said, *Hath the Lord indeed spoken only by Moses? hath he not spoken also by us?* And the Lord heard it. Esth. vi. 12. And Mordecai came again to the king's gate: *but Haman hasted to his house mourning, and having his head covered.* Ver. 13. And Haman told Zeresh his wife and all his friends every thing that had befallen him. Then said his wise men and Zeresh his wife unto him, If Mordecai be of the seed of the Jews, before whom thou hast begun to fall, thou shalt not prevail against him, but shalt surely fall before him.
x 3 John, ver. 9. I wrote unto the church: but *Diotrephes, who loveth to have the pre-*eminence among them, receiveth us not. Luke xxii. 24. And there was also *a strife among them, which of them should be accounted the greatest.*
133. y Exod. xx. 12.
z Deut. v. 16. Honour thy father and thy mother, as the Lord thy God hath commanded thee; *that thy days may be prolonged, and that it may go well with thee,* in the land which the Lord thy God giveth thee. 1 Kings viii. 25. Therefore now, Lord God of Israel, *keep with thy servant David my father that thou promisedst him,* saying, There shall not fail thee a man in my sight to sit on the throne of Israel; *so that thy children take heed to their way,* that they walk before me as thou hast walked before me. Eph. vi. 2. Honour thy father and mother, (which is the first commandment with promise,) Ver. 3. *That it may be well with thee, and thou mayest live long on the earth.*
134. a Exod. xx. 13.
135. b Eph. v. 28. So ought men to *love their wives as their own bodies;* he that loveth his wife loveth himself. Ver. 29 *For no man ever yet hated his own flesh, but nourisheth and cherisheth it,* even as the Lord the church.
c 1 Kings xviii. 4. For it was so, when Jezebel cut off the prophets of the Lord, that *Obadiah took an hundred prophets, and hid them by fifty in a cave, and fed them with bread and water,*
d Jer. xxvi. 15. But know ye for certain, that, if ye put me to death, ye shall surely bring innocent blood upon yourselves, and upon this city, and upon the inhabitants thereof: for of a truth the Lord hath sent me unto you, to speak all these words in your ears. Ver. 16. *Then said the princes and all the people unto the priests, and to the prophets, This man is not worthy to die: for* he hath spoken to us in the name of the

sions,[e] and avoiding all occasions,[f] temptations,[g] and practices, which tend to the unjust taking away the life of any;[h] by just defence thereof against violence,[i] patient bearing of the hand of God,[k] quietness of mind,[l] cheerfulness of spirit;[m] a sober use of meat,[n] drink,[o] physick,[p]

[e] Lord our God. Acts xxiii. 12. And when it was day, certain of the Jews banded together, and bound themselves under a curse, saying that they would neither eat nor drink till they had killed Paul. Ver. 16. *And when Paul's sister's son heard of their lying in wait, he went and entered into the castle and told Paul.* Ver. 17. *Then Paul called one of the centurions unto him,* and said, Bring this young man unto the chief captain: for he hath a certain thing to tell him. Ver. 21. But do not thou yield unto them: for there lie in wait for him of them more than forty men, which have bound themselves with an oath, that they will neither eat nor drink till they have killed him: and now are they ready, looking for a promise from thee. Ver. 27. This man was taken of the Jews, and should have been killed of them: *then came I with an army, and rescued him,* having understood that he was a Roman.

[e] Eph. iv. 26. Be ye angry, and sin not: *let not the sun go down upon your wrath:* Ver. 27. Neither give place to the devil.

[f] 2 Sam. ii. 22. And Abner said again to Asahel, *Turn thee aside from following me: wherefore should I smite thee to the ground?* Deut. xxii. 8. When thou buildest a new house, then *thou shalt make a battlement for thy roof, that thou bring not blood upon thine house,* if any man fall from thence.

[g] Matt. iv. 6. And saith unto him, If thou be the Son of God, cast thyself down:—Ver. 7. Jesus said unto him, *It is written again, Thou shalt not tempt the Lord thy God.* Prov. i. 10. My son, *If sinners entice thee, consent thou not.* Ver. 11. *If they say, Come with us, let us lay wait for blood,* let us lurk privily for the innocent without cause. Ver. 15. My son, *walk not thou in the way with them; refrain thy foot from their path:* Ver. 16. For their feet run to evil, and make haste to shed blood.

[h] 1 Sam. xxiv. 12. The Lord judge between me and thee, and the Lord avenge me of thee ; *but mine hand shall not be upon thee.* 1 Sam. xxvi. 9. And David said to Abishai, Destroy him not : for *who can stretch forth his hand against the Lord's anointed, and be guiltless?* Ver. 10. David said furthermore, As the Lord liveth, the Lord shall smite him ; or his day shall come to die ; or he shall descend into battle, and perish. Ver. 11. *The Lord forbid that I should stretch forth mine hand against the Lord's anointed.* Gen. xxxvii. 21. And Reuben heard it, and *he delivered him out of their hands;* and said, *Let us not kill him.* Ver. 22. And Reuben said unto them, *Shed no blood,* but cast him into this pit that is in the wilderness, and *lay no hand upon him;* that he might rid him out of their hands, to deliver him to his father again.

[i] Ps. lxxxii. 4. *Deliver the poor and needy: rid them out of the hand of the wicked.* Prov. xxiv. 11. *If thou forbear to deliver them that are drawn unto death, and those that are ready to be slain;* Ver. 12. If thou sayest, Behold, we knew it not ; doth not he that pondereth the heart consider it? and he that keepeth thy soul, doth not he know it? and shall not he render to every man according to his works? 1 Sam. xiv. 45. And the people said unto Saul, *Shall Jonathan die,* who hath wrought this great salvation in Israel? *God forbid:* as the Lord liveth, there shall not one hair of his head fall to the ground ; for he hath wrought with God this day. *So the people rescued Jonathan, that he died not.*

[k] James v. 7. *Be patient* therefore, brethren, unto the coming of the Lord. Behold, the husbandman waiteth for the precious fruit of the earth, and hath long patience for it, until he receive the early and latter rain. Ver. 8. *Be ye also patient; stablish your hearts ;* for the coming of the Lord draweth nigh. Ver. 9. *Grudge not one against another, brethren, lest ye be condemned:* behold, the Judge standeth before the door. Ver. 10. Take, my brethren, the prophets, who have spoken in the name of the Lord, for an example *of suffering affliction, and of patience.* Ver. 11. Behold, we count them happy which endure. *Ye have heard of the patience of Job,* and have seen the end of the Lord ; that the Lord is very pitiful, and of tender mercy. Heb. xii. 9. Furthermore, we have had fathers of our flesh *which corrected us, and we gave them reverence: shall we not much rather be in subjection unto the Father of spirits,* and live?

[l] 1 Thess. iv. 11. And that ye *study to be quiet,* and to do your own business, and to work with your own hands, as we commanded you. 1 Pet. iii. 3. Whose adorning, let it not be that outward adorning— Ver. 4. But let it be the hidden man of the heart, in that which is not corruptible, even *the ornament of a meek and quiet spirit,* which is in the sight of God of great price. Ps. xxxvii. 8. *Cease from anger, and forsake wrath: fret not thyself* in anywise to do evil. Ver. 9. For evil-doers shall be cut off : but those that *wait upon the Lord,* they shall inherit the earth. Ver. 10. For yet a little while, and the wicked shall not be : yea, thou shalt diligently consider his place, and it shall not be. Ver. 11. But *the meek shall inherit the earth,* and shall delight themselves in the abundance of peace.

[m] Prov. xvii. 22. *A merry heart doeth good like a medicine:* but a broken spirit drieth the bones.

[n] Prov. xxv. 16. Hast thou found *honey? eat so much as is sufficient for thee, lest thou be filled therewith, and vomit it.* Ver. 27. *It is not good to eat much honey.*

[o] 1 Tim. v. 23. *Drink no longer water,* but use a *little wine* for thy stomach's sake, and thine often infirmities.

[p] Isa. xxxviii. 21. For Isaiah had said,

sleep,q labour,r and recreations;s by charitable thoughts,t love,v compassion,w meekness, gentleness, kindness;x peaceable,y mild and courteous speeches and behaviour;z forbearance, readiness to be reconciled, patient bearing and forgiving of injuries, and requiting good for evil;a comforting and succouring the distressed, and protecting and defending the innocent.b

Q. 136. *What are the sins forbidden in the sixth commandment?*

A. The sins forbidden in the sixth commandment are, all taking

---

Let them take a lump of figs, and lay it for a plaster upon the boil, and he shall recover.

q Ps. cxxvii. 2. *It is vain for you to rise up early, to sit up late, to eat the bread of sorrows: for so he giveth his beloved sleep.*

r Eccl. v. 12. *The sleep of a labouring man is sweet,* whether he eat little or much: but the abundance of the rich will not suffer him to sleep. 2 Thess. iii. 10. For even when we were with you, this we commanded you, that *if any would not work, neither should he eat.* Ver. 12. Now them that are such we command and exhort by our Lord Jesus Christ, that with quietness *they work, and eat their own bread.* Prov. xvi. 26. *He that laboureth, laboureth for himself;* for his mouth craveth it of him.

s Eccl. iii. 4. A time to weep, *and a time to laugh:* a time to mourn, *and a time to dance.* Ver. 11. He hath made every thing beautiful in his time: also he hath set the world in their heart, &c.

t 1 Sam. xix. 4. And *Jonathan spake good of David unto Saul his father,* and said unto him, Let not the king sin against his servant,—Ver. 5. For he did put his life in his hand, and slew the Philistine, and the Lord wrought a great salvation for all Israel: thou sawest it, and didst rejoice: wherefore then wilt thou sin against innocent blood, to slay David without a cause? 1 Sam. xxii. 13. And Saul said unto him, Why have ye conspired against me, thou and the son of Jesse, in that thou hast given him bread, and a sword,—Ver. 14. Then Ahimelech answered the king, and said, *And who is so faithful among all thy servants as David,* which is the king's son-in-law, and goeth at thy bidding, and is honourable in thine house?

v Rom. xiii. 10. *Love worketh no ill to his neighbour:* therefore love is the fulfilling of the law.

w Luke x. 33. But a certain *Samaritan,* as he journeyed, came where he was: and when he saw him, *he had compassion on him,* Ver. 34. And went to him, and *bound up his wounds, pouring in oil and wine,* and *set him on his own beast,* and *brought him to an inn,* and *took care of him.*

x Col. iii. 12. *Put on* therefore, as the elect of God, holy and beloved, *bowels of mercies, kindness, humbleness of mind, meekness, long-suffering;* Ver. 13. *Forbearing one another,* and forgiving one another, if any man have a quarrel against any: even as Christ forgave you, so also do ye.

y James iii. 17. But the *wisdom that is from above* is first pure, *then peaceable, gentle,* and easy to be entreated, full of mercy and good fruits, without partiality and without hypocrisy.

z 1 Pet. iii. 8. Finally, *be ye all of one mind,* having compassion one of another; *love as brethren, be pitiful, be courteous:* Ver. 9. *Not rendering evil for evil, or railing for railing;* but contrariwise *blessing;* knowing that ye are thereunto called, that ye should inherit a blessing. Ver. 10. For he that will love life, and see good days, *let him refrain his tongue from evil, and his lips that they speak no guile:* Ver. 11. Let him eschew evil, and do good; let him seek peace, and ensue it. Prov. xv. 1. *A soft answer turneth away wrath;* but grievous words stir up anger. Judges viii. 1. And the men of Ephraim said unto him, Why hast thou served us thus, that thou calledst us not when thou wentest to fight with the Midianites? And *they did chide with him sharply.* Ver. 2. And he said unto them, What have I done now in comparison of you? Is not the gleaning of the grapes of Ephraim better than the vintage of Abi-ezer? Ver. 3. God hath delivered into your hands the princes of Midian, Oreb and Zeeb: and what was I able to do in comparison of you? *Then their anger was abated toward him when he had said that.*

a Matt. v. 24. Leave there thy gift before the altar, and go thy way; *first be reconciled to thy brother,* and then come and offer thy gift. Eph. iv. 2. With all lowliness and meekness, *with long-suffering, forbearing one another in love.* Ver. 32. And be ye kind one to another, tenderhearted, *forgiving one another,* even as God for Christ's sake hath forgiven you. Rom. xii. 17. *Recompence to no man evil for evil.*—Ver. 20. Therefore *if thine enemy hunger, feed him; if he thirst, give him drink:* for in so doing thou shalt heap coals of fire on his head. Ver. 21. Be not overcome of evil, but *overcome evil with good.*

b 1 Thess. v. 14. Now we exhort you, brethren, warn them that are unruly, *comfort the feeble-minded, support the weak,* be patient toward all men. Job xxxi. 19. *If I have seen any perish for want of clothing, or any poor without covering;* Ver. 20. If his loins have not blessed me, and if he were not warmed with the fleece of my sheep. Matt. xxv. 35. *For I was an hungered,* and ye gave me meat: *I was thirsty,* and ye gave me drink: *I was a stranger,* and ye took me in: Ver. 36. *Naked,* and ye *clothed me. I was sick,* and ye *visited me: I was in prison,* and ye came unto me. Prov. xxxi. 8. *Open thy mouth for the dumb in the cause of all such as are appointed to de-*

away the life of ourselves,c or of others,d except in case of publick justice,e lawful war,f or necessary defence;g the neglecting or withdrawing the lawful and necessary means of preservation of life;h sinful anger,i hatred,k envy,l desire of revenge;m all excessive passions,n distracting cares;o immoderate use of meat, drink,p labour,q and recreations;r provoking words,s oppression,t quarrelling,v striking, wound-

struction. Ver. 9. Open thy mouth, judge righteously, and *plead the cause of the poor and needy.*
136. e Acts xvi. 28. But *Paul cried* with a loud voice, saying, *Do thyself no harm;* for we are all here.
d Gen. ix. 6. *Whoso sheddeth man's blood, by man shall his blood be shed:* for in the image of God made he man.
e Numb. xxxv. 31. Moreover, *ye shall take no satisfaction for the life of a murderer, which is guilty of death; but he shall be surely put to death.* Ver. 33. So ye shall not pollute the land wherein ye are; for blood it defileth the land: and the land cannot be cleansed of the blood that is shed therein, but by the blood of him that shed it.
f Jer. xlviii. 10. *Cursed be he that doeth the work of the Lord deceitfully, and cursed be he that keepeth back his sword from blood.* Deut. chap. xx. throughout. Ver. 1. When thou goest out to battle against thine enemies, and seest horses and chariots, and a people more than thou, be not afraid of them: for the Lord thy God is with thee, which brought thee up out of the land of Egypt, &c.
g Exod. xxii. 2. If a thief be found *breaking up, and be smitten that he die, there shall no blood be shed for him.* Ver. 3. If the sun be risen upon him, there shall be blood shed for him; for he should make full restitution: if he have nothing, then he shall be sold for his theft.
h Matt. xxv. 42. For *I was an hungered,* and ye gave me no meat: *I was thirsty,* and ye gave me no drink: Ver. 43. *I was a stranger,* and ye took me not in: *naked,* and ye clothed me not: *sick, and in prison,* and ye visited me not. James ii. 15. *If a brother or sister be naked, and destitute of daily food,* Ver. 16. *And one of you say unto them, Depart in peace, be ye warmed and filled;* notwithstanding ye give them not *those things which are needful to the body, what doth it profit?* Eccl. vi. 1. There is an evil which I have seen under the sun, and it is common among men: Ver. 2. *A man to whom God hath given riches, wealth, and honour,* so that he wanteth nothing for his soul of all that he desireth, yet *God giveth him not power to eat thereof,* but a stranger eateth it: *this is vanity, and it is an evil disease.*
i Matt. v. 22. But I say unto you, That *whosoever is angry with his brother without a cause shall be in danger of the judgment;* and whosoever shall say to his brother, Raca, shall be *in danger of the council;* but whosoever shall say, Thou fool, shall be *in danger of hell-fire.*
k 1 John iii. 15. *Whosoever hateth his brother is a murderer:* and ye know that no murderer hath eternal life abiding in him. Lev. xix. 17. *Thou shalt not hate thy brother in thine heart:* thou shalt in any wise rebuke thy neighbour, and not suffer sin upon him.
l Prov. xiv. 30. A sound heart is the life of the flesh: but *envy is the rottenness of the bones.*
m Rom. xii. 19. Dearly beloved, *avenge not yourselves,* but rather give place unto wrath: for it is written, *Vengeance is mine;* I will repay, saith the Lord.
n Eph. iv. 31. *Let all bitterness, and wrath, and anger, and clamour,* and evil-speaking, *be put away from you,* with all malice.
o Matt. vi. 31. Therefore *take no thought, saying, What shall we eat?* or, *What shall we drink?* or, *Wherewithal shall we be clothed?* Ver. 34. *Take therefore no thought for the morrow:* for the morrow shall take thought for the things of itself. Sufficient unto the day is the evil thereof.
p Luke xxi. 34. And take heed to yourselves, *lest at any time your hearts be overcharged with surfeiting, and drunkenness,* and cares of this life, and so that day come upon you unawares. Rom. xiii. 13. Let us walk honestly, as in the day; *not in rioting and drunkenness,* not in chambering and wantonness, not in strife and envying.
q Eccl. xii. 12. And further, by these, my son, be admonished: of making many books there is no end; and *much study is a weariness of the flesh.* Eccl. ii. 22. For what hath man of all his *labour,* and of the *vexation of his heart,* wherein he hath *laboured* under the sun? Ver. 23. For *all his days are sorrows, and his travail grief; yea, his heart taketh not rest in the night. This is also vanity.*
r Isa. v. 12. And *the harp and the viol, the tabret and pipe, and wine, are in their feasts;* but they regard not the work of the Lord, neither consider the operation of his hands.
s Prov. xv. 1. A soft answer turneth away wrath; but *grievous words stir up anger.* Prov. xii. 18. *There is that speaketh like the piercings of a sword;* but the tongue of the wise is health.
t Ezek. xviii. 18. As for his father, because he cruelly oppressed, *spoiled his brother by violence,* and did that which is not good among his people, lo, even he shall *die in his iniquity.* Exod. i. 14. And *they made their lives bitter with hard bondage, in mortar, and in brick, and in all manner of service* in the field: all their service, wherein they made them serve, was with rigour.
v Gal. v. 15. But *if ye bite and devour one another,* take heed that ye be not consumed one of another. Prov. xxiii. 29.

ing,ʷ and whatsoever else tends to the destruction of the life of any.ˣ

Q. 137. *Which is the seventh commandment?*
A. The seventh commandment is, *Thou shalt not commit adultery.*ʸ

Q. 138. *What are the duties required in the seventh commandment?*
A. The duties required in the seventh commandment are, chastity in body, mind, affections,ᶻ words,ᵃ and behaviour;ᵇ and the preservation of it in ourselves and others;ᶜ watchfulness over the eyes and all the senses;ᵈ temperance,ᵉ keeping of chaste company,ᶠ modesty in apparel;ᵍ marriage by those that have not the gift of continency,ʰ conjugal love,ⁱ and cohabitation;ᵏ diligent labour in our callings;ˡ shunning all occasions of uncleanness, and resisting temptations thereunto.ᵐ

Who hath woe? who hath sorrow? who hath contentions? who hath babbling? who hath wounds without cause?
ʷ Numb. xxxv. 16. And *if he smite him with an instrument of iron, so that he die, he is a murderer: the murderer shall surely be put to death.* Ver. 17. And *if he smite him with throwing a stone, wherewith he may die, and he die, he is a murderer: the murderer shall surely be put to death.* Ver. 18. Or *if he smite him with an hand-weapon of wood, wherewith he may die, and he die, he is a murderer: the murderer shall surely be put to death.* Ver. 21. Or *in enmity smite him with his hand, that he die: he that smote him shall surely be put to death; for he is a murderer: the revenger of blood shall slay the murderer when he meeteth him.*
ˣ Exod. xxi. from verse 18. to the end. [Containing laws for smiters, for an hurt by chance, for an ox that goreth, and for him that is an occasion of harm.]
137. ʸ Exod. xx. 14.
138. ᶻ 1 Thess. iv. 4. That every one of you should know how *to possess his vessel in sanctification and honour.* Job xxxi. 1. *I made a covenant with mine eyes; why then should I think upon a maid?* 1 Cor. vii. 34. There is difference also between a wife and a virgin. *The unmarried woman careth for the things of the Lord, that she may be holy both in body and in spirit:* but she that is married careth for the things of the world, how she may please her husband.
ᵃ Col. iv. 6. *Let your speech be alway with grace, seasoned with salt,* that ye may know how ye ought to answer every man.
ᵇ 1 Pet. iii. 2. While they behold *your chaste conversation* coupled with fear.
ᶜ 1 Cor. vii. 2. Nevertheless, *to avoid fornication, let every man have his own wife, and let every woman have her own husband.* Ver. 35. And this I speak for your own profit; not that I may cast a snare upon you, but for that which is comely, and that ye may attend *upon the Lord without distraction.* Ver. 36. But if any man think that *he behaveth himself uncomely toward his virgin, if she pass the flower of her age, and need so require, let him do what he will, he sinneth not: let them marry.*
ᵈ Job xxxi. 1. *I made a covenant with mine eyes; why then should I think upon a maid?*

ᵉ Acts xxiv. 24. And after certain days, when Felix came with his wife Drusilla, which was a Jewess, he sent for Paul, and heard him concerning the faith in Christ. Ver. 25. And *as he reasoned of righteousness, temperance,* and judgment to come, Felix trembled.
ᶠ Prov. ii. 16. *To deliver thee from the strange woman, even from the stranger which flattereth with her words;* Ver. 17. Which forsaketh the guide of her youth, and forgetteth the covenant of her God: Ver. 18. For her house inclineth unto death, and her paths unto the dead. Ver. 19. *None that go unto her return again,* neither take they hold of the paths of life. Ver. 20. *That thou mayest walk in the way of good men, and keep the paths of the righteous.*
ᵍ 1 Tim. ii. 9. In like manner also, that *women adorn themselves in modest apparel, with shamefacedness and sobriety;* not with broidered hair, or gold, or pearls, or costly array.
ʰ 1 Cor. vii. 2. Nevertheless, *to avoid fornication, let every man have his own wife, and let every woman have her own husband.* Ver. 9. But *if they cannot contain, let them marry: for it is better to marry than to burn.*
ⁱ Prov. v. 19. *Let her be as the loving hind and pleasant roe;* let her breasts satisfy thee at all times: and *be thou ravished always with her love.* Ver. 20. And why wilt thou, my son, be ravished with a strange woman, and embrace the bosom of a stranger?
ᵏ 1 Pet. iii. 7. Likewise, *ye husbands, dwell with them according to knowledge,* giving honour unto the wife, as unto the weaker vessel, and as being heirs together of the grace of life; that your prayers be not hindered.
ˡ Prov. xxxi. 11. The heart of her husband doth safely trust in her, so that he shall have no need of spoil. Ver. 27. *She looketh well to the ways of her household, and eateth not the bread of idleness.* Ver. 28. Her children rise up, and call her blessed; her husband also, and he praiseth her.
ᵐ Prov. v. 8. *Remove thy way far from her, and come not nigh the door of her house.* Gen. xxxix. 8. But *he refused;* and said unto his master's wife, Behold, my master wotteth not what is with me in the house,

Q. 139. *What are the sins forbidden in the seventh commandment?*

A. The sins forbidden in the seventh commandment, besides the neglect of the duties required,[n] are, adultery, fornication,[o] rape, incest,[p] sodomy, and all unnatural lusts;[q] all unclean imaginations, thoughts, purposes, and affections;[r] all corrupt or filthy communications, or listening thereunto;[s] wanton looks,[t] impudent or light behaviour, immodest apparel;[v] prohibiting of lawful,[w] and dispensing with unlawful marriages;[x] allowing, tolerating, keeping of stews, and resorting to them;[y] entangling vows of single life,[z] undue delay of

and he hath committed all that he hath to my hand: Ver. 9. There is none greater in this house than I; neither hath he kept back any thing from me but thee, because thou art his wife : *how then can I do this great wickedness, and sin against God?* Ver. 10. And it came to pass, as she spake to Joseph day by day, that *he hearkened not unto her, to lie by her, or to be with her.*

139. n Prov. v. 7. Hear me now therefore, O ye children, and *depart not from the words of my mouth.*

o Heb. xiii. 4. Marriage is honourable in all, and the bed undefiled : but *whoremongers and adulterers God will judge.* Gal. v. 19. Now *the works of the flesh* are manifest, which are these : *Adultery, fornication, uncleanness, lasciviousness.*

p 2 Sam. xiii. 14. Howbeit he would not hearken unto her voice ; but, being stronger than she, *forced her, and lay with her.* 1 Cor. v. 1. It is reported commonly that there is fornication among you, and *such fornication* as is not so much as named among the Gentiles, that *one should have his father's wife.*

q Rom. i. 24. Wherefore God also gave them up to uncleanness, through the lusts of their own hearts, to *dishonour their own bodies between themselves.* Ver. 26. For this cause God gave them up *unto vile affections:* for even their women did change the natural use *into that which is against nature:* Ver. 27. And likewise also the men, leaving the natural use of the woman, *burned in their lust one toward another;* men with men working that which is unseemly, and receiving in themselves that recompence of their error which was meet. Lev. xx. 15. And *if a man lie with a beast, he shall surely be put to death;* and ye shall slay the beast. Ver. 16. And *if a woman approach unto any beast, and lie down thereto, thou shalt kill the woman* and the beast : they shall surely be put to death ; their blood shall be upon them.

r Matt. v. 28. But I say unto you, That *whosoever looketh on a woman to lust after her, hath committed adultery with her already in his heart.* Matt. xv. 19. For *out of the heart proceed evil thoughts,* murders, *adulteries, fornications,* thefts, false witness, blasphemies. Col. iii. 5. *Mortify* therefore your members which are upon the earth ; *fornication, uncleanness, inordinate affection, evil concupiscence,* and covetousness, which is idolatry.

s Eph. v. 3. But *fornication,* and *all uncleanness,* or covetousness, *let it not be once named among you,* as becometh saints :

Ver. 4. Neither *filthiness,* nor *foolish talking,* nor *jesting, which are not convenient;* but rather giving of thanks. Prov. vii. 5. That they may keep thee from the *strange woman,* from the stranger which flattereth with her words. Ver. 21. *With her much fair speech she caused him to yield,* with the flattering of her lips she forced him. Ver. 22. *He goeth after her straightway,* as an ox goeth to the slaughter, or as a fool to the correction of the stocks.

t Isa. iii. 16. Moreover, the Lord saith, Because the daughters of Zion are haughty, and *walk with stretched forth necks and wanton eyes,* walking and mincing as they go, and making a tinkling with their feet. 2 Pet. ii. 14. *Having eyes full of adultery,* and that cannot cease from sin ; beguiling unstable souls, &c.

v Prov. vii. 10. And, behold, there met him *a woman with the attire of an harlot,* and subtile of heart. Ver. 13. So *she caught him, and kissed him,* and *with an impudent face* said unto him, &c.

w 1 Tim. iv. 3. *Forbidding to marry,* and commanding to abstain from meats, which God hath created to be received with thanksgiving of them which believe and know the truth.

x Lev. xviii. from verse 1. to 21. Mark vi. 18. For John had said unto Herod, *It is not lawful for thee to have thy brother's wife.* Mal. ii. 11. *Judah hath dealt treacherously,* and *an abomination is committed in Israel* and in Jerusalem : for *Judah* hath profaned the holiness of the Lord which he loved, and *hath married the daughter of a strange god.* Ver. 12. The Lord will cut off the man that doeth this, the master and the scholar, out of the tabernacles of Jacob, and him that offereth an offering unto the Lord of hosts.

y 1 Kings xv. 12. And *he took away the sodomites out of the land,* and removed all the idols that his fathers had made. 2 Kings xxiii. 7. And *he brake down the houses of the sodomites,* that were by the house of the Lord, where the women wove hangings for the grove. Deut. xxiii. 17. There shall be *no whore of the daughters of Israel, nor a sodomite of the sons of Israel.* Ver. 18. *Thou shalt not bring the hire of a whore,* or the price of a dog, into the house of the Lord thy God for any vow ; for even both these are *abomination unto the Lord thy God.* Lev. xix. 29. *Do not prostitute thy daughter, to cause her to be a whore;* lest the land fall to whoredom, and the land become full of wickedness. Jer. v. 7. *How shall I pardon thee for this? thy children have*

marriage;[a] having more wives or husbands than one at the same time;[b] unjust divorce,[c] or desertion;[d] idleness, gluttony, drunkenness,[e] unchaste company;[f] lascivious songs, books, pictures, dancings, stage plays;[g] and all other provocations to, or acts of uncleanness, either in ourselves or others.[h]

forsaken me, and sworn by them that are no gods: when I had fed them to the full, *they then committed adultery, and assembled themselves by troops in the harlots' houses.* Prov. vii. 24. Hearken unto me now therefore, O ye children, and attend to the words of my mouth: Ver. 25. *Let not thine heart decline to her ways, go not astray in her paths:* Ver. 26. For she hath cast down many wounded; yea, many strong men have been slain by her. Ver. 27. Her house is the way to hell, going down to the chambers of death.

[a] Matt. xix. 10. His disciples say unto him, If the case of the man be so with his wife, it is not good to marry. Ver. 11. But he said unto them, *All men cannot receive this saying, save they to whom it is given.*

[a] 1 Cor. vii. 7. For I would that all men were even as I myself: but every man hath his proper gift of God, one after this manner, and another after that. Ver. 8. I say therefore to the unmarried and widows, It is good for them if they abide even as I. Ver. 9. But *if they cannot contain, let them marry:* for it is better to marry than to burn. Gen. xxxviii. 26. And Judah acknowledged them, and said, *She hath been more righteous than I; because that I gave her not to Shelah my son:* and he knew her again no more.

[b] Mal. ii. 14. Yet ye say, Wherefore? Because *the Lord hath been witness between thee and the wife of thy youth, against whom thou hast dealt treacherously: yet is she thy companion, and the wife of thy covenant.* Ver. 15. And did not he make one? Yet had he the residue of the Spirit. And wherefore one? That he might seek a godly seed. Therefore take heed to your spirit, *and let none deal treacherously against the wife of his youth.* Matt. xix. 5. And said, For this, cause shall a man leave father and mother, and *shall cleave to his wife: and they twain shall be one flesh.*

[c] Mal. ii. 16. For the Lord, the God of Israel, saith that *he hateth putting away:* for one covereth violence with his garment, saith the Lord of hosts; therefore take heed to your spirit, that ye deal not treacherously. Matt. v. 32. But I say unto you, That *whosoever shall put away his wife, saving for the cause of fornication, causeth her to commit adultery:* and whosoever shall marry her that is divorced committeth adultery.

[d] 1 Cor. vii. 12. But to the rest speak I, not the Lord; If any brother hath a wife that believeth not, and she be pleased to dwell with him, *let him not put her away.* Ver. 13. And the woman which hath an husband that believeth not, and *if he be pleased to dwell with her, let her not leave him.*

[e] Ezek. xvi. 49. Behold, *this was the iniquity of thy sister Sodom, pride, fulness of bread, and abundance of idleness was in her and in her daughters,* neither did she strengthen the hand of the poor and needy. Prov. xxiii. 30. *They that tarry long at the wine;* they that go to seek mixed wine. Ver. 31. *Look not thou upon the wine when it is red,* when it giveth his colour in the cup, when it moveth itself aright: Ver. 32. At the last it biteth like a serpent, and stingeth like an adder. Ver. 33. Thine eyes shall behold strange women, and thine heart shall utter perverse things.

[f] Gen. xxxix. 10. And it came to pass, as she spake to Joseph day by day, that *he hearkened not unto her, to lie by her, or to be with her.* Prov. v. 8. *Remove thy way far from her, and come not nigh the door of her house.*

[g] Eph. v. 4. *Neither filthiness, nor foolish talking, nor jesting, which are not convenient;* but rather giving of thanks. Ezek. xxiii. 14. And *that she increased her whoredoms: for when she saw men pourtrayed upon the wall, the images of the Chaldeans* pourtrayed with vermilion, Ver. 15. *Girded with girdles upon their loins, exceeding in dyed attire upon their heads, all of them princes to look to,* after the manner of the Babylonians of Chaldea, the land of their nativity: Ver. 16. *And as soon as she saw them with her eyes, she doted upon them,* and sent messengers unto them into Chaldea Isa. xxiii. 15. And it shall come to pass in that day, that Tyre shall be forgotten seventy years, according to the days of one king: after the end of seventy years shall *Tyre sing as an harlot.* Ver. 16. *Take an harp, go about the city, thou harlot* that hast been forgotten; *make sweet melody, sing many songs, that thou mayest be remembered.* Ver. 17. And it shall come to pass, after the end of seventy years, that the Lord will visit Tyre, and she shall turn to her hire, and shall commit fornication with all the kingdoms of the world upon the face of the earth. Isa. iii. 16. Moreover, the Lord saith, Because the daughters of Zion are haughty, and walk with stretched forth necks, and wanton eyes, *walking and mincing as they go,* and *making a tinkling with their feet:*— Mark vi. 22. And when *the daughter of* the said Herodias came in, *and danced, and pleased Herod,* and them that sat with him, the king said unto the damsel, Ask of me whatsoever thou wilt, and I will give it thee. Rom. xiii. 13. *Let us walk honestly,* as in the day; not in rioting and drunkenness, *not in chambering and wantonness,* not in strife and envying. 1 Pet. iv. 3. For the time past of our life may suffice us to have wrought the will of the Gentiles, *when we walked in lasciviousness, lusts, excess of wine, revellings, banquetings,* and abominable idolatries.

[h] 2 Kings ix. 30. And when Jehu was

Q. 140. *Which is the eighth commandment?*
A. The eighth commandment is, *Thou shalt not steal.*[i]

Q. 141. *What are the duties required in the eighth commandment?*
A. The duties required in the eighth commandment are, truth, faithfulness, and justice in contracts and commerce between man and man;[k] rendering to every one his due;[l] restitution of goods unlawfully detained from the right owners thereof;[m] giving and lending freely, according to our abilities, and the necessities of others;[n] moderation of our judgments, wills, and affections concerning worldly goods;[o] a provident care and study to get,[p] keep, use, and dispose these things which are necessary and convenient for the sustentation of our nature, and suitable to our condition;[q] a lawful call-

---

come to Jezreel, Jezebel heard of it; and *she painted her face, and tired her head,* and looked out at a window. Compared with Jer. iv. 30. And when thou art spoiled, what wilt thou do? Though thou clothest thyself with crimson, though thou deckest thee with ornaments of gold, though *thou rentest thy face with painting, in vain shalt thou make thyself fair;* thy lovers will despise thee, they will seek thy life. And with Ezek. xxiii. 40. And furthermore, that ye have sent for men to come from far, unto whom a messenger was sent; and, *lo, they came: for whom thou didst wash thyself, paintedst thine eyes, and deckedst thyself with ornaments.*
140. [i] Exod. xx. 15.
141. [k] Ps. xv. 2. *He that walketh uprightly, and worketh righteousness, and speaketh the truth in his heart.* Ver. 4. *He that sweareth to his own hurt, and changeth not.* Zech. vii. 4. Then came the word of the Lord of hosts unto me, saying, Ver. 10. *Oppress not the widow, nor the fatherless, the stranger, nor the poor; and let none of you imagine evil against his brother in your heart.* Zech. viii. 16. These are the things that ye shall do, *Speak ye every man the truth to his neighbour; execute the judgment of truth and peace in your gates:* Ver. 17. And *let none of you imagine evil in your hearts against his neighbour;* and *love no false oath: for all these are things that I hate,* saith the Lord.
[l] Rom. xiii. 7. *Render therefore to all their dues: tribute* to whom *tribute is due; custom* to whom *custom; fear* to whom *fear; honour* to whom *honour.*
[m] Lev. vi. 2. If a soul sin, and commit a trespass against the Lord, and lie unto his neighbour in that which was delivered him to keep, or in fellowship, or in a thing taken away by violence, or hath deceived his neighbour; Ver. 3. Or have found that which was lost, and lieth concerning it, and sweareth falsely; in any of all these that a man doeth, sinning therein: Ver. 4. Then it shall be, because he hath sinned, and is guilty, that *he shall restore that which he took violently away, or the thing which he hath deceitfully gotten, or that which was delivered him to keep, or the lost thing which he found,* Ver. 5. Or *all that about which he hath sworn falsely; he shall even restore it in the principal,* and shall *add the fifth part more thereto,* and give it unto him to whom it appertaineth, in the day of his trespass-offering. Compared with Luke xix. 8. And Zaccheus stood, and said unto the Lord, Behold, Lord, the half of my goods I give to the poor; *and if I have taken any thing from any man by false accusation, I restore him four-fold.*
[n] Luke vi. 30. *Give to every man that asketh of thee; and* of him that taketh away thy goods ask them not again. Ver. 38. *Give, and it shall be given unto you,* good measure, pressed down, and shaken together, and running over, shall men give into your bosom. For with the same measure that ye mete withal, it shall be measured to you again. 1 John iii. 17. But *whoso hath this world's good, and seeth his brother have need, and shutteth up his bowels of compassion from him, how dwelleth the love of God in him?* Eph. iv. 28. Let him that stole steal no more: but rather let him labour, working with his hands the thing which is good, *that he may have to give to him that needeth.* Gal. vi. 10. *As we have therefore opportunity, let us do good unto all men,* especially unto them who are of the household of faith.
[o] 1 Tim. vi. 6. But *godliness with contentment* is great gain. Ver. 7. For we brought nothing into this world, and it is certain we can carry nothing out. Ver. 8. And *having food and raiment, let us be therewith content.* Ver. 9. *But they that will be rich fall into temptation,* and a snare, and into many foolish and hurtful lusts, which drown men in destruction and perdition. Gal. vi. 14. But God forbid that I should glory, save in the cross of our Lord Jesus Christ, *by whom the world is crucified unto me, and I unto the world.*
[p] 1 Tim. v. 8. But *if any provide not for his own,* and *specially for those of his own house, he hath denied the faith, and is worse than an infidel.*
[q] Prov. xxvii. from verse 23. to the end. *Be thou diligent to know the state of thy flocks, and look well to thy herds;* Ver. 24. For riches are not for ever;—Eccl. ii. 24. *There is nothing better for a man, than that he should eat and drink, and that he should make his soul enjoy good in his labour.* This also I saw, that it was from the hand of God. Eccl. iii. 12. *I know that there is no good in them, but for a man to rejoice,*

ing,r and diligence in it;s frugality;ᵗ avoiding unnecessary law-suits,ᵛ and suretiship, or other like engagements;ʷ and an endeavour, by all just and lawful means, to procure, preserve, and further the wealth and outward estate of others, as well as our own.ˣ

Q. 142. *What are the sins forbidden in the eighth commandment?*

A. The sins forbidden in the eighth commandment, besides the neglect of the duties required,ʸ are, theft,ᶻ robbery,ᵃ man-stealing,ᵇ and receiving any thing that is stolen;ᶜ fraudulent dealing,ᵈ false weights

---

and *to do good in his life.* Ver. 13. And also *that every man should eat and drink, and enjoy the good of all his labour, it is the gift of God.* 1 Tim. vi. 17. Charge them that are *rich in this world,* that they be not high-minded, nor trust in uncertain riches, but in the living God, who giveth us richly all things to enjoy; Ver. 18. *That they do good, that they be rich in good works, ready to distribute, willing to communicate.* Isa. xxxviii. 1. In those days was Hezekiah sick unto death. And Isaiah the prophet, the son of Amoz, came unto him, and said unto him, Thus saith the Lord, *Set thine house in order : for thou shalt die, and not live.* Matt. xi. 8. Behold, they that *wear soft clothing are in kings' houses.*

ʳ 1 Cor. vii. 20. Let every man *abide in the same calling wherein he was called.* Gen. ii. 15. And *the Lord God took the man, and put him into the garden of Eden, to dress it, and to keep it.* Gen iii. 19. *In the sweat of thy face* shalt thou eat bread, till thou return unto the ground, &c.

ˢ Eph. iv. 28. Let him that stole steal no more : but *rather let him labour, working with his hands the thing which is good,* that he may have to give to him that needeth. Prov. x. 4. He becometh poor that dealeth with a slack hand : *but the hand of the diligent maketh rich.*

ᵗ John vi. 12. When they were filled, he said unto his disciples, *Gather up the fragments that remain,* that nothing be lost. Prov. xxi. 20. There is *treasure* to be desired and *oil in the dwelling of the wise: but a foolish man spendeth it up.*

ᵛ 1 Cor. vi. from verse 1. to 9. Dare any of you, having a matter against another, *go to law before the unjust,* and not before the saints? &c.

ʷ Prov. vi. from verse 1. to 6. My son, *if thou be surety for thy friend,* if thou hast stricken thy hand with a stranger, Ver. 2. *Thou art snared* with the words of thy mouth, &c. Prov. xi. 15. *He that is surety for a stranger shall smart for it; and he that hateth suretiship is sure.*

ˣ Lev. xxv. 35. And *if thy brother be waxen poor, and fallen in decay with thee, then thou shalt relieve him;* yea, though he be a stranger, or a sojourner : that he may live with thee. Deut. xxii. 1. *Thou shalt not see thy brother's ox or his sheep go astray, and hide thyself from them: thou shalt in any case bring them again unto thy brother.* Ver. 2. And if thy brother be not nigh unto thee, or if thou know him not, then thou shalt bring it unto thine own house, and it shall be with thee until thy brother seek

after it, and *thou shalt restore it to him again.* Ver. 3. In like manner shalt thou do with his *ass,* and so shalt thou do with his *raiment;* and with *all lost thing of thy brother's,* which he hath lost, and thou hast found, shalt thou do likewise : thou mayest not hide thyself. Ver. 4. *Thou shalt not see thy brother's ass or his ox fall down by the way, and hide thyself from them;* thou shalt surely *help him to lift them up again.* Exod. xxiii. 4. *If thou meet thine enemy's ox or his ass going astray, thou shalt surely bring it back to him again.* Ver. 5. If thou see *the ass of him that hateth thee lying under his burden,* and wouldest forbear to help him ; *thou shalt surely help with him.* Gen. xlvii. 14. And *Joseph gathered up all the money that was found in the land of Egypt, and in the land of Canaan,* for the corn which they bought : and *Joseph brought the money into Pharaoh's house.* Ver. 20. And Joseph *bought all the land of Egypt for Pharaoh;* for the Egyptians sold every man his field, because the famine prevailed over them : so the land became Pharaoh's. Phil. ii. 4. *Look not every man on his own things, but every man also on the things of others.* Matt. xxii. 39. And the second is like unto it, *Thou shalt love thy neighbour as thyself.*

142. ʸ James ii. 15. *If a brother or sister be naked, and destitute of daily food,* Ver. 16. And one of you say unto them, *Depart in peace, be ye warmed and filled; notwithstanding ye give them not those things which are needful to the body,* what doth it profit ? 1 John iii. 17. But *whoso hath this world's good, and seeth his brother have need, and shutteth up his bowels of compassion from him, how dwelleth the love of God in him ?*

ᶻ Eph. iv. 28. *Let him that stole steal no more:* but rather, &c.

ᵃ Ps. lxii. 10. Trust not in oppression, and *become not vain in robbery.*

ᵇ 1 Tim. i. 10. (The law was made) for whoremongers, for them that defile themselves with mankind, *for men-stealers,* for liars, for perjured persons, and if there be any other thing that is *contrary to sound doctrine.*

ᶜ Prov. xxix. 24. *Whoso is partner with a thief hateth his own soul:* he heareth cursing, and bewrayeth it not. Ps. l. 18. *When thou sawest a thief, then thou consentedst with him,* &c.

ᵈ 1 Thess. iv. 6. *That no man go beyond and defraud his brother in any matter:* because that the Lord *is the avenger of all such,* as we also have forewarned you, and testified.

and measures,ᵉ removing land-marks,ᶠ injustice and unfaithfulness in contracts between man and man,ᵍ or in matters of trust;ʰ oppression,ⁱ extortion,ᵏ usury,ˡ bribery,ᵐ vexatious law-suits,ⁿ unjust inclosures and depopulations;ᵒ ingrossing commodities to enhance the price;ᵖ unlawful callings,ᵠ and all other unjust or sinful ways of taking or withholding from our neighbour what belongs to him, or of enriching ourselves;ʳ covetousness;ˢ inordinate prizing and affecting worldly goods;ᵗ distrustful and distracting cares and studies in getting, keeping, and using them;ᵛ envying at the prosperity of others;ʷ as likewise idle-

e Prov. xi. 1. A *false balance is abomination to the Lord;* but a just weight is his delight. Prov. xx. 10. *Divers weights, and divers measures, both of them are alike abomination to the Lord.*

f Deut. xix. 14. *Thou shalt not remove thy neighbour's land-mark,* which they of old time have set in thine inheritance.—Prov. xxiii. 10. *Remove not the old land-mark;* and enter not into the fields of the fatherless.

g Amos viii. 5. Saying, When will the new-moon be gone, that we may sell corn? and the sabbath, that we may set forth wheat, *making the ephah small, and the shekel great,* and *falsifying the balances by deceit?* Ps. xxxvii. 21. *The wicked borroweth, and payeth not again,* &c.

h Luke xvi. 10. He that is faithful in that which is least, is faithful also in much: and *he that is unjust in the least, is unjust also in much.* Ver. 11. *If therefore ye have not been faithful in the unrighteous mammon, who will commit to your trust the true riches?* Ver. 12. And *if ye have not been faithful in that which is another man's,* who shall give you that which is your own?

i Ezek. xxii. 29. The people of the land have *used oppression,* and exercised robbery, and have vexed the poor and needy; yea, *they have oppressed the stranger wrongfully.* Lev. xxv. 17. *Ye shall not therefore oppress one another;* but thou shalt fear thy God: for I am the Lord your God.

k Matt. xxiii. 25. Woe unto you, scribes and Pharisees, hypocrites! for ye make clean the outside of the cup and of the platter, *but within they are full of extortion and excess.* Ezek. xxii. 12. In thee have they taken gifts to shed blood; thou hast taken usury and increase, and *thou hast greedily gained of thy neighbours by extortion,* and hast forgotten me, saith the Lord God.

l Ps. xv. 5. He that *putteth not out his money to usury, nor taketh reward against the innocent,* &c.

m Job xv. 34. For the congregation of hypocrites shall be desolate, and *fire shall consume the tabernacles of bribery.*

n 1 Cor. vi. 6. *But brother goeth to law with brother,* and that before the unbelievers. Ver. 7. Now therefore *there is utterly a fault among you, because ye go to law one with another.* Why do ye not rather take wrong? why do ye not rather suffer yourselves to be defrauded? Ver. 8. Nay, ye do wrong, and defraud, and that your brethren. Prov. iii. 29. *Devise not evil against thy neighbour,* seeing he dwelleth securely by thee. Ver. 30. *Strive not with a man without cause,* if he have done thee no harm.

o Isa. v. 8. *Woe unto them that join house to house, that lay field to field, till there be no place,* that they may be placed alone in the midst of the earth! Micah ii. 2. And *they covet fields, and take them by violence;* and houses, and take them away: so they oppress a man and his house, even a man and his heritage.

p Prov. xi. 26. *He that withholdeth corn, the people shall curse him;* but blessing shall be upon the head of him that selleth it.

q Acts xix. 19. *Many of them also which used curious arts* brought their books together, and *burned them* before all men: and they counted the price of them, and found it fifty thousand pieces of silver. Ver. 24. For a certain man, named Demetrius, a silversmith, which made silver shrines for Diana, brought no small gain unto the craftsmen; Ver. 25. Whom he called together with the workmen of like occupation, and said, Sirs, ye know that *by this craft we have our wealth.*

r Job xx. 19. *Because he hath oppressed and hath forsaken the poor; because he hath violently taken away an house which he builded not.* James v. 4. Behold, *the hire of the labourers which have reaped down your fields, which is of you kept back by fraud, crieth:* and the cries of them which have reaped are entered into the ears of the Lord of sabaoth. Prov. xxi. 6. *The getting of treasures by a lying tongue is a vanity* tossed to and fro of them that seek death.

s Luke xii. 15. And he said unto them, *Take heed, and beware of covetousness;* for a man's life consisteth not in the abundance of the things which he possesseth.

t 1 Tim. vi. 5. Perverse disputings of men of corrupt minds, and destitute of the truth, *supposing that gain is godliness: from such withdraw thyself.* Col. iii. 2. *Set your affection* on things above, *not on things on the earth.* Prov. xxiii. 5. *Wilt thou set thine eyes upon that which is not?* for riches certainly make themselves wings; they fly away as an eagle toward heaven. Ps. lxii. 10. *If riches increase, set not your heart upon them.*

v Matt. vi. 25. Therefore I say unto you, *Take no thought for your life,* what ye shall eat, or what ye shall *drink;* nor yet for your body, *what ye shall put on.* Is not the life more than meat, and the body than raiment? Ver. 31. Therefore *take no thought,* saying, *What shall we eat?*—Ver. 34. *Take therefore no thought for the morrow:* for the morrow shall take thought for the things

ness,ˣ prodigality, wasteful gaming; and all other ways whereby we do unduly prejudice our own outward estate,ʸ and defrauding ourselves of the due use and comfort of that estate which God hath given us.ᶻ

Q. 143. *Which is the ninth commandment?*

A. The ninth commandment is, *Thou shalt not bear false witness against thy neighbour.*ᵃ

Q. 144. *What are the duties required in the ninth commandment?*

A. The duties required in the ninth commandment are, the preserving and promoting of truth between man and man,ᵇ and the good name of our neighbour, as well as our own;ᶜ appearing and standing for the truth;ᵈ and from the heart,ᵉ sincerely,ᶠ freely,ᵍ clearly,ʰ and fully,ⁱ speaking the truth, and only the truth, in matters of judgment and justice,ᵏ and in all other things whatsoever;ˡ a charitable esteem

---

of itself. Sufficient unto the day is the evil thereof. Eccl. v. 12. The sleep of a labouring man is sweet, whether he eat little or much: but *the abundance of the rich will not suffer him to sleep.*

w Ps. lxxiii. 3. For *I was envious at the foolish, when I saw the prosperity of the wicked.* Ps. xxxvii. 1. Fret not thyself because of evil-doers, *neither be thou envious against the workers of iniquity.* Ver. 7. Rest in the Lord, and wait patiently for him: *fret not thyself because of him who prospereth in his way,* because of the man who bringeth wicked devices to pass.

x 2 Thess. iii. 11. For we hear that there are some which *walk among you disorderly, working not at all,* but are busy-bodies. Prov. xviii. 9. He also that is *slothful in his work* is brother to him that is a great waster.

y Prov. xxi. 17. He *that loveth pleasure shall be a poor man;* he that loveth *wine and oil* shall not be rich. Prov. xxiii. 20. Be not among *wine-bibbers; among riotous eaters of flesh:* Ver. 21. For *the drunkard and the glutton shall come to poverty;* and drowsiness shall clothe a man with rags. Prov. xxviii. 19. He that tilleth his land shall have plenty of bread: *but he that followeth after vain persons shall have poverty enough.*

z Eccl. iv. 8. There is one alone, and there is not a second; yea, he hath neither child nor brother: yet is there no end of all his labour; neither is his eye satisfied with riches; *neither saith he, For whom do I labour, and bereave my soul of good? This is also vanity,* yea, it is a sore travail. Eccl. vi. 2. A man *to whom God hath given riches,* wealth, and honour, so that he wanteth nothing for his soul of all that he desireth, *yet God giveth him not power to eat thereof,* but a stranger eateth it: *this is vanity,* and it is an evil disease. 1 Tim. v. 8. But *if any provide not for his own, and specially for those of his own house, he hath denied the faith,* and *is worse than an infidel.*

143. a Exod. xx. 16.

144. b Zech. viii. 16. These are the things that ye shall do, *Speak ye every man the truth to his neighbour;* execute the judgment of *truth* and peace in your gates.

c 3 John, ver. 12. *Demetrius hath good report of all men,* and of the truth itself: yea, and *we also bear record;* and ye know that our record is true.

d Prov. xxxi. 8. *Open thy mouth for the dumb* in the cause of all such as are appointed to destruction. Ver. 9. *Open thy mouth, judge righteously, and plead the cause of the poor and needy.*

e Ps. xv. 2. He that walketh uprightly, and worketh righteousness, and *speaketh the truth in his heart.*

f 2 Chron. xix. 9. And he charged them, saying, Thus shall ye do in the fear of the Lord, *faithfully, and with a perfect heart.*

g 1 Sam. xix. 4. And *Jonathan spake good of David unto Saul* his father, and said unto him, Let not the king sin against his servant, against David; because he hath not sinned against thee, and because *his works have been to thee-ward very good:* Ver. 5. For he did put his life in his hand, and slew the Philistine, and the Lord wrought a great salvation for all Israel: thou sawest it, and didst rejoice: wherefore then wilt thou sin against innocent blood, to slay David without a cause?

h Josh. vii. 19. And Joshua said unto Achan, My son, give, I pray thee, glory to the Lord God of Israel, and make confession unto him; and *tell me now what thou hast done; hide it not from me.*

i 2 Sam. xiv. 18. Then the *king* answered and said unto the woman, *Hide not from me, I pray thee, the thing that I shall ask thee.* And the woman said, Let my lord the king now speak. Ver. 19. And the king said, Is not the hand of Joab with thee in all this? And the woman answered and said, As thy soul liveth, my lord the king, none can turn to the *right hand or to the left from ought that my lord the king hath spoken:* for thy servant Joab, he bade me, and he put all these words in the mouth of thine handmaid: Ver. 20. To fetch about this form of speech hath thy servant Joab done this thing: and my lord is wise, &c.

k Lev. xix. 15. *Ye shall do no unrighteousness in judgment;* thou shalt not respect the person of the poor, nor honour the person of the mighty: but *in righteousness shalt thou judge thy neighbour.* Prov. xiv. 5. *A faithful witness will not lie;* but a false witness will utter lies. Ver. 25. A true witness delivereth souls: but *a deceitful witness speaketh lies.*

l 2 Cor. i. 17. When I therefore was thus minded, *did I use lightness?* or the things

of our neighbours;[m] loving, desiring, and rejoicing in their good name;[n] sorrowing for,[o] and covering of their infirmities;[p] freely acknowledging of their gifts and graces,[q] defending their innocency;[r] a ready receiving of a good report,[s] and unwillingness to admit of an evil report,[t] concerning them; discouraging tale-bearers,[v] flatterers,[w] and slanderers;[x] love and care of our own good name, and defending it when need requireth;[y] keeping of lawful promises;[z] studying and practising of whatsoever things are true, honest, lovely, and of good report.[a]

Q. 145. *What are the sins forbidden in the ninth commandment?*

A. The sins forbidden in the ninth commandment are, all prejudicing the truth, and the good name of our neighbours, as well as our own,[b]

---

that I purpose, do I purpose according to the flesh, that with me there should be yea, yea, and nay, nay? Ver. 18. But as God is true, our word toward you was not yea and nay. Eph. iv. 25. Wherefore, putting away lying, *speak every man truth with his neighbour;* for we are members one of another.

[m] Heb. vi. 9. But, beloved, *we are persuaded better things of you,* and things that accompany salvation, though we thus speak. 1 Cor. xiii. 7. (*Charity*) beareth all things, *believeth all things, hopeth all things,* endureth all things.

[n] Rom. I. 8. First, *I thank my God through Jesus Christ for you all, that your faith is spoken of throughout the whole world.* 2 John, ver. 4. *I rejoiced greatly that I found of thy children walking in truth,* as we have received a commandment from the Father. 3 John, ver. 3. For *I rejoiced greatly when the brethren came and testified of the truth that is in thee,* even as thou walkest in the truth. Ver. 4. I have *no greater joy than to hear that my children walk in truth.*

[o] 2 Cor. ii. 4. For *out of much affliction and anguish of heart I wrote unto you with many tears;* not that ye should be grieved, but that ye might know the love which I have more abundantly unto you. 2 Cor xii. 21. And *lest, when I come again, my God will humble me among you,* and that I shall *bewail many which have sinned already,* and have not repented of the uncleanness, and fornication, and lasciviousness which they have committed.

[p] Prov. xvii. 9. *He that covereth a transgression seeketh love;* but he that repeateth a matter separateth very friends. 1 Pet. iv. 8. And, above all things, have *fervent charity* among yourselves: for charity shall cover the multitude of sins.

[q] 1 Cor. i. 4. *I thank my God always on your behalf, for the grace of God which is given you by Jesus Christ;* Ver. 5. *That in every thing ye are enriched by him,* in all utterance, and in all knowledge. Ver. 7. So that ye *come behind in no gift;* waiting for the coming of our Lord Jesus Christ. 2 Tim. i. 4. Greatly desiring to see thee, being mindful of thy tears, *that I may be filled with joy;* Ver. 5. *When I call to remembrance the unfeigned faith that is in thee,* which dwelt first in thy grandmother Lois, and thy mother Eunice; and I am persuaded that in thee also.

[r] 1 Sam. xxii. 14. Then Ahimelech answered the king, and said, *And who is so faithful among all thy servants as David,* which is the king's son-in-law, and goeth at thy bidding, and is honourable in thine house?

[s] 1 Cor. xiii. 6. (*Charity*) rejoiceth not in iniquity, but *rejoiceth in the truth;* Ver. 7. Beareth all things, *believeth all things,* hopeth all things, endureth all things.

[t] Ps. xv. 3. He that backbiteth not with his tongue, nor doeth evil to his neighbour, *nor taketh up a reproach against his neighbour.*

[v] Prov. xxv. 23. The north wind *driveth away rain; so doth an angry countenance a backbiting tongue.*

[w] Prov. xxvi. 24. He that hateth *dissembleth with his lips,* and layeth up deceit within him: Ver. 25. *When he speaketh fair,* believe him not: for there are seven abominations in his heart.

[x] Ps. ci. 5. *Whoso privily slandereth his neighbour,* him will I cut off, &c.

[y] Prov. xxii. 1. *A good name is rather to be chosen than great riches,* and loving favour rather than silver and gold. John viii. 49. *Jesus answered, I have not a devil:* but I honour my Father, and ye do dishonour me.

[z] Ps. xv. 4. He that *sweareth* to his own hurt, *and changeth not.*

[a] Phil. iv. 8. Finally, brethren, whatsoever things are true, whatsoever things are honest, whatsoever things are just, whatsoever things are *pure,* whatsoever things are *lovely,* whatsoever things are of *good report;* if there be any virtue, and if there be any praise, *think on these things.*

145. [b] 1 Sam. xvii. 28. And Eliab his eldest brother heard when he spake unto the men: and Eliab's anger was kindled against David, and he said, Why camest thou down hither? and with whom hast thou left those few sheep in the wilderness: *I know thy pride, and the naughtiness of thine heart;* for thou art come down that thou mightest see the battle. 2 Sam. xvi. 3. And the king said, And where is thy master's son? And Ziba said unto the king, Behold, he abideth at Jerusalem: *for he said, To-day shall the house of Israel restore me the kingdom of my father.* 2 Sam. i. 9. *He said unto me again, Stand, I pray thee, upon me, and slay me;* for anguish is come upon me, because my life is yet whole in me. Ver. 10.

especially in public judicature;c giving false evidence,d suborning false witnesses,e wittingly appearing and pleading for an evil cause, out-facing and over-bearing the truth;f passing unjust sentence,g calling evil good, and good evil; rewarding the wicked according to the work of the righteous, and the righteous according to the work of the wicked;h forgery,i concealing the truth, undue silence in a just cause,k and holding our peace when iniquity calleth for either a reproof from ourselves,l or complaint to others;m speaking the truth unseason-

So I stood upon him, and slew him, because I was sure that he could not live after that he was fallen: and I took the crown that was upon his head, and the bracelet that was on his arm, and have brought them hither unto my lord. Ver. 15. And David called one of the young men, and said, Go near, and fall upon him. And he smote him that he died. Ver. 16. And David said unto him, Thy blood be upon thy head: for *thy mouth hath testified against thee,* saying, I have slain the Lord's anointed.

c Lev. xix. 15. *Ye shall do no unrighteousness in judgment;* thou shalt not respect the person of the poor, nor honour the person of the mighty: but *in righteousness shalt thou judge thy neighbour.* Hab. i. 4. Therefore the *law is slacked, and judgment doth never go forth:* for the wicked doth compass about the righteous; therefore *wrong judgment proceedeth.*

d Prov. xix. 5. *A false witness shall not be unpunished;* and he that *speaketh lies* shall not escape. Prov. vi. 16. These six things *doth the Lord hate;* yea, seven are an *abomination* unto him: Ver. 19. *A false witness that speaketh lies,* and he that soweth discord among brethren.

e Acts vi. 13. And *set up false witnesses,* which said, This man ceaseth not to speak blasphemous words against this holy place, and the law.

f Jer. ix. 3. And *they bend their tongues like their bow for lies;* but they are not valiant for the truth upon the earth: for they proceed from evil to evil, and they know not me, saith the Lord. Ver. 5. And they will deceive every one his neighbour, and *will not speak the truth:* they have *taught their tongue to speak lies,* and weary themselves to commit iniquity. Acts xxiv. 2. And when he was called forth, Tertullus began to accuse him,—Ver. 5. For *we have found this man a pestilent fellow, and a mover of sedition* among all the Jews throughout the world, and a ringleader of the sect of the Nazarenes. Ps. xii. 3. The Lord shall cut off all *flattering lips,* and the *tongue that speaketh proud things;* Ver. 4. Who have said, *With our tongue will we prevail;* our lips are our own: who is lord over us? Ps. lii. 1. Why *boastest* thou thyself in *mischief,* O mighty man? the goodness of God endureth continually. Ver. 2. Thy *tongue* deviseth mischiefs; like a sharp razor, working deceitfully. Ver. 3. Thou *lovest* evil more than good, and *lying* rather than to speak righteousness. Selah. Ver. 4. Thou *lovest all-devouring words,* O thou *deceitful tongue.*

g Prov. xvii. 15. He that *justifieth the wicked,* and he that *condemneth the just,* even they both are *abomination* to the Lord. 1 Kings xxi. from verse 9. to 14. And she (Jezebel) wrote in the letters, saying, Proclaim a fast, and set Naboth on high among the people; Ver. 10. And set two men, sons of Belial, before him, *to bear witness against him,* saying, Thou didst blaspheme God and the king: and then carry him out, and stone him, that he may die. Ver. 11. And the men of his city, even the *elders and the nobles* who were the inhabitants in his city, *did as Jezebel had sent* unto them. Ver. 13. And *(they)* stoned him with stones, that he died.

h Isa. v. 23. Which *justify the wicked* for reward, and *take away the righteousness of the righteous from him!*

i Ps. cxix. 69. The proud *have forged a lie against me:* but I will keep thy precepts with my whole heart. Luke xix. 8. And Zaccheus stood, and said unto the Lord, Behold, Lord, the half of my goods I give to the poor; and if I have taken any thing from any man *by false accusation, I restore him four-fold.* Luke xvi. 5. So he called every one of his lord's *debtors* unto him, and said unto the first, How much owest thou unto my lord? Ver. 6. And he said, An hundred measures of oil. *And he said unto him, Take thy bill,* and sit down quickly, *and write fifty.* Ver. 7. Then said he to another, And how much owest thou? &c.

k Lev. v. 1. And if a soul sin, and hear the voice of *swearing,* and is a witness, whether he hath seen or known of it ; *if he do not utter it, then he shall bear his iniquity.* Deut. xiii. 8. Thou shalt not consent unto him, nor hearken unto him ; neither shall thine eye pity him, neither shalt thou spare, *neither shalt thou conceal him.* Acts v. 3. But Peter said, Ananias, why hath Satan filled thine heart *to lie to the Holy Ghost,* and *to keep back part of the price of the land?* Ver. 8. And Peter answered unto her, Tell me whether ye sold the land for so much? *And she said, Yea, for so much.* Ver. 9. Then Peter said unto her, How is it that ye have agreed together to tempt the Spirit of the Lord? 2 Tim. iv. 16. At my first answer *no man stood with me, but all men forsook me:* I pray God that it may not be laid to their charge.

l 1 Kings i. 6. And *his father had not displeased him at any time in saying, Why hast thou done so?* Lev. xix. 17. Thou shalt *not hate* thy brother in thine heart: *thou shalt in any wise rebuke thy neighbour,* and not suffer sin upon him.

m Isa. lix. 4. *None calleth for justice,* nor

ably,ⁿ or maliciously to a wrong end,º or perverting it to a wrong meaning,ᵖ or in doubtful or equivocal expressions, to the prejudice of truth or justice;ᑫ speaking untruth,ʳ lying,ˢ slandering,ᵗ backbiting,ᵛ detracting,ʷ tale-bearing,ˣ whispering,ʸ scoffing,ᶻ reviling,ª rash,ᵇ harsh,ᶜ and partial censuring;ᵈ misconstructing intentions, words, and actions;ᵉ

any pleadeth for truth: they trust in vanity, &c.

ⁿ Prov. xxix. 11. *A fool uttereth all his mind: but a wise man keepeth it in till afterwards.*

º 1 Sam. xxii. 9. Then answered Doeg the Edomite, which was set over the servants of Saul, *and said, I saw the son of Jesse coming to Nob,* to Ahimelech the son of Ahitub. Ver. 10. And he enquired of the Lord for him, and gave him victuals, and gave him the sword of Goliath the Philistine. Compared with Ps. lii. *A Psalm of David, when Doeg the Edomite came and told Saul,* —Ver. 1. *Why boastest thou thyself in mischief,* O mighty man? &c., to verse 5.

ᵖ Ps. lvi. 5. Every day *they wrest my words:* all their thoughts are against me for evil. John ii. 19. Jesus answered and said unto them, Destroy this temple, and in three days I will raise it up. Compared with Matt. xxvi. 60. At the last came *two false witnesses,* Ver. 61. *And said, This fellow said, I am able to destroy the temple of God, and to build it in three days.*

ᑫ Gen. iii. 5. For God doth know, that in the day ye eat thereof, then *your eyes shall be opened;* and ye shall be as gods, *knowing good and evil.* Gen. xxvi. 7. And the men of the place asked him of his wife ; and he said, *She is my sister:* for he feared to say, She is my wife. Ver. 9. And Abimelech called Isaac, and said, Behold, of a surety she is thy wife ; and how saidst thou, *She is my sister?*

ʳ Isa. lix. 13. In transgressing *and lying against the Lord,* and departing away from our God, speaking oppression and revolt, *conceiving and uttering from the heart words of falsehood.*

ˢ Lev. xix. 11. Ye shall not steal, neither deal falsely, *neither lie one to another.* Col. iii. 9. *Lie not one to another,* seeing that ye have put off the old man with his deeds.

ᵗ Ps. l. 20. Thou sittest and speakest against thy brother ; *thou slanderest thine own mother's son.*

ᵛ Ps. xv. 3. *He that backbiteth not* with his tongue, &c.

ʷ James iv. 11. *Speak not evil one of another, brethren.* He that speaketh evil of his brother, and judgeth his brother, speaketh evil of the law, and judgeth the law : but if thou judge the law, thou art not a doer of the law, but a judge. Jer. xxxviii. 4. Therefore the princes said unto the king, We beseech thee, let this man be put to death ; for thus he weakeneth the hands of the men of war that remain in this city, and the hands of all the people, in speaking such words unto them : for *this man seeketh not the welfare of this people,* but the hurt.

ˣ Lev. xix. 16. *Thou shalt not go up and down as a tale-bearer among thy people;* neither shalt thou stand against the blood of thy neighbour : I am the Lord.

ʸ Rom. i. 29. Being filled with all unrighteousness, fornication, wickedness, covetousness, maliciousness ; full of envy, murder, debate, deceit, malignity ; *whisperers,* Ver. 30. Backbiters, haters of God, &c.

ᶻ Gen. xxi. 9. And Sarah saw the son of Hagar the Egyptian, which she had born unto Abraham, *mocking.* Compared with Gal. iv. 29. But as then he that was born after the flesh *persecuted him that was born after the Spirit,* even so it is now.

ª 1 Cor. vi. 10. Nor thieves, nor covetous, nor drunkards, nor *revilers,* nor extortioners, shall inherit the kingdom of God.

ᵇ Matt. vii. 1. *Judge not,* that ye be not judged.

ᶜ Acts xxviii. 4. And when the barbarians saw the venomous beast hang on his hand, they said among themselves, *No doubt this man is a murderer,* whom, though he hath escaped the sea, *yet vengeance suffereth not to live.*

ᵈ Gen. xxxviii. 24. And it came to pass, about three months after, that it was told Judah, saying, Tamar thy daughter-in-law hath played the harlot ; and also, behold, she is with child by whoredom. And *Judah said, Bring her forth, and let her be burnt.* Rom. ii. 1. Therefore thou art inexcusable, O man, whosoever thou art that judgest : for *wherein thou judgest another, thou condemnest thyself; for thou that judgest doest the same things.*

ᵉ Neh. vi. 6. Wherein was written, It is reported among the heathen, and Gashmu saith it, that thou and the Jews think to rebel : *for which cause thou buildest the wall, that thou mayest be their king,* according to these words. Ver. 7. And thou hast also appointed prophets to preach of thee at Jerusalem, saying, There is a king in Judah : and now shall it be reported to the king according to these words. Come now therefore, and let us take counsel together. Ver. 8. Then I sent unto him, saying, There are no such things done as thou sayest, but thou feignest them out of thine own heart. Rom. iii. 8. And not rather (*as we be slanderously reported, and as some affirm that we say,*) *Let us do evil, that good may come? whose damnation is just.* Ps. lxix. 10 When I wept, and chastened my soul with fasting, *that was to my reproach.* 1 Sam. i. 13. Now Hannah, she spake in her heart ; only her lips moved, but her voice was not heard : therefore *Eli thought she had been drunken.* Ver. 14. And Eli said unto her, *How long wilt thou be drunken?* put away thy wine from thee. Ver. 15. And Hannah answered and said, No, my lord ; I am a woman of a sorrowful spirit : I have drunk neither wine nor strong drink, but have

THE LARGER CATECHISM. 185

flattering,[f] vain-glorious boasting,[g] thinking or speaking too highly or too meanly of ourselves or others;[h] denying the gifts and graces of God;[i] aggravating smaller faults;[k] hiding, excusing, or extenuating of sins, when called to a free confession;[l] unnecessary discovering of infirmities;[m] raising false rumours,[n] receiving and countenancing evil reports,[o] and stopping our ears against just defence;[p] evil suspicion;[q] envying or grieving at the deserved credit of any,[r] endea-

poured out my soul before the Lord. 2 Sam. x. 3. And the princes of the children of Ammon said unto Hanun their lord, Thinkest thou that David doth honour thy father, that he hath sent comforters unto thee? *Hath not David rather sent his servants unto thee, to search the city, and to spy it out, and to overthrow it?*

f Ps. xii. 2. They speak vanity every one with his neighbour : *with flattering lips,* and with a double heart, do they speak. Ver. 3. *The Lord shall cut off all flattering lips,* and the tongue that speaketh proud things.

g 2 Tim. iii. 2. For men shall be lovers of their own selves, covetous, *boasters.*

h Luke xviii. 9. And he spake this parable unto certain which *trusted in themselves that they were righteous, and despised others.* Ver. 11. The *Pharisee* stood and prayed thus with himself, God, *I thank thee that I am not as other men are,* extortioners, unjust, adulterers, or even as this publican. Rom. xii. 16. *Mind not high things, but condescend to men of low estate.* Be not *wise in your own conceits.* 1 Cor. iv. 6. And these things, brethren, I have in a figure transferred to myself and to Apollos for your sakes ; that ye might learn in us *not to think of men above that which is written,* that no one of you be *puffed up for one against another.* Acts xii. 22. And the people gave a shout, saying, *It is the voice of a god, and not of a man.* Exod. iv. 10. And *Moses said unto the Lord, O my Lord, I am not eloquent,* neither heretofore, nor since thou hast spoken unto thy servant ; but *I am slow of speech,* and *of a slow tongue.* Ver. 11. And the Lord said unto him, Who hath made man's mouth? or who maketh the dumb, or deaf, or the seeing, or the blind? have not I the Lord? Ver. 12. Now therefore go, and I will be with thy mouth, and teach thee what thou shalt say. Ver. 13. And he said, O my Lord, send, *I pray thee, by the hand of him whom thou wilt send.* Ver. 14. And *the anger of the Lord was kindled against Moses,* &c.

i Job xxvii. 5. God forbid that I should justify you : *till I die I will not remove mine integrity from me.* Ver. 6. *My righteousness I hold fast, and will not let it go; my heart shall not reproach me so long as I live.* Job iv. 6. Is not this thy fear, *thy confidence, thy hope,* and *the uprightness of thy ways?*

k Matt. vii. 3. And *why beholdest thou the mote that is in thy brother's eye,* but considerest not the *beam* that is in thine own eye? Ver. 4. Or how wilt thou say to thy brother, Let me pull out the mote out of thine eye ; and, behold, a beam is in thine own eye? Ver. 5. Thou hypocrite, first cast out the beam out of thine own eye ; and then shalt thou see clearly to cast out the mote out of thy brother's eye.

l Prov. xxviii. 13. *He that covereth his sins shall not prosper;* but whoso confesseth and forsaketh them shall have mercy. Prov. xxx. 20. Such is the way of an adulterous woman ; she eateth, and *wipeth her mouth, and saith, I have done no wickedness.* Gen. iii. 12. And the man said, *The woman whom thou gavest to be with me, she gave me of the tree,* and I did eat. Ver. 13. And the woman said, *The serpent beguiled me,* and I did eat. Jer. ii. 35. Yet thou sayest, *Because I am innocent,* surely his anger shall turn from me : behold, I will plead with thee, *because thou sayest, I have not sinned.* 2 Kings v. 25.—And Elisha said unto him, Whence comest thou, Gehazi? And he said, *Thy servant went no whither?* Gen. iv. 9. And the Lord said unto Cain, Where is Abel thy brother? And he said, *I know not. Am I my brother's keeper?*

m Gen. ix. 22. And Ham, the father of Canaan, *saw the nakedness of his father, and told his two brethren without.* Prov. xxv. 9. Debate thy cause with thy neighbour himself, and *discover not a secret to another;* Ver. 10. Lest he that heareth it put thee to shame, and thine infamy turn not away.

n Exod. xxiii. 1. *Thou shalt not raise a false report:* put not thine hand with the wicked to be an unrighteous witness.

o Prov. xxix. 12. If a ruler *hearken to lies,* all his servants are wicked.

p Acts vii. 56. And (Stephen) said, Behold, I see the heavens opened, and the Son of man standing on the right hand of God. Ver. 57. *Then they cried out with a loud voice, and stopped their ears,*—Job xxxi. 13. *If I did despise the cause of my manservant, or of my maid-servant, when they contended with me;* Ver. 14. What then shall I do when God riseth up? and when he visiteth, what shall I answer him?

q 1 Cor. xiii. 5. (Charity) doth not behave itself unseemly, seeketh not her own, is not easily provoked, *thinketh no evil.* 1 Tim. vi. 4. He is proud, knowing nothing, but doting about questions and strifes of words, whereof cometh envy, strife, railings, *evil surmisings.*

r Numb. xi. 29. And Moses said unto him, *Enviest thou for my sake?* Would God that all the Lord's people were prophets, and that the Lord would put his Spirit upon them! Matt. xxi. 15. And when the *chief priests and scribes* saw the wonderful things that he did, and the children crying in the temple, and saying, *Hosanna* to the son of David ; *they were sore displeased.*

vouring or desiring to impair it,[s] rejoicing in their disgrace and infamy;[t] scornful contempt,[v] fond admiration;[w] breach of lawful promises;[x] neglecting such things as are of good report,[y] and practising, or not avoiding ourselves, or not hindering what we can in others, such things as procure an ill name.[z]

Q. 146. *Which is the tenth commandment?*

A. The tenth commandment is, *Thou shalt not covet thy neighbour's house, thou shalt not covet thy neighbour's wife, nor his man-servant, nor his maid-servant, nor his ox, nor his ass, nor any thing that is thy neighbour's.*[a]

Q. 147. *What are the duties required in the tenth commandment?*

A. The duties required in the tenth commandment are, such a full contentment with our own condition,[b] and such a charitable frame of the whole soul toward our neighbour, as that all our inward motions and affections touching him, tend unto, and further all that good which is his.[c]

Q. 148. *What are the sins forbidden in the tenth commandment?*

A. The sins forbidden in the tenth commandment are, discontentment with our own estate;[d] envying[e] and grieving at the good of our

---

[s] Ezra iv. 12. Be it known unto the king, that the *Jews*, which came up from thee to us are come unto Jerusalem, *building the rebellious and the bad city*, and have set up the walls thereof, and joined the foundations. Ver. 13. Be it known now unto the king, that if this city be builded, and the walls set up again, then *will they not pay toll, tribute, and custom*, and so thou shalt endamage the revenue of the kings.

[t] Jer. xlviii. 27. For *was not Israel a derision unto thee?* was he found among thieves? for *since thou spakest of him, thou skippedst for joy.*

[v] Ps. xxxv. 15. But in mine adversity they rejoiced, and gathered themselves together: yea, the abjects gathered themselves together against me,—Ver. 16. With hypocritical mockers in feasts, *they gnashed upon me with their teeth.* Ver. 21. Yea, they opened their mouth wide against me, and said, *Aha, aha! our eye hath seen it.* Matt. xxvii. 28. And they stripped him, and *put on him a scarlet robe.* Ver. 29. And when they had platted *a crown of thorns*, they put it upon his head, and a *reed* in his right hand: and *they bowed the knee before him, and mocked him, saying, Hail, king of the Jews!*

[w] Jude, ver. 16. These are murmurers, complainers, walking after their own lusts; and their mouth speaketh great swelling words, *having men's persons in admiration because of advantage.* Acts xii. 22. And *the people gave a shout, saying, It is the voice of a god, and not of a man.*

[x] Rom. i. 31. Without understanding, *covenant breakers,*—2 Tim. iii. 3. Without natural affection, *truce-breakers,* false accusers, &c.

[y] 1 Sam. ii. 24. Nay, my sons; for *it is no good report that I hear:* ye make the Lord's people to transgress.

[z] 2 Sam. xiii. 12. And she answered him, Nay, my brother, do not force me; *for no such thing ought to be done in Israel:* do not thou this folly. Ver. 13. And I, whither shall I cause my shame to go? and as for thee, *thou shalt be as one of the fools in Israel.* Now therefore, &c. Prov. v. 8. Remove thy way far from her, and *come not nigh the door of her house;* Ver. 9. Lest thou give thine honour unto others, and thy years unto the cruel. Prov. vi. 33. *A wound and dishonour shall he get; and his reproach shall not be wiped away.*

146. [a] Exod. xx. 17.

147. [b] Heb. xiii. 5. Let your conversation be without covetousness; and *be content with such things as ye have;* for he hath said, I will never leave thee, nor forsake thee. 1 Tim. vi. 6. But *godliness with contentment* is great gain.

[c] Job xxxi. 29. *If I rejoiced at the destruction of him that hated me,* or lifted up myself when evil found him. Rom. xii. 15. *Rejoice with them that do rejoice,* and *weep with them that weep.* Ps. cxxii. 7. *Peace be within thy walls,* and prosperity within thy palaces. Ver. 8. For my brethren and companions' sakes, I will now say, *Peace be within thee.* Ver. 9. Because of the house of the Lord our God, *I will seek thy good.* 1 Tim. i. 5. Now, *the end of the commandment is charity,* out of a pure heart, and of a good conscience, and of faith unfeigned. Esth. x. 3. For *Mordecai* the Jew was next unto king Ahasuerus, and great among the Jews, and accepted of the multitude of his brethren, *seeking the wealth of his people,* and speaking peace to all his seed. 1 Cor. xiii. 4. *Charity suffereth long, and is kind;* charity envieth not; charity vaunteth not itself, is not puffed up, Ver. 5. Doth not behave itself unseemly, *seeketh not her own,* is not easily provoked, thinketh no evil; Ver. 6. Rejoiceth not in iniquity, but *rejoiceth in the truth;* Ver. 7. *Beareth all things,* believeth all things, hopeth all things, *endureth all things.*

148. [d] 1 Kings xxi. 4. And *Ahab* came into his house *heavy and displeased* because

neighbour,f together with all inordinate motions and affections to any thing that is his.g

Q. 149. *Is any man able perfectly to keep the commandments of God?*

A. No man is able, either of himself,h or by any grace received in this life, perfectly to keep the commandments of God;i but doth daily break them in thought,k word, and deed.l

Q. 150. *Are all transgressions of the law of God equally heinous in themselves, and in the sight of God?*

A. All transgressions of the law of God are not equally heinous; but some sins in themselves, and by reason of several aggravations, are more heinous in the sight of God than others.m

---

of the word which Naboth the Jezreelite had spoken to him; for he had said, I will not give thee the inheritance of my fathers: and *he laid him down upon his bed, and turned away his face, and would eat no bread.* Esth. v. 13. Yet *all this availeth me nothing,* so long as I see Mordecai the Jew sitting at the king's gate. 1 Cor. x. 10. *Neither murmur ye, as some of them also murmured,* and were destroyed of the destroyer.
e Gal. v. 26. Let us not be desirous of vainglory, provoking one another, *envying one another.* James iii. 14. But if ye have *bitter envying* and strife in your hearts, glory not, and lie not against the truth. Ver. 16. For *where envying and strife is, there is confusion, and every evil work.*
f Ps. cxii. 9. He hath dispersed, he hath given to the poor; his righteousness endureth for ever; *his horn shall be exalted with honour.* Ver. 10. *The wicked shall see it, and be grieved; he shall gnash with his teeth,* and melt away: the desire of the wicked shall perish. Neh. ii. 10. When *Sanballat* the Horonite, and *Tobiah* the servant, the Ammonite, heard of it, *it grieved them exceedingly that there was come a man to seek the welfare of the children of Israel.*
g Rom. vii. 7. What shall we say then? Is the law sin? God forbid. Nay, I had not known sin but by the law: for *I had not known lust, except the law had said, Thou shalt not covet.* Ver. 8. But sin, taking occasion by the commandment, wrought in me all manner of concupiscence. For without the law sin was dead. Rom. xiii. 9. For this, Thou shalt not commit adultery, Thou shalt not kill, Thou shalt not steal, Thou shalt not bear false witness, *Thou shalt not covet;* and if there be any other commandment, it is briefly comprehended in this saying, namely, Thou shalt love thy neighbour as thyself. Col. iii. 5. Mortify therefore your members which are upon the earth; fornication, uncleanness, *inordinate affection, evil concupiscence,* and covetousness, which is idolatry. Deut. v. 21. *Neither shalt thou desire thy neighbour's wife, neither shalt thou covet thy neighbour's house,* his field, or his man-servant, or his maid-servant, his ox, or his ass, or any thing that is thy neighbour's.
149. h James iii. 2. For *in many things we offend all.* If any man offend not in word, the same is a perfect man, and able also to bridle the whole body. John xv. 5. I am the vine, ye are the branches: he that abideth in me, and I in him, the same bringeth forth much fruit; for *without me ye can do nothing.* Rom. viii. 3. For *what the law could not do, in that it was weak through the flesh,* God sending his own Son in the likeness of sinful flesh, and for sin, condemned sin in the flesh.
i Eccl. vii. 20. For *there is not a just man upon earth, that doeth good, and sinneth not.* 1 John i. 8. *If we say that we have no sin, we deceive ourselves,* and the truth is not in us. Ver. 10. *If we say that we have not sinned, we make him a liar,* and his word is not in us. Gal. v. 17. For *the flesh lusteth against the Spirit,* and the Spirit against the flesh: and these are contrary the one to the other; so *that ye cannot do the things that ye would.* Rom. vii. 18. For *I know that in me (that is, in my flesh) dwelleth no good thing:* for to will is present with me; but *how to perform that which is good I find not.* Ver. 19. For *the good that I would I do not;* but the evil which I would not, that I do.
k Gen. vi. 5. And God saw that the wickedness of man was great in the earth, and that *every imagination of the thoughts of his heart was only evil continually.* Gen. viii. 21. And the Lord said in his heart, I will not again curse the ground any more for man's sake; for *the imagination of man's heart is evil from his youth,* &c.
l Rom. iii. 9. We have before proved both *Jews and Gentiles, that they are all under sin;* Ver. 10. As it is written, *There is none righteous, no, not one.* Ver. 11. There is *none that understandeth,* there is *none that seeketh after God.* Ver. 12. They are *all gone out of the way, they are together become unprofitable;* there is *none that doeth good, no, not one.* Ver. 13. Their *throat* is an open sepulchre: with their *tongues* they have used deceit; the poison of asps is under their *lips:* Ver. 14. Whose *mouth* is full of cursing and bitterness: Ver. 15. Their *feet* are swift to shed blood: Ver. 16. Destruction and misery are in their *ways:* Ver. 17. And the way of peace have they not known: Ver. 18. There is *no fear of God* before their eyes. Ver. 19. Now we know, that what things soever the law saith, it saith to them who are under the law; that every mouth may be stopped, and *all the world may become guilty before God.* James iii. from verse 2. to 13. For *in many things we offend all,* &c.
150. m John xix. 11. Jesus answered, Thou couldest have no power at all against me, ex

Q. 151. *What are those aggravations that make some sins more heinous than others?*

A. Sins receive their aggravations,

1. From the persons offending;[n] if they be of riper age,[o] greater experience or grace,[p] eminent for profession,[q] gifts,[r] place,[s] office,[t] guides to others,[v] and whose example is likely to be followed by others.[w]

cept it were given thee from above: therefore he that delivered me unto thee *hath the greater sin*. Ezek. viii. 6. But turn thee yet again, and *thou shalt see greater abominations*. Ver. 13. Turn thee yet again, and *thou shalt see greater abominations that they do*. Ver. 15. Turn thee yet again, and *thou shalt see greater abominations than these*. 1 John v. 16. If any man see his brother *sin a sin which is not unto death*, he shall ask, and he shall give him life for them that sin not unto death. *There is a sin unto death:* I do not say that he shall pray for it. Ps. lxxviii. 17. And *they sinned yet more against him*, by provoking the most High in the wilderness. Ver. 32. *For all this they sinned still*, and believed not for his wondrous works. Ver. 56. Yet they *tempted and provoked* the most high God, and kept not his testimonies.

151. n Jer. ii. 8. *The priests said not, Where is the Lord?* and *they that handle the law knew me not:* the *pastors also transgressed* against me, and the *prophets prophesied by Baal*, and walked after things that do not profit.

o Job xxxii. 7. I said, *Days should speak, and multitude of years should teach wisdom*. Ver. 9. *Great men are not always wise;* neither do the *aged* understand *judgment*. Eccl. iv. 13. Better is a poor and a wise child than an *old and foolish king*, who will no more be admonished.

p 1 Kings xi. 4. For it came to pass, when *Solomon was old*, that his wives turned away his heart after other gods: and his heart was not perfect with the Lord his God, as was the heart of David his father. Ver. 9. And the Lord was angry with Solomon, *because his heart was turned from the Lord God of Israel, which had appeared unto him twice*.

q 2 Sam. xii. 14. Howbeit, because *by this deed thou hast given great occasion to the enemies of the Lord to blaspheme*, the child also that is born unto thee shall surely die. 1 Cor. v. 1. It is reported commonly that there is *fornication among you*, and such fornication as is not so much as named among the Gentiles, that one should have his father's wife.

r James iv. 17. Therefore *to him that knoweth to do good, and doeth it not, to him it is sin*. Luke xii. 47. And that servant, *which knew his lord's will, and prepared not himself, neither did according to his will, shall be beaten with many stripes*. Ver. 48. But he that knew not, and did commit things worthy of stripes, shall be beaten with few stripes. For *unto whomsoever much is given, of him shall be much required;* and to whom men have committed much, of him they will ask the more.

s Jer. v. 4. Therefore I said, Surely these are poor; they are foolish: for they know not the way of the Lord, nor the judgment of their God. Ver. 5. I will get me unto *the great men*, and will speak unto them; for they have known the way of the Lord, and the judgment of their God: *but these have altogether broken the yoke, and burst the bonds*.

t 2 Sam. xii. 7. And Nathan said to David, Thou art the man. Thus saith the Lord God of Israel, *I anointed thee king over Israel,—* Ver. 8. And I gave thee thy master's house, and thy master's wives into thy bosom, and gave thee the house of Israel and of Judah; and if that had been too little, I would moreover have given unto thee such and such things. Ver. 9. *Wherefore hast thou despised the commandment of the Lord*, to do evil in his sight? Ezek. viii. 11. And there stood before them seventy men of the ancients of the house of Israel, and in the midst of them stood Jaazaniah the son of Shaphan, with every man his censer in his hand: and a thick cloud of incense went up. Ver. 12. Then said he unto me, Son of man, hast thou seen *what the ancients of the house of Israel do* in the dark, every man in the chambers of his imagery? for they say, The Lord seeth us not; the Lord hath forsaken the earth.

v Rom. ii. 17. Behold, thou art called a Jew, and restest in the law, and makest thy boast of God, Ver. 18. And knowest his will,—Ver. 19. And art confident *that thou thyself art a guide of the blind, a light of them which are in darkness*, Ver. 20. An *instructer* of the foolish, a *teacher* of babes,—Ver. 21. *Thou therefore which teachest another, teachest thou not thyself? thou* that preachest a man should *not steal*, dost *thou steal?* Ver. 22. *Thou* that sayest a man *should not commit* adultery, dost *thou commit adultery? thou* that *abhorrest idols*, dost thou *commit sacrilege?* Ver. 23. Thou that *makest thy boast of the law*, through breaking the law *dishonourest thou God?* Ver. 24. For the name of God is blasphemed among the Gentiles *through you*.

w Gal. ii. 11. But when *Peter* was come to Antioch, I withstood him to the face, *because he was to be blamed*. Ver. 12. For before that certain came from James, he did eat with the Gentiles: but when they were come, he withdrew, and separated himself, fearing them which were of the circumcision. Ver. 13. And the other Jews dissembled likewise with him; *insomuch that Barnabas also was carried away with their dissimulation*. Ver. 14. But when I saw that they walked not uprightly, according to the truth of the gospel, I said unto Peter before them all, If thou, being a Jew, livest after the manner of Gentiles, and not as do the Jews, why compellest thou the Gentiles to live as do the Jews?

2. From the parties offended:ˣ if immediately against God,ʸ his attributes,ᶻ and worship;ᵃ against Christ, and his grace;ᵇ the Holy Spirit,ᶜ his witness,ᵈ and workings;ᵉ against superiors, men of eminency,ᶠ and such as we stand especially related and engaged unto;ᵍ against any of the saints,ʰ particularly weak brethren,ⁱ the souls of them, or any other,ᵏ and the common good of all or many.ˡ

x Matt. xxi. 38. But when the husbandmen *saw the son*, they said among themselves, *This is the heir; come, let us kill him*, and let us seize on his inheritance. Ver. 39. And they caught him, and cast him out of the vineyard, and slew him.

y 1 Sam. ii. 25. If one man sin against another, the judge shall judge him; but *if a man sin against the Lord, who shall entreat for him?* Acts v. 4. Thou hast not *lied* unto men, *but unto God*. Ps. li. 4. *Against thee, thee only, have I sinned*, and done this evil in thy sight; that thou mightest be justified when thou speakest, and be clear when thou judgest.

z Rom. ii. 4. Or *despisest thou the riches of his goodness, and forbearance, and longsuffering;* not knowing that the goodness of God leadeth thee to repentance?

a Mal. i. 8. And if ye *offer the blind for sacrifice*, is it not evil? and if ye *offer the lame and sick, is it not evil?* offer it now unto thy governor; will he be pleased with thee, or accept thy person? saith the Lord of hosts. Ver. 14. But cursed be the deceiver, which hath in his flock a male, and *voweth, and sacrificeth unto the Lord a corrupt thing: for I am a great King*, saith the Lord of hosts, and my name is dreadful among the heathen.

b Heb. ii. 2. For if the word spoken by *angels* was stedfast, and every transgression and disobedience received a just recompence of reward; Ver. 3. *How shall we escape, if we neglect so great salvation?*—Heb. xii. 25. See that ye refuse not him that speaketh: for if they escaped not who refused him that spake on earth, *much more shall not we escape, if we turn away from him that speaketh from heaven.*

c Heb. x. 29. *Of how much sorer punishment, suppose ye, shall he be thought worthy, who hath trodden under foot the Son of God?* Matt. xii. 31. Wherefore I say unto you, All manner of sin and blasphemy shall be forgiven unto men: but the *blasphemy against the Holy Ghost shall not be forgiven unto men*. Ver. 32. And whosoever speaketh a word against the Son of man, it shall be forgiven him: but *whosoever speaketh against the Holy Ghost, it shall not be forgiven him*, neither in this world, neither in the world to come.

d Eph. iv. 30. And *grieve not the Holy Spirit of God, whereby ye are sealed* unto the day of redemption.

e Heb. vi. 4. For *it is impossible* for those who were *once enlightened*, and have *tasted of the heavenly gift*, and were *made partakers of the Holy Ghost*, Ver. 5. And have tasted the good word of God, and the powers of the world to come, Ver. 6. *If they shall fall away, to renew them again unto repentance*, &c.

f Jude, ver. 8. Likewise also these filthy dreamers defile the flesh, *despise dominion*, and *speak evil of dignities*. Numb. xii. 8. Wherefore then were ye not afraid *to speak against my servant Moses?* Ver. 9. And the anger of the Lord was kindled against them; and he departed. Isa. iii. 5. The *child shall behave himself proudly against the ancient*, and *the base against the honourable*.

g Prov. xxx. 17. The eye that *mocketh at his father*, and *despiseth to obey his mother*, the ravens of the valley shall pick it out, and the young eagles shall eat it. 2 Cor. xii. 15. And I will very gladly spend and be spent for you; though *the more abundantly I love you, the less I be loved*. Ps. lv. 12. *For it was not an enemy that reproached me; then I could have borne it:* neither was it he that hated me that did magnify himself against me; then I would have hid myself from him: Ver. 13. *But it was thou*, a man *mine equal, my guide, and mine acquaintance*. Ver. 14. We took sweet counsel together, and walked unto the house of God in company. Ver. 15. Let death seize upon them, and let them go down quick into hell, &c.

h Zeph. ii. 8. *I have heard the reproach of Moab*, and the *revilings* of the children of *Ammon, whereby they have reproached my people*,—Ver. 10. This shall they have for their pride, because *they have reproached* and *magnified themselves against the people of the Lord of hosts*. Ver. 11. *The Lord will be terrible unto them;*—Matt. xviii. 6. But whoso shall *offend one of these little ones which believe in me*, it were better for him that a millstone were hanged about his neck, and that he were drowned in the depth of the sea. 1 Cor. vi. 8. Nay, *ye do wrong, and defraud, and that your brethren*. Rev. xvii. 6. And I saw the woman *drunken with the blood of the saints*, and with the blood *of the martyrs of Jesus*, &c.

i 1 Cor. viii. 11. And through thy knowledge *shall the weak brother perish, for whom Christ died?* Ver. 12. But when ye *sin so against the brethren, and wound their weak conscience, ye sin against Christ*. Rom. xiv. 13. Let us not therefore judge one another any more: but judge this rather, *that no man put a stumbling-block, or an occasion to fall, in his brother's way*. Ver. 15. But if thy brother be grieved with thy meat, now walkest thou not charitably. *Destroy not him with thy meat for whom Christ died*. Ver. 21. It is good neither to eat flesh, nor to drink wine, *nor any thing whereby thy brother stumbleth, or is offended, or is made weak*.

k Ezek. xiii. 19. And will ye pollute me among my people for handfuls of barley, and for pieces of bread, *to slay the souls*

3. From the nature and quality of the offence:[m] if it be against the express letter of the law,[n] break many commandments, contain in it many sins:[o] if not only conceived in the heart, but breaks forth in words and actions,[p] scandalize others,[q] and admit of no reparation:[r] if against means,[s]

[that] *should not die*, and to save the souls alive that should not live, by your lying to my people that hear your lies? 1 Cor. viii. 12. But when ye sin so against the brethren, *and wound their weak conscience*, ye sin against Christ. Rev. xviii. 12. *The merchandise of gold*,—Ver. 13. And cinnamon, and odours, and ointments, and frankincense, and wine, and oil, and fine flour, and wheat, and beasts, and sheep, and horses, and chariots, and slaves, and *souls of men*. Matt. xxiii. 15. *Woe unto you, scribes* and *Pharisees*, hypocrites! for ye compass sea and land to make one proselyte; and when he is made, *ye make him two-fold more the child of hell than yourselves.*

[l] 1 Thess. ii. 15. Who both killed the Lord Jesus and their own prophets, and have persecuted us; and they please not God, *and are contrary to all men;* Ver. 16. *Forbidding us to speak to the Gentiles*, that they might be saved,—Josh. xxii. 20. *Did not Achan* the son of Zerah *commit a trespass* in the accursed thing, *and wrath fell on all the congregation of Israel?* and that man perished not alone in his iniquity.

[m] Prov. vi. 30. Men do not despise a thief, *if he steal to satisfy his soul when he is hungry;* Ver. 31. But if he be found, he shall restore seven-fold;—Ver. 32. *But whoso committeth adultery with a woman* lacketh understanding: he that doeth it *destroyeth his own soul.* Ver. 33. A wound and dishonour shall he get; and his reproach shall not be wiped away. And so on to the end of the chapter.

[n] Ezra ix. 10. And now, O our God, what shall we say after this? for *we have forsaken thy commandments*, Ver. 11. *Which thou hast commanded by thy servants the prophets*, saying, The land, unto which ye go to possess it, is an unclean land with the filthiness of the people.—Ver. 12. Now therefore give not your daughters unto their sons, &c. 1 Kings xi. 9. And the Lord was *angry with Solomon*, because *his heart was turned* from the Lord God of Israel, *which had appeared unto him twice*, Ver. 10. *And had commanded him concerning this thing*, that he should not go after other gods: *but he kept not that which the Lord commanded.*

[o] Col. iii. 5. Mortify therefore your members which are upon the earth; fornication, uncleanness, inordinate affection, evil concupiscence, and *covetousness, which is idolatry.* 1 Tim. vi. 10. For the *love of money is the root of all evil;* which while some *coveted* after, they have *erred from the faith, and pierced themselves through with many sorrows.* Prov. v. 8. Remove thy way far from her, and come not nigh the door of her house; Ver. 9. *Lest thou give thine honour unto others, and thy years unto the cruel;* Ver. 10. *Lest strangers be filled with thy wealth*,—Ver. 11. And thou mourn at the last, when *thy flesh and thy body are consumed*, Ver. 12. And say, How have I hated instruction, and my heart despised reproof! Prov. vi. 32. But whoso *committeth adultery with a woman lacketh understanding:* he that doeth it *destroyeth his own soul.* Ver. 33. *A wound and dishonour shall he get.* Josh. vii. 21. When I saw among the spoils a goodly Babylonish garment and two hundred shekels of silver, and a wedge of gold of fifty shekels weight, then *I coveted them, and took them*, &c.

[p] James i. 14. But every man is tempted, when he is drawn away of his own lust, and enticed. Ver. 15. Then, *when lust hath conceived, it bringeth forth sin;* and sin, when it is finished, bringeth forth death. Matt. v. 22. But I say unto you, That whosoever is angry with his brother without a cause shall be in *danger of the judgment;* and whosoever shall *say to his brother, Raca*, shall be in *danger of the council;* but whosoever *shall say, Thou fool*, shall be *in danger of hell-fire.* Micah ii. 1. Woe to them that devise iniquity, and *work evil upon their beds!* when the morning is light, *they practise* it, because it is in the power of their hand.

[q] Matt. xviii. 7. Woe unto the world because of offences! for it must needs be that offences come; but *woe to that man by whom the offence cometh!* Rom. ii. 23. Thou that makest thy boast of the law, *through breaking the law dishonourest thou God?* Ver. 24. For the name of God is *blasphemed among the Gentiles through you*, as it is written.

[r] Deut. xxii. 22. If a man be found *lying with a woman married to an husband*, then they shall *both of them die*, both the man that lay with the woman, and the woman : so shalt thou put away evil from Israel. Compared with ver. 28. If a man find a *damsel that is a virgin*, which is *not betrothed*, and lay hold on her, *and lie with her*, and they be found ; Ver. 29. Then the man that lay with her shall *give unto the damsel's father fifty shekels of silver*, and she shall be his wife ; because he hath humbled her, he may not put her away all his days. Prov vi. 32. But whoso committeth adultery with a woman lacketh understanding: he that doeth it *destroyeth his own soul.* Ver. 33. A wound and dishonour shall he get; and *his reproach shall not be wiped away.* Ver. 34. For jealousy is the rage of a man ; therefore he will not spare in the day of vengeance. Ver. 35. He will *not regard any ransom ;* neither will he rest content, though thou givest many gifts.

[s] Matt. xi. 21. Woe unto thee, *Chorazin!* woe unto thee, *Bethsaida !* for *if the mighty works, which were done in you*, had been done in Tyre and Sidon, they would have repented long ago in sackcloth and ashes. Ver. 22. But I say unto you, It shall be *more tolerable for Tyre and Sidon* at the day of judgment than for you. Ver. 23. And thou, *Capernaum*, which art *exalted*

mercies,[t] judgments,[v] light of nature,[w] conviction of conscience [x] publick or private admonition,[y] censures of the church,[z] civil punishments;[a] and our prayers, purposes, promises,[b] vows,[c] covenants,[d] and engagements to God or men :[e] if done deliber-

[t] Isa. i. 3. The *ox knoweth his owner, and the ass his master's crib: but Israel doth not know,* my people doth not consider. Deut. xxxii. 6. *Do ye thus requite the Lord,* O foolish people and unwise? *is not he thy father that hath bought thee? hath he not made thee, and established thee?*

[v] Amos iv. 8. So two or three cities wandered unto one city, to drink water; *but they were not satisfied: yet have ye not returned unto me,* saith the Lord. Ver. 9. I have smitten you with *blasting and mildew:* when your gardens, and your vineyards, and your fig-trees, and your olive-trees increased, *the palmer-worm devoured them : yet have ye not returned unto me,* saith the Lord. Ver. 10. I have sent among you the *pestilence,* after the manner of Egypt: your young men have *I slain with the sword,* and have *taken away your horses;* and I have *made the stink of your camps to come up* unto your nostrils: *yet have ye not returned unto me, saith the Lord.* Ver. 11. I have *overthrown some of you,* as God overthrew Sodom and Gomorrah, and ye were as a firebrand plucked out of the burning : *yet have ye not returned unto me,* saith the Lord. Jer. v. 3. O Lord, are not thine eyes upon the truth? *thou hast stricken them, but they have not grieved;* thou hast consumed them, *but they have refused to receive correction:* they have made their faces harder than a rock ; they have refused to return.

[w] Rom. i. 26. For this cause *God gave them up unto vile affections:* for even their women did change the natural use into that which is *against nature;* Ver. 27. And likewise also the men, leaving the natural use of the woman, burned in their lust one toward another : men with men working that which is unseemly, and receiving in themselves that recompense of their error which was meet.

[x] Rom. i. 32. Who, *knowing the judgment of God, that they which commit such things are worthy of death,* not only *do the same,* but have pleasure in them that do them. Dan. v. 22. And thou his son, *O Belshazzar, hast not humbled thine heart, though thou knewest all this.* Tit. iii. 10. A man that is an heretic, after the first and second admonition, reject ; Ver. 11. Knowing that he that is such is subverted, *and sinneth, being condemned of himself.*

[y] Prov. xxix. 1. He that, *being often reproved, hardeneth his neck, shall suddenly be destroyed, and that without remedy.*

[z] Tit. iii. 10. A man that is an heretic, after the first and second admonition, reject. Matt. xviii. 17. And if he shall neglect to hear them, tell it unto the church : but if he neglect to *hear the church,* let him be unto thee as an heathen man and a publican.

[a] Prov. xxvii. 22. Though thou shouldest *bray a fool in a mortar* among wheat with a pestle, *yet will not his foolishness depart from him.* Prov. xxiii. 35. *They have stricken me,* shalt thou say, *and I was not sick: they have beaten me, and I felt it not:* when shall I awake? I will seek it yet again.

[b] Ps. lxxviii. 34. When he slew them, then they sought him ; and they returned and enquired early after God : Ver. 35. And they remembered that God was their Rock, and the high God their Redeemer. Ver. 36. Nevertheless they did flatter him with their mouth, and they lied unto him with their tongues. Ver. 37. For their heart was not right with him, *neither were they stedfast in his covenant.* Jer. ii. 20. For of old time I have broken thy yoke, and burst thy bands; and *thou saidst, I will not transgress;* when upon every high hill, and under every green tree, thou wanderest, playing the harlot. Jer. xlii. 5. Then they said to Jeremiah, The Lord be a true and faithful witness between us, if we do not even according to all things for the which the Lord thy God shall send thee to us. Ver. 6. Whether it be good, or whether it be evil, *we will obey the voice of the Lord our God,* to whom we send thee.—Ver. 20. *For ye dissembled in your hearts, when ye sent me unto the Lord your God, saying, Pray for us* unto the Lord our God ; and according unto all that the Lord our God shall say, so declare unto us, *and we will do it.* Ver. 21. And now I have this day declared it to you ; *but ye have not obeyed* the voice of the Lord your God, nor any thing for the which he hath sent me unto you.

[c] Eccl. v. 4. When thou *vowest a vow* unto God, *defer not to pay it;* for he hath no pleasure in fools: *pay that which thou hast vowed.* Ver. 5. *Better* is it that thou shouldest *not vow,* than that thou shouldest *vow and not pay.* Ver. 6. Suffer not thy mouth to cause thy flesh to sin ; neither say thou before the angel, that it was an error : wherefore should God be angry at thy voice, and destroy the work of thine hands? Prov. xx. 25. It *is a snare* to the man who *devoureth that which is holy, and after vows to make enquiry.*

[d] Lev. xxvi. 25. And I will bring a *sword* upon you, that shall *avenge the quarrel of my covenant, &c.*

[e] Prov. ii. 17. Which *forsaketh the guide of her youth,* and *forgetteth the covenant of her God.* Ezek. xvii. 18. Seeing he *despised the oath by breaking the covenant,* when, lo, he had given his hand, and hath done all these things, he shall not escape. Ver. 19. Therefore thus saith the Lord God, as I live, surely *mine oath that he hath despised,* and

ately,f wilfully,g presumptuously,h impudently,i boastingly,k maliciously,l frequently,m obstinately,n with delight,o continuance,p or relapsing after repentance.q

4. From circumstances of time,r and place;s if on the Lord's day,t or other times of divine worship;v or immediately be-

f *my covenant that he hath broken*, even *it will I recompense upon his own head.*
f Ps. xxxvi. 4. *He deviseth mischief upon his bed;* he setteth himself in a way that is not good; he abhorreth not evil.
g Jer. vi. 16. Thus saith the Lord, Stand ye in the ways, and see, and ask for the old paths, where is the good way, and walk therein, and ye shall find rest for your souls. *But they said, We will not walk therein.*
h Numb. xv. 30. But *the soul that doeth ought presumptuously* (whether he be born in the land, or a stranger,) the *same reproacheth the Lord;* and that soul shall be *cut off* from among his people. Exod. xxi. 14. But *if a man come presumptuously upon his neighbour*, to slay him with guile; thou shalt take him from mine altar, that he may die.
i Jer. iii. 3. Therefore the showers have been withholden, and there hath been no latter rain; and *thou hadst a whore's forehead, thou refusedst to be ashamed.* Prov. vii. 13. So she caught him, and kissed him, and *with an impudent face*, said unto him, &c.
k Ps. lii. 1. *Why boastest thou thyself in mischief*, O mighty man?
l 3 John, ver. 10. Wherefore, if I come, I will remember his deeds which he doeth, prating against us *with malicious words,* &c.
m Numb. xiv. 22. Because all those men which have seen my glory, and my miracles which I did in Egypt, and in the wilderness, have *tempted me now these ten times,* and have not hearkened to my voice.
n Zech. vii. 11. But they refused to hearken, and *pulled away the shoulder, and stopped their ears*, that they should not hear. Ver. 12. Yea, they *made their hearts as an adamant stone*, lest they should hear the law, and the words which the Lord of hosts hath sent in his Spirit by the former prophets: *therefore came a great wrath* from the Lord of hosts.
o Prov. ii. 14. *Who rejoice to do evil, and delight in the frowardness of the wicked.*
p Isa. lvii. 17. For the iniquity of his covetousness was I wroth, and smote him: I hid me, and was wroth, *and he went on frowardly in the way of his heart.*
q Jer. xxxiv. 8. This is the word that came unto Jeremiah from the Lord, after that the king Zedekiah had made a covenant with all the people which were at Jerusalem, *to proclaim liberty unto them;* Ver. 9. That *every man should let his man-servant, and every man his maid-servant*, being an Hebrew or an Hebrewess, *go free;* that none should serve himself of them, to wit, of a Jew his brother. Ver. 10. Now, when all the *princes*, and all the people, which had entered into the *covenant,* heard that every one should let his man-servant, and every one his maid-servant, go free, that none should serve themselves of them any more; then *they obeyed, and let them go.* Ver. 11. *But afterward they turned*, and caused the servants and the handmaids, whom they had let go free, *to return, and brought them into subjection* for servants and for handmaids. 2 Pet. ii. 20. For if *after they have escaped the pollutions of the world,* through the knowledge of the Lord and Saviour Jesus Christ, *they are again entangled* therein, and overcome, the *latter end is worse with them than the beginning.* Ver. 21. For it had been *better* for them *not to have known* the way of righteousness, *than, after they have known it, to turn from the holy commandment* delivered unto them. Ver. 22. But it is happened unto them according to the true proverb, The *dog is turned* to his own *vomit* again; and the *sow that was washed* to her *wallowing in the mire.*
r 2 Kings v. 26. And he said unto him (Gehazi), Went not mine heart with thee, when the man turned again from his chariot to meet thee? *Is it a time to receive money,* and to receive garments, and oliveyards, and vineyards, and sheep, and oxen, and men-servants, and maid-servants?
s Jer. vii. 10. And come *and stand before me in this house, which is called by my name, and say,* We are delivered to do all these abominations. Isa. xxvi. 10. Let favour be shewed to the wicked, yet will he not learn righteousness: *in the land of uprightness will he deal unjustly,* and will not behold the majesty of the Lord.
t Ezek. xxiii. 37. That they have committed adultery, and blood is in their hands, and with their idols have they committed adultery;—Ver. 38. Moreover, this they have done unto me: they have *defiled my sanctuary in the same day, and have profaned my sabbaths.* Ver. 39. For when they had slain their children to their idols, then they came *the same day* into my sanctuary to profane it; and, lo, thus have they done in the midst of mine house.
v Isa. lviii. 3. Wherefore have we fasted, say they, and thou seest not? wherefore have we afflicted our soul, and thou takest no knowledge? Behold, *in the day of your fast ye find pleasure,* and exact all your labours. Ver. 4. Behold, ye *fast for strife and debate*, and to smite with the fist of wickedness: ye shall not fast as ye do this day, to make your voice to be heard on high. Ver. 5. Is it such a fast that I have chosen? a day for a man to afflict his soul? is it to bow down his head as a bulrush, and to spread sackcloth and ashes under him? wilt thou call this a fast, and an acceptable day to the Lord? Numb. xxv. 6. And, behold, one of the children of Israel came, and brought unto his brethren a *Midianitish woman, in the sight of Moses, and in the sight of all the congregation* of the children of Israel, *who were weeping before the door of the tabernacle of the congregation.* Ver. 7. And when Phinehas, the son of Eleazar, the son of Aaron the priest, saw it, he rose

fore[w] or after these,[x] or other helps to prevent or remedy such miscarriages:[y] if in public, or in the presence of others, who are thereby likely to be provoked or defiled.[z]

Q. 152. *What doth every sin deserve at the hands of God?*

A. Every sin, even the least, being against the sovereignty,[a] goodness,[b] and holiness of God,[c] and against his righteous law,[d] deserveth his wrath and curse,[e] both in this life,[f] and that which is to come;[g] and cannot be expiated but by the blood of Christ.[h]

Q. 153. *What doth God require of us, that we may escape his wrath and curse due to us by reason of the transgression of the law?*

A. That we may escape the wrath and curse of God due to us by reason of the transgression of the law, he requireth of us repentance

up from among the congregation, and took a javelin in his hand.

w 1 Cor. xi. 20. When ye come together therefore into one place, this is not to eat the Lord's supper. Ver. 21. For in eating *every one taketh before other his own supper:* and *one is hungry*, and *another is drunken*.

x Jer. vii. 8. Behold, ye trust in lying words, that cannot profit. Ver. 9. Will ye steal, murder, and commit adultery, and swear falsely, and burn incense unto Baal, and walk after other gods whom ye know not; Ver. 10. *And come and stand before me in this house,* which is called by my name, and *say, We are delivered to do all these abominations?* Prov. vii. 14. *I have peace-offerings* with me; *this day have I paid my vows:* Ver. 15. *Therefore came I forth to meet thee,* diligently to seek thy face, and I have found thee. John xiii. 27. *And after the sop Satan entered into him.* Then said Jesus unto him, That thou doest, do quickly. Ver. 30. He then, *having received the sop, went immediately out,* &c.

y Ezra ix. 13. *And after all that is come upon us* for our evil deeds, and for our great trespass, seeing that thou our God hast punished us less than our iniquities deserve, and hast given us such deliverance as this; Ver. 14. *Should we again break thy commandments,* and join in affinity with the people of these abominations? wouldest not thou be angry with us till thou hadst consumed us?

z 2 Sam. xvi. 22. So they spread Absalom a tent upon the top of the house; and *Absalom went in unto his father's concubines in the sight of all Israel.* 1 Sam. ii. 22. Now *Eli* was very old, and heard all that his *sons did unto all Israel;* and how they *lay with the women that assembled at the door of the tabernacle* of the congregation. Ver. 23. And he said unto them, Why do ye such things? for I hear of your evil dealings by all this people. Ver. 24. Nay, my sons; for it is no good report that I hear: *ye make the Lord's people to transgress.*

152. a James ii. 10. For whosoever shall keep the whole law, *and yet offend in one point,* he is guilty of *all.* Ver. 11. For *he that said,* Do not commit adultery, *said also,* Do not kill.

b Exod. xx. 1. And God spake all these words, saying, Ver. 2. I am the Lord *thy God, which have brought thee out of the land of Egypt, out of the house of bondage.*

c Hab. i. 13. *Thou art of purer eyes than to behold evil, and canst not look on iniquity:* wherefore lookest thou upon them that deal treacherously, and holdest thy tongue when the wicked devoureth the man that is more righteous than he? Lev. x. 3. Then Moses said unto Aaron, This is it that the Lord spake, saying, *I will be sanctified in them that come nigh me,* and before all the people I will be glorified.—Lev. xi. 44. For I am the Lord your God: ye shall therefore sanctify yourselves, and *ye shall be holy; for I am holy:* neither shall ye defile yourselves with any manner of creeping thing that creepeth upon the earth. Ver. 45. For I am the Lord that bringeth you up out of the land of Egypt, to be your God: *ye shall therefore be holy; for I am holy.*

d 1 John iii. 4. Whosoever committeth sin transgresseth also the law: for *sin is the transgression of the law.* Rom. vii. 12. Wherefore *the law is holy, and the commandment holy, and just, and good.*

e Eph. v. 6. Let no man deceive you with vain words: for *because of these things cometh the wrath of God upon the children of disobedience.* Gal. iii. 10. For as many as are of the works of the law *are under the curse:* for it is written, Cursed is every one *that continueth not in all things which are written in the book of the law to do them.*

f Lam. iii. 39. *Wherefore doth a living man complain,* a man for the *punishment* of his *sins?* Deut. xxviii. from verse 15. to the end. But it shall come to pass, if thou wilt not hearken unto the voice of the Lord thy God, to observe to do all his commandments and his statutes, which I command thee this day, that *all these curses shall come upon thee,* and overtake thee. Ver. 16. *Cursed* shalt thou be in the *city,* and *cursed* shalt thou be *in the field.* Ver. 17. *Cursed* shall be *thy basket and thy store,* &c.

g Matt. xxv. 41. *Depart from me, ye cursed, into everlasting fire,* prepared for the devil and his angels.

h Heb. ix. 22. And almost all things are by the law purged with blood; and *without shedding of blood is no remission.* 1 Pet. i. 18. Forasmuch as ye know that *ye were not redeemed with corruptible things,* as silver and gold, *from your vain conversation* received by tradition from your fathers; Ver. 19. But with the *precious blood of Christ,* as of a lamb without blemish and without spot.

toward God, and faith toward our Lord Jesus Christ,[i] and the diligent use of the outward means whereby Christ communicates to us the benefits of his mediation.[k]

Q. 154. *What are the outward means whereby Christ communicates to us the benefits of his mediation?*

A. The outward and ordinary means whereby Christ communicates to his church the benefits of his mediation, are all his ordinances; especially the word, sacraments, and prayer; all which are made effectual to the elect for their salvation.[l]

Q. 155. *How is the word made effectual to salvation?*

A. The Spirit of God maketh the reading, but especially the preaching of the word, an effectual means of enlightening,[m] convincing, and humbling sinners;[n] of driving them out of themselves, and drawing them unto Christ;[o] of conforming them to his

---

153. [i] Acts xx. 21. *Testifying* both to the Jews, and also to the *Greeks, repentance toward God, and faith toward our Lord Jesus Christ.* Matt. iii. 7. But when he saw many of the Pharisees and Sadducees come to his baptism, he said unto them, O generation of vipers, who hath warned you to flee from the wrath to come? Ver. 8. *Bring forth therefore fruits meet for repentance.* Luke xiii. 3, 5. I tell you, Nay: but, except ye repent, ye shall all likewise perish. Acts xvi. 30. And (the jailer) brought them out, and said, Sirs, what must I do to be saved? Ver. 31. And they said, *Believe on the Lord Jesus Christ, and thou shalt be saved, and thy house.* John iii. 16. For God so loved the world, that he gave his only begotten Son, *that whosoever believeth in him should not perish, but have everlasting life.* Ver. 18. *He that believeth on him is not condemned:* but he that believeth not is condemned already.

[k] Prov. ii. 1. My son, *if thou wilt receive my words, and hide my commandments with thee;* Ver. 2. So that thou *incline thine ear unto wisdom,* and *apply thine heart to understanding;* Ver. 3. Yea, *if thou criest after knowledge,* and *liftest up thy voice for understanding;* Ver. 4. If thou *seekest her as silver, and searchest for her as for hid treasures;* Ver. 5. *Then shalt thou understand the fear of the Lord,* and find the knowledge of God. Prov. viii. 33. *Hear instruction, and be wise,* and refuse it not. Ver. 34. *Blessed is the man that heareth me, watching daily at my gates, waiting at the posts of my doors.* Ver. 35. For whoso findeth me *findeth life,* and shall obtain favour of the Lord. Ver. 36. But he that sinneth against me wrongeth his own soul: all they that hate me love death.

154. [l] Matt. xxviii. 19. Go ye therefore, and *teach all nations, baptizing them* in the name of the Father, and of the Son, and of the Holy Ghost; Ver. 20. *Teaching* them to observe all things whatsoever I have commanded you: and, lo, I am with you alway, even unto the end of the world. Acts ii. 42. And they *continued stedfastly* in the *apostles' doctrine* and *fellowship,* and in *breaking of bread,* and in *prayers.* Ver. 46. And they, continuing daily with one accord in the temple, and *breaking bread from house to house,* did eat their meat with gladness and singleness of heart, Ver. 47. *Praising God,* and having favour with all the people. And the Lord added to the church daily such as should be saved.

155. [m] Neh. viii. 8. So *they read in the book, in the law of God,* distinctly, and *gave the sense, and caused them to understand the reading.* Acts xxvi. 18. To *open their eyes,* and to turn them from darkness to light, and from the power of Satan unto God, that they may receive forgiveness of sins, and inheritance among them which are sanctified by faith that is in me. Ps. xix. 8. The commandment of the Lord is pure, *enlightening the eyes.*

[n] 1 Cor. xiv. 24. But if all prophesy, and there come in one that believeth not, or one unlearned, *he is convinced of all,* he is judged of all: Ver. 25. And *thus are the secrets of his heart made manifest;* and so, falling down on his face, he will worship God, and report that God is in you of a truth. 2 Chron. xxxiv. 18. Then Shaphan the scribe told the king, saying, Hilkiah the priest hath given me a book. And Shaphan read it before the king. Ver. 19. And it came to pass, when the king had heard the words of the law, that *he rent his clothes.* Ver. 26. And as for the king of Judah, who sent you to enquire of the Lord, so shall ye say unto him, Thus saith the Lord God of Israel concerning the words which thou hast heard, Ver. 27. Because *thine heart was tender,* and thou *didst humble thyself before God, when thou heardest his words against this place,* and against the inhabitants thereof, and humbledst thyself before me, and didst rend thy clothes, and weep before me; I have even heard thee also, saith the Lord. Ver. 28. Behold, I will gather thee to thy fathers, and thou shalt be gathered to thy grave in peace, &c.

[o] Acts ii. 37. Now *when they heard this, they were pricked in their heart,* and said unto Peter, and to the rest of the apostles, Men and brethren, *what shall we do?* Ver. 41. Then they that gladly received his word were baptized: and the same day there were added unto them about three thousand souls. Acts viii. from verse 27. to 39. And, behold, a man of Ethiopia, an eunuch of great authority,—Ver. 28. Was returning, and sit-

image,p and subduing them to his will;q of strengthening them against temptations and corruptions;r of building them up in grace,s and establishing their hearts in holiness and comfort through faith unto salvation.t

Q. 156. *Is the word of God to be read by all?*

A. Although all are not to be permitted to read the word publickly to the congregation,v yet all sorts of people are bound to read it apart

p 2 Cor. iii. 18. But we all, with open face beholding as in a glass the glory of the Lord, are *changed into the same image, from glory to glory,* even as by the Spirit of the Lord.

q 2 Cor. x. 4. For the *weapons of our warfare* are not carnal, but *mighty* through God *to the pulling down of strongholds;* Ver. 5. *Casting down imaginations,* and every high thing that exalteth itself against the knowledge of God, and *bringing into captivity every thought to the obedience of Christ;* Ver. 6. And having in a readiness to revenge all disobedience, when your obedience is fulfilled. Rom. vi. 17. But God be thanked, that ye were the servants of sin ; *but ye have obeyed from the heart that form of doctrine which was delivered you.*

r Matt. iv. 4. *But he answered and said, It is written,* Man shall not live by bread alone, but by every word that proceedeth out of the mouth of God. Ver. 7. *Jesus said unto him, It is written again,* Thou shalt not tempt the Lord thy God. Ver. 10. *Then saith Jesus unto him, Get thee hence, Satan: for it is written,* Thou shalt worship the Lord thy God, and him only shalt thou serve. Eph. vi. 16. Above all, *taking the shield of faith,* wherewith ye shall *be able to quench all the fiery darts of the wicked.* Ver. 17. And take the *helmet of salvation,* and the *sword of the Spirit, which is the word of God.* Ps. xix. 11. Moreover, *by them is thy servant warned;* and in keeping of them there is great reward. 1 Cor. x. 11. Now all these things happened unto them for ensamples : *and they are written for our admonition,* upon whom the ends of the world are come.

s Acts xx. 32. And now, brethren, I commend you to God, and *to the word of his grace, which is able to build you up,* and to give you an inheritance among all them which are sanctified. 2 Tim. iii. 15. And that from a child thou hast known *the holy scriptures, which are able to make thee wise unto salvation* through faith which is in

ting in his chariot, read Esaias the prophet. Ver. 29. Then the Spirit said unto Philip, Go near, and join thyself to this chariot. Ver. 30. And Philip ran thither to him, and heard him read the prophet Esaias, and said, Understandest thou what thou readest? —Ver. 35. Then Philip opened his mouth, and began at the same scripture, and *preached unto him Jesus.* Ver. 36.—And the eunuch said, See, here is water ; what doth hinder me to be baptized ? Ver. 37. And Philip said, If thou believest with all thine heart, thou mayest. And he answered and said, *I believe that Jesus Christ is the Son of God.* Ver. 38.—And they went down both into the water, both Philip and the eunuch ; and he baptized him.

Christ Jesus. Ver. 16. *All scripture is given by inspiration of God,* and is *profitable for doctrine, for reproof, for correction, for instruction in righteousness;* Ver. 17. That the man of God may be *perfect, throughly furnished unto all good works.*

t Rom. xvi. 25. Now to him that is of power *to stablish you according to my gospel, and the preaching of Jesus Christ,* according to the revelation of the mystery, which was kept secret since the world began. 1 Thess. iii. 2. And *sent Timotheus,* our brother, and minister of God, and our fellow-labourer in the gospel of Christ, *to establish you, and to comfort you concerning your faith;* Ver. 10. Night and day praying exceedingly that we might see your face, and might *perfect that which is lacking in your faith.* Ver. 11. Now God himself and our Father, and our Lord Jesus Christ, direct our way unto you. Ver. 13. *To the end he may stablish your hearts* unblameable in holiness before God, even our Father, at the coming of our Lord Jesus Christ with all his saints. Rom. xv. 4. For whatsoever things were written aforetime *were written for our learning ; that we, through patience and comfort of the scriptures, might have hope.* Rom. x. 13. For whosoever shall call upon the name of the Lord shall be saved. Ver. 14. How then shall they call on him in whom they have not believed ? and *how shall they believe in him of whom they have not heard?* and *how shall they hear without a preacher ?* Ver. 15. And how shall they preach except they be sent ? as it is written, How beautiful are the feet of them that preach the gospel of peace, and bring glad tidings of good things ! Ver. 16. But they have not all obeyed the gospel : for Esaias saith, Lord, who hath believed our report ? Ver. 17. So then *faith cometh by hearing, and hearing by the word of God.* Rom. i. 16. For I am not ashamed of *the gospel of Christ:* for *it is the power of God unto salvation to every one that believeth;* to the Jew first, and also to the Greek.

156. v Deut. xxxi. 9. And Moses wrote this law, *and delivered it unto the priests, the sons of Levi,* which bare the ark of the covenant of the Lord, and unto all the elders of Israel. Ver. 11. When all Israel is come to appear before the Lord thy God in the place which he shall choose, *thou shalt read this law before all Israel in their hearing.* Ver. 12. Gather the people together, men, and women, and children, and thy stranger that is within thy gates, that they may hear, and that they may learn, and fear the Lord your God, and observe to do all the words of this law ; Ver. 13. And that their children, which have not known any thing, may hear, and learn to fear the Lord your God,

by themselves,[w] and with their families:[x] to which end, the holy scriptures are to be translated out of the original into vulgar languages.[y]

Q. 157. *How is the word of God to be read?*

A. The holy scriptures are to be read with an high and reverent esteem of them;[z] with a firm persuasion that they are the very word

---

[w] Deut. vi. 6. And *these words*, which I command thee this day, shall be in thine heart; Ver. 7. And *thou shalt teach them diligently unto thy children*, and shalt *talk of them* when thou sittest *in thine house*, and when thou walkest by the way, and when thou liest down, and when thou risest up. Ver. 8. And thou shalt bind them for a sign upon thine hand, and they shall be as frontlets between thine eyes. Ver. 9. And thou shalt *write them upon the posts of thy house*, and on thy gates. Gen. xviii. 17. And the Lord said, Shall I hide from *Abraham* that thing which I do? Ver. 19. For I know him, *that he will command his children and his household after him*, and they shall keep the way of the Lord, &c. Ps. lxxviii. 5. For he established *a testimony* in Jacob, and appointed *a law* in Israel, *which he commanded our fathers, that they should make them known to their children;* Ver. 6. That the generation to come might know them, even the children which should be born, who should arise *and declare them to their children;* Ver. 7. That they might set their hope in God, and not forget the works of God, but keep his commandments.

as long as ye live in the land whither ye go over Jordan to possess it. Neh. viii. 2. And *Ezra the priest brought the law before the congregation*, both of men and women, and all that could hear with understanding, upon the first day of the seventh month. Ver. 3. And *he read therein* before the street that was before the water-gate, from the morning until mid-day, before the men and the women, and those that could understand: and the ears of all the people were attentive unto the book of the law. Neh. ix. 3. *And they stood up in their place, and read in the book of the law of the Lord* their God one fourth part of the day; and another fourth part they confessed, and worshipped the Lord their God. Ver. 4. Then stood up upon the stairs, of the Levites, *Jeshua, and Bani*, &c., and cried with a loud voice unto the Lord their God. Ver. 5. Then the Levites, Jeshua, and Kadmiel, &c., said, Stand up and bless the Lord your God for ever and ever; and blessed be thy glorious name, which is exalted above all blessing and praise.

[w] Deut. xvii. 19. And *it shall be with him, and he shall read therein all the days of his life;* that he may learn to fear the Lord his God, to keep all the words of this law, and these statutes, to do them. Rev. i. 3. *Blessed is he that readeth, and they that hear the words of this prophecy,* and keep those things which are written therein: for the time is at hand. John v. 39. *Search the scriptures;* for in them ye think ye have eternal life: and they are they which testify of me. Isa. xxxiv. 16. *Seek ye out of the book of the Lord, and read;* no one of these shall fail, &c.

[y] 1 Cor. xiv. 6. Now, brethren, if I come unto you speaking with tongues, what shall I profit you, except I shall speak to you either by revelation, or by knowledge, or by prophesying, or by doctrine? Ver. 9. So likewise ye, *except ye utter by the tongue words easy to be understood,* how shall it be known what is spoken? for *ye shall speak into the air.* Ver. 11. *Therefore if I know not the meaning of the voice, I shall be unto him that speaketh a barbarian,* and he that speaketh shall be a barbarian unto me. Ver. 12. Even so ye, forasmuch as ye are zealous of spiritual gifts, seek that ye may excel to the edifying of the church. Ver. 15. What is it then? I will pray with the spirit, and *I will pray with the understanding also;* I will sing with the spirit, and *I will sing with the understanding also.* Ver. 16. Else, when thou shalt bless with the spirit, *how shall he* that occupieth the room of the unlearned *say Amen* at thy giving of thanks, *seeing he understandeth not what thou sayest?* Ver. 24. But if all prophesy, and there come in one that believeth not, or one unlearned, he is convinced of all, he is judged of all. Ver. 27. *If any man speak in an unknown tongue,* let it be by two, or at the most by three, and that by course; *and let one interpret.* Ver. 28. But *if there be no interpreter, let him keep silence in the church;* and let him speak to himself, and to God.

157. [z] Ps. xix. 10. *More to be desired are they than gold,* yea, than much fine gold; *sweeter also than honey, and the honeycomb.* Neh. viii. 3. And he read therein before the street that was before the water-gate, from the morning until mid-day, before the men and the women, and those that could understand: *and the ears of all the people were attentive unto the book of the law.* Ver. 4. And Ezra the scribe stood upon a pulpit of wood, which they had made for the purpose:—Ver. 5. And Ezra opened the book in the sight of all the people; (for he was above all the people;) and, when he opened it, all the people stood up: Ver. 6. And Ezra blessed the Lord, the great God: and *all the people answered, Amen, Amen,* with *lifting up their hands; and they bowed their heads, and worshipped the Lord* with their faces to the ground, &c., to verse 10. Exod. xxiv. 7. And he (Moses) took the book of the covenant, and read in the audience of the people: *and they said, All that the Lord hath said will we do, and be obedient.* 2 Chron. xxxiv. 27. *Because thine heart was tender,* and thou didst humble *thyself before God, when thou heardest his words against this place,* and against the inhabitants thereof, and humbledst thyself before me, and didst rend thy clothes, and weep before me; *I have even heard thee also,* saith the Lord. Isa. lxvi. 2. But to

of God,ᵃ and that he only can enable us to understand them;ᵇ with desire to know, believe, and obey the will of God revealed in them;ᶜ with diligence,ᵈ and attention to the matter and scope of them;ᵉ with meditation,ᶠ application,ᵍ self-denial,ʰ and prayer.ⁱ

Q. 158. *By whom is the word of God to be preached?*

A. The word of God is to be preached only by such as are sufficiently gifted,ᵏ and also duly approved and called to that office.ˡ

---

this man will I look, even to him that is poor, and of a contrite spirit, and *trembleth at my word.*

ᵃ 2 Pet. i. 19. *We have also a more sure word of prophecy; whereunto ye do well that ye take heed, as unto a light that shineth in a dark place,* until the day dawn, and the day-star arise in your hearts: Ver. 20. *Knowing this first, that no prophecy of the scripture is of any private interpretation.* Ver. 21. For the prophecy came not in old time by the will of man; but *holy men of God spake as they were moved by the Holy Ghost.*

ᵇ Luke xxiv. 45. *Then opened he their understanding, that they might understand the scriptures.* 2 Cor. iii. 13. And not as Moses, which put a vail over his face, that the children of Israel could not stedfastly look to the end of that which is abolished: Ver. 14. But their minds were blinded: for until this day remaineth *the same vail untaken away* in the reading of the old testament; which vail is done away in Christ. Ver. 15. But even unto this day, when Moses is read, the vail is upon their heart. Ver. 16. Nevertheless, *when it shall turn to the Lord, the vail shall be taken away.*

ᶜ Deut. xvii. 19. And it shall be with him, and *he shall read therein* all the days of his life; *that he may learn to fear the Lord his God, to keep all the words of this law, and these statutes, to do them:* Ver. 20. That his heart be not lifted up above his brethren, and that he turn not aside from the commandment, to the right hand or to the left: to the end that he may prolong his days, &c.

ᵈ Acts xvii. 11. These (Bereans) were more noble than those in Thessalonica, in that they received the word with all readiness of mind, and *searched the scriptures daily, whether those things were so.*

ᵉ Acts viii. 30. And Philip ran thither to him, and heard him read the prophet Esaias, and said, Understandest thou what thou readest? Ver. 34. And *the eunuch answered Philip, and said, I pray thee, of whom speaketh the prophet this?* of himself, or of some other man? Luke x. 26. He said unto him, *What is written in the law? how readest thou?* Ver. 27. And he, answering, said, Thou shalt love the Lord thy God with all thy heart, and with all thy soul, and with all thy strength, and with all thy mind; and thy neighbour as thyself. Ver. 28. And he said unto him, Thou hast answered right: this do, and thou shalt live.

ᶠ Ps. i. 2. But his delight is in the law of the Lord; *and in his law doth he meditate day and night.* Ps. cxix. 97. O how love I thy law! it is my meditation all the day.

ᵍ 2 Chron. xxxiv. 21. *Go, enquire of the Lord for me,* and for them that are left in Israel and in Judah, *concerning the words of the book* that is found: for great is the wrath of the Lord that is poured out upon us, *because our fathers have not kept the word of the Lord,* to do after all that is written in this book.

ʰ Prov. iii. 5. Trust in the Lord with all thine heart; and *lean not unto thine own understanding.* Deut. xxxiii. 3. Yea, he loved the people; all his saints are in thy hand: and *they sat down at thy feet; every one shall receive of thy words.*

ⁱ Prov. ii. 1. My son, if thou wilt receive my words, and hide my commandments with thee; Ver. 2. So that thou incline thine ear unto wisdom, and apply thine heart to understanding; Ver. 3. Yea, *if thou criest after knowledge, and liftest up thy voice for understanding;* Ver. 4. If thou seekest her as silver, and searchest for her as for hid treasures; Ver. 5. Then shalt thou understand the fear of the Lord, and find the knowledge of God. Ver. 6. For the Lord giveth wisdom: out of his mouth cometh knowledge and understanding. Ps. cxix. 18. *Open thou mine eyes, that I may behold wondrous things out of thy law.* Neh. viii. 6. And *Ezra blessed the Lord, the great God: and all the people answered, Amen, Amen,* with lifting up their hands; and *they bowed their heads, and worshipped the Lord* with their faces to the ground. Ver. 8. *So they read in the book, in the law of God, distinctly,* &c.

158. ᵏ 1 Tim. iii. 2. *A bishop then must be blameless,* the husband of one wife, *vigilant, sober,* of *good behaviour,* given to hospitality, *apt to teach;* Ver. 6. Not a novice, lest, being lifted up with pride, he fall into the condemnation of the devil. Eph. iv. 8. Wherefore he saith, When he ascended up on high, he led captivity captive, *and gave gifts unto men.* Ver. 9. (Now that he ascended, what is it but that he also descended first into the lower parts of the earth? Ver. 10. He that descended is the same also that ascended up far above all heavens, that he might fill all things.) Ver. 11. And *he gave some, apostles;* and some, *prophets;* and some, *evangelists;* and some, *pastors* and *teachers.* Hosea iv. 6. My people are destroyed for lack of knowledge. *because thou hast rejected knowledge, I will also reject thee, that thou shalt be no priest to me:* seeing thou hast forgotten the law of thy God, I will also forget thy children. Mal. ii. 7. For *the priest's lips should keep knowledge, and they should seek the law at his mouth;* for he is the messenger of the Lord of hosts. 2 Cor. iii. 6. Who also hath *made us able*

Q. 159. *How is the word of God to be preached by those that are called thereunto?*

A. They that are called to labour in the ministry of the word, are to preach sound doctrine,^m diligently,ⁿ in season and out of season;^o plainly,^p not in the enticing words of man's wisdom, but in demonstration of the Spirit, and of power;^q faithfully,^r making known the whole counsel of God;^s wisely,^t applying themselves to the necessities and capacities of the hearers;^v zealously,^w with fervent love to God^x and the souls of his people;^y sincerely,^z

---

ministers of the new testament; not of the letter, but of the spirit: for the letter killeth, but the spirit giveth life.

l Jer. xiv. 15. Therefore thus saith the Lord concerning *the prophets that prophesy in my name,* and *I sent them not,* &c. Rom. x. 15. And *how shall they preach except they be sent?* Heb. v. 4. And *no man taketh this honour unto himself, but he that is called of God,* as was *Aaron.* 1 Cor. xii. 28. And *God hath set some in the church,* first, *apostles;* secondarily, *prophets;* thirdly, *teachers;* after that *miracles;* then *gifts of healings, helps, governments, diversities of tongues.* Ver. 29. Are all apostles? are all prophets? are all teachers? are all workers of miracles? 1 Tim. iii. 10. *And let these also first be proved;* then let them use the office of a deacon, being found blameless. 1 Tim. iv. 14. Neglect not *the gift that is in thee, which was given thee by prophecy, with the laying on of the hands of the presbytery.* 1 Tim. v. 22. *Lay hands suddenly on no man,* neither be partaker of other men's sins: keep thyself pure.

159. m Tit. ii. 1. But *speak thou the things which become sound doctrine.* Ver. 8. *Sound speech, that cannot be condemned;* that he that is of the contrary part may be ashamed, having no evil thing to say of you.

n Acts xviii. 25. This man was instructed in the way of the Lord; and, being fervent in the spirit, *he spake and taught diligently the things of the Lord,* &c.

o 2 Tim. iv. 2. Preach the word; *oe instant in season, out of season;* reprove, rebuke, exhort, with all long-suffering and doctrine.

p 1 Cor. xiv. 19. Yet in the church *I had rather speak five words with my understanding,* that by my voice I might teach others also, *than ten thousand words in an unknown tongue.*

q 1 Cor. ii. 4. And my speech and *my preaching was not with enticing words of man's wisdom,* but in demonstration of the Spirit, and of power.

r Jer. xxiii. 28. *The prophet* that hath a dream, let him tell a dream; and he that hath my word, *let him speak my word faithfully:* what is the chaff to the wheat? saith the Lord. 1 Cor. iv. 1. Let a man so account of us as of the ministers of Christ, and *stewards of the mysteries of God.* Ver. 2. Moreover, *it is required in stewards, that a man be found faithful.*

s Acts xx. 27. For I have not shunned to declare unto you *all the counsel of God.*

t Col. i. 28. Whom we preach, warning every man, and *teaching every man in all wisdom;* that we may present every man perfect in Christ Jesus. 2 Tim. ii. 15. Study to show thyself approved unto God, *a workman that needeth not to be ashamed, rightly dividing the word of truth.*

v 1 Cor. iii. 2. *I have fed you with milk, and not with meat:* for hitherto ye were not able to bear it, neither yet now are ye able. Heb. v. 12. For when for the time ye ought to be teachers, ye have need that one teach you again which be the first principles of the oracles of God; and are become *such as have need of milk, and not of strong meat.* Ver. 13. For every one that useth milk is unskilful in the word of righteousness; for he is a babe. Ver. 14. *But strong meat belongeth to them that are of full age,* even those who by reason of use have their senses exercised to discern both good and evil. Luke xii. 42. And the Lord said, *Who then is that faithful and wise steward,* whom his lord shall make ruler over his household, *to give them their portion of meat in due season?*

w Acts xviii. 25. This man was instructed in the way of the Lord; and, *being fervent in the spirit, he spake and taught diligently the things of the Lord,* &c.

x 2 Cor. v. 13. For whether we be beside ourselves, it is to God; or whether we be sober, it is for your cause. Ver. 14. *For the love of Christ constraineth us;* because we thus judge, that if one died for all, then were all dead. Phil. i. 15. Some indeed preach Christ even of envy and strife; and some also of good will. Ver. 16. The one preach Christ of contention, not sincerely, supposing to add affliction to my bonds; Ver. 17. *But the other of love,* knowing that I am set for the defence of the gospel.

y Col. iv. 12. Epaphras, who is one of you, a servant of Christ, saluteth you, always *labouring fervently for you in prayers, that ye may stand perfect and complete in all the will of God.* 2 Cor. xii. 15. And *I will very gladly spend and be spent* for you: though the more abundantly *I love you,* the less I be loved.

z 2 Cor. ii. 17. For we are not as many, which corrupt *the word of God: but as of sincerity, but as of God, in the sight of God speak we in Christ.* 2 Cor. iv. 2. But have renounced the hidden things of dishonesty, not walking in craftiness, *nor handling the word of God deceitfully;* but, by manifestation of the truth, *commending ourselves to every man's conscience in the sight of God.*

aiming at his glory,[a] and their conversion,[b] edification,[c] and salvation.[d]

Q. 160. *What is required of those that hear the word preached?*

A. It is required of those that hear the word preached, that they attend upon it with diligence,[e] preparation,[f] and prayer;[g] examine what they hear by the scriptures;[h] receive the truth with faith,[i] love,[k] meekness,[l] and readiness of mind,[m] as the word of God;[n] meditate,[o] and confer of it;[p] hide it in their hearts,[q] and bring forth the fruit of it in their lives.[r]

[a] 1 Thess. ii. 4. But as we were allowed of God to be put in trust with the gospel, even *so we speak; not as pleasing men, but God,* which trieth our hearts. Ver. 5. For neither at any time used we flattering words, as ye know, nor a cloak of covetousness; God is witness: Ver. 6. Nor of men sought we glory, neither of you, nor yet of others, when we might have been burdensome, as the apostles of Christ. John vii. 18. He that speaketh of himself seeketh his own glory: but *he that seeketh his glory that sent him, the same is true, and* no unrighteousness is in him.

[b] 1 Cor. ix. 19. For though I be free from all men, yet have I made myself servant unto all, *that I might gain the more.* Ver. 20. And unto the Jews I became as a Jew, *that I might gain the Jews;* to them that are under the law, as under the law, that I might *gain them that are under the law;* Ver. 21. To them that are without law, as without law, (being not without law to God, but under the law to Christ,) *that I might gain them that are without law.* Ver. 22. To the weak became I as weak, *that I might gain the weak:* I am *made all things to all men,* that I might *by all means save some.*

[c] 2 Cor. xii. 19. Again, think ye that we excuse ourselves unto you? we speak before God in Christ: but we *do all things,* dearly beloved, *for your edifying.* Eph. iv. 12. For the perfecting of the saints, for the work of the ministry, for *the edifying of the body of Christ.*

[d] 1 Tim. iv. 16. Take heed unto thyself, and unto the doctrine; continue in them: for in doing this thou shalt *both save thyself, and them that hear thee.* Acts xxvi. 16. But rise, and stand upon thy feet: for I have appeared unto thee for this purpose, *to make thee a minister* and a witness both of these things which thou hast seen, and of those things in the which I will appear unto thee; Ver. 17. Delivering thee from the people, and from the Gentiles, unto whom now I send thee, Ver. 18. *To open their eyes, and to turn them from darkness to light, and from the power of Satan unto God,* that they may receive *forgiveness of sins,* and *inheritance* among them which are sanctified by faith that is in me.

160. [e] Prov. viii. 34. Blessed is the man that heareth me, *watching daily at my gates, waiting at the posts of my doors.*

[f] 1 Pet. ii. 1. Wherefore, *laying aside all malice,* and all *guile,* and *hypocrisies,* and envies, and all *evil speakings,* Ver. 2. As new-born babes, *desire the sincere milk of the word,* that ye may grow thereby. Luke viii. 18. *Take heed therefore how ye hear;* for whosoever hath, to him shall be given; and whosoever hath not, from him shall be taken even that which he seemeth to have.

[g] Ps. cxix. 18. *Open thou mine eyes,* that I may behold wondrous things out of thy law. Eph. vi. 18. *Praying always with all prayer and supplication in the Spirit,* and watching thereunto with all perseverance and supplication for all saints; Ver. 19. And *for me, that utterance may be given unto me,* that I may open my mouth boldly, to make known the mystery of the gospel.

[h] Acts xvii. 11. These were *more noble* than those in Thessalonica, in that they received the word with all readiness of mind, *and searched the scriptures daily, whether those things were so.*

[i] Heb. iv. 2. For unto us was the gospel preached, as well as unto them: but *the word preached did not profit them, not being mixed with faith in them that heard it.*

[k] 2 Thess. ii. 10. And with all deceivableness of unrighteousness in them that perish; *because they received not the love of the truth,* that they might be saved.

[l] James i. 21. Wherefore, lay apart all filthiness, and superfluity of naughtiness, and *receive with meekness the ingrafted word,* which is able to save your souls.

[m] Acts xvii. 11. These were *more noble* than those in Thessalonica, in that *they received the word with all readiness of mind,* and searched the scriptures daily, whether those things were so.

[n] 1 Thess. ii. 13. For this cause also thank we God without ceasing, because, when ye received the word of God which ye heard of us, *ye received it not as the word of men, but (as it is in truth) the word of God,* which effectually worketh also in you that believe.

[o] Luke ix. 44. *Let these sayings sink down into your ears:* for the Son of man shall be delivered into the hands of men. * Heb. ii. 1. Therefore *we ought to give the more earnest heed to the things which we have heard,* lest at any time we should let them slip.

[p] Luke xxiv. 14. And *they talked together of all these things which had happened.* Deut. vi. 6. And *these words,* which I command thee this day, shall be in thine heart; Ver. 7. And thou shalt teach them diligently unto thy children, and *shalt talk of them* when thou sittest in thine house, and when thou walkest by the way, and when thou liest down, and when thou risest up.

[q] Prov. ii. 1. My son, if thou wilt receive my words, and *hide my commandments with*

Q. 161. *How do the sacraments become effectual means of salvation?*

A. The sacraments become effectual means of salvation, not by any power in themselves, or any virtue derived from the piety or intention of him by whom they are administered, but only by the working of the Holy Ghost, and the blessing of Christ, by whom they are instituted.[s]

Q. 162. *What is a sacrament?*

A. A sacrament is an holy ordinance instituted by Christ in his church,[t] to signify, seal, and exhibit[v] unto those that are within the covenant of grace,[w] the benefits of his mediation;[x] to strengthen and increase their faith, and all other graces;[y] to oblige them to obedience;[z] to testify and cherish their love and communion one with another;[a] and to distinguish them from those that are without.[b]

---

thee. Ps. cxix. 11. Thy word have *I hid in mine heart,* that I might not sin against thee.

r Luke viii. 15. But that on the good ground are they, which in an honest and good heart, having heard the word, *keep it, and bring forth fruit with patience.* James i. 25. But whoso looketh into the perfect law of liberty, and continueth therein, he being not a forgetful hearer, but a doer of the work, this man shall be blessed in his deed.

161. s 1 Pet. iii. 21. The like figure whereunto even baptism *doth also now save us, (not the putting away of the filth of the flesh,* but the answer of a good conscience toward God,) *by the resurrection of Jesus Christ.* Acts viii. 13. Then *Simon himself believed also;* and *when he was baptized,* he continued with Philip, and *wondered,* beholding the miracles and signs which were done. Compared with verse 23. For I perceive (said Peter to Simon) *that thou art in the gall of bitterness, and in the bond of iniquity.* 1 Cor. iii. 6. I have planted, Apollos watered; but *God gave the increase.* Ver. 7. So then *neither is he that planteth any thing, neither he that watereth;* but *God that giveth the increase.* 1 Cor. xii. 13. For by one *Spirit are we all baptized into one body,* whether we be Jews or Gentiles, whether we be bond or free; and have been all made to drink into one Spirit.

162. t Gen. xvii. 7. And *I will establish my covenant between me and thee, and thy seed after thee,* in their generations, *for an everlasting covenant,* to be a God unto thee, and to thy seed after thee. Ver. 10. *This is my covenant, which* ye shall keep, between me and you, and thy seed after thee; Every man-child among you shall be circumcised. Exod. chap. xii. Containing the institution of the passover. * Matt. xxviii. 19. *Go ye therefore, and teach all nations, baptizing them* in the name of the Father, and of the Son, and of the Holy Ghost. Matt. xxvi. 26. And as they were eating, *Jesus took bread, and blessed it, and brake it, and gave it to the disciples, and said, Take, eat; this is my body.* Ver. 27. And he took the cup, and gave thanks, and *gave it to them, saying, Drink ye all of it:* Ver. 28. For *this is my blood of the new testament,* which is shed for many for the remission of sins.

v Rom. iv. 11. And he received the sign of *circumcision, a seal of the righteousness of the faith which he had* yet being uncircumcised: that he might be the father of all them that believe, though they be not circumcised; that righteousness might be imputed unto them also. 1 Cor. xi. 24. And, when he had given thanks, he brake it, and said, Take, eat; *this is my body, which is broken for you: this do in remembrance of me.* Ver. 25. After the same manner also he took the cup, when he had supped, saying, *This cup is the new testament in my blood: this do ye,* as oft as ye drink it, *in remembrance of me.*

w Rom. xv. 8. Now I say, that Jesus Christ was a minister of the circumcision for the truth of God, *to confirm the promises made unto the fathers.* Exod. xii. 48. And when a stranger shall sojourn with thee, and will keep the *passover* to the Lord, *let all his males be circumcised, and then let him come near and keep it;* and he shall be as one that is born in the land: for *no uncircumcised person shall eat thereof.*

x Acts ii. 38. Then Peter said unto them, Repent, and *be baptized* every one of you in the name of Jesus Christ *for the remission of sins, and ye shall receive the gift of the Holy Ghost.* 1 Cor. x. 16. The *cup of blessing* which we bless, *is it not the communion of the blood of Christ?* the bread which we break, is it not the *communion of the body of Christ?*

y Rom. iv. 11. [See in v above.] Gal. iii. 27. For as many of you *as have been baptized into Christ have put on Christ.*

z Rom. vi. 3. Know ye not, that so many of us as were baptized into Jesus Christ *were baptized into his death?* Ver. 4. Therefore *we are buried with him by baptism into death;* that like as Christ was raised up from the dead by the glory of the Father, even so *we also should walk in newness of life.* 1 Cor. x. 21. Ye cannot *drink the cup of the Lord,* and *the cup of devils;* ye cannot *be partakers of the Lord's table, and of the table of devils*

a Eph. iv. 2. With all lowliness and meekness, with long-suffering, *forbearing one another in love;* Ver. 3. *Endeavouring to keep the unity of the Spirit in the bond of peace.* Ver. 4. There is *one body,* and *one Spirit,* even as ye are called in one hope of your calling; Ver. 5. *One Lord, one faith, one baptism.* 1 Cor. xii. 13. For *by one Spirit are we all baptized into one body,* whether we be Jews or Gentiles,

THE LARGER CATECHISM. 201

Q. 163. *What are the parts of a sacrament?*

A. The parts of a sacrament are two; the one an outward and sensible sign, used according to Christ's own appointment; the other an inward and spiritual grace thereby signified.[c]

Q. 164. *How many sacraments hath Christ instituted in his church under the New Testament?*

A. Under the New Testament Christ hath instituted in his church only two sacraments, baptism and the Lord's supper.[d]

Q. 165. *What is baptism?*

A. Baptism is a sacrament of the New Testament, wherein Christ hath ordained the washing with water in the name of the Father, and of the Son, and of the Holy Ghost,[e] to be a sign and seal of ingrafting into himself,[f] of remission of sins by his blood,[g] and regeneration by his Spirit;[h] of adoption,[i] and resurrection unto everlasting life;[k] and whereby the parties baptized are solemnly admitted into the visible church,[l] and enter into an open and professed engagement to be wholly and only the Lord's.[m]

Q. 166. *Unto whom is baptism to be administered?*

A. Baptism is not to be administered to any that are out of the visible church, and so strangers from the covenant of promise, till they profess their faith in Christ, and obedience to him,[n] but infants

whether we be bond or free; and have been all made to drink into one Spirit.
b Eph. ii. 11. Wherefore remember, that ye *being in time past Gentiles in the flesh*, who are called Uncircumcision by that which is called the Circumcision in the flesh made by hands; Ver. 12. *That at that time ye were without Christ, being aliens from the commonwealth of Israel, and strangers from the covenants of promise, having no hope*, and *without God in the world*. Gen. xxxiv. 14. And they said unto them, *We cannot do this thing, to give our sister to one that is uncircumcised; for that were a reproach unto us.*
163. c Matt. iii. 11. I indeed *baptize you with water unto repentance:* but he that cometh after me is mightier than I, whose shoes I am not worthy to bear: *he shall baptize you with the Holy Ghost, and with fire.* 1 Pet. iii. 21. The like figure whereunto *even baptism* doth also now save us, (*not the putting away of the filth* of the flesh, but *the answer of a good conscience toward God,*) *by the resurrection of Jesus Christ.* Rom. ii. 28. For he is not a Jew which is one *outwardly; neither is that circumcision which is outward in the flesh:* Ver. 29. But he is a Jew which is one *inwardly:* and *circumcision is that of the heart,* in the *spirit,* and not in the *letter;* whose praise is not of men, but of God.
164. d Matt. xxviii. 19. Go ye therefore, and teach all nations, *baptizing them* in the name of the Father, and of the Son, and of the Holy Ghost. 1 Cor. xi. 20. When ye come together therefore into one place, this is not *to eat the Lord's supper.* Ver. 23. For I have received of the Lord that which also I delivered unto you, *That the Lord Jesus, the same night in which he was betrayed, took bread.* Matt. xxvi. 26, 27, 28. [See above in t.]

165. e Matt. xxviii. 19. Go ye therefore, and teach all nations, *baptizing them in the name of the Father, and of the Son, and of the Holy Ghost.*
f Gal. iii. 27. For *as many of you as have been baptized into Christ have put on Christ.*
g Mark i. 4. John did baptize in the wilderness, and preach the *baptism of repentance for the remission of sins.* Rev. i. 5. Unto him that loved us, and *washed us from our sins in his own blood.*
h Tit. iii. 5. Not by works of righteousness which we have done, but according to his mercy he saved us, *by the washing of regeneration, and renewing of the Holy Ghost.* Eph. v. 26. That he might *sanctify and cleanse it with the washing of water by the word.*
i Gal. iii. 26. For *ye are all the children of God by faith in Christ Jesus.* Ver. 27. For as many of you *as have been baptized into Christ have put on Christ.*
k 1 Cor. xv. 29. Else what shall they do which are *baptized for the dead, if the dead rise not at all?* why are they then baptized for the dead? Rom. vi. 5. For if we have been *planted together in the likeness of his death,* we shall be also *in the likeness of his resurrection.*
l 1 Cor. xii. 13. For by one Spirit are we *all baptized into one body,* whether we be Jews or Gentiles, whether we be bond or free; and have been all made to drink into one Spirit.
m Rom. vi. 4. Therefore *we are buried with him by baptism into death;* that like as Christ was raised up from the dead by the glory of the Father, even *so we also should walk in newness of life.*
166. n Acts viii. 36. And as they went on their way they came unto a certain **water:** and the eunuch said, See, here is **water;** what doth hinder me to be baptized?

descending from parents, either both, or but one of them, professing faith in Christ, and obedience to him, are in that respect within the covenant, and to be baptized.º

Q. 167. *How is our baptism to be improved by us?*

A. The needful but much neglected duty of improving our baptism, is to be performed by us all our life long, especially in the time of temptation, and when we are present at the administration of it to others;ᵖ by serious and thankful consideration of the nature of it, and of the ends for which Christ instituted it, the privileges and benefits conferred and sealed thereby, and our solemn vow made therein;ᵠ by being humbled for our sinful defilement, our falling short of, and walking contrary to, the grace of baptism, and our engagements;ʳ by growing up to assurance of pardon of sin, and of all other blessings

---

Ver. 37. And Philip said, *If thou believest with all thine heart, thou mayest.* And he answered and said, I believe that Jesus Christ is the Son of God. Acts ii. 38. Then Peter said unto them, *Repent, and be baptized* every one of you in the name of Jesus Christ for the remission of sins, and ye shall receive the gift of the Holy Ghost.

º Gen. xvii. 7. And I will establish *my covenant between me and thee, and thy seed after thee* in their generations, for an everlasting covenant, *to be a God unto thee, and to thy seed after thee.* Ver. 9. And God said unto Abraham, Thou shalt *keep my covenant therefore, thou, and thy seed after thee,* in their generations. Compared with Gal. iii. 9. So then they which be of faith are blessed with faithful Abraham. Ver. 14. *That the blessing of Abraham might come on the Gentiles through Jesus Christ;* that we might receive the promise of the Spirit through faith. And with Col. ii. 11. *In whom also ye are circumcised* with the circumcision made without hands, in putting off the body of the sins of the flesh *by the circumcision of Christ;* Ver. 12. *Buried with him in baptism,* wherein also ye are risen with him through the faith of the operation of God, who hath raised him from the dead. And with Acts ii. 38. Then Peter said unto them, Repent, *and be baptized* every one of you in the name of Jesus Christ for the remission of sins, and ye shall receive the gift of the Holy Ghost. Ver. 39. For *the promise is unto you, and to your children,* and to all that are afar off, even as many as the Lord our God shall call. And with Rom. iv. 11. And he received *the sign of circumcision, a seal of the righteousness of the faith* which he had yet being uncircumcised: that he might be the father of all them that believe, though they be not circumcised; that righteousness might be imputed unto them also: Ver. 12. And the *father of circumcision to them who are not of the circumcision only, but who also walk in the steps of that faith of our father Abraham,* which he had being yet uncircumcised. 1 Cor. vii. 14. For the *unbelieving husband is sanctified by the wife,* and the *unbelieving wife is sanctified by the husband: else were your children unclean; but now are they holy.* Matt. xxviii. 19. Go ye therefore, and *teach all nations, baptizing them* in the name of the Father, and of the Son, and of the Holy Ghost. Luke xviii. 15. And *they brought unto him also infants,* that he would touch them: but when his disciples saw it, they rebuked them. Ver. 16. But *Jesus called them unto him, and said, Suffer little children to come unto me, and forbid them not: for of such is the kingdom of God.* Rom. xi. 16. For *if the first fruit be holy, the lump is also holy; and if the root be holy, so are the branches.*

167. ᵖ Col. ii. 11. In whom also ye are circumcised with the circumcision made without hands, *in putting off the body of the sins of the flesh by the circumcision of Christ;* Ver. 12. *Buried with him in baptism, wherein also ye are risen with him through the faith* of the operation of God, who hath raised him from the dead. Rom. vi. 4. *Therefore we are buried with him by baptism into death; that* like as Christ was raised up from the dead by the glory of the Father, *even so we also should walk in newness of life.* Ver. 6. Knowing this, that *our old man is crucified with him,* that the *body of sin might be destroyed, that henceforth we should not serve sin.* Ver. 11. Likewise *reckon ye also yourselves to be dead indeed unto sin,* but *alive unto God* through Jesus Christ our Lord.

ᵠ Rom. vi. 3. Know ye not, that so many of us as were baptized into Jesus Christ *were baptized into his death?* Ver. 4. *Therefore we are buried with him by baptism into death;* that like as Christ was raised up from the dead by the glory of the Father, *even so we also should walk in newness of life.* Ver. 5. For if we have been planted together in the likeness of his death, we shall be also in the likeness of his resurrection.

ʳ 1 Cor. i. 11. For it hath been declared unto me of you, my brethren, by them which are of the house of Chloe, that there are *contentions among you.* Ver. 12. Now this I say, that every one of you saith, I am of Paul, and I of Apollos, and I of Cephas, and I of Christ. Ver. 13. Is Christ divided? was Paul crucified for you? or *were ye baptized in the name of Paul?* Rom. vi. 2. *God forbid. How shall we, that are dead to sin, live any longer therein?* Ver. 3. Know ye not, that so many of us as were baptized into Jesus Christ were *baptized into his death?*

sealed to us in that sacrament;[s] by drawing strength from the death and resurrection of Christ, into whom we are baptized, for the mortifying of sin, and quickening of grace;[t] and by endeavouring to live by faith,[v] to have our conversation in holiness and righteousness,[w] as those that have therein given up their names to Christ;[x] and to walk in brotherly love, as being baptized by the same Spirit into one body.[y]

Q. 168. *What is the Lord's supper?*

A. The Lord's supper is a sacrament of the New Testament,[z] wherein, by giving and receiving bread and wine according to the appointment of Jesus Christ, his death is shewed forth; and they that worthily communicate feed upon his body and blood, to their spiritual nourishment and growth in grace;[a] have their union and communion with him confirmed;[b] testify and renew their thankfulness,[c] and engagement to God,[d] and their mutual love and fellowship each with other, as members of the same mystical body.[o]

Q. 169. *How hath Christ appointed bread and wine to be given and received in the sacrament of the Lord's supper?*

A. Christ hath appointed the ministers of his word, in the administration of this sacrament of the Lord's supper, to set apart the bread and wine from common use, by the word of institution, thanksgiving, and prayer; to take and break the bread, and to give both the

[s] Rom. iv. 11. And he received the sign of *circumcision, a seal of the righteousness of the faith* which he had yet being uncircumcised: that he might be *the father of all them that believe,* though they be not circumcised; *that righteousness might be imputed unto them also:* Ver. 12. And the father of circumcision to them who are not of the circumcision only, but who also walk in the steps of that faith of our father Abraham, which he had being yet uncircumcised. 1 Pet. iii. 21. The like figure whereunto *even baptism doth also now save us,* (not the putting away of the filth of the flesh, but *the answer of a good conscience toward God,*) by the resurrection of Jesus Christ.

[t] Rom. vi. 3, 4, 5. [See above in q.]

[v] Gal. iii. 26. *For ye are all the children of God by faith in Christ Jesus.* Ver. 27. For as many of you as have been *baptized into Christ have put on Christ.*

[w] Rom. vi. 22. *But now, being made free from sin,* and become servants to God, ye *have your fruit unto holiness,* and the end everlasting life.

[x] Acts ii. 38. Then Peter said unto them, Repent, *and be baptized every one of you in the name of Jesus Christ* for the remission of sins, and ye shall receive the gift of the Holy Ghost.

[y] 1 Cor. xii. 13. *For by one Spirit are we all baptized into one body,* whether we be Jews or Gentiles, whether we be bond or free; and have been all made to drink into one Spirit. Ver. 25. *That there should be no schism in the body; but that the members should have the same care one for another.* Ver. 26. And whether *one member suffer, all the members suffer with it;* or *one member be honoured, all the members rejoice with it.* Ver. 27. Now ye are the body of Christ, and members in particular.

168. [z] Luke xxii. 20. Likewise also the cup after supper, saying, *This cup is the new testament in my blood,* which is shed for you.

[a] Matt. xxvi. 26. And as they were eating, *Jesus took bread,* and blessed it, and brake it, and *gave it to the disciples,* and said, *Take, eat: this is my body.* Ver. 27. And he *took the cup,* and gave thanks, and *gave it to them,* saying, *Drink ye all of it:* Ver. 28. For *this is my blood of the new testament,* which is shed for many for the remission of sins. 1 Cor. xi. 23. For *I have received of the Lord* that which also *I delivered* unto you, That *the Lord Jesus,* the same night in which he was betrayed, *took bread:* Ver. 24. And, when he had given thanks, he brake it, and said, *Take, eat; this is my body, which is broken for you: this do in remembrance of me.* Ver. 25. After the same manner also *he took the cup,* when he had supped, saying, *This cup is the new testament in my blood: this do ye,* as oft as ye drink it, *in remembrance of me.* Ver. 26. For as often as ye eat this *bread,* and drink this *cup, ye do shew the Lord's death till he come.*

[b] 1 Cor. x. 16. The *cup of blessing* which we bless, *is it not the communion of the blood of Christ?* the *bread* which we break, *is it not the communion of the body of Christ?*

[c] 1 Cor. xi. 24. [See above in a.]

[d] 1 Cor. x. 14. Wherefore, my dearly beloved, flee from idolatry. Ver. 15. I speak as to wise men; judge ye what I say. Ver. 16. The *cup of blessing* which we bless, is it not *the communion of the blood of Christ?* the *bread* which we break, is it not *the communion of the body of Christ?* Ver. 21. *Ye cannot drink the cup of the Lord, and the cup of devils; ye* cannot be *partakers of the Lord's table,* and of the *table of devils.*

[e] 1 Cor. x. 17. For we, *being many, are*

bread and the wine to the communicants: who are, by the same appointment, to take and eat the bread, and to drink the wine, in thankful remembrance that the body of Christ was broken and given, and his blood shed, for them.^f

Q. 170. *How do they that worthily communicate in the Lord's supper feed upon the body and blood of Christ therein?*

A. As the body and blood of Christ are not corporally or carnally present in, with, or under the bread and wine in the Lord's supper,^g and yet are spiritually present to the faith of the receiver, no less truly and really than the elements themselves are to their outward senses;^h so they that worthily communicate in the sacrament of the Lord's supper, do therein feed upon the body and blood of Christ, not after a corporal and carnal, but in a spiritual manner; yet truly and really,ⁱ while by faith they receive and apply unto themselves Christ crucified, and all the benefits of his death.^k

Q. 171. *How are they that receive the sacrament of the Lord's supper to prepare themselves before they come unto it?*

A. They that receive the sacrament of the Lord's supper are, before they come, to prepare themselves thereunto, by examining themselves^l of their being in Christ,^m of their sins and wants;ⁿ of the truth and measure of their knowledge,^o faith,^p repentance;^q love to God and

one bread, and one body: for we are all partakers of that one bread.
109. f 1 Cor. xi. 23, 24. [See before under r.] Matt. xxvi. 26, 27, 28. [See before at s.] Mark xiv. 22. And as they did eat, *Jesus took bread,* and *blessed,* and *brake it,* and *gave to them,* and said, *Take, eat: this is my body.* Ver. 23. And he *took the cup,* and when he had given thanks, he *gave it to them;* and they *all drank of it.* Ver. 24. And he said unto them, This is my blood of the new testament, which is shed for many. Luke xxii. 19. And he *took bread,* and *gave thanks,* and *brake it,* and *gave unto them,* saying, This is my body, which is given for you: *this do in remembrance of me.* Ver. 20. Likewise also the cup after supper, saying, *This cup is the new testament in my blood,* which is shed for you.
170. g Acts iii. 21. *Whom the heaven must receive until the times of restitution of all things,* which God hath spoken by the mouth of all his holy prophets since the world began.
h Matt. xxvi. 26. And as they were eating, Jesus took bread, and blessed it, and brake it, and gave it to the disciples, and said, Take, eat; *this is my body.* Ver. 28. For *this is my blood of the new testament,* which *is shed for many* for the remission of sins.
i 1 Cor. xi. 24. And, when he had given thanks, he brake it, and said, *Take, eat; this is my body,* which is broken for you: this do in remembrance of me. Ver. 25. After the same manner also he took the cup, when he had supped, saying, *This cup is the new testament in my blood:* this do ye, as oft as ye drink it, in remembrance of me. Ver. 26. For as often as ye eat this bread, and drink this cup, ye do shew the Lord's death till he come. Ver. 27. Wherefore, *whosoever shall eat this bread, and drink this cup of the Lord, unworthily,* shall be *guilty of the body and blood of the Lord.* Ver. 28. But let a man examine himself, and so let him eat of that bread, and drink of that cup. Ver. 29. For he that eateth and drinketh unworthily, eateth and drinketh damnation to himself, *not discerning the Lord's body.*
k 1 Cor. x. 16. The *cup of blessing* which we bless, *is it not the communion of the blood of Christ?* the *bread* which we break, *is it not the communion of the body of Christ?*
171. l 1 Cor. xi. 28. But let *a man examine himself,* and so let him eat of that bread, and drink of that cup.
m 2 Cor. xiii. 5 *Examine yourselves, whether ye be in the faith;* prove your own selves : *know ye not your own selves, how that Jesus Christ is in you, except ye be reprobates?*
n 1 Cor. v. 7. *Purge out therefore the old leaven,* that ye may be a new lump, as ye are unleavened. For even Christ our passover is sacrificed for us. Compared with Exod. xii. 15. *Seven days shall ye eat unleavened bread;* even *the first day ye shall put away leaven out of your houses:* for whosoever eateth leavened bread, from the first day until the seventh day, that soul shall be cut off from Israel.
o 1 Cor. xi. 29. For he that eateth and drinketh unworthily, *eateth and drinketh damnation* to himself, *not discerning the Lord's body.*
p 1 Cor. xiii. 5. [See above in letter m.] Matt. xxvi. 28. For this is my blood of the new testament, which is shed for many for the remission of sins.
q Zech. xii. 10. And I will pour upon the house of David, and upon the inhabitants of Jerusalem, the spirit of grace and of supplications; and *they shall look upon me whom they have pierced,* and *they shall*

the brethren,ʳ charity to all men,ˢ forgiving those that have done them wrong;ᵗ of their desires after Christ,ᵛ and of their new obedience;ʷ and by renewing the exercise of these graces,ˣ by serious meditation,ʸ and fervent prayer.ᶻ

Q. 172. *May one who doubteth of his being in Christ, or of his due preparation, come to the Lord's supper?*

A. One who doubteth of his being in Christ, or of his due preparation to the sacrament of the Lord's supper, may have true interest in Christ, though he be not yet assured thereof;ᵃ and in God's account hath it, if he be duly affected with the apprehension of the want of

---

mourn *for him*, as one mourneth for his only son, and shall be in bitterness for him, as one that is in bitterness for his first-born. 1 Cor. xi. 31. For if *we would judge ourselves*, we should not be *judged*.

ʳ 1 Cor. x. 16. The *cup of blessing* which we bless, is it not *the communion of the blood of Christ?* the *bread which we break*, is it not *the communion of the body of Christ?* Ver. 17. *For we, being many, are one bread, and one body:* for we are all partakers of that one bread. Acts ii. 46. And they, continuing daily *with one accord* in the temple, and *breaking bread from house to house*, did eat their meat with gladness and *singleness of heart*, Ver. 47. *Praising God*, and having favour with all the people. And the Lord added to the church daily such as should be saved.

ˢ 1 Cor. v. 8. Therefore *let us keep the feast*, not with old leaven, *neither with the leaven of malice and wickedness; but with the unleavened bread of sincerity and truth.* 1 Cor. xi. 18. For first of all, *when ye come together in the church*, I hear that there be divisions among you; and I partly believe it. Ver. 20. When ye come together therefore into one place, *this is not to eat the Lord's supper.*

ᵗ Matt. v. 23. Therefore, if thou bring *thy gift to the altar*, and there rememberest that thy *brother* hath ought against thee; Ver. 24. Leave there thy gift before the altar, and go thy way; *first be reconciled to thy brother, and then come and offer thy gift.*

ᵛ Isa. lv. 1. Ho, every one *that thirsteth*, come ye to the waters, and he that hath no money: come ye, buy and eat; yea, come, buy wine and milk without money, and without price. John vii. 37. In the last day, that great day of the feast, Jesus stood and cried, saying, *If any man thirst*, let him come unto me, and drink.

ʷ 1 Cor. v. 7. Purge out therefore *the old leaven*, that ye may be a *new lump*, as ye are unleavened. *For even Christ our passover is sacrificed for us;* Ver. 8. Therefore, *let us keep the feast, not with old leaven*, neither with the leaven of malice and wickedness; but *with the unleavened bread of sincerity and truth.*

ˣ 1 Cor. xi. 25. After the same manner also he took the cup, when he had supped, saying, This cup is the new testament in my blood : *this do ye, as oft as ye drink it, in remembrance of me.* Ver. 26. For as *often as* ye eat this bread, and drink this cup, ye *do shew the Lord's death* till he come.

Ver. 28. But *let a man examine himself*, and so let him eat of that bread, and drink of that cup. Heb. x. 21. And having an high priest over the house of God ; Ver. 22. *Let us draw near with a true heart, in full assurance of faith*, having our *hearts sprinkled from an evil conscience*, and our *bodies washed with pure water.* Ver. 24. And let us *consider one another, to provoke unto love and to good works.* Ps. xxvi. 6. *I will wash mine hands in innocency: so will I compass thine altar, O Lord.*

ʸ 1 Cor. xi. 24. And, when he had given thanks, he brake it, and said, Take, eat; this is my body, which is broken for you: *this do in remembrance of me.* Ver. 25. After the same manner also he took the cup, when he had supped, saying, This cup is the new testament in my blood : *this do ye, as oft as ye drink it, in remembrance of me.*

ᶻ 2 Chron. xxx. 18. For a multitude of the people, even many of Ephraim, and Manasseh, Issachar, and Zebulun, had not cleansed themselves, yet did *they eat the passover* otherwise than it was written : but *Hezekiah prayed for them*, saying, The good Lord pardon every one Ver. 19. That prepareth his heart to seek God, the Lord God of his fathers, though he be not cleansed according to the purification of the sanctuary. Matt. xxvi. 26. And as they were eating, *Jesus* took bread, *and blessed it*, and brake it, and gave it to the disciples, and said, Take, eat ; this is my body.

172. ᵃ Isa. l. 10. Who is among you that feareth the Lord, that obeyeth the voice of his servant, *that walketh in darkness, and hath no light ? let him trust in the name of the Lord, and stay upon his God.* 1 John v. 13. These things have I written *unto you that believe* on the name of the Son of God, *that ye may know that ye have eternal life*, and *that ye may believe* on the name of the Son of God. Ps. lxxxviii. throughout. Ps. lxxvii. to verse 12. Ver. 1. I cried unto God with my voice, even unto God with my voice ; and he gave ear unto me. Ver. 2. In the day of my trouble I sought the Lord : my sore ran in the night, and ceased not : my soul refused to be comforted. Ver. 3. I remembered God, *and was troubled:* I complained, and *my spirit was overwhelmed.* Selah. Ver. 4. *Thou holdest mine eyes waking:* I am so troubled that I cannot speak, &c. Ver. 7. *Will the Lord cast off for ever ?* and *will he be favourable no more ?* Ver. 8. *Is his mercy clean gone for ever ?* doth *his promise fail for evermore ?* Ver. 9.

it,[b] and unfeignedly desires to be found in Christ,[c] and to depart from iniquity:[d] in which case (because promises are made, and this sacrament is appointed, for the relief even of weak and doubting Christians [e]) he is to bewail his unbelief,[f] and labour to have his doubts resolved;[g] and, so doing, he may and ought to come to the Lord's supper, that he may be further strengthened.[h]

Q. 173. *May any who profess the faith, and desire to come to the Lord's supper, be kept from it?*

A. Such as are found to be ignorant or scandalous, notwithstanding their profession of the faith, and desire to come to the Lord's sup-

---

Hath God *forgotten to be gracious?* hath he *in anger shut up his tender mercies?* Ver. 10. And I said, *This is my infirmity:* but I will remember the years of the right hand of the Most High. Jonah ii. 4. Then I said, *I am cast out of thy sight;* yet I will look again toward thy holy temple. Ver. 7. When *my soul fainted within me* I remembered the Lord; and my prayer came in unto thee, into thine holy temple.

[b] Isa. liv. 7. For *a small moment have I forsaken thee;* but *with great mercies will I gather thee.* Ver. 8. In a little wrath *I hid my face* from thee for a moment; but with everlasting kindness *will I have mercy on thee, saith the Lord thy Redeemer.* Ver. 9. For this is as the waters of Noah unto me ; for as I have sworn that the waters of Noah should no more go over the earth ; so have I sworn that I would not be wroth with thee, nor rebuke thee. Ver. 10. For the mountains shall depart, and the hills be removed ; but *my kindness shall not depart from thee, neither shall the covenant of my peace be removed,* saith the Lord that hath mercy on thee. Matt. v. 3. *Blessed are the poor in spirit;* for theirs is the kingdom of heaven. Ver. 4. *Blessed are they that mourn;* for they shall be comforted. Ps. xxxi. 22. For *I said in my haste, I am cut off from before thine eyes; nevertheless thou heardest the voice of my supplications* when I cried unto thee. Ps. lxxiii. 13. *Verily I have cleansed my heart in vain,* and washed my hands in innocency. Ver. 22. *So foolish was I, and ignorant:* I was as a beast before thee. Ver. 23. *Nevertheless I am continually with thee; thou hast holden me by my right hand.*

[c] Phil. iii. 8. Yea doubtless, and I count all things but loss for the excellency of the knowledge of Christ Jesus my Lord : for whom I have suffered the loss of all things, and *do count them but dung, that I may win Christ,* Ver. 9. *And be found in him,* not having mine own righteousness, which is of the law, but that which is through the faith of Christ, the righteousness which is of God by faith. Ps. x. 17. Lord, *thou hast heard the desire of the humble;* thou wilt prepare their heart, thou wilt cause thine ear to hear. *Ps. xlii. 1. As the hart panteth after the water-brooks, so panteth my soul after thee, O God. Ver. 2. My soul thirsteth for God, for the living God : when shall I come and appear before God? Ver. 5. Why art thou cast down, O my soul? and why art thou disquieted in me? hope thou in God;* for I shall yet praise him for the help of his countenance. Ver. 11. *Why art thou cast down, O my soul?* and why art thou disquieted within me ? *hope thou in God; for I shall yet praise him,* who is the health of my countenance, and my God.

[d] 2 Tim. ii. 19. Nevertheless the foundation of God standeth sure, having this seal, The Lord knoweth them that are his. And, *Let every one that nameth the name of Christ depart from iniquity.* Isa. l. 10. Who is among you *that feareth the Lord, that obeyeth the voice of his servant,* that walketh in darkness, and hath no light? *let him trust in the name of the Lord,* and stay upon his God. Ps. lxvi. 18. *If I regard iniquity in my heart, the Lord will not hear me;* Ver. 19. But verily *God hath heard me;* he hath attended to the voice of my prayer. Ver. 20. Blessed be God, which hath not turned away my prayer, nor his mercy from me.

[e] Isa. xl. 11. He shall feed his flock like a shepherd ; *he shall gather the lambs with his arm, and carry them in his bosom,* and shall *gently lead those that are with young.* Ver. 29. *He giveth power to the faint; and to them that have no might he increaseth strength.* Ver. 31. But *they that wait upon the Lord shall renew their strength;* they shall mount up with wings as eagles ; they shall run, and not be weary ; and they shall walk, and not faint. Matt. xi. 28. *Come unto me, all ye that labour and are heavy laden, and I will give you rest.* Matt. xii. 20. *A bruised reed shall he not break, and smoking flax shall he not quench,* till he send forth judgment unto victory. Matt. xxvi. 28. For this is *my blood of the new testament,* which is *shed for many for the remission of sins.*

[f] Mark ix. 24. And straightway the father of the child cried out, and said with tears, Lord, *I believe; help thou mine unbelief.*

[g] Acts ii. 37. Now when they heard this, they were pricked in their heart, and said unto Peter, and to the rest of the apostles, *Men and brethren, what shall we do?* Acts xvi. 30. And brought them out, and said, *Sirs, what must I do to be saved?*

[h] Rom. iv. 11. And he received *the sign of circumcision, a seal of the righteousness of the faith which he had yet being uncircumcised:* that he might be the father of all them that believe, though they be not circumcised ; that righteousness might be imputed unto them also. 1 Cor. xi. 28. But *let a man examine himself, and so let him eat* of that *bread,* and drink of that *cup.*

per, may and ought to be kept from that sacrament, by the power which Christ hath left in his church,[i] until they receive instruction, and manifest their reformation.[k]

Q. 174. *What is required of them that receive the sacrament of the Lord's supper in the time of the administration of it?*

A. It is required of them that receive the sacrament of the Lord's supper, that, during the time of the administration of it, with all holy reverence and attention they wait upon God in that ordinance,[l] diligently observe the sacramental elements and actions,[m] heedfully discern the Lord's body,[n] and affectionately meditate on his death and sufferings,[o] and thereby stir up themselves to a vigorous exercise of their graces;[p] in judging themselves,[q] and sorrowing for sin;[r] in earnest hungering and thirsting after Christ,[s] feeding on him by faith,[t] receiving of his fulness,[v] trusting in his merits,[w] rejoicing in his

---

173. [i] 1 Cor. xi. 27. to the end. Wherefore, *whosoever shall eat this bread, and drink this cup of the Lord, unworthily, shall be guilty of the body and blood of the Lord.* Ver. 28. *But let a man examine himself,* and so let him eat of that bread, and drink of that cup. Ver. 29. For he that eateth and drinketh *unworthily,* eateth and drinketh damnation to himself, *not discerning the Lord's body.* Ver. 30. *For this cause many are weak and sickly among you,* and many sleep. Ver. 31. For *if we would judge ourselves, we should not be judged,* &c., to the end of the chapter. Compared with Matt. vii. 6. *Give not that which is holy unto the dogs, neither cast ye your pearls before swine,* lest they trample them under their feet, and turn again and rend you. And with 1 Cor. chapter v. to the end. And with Jude, ver. 23. And *others save with fear, pulling them out of the fire;* hating even the garment spotted by the flesh. And with 1 Tim. v. 22. *Lay hands suddenly on no man, neither be partaker of other men's sins: keep thyself pure.*

[k] 2 Cor. ii. 7. So that contrariwise *ye ought rather to forgive him, and comfort him, lest perhaps such an one should be swallowed up with over-much sorrow.*

174. [l] Lev. x. 3. Then Moses said unto Aaron, This is it that the Lord spake, saying, *I will be sanctified in them that come nigh me,* and before all the people I will be glorified. Heb. xii. 28. Wherefore, we receiving a kingdom which cannot be moved, let us have grace, whereby we may *serve God acceptably with reverence and godly fear.* Ps. v. 7. But as for me, I will come into thy house in the multitude of thy mercy; and *in thy fear will I worship toward thy holy temple.* 1 Cor. xi. 17. Now in this that I declare unto you I praise you not, *that ye come together not for the better, but for the worse.* Ver. 26. For as often as ye eat this bread, and drink this cup, ye do shew the Lord's death till he come. Ver. 27. Wherefore, *whosoever shall eat this bread, and drink this cup of the Lord, unworthily, shall be guilty* of the body and blood of the Lord.

[m] Exod. xxiv. 8. And Moses took the blood, and sprinkled it on the people, and said, *Behold the blood of the covenant,* which the Lord hath made with you concerning all these words. Compared with Matt. xxvi. 28. For *this is my blood of the new testament,* which is shed for many for the remission of sins.

[n] 1 Cor. xi. 29. For he that eateth and drinketh *unworthily,* eateth and drinketh damnation to himself, *not discerning the Lord's body.*

[o] Luke xxii. 19. And he took bread, and gave thanks, and brake it, and gave unto them, saying, This is my body, which is given for you: *this do in remembrance of me.*

[p] 1 Cor. xi. 26. For as often as ye eat this bread, and drink this cup, *ye do shew the Lord's death till he come.* 1 Cor. x. 3. And did *all eat the same spiritual meat;* Ver. 4. And did *all drink the same spiritual drink;* (for they drank of that *spiritual Rock* that followed them; and *that Rock was Christ:*) Ver. 5. But with many of them God was *not well pleased;* for they were overthrown in the wilderness. Ver. 11. Now all *these things happened unto them for ensamples:* and they are written for our admonition, upon whom the ends of the world are come. Ver. 14. *Wherefore,* my dearly beloved, *flee from idolatry.*

[q] 1 Cor. xi. 31. For if we would *judge ourselves,* we should not be judged.

[r] Zech. xii. 10. And I will pour upon the house of David, and upon the inhabitants of Jerusalem, the spirit of grace and of supplications; and *they shall look upon me whom they have pierced, and they shall mourn for him,* as one mourneth for his only son, and shall *be in bitterness* for him, as one that is in bitterness for his first-born.

[s] Rev. xxii. 17. And the Spirit and the bride say, Come. And let him that heareth say, Come. And *let him that is athirst come.* And whosoever will, let him take the water of life freely.

[t] John vi. 35. And *Jesus* said unto them, *I am the bread of life: he that cometh to me shall never hunger; and he that believeth on me shall never thirst.*

[v] John i. 16. And *of his fulness have all we received,* and grace for grace.

[w] Phil. iii. 9. And be found in him, not having mine own righteousness, which is of the law, but *that which is through the faith of Christ, the righteousness which is of God by faith.*

love,[x] giving thanks for his grace;[y] in renewing of their covenant with God,[z] and love to all the saints.[a]

Q. 175. *What is the duty of Christians, after they have received the sacrament of the Lord's supper?*

A. The duty of Christians, after they have received the sacrament of the Lord's supper, is seriously to consider how they have behaved themselves therein, and with what success;[b] if they find quickening and comfort, to bless God for it,[c] beg the continuance of it,[d] watch against relapses,[e] fulfil their vows,[f] and encourage themselves to a frequent attendance on that ordinance:[g] but if they find no present benefit, more exactly to review their preparation to, and carriage at, the sacrament;[h] in both which, if they can approve themselves to

---

[x] Ps. lxiii. 4. *Thus will I bless thee while I live:* I will lift up my hands in thy name. Ver. 5. *My soul shall be satisfied as with marrow and fatness; and my mouth shall praise thee with joyful lips.* 2 Chron. xxx. 21. And the children of Israel, that were present at Jerusalem, *kept the feast of unleavened bread* seven days *with great gladness:* and the Levites and the priests praised the Lord day by day, *singing with loud instruments unto the Lord.*

[y] Ps. xxii. 26. *The meek shall eat and be satisfied; they shall praise the Lord* that seek him: your heart shall live for ever.

[z] Jer. l. 5. They shall ask the way to Zion, with their faces thitherward, saying, *Come, and let us join ourselves to the Lord in a perpetual covenant* that shall not be forgotten. Ps. l. 5. Gather my saints together unto me; *those that have made a covenant with me by sacrifice.*

[a] Acts ii. 42. And they *continued stedfastly* in the *apostles' doctrine and fellowship,* and in breaking of bread, and in prayers.

175. [b] Ps. xxviii. 7. The Lord is my strength and my shield; *my heart trusted in him, and I am helped:* therefore my heart greatly rejoiceth; and with my song will I praise him. Ps. lxxxv. 8. *I will hear what God the Lord will speak:* for he will speak peace unto his people, and to his saints; but let them not turn again to folly. 1 Cor. xi. 17. Now in this that I declare unto you I praise you not, *that ye come together not for the better, but for the worse.* Ver. 30. For this cause many are weak and sickly among you, and many sleep. Ver. 31. For *if we would judge ourselves,* we should not be judged.

[c] 2 Chron. xxx. 21, 22, 23, 25, 26. Ver. 21. And the children of Israel, that were present at Jerusalem, *kept the feast of* unleavened bread seven days *with great gladness:* and the Levites and the priests *praised the Lord* day by day, *singing* with loud instruments *unto the Lord,* &c. Acts ii. 42. And they *continued* stedfastly in the apostles' doctrine and fellowship, and in *breaking of bread, and in prayers.* Ver. 46. And they, continuing daily with one accord in the temple, and *breaking bread* from house to house, *did eat their meat with gladness and singleness of heart,* Ver. 47. *Praising* God, and having favour with all the people, &c.

[d] Ps. xxxvi. 10. *O continue thy loving-*kindness unto them that know thee; and thy righteousness to the upright in heart. Cant. iii. 4. It was but a little that I passed from them, but I found him whom my soul loveth: *I held him, and would not let him go,* until I had brought him into my mother's house, and into the chamber of her that conceived me. 1 Chron. xxix. 18. *O Lord God* of Abraham, Isaac, and of Israel, our fathers, *keep this for ever in the imagination of the thoughts of the heart of thy people,* and prepare their heart unto thee.

[e] 1 Cor. x. 3. And *did all eat the same spiritual meat;* Ver. 4. And *did all drink the same spiritual drink;* (for they drank of that spiritual Rock that followed them; and that Rock was Christ:) Ver. 5. *But with many of them God was not well pleased;* for they were overthrown in the wilderness. Ver. 12. *Wherefore, let him that thinketh he standeth take heed lest he fall.*

[f] Ps. l. 14. *Offer unto God thanksgiving; and pay thy vows unto the most High.*

[g] 1 Cor. xi. 25. After the same manner also he took the cup, when he had supped, saying, This cup is the new testament in my blood: *this do ye, as oft as ye drink it,* in remembrance of me. Ver. 26. For *as often* as ye eat this bread, and drink this cup, ye do shew the Lord's death till he come. Acts ii. 42. And *they continued stedfastly in the apostles' doctrine and fellowship, and in breaking of bread, and in prayers.* Ver. 46. And *they, continuing daily with one accord in the temple, and breaking bread* from house to house, did eat their meat with gladness and singleness of heart.

[h] * Cant. v. 1. I am come into my garden, my sister, my spouse: I have gathered my myrrh with my spice; I have eaten my honey-comb with my honey; I have drunk my wine with my milk: eat, O friends; drink, yea, drink abundantly, O beloved. Ver. 2. *I sleep, but my heart waketh:* it is the voice of my beloved that knocketh, saying, Open to me, my sister, my love, my dove, my undefiled: for my head is filled with dew, and my locks with the drops of the night. Ver. 3. *I have put off my coat; how shall I put it on? I have washed my feet; how shall I defile them?* Ver. 4. My beloved put in his hand by the hole of the door, and my bowels were moved for him. Ver. 5. *I rose up to open to my beloved;* and my hands dropped with myrrh, and my fingers with sweet

God and their own consciences, they are to wait for the fruit of it in due time:¹ but, if they see they have failed in either, they are to be humbled,ᵏ and to attend upon it afterwards with more care and diligence.¹

Q. 176. *Wherein do the sacraments of baptism and the Lord's supper agree?*

A. The sacraments of baptism and the Lord's supper agree, in that the author of both is God;ᵐ the spiritual part of both is Christ and his benefits;ⁿ both are seals of the same covenant,º are to be dispensed

---

smelling myrrh, upon the handles of the lock. Ver. 6. *I opened to my beloved; but my beloved had withdrawn himself, and was gone: my soul failed when he spake: I sought him, but I could not find him; I called him, but he gave me no answer.* Eccles. v. 1. *Keep thy foot when thou goest to the house of God, and be more ready to hear, than to give the sacrifice of fools: for they consider not that they do evil.* Ver. 2. *Be not rash with thy mouth,* and let not thine heart be hasty to utter any thing before God: for God is in heaven, and thou upon earth: therefore let thy words be few. Ver. 3. *For a dream cometh through the multitude of business; and a fool's voice is known by multitude of words.* Ver. 4. When thou vowest a *vow* unto God, *defer not to pay it;* for he hath no pleasure in fools: pay that which thou hast vowed. Ver. 5. Better is it that thou shouldest not vow, than that thou shouldest vow and not pay. Ver. 6. Suffer not thy mouth to cause thy flesh to sin; *neither say thou before the angel, that it was an error:* wherefore should God be angry at thy voice, and destroy the work of thine hands?
¹ Ps. cxxiii. 1. *Unto thee lift I up mine eyes,* O thou that dwellest in the heavens.
* Ver. 2. Behold, as the eyes of servants look unto the hand of their masters, and as the eyes of a maiden unto the hand of her mistress; *so our eyes wait upon the Lord our God,* until that he have mercy upon us. Ps. xlii. 5. Why art thou cast down, O my soul? and why art thou disquieted in me? *hope thou in God; for I shall yet praise him* for the help of his countenance. Ver. 8. Yet the Lord will command his loving-kindness in the day-time, and in the night his song shall be with me, and my prayer unto the God of my life. Ps. xliii. 3. O send out thy light and thy truth: let them lead me, let them bring me unto thy holy hill, and to thy tabernacles. Ver. 4. Then will I go unto the altar of God, unto God my exceeding joy: yea, upon the harp will I praise thee, O God, my God. Ver. 5. Why art thou cast down, O my soul? and why art thou disquieted within me? *hope in God; for I shall yet praise him,* who is the health of my countenance, and my God.
ᵏ 2 Chron. xxx. 18. For a multitude of the people, even many of Ephraim, and Manasseh, Issachar, and Zebulun, *had not cleansed themselves, yet did they eat the passover* otherwise than it was written: but Hezekiah prayed for them, saying, *The good Lord pardon every one* Ver. 19. *That prepareth his heart to seek God, the Lord God of his fathers, though he be not cleansed according to the purification of the sanctuary.* Isa. l. 16. *Wash you, make you clean; put away the evil of your doings* from before mine eyes; cease to do evil. Ver. 18. *Come now, and let us reason together,* saith the Lord: Though your sins be as *scarlet,* they shall be as white as *snow:* though they be *red like crimson,* they shall be *as wool.*
¹ 2 Cor. vii. 11. For, behold, this selfsame thing, that ye sorrowed after a godly sort, *what carefulness it wrought in you,* yea, what clearing of yourselves, yea, what indignation, yea, what fear, yea, what *vehement desire,* yea, *what zeal,* yea, what revenge! In all things ye have approved yourselves to be clear in this matter. 1 Chron. xv. 12. And (David) said unto them, Ye are the chief of the fathers of the Levites: *sanctify yourselves,* both ye and your brethren, that ye may bring up the ark of the Lord God of Israel unto the place that I have prepared for it. Ver. 13. *For because ye did it not at the first,* the Lord our God *made a breach upon us,* for that we *sought him not after the due order.* Ver. 14. *So the priests and the Levites sanctified themselves to* bring up the ark of the Lord God of Israel.
176. ᵐ Matt. xxviii. 19. *Go ye therefore, and teach all nations, baptizing them* in the name of the Father, and of the Son, and of the Holy Ghost. 1 Cor. xi. 23. For *I have received of the Lord that which also I delivered unto you,* That the Lord Jesus, the same night in which he was betrayed, took bread.
ⁿ Rom. vi. 3. Know ye not, that so many of us as were *baptized into Jesus Christ were baptized into his death?* Ver. 4. Therefore we are buried with him by baptism into death; that *like as Christ was raised* up from the dead by the glory of the Father, even *so we also should walk in newness of life.* 1 Cor. x. 16. The *cup of blessing* which we bless, is it not the *communion of the blood of Christ?* the *bread which we break,* is it not the *communion of the body of Christ?*
º Rom. iv. 11. And he received *the sign of circumcision, a seal of the righteousness of the faith* which he had yet being uncircumcised: that he might be the father of all them *that believe,* though they be not circumcised; that righteousness might be imputed unto them also. Compared with Col. ii. 12. *Buried with him in baptism,* wherein also ye *are risen with him* through the *faith* of the operation of God, who hath raised him from the dead. Matt. xxvi. 27. And he took the cup, and gave thanks, and gave it to them, saying, Drink ye all of it: Ver. 28. For *this is my blood of the new*

by ministers of the gospel, and by none other;[p] and to be continued in the church of Christ until his second coming.[q]

Q. 177. *Wherein do the sacraments of baptism and the Lord's supper differ?*

A. The sacraments of baptism and the Lord's supper differ, in that baptism is to be administered but once, with water, to be a sign and seal of our regeneration and ingrafting into Christ,[r] and that even to infants;[s] whereas the Lord's supper is to be administered often, in the elements of bread and wine, to represent and exhibit Christ as spiritual nourishment to the soul,[t] and to confirm our continuance and growth in him,[v] and that only to such as are of years and ability to examine themselves.[w]

Q. 178. *What is prayer?*

A. Prayer is an offering up of our desires unto God,[x] in the name of Christ,[y] by the help of his Spirit;[z] with confession of our sins,[a] and thankful acknowledgment of his mercies.[b]

---

testament, which is shed for many for the remission of sins.

[p] John i. 33. And I knew him not: but *he that sent me to baptize with water*, the same said unto me, Upon whom thou shalt see the Spirit descending, and remaining on him, the same is he which baptizeth with the Holy Ghost. Matt. xxviii. 19. *Go ye therefore, and teach all nations, baptizing them* in the name of the Father, and of the Son, and of the Holy Ghost. 1 Cor. xi. 23. For *I have received of the Lord that which also I delivered unto you*, That the Lord Jesus, the same night in which he was betrayed, took bread. 1 Cor. iv. 1. Let a man so account of us as of the *ministers of Christ, and stewards of the mysteries of God*. Heb. v. 4. And *no man taketh this honour unto himself, but he that is called* of God, as was Aaron.

[q] Matt. xxviii. 19. *Go ye therefore, and teach all nations, baptizing them* in the name of the Father, and of the Son, and of the Holy Ghost; Ver. 20. *Teaching them* to observe all things whatsoever I have commanded you; *and, lo, I am with you alway, even unto the end of the world.* Amen. 1 Cor. xi. 26. For as often as ye eat this bread, and drink this cup, *ye do shew the Lord's death till he come.*

177. [r] Matt. iii. 11. I indeed *baptize you with water unto repentance:* but he that cometh after me is mightier than I, whose shoes I am not worthy to bear: he shall baptize you with the Holy Ghost, and with fire. Tit. iii. 5. Not by works of righteousness which we have done, but according to his mercy he saved us, *by the washing of regeneration,* and renewing of the Holy Ghost. Gal. iii. 27. For as many of you *as have been baptized into Christ have put on Christ.*

[s] Gen. xvii. 7. And *I will establish my covenant between me and thee, and thy seed after thee, in their generations,* for an everlasting covenant, *to be a God unto thee, and to thy seed after thee.* Ver. 9. And God said unto Abraham, Thou shalt keep my covenant therefore, *thou,* and *thy seed after thee,* in their generations. Acts ii. 38. Then Peter said unto them, Repent, and be baptized every one of you in the name of Jesus Christ for the remission of sins, and ye shall receive the gift of the Holy Ghost. Ver. 39. *For the promise is unto you, and to your children,* and to all that are afar off, even as many as the Lord our God shall call. 1 Cor. vii. 14. For the unbelieving husband is sanctified by the wife, and the unbelieving wife is sanctified by the husband: *else were your children unclean; but now are they holy.*

[t] 1 Cor. xi. 23. For I have received of the Lord that which also I delivered unto you, That the Lord Jesus, the same night in which he was betrayed, *took bread:* Ver. 24. And, when he had given thanks, he brake it, and said, Take, eat; *this is my body,* which is broken for you: this do in remembrance of me. Ver. 25. After the same manner also he took the *cup,* when he had supped, saying, *This cup is the new testament* in my blood: this do ye, *as oft as ye drink it,* in remembrance of me. Ver. 26. For *as often as ye eat this bread, and drink this cup,* ye do shew the Lord's death till he come.

[v] 1 Cor. x. 16. The *cup of blessing* which we bless, is it not the *communion of the blood of Christ?* the bread which *we break,* is it not the *communion of the body of Christ?*

[w] 1 Cor. xi. 28. But *let a man examine himself,* and so let him eat of that *bread,* and drink of that *cup.* Ver. 29. For he that eateth and drinketh *unworthily,* eateth and drinketh damnation to himself, *not discerning the Lord's body.*

178. [x] Ps. lxii. 8. Trust in him at all times; ye people, *pour out your heart before him:* God is a refuge for us. Selah.

[y] John xvi. 23. And in that day ye shall ask me nothing. Verily, verily, I say unto you, Whatsoever ye shall *ask the Father in my name,* he will give it you.

[z] Rom. viii. 26. Likewise *the Spirit also helpeth our infirmities:* for we know not what we should pray for as we ought; but the *Spirit itself maketh intercession for us* with groanings which cannot be uttered.

[a] Ps. xxxii. 5. *I acknowledged my sin unto*

Q. 179. *Are we to pray unto God only?*

A. God only being able to search the hearts,^c hear the requests,^d pardon the sins,^e and fulfil the desires of all;^f and only to be believed in,^g and worshipped with religious worship;^h prayer, which is a special part thereof,ⁱ is to be made by all to him alone,^k and to none other.^l

Q. 180. *What is it to pray in the name of Christ?*

A. To pray in the name of Christ is, in obedience to his command, and in confidence on his promises, to ask mercy for his sake;^m not by bare mentioning of his name,ⁿ but by drawing our encouragement to pray, and our boldness, strength, and hope of acceptance in prayer, from Christ and his mediation.^o

Q. 181. *Why are we to pray in the name of Christ?*

A. The sinfulness of man, and his distance from God by reason thereof, being so great, as that we can have no access into his presence without a mediator;^p and there being none in heaven or earth appointed

---

thee, and mine iniquity have I not hid. I said, I will confess my transgressions unto the Lord; and thou forgavest the iniquity of my sin. Selah. Ver. 6. *For this shall every one that is godly pray unto thee in a time when thou mayest be found.* Dan. ix. 4. *And I prayed unto the Lord my God, and made my confession,* and said, O Lord, the great and dreadful God, &c.

b Phil. iv. 6. Be careful for nothing: but in every thing *by prayer and supplication, with thanksgiving, let your requests be made known unto God.*

179. c 1 Kings viii. 39. Then hear thou in heaven thy dwelling-place, and forgive, and do, and give to every man according to his ways, *whose heart thou knowest;* (for thou, *even thou only, knowest the hearts of all the children of men.*) Acts i. 24. And they prayed, and said, *Thou, Lord, which knowest the hearts of all men,* shew whether of these two thou hast chosen. Rom. viii. 27. And *he that searcheth the hearts knoweth* what is the mind of the Spirit, because he maketh intercession for the saints according to the will of God.

d Ps. lxv. 2. O thou *that hearest prayer,* unto thee shall all flesh come.

e Micah vii. 18. Who is a God like unto thee, *that pardoneth iniquity, and passeth by the transgression* of the remnant of his heritage? he retaineth not his anger for ever, because he delighteth in mercy.

f Ps. cxlv. 18. The Lord is nigh unto all them that call upon him, to all that call upon him in truth. Ver. 19. He will *fulfil the desire of them that fear him:* he also will hear their cry, and will save them.

g Rom. x. 14. *How then shall they call on him in whom they have not believed?*

h Matt. iv. 10. Then saith Jesus unto him, Get thee hence, Satan: for it is written, *Thou shalt worship the Lord thy God, and him only shalt thou serve.*

i 1 Cor. i. 2. Unto the church of God which is at Corinth, to them that are sanctified in Christ Jesus, called to be saints, with *all that in every place call upon the name of Jesus Christ our Lord,* both theirs and ours.

k Ps. l. 15. And *call upon me* in the day of trouble; I will deliver thee, and thou shalt glorify me.

l Rom. x. 14. How then shall they call *on him in whom they have not believed?*

180. m John xiv. 13. And whatsoever ye shall *ask in my name,* that will I do, that the Father may be glorified in the Son. Ver. 14. If ye shall *ask any thing* in my name, I will do it. John xvi. 24. Hitherto have ye *asked nothing in my name:* ask, and ye shall receive, that your joy may be full. Dan. ix. 17. Now therefore, O our God, hear the prayer of thy servant, and his supplications, and cause thy face to shine upon thy sanctuary that is desolate, *for the Lord's sake.*

n Matt. vii. 21. *Not every one that saith unto me, Lord, Lord,* shall enter into the kingdom of heaven; but he that doeth the will of my Father which is in heaven.

o Heb. iv. 14. *Seeing then that we have a great high priest,* that is passed into the heavens, *Jesus* the Son of God, let us hold fast our profession. Ver. 15. For we have not an high priest which cannot be touched with the feeling of our infirmities; but was in all points tempted like as we are, yet without sin. Ver. 16. *Let us therefore come boldly unto the throne of grace,* that we may obtain mercy, and find grace to help in time of need. 1 John v. 13. These things have I written unto you that believe on the name of the Son of God, that *ye may know that* ye have eternal life, and *that ye may believe on the name of the Son of God.* Ver. 14. *And this is the confidence that we have in him, that, if we ask any thing according to his will, he heareth us.* Ver. 15. And if we know that he hear us, *whatsoever we ask, we know* that we have *the petitions that we desired of him.*

181. p John xiv. 6. Jesus saith unto him, I am *the way,* and the truth, and the life: *no man cometh unto the Father, but by me.* Isa. lix. 2. But *your iniquities have separated between you and your God,* and your sins have hid his face from you, that he will not hear. Eph. iii. 12. *In whom we*

to, or fit for, that glorious work but Christ alone,^q we are to pray in no other name but his only.^r

Q. 182. *How doth the Spirit help us to pray?*

A. We not knowing what to pray for as we ought, the Spirit helpeth our infirmities, by enabling us to understand both for whom, and what, and how prayer is to be made; and by working and quickening in our hearts (although not in all persons, nor at all times, in the same measure) those apprehensions, affections, and graces which are requisite for the right performance of that duty.^s

Q. 183. *For whom are we to pray?*

A. We are to pray for the whole church of Christ upon earth;^t for magistrates,^v and ministers;^w for ourselves,^x our brethren,^y yea, our enemies;^z and for all sorts of men living,^a or that shall live hereafter;^b but not for the dead,^c nor for those that are known to have sinned the sin unto death.^d

---

have boldness and *access with confidence by the faith of him.*

q John vi. 27. Labour not for the meat which perisheth, but for that meat which endureth unto everlasting life, which the Son of man shall give unto you: for *him hath God the Father sealed.* Heb. vii. 25. Wherefore he is *able also to save them to the uttermost that come unto God by him,* seeing he *ever liveth* to make intercession for them. Ver. 26. For such an high priest became us, who is holy, harmless, undefiled, separate from sinners, and made higher than the heavens; Ver. 27. Who needeth not daily, as those high priests, to offer up sacrifice, first for his own sins, and then for the people's: for this he did once, when he offered up himself. 1 Tim. ii. 5. For there is one God, and *one mediator between God and men, the man Christ Jesus.*

r Col. iii. 17. And whatsoever ye do in word or deed, *do all in the name of the Lord Jesus, giving thanks to God* and the Father *by him.* Heb. xiii. 15. *By him therefore let us offer the sacrifice of praise to God continually,* that is, the fruit of our lips, *giving thanks to his name.*

182. s Rom. viii. 26. Likewise *the Spirit also helpeth our infirmities:* for *we know not what we should pray for as we ought;* but the *Spirit itself* maketh intercession for us with groanings which cannot be uttered. Ver. 27. And he that searcheth the hearts knoweth what is the mind of the Spirit, because *he maketh intercession for the saints according to the will of God.* Ps. x. 17. Lord, thou hast heard the desire of the humble: *thou wilt prepare their heart,* thou wilt cause thine ear to hear. Zech. xii. 10. And *I will pour upon the house of David,* and upon the inhabitants of Jerusalem, *the spirit of grace and of supplications;* and they shall look upon me whom they have pierced, and they shall mourn, &c.

183. t Eph. vi. 18. Praying always with all prayer and supplication in the Spirit, and watching thereunto with all perseverance and supplication for *all saints.* Ps. xxviii. 9. Save *thy people,* and bless *thine inheritance:* feed them also, and lift them up for ever.

v 1 Tim. ii. 1. I exhort therefore, that, first of all, supplications, prayers, intercessions, and giving of thanks, be made for *all men;* Ver. 2. For *kings,* and for *all that are in authority;* that we may lead a quiet and peaceable life in all godliness and honesty.

w Col. iv. 3. Withal praying also for us, that God would open unto us a door of utterance, to speak the mystery of Christ, for which I am also in bonds.

x Gen. xxxii. 11. Deliver *me,* I pray thee, from the hand of my brother, from the hand of Esau: for I fear him, lest he will come and smite me, and the mother with the children.

y James v. 16. Confess your faults one to another, and pray *one for another,* that ye may be healed. The effectual fervent prayer of a righteous man availeth much.

z Matt. v. 44. But I say unto you, Love your enemies, bless them that curse you, do good to them that hate you, and *pray for them which despitefully use you,* and persecute you.

a 1 Tim. ii. 1, 2. [See above in v.]

b John xvii. 20. Neither pray I for these alone, but for *them also which shall believe on me through their word.* 2 Sam. vii. 29. Therefore now let it please thee to bless *the house of thy servant, that it may continue for ever before thee:* for thou, O Lord God, hast spoken it; and with thy blessing *let the house of thy servant be blessed for ever.*

c 2 Sam. xii. 21. Then said his servants unto him, What thing is this that thou hast done? Thou didst fast and weep for the child, while it was alive; but when the child was dead, thou didst rise and eat bread. Ver. 22. And he said, While the child was yet alive, I fasted and wept: for I said, Who can tell whether God will be gracious to me, that the child may live? Ver. 23. But *now he is dead, wherefore should I fast?* can I bring him back again? I shall go to him, but he shall not return to me.

d 1 John v. 16. If any man see his brother sin a sin which is not unto death, he shall ask, and he shall give him life for them that sin not unto death. There is a sin unto death: *I do not say that he shall pray for it.*

Q. 184. *For what things are we to pray?*

A. We are to pray for all things tending to the glory of God,^e the welfare of the church,^f our own^g or others good;^h but not for any thing that is unlawful.ⁱ

Q. 185. *How are we to pray?*

A. We are to pray with an awful apprehension of the majesty of God,^k and deep sense of our own unworthiness,^l necessities,^m and sins;ⁿ with penitent,^o thankful,^p and enlarged hearts;^q with understanding,^r faith,^s sincerity,^t fervency,^v love,^w and perseverance,^x waiting upon him,^y with humble submission to his will.^z

Q. 186. *What rule hath God given for our direction in the duty of prayer?*

A. The whole word of God is of use to direct us in the duty of prayer;^a but the special rule of direction is that form of prayer which our Saviour Christ taught his disciples, commonly called *The Lord's prayer.*^b

---

184. ^e Matt. vi. 9. After this manner therefore pray ye: Our Father which art in heaven, *Hallowed be thy name.*
^f Ps. li. 18. Do good in thy good pleasure unto *Zion:* build thou the walls of *Jerusalem.* Ps. cxxii. 6. Pray for *the peace of Jerusalem:* they shall prosper that love thee.
^g Matt. vii. 11. If ye then, being evil, know how to give good gifts unto your children, how much more shall your Father which is in heaven give *good things to them that ask him?*
^h Ps. cxxv. 4. Do *good,* O Lord, unto *those that be good,* and to them that are upright in their hearts.
ⁱ 1 John v. 14. And this is the confidence that we have in him, that, if we ask *any thing according to his will,* he heareth us.
185. ^k Eccl. v. 1. *Keep thy foot when thou goest to the house of God,* and be more ready to hear than to give the sacrifice of fools: for they consider not that they do evil.
^l Gen. xviii. 27. And Abraham answered and said, Behold now, I have taken upon me to speak unto the Lord, which am *but dust and ashes.* Gen. xxxii. 10. I am *not worthy of the least of all the mercies,* and of all the truth, which thou hast shewed unto thy servant, &c.
^m Luke xv. 17. And when he came to himself, he said, How many hired servants of my father's have bread enough, and to spare, and *I perish with hunger!* Ver. 18 I will arise and go to my father, and will say unto him, Father, *I have sinned against Heaven, and before thee,* Ver. 19. And am *no more worthy to be called thy son:* make me as one of thy hired servants.
ⁿ Luke xviii. 13. And the publican, standing afar off, would not lift up so much as his eyes unto heaven, but smote upon his breast, saying, God be merciful to me *a sinner.* Ver. 14. I tell you, this man went down to his house justified rather than the other: for every one that exalteth himself shall be abased; and he that humbleth himself shall be exalted.
^o Ps. li. 17. The sacrifices of God are *a broken spirit: a broken and a contrite heart,* O God, thou wilt not despise.

^p Phil. iv. 6. Be careful for nothing: but in every thing by prayer and supplication, *with thanksgiving,* let your requests be made known unto God.
^q 1 Sam. i. 15. And Hannah answered and said, No, my lord; I am a woman of a sorrowful spirit: I have drunk neither wine nor strong drink, but *have poured out my soul before the Lord.* 1 Sam. ii. 1. And Hannah prayed, and said, *My heart rejoiceth* in the Lord; mine horn is exalted in the Lord; *my mouth is enlarged* over mine enemies; because I rejoice in thy salvation.
^r 1 Cor. xiv. 15. What is it then? I will pray with the spirit, and I will pray *with the understanding* also, &c.
^s Mark xi. 24. Therefore I say unto you, What things soever ye desire, when ye pray, *believe that ye receive them,* and ye shall have them. James i. 6. But let him *ask in faith, nothing wavering:* for he that wavereth is like a wave of the sea driven with the wind and tossed.
^t Ps. cxlv. 18. The Lord is nigh unto all them that call upon him, to all that call upon him *in truth.* Ps. xvii. 1. Hear the right, O Lord, attend unto my cry; give ear unto my prayer, *that goeth not out of feigned lips.*
^v James v. 16. The *effectual fervent* prayer of a righteous man availeth much.
^w 1 Tim. ii. 8. I will therefore that men *pray* every where, lifting up holy hands, *without wrath* and doubting.
^x Eph. vi. 18. *Praying* always with all prayer and supplication in the Spirit, and *watching thereunto with all perseverance* and supplication for all saints.
^y Micah vii. 7. Therefore I will look unto the Lord; I will *wait for the God of my salvation:* my God will hear me.
^z Matt. xxvi. 39. And he went a little farther, and fell on his face, and *prayed,* saying, O my Father, if it be possible, let this cup pass from me: nevertheless, *not as I will, but as thou wilt.*
186. ^a 1 John v. 14. And this is the confidence that we have in him, that, *if we ask any thing according to his will,* he heareth us.
^b Matt. vi. 9-13. After this manner there-

Q. 187. *How is the Lord's prayer to be used?*

A. The Lord's prayer is not only for direction, as a pattern, according to which we are to make other prayers; but may also be used as a prayer, so that it be done with understanding, faith, reverence, and other graces necessary to the right performance of the duty of prayer.[c]

Q. 188. *Of how many parts doth the Lord's prayer consist?*

A. The Lord's prayer consists of three parts; a preface, petitions, and a conclusion.

Q. 189. *What doth the preface of the Lord's prayer teach us?*

A. The preface of the Lord's prayer (contained in these words, *Our Father which art in heaven*,[d]) teacheth us, when we pray, to draw near to God with confidence of his fatherly goodness, and our interest therein;[e] with reverence, and all other child-like dispositions,[f] heavenly affections,[g] and due apprehensions of his sovereign power, majesty, and gracious condescension:[h] as also, to pray with and for others.[i]

Q. 190. *What do we pray for in the first petition?*

A. In the first petition, (which is, *Hallowed be thy name*,[k]) acknowledging the utter inability and indisposition that is in ourselves and all men to honour God aright,[l] we pray, that God would by his grace enable and incline us and others to know, to acknowledge, and highly to esteem him,[m] his titles,[n] attributes,[o] ordinances, word,[p]

---

fore pray ye: *Our Father, &c.* Luke xi. 2, 3, 4. And he said unto them, When ye pray, say, *Our Father, &c.*
187. [c] Matt. vi. 9. Compared with Luke xi. 2. [See above in letter b.]
189. [d] Matt. vi. 9.
[e] Luke xi. 13. If ye then, being evil, know how to give good gifts unto your children; *how much more shall your heavenly Father give the Holy Spirit to them that ask him?* Rom. viii. 15. For ye have not received the spirit of bondage again to fear; but ye have received the Spirit of adoption, *whereby we cry, Abba, Father.*
[f] Isa. lxiv. 9. Be not wroth very sore, O Lord, neither remember iniquity for ever: *behold, see, we beseech thee, we are all thy people.*
[g] Ps. cxxiii. 1. *Unto thee lift I up mine eyes,* O thou that dwellest in the heavens. Lam. iii. 41. *Let us lift up our heart with our hands unto God* in the heavens.
[h] Isa. lxiii. 15. Look down from heaven, and behold from the habitation of thy holiness and of thy glory: *where is thy zeal and thy strength, the sounding of thy bowels and of thy mercies toward me?* are they restrained? Ver. 16. Doubtless thou art our Father, though Abraham be ignorant of us, and Israel acknowledge us not: *thou, O Lord, art our Father, our Redeemer; thy name is from everlasting.* Neh. i. 4. And it came to pass, when I heard these words, that I sat down and wept, and mourned certain days, and fasted, and *prayed* before the God of heaven, Ver. 5. And said, I beseech thee, *O Lord God of heaven*, the great and terrible God, *that keepeth covenant and mercy for them that love him, and observe his commandments:* Ver. 6. Let thine ear now be attentive, and thine eyes open, that thou mayest hear the prayer of thy servant, which I pray before thee now, day and night, for the children of Israel thy servants, and confess the sins of the children of Israel, which we have sinned against thee: both I and my father's house have sinned.
[i] Acts xii. 5. Peter therefore was kept in prison; but *prayer was made without ceasing of the church unto God for him.*
190. [k] Matt. vi. 9.
[l] 2 Cor. iii. 5. *Not that we are sufficient of ourselves to think any thing as of ourselves;* but our sufficiency is of God. Ps. li. 15. *O Lord, open thou my lips;* and my mouth shall shew forth thy praise.
[m] Ps. lxvii. 2. *That thy way may be known upon earth, thy saving health among all nations.* Ver. 3. *Let the people praise thee,* O God; let all the people praise thee.
[n] Ps. lxxxiii. 18. *That men may know that thou, whose name alone is JEHOVAH,* art the most High over all the earth.
[o] Ps. lxxxvi. 10. For *thou art great,* and *doest wondrous things;* thou art God alone. Ver. 11. Teach me thy way, O Lord; I will walk in thy truth: unite my heart to fear thy name. Ver. 12. *I will praise thee,* O Lord my God, with all my heart; and I will glorify thy name for evermore. Ver. 13. *For great is thy mercy* toward me; and thou hast delivered my soul from the lowest hell. Ver. 15. But thou, O Lord, art *a God full of compassion, and gracious, long-suffering, and plenteous in mercy and truth.*
[p] 2 Thess. iii. 1. Finally, brethren, *pray for us, that the word of the Lord may have free course, and be glorified,* even as it is with you. Ps. cxlvii. 19. He *sheweth his word unto Jacob, his statutes and his judgments unto Israel.* Ver. 20. He hath not dealt so with any nation: and as for his judgments, they have not known them. *Praise ye the Lord.* Ps. cxxxviii. 1. *I will praise thee with my whole heart;* before the gods will I sing praise unto thee. Ver. 2

works, and whatsoever he is pleased to make himself known by;^q and to glorify him in thought, word,^r and deed:^s that he would prevent and remove atheism,^t ignorance,^v idolatry,^w profaneness,^x and whatsoever is dishonourable to him;^y and, by his over-ruling providence, direct and dispose of all things to his own glory.^z

Q. 191. *What do we pray for in the second petition?*

A. In the second petition, (which is, *Thy kingdom come*,^a) acknowledging ourselves and all mankind to be by nature under the dominion of sin and Satan,^b we pray, that the kingdom of sin and Satan may be destroyed,^c the gospel propagated throughout the

---

I will worship toward thy holy temple, and *praise thy name for thy loving-kindness, and for thy truth: for thou hast magnified thy word above all thy name.* Ver. 1. In the day when I cried thou answeredst me, and strengthenedst me with strength in my soul. 2 Cor. ii. 14. Now *thanks be unto God,* which always causeth us to triumph in Christ, and *maketh manifest the savour of his knowledge by us in every place.* Ver. 15. For we are unto God a sweet savour of Christ, in them that are saved, and in them that perish.

q Ps. cxlv. throughout. *I will extol thee, my God, O King,* &c. Ps. viii. throughout. O Lord our Lord, *how excellent is thy name* in all the earth! &c.

r Ps. ciii. 1. *Bless the Lord, O my soul; and all that is within me,* bless his holy name. Ps. xix. 14. *Let the words of my mouth, and the meditation of my heart,* be acceptable in thy sight, O Lord, my strength, and my redeemer.

s Phil. i. 9. *And this I pray, that your love may abound yet more and more* in knowledge and in all judgment; Ver. 11. *Being filled with the fruits of righteousness,* which are by Jesus Christ, *unto the glory and praise of God.*

t Ps. lxvii. 1. God be merciful unto us, and bless us; and cause his face to shine upon us. Selah. Ver. 2. *That thy way may be known upon earth,* thy saving health among all nations. Ver. 3. *Let the people praise thee, O God;* let all the people praise thee. Ver. 4. O let the nations be glad, and sing for joy: for thou shalt judge the people righteously, and govern the nations upon earth. Selah.

v Eph. i. 17. That the God of our Lord Jesus Christ, the Father of glory, *may give unto you the spirit of wisdom and revelation in the knowledge of him:* Ver. 18. *The eyes of your understanding being enlightened; that ye may know* what is the hope of his calling, and what the riches of the glory of his inheritance in the saints.

w Ps. xcvii. 7. *Confounded be all they that serve graven images,* that *boast* themselves of *idols:* worship him, all ye gods.

x Ps. lxxiv. 18. *Remember this,* that the *enemy hath reproached, O Lord, and that the foolish people have blasphemed thy name.* Ver. 22. *Arise,* O God, plead thine own cause: *remember how the foolish man reproacheth thee daily.* Ver. 23. Forget not the voice of thine enemies: *the tumult of those that rise up against thee* increaseth continually.

y 2 Kings xix. 15. And Hezekiah prayed before the Lord, and said, O Lord God of Israel, which dwellest between the cherubims, thou art the God, even thou alone, of all the kingdoms of the earth; thou hast made heaven and earth. Ver. 16. Lord, bow down thine ear, and hear; open, Lord, thine eyes, and see; *and hear the words of Sennacherib, which hath sent him to reproach the living God.*

z 2 Chron. xx. 6. And (Jehoshaphat) said, O Lord God of our fathers, *art not thou God in heaven? and rulest not thou over all the kingdoms of the heathen?* and in thine hand is there not power and might, so that none is able to withstand thee? Ver. 10. *And now, behold, the children of Ammon,* and *Moab,* and *mount Seir,* whom thou wouldest not let Israel invade, when they came out of the land of Egypt, but they turned from them, and destroyed them not; Ver. 11. *Behold,* I say, how they reward us, to come *to cast us out of thy possession, which thou hast given us* to inherit. Ver. 12. *O our God, wilt thou not judge them?* for we have no might against this great company that cometh against us; neither know we what to do: *but our eyes are upon thee.* Ps. lxxxiii. throughout. Keep not thou silence, O God: hold not thy peace, &c. Ps. cxl. 4. Keep me, O Lord, from the hands of the wicked; preserve me from the violent man, who have purposed to overthrow my goings. Ver. 8. *Grant not, O Lord, the desires of the wicked;* further not his wicked device, *lest they exalt themselves.* Selah.

191. a Matt. vi. 10.

b Eph. ii. 2. *Wherein in time past ye walked according to the course of this world, according to the prince of the power of the air, the spirit that now worketh in the children of disobedience:* Ver. 3. Among whom also we all had our conversation in times past in the lusts of our flesh, *fulfilling the desires of the flesh* and of the mind; and *were by nature the children of wrath,* even as others.

c Ps. lxviii. 1. *Let God arise, let his enemies be scattered:* let them also that hate him flee before him. Ver. 18. Thou hast ascended on high, thou hast *led captivity captive:* thou hast received gifts for men; yea, for the rebellious also, that the Lord God might dwell among them. Rev. xii. 10. And I heard a loud voice saying in heaven, *Now is come salvation, and strength, and the kingdom of our God, and the power of his Christ:* for the accuser of our brethren

world,[d] the Jews called,[e] the fulness of the Gentiles brought in;[f] the church furnished with all gospel-officers and ordinances,[g] purged from corruption,[h] countenanced and maintained by the civil magistrate:[i] that the ordinances of Christ may be purely dispensed, and made effectual to the converting of those that are yet in their sins, and the confirming, comforting, and building up of those that are already converted:[k] that Christ would rule in our hearts here,[l] and hasten the time of his second coming, and our reigning with him for ever:[m] and that he would be pleased so to exercise the kingdom of his power in all the world, as may best conduce to these ends.[n]

---

is cast down, which accused them before our God day and night. Ver. 11. And *they overcame him by the blood of the Lamb*, and by the word of their testimony; and they loved not their lives unto the death.

[d] 2 Thess. iii. 1. Finally, brethren, *pray for us, that the word of the Lord may have free course, and be glorified*, even as it is with you.

[e] Rom. x 1. Brethren, *my heart's desire and prayer to God for Israel is, that they might be saved*.

[f] John xvii. 9. I pray for them: I pray not for the world, but for them which thou hast given me; for they are thine. Ver. 20. *Neither pray I for these alone, but for them also which shall believe on me through their word*. Rom. xi. 25. For I would not, brethren, that ye should be ignorant of this mystery, (lest ye should be wise in your own conceits,) that blindness in part is happened to Israel, *until the fulness of the Gentiles be come in*. Ver. 26. And so all Israel shall be saved; as it is written, There shall come out of Zion the Deliverer, and shall turn away ungodliness from Jacob. Ps. lxvii. throughout. God be merciful unto us, and bless us; and cause his face to shine upon us, &c.

[g] Matt. ix. 38. *Pray ye therefore the Lord of the harvest, that he will send forth labourers into his harvest*. 2 Thess. iii. 1. Finally, brethren, *pray for us, that the word of the Lord may have free course, and be glorified*, even as it is with you.

[h] Mal. i. 11. For from the rising of the sun, even unto the going down of the same, my name shall be great among the Gentiles; and in every place *incense shall be offered unto my name, and a pure offering: for my name shall be great among the heathen*, saith the Lord of hosts. Zeph. iii. 9. For then *will I turn to the people a pure language*, that they may all call upon the name of the Lord, to serve him with one consent.

[i] 1 Tim. ii. 1. I exhort therefore, that, first of all, supplications, prayers, intercessions, and giving of thanks, be made for all men; Ver. 2. *For kings, and for all that are in authority; that we may lead a quiet and peaceable life in all godliness and honesty*.

[k] Acts iv. 29. And now, Lord, behold their threatenings: *and grant unto thy servants, that with all boldness they may speak thy word*. Ver. 30. By stretching forth thine hand to heal; *and that signs and wonders may be done* by the name of thy holy child Jesus. Eph. vi. 18. *Praying* always with all prayer and supplication in the Spirit, and watching thereunto with all perseverance and supplication for all saints; Ver. 19. And *for me, that utterance may be given unto me, that I may open my mouth boldly, to make known the mystery of the gospel*. Ver. 20. For which I am an ambassador in bonds; that therein I may *speak boldly, as I ought to speak*. Rom. xv. 29. And I am sure that, when I come unto you, I shall come in the fulness of the blessing of the gospel of Christ. Ver. 30. Now I beseech you, brethren, for the Lord Jesus Christ's sake, and for the love of the Spirit, that ye *strive together with me in your prayers to God for me;* Ver. 32. *That I may come unto you with joy* by the will of God, and may with you be refreshed. 2 Thess. i. 11. Wherefore also *we pray always for you, that our God would count you worthy of this calling, and fulfil all the good pleasure of his goodness, and the work of faith with power*. 2 Thess. ii. 16. Now our *Lord Jesus Christ* himself, and *God*, even our Father, which hath loved us, and hath given us everlasting consolation, and good hope through grace, Ver. 17. *Comfort your hearts, and stablish you in every good word and work*.

[l] Eph. iii. 14. For this cause *I bow my knees* unto the Father of our Lord Jesus Christ, Ver. 15. Of whom the whole family in heaven and earth is named, Ver. 16. That he would *grant you*, according to the riches of his glory, *to be strengthened with might by his Spirit in the inner man;* Ver. 17. *That Christ may dwell in your hearts by faith;* that ye, being rooted and grounded in love, Ver. 18. May be able to comprehend with all saints what is the breadth, and length, and depth, and height; Ver. 19. And *to know the love of Christ*, which passeth knowledge, that ye might *be filled with all the fulness of God*. Ver. 20. Now unto him that is able to do exceeding abundantly above all that we ask or think, according to the power that worketh in us.

[m] Rev. xxii. 20. He which testifieth these things saith, *Surely I come quickly: Amen. Even so, come, Lord Jesus*.

[n] Isa. lxiv. 1. Oh that *thou wouldest rend the heavens, that thou wouldest come down*, that the mountains might flow down at thy presence; Ver. 2. As when the melting fire burneth, the fire causeth the waters to boil; *to make thy name known to thine adversaries, that the nations may tremble at thy presence!* Rev. iv. 8. And the four beasts had each of them six wings about

Q. 192 *What do we pray for in the third petition?*

A. In the third petition, (which is, *Thy will be done in earth, as it is in heaven,*[o]) acknowledging, that by nature we and all men are not only utterly unable and unwilling to know and do the will of God,[p] but prone to rebel against his word,[q] to repine and murmur against his providence,[r] and wholly inclined to do the will of the flesh, and of the devil:[s] we pray, that God would by his Spirit take away from ourselves and others all blindness,[t] weakness,[v] indisposedness,[w] and perverseness of heart;[x] and by his grace make us able and willing to know, do, and submit to his will in all things,[y] with the like humility,[z] cheerfulness,[a] faithfulness,[b]

him; and they were full of eyes within: and they rest not day and night, saying, Holy, holy, holy, Lord God Almighty, which was, and is, and is to come. Ver. 9. And when *those beasts give glory, and honour, and thanks, to him* that sat on the throne, who liveth for ever and ever, Ver. 10. The four and twenty elders fall down before him that sat on the throne, and worship him that liveth for ever and ever, and cast their crowns before the throne, saying, Ver. 11. *Thou art worthy, O Lord, to receive glory,* and honour, and power: for thou hast created all things, and for thy pleasure they are and were created.

192. o Matt. vi. 10.

p Rom. vii. 18. For *I know that in me (that is, in my flesh) dwelleth no good thing:* for to will is present with me; but *how to perform that which is good I find not.* Job xxi. 14. Therefore they say unto God, Depart from us; for *we desire not the knowledge of thy ways.* 1 Cor. ii. 14. But the natural man *receiveth not the things of the Spirit of God:* for they are foolishness unto him; *neither can he know them,* because they are spiritually discerned.

q Rom. viii. 7. Because *the carnal mind is enmity against God; for it is not subject to the law* of God, *neither indeed can be.*

r Exod. xvii. 7. And he called the name of the place Massah, and Meribah, because of *the chiding of the children of Israel,* and because they *tempted the Lord,* saying, Is the Lord among us, or not? Numb. xiv. 2. And *all the children of Israel murmured against Moses and against Aaron;* and the whole congregation said unto them, Would God that we had died in the land of Egypt! or, would God we had died in this wilderness!

s Eph. ii. 2. Wherein in time past *ye walked according to the course of this world, according to the prince of the power of the air, the spirit that now worketh in the children of disobedience.*

t Eph. i. 17. That the God of our Lord Jesus Christ, the Father of glory, may *give unto you the spirit of wisdom and revelation in the knowledge of him:* Ver. 18. *The eyes of your understanding being enlightened;* that ye may know what is the hope of his calling, and what the riches of the glory of his inheritance in the saints.

v Eph. iii 16. That he would *grant you,* according to the riches of his glory, *to be strengthened with might by his Spirit in the inner man.*

w Matt. xxvi. 40. And he cometh unto the disciples, and findeth them asleep, and saith unto Peter, What! could ye not watch with me one hour? Ver. 41. *Watch and pray,* that ye enter not into temptation: the spirit indeed is willing, *but the flesh is weak.*

x Jer. xxxi. 18. I have surely heard Ephraim bemoaning himself thus; Thou hast chastised me, and I was chastised, *as a bullock unaccustomed to the yoke: turn thou me, and I shall be turned;* for thou art the Lord my God. Ver. 19. Surely after that I was turned, I repented; and after that I was instructed, I smote upon my thigh: I was ashamed, yea, even confounded, because I did bear the reproach of my youth.

y Ps. cxix. 1. Blessed are the undefiled in the way, who walk in the law of the Lord. Ver. 8. I will keep thy statutes: O forsake me not utterly. Ver. 35. *Make me to go in the path of thy commandments;* for therein do I delight. Ver. 36. *Incline my heart unto thy testimonies,* and not to covetousness. Acts xxi. 14. And when he would not be persuaded, we ceased, saying, *The will of the Lord be done.*

z Micah vi. 8. He hath shewed thee, O man, what is good; and what doth the Lord require of thee, but to do justly, and to love mercy, and *to walk humbly with thy God?*

a Ps. c. 2. *Serve the Lord with gladness;* come before his presence *with singing.* Job i. 21. And (Job) said, Naked came I out of my mother's womb, and naked shall I return thither: the Lord gave, and the Lord hath taken away; *blessed be the name of the Lord.* 2 Sam. xv. 25. And the king said unto Zadok, Carry back the ark of God into the city: if I shall find favour in the eyes of the Lord, he will bring me again, and shew me both it and his habitation. * Ver. 26. But if he thus say, I have no delight in thee; *behold, here am I, let him do to me as seemeth good unto him.*

b Isa. xxxviii. 3. And said, Remember now, O Lord, I beseech thee, how *I have walked before thee in truth, and with a perfect heart,* and have done that which is good in thy sight: and Hezekiah wept sore.

diligence,[c] zeal,[d] sincerity,[e] and constancy,[f] as the angels do in heaven.[g]

Q. 193. *What do we pray for in the fourth petition?*

A. In the fourth petition, (which is, *Give us this day our daily bread,*[h]) acknowledging, that in Adam, and by our own sin, we have forfeited our right to all the outward blessings of this life, and deserve to be wholly deprived of them by God, and to have them cursed to us in the use of them;[i] and that neither they of themselves are able to sustain us,[k] nor we to merit,[l] or by our own industry to procure them;[m] but prone to desire,[n] get,[o] and use them unlawfully:[p] we pray for ourselves and others, that both they and we, waiting upon the providence of God from day to day in the use of lawful means, may, of his free gift, and as to his fatherly wisdom shall seem best, enjoy a competent portion of them;[q] and have the same continued and blessed

---

[c] Ps. cxix. 4. Thou hast commanded us to *keep thy precepts diligently.* Ver. 5. *O that my ways were directed* to keep thy statutes!

[d] Rom. xii. 11. Not slothful in business; *fervent in spirit; serving the Lord.*

[e] Ps. cxix. 80. Let *my heart be sound in thy statutes,* that I be not ashamed.

[f] Ps. cxix. 112. I have inclined mine heart *to perform thy statutes alway, even unto the end.*

[g] Isa. vi. 2. Above it stood the *seraphims:* each one had six wings; with twain he covered his face, and with twain he covered his feet, and with twain he did fly. Ver. 3. And *one cried unto another, and said, Holy, holy, holy is the Lord of hosts:* the whole earth is full of his glory. Ps. ciii. 20. *Bless the Lord, ye his angels,* that excel in strength, that *do his commandments, hearkening unto the voice of his word.* Ver. 21. Bless ye the Lord, all *ye his hosts; ye ministers of his, that do his pleasure.* Matt. xviii. 10. Take heed that ye despise not one of these little ones: for I say unto you, That in heaven *their angels do always behold the face of my Father which is in heaven.*

193. [h] Matt. vi. 11.

[i] Gen. ii. 17. But of the tree of the knowledge of good and evil, thou shalt not eat of it: for *in the day that thou eatest thereof thou shalt surely die.* Gen. iii. 17. And unto Adam he said, Because thou hast hearkened unto the voice of thy wife, and hast eaten of the tree, of which I commanded thee, saying, Thou shalt not eat of it: *cursed is the ground for thy sake; in sorrow shalt thou eat of it* all the days of thy life. Rom. viii. 20. For *the creature was made subject to vanity,* not willingly, but by reason of him who hath subjected the same in hope; Ver. 21. Because the creature itself also shall be delivered from the bondage of corruption into the glorious liberty of the children of God. Ver. 22. For we know that the whole creation groaneth and travaileth in pain together until now. Jer. v. 25. *Your iniquities have turned away these things, and your sins have withholden good things from you.* Deut. xxviii. from verse 15. to the end of the chapter. Ver. 15. But it shall come to pass, *if thou wilt not hearken unto the voice of the Lord thy God,* to observe to do all his commandments and his statutes, which I command thee this day, that *all these curses shall come upon thee, and overtake thee.* Ver. 16. *Cursed* shalt thou be in the *city,* and *cursed* shalt thou be in the *field.* Ver. 17. *Cursed* shall be thy *basket* and thy *store,* &c.

[k] Deut. viii. 3. And he humbled thee, and suffered thee to hunger, and fed thee with manna, which thou knewest not, neither did thy fathers know; that he might make thee know *that man doth not live by bread only, but by every word that proceedeth out of the mouth of the Lord doth man live.*

[l] Gen. xxxii. 10. *I am not worthy of the least of all the mercies,* and of all the truth, which thou hast shewed unto thy servant, &c.

[m] Deut. viii. 17. And *thou say in thine heart, My power, and the might of mine hand, hath gotten me this wealth.* Ver. 18. But thou shalt remember *the Lord thy God;* for *it is he that giveth thee power to get wealth,* that he may establish his covenant which he sware unto thy fathers, as it is this day.

[n] Jer. vi. 13. For from the least of them even unto the greatest of them, *every one is given to covetousness;* and from the prophet even unto the priest, every one dealeth falsely. Mark vii. 21. For *from within, out of the heart of men, proceed evil thoughts,* adulteries, fornications, murders, Ver. 22. Thefts, *covetousness,* wickedness, deceit, &c.

[o] Hos. xii. 7. He is a merchant, the *balances of deceit are in his hand: he loveth to oppress.*

[p] James iv. 3. Ye ask, and receive not, because ye ask amiss, *that ye may consume it upon your lusts.*

[q] Gen. xliii. 12. And *take double money in your hand;* and the money that was brought again in the mouth of your sacks, carry it again in your hand; peradventure it was an oversight. Ver. 13. *Take also your brother,* and arise, go again unto the man: Ver. 14. And *God Almighty give you mercy before the man.* Gen. xxviii. 20. And Jacob vowed a vow, saying, *If God will be with me, and will keep me in this way that I go, and will give me bread to eat, and raiment to put on.* Eph. iv. 28. Let him that stole steal no more: but rather let him labour,

unto us in our holy and comfortable use of them,[r] and contentment in them;[s] and be kept from all things that are contrary to our temporal support and comfort.[t]

Q. 194. *What do we pray for in the fifth petition?*

A. In the fifth petition, (which is, *Forgive us our debts, as we forgive our debtors*,[v]) acknowledging, that we and all others are guilty both of original and actual sin, and thereby become debtors to the justice of God; and that neither we, nor any other creature, can make the least satisfaction for that debt:[w] we pray for ourselves and others, that God of his free grace would, through the obedience and satisfaction of Christ, apprehended and applied by faith, acquit us both from the guilt and punishment of sin,[x] accept us in his Beloved;[y] continue his favour and grace to us,[z] pardon our daily failings,[a] and fill us with peace and joy, in giving us daily more and more assurance of forgiveness;[b] which we are the rather emboldened to ask, and encouraged to expect, when

working with his hands the thing which is good, that he may have to give to him that needeth. 2 Thess. iii. 11. For we hear that there are some which *walk among you disorderly, working not at all,* but are busybodies. Ver. 12. Now them that are such *we command and exhort* by our Lord Jesus Christ, *that with quietness they work, and eat their own bread.* Phil. iv. 6. *Be careful for nothing:* but in every thing by prayer and supplication, with thanksgiving, let your requests be made known unto God.

[r] 1 Tim. iv. 3. Forbidding to marry, and commanding to abstain from *meats,* which God hath created to be received with thanksgiving of them which believe and know the truth. Ver. 4. *For every creature of God is good, and nothing to be refused, if it be received with thanksgiving:* Ver. 5. *For it is sanctified by the word of God and prayer.*

[s] 1 Tim. vi. 6. But godliness with contentment is great gain. Ver. 7. For we brought nothing into this world, and it is certain we can carry nothing out. Ver. 8. And *having food and raiment, let us be therewith content.*

[t] Prov. xxx. 8. Remove far from me vanity and lies; *give me neither poverty nor riches; feed me with food convenient for me.* Ver. 9. *Lest I be full,* and deny thee, and say, Who is the Lord? or *lest I be poor,* and steal, and take the name of my God in vain.

194. [v] Matt. vi. 12.

[w] Rom. iii. from verse 9. to 22. Ver. 9. What then? are we better than they? No, in no wise: for we have before proved both Jews and Gentiles, *that they are all under sin;* Ver. 10. As it is written, There is *none righteous, no, not one:* Ver. 11. There is none that understandeth, there is none that seeketh after God: Ver. 12. They are all gone out of the way, they are together become unprofitable; there is none that doeth good, no, not one, &c. Ver. 19. That every mouth may be stopped, and *all the world may become guilty before God,* &c. Matt. xviii. 24. And when he had begun to reckon, one was brought unto him which owed him ten thousand talents. Ver. 25. But *forasmuch as he had not to pay,* his lord commanded him to be sold, and his wife and children, and all that he had, and payment to be made. Ps. cxxx. 3. *If thou, Lord, shouldest mark iniquities, O Lord, who shall stand?* Ver. 4. But there is forgiveness with thee, that thou mayest be feared.

[x] Rom. iii. 24. Being *justified freely by his grace, through the redemption that is in Christ Jesus;* Ver. 25. Whom God hath set forth to be *a propitiation through faith in his blood,* to declare his righteousness *for the remission of sins that are past,* through the forbearance of God; Ver. 26. To declare, I say, at this time his *righteousness;* that he might be just, and *the justifier of him which believeth in Jesus.* Heb. ix. 22. And almost all things are by the law *purged with blood;* and *without shedding of blood is no remission.*

[y] Eph. i. 6. To the praise of the glory of his grace, wherein he hath *made us accepted in the Beloved:* Ver. 7. In whom we have redemption through his blood, the forgiveness of sins, according to the riches of his grace.

[z] 2 Pet. i. 2. *Grace and peace be multiplied unto you* through the knowledge of God, and of Jesus our Lord.

[a] Hosea xiv. 2. Take with you words, and turn to the Lord: *say unto him, Take away all iniquity,* and receive us graciously: so will we render the calves of our lips. Jer. xiv. 7. O Lord, *though our iniquities testify against us, do thou it for thy name's sake:* for our *backslidings are many; we have sinned against thee.*

[b] Rom. xv. 13. Now the God of hope *fill you with all joy and peace in believing,* that ye may *abound in hope,* through the power of the Holy Ghost. Ps. li. 7. Purge me with hyssop, and I shall be clean; wash me, and I shall be whiter than snow. Ver. 8. *Make me to hear joy and gladness;* that the bones which thou hast broken may rejoice. Ver. 9. Hide thy face from my sins, and blot out all mine iniquities. Ver. 10. Create in me a clean heart, O God; and renew a right spirit within me. Ver. 12. *Restore unto me the joy of thy salvation;* and uphold me with thy free spirit.

we have this testimony in ourselves that we from the heart forgive others their offences.c

Q. 195. *What do we pray for in the sixth petition?*

A. In the sixth petition, (which is, *And lead us not into temptation, but deliver us from evil*,d) acknowledging, that the most wise, righteous, and gracious God, for divers holy and just ends, may so order things, that we may be assaulted, foiled, and for a time led captive by temptations;e that Satan,f the world,g and the flesh, are ready powerfully to draw us aside, and ensnare us;h and that we, even after the pardon of our sins, by reason of our corruption,i weakness, and want of watchfulness,k are not only subject to be tempted, and forward to expose ourselves unto temptations,l but also of ourselves unable and unwilling to resist them, to recover out of them, and to improve them;m and worthy to be left under the

---

c Luke xi. 4. And *forgive us our sins; for we also forgive every one that is indebted to us.* Matt. vi. 14. For *if ye forgive men their trespasses, your heavenly Father will also forgive you;* Ver. 15. But if ye forgive not men their trespasses, neither will your Father forgive your trespasses. Matt. xviii. 35. So *likewise* shall my heavenly Father do also unto you, *if ye from your hearts forgive not every one his brother their trespasses.*

195. d Matt. vi. 13.

e 2 Chron. xxxii. 31. Howbeit *in the business of the ambassadors of the princes of Babylon,* who sent unto him to enquire of the wonder that was done in the land, *God left him, to try him,* that he might know all that was in his heart.

f 1 Chron. xxi. 1. And *Satan stood up against Israel, and provoked David to number Israel.*

g Luke xxi. 34. And take heed to yourselves, *lest at any time your hearts be overcharged with surfeiting, and drunkenness, and cares of this life,* and so that day come upon you unawares. Mark iv. 19. *And the cares of this world, and the deceitfulness of riches,* and the lusts of other things entering in, *choke the word,* and it becometh unfruitful.

h James i. 14. But every man is tempted, when *he is drawn away of his own lust, and enticed.*

i Gal. v. 17. For *the flesh lusteth against the Spirit,* and the Spirit against the flesh: and these are contrary the one to the other; so that ye cannot do the things that ye would.

k Matt. xxvi. 41. *Watch and pray, that ye enter not into temptation:* the spirit indeed is willing, *but the flesh is weak.*

l Matt. xxvi. 69. Now Peter sat without in the palace: and a damsel came unto him, saying, Thou also wast with Jesus of Galilee. Ver. 70. *But he denied before them all,* saying, I know not what thou sayest. Ver. 71. And when he was gone out into the porch, another maid saw him, and said unto them that were there, This fellow was also with Jesus of Nazareth. Ver. 72. And *again he denied with an oath,* I do not know the man. Gal. ii. 11. But when *Peter* was come to Antioch, I withstood him to the face, *because he was to be blamed.* Ver. 12. For before that certain came from James, he did eat with the Gentiles: but when they were come, he withdrew, and *separated himself fearing them which were of the circumcision.* Ver. 13. And *the other Jews dissembled likewise with him;* insomuch that *Barnabas also was carried away with their dissimulation.* Ver. 14. But when I saw that *they walked not uprightly, according to the truth of the gospel,* I said unto Peter, &c. 2 Chron. xviii. 3. And Ahab king of Israel said unto Jehoshaphat king of Judah, *Wilt thou go with me to Ramoth-gilead?* And he answered him, *I am as thou art, and my people as thy people;* and we will be with thee in the war. Compared with 2 Chron. xix. 2. And Jehu the son of Hanani *the seer* went out to meet him, and *said to king Jehoshaphat, Shouldest thou help the ungodly, and love them that hate the Lord?* therefore is wrath upon thee from before the Lord.

m Rom. vii. 23. But I see *another law in my members* warring against the law of my mind, and *bringing me into captivity to the law of sin* which is in my members. Ver. 24. *O wretched man that I am! who shall deliver me from the body of this death?* 1 Chron. xxi. 1. And *Satan stood up* against Israel, and *provoked David to number Israel.* Ver. 2. *And David said to Joab, and to the rulers of the people, Go, number Israel from Beersheba even to Dan;* and bring the number of them to me, that I may know it. Ver. 3. And *Joab answered,* The Lord make his people an hundred times so many more as they be: but, my lord the king, are they not all my lord's servants? *why then doth my lord require this thing? why will he be a cause of trespass to Israel?* Ver. 4. Nevertheless the king's word prevailed against Joab: wherefore Joab departed, &c. 2 Chron. xvi. 7. And at that time Hanani the seer came to Asa king of Judah, and said unto him, Because thou hast relied on the king of Syria, and not relied on the Lord thy God, therefore is the host of the king of Syria escaped out of thine hand. Ver. 8. Were not the Ethiopians and the Lubims a huge host, with very many chariots and horsemen? yet, because thou didst rely on the Lord, he delivered them into thine hand.

power of them:ᵘ we pray, that God would so over-rule the world and all in it,ᵒ subdue the flesh,ᵖ and restrain Satan,ᵠ order all things,ʳ bestow and bless all means of grace,ˢ and quicken us to watchfulness in the use of them, that we and all his people may by his providence be kept from being tempted to sin;ᵗ or, if tempted, that by his Spirit we may be powerfully supported and enabled to stand in the hour of temptation;ᵛ or when fallen, raised again and recovered out of it,ʷ and have a sanctified use and improvement thereof:ˣ that our sanctification and salvation may be perfected,ʸ Satan trodden under our feet,ᶻ and we fully freed from sin, temptation, and all evil, for ever.ᵃ

Q. 196. *What doth the conclusion of the Lord's prayer teach us?*
A. The conclusion of the Lord's prayer, (which is, *For thine is the*

Ver. 9. For the eyes of the Lord run to and fro throughout the whole earth, to shew himself strong in the behalf of them whose heart is perfect towards him. Herein thou hast done foolishly; therefore from henceforth thou shalt have wars. Ver. 10. *Then Asa was wroth with the seer, and put him in a prison-house; for he was in a rage with him because of this thing. And Asa oppressed some of the people the same time.*
n Ps. lxxxi. 11. *But my people would not hearken to my voice;* and Israel would none of me. Ver. 12. *So I gave them up unto their own hearts' lust:* and they walked in their own counsels.
o John xvii. 15. I *pray not that thou shouldest take them out of the world, but that thou shouldest keep them from the evil.*
p Ps. li. 10. *Create in me a clean heart, O God; and renew a right spirit within me.* Ps. cxix. 133. Order my steps in thy word: and *let not any iniquity have dominion over me.*
q 2 Cor. xii. 7. And lest I should be exalted above measure through the abundance of the revelations, *there was given to me a thorn in the flesh, the messenger of Satan to buffet me,* lest I should be exalted above measure. Ver. 8. For this thing *I besought the Lord thrice, that it might depart from me.*
r 1 Cor. x. 12. Wherefore, let him that thinketh he standeth take heed lest he fall. Ver. 13. There hath no temptation taken you but such as is common to man: but God is faithful, *who will not suffer you to be tempted above that ye are able; but will with the temptation also make a way to escape,* that ye may be able to bear it.
s Heb. xiii. 20. Now the God of peace, that brought again from the dead our Lord Jesus, that great shepherd of the sheep, through the blood of the everlasting covenant, Ver. 21. *Make you perfect in every good work to do his will,* working in you that which is well-pleasing in his sight, through Jesus Christ, &c.
t Matt. xxvi. 41. *Watch and pray, that ye enter not into temptation.* Ps. xix. 13. *Keep back thy servant also from presumptuous sins;* let them not have dominion over me: then shall I be upright, and I shall be innocent from the great transgression.
v Eph. iii. 14. For this cause I bow my knees unto the Father of our Lord Jesus Christ, Ver. 15. Of whom the whole family in heaven and earth is named, Ver. 16. *That he would grant you,* according to the riches of his glory, *to be strengthened with might by his Spirit in the inner man;* Ver. 17. That Christ may dwell in your hearts by faith. 1 Thess. iii. 13. To the end he may *stablish your hearts unblameable in holiness before God,* even our Father, at the coming of our Lord Jesus Christ with all his saints. Jude, ver. 24. Now unto him *that is able to keep you from falling,* and to present you faultless before the presence of his glory with exceeding joy
w Ps. li. 12. *Restore unto me the joy of thy salvation;* and uphold me with thy free Spirit.
x 1 Pet. v. 8. *Be sober, be vigilant;* because your adversary the *devil,* as a roaring lion, walketh about, seeking whom he may devour: Ver. 9. *Whom resist stedfast in the faith,* knowing that the same afflictions are accomplished in your brethren that are in the world. Ver. 10. But *the God* of all grace, who hath called us unto his eternal glory by Christ Jesus, *after that ye have suffered a while, make you perfect, stablish, strengthen, settle you.*
y 2 Cor. xiii. 7. Now I pray to God that ye do no evil; not that we should appear approved, but that ye should do that which is honest, though we be as reprobates. Ver. 9. For we are glad when we are weak, and ye are strong: and *this also we wish, even your perfection.*
z Rom. xvi. 20. And the God of peace shall *bruise Satan under your feet shortly.* Zech. iii. 2. And *the Lord said unto Satan, The Lord rebuke thee, O Satan;* even the Lord that hath chosen Jerusalem rebuke thee: is not this a brand plucked out of the fire? Luke xxii. 31. And the Lord said, *Simon, Simon, behold, Satan hath desired to have you, that he may sift you as wheat:* Ver. 32. *But I have prayed for thee, that thy faith fail not:* and when thou art converted, strengthen thy brethren.
a John xvii. 15. *I pray not that thou shouldest take them out of the world, but that thou shouldest keep them from the evil.* 1 Thess. v. 23. And the very *God* of peace *sanctify you wholly:* and *I pray God your whole spirit, and soul, and body, be preserved blameless unto the coming of our Lord Jesus Christ.*

kingdom, and the power, and the glory, for ever. Amen.[b]) teacheth us to enforce our petitions with arguments,[c] which are to be taken, not from any worthiness in ourselves, or in any other creature, but from God;[d] and with our prayers to join praises,[e] ascribing to God alone eternal sovereignty, omnipotency, and glorious excellency;[f] in regard whereof, as he is able and willing to help us,[g] so we by faith are emboldened to plead with him that he would,[h] and quietly to rely upon him, that he will fulfil our requests.[i] And, to testify this our desire and assurance, we say, *Amen.*[k]

196. [b] Matt. vi. 13.

[c] Rom. xv. 30. Now I beseech you, brethren, for the Lord Jesus Christ's sake, and for the love of the Spirit, that ye *strive together with me in your prayers to God for me.*

[d] Dan. ix. 4. And *I prayed unto the Lord my God,* and made my confession, and said, *O Lord, the great and dreadful God, keeping the covenant* and mercy to them that love him, and to them that keep his commandments;—Ver. 7. O Lord, *righteousness belongeth unto thee,* but unto us confusion of faces, as at this day;—Ver. 8. O Lord, to us belongeth confusion of face, to our kings, to our princes, and to our fathers, because we have sinned against thee. Ver. 9. *To the Lord our God belong mercies and forgivenesses,* though we have rebelled against him. Ver. 16. *O Lord, according to all thy righteousness, I beseech thee,* let thine anger and thy fury be turned away from thy city Jerusalem,—Ver. 17. Now therefore, O our God, hear the prayer of thy servant, and his supplications, and cause thy face to shine upon thy sanctuary that is desolate, *for the Lord's sake.* Ver. 18. *O my God, incline thine ear, and hear; open thine eyes, and behold our desolations, and the city which is called by thy name:* for we do not present our supplications before thee for our righteousnesses, *but for thy great mercies.* Ver. 19. O Lord, hear; O Lord, forgive; O Lord, hearken and do; *defer not, for thine own sake, O my God: for thy city and thy people are called by thy name.*

[e] Phil. iv. 6. Be careful for nothing: but in every thing *by prayer and supplication, with thanksgiving, let your requests be made known unto God,* &c.

[f] 1 Chron. xxix. 10. Wherefore David blessed the Lord before all the congregation: and David said, Blessed be thou, Lord God of Israel our father, for ever and ever. Ver. 11. *Thine, O Lord, is the greatness, and the power, and the glory, and the victory, and the majesty: for all that is in the heaven* and *in the earth is thine; thine is the kingdom, O Lord, and thou art exalted as head above all.* Ver. 12. Both *riches and honour come of thee,* and *thou reignest over all, and in thine hand is power and might;* and in thine hand it is to make great, and to give strength unto all. Ver. 13. Now therefore, our God, *we thank thee, and praise thy glorious name.*

[g] Eph. iii. 20. Now unto him *that is able to do exceeding abundantly above all that we ask or think,* according to the power that worketh in us, Ver. 21. Unto him be glory in the church by Christ Jesus throughout all ages, world without end. Amen. Luke xi. 13. If ye then, being evil, know how to give good gifts unto your children; *how much more shall your heavenly Father give the Holy Spirit to them that ask him?*

[h] 2 Chron. xx. 6. And (Jehoshaphat) said, *O Lord God of our fathers, art not thou God in heaven? and rulest not thou over all the kingdoms of the heathen?* and *in thine hand is there not power and might,* so that none is able to withstand thee? Ver. 11. *Behold, I say, how they reward us,* to come to cast us out of thy possession, which thou hast given us to inherit.

[i] 2 Chron. xiv. 11. And Asa cried unto the Lord his God, and said, Lord, it is nothing with thee to help, whether with many, or with them that have no power: *help us, O Lord our God; for we rest on thee, and in thy name we go against this multitude.* O Lord, thou art our God; let not man prevail against thee.

[k] 1 Cor. xiv. 16. Else, when thou shalt bless with the spirit, *how shall he that occupieth the room of the unlearned say Amen at thy giving of thanks,* seeing he understandeth not what thou sayest? Rev. xxii. 20. He which testifieth these things saith, Surely I come quickly: *Amen.* Even so come, Lord Jesus. Ver. 21. The grace of our Lord Jesus Christ be with you all. *AMEN.*

THE SHORTER CATECHISM;

AGREED UPON BY

THE ASSEMBLY OF DIVINES AT WESTMINSTER,

WITH THE ASSISTANCE OF

COMMISSIONERS FROM THE CHURCH OF SCOTLAND,

AS

A PART OF THE COVENANTED UNIFORMITY IN RELIGION BETWIXT THE CHURCHES OF CHRIST IN THE KINGDOMS OF SCOTLAND, ENGLAND, AND IRELAND.

And Approved Anno 1648, by the General Assembly of the Church of Scotland, to be a Directory for Catechising such as are of weaker Capacity, with the Proofs from the Scripture.

ASSEMBLY AT EDINBURGH, July 28, 1648. Sess. 19.

Act approving the SHORTER CATECHISM.

THE General Assembly having seriously considered the SHORTER CATECHISM agreed upon by the Assembly of Divines sitting at Westminster, with assistance of Commissioners from this Kirk; do find, upon due examination thereof, that the said Catechism is agreeable to the word of God, and in nothing contrary to the received doctrine, worship, discipline, and government of this Kirk. And therefore approve the said Shorter Catechism, as a part of the intended uniformity, to be a Directory for catechising such as are of weaker capacity.

A. KER.

THE SHORTER CATECHISM.

QUEST. 1. *WHAT is the chief end of man?*
Ans. Man's chief end is to glorify God,[a] and to enjoy him for ever.[b]

Q. 2. *What rule hath God given to direct us how we may glorify and enjoy him?*
A. The word of God, which is contained in the scriptures of the Old and New Testaments,[c] is the only rule to direct us how we may glorify and enjoy him.[d]

Q. 3. *What do the scriptures principally teach?*
A. The scriptures principally teach what man is to believe concerning God, and what duty God requires of man.[e]

Q. 4. *What is God?*
A. God is a Spirit,[f] infinite,[g] eternal,[h] and unchangeable,[i] in his being,[k] wisdom,[l] power,[m] holiness,[n] justice, goodness, and truth.[o]

---

1. [a] 1 Cor. x. 31. Whether therefore ye eat, or drink, or whatsoever ye do, *do all to the glory of God.* Rom. xi. 36. For of him, and through him, and to him, are all things: *to whom be glory for ever. Amen.*
[b] Ps. lxxiii. 25. *Whom have I in heaven but thee?* and there is none upon earth *that I desire besides thee.* Ver. 26. My flesh and my heart faileth: but God is the strength of my heart *and my portion for ever.* Ver. 27. For, lo, they that are far from thee shall perish: thou hast destroyed all them that go a-whoring from thee. Ver. 28. *But it is good for me to draw near to God: I have put my trust in the Lord God, that I may declare all thy works.*

2. [c] 2 Tim. iii. 16. *All scripture is given by inspiration of God,* and is profitable for doctrine, for reproof, for correction, for instruction in righteousness. Eph. ii. 20. And are built upon *the foundation of the apostles and prophets, Jesus Christ himself being the chief corner-stone.*
[d] 1 John i. 3. That which we have seen and heard declare we unto you, *that ye also may have fellowship with us:* and truly our fellowship is with the Father, and with his Son Jesus Christ. Ver. 4. And these things write we unto you, *that your joy may be full.*

3. [e] 2 Tim. i. 13. Hold fast the form of sound words, which thou hast heard of me, *in faith and love which is in Christ Jesus.* 2 Tim. iii. 16. [See in letter c.]

4. [f] John iv. 24. *God is a Spirit:* and they that worship him must *worship him in spirit and in truth.*
[g] Job xi. 7. *Canst thou by searching find out God? canst thou find out the Almighty unto perfection?* Ver. 8. It is as *high as heaven;* what canst thou do? *deeper than hell;* what canst thou know? Ver. 9. The measure thereof is *longer than the earth, and broader than the sea.*
[h] Ps. xc. 2. Before the mountains were brought forth, or ever thou hadst formed the earth and the world, *even from everlasting to everlasting thou art God.*
[i] James i. 17. Every good gift and every perfect gift is from above, and cometh down from the Father of lights, with whom is *no variableness, neither shadow of turning.*
[k] Exod. iii. 14. And God said unto Moses, *I AM THAT I AM:* and he said, Thus shalt thou say unto the children of Israel, *I AM hath sent me unto you.*
[l] Ps. cxlvii. 5. Great is our Lord, and of great power: *his understanding is infinite.*
[m] Rev. iv. 8. And the four beasts had each of them six wings about him; and they were full of eyes within: and they rest not day and night, saying, *Holy, holy, holy, Lord God Almighty, which was, and is, and is to come.*
[n] Rev. xv. 4. Who shall not fear thee, O Lord, and glorify thy name? *for thou only art holy:* for all nations shall come and worship before thee; *for thy judgments are made manifest.*
[o] Exod. xxxiv. 6. And the Lord passed by before him, and proclaimed, *The Lord, The Lord God, merciful and gracious, long-suffering, and abundant in goodness and truth,* Ver. 7. Keeping mercy for thousands, forgiving iniquity, and transgression, and

Q. 5. Are there more Gods than one?

A. There is but One only, the living and true God.ᵖ

Q. 6. How many persons are there in the Godhead?

A. There are three persons in the Godhead; the Father, the Son, and the Holy Ghost; and these three are one God, the same in substance, equal in power and glory.ᑫ

Q. 7. What are the decrees of God?

A. The decrees of God are, his eternal purpose, according to the counsel of his will, whereby, for his own glory, he hath foreordained whatsoever comes to pass.ʳ

Q. 8. How doth God execute his decrees?

A. God executeth his decrees in the works of creation and providence.

Q. 9. What is the work of creation?

A. The work of creation is, God's making all things of nothing, by the word of his power, in the space of six days, and all very good.ˢ

Q. 10. How did God create man?

A. God created man male and female, after his own image, in knowledge, righteousness, and holiness, with dominion over the creatures.ᵗ

Q. 11. What are God's works of providence?

A. God's works of providence are, his most holy,ᵛ wise,ʷ and powerful preserving ˣ and governing all his creatures, and all their actions.ʸ

Q. 12. What special act of providence did God exercise toward man in the estate wherein he was created?

sin, and that will by no means *clear the guilty; visiting the iniquity of the fathers upon the children, and upon the children's children,* unto the third and to the fourth generation.

5. ᵖ Deut. vi. 4. Hear, O Israel; *The Lord our God is one Lord.* Jer. x. 10. But *the Lord is the true God, he is the living God, and an everlasting King:* at his wrath the earth shall tremble, and the nations shall not be able to abide his indignation.

6. ᑫ 1 John v. 7. *For there are three that bear record in heaven, the Father, the Word, and the Holy Ghost: and these three are one.* Matt. xxviii. 19. Go ye therefore, and teach all nations, baptizing them *in the name of the Father, and of the Son, and of the Holy Ghost.*

7. ʳ Eph. i. 4. According as he hath *chosen us in him before the foundation of the world,* that we should be *holy and without blame before him in love.* Ver. 11. In whom also we have obtained an inheritance, being *predestinated according to the purpose of him who worketh all things after the counsel of his own will.* Rom. ix. 22. What if God, willing to shew his wrath, and to make his power known, endured *with much long-suffering* the vessels of wrath fitted to destruction; Ver. 23. And that he might make known the *riches of his glory* on the vessels of mercy, *which he had afore prepared unto glory?*

9. ˢ Gen. i. throughout. Heb. xi. 3. Through faith we understand that the *worlds were framed by the word of God;* so that *things which are seen were not made of things which do appear.*

10. ᵗ Gen. i. 26. And God said, Let us *make man in our image, after our likeness;* and *let them have dominion over the fish of the sea,* and *over the fowl of the air,* and *over the cattle,* and *over all the earth,* and *over every creeping thing that creepeth upon the earth.* Ver. 27. So God created man in his *own image:* in the *image of God created he him;* male and female created he them. Ver. 28. And God blessed them: and God said unto them, *Be fruitful, and multiply, and replenish the earth, and subdue it;* and have *dominion over the fish of the sea,* and over the *fowl of the air,* and over *every living thing that moveth upon the earth.* Col. iii. 10. And have put on the new man, which is renewed in knowledge after the *image of him that created him.* Eph. iv. 24. And that ye put on the new man, which after God is *created in righteousness and true holiness.*

11. ᵛ Ps. cxlv. 17. The Lord is righteous in all his ways, and *holy in all his works.*

ʷ Ps. civ. 24. O Lord, how manifold are thy works! *in wisdom hast thou made them all:* the earth is full of thy riches. Isa. xxviii. 29. This also cometh forth from the Lord of hosts, which is *wonderful in counsel, and excellent in working.*

ˣ Heb. i. 3. Who, being the brightness of his glory, and the express image of his person, and *upholding all things by the word of his power,* when he had by himself purged our sins, sat down on the right hand of the Majesty on high.

ʸ Ps. ciii. 19. The Lord hath prepared his throne in the heavens; and *his kingdom ruleth over all.* Matt. x. 29. Are not two sparrows sold for a farthing? and one of them *shall not fall on the ground without your Father.* Ver. 30. But the very hairs *of your head are all numbered.* Ver 31.

A. When God had created man, he entered into a covenant of life with him, upon condition of perfect obedience; forbidding him to eat of the tree of the knowledge of good and evil, upon the pain of death.ᶻ

Q. 13. *Did our first parents continue in the estate wherein they were created?*

A. Our first parents, being left to the freedom of their own will, fell from the estate wherein they were created, by sinning against God.ᵃ

Q. 14. *What is sin?*

A. Sin is any want of conformity unto, or transgression of, the law of God.ᵇ

Q. 15. *What was the sin whereby our first parents fell from the estate wherein they were created?*

A. The sin whereby our first parents fell from the estate wherein they were created, was their eating the forbidden fruit.ᶜ

Q. 16. *Did all mankind fall in Adam's first transgression?*

A. The covenant being made with Adam, not only for himself, but for his posterity; all mankind, descending from him by ordinary generation, sinned in him, and fell with him, in his first transgression.ᵈ

Q. 17. *Into what estate did the fall bring mankind?*

A. The fall brought mankind into an estate of sin and misery.ᵉ

Q. 18. *Wherein consists the sinfulness of that estate whereinto man fell?*

A. The sinfulness of that estate whereinto man fell, consists in the guilt of Adam's first sin, the want of original righteousness, and the corruption of his whole nature, which is commonly called Original Sin; together with all actual transgressions which proceed from it.ᶠ

Fear ye not therefore, ye are of *more value than many sparrows.*

12. ᶻ Gal. iii. 12. And the law is not of faith: but, The man that doeth them *shall live in them.* Gen. ii. 17. *But of the tree of the knowledge of good and evil, thou shalt not eat of it:* for in the day that thou eatest thereof *thou shalt surely die.*

13. ᵃ Gen. iii. 6. And when the woman saw that the tree was good for food, and that it was pleasant to the eyes, and a tree to be desired to make one wise, *she took of the fruit thereof, and did eat; and gave also unto her husband with her, and he did eat.* Ver. 7. And the eyes of them both were opened, and they knew that they were naked; and they sewed fig-leaves together, and made themselves aprons. Ver. 8. And they heard the voice of the Lord God walking in the garden in the cool of the day: and *Adam and his wife hid themselves from the presence of the Lord God* amongst the trees of the garden. Ver. 13. And the Lord God said unto the woman, What is this that thou hast done? And the woman said, *The serpent beguiled me, and I did eat.* Eccl. vii. 29. Lo, this only have I found, that God hath made man upright; but *they have sought out many inventions*

14. ᵇ 1 John iii. 4. Whosoever committeth sin transgresseth also the law: for *sin is the transgression of the law.*

15. ᶜ Gen. iii. 6. [See in letter a.] Ver. 12. The woman whom thou gavest to be with me, she gave me of the tree, and *I did eat.*

16. ᵈ Gen. ii. 16. And *the Lord God commanded the man, saying,* Of every tree of the garden thou mayest freely eat. Ver. 17. But of the tree of the knowledge of good and evil, thou shalt not eat of it: for in the day that thou eatest thereof thou shalt surely die. Rom. v. 12. Wherefore, as by one man sin entered into the world, and death by sin; and so death passed upon all men, *for that all, have sinned.* 1 Cor. xv. 21. For *since by man came death,* by man came also the resurrection of the dead. Ver. 22. For as *in Adam all die,* even so in Christ shall all be made alive.

17. ᵉ Rom. v. 12. Wherefore, as by one man *sin entered into the world,* and *death by sin;* and so *death passed upon all men,* for that *all have sinned.*

18. ᶠ Rom. v. 12. Wherefore, as by one man *sin entered into the world,* and *death by sin;* and so *death passed upon all men,* for that *all have sinned.* Ver. 19. For as by one man's disobedience many were made sinners; so by the obedience of one shall many be made righteous. Rom. v. from ver. 10. to the 20. Eph. ii. 1. And you hath he quickened, who were *dead in trespasses and sins;* Ver. 2. Wherein *in time past ye walked according to the course of this world,* according to the prince of the power of the air, *the spirit that now worketh in the children of disobedience:* Ver. 3. Among whom also we all had our conversation in times past, in the lusts of our flesh, fulfilling the desires of the flesh and of the mind; and

Q. 19. *What is the misery of that estate whereinto man fell?*

A. All mankind by their fall lost communion with God,[g] are under his wrath and curse,[h] and so made liable to all miseries in this life, to death itself, and to the pains of hell for ever.[i]

Q. 20. *Did God leave all mankind to perish in the estate of sin and misery?*

A. God having, out of his mere good pleasure, from all eternity, elected some to everlasting life,[k] did enter into a covenant of grace, to deliver them out of the estate of sin and misery, and to bring them into an estate of salvation by a Redeemer.[l]

Q. 21. *Who is the Redeemer of God's elect?*

A. The only Redeemer of God's elect is the Lord Jesus Christ,[m] who, being the eternal Son of God, became man,[n] and so was, and continueth to be, God and man in two distinct natures, and one person, for ever.[o]

Q. 22. *How did Christ, being the Son of God, become man?*

A. Christ, the Son of God, became man, by taking to himself a true

---

were by nature the children of wrath, even as others. James i. 14. But every man is tempted, *when he is drawn away of his own lust, and enticed.* Ver. 15. Then, when lust hath conceived, it bringeth forth sin; and sin, when it is finished, bringeth forth death. Matt. xv. 19. For *out of the heart proceed evil thoughts, murders, adulteries, fornications, thefts, false witness, blasphemies.*

19. g Gen. iii. 8. And they heard the voice of the Lord God walking in the garden in the cool of the day: and Adam and his wife *hid themselves from the presence of the Lord God* amongst the trees of the garden. Ver. 10. And he said, I heard thy voice in the garden, and I was afraid, *because I was naked; and I hid myself.* Ver. 24. So he drove out the man: *and he placed at the east of the garden of Eden cherubims and a flaming sword which turned every way, to keep the way of the tree of life.*

h Eph. ii. 2. Wherein in time past ye walked according to the course of this world, according to the prince of the power of the air, the spirit that now worketh in the children of disobedience: Ver. 3. Among whom also we all had our conversation in times past in the lusts of our flesh, fulfilling the desires of the flesh and of the mind; *and were by nature the children of wrath, even as others.* Gal. iii. 10. For *as many as are of the works of the law are under the curse: for it is written, Cursed is every one that continueth not in all things which are written in the book of the law to do them.*

i Lam. iii. 39. Wherefore doth a living man complain, *a man for the punishment of his sins?* *Rom. vi. 23. For *the wages of sin is death;* but the gift of God is eternal life through Jesus Christ our Lord. Matt. xxv. 41. Then shall he say also unto them on the left hand, *Depart from me, ye cursed, into everlasting fire, prepared for the devil and his angels.* Ver. 46. And *these shall go away into everlasting punishment:* but the righteous into life eternal.

20. k Eph. i. 4. According as he hath *chosen us in him before the foundation of the world, that we should be holy and without blame before him in love.*

l Rom. iii. 20. Therefore by the deeds of the law there shall no flesh be justified in his sight: for by the law is the knowledge of sin. Ver. 21. But now *the righteousness of God without the law is manifested,* being witnessed by the law and the prophets; Ver. 22. Even *the righteousness of God which is by faith of Jesus Christ unto all and upon all them that believe;* for there is no difference. Gal. iii. 21. Is the law then against the promises of God? God forbid: for if there had been a law given which could have given life, verily righteousness should have been by the law. Ver. 22. But the scripture hath concluded all under sin, *that the promise by faith of Jesus Christ might be given to them that believe.*

21. m 1 Tim. ii. 5. For there is *one God, and one mediator between God and men, the man Christ Jesus;* Ver. 6. Who gave himself *a ransom for all,* to be testified in due time.

n John i. 14. And *the Word was made flesh* and *dwelt among us,* (and we beheld his glory, *the glory as of the only begotten of the Father,) full of grace and truth.* Gal. iv. 4. But when the fulness of the time was come, *God sent forth his Son, made of a woman, made under the law.*

o Rom. ix. 5. Whose are the fathers, and of whom, as concerning the flesh, Christ came, *who is over all, God blessed for ever.* Amen. Luke i. 35. And the angel answered and said unto her, The Holy Ghost shall come upon thee, and the power of the Highest shall overshadow thee: therefore also that holy thing, which shall be born of thee, shall be called *the Son of God.* Col. ii. 9. For in him *dwelleth all the fulness of the Godhead bodily.* Heb. vii. 24. But this man, because he continueth ever, hath an unchangeable priesthood. Ver. 25. Wherefore he is able also to save them to the uttermost that come unto God by him, *seeing he ever liveth to make intercession for them.*

body,p and a reasonable soul,q being conceived by the power of the Holy Ghost, in the womb of the Virgin Mary, and born of her,r yet without sin.s

Q. 23. *What offices doth Christ execute as our Redeemer?*
A. Christ, as our Redeemer, executeth the offices of a prophet, of a priest, and of a king, both in his estate of humiliation and exaltation.t

Q. 24. *How doth Christ execute the office of a prophet?*
A. Christ executeth the office of a prophet, in revealing to us, by his word and Spirit, the will of God for our salvation.v

22. p Heb. ii. 14. Forasmuch then as the children are partakers of flesh and blood, he also *himself likewise took part of the same;* that through death he might destroy him that had the power of death, that is, the devil. Ver. 16. For verily he took not on him the nature of angels; but he *took on him the seed of Abraham.* Heb. x. 5. Wherefore, when he cometh into the world, he saith, Sacrifice and offering thou wouldest not, but *a body hast thou prepared me.* q Matt. xxvi. 38. Then saith he unto them, *My soul is exceeding sorrowful, even unto death:* tarry ye here, and watch with me. r Luke i. 27. To a virgin espoused to a man, whose name was Joseph, of the house of David; and the virgin's name was Mary. Ver. 31. And, behold, thou *shalt conceive in thy womb, and bring forth a son,* and shalt call his name *JESUS.* Ver. 35. And the angel answered and said unto her, The Holy Ghost shall come upon thee, and the power of the Highest shall overshadow thee: therefore also that holy thing, which shall be born of thee, shall be called the Son of God. Ver. 42. And she spake out with a loud voice, and said, Blessed art thou among women, and *blessed is the fruit of thy womb.* Gal. iv. 4. [See in the preceding question, letter n.] s Heb. iv. 15. For we have not an high priest which cannot be touched with the feeling of our infirmities; but was in all points tempted like as we are, *yet without sin.* Heb. vii. 26. For such an high priest became us, who is holy, harmless, undefiled, *separate from sinners,* and made higher than the heavens. 23. t Acts iii. 21. Whom the heaven must receive until the times of restitution of all things, which God hath spoken by the mouth of all his holy prophets since the world began. Ver. 22. For Moses truly said unto the fathers, *A prophet shall the Lord your God raise up unto you of your brethren,* like unto me; him shall ye hear in all things whatsoever he shall say unto you. Heb. xii. 25. See that ye refuse not him that speaketh: for if they escaped not who refused him that spake on earth, much more shall not we escape, if we turn away from him *that speaketh from heaven.* Compared with 2 Cor. xiii. 3. Since ye seek a proof of *Christ speaking in me,* which to you-ward is not weak, but is mighty in you. Heb. v. 5. So also Christ glorified not himself *to be made an high priest;* but he that said unto him, Thou art my Son, to-day have I begotten thee. Ver. 6. *As he saith also in another place,* Thou art a priest for ever, after the order of Melchisedec. Ver. 7. Who in the days of his flesh, *when he had offered up prayers* and supplications, with strong crying and tears, unto him that was able to save him from death, and was heard in that he feared. Heb. vii. 25. Wherefore he is able also to save them to the uttermost that come unto God by him, seeing he ever liveth to make intercession for them. Ps. ii. 6. Yet *have I set my King* upon my holy hill of Zion. Isa. ix. 6. For unto us a child is born, unto us a son is given; and *the government shall be upon his shoulder:* and his name shall be called Wonderful, Counsellor, The mighty God, The everlasting Father, *The Prince of Peace.* Ver. 7. Of the increase of *his government* and peace there shall be no end, upon the throne of David, and upon *his kingdom,* to order it, and to establish it with judgment and with justice from henceforth even for ever. The zeal of the Lord of hosts will perform this. Matt. xxi. 5. Tell ye the daughter of Sion, *Behold, thy King cometh* unto thee, meek, and sitting upon an ass, and a colt the foal of an ass. Ps. ii. 8. Ask of me, and I shall give thee the heathen for thine inheritance, and the uttermost parts of the earth for thy possession. Ver. 9. *Thou shalt break them with a rod of iron; thou shalt dash them in pieces* like a potter's vessel. Ver. 10. Be wise now therefore, O ye kings; be instructed, ye judges of the earth. Ver. 11. *Serve the Lord* with fear, and rejoice with trembling. 24. v John i. 18. No man hath seen God at any time; the only begotten Son, which is in the bosom of the Father, *he hath declared him.* 1 Pet. i. 10. Of which salvation the prophets have enquired and searched diligently, who prophesied of the grace that should come unto you: Ver. 11. Searching what, or *what manner of time, the Spirit of Christ which was in them* did signify, when it testified beforehand the sufferings of Christ, and the glory that should follow. Ver. 12. Unto *whom it was revealed,* that not unto themselves, but unto us, they did minister the things which are now reported unto you by them that have preached the gospel unto you *with the Holy Ghost* sent down from heaven; which things the angels desire to look into. John xv. 15. Henceforth I call you not servants; for the servant knoweth not what his lord doeth: but I have called you friends; for all things that I have heard of my Father *I have made known unto you.* John xx. 31. But *these are written, that ye might believe that Jesus is the Christ,* the Son of God; and that believing ye might have life through his name.

Q. 25. *How doth Christ execute the office of a priest?*

A. Christ executeth the office of a priest, in his once offering up of himself a sacrifice to satisfy divine justice,[w] and reconcile us to God;[x] and in making continual intercession for us.[y]

Q. 26. *How doth Christ execute the office of a king?*

A. Christ executeth the office of a king, in subduing us to himself,[z] in ruling[a] and defending us,[b] and in restraining and conquering all his and our enemies.[c]

Q. 27. *Wherein did Christ's humiliation consist?*

A. Christ's humiliation consisted in his being born, and that in a low condition,[d] made under the law,[e] undergoing the miseries of this life,[f] the wrath of God,[g] and the cursed death of the cross;[h] in being buried,[i] and continuing under the power of death for a time.[k]

Q. 28. *Wherein consisteth Christ's exaltation?*

A. Christ's exaltation consisteth in his rising again from the dead

---

25. [w] Heb. ix. 14. How much more shall *the blood of Christ, who* through the eternal Spirit *offered himself without spot to God,* purge your conscience from dead works, to serve the living God? Ver. 28. So *Christ was once offered* to bear the sins of many; and unto them that look for him shall he appear the second time, without sin, unto salvation.

[x] Heb. ii. 17. Wherefore in all things it behoved him to be made like unto his brethren, that he might be a merciful and faithful high priest in things pertaining to God, *to make reconciliation for the sins of the people.*

[y] Heb. vii. 24. But this man, because he continueth ever, hath an unchangeable priesthood. Ver. 25. Wherefore he is able also to save them to the uttermost that come unto God by him, seeing *he ever liveth to make intercession for them.*

26. [z] Acts xv. 14. Simeon hath declared how God at the first did visit the Gentiles, *to take out of them a people for his name.* Ver. 15. And to this agree the words of the prophets; as it is written, Ver. 16. After this I will return, and will *build again the tabernacle* of David, which is fallen down; and I will build again the ruins thereof, and I will set it up.

[a] Isa. xxxiii. 22. For the Lord is our judge, the *Lord is our lawgiver, the Lord is our king;* he will save us.

[b] Isa. xxxii. 1. Behold, a king shall reign in righteousness, and princes shall rule in judgment. Ver. 2. And *a man shall be as an hiding-place from the wind,* and a covert from the tempest; as rivers of water in a dry place; as the shadow of a great rock in a weary land.

[c] 1 Cor. xv. 25. For he must reign, *till he hath put all enemies under his feet.* Ps. cx. throughout.

27. [d] Luke ii. 7. And she brought forth her first-born son, and wrapped him in swaddling clothes, and *laid him in a manger;* because there was no room for them in the inn.

[e] Gal. iv. 4. But when the fulness of the time was come, God sent forth his Son, made of a woman, *made under the law.*

[f] Heb. xii. 2. Looking unto Jesus, the author and finisher of our faith; who, for the joy that was set before him, *endured the cross,* despising the shame, and is set down at the right hand of the throne of God. Ver. 3. For consider *him that endured such contradiction of sinners* against himself, lest ye be wearied and faint in your minds. Isa. liii. 2. For he shall grow up before him as a tender plant, and as a root out of a dry ground: he hath no form nor comeliness; and when we shall see him, *there is no beauty that we should desire him.* Ver. 3. *He is despised and rejected of men; a man of sorrows, and acquainted with grief;* and *we hid as it were our faces from him: he was despised, and we esteemed him not.*

[g] Luke xxii. 44. And, *being in an agony,* he prayed more earnestly: and his sweat was as it were great drops of blood falling down to the ground. Matt. xxvii. 46. And about the ninth hour Jesus cried with a loud voice, saying, Eli, Eli, lama sabachthani? that is to say, *My God, my God, why hast thou forsaken me?*

[h] Phil. ii. 8. And being found in fashion as a man, he humbled himself, and became *obedient unto death, even the death of the cross.*

[i] 1 Cor. xv. 3. For I delivered unto you first of all that which I also received, how that Christ died for our sins according to the scriptures; Ver. 4. And that *he was buried,* and that he rose again the third day according to the scriptures.

[k] Acts ii. 24. *Whom God hath raised up, having loosed the pains of death:* because it was not possible that he should be holden of it. Ver. 25. For David speaketh concerning him, I foresaw the Lord always before my face; for he is on my right hand, that I should not be moved: Ver. 26. Therefore did my heart rejoice, and my tongue was glad; moreover also, my flesh shall rest in hope: Ver. 27. Because *thou wilt not leave my soul in hell, neither wilt thou suffer thine Holy One to see corruption.* Ver. 31 He, seeing this before, spake of the resurrection of Christ, that *his soul was not left in hell,* neither *his flesh did see corruption*

on the third day,¹ in ascending up into heaven,ᵐ in sitting at the right hand of God the Father,ⁿ and in coming to judge the world at the last day.º

Q. 29. *How are we made partakers of the redemption purchased by Christ?*

A. We are made partakers of the redemption purchased by Christ, by the effectual application of it to usᵖ by his Holy Spirit.ᑫ

Q. 30. *How doth the Spirit apply to us the redemption purchased by Christ?*

A. The Spirit applieth to us the redemption purchased by Christ, by working faith in us,ʳ and thereby uniting us to Christ in our effectual calling.ˢ

Q. 31. *What is effectual calling?*

A. Effectual calling is the work of God's Spirit,ᵗ whereby, convincing us of our sin and misery,ᵛ enlightening our minds in the knowledge of Christ,ʷ and renewing our wills,ˣ he doth persuade and enable us to embrace Jesus Christ, freely offered to us in the gospel.ʸ

Q. 32. *What benefits do they that are effectually called partake of in this life?*

---

28. ¹ 1 Cor. xv. 4. And that he was buried, and that *he rose again the third day according to the scriptures.*
ᵐ Mark xvi. 19. So then, after the Lord had spoken unto them, *he was received up into heaven, and sat on the right hand of God.*
ⁿ Eph. i. 20. Which he wrought in Christ, when he raised him from the dead, and *set him at his own right hand in the heavenly places.*
º Acts i. 11. Which also said, Ye men of Galilee, why stand ye gazing up into heaven? this same Jesus, which is taken up from you into heaven, *shall so come in like manner as ye have seen him go into heaven.* Acts xvii. 31. Because he hath *appointed a day,* in the which he will *judge the world in righteousness by that man* whom he hath ordained; whereof he hath given assurance unto all men, in that he hath *raised him from the dead.*

29. ᵖ John i. 11. He came unto his own, and his own received him not. Ver. 12. But *as many as received him, to them gave he power to become the sons of God, even to them that believe on his name.*
ᑫ Tit. iii. 5. Not by works of righteousness which we have done, but according to *his mercy he saved us, by the washing of regeneration, and renewing of the Holy Ghost;* Ver. 6. *Which he shed on us abundantly through Jesus Christ our Saviour.*

30. ʳ Eph. i. 13. In whom ye also trusted, after that ye heard the word of truth, the gospel of your salvation: in whom also, after *that ye believed,* ye were *sealed with that Holy Spirit of promise,* Ver. 14. Which is the earnest of our inheritance, until the redemption of *the purchased possession,* unto the praise of his glory. John vi. 37. All that the Father giveth me shall come to me: and him that cometh to me I will in no wise cast out. Ver. 39. And this is the Father's will which hath sent me, that of *all which he hath given me I should lose* nothing, but should *raise it up again at the last day.* Eph. ii. 8. For *by grace are ye saved through faith;* and that not of yourselves: *it is the gift of God.*
ˢ Eph. iii. 17. That *Christ may dwell in your hearts by faith;* that ye, being *rooted and grounded in love,* &c. 1 Cor. i. 9. God is faithful, by whom ye were called unto *the fellowship of his Son Jesus Christ our Lord.*

31. ᵗ 2 Tim. i. 9. Who hath saved us, and called us with an holy calling, not according to our works, but *according to his own purpose and grace, which was given us in Christ Jesus* before the world began. 2 Thess. ii. 13. But we are bound to give thanks alway to God for you, brethren beloved of the Lord, because God hath from the beginning chosen you to salvation *through sanctification of the Spirit,* and belief of the truth. Ver. 14. Whereunto *he called you* by our gospel, to the obtaining of the glory of our Lord Jesus Christ.
ᵛ Acts ii. 37. Now when they heard this, *they were pricked in their heart,* and said unto Peter, and to the rest of the apostles, Men and brethren, *what shall we do?*
ʷ Acts xxvi. 18. *To open their eyes, and to turn them from darkness to light,* and from the power of Satan unto God, that they may receive forgiveness of sins, and inheritance among them which are sanctified by faith that is in me.
ˣ Ezek. xxxvi. 26. *A new heart also will I give you,* and a new spirit will I put within you; and I will take away the stony heart out of your flesh, and I will give you an heart of flesh. Ver. 27. And I will put my Spirit within you, and *cause you to walk in my statutes,* and ye shall keep my judgments, and do them.
ʸ John vi. 44. No man *can come to me,* except the Father, which hath sent me, draw him: and I will raise him up at the last day. Ver. 45. It is written in the prophets, And they shall be all taught of God. Every man

A. They that are effectually called do in this life partake of justification,[z] adoption,[a] and sanctification, and the several benefits which in this life do either accompany or flow from them.[b]

Q. 33. *What is justification?*

A. Justification is an act of God's free grace, wherein he pardoneth all our sins,[c] and accepteth us as righteous in his sight,[d] only for the righteousness of Christ imputed to us,[e] and received by faith alone.[f]

Q. 34. *What is adoption?*

A. Adoption is an act of God's free grace,[g] whereby we are received into the number, and have a right to all the privileges of the sons of God.[h]

Q. 35. *What is sanctification?*

A. Sanctification is the work of God's free grace,[i] whereby we are renewed in the whole man after the image of God,[k] and are enabled more and more to die unto sin, and live unto righteousness.[l]

Q. 36. *What are the benefits which in this life do accompany or flow from justification, adoption, and sanctification?*

A. The benefits which in this life do accompany or flow from justi-

therefore that hath heard, and hath learned of the Father, *cometh unto me.* Phil. ii. 13. For it is *God which worketh in you, both to will and to do* of his good pleasure.

32. ᵃ Rom. viii. 30. Moreover, whom he did predestinate, them he also called; and *whom he called, them he also justified;* and whom he justified, them he also glorified.

ᵃ Eph. i. 5. Having predestinated us unto *the adoption of children* by Jesus Christ to himself, according to the good pleasure of his will.

ᵇ 1 Cor. i. 26. For ye see your calling, brethren, how that not many wise men after the flesh, not many mighty, not many noble, are called. Ver. 30. But of him are ye in Christ Jesus, who of God is made *unto us wisdom, and righteousness, and sanctification, and redemption.*

33. ᶜ Rom. iii. 24. Being justified freely by his grace, through the redemption that is in Christ Jesus; Ver. 25. Whom God hath set forth to be a propitiation through faith in his blood, to declare his righteousness *for the remission of sins* that are past, through the forbearance of God. Rom. iv. 6. Even as David also describeth the blessedness of the man, unto whom God imputeth righteousness without works, Ver. 7. Saying, Blessed are they *whose iniquities are forgiven, and whose sins are covered.* Ver. 8. Blessed is the man *to whom the Lord will not impute sin.*

ᵈ 2 Cor. v. 19. To wit, that God was in Christ, reconciling the world unto himself, *not imputing their trespasses unto them;* and hath committed unto us the word of reconciliation. Ver. 21. For he hath made him to be sin for us, who knew no sin; *that we might be made the righteousness of God in him.*

ᵉ Rom. v. 17. For if by one man's offence death reigned by one; much more they which receive abundance of grace, and *of the gift of righteousness,* shall reign in life by one, Jesus Christ. Ver. 18. Therefore, as by the offence of one judgment came upon all men to condemnation; even so *by the righteousness of one the free gift came upon all men unto justification of life.* Ver. 19. For as by one man's disobedience many were made sinners; so *by the obedience of one shall many be made righteous.*

ᶠ Gal. ii. 16. Knowing that a man is not justified by the works of the law, but *by the faith of Jesus Christ,* even *we have believed in Jesus Christ, that we might be justified by the faith of Christ,* and not by the works of the law: for by the works of the law shall no flesh be justified. Phil. iii. 9. And be found in him, not having mine own righteousness, which is of the law, but *that which is through the faith of Christ,* the righteousness which is *of God by faith.*

34. ᵍ 1 John iii. 1. Behold *what manner of love the Father hath bestowed upon us, that we should be called the sons of God:* therefore the world knoweth us not, because it knew him not.

ʰ John i. 12. But as many as received him, *to them gave he power to become the sons of God,* even to them that believe on his name. Rom. viii. 17. And *if children, then heirs; heirs of God, and joint-heirs with Christ:* if so be that we suffer with him, that we may be also glorified together.

35. ⁱ 2 Thess. ii. 13. God hath from the beginning chosen you to salvation *through sanctification of the Spirit,* and belief of the truth.

ᵏ Eph. iv. 23. And be *renewed in the spirit of your mind;* Ver. 24. And that ye put on the new man, *which after God is created in righteousness and true holiness.*

ˡ Rom. vi. 4. Therefore we are buried *with him by baptism into death;* that like as Christ was raised up from the dead by the glory of the Father, even so we also should walk in newness of life. Ver. 6. Knowing this, that our old man is crucified with him, that the body of sin might be destroyed, *that henceforth we should not serve sin.* Rom. viii. 1. There is therefore now no condemnation to them which are in

fication, adoption, and sanctification, are, assurance of God's love, peace of conscience,[m] joy in the Holy Ghost,[n] increase of grace,[o] and perseverance therein to the end.[p]

Q. 37. *What benefits do believers receive from Christ at death?*

A. The souls of believers are at their death made perfect in holiness,[q] and do immediately pass into glory;[r] and their bodies, being still united to Christ,[s] do rest in their graves[t] till the resurrection.[v]

Q. 38. *What benefits do believers receive from Christ at the resurrection?*

A. At the resurrection, believers being raised up in glory,[w] shall be openly acknowledged and acquitted in the day of judgment,[x] and made perfectly blessed in the full enjoying of God[y] to all eternity.[z]

Q. 39. *What is the duty which God requireth of man?*

A. The duty which God requireth of man, is obedience to his revealed will.[a]

Q. 40. *What did God at first reveal to man for the rule of his obedience?*

Christ Jesus, *who walk not after the flesh, but after the Spirit.*

36. m Rom. v. 1. Therefore, *being justified by faith, we have peace with God, through our Lord Jesus Christ:* Ver. 2. By whom also we have access by faith into this grace wherein we stand, and *rejoice in hope of the glory of God.* Ver. 5. And *hope maketh not ashamed; because the love of God is shed abroad in our hearts* by the Holy Ghost, which is given unto us.

n Rom. xiv. 17. For *the kingdom of God is not meat and drink; but righteousness, and peace, and joy in the Holy Ghost.*

o Prov. iv. 18. But *the path of the just is as the shining light, that shineth more and more unto the perfect day.*

p 1 John v. 13. These things have I written unto you that believe on the name of the Son of God, that *ye may know that ye have eternal life,* and that ye may believe on the name of the Son of God. 1 Pet. i. 5. Who *are kept* by the power of God through faith *unto salvation,* ready to be revealed in the last time.

37. q Heb. xii. 23. To the general assembly and church of the first-born, which are written in heaven, and *to the spirits of just men made perfect.*

r 2 Cor. v. 1. For we know, that, if our earthly house of this tabernacle *were dissolved, we have a building of God,* an house not made with hands, eternal in the heavens. Ver. 6. Therefore we are always confident, knowing that, whilst we are at *home in the body, we are absent from the Lord:* Ver. 8. We are confident, I say, and willing rather to be *absent from the body, and to be present with the Lord.* Phil. i. 23. For I am in a strait betwxt two, having a desire *to depart, and to be with Christ;* which is far better. Luke xxiii. 43. And Jesus said unto him, Verily I say unto thee, *To-day shalt thou be with me in paradise.*

s 1 Thess. iv. 14. For if we believe that Jesus died, and rose again, even so them

also *which sleep in Jesus* will God bring with him.

t Isa. lvii. 2. He shall enter into peace: *they shall rest in their beds,* each one walking in his uprightness.

v Job xix. 26. And though after my skin worms destroy this body, yet *in my flesh shall I see God:* Ver. 27. *Whom I shall see for myself,* and mine eyes shall behold, and not another; though my reins be consumed within me.

38. w 1 Cor. xv. 43. It is sown in dishonour, *it is raised in glory:* it is sown in weakness, it is raised in power.

x Matt. xxv. 23. His lord said unto him, *Well done, good and faithful servant;* thou hast been faithful over a few things, I will make thee ruler over many things: enter thou into the joy of thy lord. Matt. x. 32. Whosoever therefore shall confess me before men, *him will I confess also before my Father which is in heaven.*

y 1 John iii. 2. Beloved, now are we the sons of God; and it doth not yet appear what we shall be: but we know that, when he shall appear, we shall be like him; for *we shall see him as he is.* 1 Cor. xiii. 12. For now we see through a glass, darkly; but *then face to face:* now I know in part; but *then shall I know even as also I am known.*

z 1 Thess. iv. 17. Then we which are alive and remain shall be caught up together with them in the clouds, to meet the Lord in the air: and *so shall we ever be with the Lord.* Ver. 18. Wherefore comfort one another with these words.

39. a Micah vi. 8. He hath shewed thee, O man, what is good; and *what doth the Lord require of thee, but to do justly, and to love mercy, and to walk humbly with thy God?* 1 Sam. xv. 22. And Samuel said, Hath the Lord as great delight in burnt-offerings and sacrifices, as in obeying the voice of the Lord? Behold, *to obey is better than sacrifice,* and to hearken than the fat of rams.

A. The rule which God at first revealed to man for his obedience, was the moral law.[b]

Q. 41. *Where is the moral law summarily comprehended?*

A. The moral law is summarily comprehended in the ten commandments.[c]

Q. 42. *What is the sum of the ten commandments?*

A. The sum of the ten commandments is, To love the Lord our God with all our heart, with all our soul, with all our strength, and with all our mind; and our neighbour as ourselves.[d]

Q. 43. *What is the preface to the ten commandments?*

A. The preface to the ten commandments is in these words, *I am the Lord thy God, which have brought thee out of the land of Egypt, out of the house of bondage.*[e]

Q. 44. *What doth the preface to the ten commandments teach us?*

A. The preface to the ten commandments teacheth us, That because God is the Lord, and our God, and Redeemer, therefore we are bound to keep all his commandments.[f]

Q. 45. *Which is the first commandment?*

A. The first commandment is, *Thou shalt have no other gods before me.*[g]

Q. 46. *What is required in the first commandment?*

A. The first commandment requireth us to know and acknowledge God to be the only true God, and our God;[h] and to worship and glorify him accordingly.[i]

Q. 47. *What is forbidden in the first commandment?*

A. The first commandment forbiddeth the denying,[k] or not wor-

---

40. [b] Rom. ii. 14. For when the Gentiles, which have not the law, do by nature the things contained in the law, these, having not the law, *are a law unto themselves;* Ver. 15. Which shew *the work of the law written* in their hearts, their conscience also bearing witness, and their thoughts the mean while accusing or else excusing one another. Rom. x. 5. For Moses describeth the righteousness which is *of the law, That the man which doeth those things shall live by them.*

41. [c] Deut. x. 4. And he wrote on the tables, according to the *first writing, the ten commandments,* which the Lord spake unto you in the mount, out of the midst of the fire, in the day of the assembly: and the Lord gave them unto me. Matt. xix. 17. And he said unto him, Why callest thou me good? there is none good but one, that is, God: but if thou wilt enter into life, *keep the commandments.*

42. [d] Matt. xxii. 37. Jesus said unto him, *Thou shalt love the Lord thy God with all thy heart, and with all thy soul, and with all thy mind.* Ver. 38. This is the first and great commandment. Ver. 39. And the second is like unto it, *Thou shalt love thy neighbour as thyself.* Ver. 40. *On these two commandments hang all the law and the prophets.*

43. [e] Exod. xx. 2.

44. [f] Luke i. 74. That he would grant unto us, that we, *being delivered out of the hand of our enemies, might serve him* without fear, Ver. 75. In holiness and righteousness before him, all the days of our life. 1 Pet. i. 15. But as he which hath called you is holy, *so be ye holy* in all manner of conversation; Ver. 16. Because it is written, *Be ye holy; for I am holy.* Ver. 17. And if ye call on the Father, who without respect of persons judgeth according to every man's work, pass the time of your sojourning here in fear: Ver. 18. Forasmuch as ye know that ye were not redeemed with corruptible things, as silver and gold, from your vain conversation received by tradition from your fathers; Ver. 19. *But with the precious blood of Christ,* as of a lamb without blemish and without spot.

45. [g] Exod. xx. 3.

46. [h] 1 Chron. xxviii. 9. And thou, Solomon my son, *know thou the God of thy father,* and serve him with a perfect heart, and with a willing mind; for the Lord searcheth all hearts, and understandeth all the imaginations of the thoughts: if thou seek him, he will be found of thee; but if thou forsake him, he will cast thee off for ever. Deut. xxvi. 17. *Thou hast avouched the Lord this day to be thy God,* and to walk in his ways, and to keep his statutes, and his commandments, and his judgments, and to hearken unto his voice.

[i] Matt. iv. 10. Then saith Jesus unto him, Get thee hence, Satan: for it is written, *Thou shalt worship the Lord thy God,* and him only shalt thou serve. Ps. xxix. 2 *Give unto the Lord the glory due unto his name; worship the Lord* in the beauty of holiness.

47. [k] Ps. xiv. 1. *The fool hath said* in his heart, *There is no God.* They are corrupt;

shipping and glorifying the true God as God,^{l} and our God;^{m} and the giving of that worship and glory to any other, which is due to him alone.^{n}

Q. 48. *What are we specially taught by these words* [before me] *in the first commandment?*

A. These words [*before me*] in the first commandment teach us, That God, who seeth all things, taketh notice of, and is much displeased with, the sin of having any other god.^{o}

Q. 49. *Which is the second commandment?*

A. The second commandment is, *Thou shalt not make unto thee any graven image, or any likeness of any thing that is in heaven above, or that is in the earth beneath, or that is in the water under the earth: thou shalt not bow down thyself to them, nor serve them: for I the Lord thy God am a jealous God, visiting the iniquity of the fathers upon the children unto the third and fourth generation of them that hate me; and shewing mercy unto thousands of them that love me, and keep my commandments.*^{p}

Q. 50. *What is required in the second commandment?*

A. The second commandment requireth the receiving, observing, and keeping pure and entire, all such religious worship and ordinances as God hath appointed in his word.^{q}

Q. 51. *What is forbidden in the second commandment?*

A. The second commandment forbiddeth the worshipping of God by images,^{r} or any other way not appointed in his word.^{s}

they have done abominable works; there is none that doeth good.
l Rom. i. 21. Because that, when they knew God, *they glorified him not as God,* neither were thankful; but became vain in their imaginations, and their foolish heart was darkened.
m Ps. lxxxi. 10. *I am the Lord thy God,* which brought thee out of the land of Egypt: open thy mouth wide, and I will fill it. Ver. 11. But *my people would not hearken to my voice;* and Israel would none of me.
n Rom. i. 25. Who changed the truth of God into a lie, and *worshipped and served the creature more than the Creator,* who is blessed for ever. Amen. Ver. 26. For this cause God gave them up unto vile affections: for even their women did change the natural use into that which is against nature.
48. o Ezek. viii. 5. Then said he unto me, Son of man, lift up thine eyes now the way toward the north. So I lifted up mine eyes the way toward the north, and behold northward at the gate of the altar this image of jealousy in the entry. Ver. 6. He said furthermore unto me, Son of man, seest thou what they do? even *the great abominations* that the house of Israel committeth here, that I should go far off from my sanctuary? But turn thee yet again, and thou shalt see greater abominations, &c., to the end of the chapter. Ps. xliv. 20. If we have forgotten the name of our God, *or stretched out our hands to a strange god;* Ver. 21. *Shall not God search this out?* for he knoweth the secrets of the heart.
49. p Exod. xx. 4, 5, 6.
50. q Deut. xxxii. 46. And he said unto them. Set your hearts unto all the words which I testify among you this day, which ye shall command your children *to observe to do, all the words of this law.* Matt. xxviii. 20. *Teaching them to observe all things whatsoever I have commanded you;* and, lo, I am with you alway, even unto the end of the world. Amen. Acts ii. 42. And they continued *stedfastly in the apostles' doctrine* and fellowship, and in breaking of bread, and in prayers.
51. r Deut. iv. 15. Take ye therefore good heed unto yourselves, (for ye saw no manner of similitude on the day that the Lord spake unto you in Horeb out of the midst of the fire,) Ver. 16. Lest ye corrupt yourselves, and *make you a graven image, the similitude of any figure, the likeness of male or female;* Ver. 17. *The likeness of any beast that is on the earth, the likeness of any winged fowl that flieth in the air;* Ver. 18. *The likeness of any thing that creepeth on the ground, the likeness of any fish that is in the waters beneath the earth:* Ver. 19. And lest thou lift up thine eyes unto heaven, and when thou seest the sun, and the moon, and the stars, even all the host of heaven, *shouldest be driven to worship them, and serve them,* which the Lord thy God hath divided unto all nations under the whole heaven. Exod. xxxii. 5. And when Aaron saw it, he built an altar before it; and Aaron made proclamation, and said, To-morrow is a feast to the Lord. Ver. 8. They have turned aside quickly out of the way which I commanded them: *they have made them a molten calf, and have worshipped it,* and have sacrificed thereunto, and said, These be thy gods, O Israel, which have brought thee up out of the land of Egypt.
s Deut. xii. 31. Thou shalt not do so unto

Q. 52. *What are the reasons annexed to the second commandment?*

A. The reasons annexed to the second commandment are, God's sovereignty over us,[t] his propriety in us,[v] and the zeal he hath to his own worship.[w]

Q. 53. *Which is the third commandment?*

A. The third commandment is, *Thou shalt not take the name of the Lord thy God in vain: for the Lord will not hold him guiltless that taketh his name in vain.*[x]

Q. 54. *What is required in the third commandment?*

A. The third commandment requireth the holy and reverent use of God's names,[y] titles,[z] attributes,[a] ordinances,[b] word,[c] and works.[d]

Q. 55. *What is forbidden in the third commandment?*

A. The third commandment forbiddeth all profaning or abusing of any thing whereby God maketh himself known.[e]

Q. 56. *What is the reason annexed to the third commandment?*

A. The reason annexed to the third commandment is, That however the breakers of this commandment may escape punishment from men, yet the Lord our God will not suffer them to escape his righteous judgment.[f]

the Lord thy God: for every *abomination to the Lord which he hateth* have they done unto their gods; for even *their sons and their daughters they have burnt in the fire to their gods.* Ver. 32. What thing soever I command you, observe to do it: thou shalt not add thereto, nor diminish from it.

52. t Ps. xcv. 2. *Let us come before his presence* with thanksgiving, and *make a joyful noise* unto him with psalms. Ver. 3. *For the Lord is a great God,* and *a great King above all gods.* Ver. 6. *O come, let us worship* and bow down; let us kneel before *the Lord our Maker.*

v Ps. xlv. 11. So shall the King greatly desire thy beauty: for *he is thy Lord, and worship thou him.*

w Exod. xxxiv. 13. But ye shall destroy their altars, break their images, and cut down their groves. Ver. 14. *For thou shalt worship no other god: for the Lord,* whose name is Jealous, *is a jealous God.*

53. x Exod. xx. 7.

54. y Matt. vi. 9. After this manner therefore pray ye: Our Father which art in heaven, *Hallowed be thy name.* Deut. xxviii. 58. If thou wilt not observe to do all the words of this law that are written in this book, that *thou mayest fear this glorious and fearful name, THE LORD THY GOD.*

z Ps. lxviii. 4. Sing unto God, sing praises to his name: *extol him* that rideth upon the heavens *by his name JAH,* and rejoice before him.

a Rev. xv. 3. And they sing the song of Moses the servant of God, and the song of the Lamb, saying, Great and marvellous are thy works, *Lord God Almighty; just and true* are thy ways, *thou King of saints.* Ver. 4. Who shall not fear thee, O Lord, and glorify thy name? for *thou only art holy:* for all nations shall come and worship before thee; for thy judgments are made manifest.

b Mal. i. 11. For from the rising of the sun, even unto the going down of the same, my name shall be great among the Gentiles; and in every place *incense shall be offered* unto my name, and *a pure offering:* for my name shall be great among the heathen, saith the Lord of hosts. Ver. 14. But *cursed be the deceiver, which hath in his flock a male,* and voweth, and *sacrificeth unto the Lord a corrupt thing:* for I am a great King, saith the Lord of hosts, and my name is dreadful among the heathen.

c Ps. cxxxviii. 1. I will praise thee with my whole heart: before the gods will I sing praise unto thee. Ver. 2. *I will worship* toward thy holy temple, and praise thy name for thy loving-kindness, and *for thy truth:* for *thou hast magnified thy word above all thy name.*

d Job xxxvi. 24. Remember *that thou magnify his work,* which men behold.

55. e Mal. i. 6. A son honoureth his father, and a servant his master: if then I be a father, *where is mine honour?* and if I be a master, *where is my fear?* saith the Lord of hosts *unto you,* O priests, *that despise my name.* And ye say, Wherein have we despised thy name? Ver. 7. *Ye offer polluted bread upon mine altar;* and ye say, Wherein have we polluted thee? In that ye say, The table of the Lord is contemptible. Ver. 12. But *ye have profaned it,* in that ye say, The table of the Lord is polluted; and the fruit thereof, even his meat, is contemptible. Mal. ii. 2. *If ye will not hear,* and if ye will not lay it to heart, *to give glory unto my name,* saith the Lord of hosts, *I will even send a curse* upon you, and I will curse your blessings; yea, I have cursed them already, because ye do not lay it to heart. Mal. iii. 14. Ye have said, It is vain to serve God; and *what profit is it that we have kept his ordinance,* and that we have walked mournfully before the Lord of hosts?

56. f 1 Sam. ii. 12. Now the sons of Eli were sons of Belial; they knew not the

Q. 57. *Which is the fourth commandment?*
A. The fourth commandment is, *Remember the sabbath-day, to keep it holy. Six days shalt thou labour, and do all thy work: but the seventh day is the sabbath of the Lord thy God: in it thou shalt not do any work, thou, nor thy son, nor thy daughter, thy man-servant, nor thy maid-servant, nor thy cattle, nor thy stranger that is within thy gates: for in six days the Lord made heaven and earth, the sea, and all that in them is, and rested the seventh day: wherefore the Lord blessed the sabbath-day, and hallowed it.*g

Q. 58. *What is required in the fourth commandment?*
A. The fourth commandment requireth the keeping holy to God such set times as he hath appointed in his word; expressly one whole day in seven, to be a holy sabbath to himself.h

Q. 59. *Which day of the seven hath God appointed to be the weekly sabbath?*
A. From the beginning of the world to the resurrection of Christ, God appointed the seventh day of the week to be the weekly sabbath; and the first day of the week ever since, to continue to the end of the world, which is the Christian sabbath.i

Q. 60. *How is the sabbath to be sanctified?*
A. The sabbath is to be sanctified by a holy resting all that day,k even from such worldly employments and recreations as are lawful on other days;l and spending the whole time in the publick and private

---

Lord. Ver. 17. Wherefore *the sin of the young men was very great before the Lord; for men abhorred the offering of the Lord.* Ver. 22. Now Eli was very old, and heard all that his sons did unto all Israel; and how they lay with the women that assembled at the door of the tabernacle of the congregation. Ver. 29. Wherefore kick ye at my sacrifice, and at mine offering, which I have commanded in my habitation; and honourest thy sons above me, to make yourselves fat with the chiefest of all the offerings of Israel my people? 1 Sam. iii. 13. For I have told him, that *I will judge his house for ever, for the iniquity which he knoweth; because his sons made themselves vile, and he restrained them not.* Deut. xxviii. 58. *If thou wilt not observe to do all the words of this law* that are written in this book, that thou mayest fear this glorious and fearful name, THE LORD THY GOD; Ver. 59. *Then the Lord will make thy plagues wonderful,* and the plagues of thy seed, even great plagues, and of long continuance, and sore sicknesses, and of long continuance.

57. g Exod. xx. 8–11.
58. h Deut. v. 12. *Keep the sabbath-day* to sanctify it, *as the Lord thy God hath commanded thee.* Ver. 13. Six days thou shalt labour, and do all thy work; Ver. 14. But *the seventh day is the sabbath of the Lord thy God: in it thou shalt not do any work,* thou, nor thy son, nor thy daughter, nor thy man-servant, nor thy maid-servant, nor thine ox, nor thine ass, nor any of thy cattle, nor thy stranger that is within thy gates; that thy man-servant and thy maid-servant may rest as well as thou.
59. i Gen. ii. 2. And on the seventh day God ended his work which he had made; and *he rested on the seventh day from all his work* which he had made. Ver. 3. And *God blessed the seventh day, and sanctified it;* because that in it he had rested from all his work which God created and made. 1 Cor. xvi. 1. Now concerning the collection for the saints, as I have given order to the churches of Galatia, *even so do ye.* Ver. 2. *Upon the first day of the week* let every one of you lay by him in store, as God hath prospered him, that there be no gatherings when I come. Acts xx. 7. *And upon the first day of the week, when the disciples came together to break bread,* Paul preached unto them, ready to depart on the morrow; and continued his speech until midnight.
60. k Exod. xx. 8. Remember *the sabbath-day, to keep it holy.* Ver. 10. But the seventh day is *the sabbath of the Lord thy God: in it thou shalt not do any work,* thou, nor thy son, &c. Exod. xvi. 25. And Moses said, Eat that to-day; for to-day is a sabbath unto the Lord: to-day ye shall not find it in the field. Ver. 26. Six days ye shall gather it; but on the seventh day, which is the sabbath, in it there shall be none. Ver. 27. And it came to pass, that there went out some of the people on the seventh day for to gather, and they found none. Ver. 28. And the Lord said unto Moses, How long refuse ye to keep my commandments and my laws?
l Neh. xiii. 15. In those days saw I in Judah some *treading wine-presses on the sabbath, and bringing in sheaves, and lading asses; as also wine, grapes, and figs, and all manner of burdens,* which they brought into Jerusalem on the sabbath-day: and *I testified against them in the day wherein they sold victuals.* Ver. 16. There

exercises of God's worship,^m except so much as is to be taken up in the works of necessity and mercy.ⁿ

Q. 61. *What is forbidden in the fourth commandment?*

A. The fourth commandment forbiddeth the omission or careless performance of the duties required,^o and the profaning the day by idleness,^p or doing that which is in itself sinful,^q or by unnecessary thoughts, words, or works, about our worldly employments or recreations.^r

Q. 62. *What are the reasons annexed to the fourth commandment?*

A. The reasons annexed to the fourth commandment are, God's allowing us six days of the week for our own employments,^s his challenging a special propriety in the seventh, his own example, and his blessing the sabbath-day.^t

dwelt men of Tyre also therein, *which brought fish, and all manner of ware, and sold on the sabbath* unto the children of Judah, and in Jerusalem. Ver. 17. *Then I contended with the nobles of Judah,* and said unto them, *What evil thing is this that ye do, and profane the sabbath-day?* Ver. 18. Did not your fathers thus, and did not our God bring all this evil upon us, and upon this city? yet ye bring more wrath upon Israel, by profaning the sabbath. Ver. 19. And it came to pass, that when the gates of Jerusalem began to be dark before the sabbath, I commanded that the gates should be shut, and charged that they should not be opened till after the sabbath: and some of my servants set I at the gates, that there should no burden be brought in on the sabbath-day. Ver. 21. Then I testified against them, and said unto them, *Why lodge ye about the wall?* if ye do so again, I will lay hands on you. From that time forth *came they no more on the sabbath.* Ver. 22. And I commanded the Levites, that they should cleanse themselves, and that they should come and keep the gates, to sanctify the sabbath-day. Remember me, O my God, concerning this also, and spare me according to the greatness of thy mercy.

^m Luke iv. 16. And he came to Nazareth, where he had been brought up: and, as his custom was, he went into the synagogue *on the sabbath-day,* and *stood up for to read.* Acts xx. 7. And upon the first day of the week, &c. [See letter l.] Ps. xcii. [title, A psalm or song for the sabbath-day.] Isa. lxvi. 23. And it shall come to pass, that from one new-moon to another, and *from one sabbath to another, shall all flesh come to worship before me,* saith the Lord.

ⁿ Matt. xii. from verse 1. to 31. At that time Jesus went on the sabbath-day through the corn; and his disciples were an hungered, and began to pluck the ears of corn, and to eat. Ver. 2. But when the Pharisees, &c. Ver. 12. *It is lawful to do well on the sabbath-days.*

61. ^o Ezek. xxii. 26. *Her priests have violated my law,* and have profaned mine holy things: they have put no difference between the holy and profane, neither have they shewed difference between the unclean and the clean, and *have hid their eyes from my sabbaths,* and I am profaned among them.

Amos viii. 5. Saying, When will the new-moon be gone, that we may sell corn? and *the sabbath, that we may set forth wheat,* making the ephah small, and the shekel great, and falsifying the balances by deceit? Mal. i. 13. Ye said also, Behold, *what a weariness is it!* and ye have snuffed at it, saith the Lord of hosts: and ye brought that which was torn, and the lame, and the sick; thus ye brought an offering: should I accept this of your hand? saith the Lord.

^p Acts xx. 7. And upon the first day of the week, when the disciples came together to break bread, Paul preached unto them, ready to depart on the morrow; and continued his speech until midnight. Ver. 9. And there sat in a window a certain young man named Eutychus, being *fallen into a deep sleep:* and as Paul was long preaching, he sunk down with sleep, and fell down from the third loft, and was taken up dead.

^q Ezek. xxiii. 38. Moreover, this they have done unto me: they have defiled my sanctuary in the same day, and *have profaned my sabbaths.*

^r Jer. xvii. 24. And it shall come to pass, if ye diligently hearken unto me, saith the Lord, *to bring in no burden* through the gates of this city *on the sabbath-day,* but hallow the sabbath-day, *to do no work therein;* Ver. 25. Then shall there enter into the gates of this city kings and princes sitting upon the throne of David, riding in chariots and on horses, they, and their princes, the men of Judah, and the inhabitants of Jerusalem; and this city shall remain for ever. Ver. 26. And they shall come from the cities of Judah, and from the places about Jerusalem, and from the land of Benjamin, and from the plain, and from the mountains, and from the south, bringing burnt-offerings, and sacrifices, and meat-offerings, and incense, and bringing sacrifices of praise, unto the house of the Lord. Isa. lviii. 13. If thou turn away thy foot from the Sabath, *from doing thy pleasure on my holy day,* and call the sabbath a delight, the holy of the Lord, honourable; and shalt honour him, *not doing thine own ways, nor finding thine own pleasure, nor speaking thine own words.*

62. ^s Exod. xx. 9. *Six days shalt thou labour,* and do all thy work.

^t Exod. xx. 11. For in six days the Lord made heaven and earth, the sea, and all that

Q. 63. *Which is the fifth commandment?*

A. The fifth commandment is, *Honour thy father and thy mother; that thy days may be long upon the land which the Lord thy God giveth thee.*[v]

Q. 64. *What is required in the fifth commandment?*

A. The fifth commandment requireth the preserving the honour, and performing the duties, belonging to every one in their several places and relations, as superiors,[w] inferiors,[x] or equals.[y]

Q. 65. *What is forbidden in the fifth commandment?*

A. The fifth commandment forbiddeth the neglecting of, or doing any thing against, the honour and duty which belongeth to every one in their several places and relations.[z]

Q. 66. *What is the reason annexed to the fifth commandment?*

A. The reason annexed to the fifth commandment, is a promise of long life and prosperity (as far as it shall serve for God's glory and their own good) to all such as keep this commandment.[a]

Q. 67. *Which is the sixth commandment?*

A. The sixth commandment is, *Thou shalt not kill.*[b]

Q. 68. *What is required in the sixth commandment?*

A. The sixth commandment requireth all lawful endeavours to preserve our own life,[c] and the life of others.[d]

Q. 69. *What is forbidden in the sixth commandment?*

A. The sixth commandment forbiddeth the taking away of our own life, or the life of our neighbour unjustly, or whatsoever tendeth thereunto.[e]

Q. 70. *Which is the seventh commandment?*

A. The seventh commandment is, *Thou shalt not commit adultery.*[f]

Q. 71. *What is required in the seventh commandment?*

in them is, and rested the seventh day: wherefore the Lord *blessed the sabbath-day,* and hallowed it.

63. v Exod. xx. 12.

64. w Eph. v. 21. *Submitting yourselves one to another* in the fear of God. x 1 Pet. ii. 17. *Honour all men. Love the brotherhood. Fear God. Honour the king.* y Rom. xii. 10. *Be kindly affectioned one to another* with brotherly love; *in honour preferring one another.*

65. z Matt. xv. 4. For God commanded, saying, Honour thy father and mother: and, *He that curseth father or mother, let him die the death.* Ver. 5. But ye say, *Whosoever shall say to his father* or his mother, It is a gift, by whatsoever thou mightest be profited by me, Ver. 6. And honour not his father or his mother, he shall be free. *Thus have ye made the commandment of God of none effect* by your tradition. Ezek. xxxiv. 2. Son of man, prophesy against the shepherds of Israel, prophesy, and say unto them, Thus saith the Lord God unto the shepherds, *Woe be to the shepherds of Israel that do feed themselves!* should not the shepherds feed the flocks? Ver. 3. Ye eat the fat, and ye clothe you with the wool, ye kill them that are fed: but *ye feed not the flock.* Ver. 4. *The diseased have ye not strengthened, neither have ye healed that which was sick, neither have ye bound up that which was broken, neither have ye brought again that* which was driven away, neither have ye sought that which was lost; but with force and with cruelty have ye ruled them. Rom. xiii. 8. *Owe no man any thing,* but to love one another: for he that loveth another hath fulfilled the law.

66. a Deut. v. 16. Honour thy father and thy mother, as the Lord thy God hath commanded thee; *that thy days may be prolonged, and that it may go well with thee, in the land* which the Lord thy God giveth thee. Eph. vi. 2. Honour thy father and mother, (which is the first commandment with promise,) Ver. 3. *That it may be well with thee, and thou mayest live long on the earth.*

67. b Exod. xx. 13.

68. c Eph. v. 28. So ought men to love their wives *as their own bodies:* he that loveth his wife loveth himself. Ver. 29. For no man ever yet hated *his own flesh;* but nourisheth and cherisheth it, even as the Lord the church.

d 1 Kings xviii. 4. For it was so, when Jezebel cut off the prophets of the Lord, that *Obadiah took an hundred prophets, and hid them by fifty in a cave, and fed them with bread and water.*

69. e Acts xvi. 28. But *Paul cried* with a loud voice, saying, *Do thyself no harm;* for we are all here. Gen. ix. 6. *Whoso sheddeth man's blood, by man shall his blood be shed:* for in the image of God made he man.

70. f Exod. xx. 41.

A. The seventh commandment requireth the preservation of our own and our neighbour's chastity, in heart, speech, and behaviour.g

Q. 72. *What is forbidden in the seventh commandment?*
A. The seventh commandment forbiddeth all unchaste thoughts, words, and actions.h

Q. 73. *Which is the eighth commandment?*
A. The eighth commandment is, *Thou shalt not steal.*i

Q. 74. *What is required in the eighth commandment?*
A. The eighth commandment requireth the lawful procuring and furthering the wealth and outward estate of ourselves and others.k

Q. 75. *What is forbidden in the eighth commandment?*
A. The eighth commandment forbiddeth whatsoever doth or may unjustly hinder our own or our neighbour's wealth or outward estate.l

Q. 76. *Which is the ninth commandment?*

71. g 1 Cor. vii. 2. Nevertheless, *to avoid fornication,* let every man have his own wife, and let every woman have her own husband. Ver. 3. *Let the husband render unto the wife due benevolence: and likewise also the wife unto the husband.* Ver. 5. *Defraud ye not one the other,* except it be with consent for a time, that ye may give yourselves to fasting and prayer; and come together again, that Satan tempt you not for your incontinency Ver. 34. There is difference also between a wife and a virgin. The unmarried woman careth for the things of the Lord, *that she may be holy both in body and in spirit:* but she that is married careth for the things of the world, how she may please her husband. Ver. 36. But if any man think that he behaveth himself uncomely toward his virgin, if she pass the flower of her age, and need so require, let him do what he will, he sinneth not; *let them marry.* Col. iv. 6. *Let your speech be alway with grace, seasoned with salt,* that ye may know how ye ought to answer every man. 1 Pet. iii. 2. While they behold *your chaste conversation* coupled with fear.

72. h Matt. xv. 19. For *out of the heart* proceed evil thoughts, murders, *adulteries, fornications,* thefts, false witness, blasphemies. Matt. v. 28. But I say unto you, That whosoever looketh on a woman *to lust after her, hath committed adultery* with her already in his heart. Eph. v. 3. But *fornication, and all uncleanness,* or covetousness, *let it not be once named among you,* as becometh saints; Ver. 4. *Neither filthiness, nor foolish talking,* nor jesting, which are not convenient; but rather giving of thanks.

73. i Exod. xx. 15.

74. k Gen. xxx. 30. For it was little which thou hadst before I came, and it is now increased unto a multitude; and the Lord hath blessed thee since my coming: and now, *when shall I provide for mine own house also?* 1 Tim. v. 8. But *if any provide not for his own, and specially for those of his own house, he hath denied the faith,* and is worse than an infidel. Lev. xxv. 35. And if thy brother be waxen poor, and fallen in decay with thee, then *thou shalt relieve him;* yea, though he be a stranger, or a sojourner: that he may live with thee. Deut. xxii. 1. Thou shalt not see thy brother's ox or his sheep go astray, and *hide thyself from them: thou shalt in any case bring them again unto thy brother.* Ver. 2. And if thy brother be not nigh unto thee, or if thou know him not; then *thou shalt bring it unto thine own house,* and it shall be with thee until thy brother seek after it, and *thou shalt restore it to him again.* Ver. 3. *In like manner shalt thou do with his ass,* and so shalt thou do with his raiment; and with all lost thing of thy brother's, which he hath lost, and thou hast found, shalt thou do likewise: thou mayest not hide thyself. Ver. 4. Thou shalt not see thy brother's ass or his ox fall down by the way, and hide thyself from them; *thou shalt surely help him to lift them up again.* Ver. 5. The woman shall not wear that which pertaineth unto a man, neither shall a man put on a woman's garment: for all that do so are abomination unto the Lord thy God. Exod. xxiii. 4. If thou meet thine enemy's ox or his ass going astray, *thou shalt surely bring it back to him again.* Ver. 5. If thou see the ass of him that hateth thee lying under his burden, and wouldest forbear to help him; *thou shalt surely help with him.* Gen. xlvii. 14. *And Joseph gathered up all the money* that was found in the land of Egypt, and in the land of Canaan, *for the corn which they bought:* and Joseph brought the money into Pharaoh's house. Ver. 20. *And Joseph bought all the land of Egypt* for Pharaoh; for the Egyptians sold every man his field, because the famine prevailed over them: so the land became Pharaoh's.

75. l Prov. xxi. 17. He that loveth pleasure shall be a poor man; he that loveth wine and oil shall not be rich. Prov. xxiii. 20. *Be not among wine-bibbers; among riotous eaters of flesh.* Ver. 21. For the drunkard and the glutton shall come to poverty; and drowsiness shall clothe a man with rags. Prov. xxviii. 19. He that tilleth his land shall have plenty of bread: but he that followeth after vain persons shall have poverty enough. Eph. iv. 28. *Let him* that stole *steal no more;* but rather let him labour,

A. The ninth commandment is, *Thou shalt not bear false witness against thy neighbour.*ᵐ

Q. 77. *What is required in the ninth commandment?*

A. The ninth commandment requireth the maintaining and promoting of truth between man and man,ⁿ and of our own and our neighbour's good name,ᵒ especially in witness-bearing.ᵖ

Q. 78. *What is forbidden in the ninth commandment?*

A. The ninth commandment forbiddeth whatsoever is prejudicial to truth, or injurious to our own or our neighbour's good name.ᑫ

Q. 79. *Which is the tenth commandment?*

A. The tenth commandment is, *Thou shalt not covet thy neighbour's house, thou shalt not covet thy neighbour's wife, nor his man-servant, nor his maid-servant, nor his ox, nor his ass, nor any thing that is thy neighbour's.*ʳ

Q. 80. *What is required in the tenth commandment?*

A The tenth commandment requireth full contentment with our own condition,ˢ with a right and charitable frame of spirit toward our neighbour, and all that is his.ᵗ

Q. 81. *What is forbidden in the tenth commandment?*

A. The tenth commandment forbiddeth all discontentment with our own estate,ᵛ envying or grieving at the good of our neighbour,ʷ and all inordinate motions and affections to any thing that is his.ˣ

working with his hands the thing which is good, that he may have to give to him that needeth.

76. ᵐ Exod. xx. 16.

77. ⁿ Zech. viii. 16. These are the things that ye shall do, *Speak ye every man the truth to his neighbour; execute the judgment of truth* and peace in your gates.

ᵒ 3 John, ver. 12. Demetrius hath good report of all men, and of the truth itself: yea, and *we also bear record;* and ye know that our record is true.

ᵖ Prov. xiv. 5. *A faithful witness will not lie;* but a false witness will utter lies. Ver. 25. *A true witness delivereth souls;* but a deceitful witness speaketh lies.

78. ᑫ 1 Sam. xvii. 28. And Eliab his eldest brother heard when he spake unto the men: and Eliab's anger was kindled against David, and he said, Why camest thou down hither? and with whom hast thou left those few sheep in the wilderness? *I know thy pride, and the naughtiness of thine heart;* for thou art come down that thou mightest see the battle. Lev. xix. 16. *Thou shalt not go up and down as a tale-bearer* among thy people; *neither shalt thou stand against the blood of thy neighbour;* I am the Lord. Ps. xv. 3. *He that backbiteth not with his tongue,* nor doeth evil to his neighbour, *nor taketh up a reproach against his neighbour.*

79. ʳ Exod. xx. 17.

80. ˢ Heb. xiii. 5. Let your conversation be without covetousness; and *be content with such things as ye have;* for he hath said, I will never leave thee, nor forsake thee. 1 Tim. vi. 6. But godliness *with contentment* is great gain.

ᵗ Job xxxi. 29. *If I rejoiced at the destruction of him* that hated me, or *lifted up myself when evil found him.* Rom. xii. 15. *Rejoice with them that do rejoice, and weep with them that weep.* 1 Tim. i. 5. *Now, the end of the commandment is charity, out of a pure heart,* and of a good conscience, and of faith unfeigned. 1 Cor. xiii. 4. *Charity suffereth long,* and is kind; *charity envieth not; charity vaunteth not itself,* is not puffed up, Ver. 5. *Doth not behave itself unseemly,* seeketh not her own, is not easily provoked, thinketh no evil; Ver. 6. Rejoiceth not in iniquity, but rejoiceth in the truth; Ver. 7. *Beareth all things,* believeth all things, hopeth all things, *endureth all things.*

81. ᵛ 1 Kings xxi. 4. And Ahab came into his house *heavy and displeased* because of the word which Naboth the Jezreelite had spoken to him; for he had said, I will not give thee the inheritance of my fathers: and *he laid him down upon his bed, and turned away his face, and would eat no bread.* Esther v. 13. *Yet all this availeth me no thing,* so long as I see Mordecai the Jew sitting at the king's gate. 1 Cor. x. 10. *Neither murmur ye,* as some of them also murmured, and were destroyed of the destroyer.

ʷ Gal. v. 26. Let us not be desirous of vainglory, provoking one another, *envying one another.* James iii. 14. But *if ye have bitter envying* and strife in your hearts, glory not, and lie not against the truth. Ver. 16. For *where envying and strife is,* there is confusion, and every evil work.

ˣ Rom. vii. 7. What shall we say then? Is the law sin? God forbid. Nay, I had not known sin but by the law: for *I had not known lust, except the law had said, Thou shalt not covet.* Ver. 8. But sin, taking occasion by the commandment, *wrought in me all manner of concupiscence.* For without the law sin was dead. Rom. xiii. 9. For this, Thou shalt not commit adultery, Thou shalt not kill, Thou shalt not steal, Thou shalt not bear false witness, *Thou shalt not*

Q. 82. *Is any man able perfectly to keep the commandments of God?*
A. No mere man since the fall is able in this life perfectly to keep the commandments of God,y but doth daily break them in thought, word, and deed.z

Q. 83. *Are all transgressions of the law equally heinous?*
A. Some sins in themselves, and by reason of several aggravations, are more heinous in the sight of God than others.a

Q. 84. *What doth every sin deserve?*
A. Every sin deserveth God's wrath and curse, both in this life, and that which is to come.b

Q. 85. *What doth God require of us, that we may escape his wrath and curse due to us for sin?*
A. To escape the wrath and curse of God due to us for sin, God requireth of us faith in Jesus Christ, repentance unto life,c with the diligent use of all the outward means whereby Christ communicateth to us the benefits of redemption.d

covet; and if there be any other commandment, it is briefly comprehended in this saying, namely, Thou shalt love thy neighbour as thyself. Deut. v. 21. *Neither shalt thou desire thy neighbour's wife, neither shalt thou covet thy neighbour's house, his field, or his man-servant, or his maid-servant, his ox, or his ass, or any thing that is thy neighbour's.*

82. y Eccl. vii. 20. For there is not a just man upon earth, *that doeth good, and sinneth not.* 1 John i. 8. *If we say that we have no sin, we deceive ourselves,* and the truth is not in us. Ver. 10. *If we say that we have not sinned,* we make him a liar, and his word is not in us. Gal. v. 17. For *the flesh lusteth against the Spirit,* and the Spirit against the flesh: and these are contrary the one to the other; so that *ye cannot do the things that ye would.*

z Gen. vi. 5. And God saw that the wickedness of man was great in the earth, and *that every imagination of the thoughts of his heart was only evil continually.* Gen. viii. 21. And the Lord smelled a sweet savour; and the Lord said in his heart, I will not again curse the ground any more for man's sake; for *the imagination of man's heart is evil from his youth;* neither will *I* again smite any more every thing living, as I have done. Rom. iii. 9. What then? are we better than they? No, in no wise: for we have before proved both Jews and Gentiles, *that they are all under sin.*—And so on to verse 21. James iii. 2. For *in many things we offend all. If any man offend not in word, the same is a perfect man,* and able also to bridle the whole body.—And so on to verse 13

83. a Ezek. viii. 6. He said furthermore unto me, Son of man, seest thou what they do? even the great abominations that the house of Israel committeth here, that I should go far off from my sanctuary? But turn thee yet again, and *thou shalt see greater abominations.* Ver. 13. He said also unto me, Turn thee yet again, and *thou shalt see greater abominations that they do.* Ver. 15. Then said he unto me, Hast thou seen this, O son of man? Turn thee yet again, and thou shalt see greater abominations than these. 1 John v. 16. If any man see his brother sin a sin which is not unto death, he shall ask, and he shall give him life for them that sin not unto death. *There is a sin unto death:* I do not say that he shall pray for it. Ps. lxxviii. 17. And *they sinned yet more* against him, by provoking the most High in the wilderness. Ver. 32. *For all this they sinned still, and believed not for his wondrous works.* Ver. 56. *Yet they tempted and provoked the most high God,* and kept not his testimonies.

84. b Eph. v. 6. Let no man deceive you with vain words: for *because of these things cometh the wrath of God upon the children of disobedience.* Gal. iii. 10. For as many as are of the works of the law are under the curse: for it is written, *Cursed is every one that continueth not in all things which are written in the book of the law to do them.* Lam. iii. 39. Wherefore doth a living man complain, *a man for the punishment of his sins?* Matt. xxv. 41. Then shall he say also unto them on the left hand, *Depart from me, ye cursed,* into everlasting fire, prepared for the devil and his angels.

85. c Acts xx. 21. Testifying both to the Jews, and also to the Greeks, *repentance toward God, and faith toward our Lord Jesus Christ.*

d Prov. ii. 1. *My son, if thou wilt receive my words, and hide my commandments with thee;* Ver. 2. So that thou incline thine ear unto wisdom, and apply thine heart to understanding; Ver. 3. Yea, if thou criest after knowledge, and liftest up thy voice for understanding; Ver. 4. If thou seekest her as silver, and searchest for her as for hid treasures; Ver. 5. *Then shalt thou understand the fear of the Lord, and find the knowledge of God.* Prov. viii. 33. *Hear instruction, and be wise, and refuse it not.* Ver. 34. Blessed is the man that heareth me, watching daily at my gates, waiting at the posts of my doors. Ver. 35. For *whoso findeth me findeth life, and shall obtain favour of the Lord.* Ver. 36. But he that sinneth against me wrongeth his own soul: all they that hate me love death. Isa. lv.

Q. 86. *What is faith in Jesus Christ?*
A. Faith in Jesus Christ is a saving grace,[e] whereby we receive and rest upon him alone for salvation, as he is offered to us in the gospel.[f]

Q. 87. *What is repentance unto life?*
A. Repentance unto life is a saving grace,[g] whereby a sinner, out of a true sense of his sin,[h] and apprehension of the mercy of God in Christ,[i] doth, with grief and hatred of his sin, turn from it unto God,[k] with full purpose of, and endeavour after, new obedience.[l]

Q. 88. *What are the outward means whereby Christ communicateth to us the benefits of redemption?*
A. The outward and ordinary means whereby Christ communicateth to us the benefits of redemption, are his ordinances, especially the word, sacraments, and prayer; all which are made effectual to the elect for salvation.[m]

Q. 89. *How is the word made effectual to salvation?*
A. The Spirit of God maketh the reading, but especially the preaching of the word, an effectual means of convincing and converting sinners, and of building them up in holiness and comfort, through faith, unto salvation.[n]

---

3. Incline your ear, and come unto me: hear, and *your soul shall live;* and I will make an everlasting covenant with you, even the sure mercies of David.

86. e Heb. x. 39. But we are not of them who draw back unto perdition; but of them that *believe to the saving of the soul.*

f John i. 12. But *as many as received him,* to them gave he power to become the sons of God, even to them that believe on his name. Isa. xxvi. 3. Thou wilt keep him in perfect peace, whose *mind is stayed on thee; because he trusteth in thee.* Ver. 4. Trust ye in the Lord for ever: for in the Lord JEHOVAH is everlasting strength. Phil. iii. 9. And be found in him, not having mine own righteousness, which is of the law, but *that which is through the faith of Christ,* the righteousness which is of God by faith. Gal. ii. 16. Knowing that a man is not justified by the works of the law, but *by the faith of Jesus Christ, even we have believed in Jesus Christ, that we might be justified* by the faith of Christ, and not by the works of the law: for by the works of the law shall no flesh be justified.

87. g Acts xi. 18. When they heard these things, they held their peace, and glorified God, saying, Then hath God also to the Gentiles granted *repentance unto life.*

h Acts ii. 37. Now when they heard this, *they were pricked in their heart,* and said unto Peter, and to the rest of the apostles, Men and brethren, what shall we do? Ver. 38. Then Peter said unto them, *Repent,* and be baptized every one of you in the name of Jesus Christ for the remission of sins, and ye shall receive the gift of the Holy Ghost.

i Joel ii. 12. Therefore also now, saith the Lord, *Turn ye even to me* with all your heart, and with fasting, and with weeping, and with mourning. Jer. iii. 22. Return, ye backsliding children, and I will heal your backslidings. Behold, *we come unto thee; for thou art the Lord our God.*

k Jer. xxxi. 18. I have surely heard *Ephraim bemoaning himself* thus; Thou hast chastised me, and I was chastised, as a bullock unaccustomed to the yoke: turn thou me, and I shall be turned; for thou art the Lord my God. Ver. 19. Surely after that I was turned, *I repented;* and after that I was instructed, *I smote upon my thigh: I was ashamed,* yea, even confounded, because I did bear the reproach of my youth. Ezek. xxxvi. 31. Then shall ye remember your own evil ways, and your doings that were not good, and *shall loathe yourselves in your own sight, for your iniquities,* and for your abominations.

l 2 Cor. vii. 11. For, behold, this selfsame thing, that ye sorrowed after a godly sort, what carefulness it wrought in you, yea, what clearing of yourselves, yea, what indignation, yea, what fear, yea, *what vehement desire, yea, what zeal,* yea, what revenge! In all things ye have approved yourselves to be clear in this matter. Isa. i. 16. Wash you, make you clean; put away the evil of your doings from before mine eyes; *cease to do evil;* Ver. 17. *Learn to do well;* seek judgment; relieve the oppressed; judge the fatherless; plead for the widow.

88. m Matt. xxviii. 19. Go ye therefore, and *teach all nations, baptizing them* in the name of the Father, and of the Son, and of the Holy Ghost; Ver. 20. *Teaching them to observe all things* whatsoever I have commanded you: and, lo, I am with you alway, even unto the end of the world. Amen. Acts ii. 42. And they continued stedfastly *in the apostles' doctrine and fellowship, and in breaking of bread, and in prayers.* Ver. 46. And they, continuing daily with one accord *in the temple,* and *breaking bread from house to house,* did eat their meat with gladness and singleness of heart, Ver. 47. Praising God, and having favour with all the people. And *the Lord added to the church daily such as should be saved.*

89. n Neh. viii. 8. So they *read in the*

Q. 90. *How is the word to be read and heard, that it may become effectual to salvation?*

A. That the word may become effectual to salvation, we must attend thereunto with diligence,º preparation,ᵖ and prayer;ᵠ receive it with faith and love,ʳ lay it up in our hearts,ˢ and practise it in our lives.ᵗ

Q. 91. *How do the sacraments become effectual means of salvation?*

A. The sacraments become effectual means of salvation, not from any virtue in them, or in him that doth administer them; but only by the blessing of Christ,ᵛ and the working of his Spirit in them that by faith receive them.ʷ

Q. 92. *What is a sacrament?*

A. A sacrament is an holy ordinance instituted by Christ; wherein, by sensible signs, Christ, and the benefits of the new covenant, are represented, sealed, and applied to believers.ˣ

book, *in the law of God, distinctly,* and gave the sense, and caused them to understand the reading. 1 Cor. xiv. 24. *But if all prophesy,* and there come in one that believeth not, or one unlearned, *he is convinced of all, he is judged of all;* Ver. 25. And thus are the secrets of his heart made manifest; and so, falling down on his face, *he will worship God,* and report that God is in you of a truth. Acts xxvi. 18. *To open their eyes, and to turn them from darkness to light,* and from the power of Satan unto God, that they may receive forgiveness of sins, and inheritance among them which are sanctified by faith that is in me. Ps. xix. 8. *The statutes of the Lord are right, rejoicing the heart:* the commandment of the Lord is pure, *enlightening the eyes.* Acts xx. 32. And now, brethren, I commend you to God, and *to the word of his grace, which is able to build you up, and to give you an inheritance among all them which are sanctified.* Rom. xv. 4. For whatsoever things were written aforetime were *written for our learning;* that we, through patience and comfort of *the scriptures, might have hope.* 2 Tim. iii. 15. And that from a child thou hast known *the holy scriptures, which are able to make thee wise unto salvation* through faith which is in Christ Jesus. Ver. 16. All scripture is given by inspiration of God, and *is profitable for doctrine, for reproof, for correction, for instruction in righteousness;* Ver. 17. *That the man of God may be perfect,* throughly furnished unto all good works. Rom. x. 13. For whosoever shall call upon the name of the Lord shall be saved. Ver. 14. How then shall they call on him in whom they have not believed? and *how shall they believe in him of whom they have not heard? and how shall they hear without a preacher?* Ver. 15. And how shall they preach except they be sent? as it is written, How beautiful are the feet of them that preach the gospel of peace, and bring glad tidings of good things! Ver. 16. But they have not all obeyed the gospel: for Esaias saith, Lord, who hath believed our report? Ver. 17. So then faith cometh by hearing, and hearing by the word of God. Rom. i. 16. For I am not ashamed of the gospel of Christ: for *it is the power of God unto salvation* to every one that believeth; to the Jew first, and also to the Greek.

90. º Prov. viii. 34. Blessed is the man that heareth me, watching daily at my gates, *waiting at the posts of my doors.*

ᵖ 1 Pet. ii. 1. Wherefore, *laying aside all malice, and all guile, and hypocrisies, and envies, and all evil speakings,* Ver. 2. As new-born babes, *desire the sincere milk of the word,* that ye may grow thereby.

ᵠ Ps. cxix. 18. *Open thou mine eyes, that I may behold wondrous things out of thy law.*

ʳ Heb. iv. 2. For unto us was the gospel preached, as well as unto them: but the word preached did not profit them, *not being mixed with faith in them that heard it.* 2 Thess. ii. 10. And with all deceivableness of unrighteousness in them that perish; *because they received not the love of the truth,* that they might be saved.

ˢ Ps. cxix. 11. *Thy word have I hid in mine heart,* that I might not sin against thee.

ᵗ Luke viii. 15. But that on the good ground are they, which *in an honest and good heart, having heard the word, keep it,* and bring forth fruit with patience. James i. 25. But whoso looketh into the perfect law of liberty, and *continueth therein,* he being not a forgetful hearer, but a doer of the work, this man shall be blessed in his deed.

91. ᵛ 1 Pet. iii. 21. The like figure whereunto even baptism doth also now save us, (*not the putting away of the filth of the flesh, but the answer of a good conscience toward God,*) by the resurrection of Jesus Christ. Matt. iii. 11. I indeed baptize you with water unto repentance: but he that cometh after me is mightier than I, whose shoes I am not worthy to bear: *he shall baptize you with the Holy Ghost,* and with fire. 1 Cor. iii. 6. I have planted, Apollos watered; but *God gave the increase.* Ver. 7. So then neither is he that planteth any thing, neither he that watereth; but God that giveth the increase.

ʷ 1 Cor. xii. 13. For *by one Spirit are we all baptized into one body,* whether we be Jews or Gentiles, whether we be bond or free; and *have been all made to drink into one Spirit.*

92. ˣ Gen. xvii. 7. And I will establish my

Q. 93. *Which are the sacraments of the New Testament?*
A. The sacraments of the New Testament are, Baptism,[y] and the Lord's supper.[z]

Q. 94. *What is baptism?*
A. Baptism is a sacrament, wherein the washing with water in the name of the Father, and of the Son, and of the Holy Ghost,[a] doth signify and seal our ingrafting into Christ, and partaking of the benefits of the covenant of grace, and our engagement to be the Lord's.[b]

Q. 95. *To whom is baptism to be administered?*
A. Baptism is not to be administered to any that are out of the visible church, till they profess their faith in Christ, and obedience to him;[c] but the infants of such as are members of the visible church are to be baptized.[d]

Q. 96. *What is the Lord's supper?*
A. The Lord's supper is a sacrament, wherein, by giving and receiving bread and wine, according to Christ's appointment, his death is shewed forth; and the worthy receivers are, not after a corporal and carnal manner, but by faith, made partakers of his body and blood, with all his benefits, to their spiritual nourishment, and growth in grace.[e]

Q. 97. *What is required to the worthy receiving of the Lord's supper?*
A. It is required of them that would worthily partake of the Lord's

covenant between me and thee, and thy seed after thee, in their generations, for an everlasting covenant, to be a God unto thee, and to thy seed after thee. Ver. 10. *This is my covenant, which ye shall keep, between me and you, and thy seed after thee; Every man-child among you shall be circumcised.* Exod. xii. throughout. 1 Cor. xi. 23. For I have received of the Lord that which also I delivered unto you, That *the Lord Jesus,* the same night in which he was betrayed, *took bread.* Ver. 26. For as often as ye eat this *bread, and drink this cup,* ye do shew the Lord's death till he come.
93. y Matt. xxviii. 19. Go ye therefore, and teach all nations, *baptizing them* in the name of the Father, and of the Son, and of the Holy Ghost.
z Matt. xxvi. 26. And as they were eating, *Jesus took bread,* and blessed it, and brake it, and gave it to the disciples, and said, Take, eat; this is my body. Ver. 27. And *he took the cup,* and gave thanks, and gave it to them, saying, Drink ye all of it: Ver. 28. For this is my blood of the new testament, which is shed for many for the remission of sins.
94. a Matt. xxviii. 19. [See in letter y.]
b Rom. vi. 4. Therefore we are *buried with him by baptism into death;* that like as Christ was raised up from the dead by the glory of the Father, even *so we also should walk in newness of life.* Gal. iii. 27. For as many of you *as have been baptized into Christ have put on Christ.*
95. c Acts viii. 36. And as they went on their way, they came unto a certain water: and the eunuch said, See, here is water; what doth hinder me to be baptized? Ver. 37. And Philip said, *If thou believest with all thine heart, thou mayest.* And he answered and said, I believe that Jesus Christ is the Son of God. Acts ii. 38. Then Peter said unto them, *Repent, and be baptized every one of you* in the name of Jesus Christ for the remission of sins, and ye shall receive the gift of the Holy Ghost.
d Acts ii. 38. [See before.] Ver. 39. *For the promise is unto you, and to your children,* and to all that are afar off, even as many as the Lord our God shall call. Gen. xvii. 10. [See in letter x.] Compared with Col. ii. 11. In whom also ye are *circumcised with the circumcision* made without hands, in putting off the body of the sins of the flesh by the circumcision of Christ; Ver. 12. *Buried with him in baptism,* wherein also ye are risen with him through the faith of the operation of God, who hath raised him from the dead. 1 Cor. vii. 14. For the unbelieving husband is sanctified by the wife, and the unbelieving wife is sanctified by the husband; else were your children unclean; but *now are they holy.*
96. e 1 Cor. xi. 23. For I have received of the Lord that which also I delivered unto you, That the Lord Jesus, the same night in which he was betrayed, took bread: Ver. 24. And, when he had given thanks, he brake it, and said, Take, eat; this is my body, which is broken for you: *this do in remembrance of me.* Ver. 25. After the same manner also he took the cup, when he had supped, saying, This cup is the new testament in my blood: this do ye, as oft as ye drink it, in remembrance of me. Ver. 26. For as often as ye eat this bread, and drink this cup, *ye do shew the Lord's death till he come.* 1 Cor. x. 16. *The cup of blessing* which we bless, *is it not the communion*

supper, that they examine themselves of their knowledge to discern the Lord's body,[f] of their faith to feed upon him,[g] of their repentance,[h] love,[i] and new obedience;[k] lest, coming unworthily, they eat and drink judgment to themselves.[l]

Q. 98. *What is prayer?*

A. Prayer is an offering up of our desires unto God,[m] for things agreeable to his will,[n] in the name of Christ,[o] with confession of our sins,[p] and thankful acknowledgment of his mercies.[q]

Q. 99. *What rule hath God given for our direction in prayer?*

A. The whole word of God is of use to direct us in prayer;[r] but the special rule of direction is that form of prayer which Christ taught his disciples, commonly called *The Lord's prayer*.[s]

Q. 100. *What doth the preface of the Lord's prayer teach us?*

A. The preface of the Lord's prayer (which is, *Our Father which art in heaven*[t]) teacheth us to draw near to God with all holy reverence and confidence, as children to a father, able and ready to help us;[v] and that we should pray with and for others.[w]

Q. 101. *What do we pray for in the first petition?*

A. In the first petition (which is, *Hallowed be thy name*[x]) we pray, That God would enable us and others to glorify him in all that where-

of the blood of Christ? the bread which we break, is it not the communion of the body of Christ?

97. f 1 Cor. xi. 28. But *let a man examine himself, and so let him eat of that bread, and drink of that cup.* Ver. 29. For he that eateth and drinketh unworthily, eateth and drinketh damnation to himself, *not discerning the Lord's body.*

g 2 Cor. xiii. 5. *Examine yourselves, whether ye be in the faith; prove your own selves:* know ye not your own selves, how that Jesus Christ is in you, except ye be reprobates?

h 1 Cor. xi. 31. For *if we would judge ourselves,* we should not be judged.

i 1 Cor. x. 16. The cup of blessing which we bless, *is it not the communion* of the blood of Christ? the bread which we break, *is it not the communion of* the body of Christ? Ver. 17. *For we, being many, are one bread,* and one body: *for we are all partakers of that one bread.*

k 1 Cor. v. 7. Purge out therefore the old leaven, *that ye may be a new lump*, as ye are unleavened. For even Christ our passover is sacrificed for us: Ver. 8. Therefore *let us keep the feast,* not with old leaven, neither with the leaven of malice and wickedness ; but *with the unleavened bread of sincerity and truth.*

l 1 Cor. xi. 28, 29. [See in letter f.]

98. m Ps. lxii. 8. Trust in him at all times; ye people, *pour out your heart before him:* God is a refuge for us. Selah.

n 1 John v. 14. And this is the confidence that we have in him, that, *if we ask any thing according to his will,* he heareth us.

o John xvi. 23. And in that day ye shall ask me nothing. Verily, verily, I say unto you, *Whatsoever ye shall ask the Father in my name,* he will give it you.

p Ps. xxxii. 5 *I acknowledged my sin unto thee,* and mine iniquity have I not hid. *I said, I will confess my transgressions* unto the Lord ; and thou forgavest the iniquity of my sin. Selah. Ver. 6. *For this shall every one that is godly pray unto thee* in a time when thou mayest be found: surely in the floods of great waters they shall not come nigh unto him. Dan. ix. 4. And *I prayed unto the Lord* my God, and *made my confession,* and said, O Lord, the great and dreadful God, keeping the covenant and mercy to them that love him, and to them that keep his commandments.

q Phil. iv. 6. Be careful for nothing : but in every thing *by prayer and supplication, with thanksgiving,* let your requests be made known unto God.

99. r 1 John v. 14. And this is the confidence that we have in him, that, if we *ask any thing according to his will,* he heareth us.

s Matt. vi. 9-13. After this manner therefore pray ye : Our Father, &c. Compared with Luke xi. 2, 3, 4. And he said unto them, *When ye pray, say,* Our Father, &c.

100. t Matt. vi. 9.

v Rom. viii. 15. For ye have not received the spirit of bondage again to fear; but ye have received the spirit of adoption, whereby *we cry, Abba, Father.* Luke xi. 13. If ye then, being evil, know how to give good gifts unto your children; *how much more shall your heavenly Father* give the Holy Spirit to them that ask him?

w Acts xii. 5. Peter therefore was kept in prison ; but *prayer was made* without ceasing of the church unto God *for him.* 1 Tim. ii. 1. I exhort therefore, that, first of all, *supplications, prayers, intercessions,* and giving of thanks, be made for all men ; Ver. 2. *For kings, and for all that are in authority;* that we may lead a quiet and peaceable life in all godliness and honesty

101. x Matt. vi. 9.

by he maketh himself known;^y and that he would dispose all things to his own glory.^z

Q. 102. *What do we pray for in the second petition?*

A. In the second petition (which is, *Thy kingdom come*^a) we pray, That Satan's kingdom may be destroyed;^b and that the kingdom of grace may be advanced,^c ourselves and others brought into it, and kept in it;^d and that the kingdom of glory may be hastened.^e

Q. 103. *What do we pray for in the third petition?*

A. In the third petition (which is, *Thy will be done in earth, as it is in heaven*^f) we pray, That God, by his grace, would make us able and willing to know, obey, and submit to his will in all things,^g as the angels do in heaven.^h

Q. 104. *What do we pray for in the fourth petition?*

A. In the fourth petition (which is, *Give us this day our daily bread*ⁱ) we pray, That of God's free gift we may receive a competent portion of the good things of this life, and enjoy his blessing with them.^k

Q. 105. *What do we pray for in the fifth petition?*

A. In the fifth petition (which is, *And forgive us our debts, as we forgive our debtors*^l) we pray, That God, for Christ's sake, would freely pardon all our sins;^m which we are the rather encouraged to ask,

---

^y Ps. lxvii. 2. That thy way may be known upon earth, thy saving health among all nations. Ver. 3. Let the people praise thee, O God; let all the people praise thee.

^z Ps. lxxxiii. throughout.

102. ^a Matt. vi. 10.

^b Ps. lxviii. 1. Let God arise, *let his enemies be scattered: let them also that hate him flee before him.* Ver. 18. Thou hast ascended on high, *thou hast led captivity captive:* thou hast received gifts for men; yea, for the rebellious also, that the Lord God might dwell among them.

^c Rev. xii. 10. And I heard a loud voice saying in heaven, *Now is come salvation, and strength, and the kingdom of our God, and the power of his Christ:* for the accuser of our brethren is cast down, which accused them before our God day and night. Ver. 11. And they overcame him by the blood of the Lamb, and by the word of their testimony; and they loved not their lives unto the death.

^d 2 Thess. iii. 1. Finally, brethren, *pray for us, that the word of the Lord may have free course, and be glorified,* even as it is with you. Rom. x. 1. Brethren, my heart's desire and *prayer to God* for Israel is, *that they might be saved.* John xvii. 9. *I pray for them:* I pray not for the world, but for them which thou hast given me; for they are thine. Ver. 20. *Neither pray I for these alone, but for them also which shall believe* on me through their word.

^e Rev. xxii. 20. He which testifieth these things saith, Surely I come quickly: Amen. Even so, *come, Lord Jesus.*

103. ^f Matt. vi. 10.

^g Ps. lxvii. throughout. Ps. cxix. 36. *Incline my heart unto thy testimonies,* and not to covetousness. Matt. xxvi 39. And he went a little farther, and fell on his face, and prayed, saying, O my Father, if it be possible, let this cup pass from me: *nevertheless, not as I will, but as thou wilt.* 2 Sam. xv. 25. And the king said unto Zadok, Carry back the ark of God into the city; *if I shall find favour in the eyes of the Lord,* he will bring me again, and shew me both it and his habitation. Job i. 21. And (Job) said, Naked came I out of my mother's womb, and naked shall I return thither: *the Lord gave, and the Lord hath taken away; blessed be the name of the Lord.*

^h Ps. ciii. 20. Bless the Lord, ye his angels, that excel in strength, that do his commandments, *hearkening unto the voice of his word.* Ver. 21. Bless ye the Lord, all ye his hosts; *ye ministers of his, that do his pleasure.*

104. ⁱ Matt. vi. 11.

^k Prov. xxx. 8. Remove far from me vanity and lies; give me neither poverty nor riches; *feed me with food convenient for me:* Ver. 9. Lest I be full, and deny thee, and say, Who is the Lord? or lest I be poor, and steal, and take the name of my God in vain. Gen. xxviii. 20. And Jacob vowed a vow, saying If God will be with me, and will keep me in this way that I go, and *will give me bread to eat, and raiment to put on.* 1 Tim. iv. 4. For every creature of God is good, and nothing to be refused, if it be received with thanksgiving: Ver. 5. For *it is sanctified by* the word of God and *prayer.*

105. ^l Matt. vi. 12.

^m Ps. li. 1. *Have mercy upon me,* O God, according to thy loving-kindness; according unto the multitude of thy tender mercies *blot out my transgressions.* Ver. 2. *Wash me throughly from mine iniquity, and cleanse me from my sin.* Ver. 7. *Purge me* with hyssop, and I shall be clean; *wash me,* and I shall be whiter than snow. Ver. 9. *Hide thy face from my sins, and blot out*

because by his grace we are enabled from the heart to forgive others.[n]

Q. 106. *What do we pray for in the sixth petition?*

A. In the sixth petition (which is, *And lead us not into temptation, but deliver us from evil*[o]) we pray, That God would either keep us from being tempted to sin,[p] or support and deliver us when we are tempted.[q]

Q. 107. *What doth the conclusion of the Lord's prayer teach us?*

A. The conclusion of the Lord's prayer (which is, *For thine is the kingdom, and the power, and the glory, for ever, Amen*[r]) teacheth us to take our encouragement in prayer from God only,[s] and in our prayers to praise him, ascribing kingdom, power, and glory to him.[t] And, in testimony of our desire, and assurance to be heard, we say, *Amen*.[v]

all mine iniquities. Dan. ix. 17. Now therefore, O our God, hear the prayer of thy servant, and his supplications, and cause thy face to shine upon thy sanctuary that is desolate, for the Lord's sake. Ver. 18. O my God, incline thine ear, and hear; open thine eyes, and behold our desolations, and the city which is called by thy name: for we do not present our supplications before thee for our righteousness, but for thy great mercies. Ver. 19. *O Lord, hear; O Lord, forgive;* O Lord, hearken and do; defer not, *for thine own sake, O my God;* for thy city and thy people are called by thy name.

[n] Luke xi. 4. And forgive us our sins; *for we also forgive every one that is indebted to us.* Matt. xviii. 35. So likewise shall my heavenly Father do also unto you, *if ye from your hearts forgive not every one his brother their trespasses.*

106. [o] Matt. vi. 13.

[p] Matt. xxvi. 41. Watch and *pray, that ye enter not into temptation:* the spirit indeed is willing, but the flesh is weak.

[q] 2 Cor. xii. 7. And lest I should be exalted above measure through the abundance of the revelations, there was given to me a thorn in the flesh, the messenger of Satan to buffet me, lest I should be exalted above measure. Ver. 8. *For this thing I besought the Lord* thrice, that it might depart from me.

107. [r] Matt. vi. 13.

[s] Dan. ix. 4. And I prayed unto the Lord my God, and made my confession, and said, O Lord, the great and dreadful God, keeping the covenant and mercy to them that love him, and to them that keep his commandments. Ver. 7. O Lord, righteousness belongeth unto thee, but unto us confusion of faces, as at this day; to the men of Judah, and to the inhabitants of Jerusalem, and unto all Israel, that are near, and that are far off, through all the countries whither thou hast driven them, because of their trespass that they have trespassed against thee. Ver. 8. O Lord, to us belongeth confusion of face, to our kings, to our princes, and to our fathers, because we have sinned against thee. Ver. 9. *To the Lord our God belong mercies and forgivenesses,* though we have rebelled against him. Ver. 16. *O Lord, according to all thy righteousness,* I beseech thee, let thine anger and thy fury be turned away from thy city Jerusalem, thy holy mountain: because for our sins, and for the iniquities of our fathers, Jerusalem and thy people are become a reproach to all that are about us. Ver. 17. Now therefore, O our God, hear the prayer of thy servant, and his supplications, and cause thy face to shine upon thy sanctuary that is desolate. *for the Lord's sake.* Ver. 18. O my God, incline thine ear, and hear; open thine eyes, and behold our desolations, and the city which is called by thy name: for *we do not present our supplications* before thee for our righteousnesses, *but for thy great mercies.* Ver. 19. O Lord, hear; O Lord, forgive; O Lord, hearken and do; *defer not, for thine own sake,* O my God: for thy city and thy people are called by thy name.

[t] 1 Chron. xxix. 10. Wherefore David blessed the Lord before all the congregation: and David said, Blessed be thou, Lord God of Israel our father, for ever and ever. Ver. 11. *Thine, O Lord, is the greatness, and the power, and the glory, and the victory, and the majesty:* for all that is in the heaven and in the earth is thine; thine is the kingdom, O Lord, and thou art exalted as head above all. Ver. 12. Both riches and honour come of thee, and thou reignest over all; *and in thine hand is power and might;* and in thine hand it is to make great, and to give strength unto all. Ver. 13. Now therefore, our God, we thank thee, and praise thy glorious name.

[v] 1 Cor. xiv. 16. Else, when thou shalt bless with the spirit, *how shall he* that occupieth the room of the unlearned *say Amen* at thy giving of thanks, seeing he understandeth not what thou sayest? Rev. xxii. 20. He which testifieth these things saith, Surely I come quickly: *Amen.* Even so, come, Lord Jesus. Ver. 21. The grace of our Lord Jesus Christ be with you all *Amen.*

THE TEN COMMANDMENTS.
Exod. xx.

GOD spake all these words, saying, I am the Lord thy God, which have brought thee out of the land of Egypt, out of the house of bondage.

I. Thou shalt have no other gods before me.

II. Thou shalt not make unto thee any graven image, or any likeness of any thing that is in heaven above, or that is in the earth beneath, or that is in the water under the earth: Thou shalt not bow down thyself to them, nor serve them; for I the Lord thy God am a jealous God, visiting the iniquity of the fathers upon the children unto the third and fourth generation of them that hate me; and shewing mercy unto thousands of them that love me, and keep my commandments.

III. Thou shalt not take the name of the Lord thy God in vain: for the Lord will not hold him guiltless that taketh his name in vain.

IV. Remember the sabbath-day, to keep it holy. Six days shalt thou labour and do all thy work: But the seventh day is the sabbath of the Lord thy God: in it thou shalt not do any work, thou, nor thy son, nor thy daughter, thy man-servant, nor thy maid-servant, nor thy cattle, nor thy stranger that is within thy gates: For in six days the Lord made heaven and earth, the sea, and all that in them is, and rested the seventh day: wherefore the Lord blessed the sabbath-day, and hallowed it.

V. Honour thy father and thy mother; that thy days may be long upon the land which the Lord thy God giveth thee.

VI. Thou shalt not kill.

VII. Thou shalt not commit adultery.

VIII. Thou shalt not steal.

IX. Thou shalt not bear false witness against thy neighbour.

X. Thou shalt not covet thy neighbour's house, thou shalt not covet thy neighbour's wife, nor his man-servant, nor his maid-servant, nor his ox, nor his ass, nor any thing that is thy neighbour's.

THE LORD'S PRAYER.
Matt. vi.

OUR Father which art in heaven, Hallowed be thy name. Thy kingdom come. Thy will be done in earth, as it is in heaven. Give us this day our daily bread. And forgive us our debts, as we forgive our debtors. And lead us not into temptation; but deliver us from evil: For thine is the kingdom, and the power, and the glory, for ever. Amen.

THE CREED.

I BELIEVE in God the Father Almighty, maker of heaven and earth; and in Jesus Christ, his only Son, our Lord, which was conceived by the Holy Ghost, born of the Virgin Mary, suffered under Pontius Pilate, was crucified, dead, and buried: he descended into hell;* the third day he arose again from the dead; he ascended into heaven, and sitteth on the right hand of God the Father Almighty, from thence he shall come to judge the quick and the dead. I believe in the Holy Ghost; the holy catholick church; the communion of saints; the forgiveness of sins; the resurrection of the body; and the life everlasting. Amen.

* *i. e.* Continued in the state of the dead, and under the power of death till the third day.

SO much of every question, both in the Larger and Shorter Catechism, is repeated in the answer, as maketh every answer an entire proposition or sentence in itself; to the end the learner may further improve it upon all occasions, for his increase in knowledge and piety, even out of the course of catechising, as well as in it.

And albeit the substance of the doctrine comprised in that abridgment, commonly called *The Apostles' Creed*, be fully set forth in each of the Catechisms, so as there is no necessity of inserting the Creed itself; yet it is here annexed, not as though it were composed by the Apostles, or ought to be esteemed canonical scripture, as the Ten Commandments, and the Lord's Prayer, (much less a prayer, as ignorant people have been apt to make both it and the Decalogue,) but because it is a brief sum of the Christian faith, agreeable to the word of God, and anciently received in the churches of Christ.

THE SUM OF SAVING KNOWLEDGE:

OR,

A BRIEF SUM OF CHRISTIAN DOCTRINE,

CONTAINED IN THE HOLY SCRIPTURES, AND HOLDEN FORTH
IN THE FORESAID CONFESSION OF FAITH
AND CATECHISMS;

TOGETHER WITH

THE PRACTICAL USE THEREOF.

JOHN vi 37.—All that the Father giveth me shall come to me; and him that cometh to me I will in no wise cast out.

CONTENTS.

HEADS.

I. Our woeful condition by nature.
II. The remedy provided in Christ Jesus.
III. The means provided in the covenant of grace.
IV. The blessings conveyed by these means.

The Use of Saving Knowledge.

1. For convincing of sin by the law.
2. Of righteousness by the law.
3. Of judgment by the law.
4. For convincing of sin, righteousness, and judgment by the gospel.
Of righteousness to be had only by faith in Christ.
For strengthening a man's faith, &c.

Warrants and Motives to Believe.

1. God's hearty invitation.
2. His earnest request to be reconciled.
3. His command, charging all to believe.
4. Much assurance of life given to believers, &c.

Evidences of true Faith.

1. Conviction of the believer's obligation to keep the moral law.
2. That the believer practise the rules of godliness and righteousness.
3. That obedience to the law run in the right channel of faith in Christ.
4. The keeping of strait communion with Christ, the fountain of all grace and good works.
For strengthening the believer in faith and obedience, by these evidences.

THE
SUM OF SAVING KNOWLEDGE, &c.

The Sum of Saving Knowledge may be taken up in these four heads:—1. The woeful condition wherein all men are by nature, through breaking of the covenant of works. 2. The remedy provided for the elect in Jesus Christ by the covenant of grace. 3. The means appointed to make them partakers of this covenant. 4. The blessings which are effectually conveyed unto the elect by these means.—Which four heads are set down each of them in some few propositions.

HEAD I.

Our woeful condition by nature, through breaking the covenant of works. Hos. xiii. 9. O Israel, thou hast destroyed thyself.

I. THE almighty and eternal God, the Father, the Son, and the Holy Ghost, three distinct persons in the one and the same undivided Godhead, equally infinite in all perfections, did, before time, most wisely decree, for his own glory, whatsoever cometh to pass in time: and doth most holily and infallibly execute all his decrees, without being partaker of the sin of any creature.

II. This God, in six days, made all things of nothing, very good in their own kind: in special, he made all the angels holy; and he made our first parents, Adam and Eve, the root of mankind, both upright and able to keep the law written in their heart. Which law they were naturally bound to obey under pain of death; but God was not bound to reward their service, till he entered into a covenant or contract with them, and their posterity in them, to give them eternal life, upon condition of perfect personal obedience; withal threatening death in case they should fail. This is the covenant of works.

III. Both angels and men were subject to the change of their own freewill, as experience proved, (God having reserved to himself the incommunicable property of being naturally unchangeable:) for many angels of their own accord fell by sin from their first estate, and became devils. Our first parents, being enticed by Satan, one of these devils speaking in a serpent, did break the covenant of works, in eating the forbidden fruit; whereby they, and their posterity, being in their loins, as branches in the root, and comprehended in the same covenant with them, became not only liable to eternal death, but also lost all ability to please God; yea, did become by nature enemies to God, and to all spiritual good, and inclined only to evil continually. This is our original sin, the bitter root of all our actual transgressions, in thought, word, and deed.

HEAD II.

The remedy provided in Jesus Christ for the elect by the covenant of grace. Hos. xiii. 9. O Israel, thou hast destroyed thyself; but in me is thine help.

I. ALBEIT man, having brought himself into this woeful condition, be neither able to help himself, nor willing to be helped by God out of it, but rather inclined to lie still, insensible of it, till he perish; yet God, for the glory of his rich grace, hath revealed in his word a way to save sinners, viz. by faith in Jesus Christ, the eternal Son of God, by virtue of, and according to the tenor of the covenant of redemption, made and agreed upon between God the Father and God the Son, in the council of the Trinity, before the world began.

II. The sum of the covenant of redemption is this: God having freely chosen unto life a certain number of lost mankind, for the glory of his rich grace, did give them, before the world began, unto God the Son, appointed Redeemer, that, upon condition he would humble himself so far as to assume the human nature, of a soul and a body, unto personal union with his divine nature, and submit himself to the law, as surety for them, and satisfy justice for them, by giving obedience in their name, even unto the suffering of the cursed death of the cross, he should ransom and redeem them all from sin and death, and purchase unto them righteousness and eternal life, with all saving graces leading thereunto, to be effectually, by means of his own appointment, applied in due time to every one of them. This condition the Son of God (who is Jesus Christ our Lord) did accept before the world began, and in the fulness of time came into the world, was born of the Virgin Mary, subjected himself to the law, and completely paid the ransom on the cross: But by virtue of the foresaid bargain made before the world began, he is in all ages, since the fall of Adam, still upon the work of applying actually the purchased benefits unto the elect; and that he doth by way of entertaining a covenant of free grace and reconciliation with them, through faith in himself; by which covenant, he makes over to every believer a right and interest to himself, and to all his blessings.

III. For the accomplishment of this covenant of redemption, and making the elect partakers of the benefits thereof in the covenant of grace, Christ Jesus was clad with the threefold office of Prophet, Priest, and King: made a Prophet, to reveal all saving knowledge to his people, and to persuade them to believe and obey the same; made a Priest, to offer up himself a sacrifice once for them all, and to intercede continually with the Father, for making their persons and services acceptable to him; and made a King, to subdue them to himself, to feed and rule them by his own appointed ordinances, and to defend them from their enemies.

HEAD III.

The outward means appointed to make the elect partakers of this covenant, and all the rest that are called, to be inexcusable. Matt. xxii. 14. Many are called.

I. THE outward means and ordinances, for making men partakers of the covenant of grace, are so wisely dispensed, as that the elect shall be infallibly converted and saved by them; and the reprobate, among whom they are, not to be justly stumbled. The means are especially these four. 1. The word of God. 2. The sacraments. 3. Kirk-government. 4. Prayer. In the word of God preached by sent messengers, the Lord makes offer of grace to all sinners, upon condition of faith in Jesus Christ; and whosoever do confess their sin, accept of Christ offered, and submit themselves to his ordinances, he will have both them and their children received into the honour and privileges of the covenant of grace. By the sacraments, God will have the covenant sealed for confirming the bargain on the foresaid condition. By kirk-government, he will have them hedged in, and helped forward unto the keeping of the covenant. And by prayer, he will have his own glorious grace, promised in the covenant, to be daily drawn forth, acknowledged, and employed. All which means are followed either really, or in profession only, according to the quality of the covenanters, as they are true or counterfeit believers.

II. The covenant of grace, set down in the Old Testament before Christ came, and in the New since he came, is one and the same in substance, albeit different in outward administration: For the covenant in the Old Testament, being sealed with the sacraments of circumcision and the paschal lamb, did set forth Christ's death to come, and the benefits purchased thereby, under the shadow of bloody sacrifices, and sundry ceremonies: but since Christ came, the covenant being sealed by the sacraments of baptism and the Lord's supper, doth clearly hold forth Christ already crucified before our eyes, victorious over death and the grave, and gloriously ruling heaven and earth, for the good of his own people.

HEAD IV.

The blessings which are effectually conveyed by these means to the Lord's elect, or chosen ones. Matt. xxii. 14. Many are called, but few are chosen.

I. BY these outward ordinances, as our Lord makes the reprobate inexcusable, so, by the power of his Spirit, he applies unto the elect, effectually, all saving graces purchased to them in the covenant of redemption, and maketh a change in their persons. In particular, 1. He doth convert or regenerate them, by giving spiritual life to them, in opening their understandings, renewing their wills, affections, and faculties, for giving spiritual obedience to his commands. 2. He gives them saving faith, by making them, in the sense of deserved condemnation, to give their consent heartily to the covenant of grace, and to embrace Jesus Christ unfeignedly. 3. He gives them repentance, by making them, with godly sorrow, in the hatred of sin, and love of righteousness, turn from all iniquity to the service of God. And, 4. He sanctifies them, by making them go on and persevere in faith and spiritual obedience to the law of God, manifested by fruitfulness in all duties, and doing good works, as God offereth occasion.

II. Together with this inward change of their persons, God changes also their state: for, so soon as they are brought by faith into the covenant of grace, 1. He justifies them, by imputing unto them that perfect obedience which Christ gave to the law, and the satisfaction also which upon the cross Christ gave unto justice in their name. 2. He reconciles them, and makes them friends to God, who were before enemies to God. 3. He adopts them, that they shall be no more children of Satan, but children of God, enriched with all spiritual privileges of his sons. And, last of all, after their warfare in this life is ended, he perfects their holiness and blessedness, first of their souls at their death, and then both of their souls and their bodies, being joyfully joined together again in the resurrection, at the day of his glorious coming to judgment, when all the wicked shall be sent away to hell, with Satan whom they have served: but Christ's own chosen and redeemed ones, true believers, students of holiness, shall remain with himself for ever, in the state of glorification.

THE PRACTICAL USE OF SAVING KNOWLEDGE,

Contained in SCRIPTURE, *and holden forth briefly in the foresaid* CONFESSION OF FAITH *and* CATECHISMS.

THE chief general use of Christian doctrine is, to convince a man of sin, and of righteousness, and of judgment, John xvi. 8. partly by the law or covenant of works, that he may be humbled and become penitent; and partly by the gospel or covenant of grace, that he may become an unfeigned believer in Jesus Christ, and be strengthened in his faith upon solid grounds and warrants, and give evidence of the truth of his faith by good fruits, and so be saved.

The sum of the covenant of works, or of the law, is this: "If thou do all that is commanded, and not fail in any point, thou shalt be saved: but if thou fail, thou shalt die." Rom. x. 5. Gal. iii. 10, 12.

The sum of the gospel, or covenant of grace and reconciliation, is this: "If thou flee from deserved wrath to the true Redeemer Jesus Christ, (who is able to save to the uttermost all that come to God through him,) thou shalt not perish, but have eternal life." Rom. x. 8, 9, 11.

For convincing a man of sin, of righteousness, and of judgment by the law, or covenant of works, let these scriptures, among many more, be made use of.

I. For convincing a man of sin by the law, consider *Jer.* xvii. 9, 10.

The heart is deceitful above all things, and desperately wicked: who can know it? I the Lord search the heart, I try the reins, even to give every man according to his ways, and according to the fruit of his doings.

Here the Lord teacheth these two things:

1. That the fountain of all our miscarriage, and actual sinning against God, is in the heart, which comprehendeth the mind, will, affections, and all the powers of the soul, as they are corrupted and defiled with original sin; the mind being not only ignorant and incapable of saving truth, but also full of error and enmity against God; and the will and affections being obstinately disobedient unto all God's directions, and bent toward that only which is evil: "The heart (saith he) is deceitful above all things, and desperately wicked;" yea, and unsearchably wicked, so that no man *can know it;* and Gen. vi. 5. "Every imagination of the thoughts of man's heart is only evil continually," saith the Lord, whose testimony we must trust in this and all other matters; and experience also may teach us, that, till God make us deny ourselves, we never look to God in any thing, but fleshly self-interest alone doth rule us, and move all the wheels of our actions.

2. That the Lord bringeth our original sin, or wicked inclination, with all the actual fruits thereof, unto reckoning before his judgment-seat; "For he searcheth the heart, and trieth the reins, to give every man according to his ways, and according to the fruit of his doings."

Hence let every man reason thus:

"What God and my guilty conscience beareth witness of, I am convinced that it is true:

"But God and my guilty conscience beareth witness, that my heart is deceitful above all things, and desperately wicked; and that all the imaginations of my heart, by nature, are only evil continually:

"Therefore I am convinced that this is true."

Thus a man may be convinced of sin by the law.

II. For convincing a man of righteousness by the law, consider *Gal.* iii. 10.

As many as are of the works of the law are under the curse; for it is written, Cursed is every one that continueth not in all things which are written in the book of the law to do them.

Here the apostle teacheth us three things:

1. That, by reason of our natural sinfulness, the impossibility of any man's being justified by the works of the law is so certain, that whosoever do seek justification by the works of the law, are liable to the curse of God for breaking of the law; "For as many as are of the works of the law are under the curse," saith he.

2. That, unto the perfect fulfilling of the law, the keeping of one or two of the precepts, or doing of some, or of all duties (if it were possible) for a time, is not sufficient; for the law requireth, that "a man continue in all things which are written in the book of the law to do them."

3. That, because no man can come up to this perfection, every man by nature is under the curse; for the law saith, "Cursed is every one that continueth not in all things which are written in the book of the law to do them."

Now, to be under the curse, comprehendeth all the displeasure of God, with the danger of the breaking forth more and more of his wrath upon soul and body, both in this life, and after death perpetually, if grace do not prevent the full execution thereof.

Hence let every man reason thus:

"Whosoever, according to the covenant of works, is liable to the curse of God for breaking the law, times and ways out of number, cannot be justified, or find righteousness by the works of the law:

"But I, (may every man say,) according to the covenant of works, am liable to the curse of God, for breaking the law times and ways without number:

"Therefore I cannot be justified, or have righteousness by the works of the law."

Thus may a man be convinced of righteousness, that it is not to be had by his own works, or by the law.

III. For convincing a man of judgment by the law, consider 2 *Thess.* i. 7.

The Lord Jesus shall be revealed from heaven with his mighty angels, Ver. 8. *In flaming fire, taking vengeance on them that know not God, and that obey not the gospel of our Lord Jesus Christ:* Ver. 9. *Who shall be punished with everlasting destruction from the presence of the Lord, and from the glory of his power;* Ver. 10. *When he shall come to be glorified in his saints, and to be admired in all them that believe.*

Wherein we are taught, that our Lord Jesus, who now offers to be Mediator for them who believe in him, shall, at the last day, come armed with flaming fire, to judge, condemn, and destroy all them who have not believed God, have not received the offer of grace made in the gospel, nor obeyed the doctrine thereof; but remain in their natural state, under the law or covenant of works.

Hence let every man reason thus:

"What the righteous Judge hath forewarned me shall be done at the last day, I am sure is just judgment:

"But the righteous Judge hath forewarned me, that if I do not believe God in time, and obey not the doctrine of the gospel, I shall be secluded from his presence and his glory at the last day, and be tormented in soul and body for ever:

"Therefore I am convinced that this is a just judgment:

"And I have reason to thank God heartily, who hath forewarned me to flee from the wrath which is to come."

Thus every man may be, by the law or covenant of works, convinced of judgment, if he shall continue under the covenant of works, or shall not obey the gospel of our Lord Jesus.

IV. For convincing a man of sin, righteousness, and judgment, by the gospel.

As for convincing a man of sin, and righteousness, and judgment, by the gospel, or covenant of grace, he must understand three things: 1. That not believing in Jesus Christ, or refusing of the covenant of grace offered in him, is a greater and more dangerous sin than all other sins against the law; because the hearers of the gospel, not believing in Christ, do reject God's mercy in Christ, the only way of freedom from sin and wrath, and will not yield to be reconciled to God. 2. Next, he must understand, that perfect remission of sin, and true righteousness, is to be had only by faith in Jesus; because God requireth no other conditions but faith; and testifies from heaven, that he is well pleased to justify sinners upon this condition. 3. He must understand, that upon righteousness received by faith, judgment shall follow, on the one hand, to the destroying of the works of the devil in the believer, and to the perfecting of the work of sanctification in him, with power: and that, upon refusing to take righteousness by faith in Jesus Christ, judgment shall follow, on the other hand, to the condemnation of the misbeliever, and destroying of him with Satan and his servants for ever.

For this end, let these passages of scripture, among many others, serve to make the greatness of the sin of not believing in Christ appear; or, to make the greatness of the sin of refusing of the covenant of grace offered to us, in the offering of Christ unto us appear, let the fair offer of grace be looked upon as it is made, Isa. lv. 3. *Incline your ear, and come unto me,* (saith the Lord :) *hear, and your soul shall live; and I will make an everlasting covenant with you, even the sure mercies of David.* That is, If ye will believe me, and be reconciled to me, I will, by covenant, give unto you Christ, and all saving graces in him : repeated Acts xiii. 34.

Again, consider, that this general offer in substance is equivalent to a special offer made to every one in particular; as appeareth by the apostle's making use of it, Acts xvi. 31. *Believe on the Lord Jesus Christ, and thou shalt be saved, and thy house.* The reason of which offer is given, John iii. 16. *For God so loved the world, that he gave his only begotten Son, that whosoever believeth in him should not perish, but have everlasting life.* Seeing then this great salvation is offered in the Lord Jesus, whosoever believeth not in him, but looks for happiness some other way, what doth he else but *observe lying vanities, and forsake his own mercy,* which he might have had in Christ? Jonah ii. 8, 9. What doth he else but blaspheme God in his heart? as it is said, 1 John v. 10, 11. *He that believeth not God hath made him a liar; because he believeth not the record that God gave of his Son. And this is the record, that God hath given to us eternal life; and this life is in his Son.* And that no sin against the law is like unto this sin, Christ testifies, John xv. 22. *If I had not come and spoken unto them, they had not had sin; but now they have no cloak for their sin.* This may convince a man of the greatness of this sin of not believing in Christ.

For convincing a man of righteousness to be had only by faith in Jesus Christ, consider how, *Rom.* x. 3, 4.

It is said, that the Jews, *being ignorant of God's righteousness, and going about to establish their own righteousness, have not submitted themselves unto the righteousness of God,* (and so they perished.) *For Christ is the end of the law for righteousness to every one that believeth.* And Acts xiii. 39. *By him all that believe are justified from all things, from which ye could not be justified by the law of Moses.* And 1 John i. 7. *The blood of Jesus Christ his Son cleanseth us from all sin.*

For convincing a man of judgment, if a man embrace this righteousness, consider 1 John iii. 8. *For this purpose the Son of God was manifested, that he might destroy the works of the devil.* And Heb. ix. 14. *How much more shall the blood of Christ, who through the eternal Spirit offered himself without spot to God, purge your conscience from dead works to serve the living God?*

But if a man embrace not this righteousness, his doom is pronounced, John iii. 18, 19. *He that believeth not is condemned already, because he hath not believed in the name of the only begotten Son of God. And this is the condemnation, that light is come into the world, and men loved darkness rather than light.*

Hence let the penitent, desiring to believe, reason thus:
"What doth suffice to convince all the elect in the world of the greatness of the sin of
" not believing in Christ, or refusing to flee to him for relief from sins done against the
" law, and from wrath due thereto; and what sufficeth to convince them that righteous-
" ness and eternal life is to be had by faith in Jesus Christ, or by consenting to the cove-
" nant of grace in him; and what sufficeth to convince them of judgment to be exercised
" by Christ, for destroying the works of the devil in the man, and sanctifying and saving
" all that believe in him, may suffice to convince me also:
" But what the Spirit hath said, in these or other like scriptures, sufficeth to convince
" the elect world of the foresaid sin, and righteousness, and judgment:
" Therefore what the Spirit hath said, in these and other like scriptures, serveth to
" convince me thereof also."

Whereupon let the penitent desiring to believe take with him words, and say heartily to the Lord, Seeing thou sayest, *Seek ye my face;* my soul answereth unto thee, *Thy face, Lord, will I seek.* I have hearkened unto the offer of an everlasting covenant of all saving mercies to be had in Christ, and I do heartily embrace thy offer. Lord, let it be a bargain; *Lord, I believe; help my unbelief:* Behold, I give myself to thee, to serve thee in all things for ever; and I hope *thy right hand shall save me:* the Lord will perfect that which concerneth me: thy mercy, O Lord, endureth for ever; forsake not the *works of thine own hands.*

Thus may a man be made an unfeigned believer in Christ.

For strengthening the man's faith who hath agreed unto the covenant of grace.

BECAUSE many true believers are weak, and do much doubt if ever they shall be sure of the soundness of their own faith and effectual calling, or made certain of their justification and salvation, when they see that many, who profess faith, are found to deceive themselves; let us see how every believer may be made strong in the faith, and sure of his own election and salvation upon solid grounds, by sure warrants, and true evidences of faith. To this end, among many other scriptures, take these following.

1. For laying solid grounds of Faith, consider 2 Peter i. 10. *Wherefore the rather, brethren, give diligence to make your calling and election sure: for if ye do these things ye shall never fall.*

In which words, the apostle teacheth us these four things, for help and direction how to be made strong in the faith.

1. That such as believe in Christ Jesus, and are fled to him for relief from sin and wrath, albeit they be weak in the faith, yet they are indeed children of the same Father with the apostles; for so he accounteth of them, while he calleth them *brethren.*

2. That albeit we be not sure, for the time, of our effectual calling and election, yet we may be made sure of both, if we use diligence; for this he presupposeth, saying, "Give " diligence to make your calling and election sure."

3. That we must not be discouraged, when we see many seeming believers prove rotten branches, and make defection; but we must the rather take the better heed to ourselves: "Wherefore the rather, brethren, (saith he,) give all diligence."

4. That the way to be sure both of our effectual calling and election, is to make sure work of our faith, by laying the grounds of it solidly, and bringing forth the fruits of our faith in new obedience constantly: "For if ye do these things, (saith he,) ye shall never " fall;" understanding by *these things,* what he had said of sound faith, Ver. 1, 2, 3, 4, and what he had said of the bringing out of the fruits of faith, Ver. 5, 6, 7, 8, 9.

2. To this same purpose, consider Rom. viii. 1. *There is therefore now no condemnation to them which are in Christ Jesus, who walk not after the flesh, but after the Spirit.* Ver. 2. *For the law of the Spirit of life in Christ Jesus hath made me free from the law of sin and death.* Ver. 3. *For what the law could not do, in that it was weak through the flesh, God sending his own Son in the likeness of sinful flesh, and for sin, condemned sin in the flesh;* Ver. 4. *That the righteousness of the law might be fulfilled in us, who walk not after the flesh, but after the Spirit.*

Wherein the apostle teacheth us these four things, for laying of the ground of faith solidly:

1. That every one is a true believer, who, in the sense of his sin, and fear of God's wrath, doth flee for full relief from both unto Jesus Christ alone, as the only Mediator and all-sufficient Redeemer of men; and, being fled to Christ, doth strive against his own flesh, or corrupt inclination of nature, and studieth to follow the rule of God's Spirit, set down in his word: for the man, whom the apostle doth here bless as a true believer, is a man in Christ Jesus, "who doth not walk after the flesh, but after the Spirit."

2. That all such persons as are fled to Christ, and do strive against sin, howsoever they may be possibly exercised under the sense of wrath, and fear of condemnation, yet they are in no danger; for "there is no condemnation (saith he) to them that are in Christ "Jesus, who walk not after the flesh, but after the Spirit."

3. That albeit the apostle himself, (brought in here for example's cause,) and all other true believers in Christ, be by nature under the law of sin and death, or under the covenant of works, (called the law of sin and death, because it bindeth sin and death upon us, till Christ set us free;) yet the law of the Spirit of life in Christ Jesus, or the covenant of grace, (so called, because it doth enable and quicken a man to a spiritual life through Christ,) doth set the apostle, and all true believers, free from the covenant of works, or the law of sin and death: so that every man may say with him, "The law of the Spirit "of life," or the covenant of grace, "hath made me free from the law of sin and death," or covenant of works.

4. That the fountain and first ground, from whence our freedom from the curse of the law doth flow, is the covenant of redemption, passed betwixt God and God the Son as incarnate, wherein Christ takes the curse of the law upon him for sin, that the believer, who could not otherwise be delivered from the covenant of works, may be delivered from it. And this doctrine the apostle holdeth forth in these four branches: (1.) That it was utterly impossible for the law, or the covenant of works, to bring righteousness and life to a sinner, because it was weak. (2.) That this weakness and inability of the law, or covenant of works, is not the fault of the law, but the fault of sinful flesh, which is neither able to pay the penalty of sin, nor to give perfect obedience to the law, (presuppose bygone sins were forgiven:) "The law was weak (saith he) through the flesh." (3.) That the righteousness and salvation of sinners, which was impossible to be brought about by the law, is brought to pass by sending God's own Son, Jesus Christ, in the flesh, in whose flesh sin is condemned and punished, for making satisfaction in the behalf of the elect, that they might be set free. (4.) That by his means the law loseth nothing, because the righteousness of the law is best fulfilled this way; first, by Christ's giving perfect active obedience in our name unto it in all things; next, by his paying in our name the penalty due to our sins in his death: and, lastly, by his working of sanctification in us, who are true believers, who strive to give new obedience unto the law, and "walk not after the "flesh, but after the Spirit."

WARRANTS TO BELIEVE.

FOR building our confidence upon this sure ground, these four Warrants and special Motives to believe in Christ may serve.

The first whereof is *God's hearty invitation* given forth, *Isa.* lv. 1, 2, 3, 4, 5.

Ho, every one that thirsteth, come ye to the waters, and he that hath no money: come ye, buy and eat; yea, come, buy wine and milk without money, and without price. Ver. 2. *Wherefore do ye spend money for that which is not bread? and your labour for that which satisfieth not? Hearken diligently unto me, and eat ye that which is good, and let your soul delight itself in fatness.* Ver. 3. *Incline your ear, and come unto me: hear, and your soul shall live; and I will make an everlasting covenant with you, even the sure mercies of David.* Ver. 4. *Behold, I have given him for a witness to the people, a leader and commander to the people,* &c.

Here (after setting down the precious ransom of our redemption by the sufferings of Christ, and the rich blessings purchased to us thereby, in the two former chapters) the Lord, in this chapter,

1. Maketh open offer of Christ and his grace, by proclamation of a free and gracious market of righteousness and salvation, to be had through Christ to every soul, without exception, that truly desires to be saved from sin and wrath: "Ho, every one that "thirsteth," saith he

2. He inviteth all sinners, that for any reason stand at a distance from God, to come and take from him riches of grace, running in Christ as a river, to wash away sin, and to slocken wrath: "Come ye to the waters," saith he.

3. Lest any should stand aback in the sense of his own sinfulness or unworthiness, and inability to do any good, the Lord calleth upon such persons in special, saying, "He "that hath no money, come."

R

4. He craveth no more of his merchant, but that he be pleased with the wares offered, which are grace, and more grace; and that he heartily consent unto, and embrace this offer of grace, that so he may close a bargain, and a formal covenant with God; "Come, "buy without money, (saith he,) come, eat;" that is, consent to have, and take unto you all saving graces; make the wares your own, possess them, and make use of all blessings in Christ; whatsoever maketh for your spiritual life and comfort, use and enjoy it freely, without paying any thing for it: "Come, buy wine and milk without money, and without "price," saith he.

5. Because the Lord knoweth how much we are inclined to seek righteousness and life by our own performances and satisfaction, to have righteousness and life as it were by the way of works, and how loath we are to embrace Christ Jesus, and to take life by way of free grace through Jesus Christ, upon the terms whereupon it is offered to us; therefore the Lord lovingly calls us off this our crooked and unhappy way with a gentle and timeous admonition, giving us to understand, that we shall but lose our labour in this our way: "Wherefore do ye spend your money (saith he) for that which is not bread? "and your labour for that which satisfieth not?"

6. The Lord promiseth to us solid satisfaction in the way of betaking ourselves unto the grace of Christ, even true contentment, and fulness of spiritual pleasure, saying, "Hearken diligently unto me, and eat ye that which is good, and let your soul delight "itself in fatness."

7. Because faith cometh by hearing, he calleth for audience unto the explication of the offer, and calleth for believing of, and listening unto the truth, which is able to beget the application of saving faith, and to draw the soul to trust it. God: "Incline your ear, "and come unto me," saith he. To which end, the Lord promises, that this offer being received, shall quicken the dead sinner; and that, upon the welcoming of this offer, he will close the covenant of grace with the man that shall consent unto it, even an indissolvable covenant of perpetual reconciliation and peace: "Hearken, and your soul shall "live; and I will make an everlasting covenant with you." Which covenant, he declareth, shall be in substance the assignation, and the making over, of all the saving graces which David (who is Jesus Christ, Acts xiii. 34.) hath bought for us in the covenant of redemption: "I will make a covenant with you, (saith he,) even the sure mercies "of David." By *sure mercies*, he means saving graces, such as are righteousness, peace, and joy in the Holy Ghost, adoption, sanctification, and glorification, and whatsoever belongs to godliness and life eternal.

8. To confirm and assure us of the real grant of these saving mercies, and to persuade us of the reality of the covenant betwixt God and the believer of this word, the Father hath made a fourfold gift of his eternal and only begotten Son:

First, To be incarnate and born for our sake, of the seed of David his type; for which cause he is called here, and Acts xiii. 34. DAVID, the true and everlasting King of Israel. This is the great gift of God to man, John iv. 10. And here, *I have given him to be David, or born of David, to the people.*

Secondly, He hath made a gift of Christ to be a witness to the people, both of the sure and saving mercies granted to the redeemed in the covenant of redemption; and also of the Father's willingness and purpose to apply them, and to make them fast in the covenant of reconciliation made with such as embrace the offer: "I have given him (saith "the Lord here) to be a witness to the people." And truly he is a sufficient witness in this matter in many respects: 1*st*, Because he is one of the blessed Trinity, and party-contractor for us, in the covenant of redemption, before the world was. 2*dly*, He is by office, as Mediator, the Messenger of the covenant, and hath gotten commission to reveal it. 3*dly*, He began actually to reveal it in paradise, where he promised, that the seed of the woman should bruise the head of the serpent. 4*thly*, He set forth his own death and sufferings, and the great benefit should come thereby to us, in the types and figures of sacrifices and ceremonies before his coming. 5*thly*, He gave more and more light about this covenant, speaking by his Spirit, from age to age, in the holy prophets. 6*thly*, He came himself, in the fulness of time, and did bear witness of all things belonging to this covenant, and of God's willing mind to take believers into it; partly, by uniting our nature in one person with the divine nature; partly, by preaching the good tidings of the covenant with his own mouth; partly, by paying the price of redemption on the cross; and partly, by dealing still with the people, from the beginning to this day, to draw in, and to hold in the redeemed in this covenant.

Thirdly, God hath made a gift of Christ, as a leader to the people, to bring us through all difficulties, all afflictions and temptations, unto life, by this covenant: and he it is, and no other, who doth indeed lead his own unto the covenant; and, in the covenant, all the way on unto salvation: 1. By the direction of his word and Spirit. 2. By the example of his own life, in faith and obedience, even to the death of the cross. 3. By his powerful working, bearing his redeemed ones in his arms, and causing them to lean on him, while they go up through the wilderness.

Fourthly, God hath made a gift of Christ unto his people, as a commander; which office he faithfully exerciseth, by giving to his kirk and people laws and ordinances, pastors and governors, and all necessary officers; by keeping courts and assemblies among them, to see that his laws be obeyed; subduing, by his word, Spirit, and discipline, his people's corruptions; and, by his wisdom and power, guarding them against all their enemies whatsoever.

Hence he who hath closed bargain with God may strengthen his faith, by reasoning after this manner:

"Whosoever doth heartily receive the offer of free grace, made here to sinners, thirsting for righteousness and salvation: unto him, by an everlasting covenant, belongeth Christ, the true David, with all his sure and saving mercies:

"But I (may the weak believer say) do heartily receive the offer of free grace made here to sinners, thirsting for righteousness and salvation:

"Therefore unto me, by an everlasting covenant, belongeth Christ Jesus, with all his sure and saving mercies."

The second Warrant and special Motive to embrace Christ, and believe in him, is the *earnest request* that God maketh to us to be reconciled to him in Christ; holden forth, 2 Cor. v. 19, 20, 21.

God was in Christ, reconciling the world unto himself, not imputing their trespasses unto them; and hath committed unto us the word of reconciliation. Ver. 20. *Now then, we are ambassadors for Christ, as though God did beseech you by us: we pray you in Christ's stead, be ye reconciled to God.* Ver. 21. *For he hath made him to be sin for us, who knew no sin; that we might be made the righteousness of God in him.*

Wherein the apostle teacheth us these nine doctrines:

1. That the elect world, or world of redeemed souls, are by nature in the estate of enmity against God: this is presupposed in the word *reconciliation;* for reconciliation, or renewing of friendship, cannot be, except betwixt those that have been at enmity.

2. That in all the time bypast, since the fall of Adam, Christ Jesus, the eternal Son of God, as Mediator, and the Father in him, hath been about the making friendship (by his word and Spirit) betwixt himself and the elect world: "God (saith he) was in Christ "reconciling the world to himself."

3. That the way of reconciliation was in all ages one and the same in substance, *viz.* by forgiving the sins of them who do acknowledge their sins and their enmity against God, and do seek reconciliation and remission of sins in Christ: "For God (saith he) was "in Christ reconciling the world unto himself," by way of "not imputing their trespasses "unto them."

4. That the end and scope of the gospel, and whole word of God, is threefold: (1.) It serveth to make people sensible of their sins, and of their enmity against God, and of their danger, if they should stand out, and not fear God's displeasure. (2.) The word of God serveth to make men acquainted with the course which God hath prepared for making friendship with them through Christ, *viz.* That if men shall acknowledge the enmity, and shall be content to enter into a covenant of friendship with God through Christ, then God will be content to be reconciled with them freely. (3.) The word of God serveth to teach men how to carry themselves towards God, as friends, after they are reconciled to him, *viz.* to be loath to sin against him, and to strive heartily to obey his commandments: and therefore the word of God here is called *the word of reconciliation,* because it teacheth us what need we have of reconciliation, and how to make it, and how to keep the reconciliation of friendship, being made with God through Christ.

5. That albeit the hearing, believing, and obeying of this word, doth belong to all those to whom this gospel doth come; yet the office of preaching of it with authority belongeth to none, but to such only as God doth call to his ministry, and sendeth out with commission for this work. This the apostle holdeth forth, Ver. 19. in these words, "He hath 'committed to us the word of reconciliation.'

6. That the ministers of the gospel should behave themselves as Christ's messengers, and should closely follow their commission laid down in the word, Matt. xxviii. 19, 20; and when they do so, they should be received by the people as ambassadors from God; for here the apostle, in all their names, saith, "We are ambassadors for Christ, as though "God did beseech you by us."

7. That ministers, in all earnestness of affections, should deal with people to acknowledge their sins, and their natural enmity against God, more and more seriously; and to consent to the covenant of grace and embassage of Christ more and more heartily; and to evidence more and more clearly their reconciliation, by a holy carriage before God. This he holdeth forth, when he saith, "We pray you, be ye reconciled to God."

8. That in the ministers' affectionate dealing with the people, the people should consider that they have to do with God and Christ, requesting them, by the ministers, to be reconciled. Now, there cannot be a greater inducement to break a sinner's hard heart, than God's making a request to him for friendship; for when it became us, who have done so many wrongs to God, to seek friendship of God, he preventeth us: and (O wonder of wonders!) he requesteth us to be content to be reconciled to him; and therefore most fearful wrath must abide them who do set light by this request, and do not yield when they hear ministers with commission, saying, "We are ambassadors for Christ, as though "God did beseech you by us: we pray you in Christ's stead, be ye reconciled to God."

9. To make it appear how it cometh to pass that the covenant of reconciliation should be so easily made up betwixt God and a humble sinner fleeing to Christ, the apostle leads us unto the cause of it, holden forth in the covenant of redemption, the sum whereof is this: "It is agreed betwixt God and the Mediator Jesus Christ the Son of God, surety "for the redeemed, as parties-contractors, that the sins of the redeemed should be im

"puted to innocent Christ, and he both condemned and put to death for them, upon
" this very condition, that whosoever heartily consents unto the covenant of reconcilia-
" tion offered through Christ, shall, by the imputation of his obedience unto them, be
" justified and holden righteous before God; for God hath made Christ, *who knew no sin,
" to be sin for us,* saith the apostle, *that we might be made the righteousness of God in
" him.*"

Hence may a weak believer strengthen his faith, by reasoning from this ground after this manner:

" He that, upon the loving request of God and Christ, made to him by the mouth of
" ministers, (having commission to that effect,) hath embraced the offer of perpetual re-
" conciliation through Christ, and doth purpose, by God's grace, as a reconciled person,
" to strive against sin, and to serve God to his power constantly, may be as sure to have
" righteousness and eternal life given to him, for the obedience of Christ imputed to him,
" as it is sure that Christ was condemned and put to death for the sins of the redeemed
" imputed to him:

" But I (may the weak believer say) upon the loving request of God and Christ, made
" to me by the mouth of his ministers, have embraced the offer of perpetual reconciliation
" through Christ, and do purpose, by God's grace, as a reconciled person, to strive against
' sin, and to serve God to my power constantly:

" Therefore I may be as sure to have righteousness and eternal life given to me, for
" the obedience of Christ imputed to me, as it is sure that Christ was condemned and
" put to death for the sins of the redeemed imputed to him."

The third Warrant and special Motive to believe in Christ, is the strait and *awful command of God,* charging all the hearers of the gospel to approach to Christ in the order set down by him, and to believe in him; holden forth, 1 *John* iii. 23.

This is his commandment, That we should believe on the name of his Son Jesus Christ, and love one another, as he gave us commandment.

Wherein the apostle giveth us to understand these five doctrines:

1. That if any man shall not be taken with the sweet invitation of God, nor with the humble and loving request of God, made to him to be reconciled, he shall find he hath to do with the sovereign authority of the highest Majesty; for "this is his commandment, " that we believe in him," saith he.

2. That if any man look upon this commandment as he hath looked heretofore upon the neglected commandments of the law, he must consider that this is a command of the gospel, posterior to the law, given for making use of the remedy of all sins; which, if it be disobeyed, there is no other command to follow but this, " Go, ye cursed, into the " everlasting fire of hell;" for "this is his commandment;" the obedience of which is most pleasant in his sight, Ver. 22. and without which it is impossible to please him, Heb. xi. 6.

3. That every one who heareth the gospel, must make conscience of the duty of lively faith in Christ; the weak believer must not think it presumption to do what is commanded; the person inclined to desperation must take up himself, and think upon obedience unto this sweet and saving command; the strong believer must dip yet more in the sense of his need he hath of Jesus Christ, and more and more grow in the obedience of this command; yea, the most impenitent, profane, and wicked person must not thrust out himself, or be thrust out by others, from orderly aiming at this duty, how desperate soever his condition seems to be; for he that commands all men to believe in Christ, doth thereby command all men to believe that they are damned and lost without Christ: he thereby commands all men to acknowledge their sins, and their need of Christ, and in effect commands all men to repent, that they may believe in him. And whosoever do refuse to repent of their bygone sins, are guilty of disobedience to this command given to all hearers, but especially to those that are within the visible church: for " this is his " commandment, that we should believe on the name of his Son Jesus Christ," saith he.

4. That he who obeyeth this commandment hath built his salvation on a solid ground: for, 1st, He hath found the promised Messiah, completely furnished with all perfections unto the perfect execution of the offices of Prophet, Priest, and King; for he is that Christ in whom the man doth believe. 2d, He hath embraced a Saviour, who is able to save to the uttermost, yea, and who doth effectually save every one that cometh to God through him; for he is Jesus, the true Saviour of his people from their sins. 3d, He that obeyeth this command hath built his salvation on the Rock, that is, on the Son of God, to whom it is no robbery to be called equal to the Father, and who is worthy to be the object of saving faith, and of spiritual worship: for "this is his command, (saith he,) " that we believe in the name of his Son Jesus Christ."

5. That he who hath believed on Jesus Christ, though he be freed from the curse of the law, is not freed from the command and obedience of the law, but tied thereunto by a new obligation, and a new command from Christ; which new command from Christ importeth help to obey the command; unto which command from Christ, the Father addeth his authority and command also; for " this is his commandment, (saith John,' " that we believe on the name of his Son Jesus Christ, and love one another, as he hath " commanded us." The first part of which command, enjoining belief in him, necessarily

implieth love to God, and so obedience to the first table; for believing in God, and loving God, are inseparable; and the second part of the command enjoineth love to our neighbour, (especially to the household of faith,) and so obedience to the second table of the law.

Hence may a weak believer strengthen himself, by reasoning from this ground after this manner:

"Whosoever, in the sense of his own sinfulness, and fear of God's wrath, at the com-
"mand of God, is fled to Jesus Christ, the only remedy of sin and misery, and hath en-
"gaged his heart to the obedience of the law of love, his faith is not presumptuous or
"dead, but true and saving faith:

"But I, (may the weak believer say,) in the sense of my own sinfulness, and fear of
"God's wrath, am fled to Jesus Christ, the only remedy of sin and misery, and have
"engaged my heart to the obedience of the law of love:

"Therefore my faith is not a presumptuous and dead faith, but true and saving faith."

The fourth Warrant and special Motive to believe in Christ, is *much assurance of life* given, in case men shall obey the command of believing; and a *fearful certification* of destruction, in case they obey not; holden forth, *John* iii. 35.

The Father loveth the Son, and hath given all things into his hand. Ver. 36. *He that believeth on the Son hath everlasting life: and he that believeth not the Son shall not see life; but the wrath of God abideth on him.*

Wherein are holden forth to us these five following doctrines:

1. That the Father is well satisfied with the undertakings of the Son, entered Redeemer and Surety, to pay the ransom of believers and to perfect them in holiness and salvation: "The Father loveth the Son," saith he; *viz.* as he standeth Mediator in our name, undertaking to perfect our redemption in all points: The Father loveth him, that is, doth heartily accept his offer to do the work, and is well pleased with him: his soul delighteth in him, and resteth upon him, and maketh him, in this his office, the "receptacle of love, "and grace, and good will," to be conveyed by him to believers in him.

2. That, for fulfilling of the covenant of redemption, the Father hath given to the Son (as he standeth in the capacity of the Mediator, or as he is God incarnate, the Word made flesh) all authority in heaven and earth, all furniture of the riches of grace, and of spirit and life, with all power and ability, which the union of the divine nature with the human, or which the fulness of the Godhead dwelling substantially in his human nature, or which the indivisible all-sufficiency and omnipotency of the inseparable, every where present Trinity doth import, or the work of redemption can require: "The Father (saith "he) hath given all things into the Son's hand," to wit, for accomplishing his work.

3. Great assurance of life is holden forth to all who shall heartily receive Christ, and the offer of the covenant of grace and reconciliation through him: "He that believeth "on the Son (saith he) hath everlasting life;" for it is made fast unto him, 1*st*, In God's purpose and irrevocable decree, as the believer is a man elected to life. 2*d*, By effectual calling of him unto life by God, who, as he is faithful, so will he do it. 3*d*, By promise and everlasting covenant, sworn by God, to give the believer strong consolation in life and death, upon immutable grounds. 4*th*, By a pawn and infeftment under the great seal of the sacrament of the Lord's supper, so oft as the believer shall come to receive the symbols and pledges of life. 5*th*, In Christ the fountain and head of life, who is entered in possession, as attorney for believers; in whom our life is so laid up, that it cannot be taken away. 6*th*, By begun possession of spiritual life and regeneration, and a kingdom consisting in righteousness, peace, and joy in the Holy Ghost, erected within the believer, as earnest of the full possession of everlasting life.

4. A fearful certification is given, if a man receive not the doctrine concerning righteousness and eternal life to be had by Jesus Christ: "He that believeth not the Son shall "not see life," that is, not so much as understand what it meaneth.

5. He further certifieth, that if a man receive not the doctrine of the Son of God, he shall be burdened twice with the wrath of God; once, as a born rebel by nature, he shall bear the curse of the law, or the covenant of works; and next, he shall endure a greater condemnation, in respect that light being come into the world, and offered to him, he hath rejected it, and loveth darkness rather than light: and this double wrath shall be fastened and fixed immovably upon him, so long as he remaineth in the condition of misbelief: "The wrath of God abideth on him," saith he.

Hence may the weak believer strengthen his faith, by reasoning from this ground after this manner:

"Whosoever believeth the doctrine delivered by the Son of God, and findeth himself
"partly drawn powerfully to believe in him, by the sight of life in him, and partly
"driven, by the fear of God's wrath to adhere unto him, may be sure of right and
"interest to life eternal through him.

"But sinful and unworthy I (may the weak believer say) do believe the doctrine deli-
"vered by the Son of God, and do feel myself partly drawn powerfully to believe in him,
"by the sight of life in him, and partly driven, by the fear of God's wrath, to adhere
"unto him:

"Therefore I may be sure of my right and interest unto eternal life through him."

THE EVIDENCES OF TRUE FAITH.

SO much for the laying the grounds of faith, and warrants to believe. Now, for evidencing of true faith by fruits, these four things are requisite: 1. That the believer be soundly convinced, in his judgment, of his obligation to keep the whole moral law, all the days of his life; and that not the less, but so much the more, as he is delivered by Christ from the covenant of works, and curse of the law. 2. That he endeavour to grow in the exercise and daily practice of godliness and righteousness. 3. That the course of his new obedience run in the right channel, that is through faith in Christ, and through a good conscience, to all the duties of love towards God and man. 4. That he keep strait communion with the fountain Christ Jesus, from whom grace must run along, for furnishing of good fruits.

For the first, viz. To convince the believer, in his judgment, of his obligation to keep the moral law, among many passages, take *Matt* v. 16.

Let your light so shine before men, that they may see your good works, and glorify your Father which is in heaven. Ver. 17. *Think not that I am come to destroy the law or the prophets: I am not come to destroy, but to fulfil.* Ver. 18. *For verily I say unto you, Till heaven and earth pass, one jot or one tittle shall in no wise pass from the law, till all be fulfilled.* Ver. 19. *Whosoever therefore shall break one of these least commandments, and shall teach men so, he shall be called the least in the kingdom of heaven: but whosoever shall do and teach them, the same shall be called great in the kingdom of heaven.* Ver. 20. *For I say unto you, That except your righteousness shall exceed the righteousness of the scribes and Pharisees, ye shall in no case enter into the kingdom of heaven.*

Wherein our Lord,

1. Giveth commandment to believers, justified by faith, to give evidence of the grace of God in them before men, by doing good works: "Let your light so shine before men, " (saith he,) that they may see your good works."

2. He induceth them so to do, by shewing, that albeit they be not justified by works, yet spectators of their good works may be converted or edified; and so glory may redound to God by their good works, when the witnesses thereof "shall glorify your Father which is " in heaven."

3. He gives them no other rule for their new obedience than the moral law, set down and explicated by Moses and the prophets: "Think not (saith he) that I am come to " destroy the law or the prophets."

4. He gives them to understand, that the doctrine of grace, and freedom from the curse of the law by faith in him, is readily mistaken by men's corrupt judgments, as if it did loose or slacken the obligation of believers to obey the commands, and to be subject to the authority of the law; and that this error is indeed a destroying of the law and of the prophets, which he will in no case ever endure in any of his disciples, it is so contrary to the end of his coming, which is first to sanctify, and then to save believers: "Think not " (saith he) that I am come to destroy the law or the prophets.'

5. He teacheth, that the end of the gospel and covenant of grace is to procure men's obedience unto the moral law: "I am come (saith he) to fulfil the law and the prophets."

6. That the obligation of the moral law, in all points, unto all holy duties, is perpetual, and shall stand to the world's end, that is, "till heaven and earth pass away."

7. That as God hath had a care of the Scriptures from the beginning, so shall he have a care of them still to the world's end, that there shall not one jot or one tittle of the substance thereof be taken away; so saith the text, Ver. 18.

8. That as the breaking of the moral law, and defending the transgressions thereof to be no sin, doth exclude men both from heaven, and justly also from the fellowship of the true kirk; so the obedience of the law, and teaching others to do the same, by example, counsel, and doctrine, according to every man's calling, proveth a man to be a true believer, and in great estimation with God, and worthy to be much esteemed of by the true church, Ver. 19.

9. That the righteousness of every true Christian must be more than the righteousness of the scribes and Pharisees; for the scribes and Pharisees, albeit they took great pains to discharge sundry duties of the law, yet they cutted short the exposition thereof, that it might the less condemn their practice; they studied the outward part of the duty, but neglected the inward and spiritual part; they discharged some meaner duties carefully, but neglected judgment, mercy, and the love of God: in a word, they went about to establish their own righteousness, and rejected the righteousness of God by faith in Jesus. But a true Christian must have more than all this; he must acknowledge the full extent of the spiritual meaning of the law, and have a respect to all the commandments, and labour to cleanse himself from all filthiness of flesh and spirit, and "not lay " weight upon what service he hath done, or shall do," but clothe himself with the imputed righteousness of Christ, which only can hide his nakedness, or else he cannot be saved; so saith the text, "Except your righteousness," &c.

The second thing requisite to evidence true faith is, that the believer endeavour to put the rules of godliness and righteousness in practice, and to grow in the daily exercise thereof; holden forth, 2 *Pet.* i. 5.

And besides this, giving all diligence, add to your faith, virtue; and to virtue, knowledge; Ver. 6. *And to knowledge, temperance; and to temperance, patience; and to patience, godliness;* Ver. 7. *And to godliness, brotherly-kindness; and to brotherly-kindness, charity.* Ver. 8. *For if these things be in you, and abound, they make you that ye shall neither be barren nor unfruitful in the knowledge of our Lord Jesus Christ.*

Wherein, 1. The apostle teacheth believers, for evidencing of precious faith in themselves, to endeavour to add to their faith seven other sister graces. The first is Virtue, or the active exercise and practice of all moral duties, that so faith may not be idle, but put forth itself in work. The second is Knowledge, which serves to furnish faith with information of the truth to be believed, and to furnish virtue with direction what duties are to be done, and how to go about them prudently. The third is Temperance, which serveth to moderate the use of all pleasant things, that a man be not clogged therewith, nor made unfit for any duty whereto he is called. The fourth is Patience, which serveth to moderate a man's affections, when he meeteth with any difficulty or unpleasant thing; that he neither weary for pains required in well-doing, nor faint when the Lord chastiseth him, nor murmur when he crosseth him. The fifth is Godliness, which may keep him up in all the exercises of religion, inward and outward; whereby he may be furnished from God for all other duties which he hath to do. The sixth is Brotherly-kindness, which keepeth estimation of, and affection to, all the household of faith, and to the image of God in every one wheresoever it is seen. The seventh is Love, which keepeth the heart in readiness to do good to all men, whatsoever they be, upon all occasions which God shall offer.

2. Albeit it be true, that there is much corruption and infirmity in the godly; yet the apostle will have men uprightly endeavouring, and doing their best, as they are able, to join all these graces one to another, and to grow in the measure of exercising them : " Giving all diligence, (saith he,) add to your faith," &c.

3. He assureth all professed believers, that as they shall profit in the obedience of this direction, so they shall profitably prove the soundness of their own faith ; and, if they want these graces, that they shall be found blind deceivers of themselves, Ver. 9.

The third thing requisite to evidence true faith is, that obedience to the law run in the right channel, that is, through faith in Christ, &c., holden forth,1 *Tim.* i. 5.

Now, the end of the commandment is love, out of a pure heart, and of a good conscience, and of faith unfeigned.

Wherein the apostle teacheth these seven doctrines :
1. That the obedience of the law must flow from love, and love from a pure heart, and a pure heart from a good conscience, and a good conscience from faith unfeigned : this he makes the only right channel of good works: " The end of the law is love," &c.
2. That the end of the law is not, that men may be justified by their obedience of it, as the Jewish doctors did falsely teach ; for it is impossible that sinners can be justified by the law, who, for every transgression, are condemned by the law: " For the end of the " law is (not such as the Jewish doctors taught, but) love, out of a pure heart," &c.
3. That the true end of the law, preached unto the people, is, that they, by the law, being made to see their deserved condemnation, should flee to Christ unfeignedly, to be justified by faith in him ; so saith the text, while it maketh love to flow through faith in Christ.
4. That no man can set himself in love to obey the law, excepting as far as his conscience is quieted by faith, or is seeking to be quieted in Christ ; for " the end of the law " is love, out of a good conscience, and faith unfeigned."
5. That feigned faith goeth to Christ without reckoning with the law, and so wants an errand ; but unfeigned faith reckoneth with the law, and is forced to flee for refuge unto Christ, as the end of the law for righteousness, so often as it finds itself guilty for breaking of the law: " For the end of the law is faith unfeigned."
6. That the fruits of love may come forth in act particularly, it is necessary that the heart be brought to the hatred of all sin and uncleanness, and to a stedfast purpose to follow all holiness universally : " For the end of the law is love, out of a pure heart."
7. That unfeigned faith is able to make the conscience good, and the heart pure, and the man lovingly obedient to the law; for when Christ's blood is seen by faith to quiet justice, then the conscience becometh quiet also, and will not suffer the heart to entertain the love of sin, but sets the man on work to fear God for his mercy, and to obey all his commandments, out of love to God, for his free gift of justification, by grace bestowed on him : " For this is the end of the law indeed," whereby it obtaineth of a man more obedience than any other way.

The fourth thing requisite to evidence true faith is, the *keeping strait communion with Christ,* the fountain of all graces, and of all good works; holden forth, *John* xv. 5.

I am the vine, ye are the branches: he that abideth in me, and I in him, the same bringeth forth much fruit; for without me ye can do nothing.

Wherein Christ, in a similitude from a vine-tree, teacheth us,

1. That by nature we are wild barren briers, till we be changed by coming unto Christ, and that Christ is that noble vine-tree, having all life and sap of grace in himself, and able to change the nature of every one that cometh to him, and to communicate spirit and life to as many as shall believe in him: "I am the vine, (saith he,) and ye are the "branches."

2. That Christ loveth to have believers so united unto him, as that they be not separated at any time by unbelief: and that there may be a mutual inhabitation of them in him, by faith and love; and of him in them, by his word and Spirit; for he joineth these together, "If ye abide in me, and I in you," as things inseparable.

3. That except a man be ingrafted into Christ, and united to him by faith, he cannot do any the least good works of his own strength; yea, except in as far as a man doth draw spirit and life from Christ by faith, the work which he doth is naughty and null in point of goodness in God's estimation: "For without me (saith he) ye can do nothing."

4. That this mutual inhabitation is the fountain and infallible cause of constant continuing and abounding in well-doing: For "he that abideth in me, and I in him, (saith "he,) the same beareth much fruit." Now, as our abiding in Christ presupposeth three things; 1*st*, That we have heard the joyful sound of the gospel, making offer of Christ to us, who are lost sinners by the law; 2*d*, That we have heartily embraced the gracious offer of Christ; 3*d*, That by receiving of him we are become the sons of God, *John* i. 12. and are incorporated into his mystical body, that he may dwell in us, as his temple, and we dwell in him, as in the residence of righteousness and life: so our abiding in Christ importeth other three things, (1.) An employing of Christ in all our addresses to God, and in all our undertakings of whatsoever piece of service to him. (2.) A contentedness with his sufficiency, without going out from him to seek righteousness, or life, or furniture in any case, in our own or any of the creature's worthiness. (3.) A fixedness in our believing in him, a fixedness in our employing and making use of him, and a fixedness in our contentment in him, and adhering to him, so that no allurement, no temptation of Satan or the world, no terror nor trouble, may be able to drive our spirits from firm adherence to him, or from the constant avowing of his truth, and obeying his commands, who hath loved us, and given himself for us; and in whom not only our life is laid up, but also the fulness of the Godhead dwelleth bodily, by reason of the substantial and personal union of the divine and human nature in him.

Hence let every watchful believer, for strengthening himself in faith and obedience, reason after this manner:

"Whosoever doth daily employ Christ Jesus for cleansing his conscience and affections "from the guiltiness and filthiness of sins against the law, and for enabling him to give "obedience to the law in love, he hath the evidence of true faith in himself:

"But I (may every watchful believer say) do daily employ Jesus Christ for cleansing "my conscience and affections from the guiltiness and filthiness of sins against the law, "and for enabling of me to give obedience to the law in love:

"Therefore I have the evidence of true faith in myself."

And hence also let the sleepy and sluggish believer reason, for his own upstirring, thus:
"Whatsoever is necessary for giving evidence of true faith, I study to do it, except I "would deceive myself and perish:

"But to employ Christ Jesus daily for cleansing of my conscience and affections from "the guiltiness and filthiness of sins against the law, and for enabling me to give obedi-"ence to the law in love, is necessary for evidencing of true faith in me:

"Therefore this I must study to do, except I would deceive myself and perish."

And, *lastly*, Seeing Christ himself hath pointed this forth, as an undoubted evidence of a man elected of God unto life, and given to Jesus Christ to be redeemed, "if he come unto "him," that is, close covenant, and keep communion with him, as he teacheth us, John vi. 37. saying, "All that the Father hath given me shall come to me; and him that "cometh to me I will in no wise cast out;" let every person, who doth not in earnest make use of Christ for remission of sin, and amendment of life, reason hence, and from the whole premises, after this manner, that his conscience may be awakened:

"Whosoever is neither by the law, nor by the gospel, so convinced of sin, righteous "ness, and judgment, as to make him come to Christ, and employ him daily for remission "of sin, and amendment of life; he wanteth not only all evidence of saving faith, but "also all appearance of his election, so long as he remaineth in this condition:

"But I (may every impenitent person say) am neither by the law nor gospel so con-"vinced of sin, righteousness, and judgment, as to make me come to Christ, and employ "him daily for remission of sin, and amendment of life:

"Therefore I want not only all evidence of saving faith, but also all appearance of my "election, so long as I remain in this condition."

THE CONFESSION OF FAITH

OF

THE KIRK OF SCOTLAND:

OR,

THE NATIONAL COVENANT,

WITH A DESIGNATION OF SUCH ACTS OF PARLIAMENT AS ARE EXPEDIENT FOR JUSTIFYING THE UNION AFTERMENTIONED.

JOSHUA xxiv. 25.—So Joshua made a covenant with the people that day, and set them a statute and an ordinance in Shechem.

2 KINGS xi. 17.—And Jehoiada made a covenant between the Lord and the king and the people, that they should be the Lord's people; between the king also and the people.

ISAIAH xliv. 5.—One shall say, I am the Lord's; and another shall call himself by the name of Jacob; and another shall subscribe with his hand unto the Lord and surname himself by the name of Israel.

ASSEMBLY AT EDINBURGH, August 30, 1639.   Sess. 23.

ACT *ordaining, by Ecclesiastical Authority, the Subscription of the* CONFESSION OF FAITH AND COVENANT, *with the* ASSEMBLY'S *Declaration.*

THE General Assembly considering the great happiness which may flow from a full and perfect union of this kirk and kingdom, by joining of all in one and the same Covenant with God, with the King's Majesty, and amongst ourselves; having by our great oath, declared the uprightness and loyalty of our intentions in all our proceedings; and having withal supplicated his Majesty's high Commissioner, and the Lords of his Majesties honourable Privy Council, to enjoin, by Act of Council, all the lieges in time coming to subscribe the Confession of Faith and Covenant; which, as a testimony of our fidelity to God, and loyalty to our King, we have subscribed: And seeing his Majesty's high Commissioner, and the Lords of his Majesty's honourable Privy Council, have granted the desire of our supplication, ordaining, by civil authority, all his Majesty's lieges, in time coming, to subscribe the foresaid Covenant: that our union may be the more full and perfect, we, by our act and constitution ecclesiastical, do approve the foresaid Covenant in all the heads and clauses thereof; and ordain of new, under all ecclesiastical censure, That all the masters of universities, colleges, and schools, all scholars at the passing of their degrees, all persons suspected of Papistry, or any other error; and finally, all the members of this kirk and kingdom, subscribe the same, with these words prefixed to their subscription, "The Article of this Covenant, which was at the first subscription referred to the determination of the General Assembly, being determined ; and thereby the five articles of Perth, the government of the kirk by bishops, the civil places and power of kirkmen, upon the reasons and grounds contained in the acts of the General Assembly, declared to be unlawful within this kirk; we subscribe according to the determination foresaid." And ordain the Covenant, with this declaration, to be insert in the registers of the Assemblies of this kirk, general, provincial, and presbyterial, *ad perpetuam rei memoriam.* And in all humility supplicate his Majesty's high Commissioner, and the honourable estates of Parliament, by their authority, to ratify and enjoin the same, under all civil pains; which will tend to the glory of God, preservation of religion, the King's Majesty's honour, and perfect peace of this kirk and kingdom.

CHARLES I. Parl. 2. Act 5.

ACT *anent the Ratification of the* COVENANT, *and of the Assembly's Supplication, Act of Council, and Act of Assembly concerning the Covenant.*

AT EDINBURGH, June 11, 1640.

THE Estates of Parliament, presently convened by his Majesty's special authority, considering the supplication of the General Assembly at Edinburgh, the 12th of August 1639, to his Majesty's high Commissioner, and the Lords of his Majesty's honourable Privy Council; and the act of Council of the 30th of August 1639, containing the answer of the said supplication; and the act of the said General Assembly, ordaining, by their ecclesiastical constitution, the subscription of the Confession of Faith and Covenant mentioned in their supplication: and withal, having supplicated his Majesty to ratify and enjoin the same by his royal authority, under all civil pains, as tending to the glory of God, the preservation of religion, the King's Majesty's honour, and the perfect peace of this kirk and kingdom; do ratify and approve the said supplication, act of Council and act of Assembly; and, conform thereto, ordain and command the said Confession and Covenant to be subscribed by all his Majesty's subjects of what rank and quality soever, under all civil pains; and ordain the said supplication, act of Council, and act of the Assembly, with the whole Confession and Covenant itself, to be insert and registrate in the acts and books of Parliament; and also ordain the samen to be presented at the entry of every Parliament, and, before they proceed to any other act, that the same be publickly read, and sworn by the whole members of Parliament, claiming voice therein; otherwise the refusers to subscribe and swear the same shall have no place nor voice in Parliament: And sicklike, ordain all judges, magistrates, or other officers, of whatsoever place, rank, or quality, and ministers at their entry, to swear and subscribe the samen Covenant, whereof the the tenor follows.

THE

NATIONAL COVENANT;

OR,

THE CONFESSION OF FAITH:

Subscribed at first by the King's Majesty, and his Household, in the year 1580; thereafter by persons of all ranks in the year 1581, by ordinance of the Lords of Secret Council, and acts of the General Assembly; subscribed again by all sorts of persons in the year 1590, by a new ordinance of Council, at the desire of the General Assembly: with a general bond for the maintaining of the true Christian religion, and the King's person; and, together with a resolution and promise, for the causes after expressed, to maintain the true religion, and the King's Majesty, according to the foresaid Confession and acts of Parliament, subscribed by Barons, Nobles, Gentlemen, Burgesses, Ministers, and Commons, in the year 1638: approven by the General Assembly 1638 and 1639; and subscribed again by persons of all ranks and qualities in the year 1639, by an ordinance of Council, upon the supplication of the General Assembly, and act of the General Assembly, ratified by an act of Parliament 1640: and subscribed by King *Charles II.* at *Spey, June* 23, 1650, and *Scoon, January* 1, 1651.

WE all and every one of us under-written, protest, That, after long and due examination of our own consciences in matters of true and false religion, we are now thoroughly resolved in the truth by the word and Spirit of God: and therefore we believe with our hearts, confess with our mouths, subscribe with our hands, and constantly affirm, before God and the whole world, that this only is the true Christian faith and religion, pleasing God, and bringing salvation to man, which now is, by the mercy of God, revealed to the world by the preaching of the blessed evangel; and is received, believed, and defended by many and sundry notable kirks and realms, but chiefly by the kirk of Scotland, the King's Majesty, and three estates of this realm, as God's eternal truth, and only ground of our salvation; as more particularly is expressed in the Confession of our Faith, established and publickly confirmed by sundry acts of Parliaments, and now of a long time hath been openly professed by the King's Majesty, and whole body of this realm both in burgh and land. To the which Confession and Form of Religion we willingly agree in our conscience in all points, as unto God's undoubted truth and verity, grounded only upon his written word. And therefore we abhor and detest all contrary religion and doctrine; but chiefly all kind of Papistry in general and particular heads, even as they are now damned and confuted by the word of God and Kirk of Scotland. But, in special, we detest and refuse the usurped authority of that Roman Antichrist upon the scriptures of God, upon the kirk, the civil magistrate, and consciences of men; all his tyrannous laws made upon indifferent things against our Christian liberty; his erroneous doctrine against the sufficiency of the written word, the perfection of the law, the office of Christ, and his blessed evangel; his corrupted doctrine concerning original sin, our natural inability and rebellion to God's law, our justification by faith only, our imperfect sanctification and obedience to the law; the nature, number, and use of the holy sacraments; his five bastard sacraments, with all his rites, ceremonies, and false doctrine, added to the ministration of the true sacraments without the word of God; his cruel judgment against infants departing without the sacrament; his absolute necessity of baptism; his blasphemous opinion of transubstantiation, or real presence of Christ's body in the elements, and receiving of the same by the wicked, or bodies of men; his dispensations with solemn oaths, perjuries, and degrees of marriage forbidden in the word; his cruelty against the innocent divorced; his devilish mass; his blasphemous priesthood; his profane sacrifice for sins of the dead and the quick; his canonization of men; calling upon angels or saints departed, worshipping of imagery, relicks, and crosses; dedicating of kirks, altars, days; vows to creatures; his purgatory, prayers for the dead; praying or speaking in a strange language, with his processions, and blasphemous litany and multitude of advocates or mediators; his manifold orders, auricular confession; his desperate and uncertain repentance; his general and doubtsome faith; his satisfactions of men for their sins; his justification by works, *opus operatum*, works of supererogation, merits, pardons, peregrinations, and stations; his holy water, baptizing of bells, conjuring of spirits, crossing, sayning, anointing, conjuring, hallowing of God's good creatures, with the superstitious opinion joined therewith; his worldly monarchy, and wicked hierarchy; his three solemn vows, with all his shavelings of sundry sorts; his erroneous and bloody decrees made at Trent, with all the subscribers or approvers of that cruel and bloody band, conjured against the kirk of God. And finally, we detest all his vain allegories, rites, signs, and traditions brought in the kirk, without or against the word of God, and doctrine of this true reformed kirk; to the which we join ourselves willingly, in doctrine, faith, religion, discipline, and use of the holy sacraments, as lively members of the same in Christ our Head: promising and swearing, by the great name of the LORD our GOD, that we shall continue in the obedience of the doctrine and discipline of this kirk,* and shall defend the same, according to our vocation and power, all the days of our lives; under the pains contained in the law, and danger both of body and soul in the day of God's fearful judgment.

And seeing that many are stirred up by Satan, and that Roman Antichrist, to promise, swear, subscribe, and for a time use the holy sacraments in the kirk deceitfully, against their own conscience; minding hereby, first, under the external cloak of religion, to corrupt and subvert secretly God's true religion within the kirk; and afterward, when time may serve, to become open enemies and persecutors of the same, under vain hope of the Pope's dispensation, devised against the word of God, to his greater confusion, and their double condemnation in the day of the Lord Jesus: we therefore, willing to take away all suspicion of hypocrisy, and of such double dealing with God, and his kirk, protest, and call the Searcher of all hearts for witness, that our minds and hearts do fully agree with this our Confession, promise, oath, and subscription: so that we are not moved with any worldly respect, but are persuaded only in our conscience, through the knowledge and love of God's true religion imprinted in our hearts by the Holy Spirit, as we shall answer to him in the day when the secrets of all hearts shall be disclosed.

And because we perceive, that the quietness and stability of our religion and kirk doth depend upon the safety and good behaviour of the King's Majesty, as upon a comfortable instrument of God's mercy granted to this country, for the maintaining of his kirk, and ministration of justice amongst us; we protest and promise with our hearts, under the same oath, hand-writ, and pains, that we shall defend his person and authority with our goods, bodies, and lives, in the defence of Christ, his evangel, liberties of our country, ministration of justice, and punishment of iniquity, against all enemies within this realm or without, as we desire our God to be a strong and merciful defender to us in the day of our death, and coming of our Lord Jesus Christ; to whom, with the Father, and the Holy Spirit, be all honour and glory eternally. *Amen.*

LIKEAS many Acts of Parliament, not only in general do abrogate, annul, and rescind all laws, statutes, acts, constitutions, canons civil or municipal, with all other ordinances, and practique penalities whatsoever, made in prejudice of the true religion, and professors thereof; or of the true kirk, discipline, jurisdiction, and freedom thereof; or in favours of idolatry and superstition, or of the Papistical kirk: As Act 3, Act 31, Parl. 1; Act 23, Parl. 11; Act 114, Parl. 12 of King James VI., That Papistry and superstition may be utterly suppressed, according to the intention of the Acts of Parliament, repeated in the fifth Act, Parl. 20, King James VI. And to that end they ordain all Papists and Priests to be punished with manifold civil and ecclesiastical pains, as adversaries to God's true religion, preached, and by law established, within this realm, Act 24, Parl. 11, King James VI.; as common enemies to all Christian government, Act 18, Parl. 16, King James

---

* The Confession which was subscribed at Halyrud-house the 25th of February 1587-8, by the King, Lennox, Huntly, the Chancellor, and about ninety-five other persons, hath here added, "Agreeing to the word." Sir John Maxwell of Pollock hath the original parchment.

VI.; as rebellers and gainstanders of our Sovereign Lord's authority, Act 47, Parl. 3, King James VI.; and as idolaters, Act 104, Parl. 7, King James VI. But also in particular, by and attour the Confession of Faith, do abolish and condemn the Pope's authority and jurisdiction out of this land, and ordains the maintainers thereof to be punished, Act 2, Parl. 1; Act 51, Parl. 3; Act 106, Parl. 7; Act 114, Parl. 12, King James VI.: do condemn the Pope's erroneous doctrine, or any other erroneous doctrine repugnant to any of the articles of the true and Christian religion, publickly preached, and by law established, in this realm; and ordains the spreaders and makers of books or libels, or letters or writs of that nature, to be punished, Act 46, Parl. 3; Act 106, Parl. 7; Act 24, Parl. 11, King James VI.: do condemn all baptism conform to the Pope's kirk, and the idolatry of the mass; and ordains all sayers, wilful hearers, and concealers of the mass, the maintainers and resetters of the priests, Jesuits, trafficking Papists, to be punished without any exception or restriction, Act 5, Parl. 1; Act 120, Parl. 12; Act 164, Parl. 13; Act 193, Parl. 14; Act 1, Parl. 19; Act 5, Parl. 20, King James VI.: do condemn all erroneous books and writs containing erroneous doctrine against the religion presently professed, or containing superstitious rites and ceremonies Papistical, whereby the people are greatly abused; and ordains the home-bringers of them to be punished, Act 25, Parl. 11, King James VI.: do condemn the monuments and dregs of bygone idolatry, as going to crosses, observing the festival days of saints, and such other superstitious and Papistical rites, to the dishonour of God, contempt of true religion, and fostering of great error among the people; and ordains the users of them to be punished for the second fault, as idolaters, Act 104, Parl. 7, King James VI.

Likeas many Acts of Parliament are conceived for maintenance of God's true and Christian religion, and the purity thereof, in doctrine and sacraments of the true church of God, the liberty and freedom thereof, in her national, synodal assemblies, presbyteries, sessions, policy, discipline, and jurisdiction thereof; as that purity of religion, and liberty of the church was used, professed, exercised, preached, and confessed, according to the reformation of religion in this realm: As for instance, the 99th Act, Parl. 7; Act 25, Parl. 11; Act 114, Parl. 12; Act 160, Parl. 13 of King James VI. ratified by the 4th Act of King Charles. So that the 6th Act, Parl. 1, and 68th Act, Parl. 6 of King James VI. in the year of God 1579, declare the ministers of the blessed evangel, whom God of his mercy had raised up, or hereafter should raise, agreeing with them that then lived, in doctrine and administration of the sacraments; and the people that professed Christ, as he was then offered in the evangel, and doth communicate with the holy sacraments (as in he reformed kirks of this realm they were presently administrate) according to the Confession of Faith, to be the true and holy kirk of Christ Jesus within this realm. And decerns and declares all and sundry, who either gainsay the word of the evangel received and approved as the heads of the Confession of Faith, professed in Parliament in the year of God 1560, specified also in the first Parliament of King James VI., and ratified in this present Parliament, more particularly do express; or that refuse the administration of the holy sacraments, as they were then ministrated; to be no members of the said kirk within this realm, and true religion presently professed, so long as they keep themselves so divided from the society of Christ's body. And the subsequent Act 69, Parl. 6 of King James VI. declares, that there is no other face of kirk, nor other face of religion, than was presently at that time, by the favour of God, established within this realm: " Which therefore is ever styled God's " true religion, Christ's true religion, the true and Christian religion, and a " perfect religion;" which, by manifold Acts of Parliament, all within this realm are bound to profess, to subscribe the articles thereof, the Confession of Faith, to recant all doctrine and errors repugnant to any of the said articles, Act 4 and 9, Parl. 1; Acts 45, 46, 47, Parl. 3; Act 71, Parl. 6; Act 106, Parl. 7; Act 24, Parl. 11; Act 123, Parl. 12; Act 194 and 197, Parl. 14 of King James VI. And all magistrates, sheriffs, &c. on the one part, are ordained to search, apprehend, and punish all contraveners: For instance, Act 5, Parl. 1; Act 104, Parl. 7; Act 25, Parl. 11, King James VI.; and that notwithstanding of the King's Majesty's licences on the contrary, which are discharged.

and declared to be of no force, in so far as they tend in any wise to the prejudice and hinder of the execution of the Acts of Parliament against Papists and adversaries of true religion, Act 106, Parl. 7, King James VI. On the other part, in the 47th Act, Parl. 3, King James VI., it is declared and ordained, Seeing the cause of God's true religion and his Highness's authority are so joined, as the hurt of the one is common to both; that none shall be reputed as loyal and faithful subjects to our sovereign Lord, or his authority, but be punishable as rebellers and gainstanders of the same, who shall not give their confession, and make their profession of the said true religion: and that they who, after defection, shall give the confession of their faith of new, they shall promise to continue therein in time coming, to maintain our sovereign Lord's authority, and at the uttermost of their power to fortify, assist, and maintain the true preachers and professors of Christ's religion, against whatsoever enemies and gainstanders of the same; and namely, against all such, of whatsoever nation, estate, or degree they be of, that have joined or bound themselves, or have assisted, or assist, to set forward and execute the cruel decrees of the council of Trent, contrary to the true preachers and professors of the word of God; which is repeated, word by word, in the articles of pacification at Perth, the 23d of February 1572, approved by Parliament the last of April 1573, ratified in Parliament 1587, and related Act 123, Parl. 12 of King James VI.; with this addition, "That they are bound to resist all "treasonable uproars and hostilities raised against the true religion, the "King's Majesty, and the true professors."

Likeas, all lieges are bound to maintain the King's Majesty's royal person and authority, the authority of Parliaments, without the which neither any laws or lawful judicatories can be established, Act 130 and 131, Parl. 8, King James VI., and the subjects' liberties, who ought only to live and be governed by the King's laws, the common laws of this realm allenarly, Act 48, Parl. 3, King James I.; Act 79, Parl. 6, King James IV.; repeated in the Act 131, Parl. 8, King James VI.; which if they be innovated and prejudged, "the "commission anent the union of the two kingdoms of Scotland and England, "which is the sole act of the 17th Parl. of King James VI., declares," such confusion would ensue as this realm could be no more a free monarchy: because, by the fundamental laws, ancient privileges, offices, and liberties of this kingdom, not only the princely authority of his Majesty's royal descent hath been these many ages maintained, but also the people's security of their lands, livings, rights, offices, liberties, and dignities preserved. And therefore, for the preservation of the said true religion, laws, and liberties of this kingdom, it is statute by the 8th Act, Parl. 1, repeated in the 99th Act, Parl. 7, ratified in the 23d Act, Parl. 11, and 114th Act, Parl. 12, of King James VI., and 4th Act, Parl. 1, of King Charles I. "That all Kings and Princes at their coro"nation, and reception of their princely authority, shall make their faithful "promise by their solemn oath, in the presence of the eternal God, that, "enduring the whole time of their lives, they shall serve the same eternal God, "to the uttermost of their power, according as he hath required in his most "holy word, contained in the Old and New Testament; and according to the "same word, shall maintain the true religion of Christ Jesus, the preaching "of his holy word, the due and right ministration of the sacraments now "received and preached within this realm, (according to the Confession of "Faith immediately preceding,) and shall abolish and gainstand all false "religion contrary to the same; and shall rule the people committed to their "charge, according to the will and command of God revealed in his foresaid "word, and according to the laudable laws and constitutions received in this "realm, nowise repugnant to the said will of the eternal God; and shall pro"cure, to the uttermost of their power, to the kirk of God, and whole Christian "people, true and perfect peace in all time coming: and that they shall be "careful to root out of their empire all hereticks and enemies to the true "worship of God, who shall be convicted by the true kirk of God of the "foresaid crimes." Which was also observed by his Majesty, at his coronation in Edinburgh 1633, as may be seen in the order of the coronation.

In obedience to the commandment of God, conform to the practice of the godly in former times, and according to the laudable example of our worthy and religious progenitors, and of many yet living amongst us, which was warranted also by act of Council, commanding a general band to be made and subscribed by his Majesty's subjects of all ranks for two causes: one was, For defending the true religion, as it was then reformed, and is expressed in the Confession of Faith above written, and a former large Confession established by sundry acts of lawful General Assemblies and of Parliaments, unto which it hath relation, set down in publick Catechisms; and which hath been for many years, with a blessing from heaven, preached and professed in this kirk and kingdom, as God's undoubted truth, grounded only upon his written word. The other cause was, For maintaining the King's Majesty, his person and estate; the true worship of God and the King's authority being so straitly joined, as that they had the same friends and common enemies, and did stand and fall together. And finally, being convinced in our minds, and confessing with our mouths, that the present and succeeding generations in this land are bound to keep the foresaid national oath and subscription inviolable.

We Noblemen, Barons, Gentlemen, Burgesses, Ministers, and Commons under-subscribing, considering divers times before, and especially at this time, the danger of the true reformed religion, of the King's honour, and of the publick peace of the kingdom, by the manifold innovations and evils, generally contained, and particularly mentioned in our late supplications, complaints, and protestations; do hereby profess, and before God, his angels, and the world, solemnly declare, That with our whole heart we agree, and resolve all the days of our life constantly to adhere unto and to defend the foresaid true religion, and (forbearing the practice of all innovations already introduced in the matters of the worship of God, or approbation of the corruptions of the publick government of the kirk, or civil places and power of kirkmen, till they be tried and allowed in free Assemblies and in Parliament) to labour, by all means lawful, to recover the purity and liberty of the Gospel, as it was established and professed before the foresaid novations. And because, after due examination, we plainly perceive, and undoubtedly believe, that the innovations and evils contained in our supplications, complaints, and protestations, have no warrant of the word of God, are contrary to the articles of the foresaid Confession, to the intention and meaning of the blessed reformers of religion in this land, to the above-written acts of Parliament; and do sensibly tend to the re-establishing of the Popish religion and tyranny, and to the subversion and ruin of the true reformed religion, and of our liberties, laws, and estates; we also declare, That the foresaid Confessions are to be interpreted, and ought to be understood of the foresaid novations and evils, no less than if every one of them had been expressed in the foresaid Confessions; and that we are obliged to detest and abhor them, amongst other particular heads of Papistry abjured therein. And therefore, from the knowledge and conscience of our duty to God, to our King and country, without any worldly respect or inducement, so far as human infirmity will suffer, wishing a further measure of the grace of God for this effect; we promise and swear, by the GREAT NAME OF THE LORD OUR GOD, to continue in the profession and obedience of the foresaid religion; and that we shall defend the same, and resist all these contrary errors and corruptions, according to our vocation, and to the uttermost of that power that God hath put in our hands, all the days of our life.

And in like manner, with the same heart, we declare before God and men, That we have no intention nor desire to attempt any thing that may turn to the dishonour of God, or to the diminution of the King's greatness and authority; but, on the contrary, we promise and swear, That we shall, to the uttermost of our power, with our means and lives, stand to the defence of our dread sovereign the King's Majesty, his person and authority, in the defence and preservation of the foresaid true religion, liberties, and laws of the kingdom; as also to the mutual defence and assistance every one of us of another, in the same cause of maintaining the true religion, and his Majesty's authority, with our best counsel, our bodies, means, and whole power, against all sorts of persons whatsoever; so that whatsoever shall be done to the least of us for that cause, shall be taken as done to us all in general, and to every one of us in particular. And that we shall neither directly nor indirectly suffer ourselves to be divided or withdrawn, by whatsoever suggestion, combination, allurement, or terror, from this blessed and loyal conjunction; nor shall cast in any let or impediment that may stay or hinder any such resolution as by common consent shall be found to conduce for so good ends; but, on the contrary, shall by all lawful means labour to further and promote the same: and if any such dangerous and divisive motion be made to us by word or writ, we, and every one of us, shall either suppress it, or, if need be, shall incontinent make the same known, that it may be timeously obviated. Neither do we fear the foul aspersions of rebellion, combination, or what else our adversaries, from their craft and malice, would put upon us; seeing what we do is so well warranted, and ariseth from an unfeigned desire to maintain the true worship of God, the majesty of our King, and the peace of the kingdom, for the common happiness of ourselves and our posterity.

And because we cannot look for a blessing from God upon our proceedings, except with our profession and subscription we join such a life and conversation as beseemeth Christians who have renewed their covenant with God; we therefore faithfully promise for ourselves, our followers, and all others under us, both in publick, and in our particular families, and personal carriage, to endeavour to keep ourselves within the bounds of Christian liberty, and to be good examples to others of all godliness, soberness, and righteousness, and of every duty we owe to God and man.

And, that this our union and conjunction may be observed without violation, we call the LIVING GOD, THE SEARCHER OF OUR HEARTS, to witness, who knoweth this to be our sincere desire and unfeigned resolution, as we shall answer to JESUS CHRIST in the great day, and under the pain of God's everlasting wrath, and of infamy and loss of all honour and respect in this world: most humbly beseeching the LORD to strengthen us by his HOLY SPIRIT for this end, and to bless our desires and proceedings with a happy success; that religion and righteousness may flourish in the land, to the glory of GOD, the honour of our King, and peace and comfort of us all. In witness whereof, we have subscribed with our hands all the premises.

THE article of this Covenant, which was at the first subscription referred to the determination of the General Assembly, being now determined; and thereby the five articles of Perth, the government of the kirk by bishops, and the civil places and power of kirkmen, upon the reasons and grounds contained in the Acts of the General Assembly, declared to be unlawful within this kirk we subscribe according to the determination aforesaid.

THE

SOLEMN LEAGUE AND COVENANT

FOR

REFORMATION AND DEFENCE OF RELIGION, THE HONOUR AND
HAPPINESS OF THE KING, AND THE PEACE AND SAFETY
OF THE THREE KINGDOMS OF SCOTLAND,
ENGLAND, AND IRELAND.

Taken and Subscribed several times by King Charles II., and by all ranks in the said three kingdoms.

WITH

AN ACT OF THE GENERAL ASSEMBLY 1643 AND AN ACT OF PARLIAMENT 1644,
RATIFYING AND APPROVING THE SAID LEAGUE AND COVENANT.

JER. l. 5.—Come, and let us join ourselves to the Lord in a perpetual Covenant that shall not be forgotten.

PROV. xxv. 5.—Take away the wicked from before the king, and his throne shall be established in righteousness.

2 CHRON. xv. 15.—And all Judah rejoiced at the oath; for they had sworn with all their heart.

GAL. iii. 15.—Though it be but a man's covenant, yet if it be confirmed by an oath, no man disannulleth or addeth thereto.

Assembly at EDINBURGH, August 17, 1643. Sess. 14.

The General Assembly's Approbation of the SOLEMN LEAGUE AND COVENANT.

THE Assembly having recommended unto a Committee appointed by them to join with the Committee of the Honourable Convention of Estates, and the Commissioners of the Honourable Houses of the Parliament of England, for bringing the kingdoms to a more near conjunction and union, received from the foresaid Committees the Covenant after mentioned, as the result of their consultations : and having taken the same, as a matter of so publick concernment and so deep importance doth require, unto their gravest consideration, did, with all their hearts, and with the beginnings of the feelings of that joy, which they did find in so great measure upon the renovation of the National Covenant of this kirk and kingdom All with one voice approve and embrace the same, as the most powerful mean, by the blessing of GOD, for settling and preserving the true Protestant religion with perfect peace in his Majesty's dominions, and propagating the same to other nations, and for establishing his Majesty's throne to all ages and generations. And therefore, with their best affections, recommend the same to the Honourable Convention of Estates, that, being examined and approved by them, it may be sent with all diligence to the kingdom of England, that, being received and approven there, the same may be, with publick humiliation, and all religious and answerable solemnity, sworn and subscribed by all true professors of the reformed religion, and all his Majesty's good subjects in both kingdoms.

A. JOHNSTOUN.

CHARLES I. Parl. 3. Sess. 1. Act 5.

ACT *anent the Ratification of the calling of the Convention, Ratification of the League and Covenant, Articles of Treaty betwixt the Kingdoms of Scotland and England, and remanent Acts of the Convention of Estates, and Committee thereof.*

AT EDINBURGH, July 15, 1644.

THE Estates of Parliament, presently convened by virtue of the last act of the last Parliament, holden by his Majesty, and the three Estates, in *anno* 1641, considering, that the Lords of his Majesty's Privy Council, and Commissioners for conserving the articles of the treaty, having, according to their interests and trust committed to them by his Majesty and Estates of Parliament, used all means, by supplications, remonstrances, and sending of Commissioners, for securing the peace of this kingdom, and removing the unhappy distractions betwixt his Majesty and his subjects in England, in such a way as might serve most for his Majesty's honour, and good of both kingdoms; and their humble and dutiful endeavours for so good ends having proven ineffectual, and their offer of mediation and intercession being refused by his Majesty; and thereby finding the weight and difficulty of affairs, and the charge lying on them to be greater than they could bear; did therefore, in the month of May 1643, meet together with the Commissioners for the common burdens, that, by joint advice, some resolution might be taken therein; and in respect of the danger imminent to the true Protestant religion, his Majesty's honour, and peace of thir kingdoms, by the multitude of Papists and their adherents in arms in England and Ireland, and of many other publick and important affairs, which could not admit delay, and did require the advice of the representative body of the kingdom; appointed and caused indict a meeting of the Convention of Estates (his Majesty having formerly refused their humble desires for a Parliament) to be on the 22d of June following; which diet being frequently kept by the Noblemen, Commissioners of shires and burghs, and they finding these dangers against this kirk and state still increasing, resolved, after serious deliberation and advice of the General Assembly, and joint concurrence of the Commissioners authorized by the Parliament of England, that one of the chiefest remedies for preventing of these and the like dangers, for preservation of religion, and both kingdoms from ruin and destruction, and for procuring of peace, That both kingdoms should, for these ends, enter into Covenant; which was accordingly drawn up, and cheerfully embraced and allowed.—And at last a treaty was agreed unto by both kingdoms, concerning the said Covenant, and assistance craved from this kingdom by the kingdom of England, in pursuance of the ends expressed therein :—And the Estates being still desirous to use all good means, that, without the effusion of more blood, there may be such a blessed pacification betwixt his Majesty and his subjects, as may tend to the good of religion, his Majesty's true honour and safety, and happiness of his people, did therefore give commission to John Earl of Loudoun, Lord Chancellor, Lord Maitland, Lord Warristoun, and Mr Robert Barclay, to repair to England, and endeavour the effectuating of these ends contained in the covenant of treaties, conform to their instructions.—

And the said Estates having taken the proceedings above written to their consideration, do find and declare, That the Lords of Council, and conservers of peace, did behave themselves as faithful counsellors, loyal subjects, and good patriots, in tendering their humble endeavours for removing the distractions betwixt his Majesty and his subjects, and in calling the Commissioners for the common burdens, and, by joint advice, appointing the late meeting of Convention, wherein they have approven themselves answerable to the duty of their places, and that trust committed to them; and therefore ratifies and approves their whole proceedings therein, and declares the said Convention was lawful, called, and also full and free in itself, consisting of all the members thereof, as any Convention hath been at any time bygone; and ratifies and approves the several acts made by them, or their committee, for enjoining the Covenant.——And also, the said estates of Parliament (but prejudice of the premises, and of the general ratification above mentioned) ratify, approve, and confirm the foresaid mutual League and Covenant, concerning the reformation and defence of religion, the honour and happiness of the King, and the peace and safety of the three kingdoms of Scotland, England, and Ireland; together with the acts of the Kirk and Estate authorizing the same League and Covenant; together also with the foresaid articles of treaty agreed upon betwixt the said Commissioners of the Convention of Estates of Scotland and the Commissioners of both the Houses of Parliament of England, concerning the said Solemn League and Covenant.——And the said Estates ordain the same acts, with the League and Covenant above specified, acts authorizing the same, and the articles of treaty foresaid, to have the full force and strength of perfect laws and acts of Parliament, and to be observed by all his Majesty's lieges, conform to the tenors thereof respective. Of the which League and Covenant, the tenor follows:

THE
SOLEMN LEAGUE AND COVENANT

FOR

Reformation and Defence of Religion, the Honour and Happiness of the King, and the Peace and Safety of the Three Kingdoms of Scotland, England, and Ireland; agreed upon by Commissioners from the Parliament and Assembly of Divines in England, with Commissioners of the Convention of Estates, and General Assembly in Scotland; approved by the General Assembly of the Church of Scotland, and by both Houses of Parliament and Assembly of Divines in England, and taken and subscribed by them, *Anno* 1643; and thereafter, by the said authority, taken and subscribed by all Ranks in Scotland and England the same Year; and ratified by Act of the Parliament of Scotland, *Anno* 1644: And again renewed in Scotland, with an Acknowledgment of Sins, and Engagement to Duties, by all Ranks, *Anno* 1648, and by Parliament 1649; and taken and subscribed by *King Charles II.* at *Spey, June* 23, 1650; and at *Scoon, January* 1, 1651.

WE Noblemen, Barons, Knights, Gentlemen, Citizens, Burgesses, Ministers of the Gospel, and Commons of all sorts, in the kingdoms of Scotland, England, and Ireland, by the providence of GOD, living under one King, and being of one reformed religion, having before our eyes the glory of GOD, and the advancement of the kingdom of our Lord and Saviour JESUS CHRIST, the honour and happiness of the King's Majesty and his posterity, and the true publick liberty, safety, and peace of the kingdoms, wherein every one's private condition is included: And calling to mind the treacherous and bloody plots, conspiracies, attempts, and practices of the enemies of GOD, against the true religion and professors thereof in all places, especially in these three kingdoms, ever since the reformation of religion; and how much their rage, power, and presumption are of late, and at this time, increased and exercised, whereof the deplorable state of the church and kingdom of Ireland, the distressed estate of the church and kingdom of England, and the dangerous estate of the church and kingdom of Scotland, are present and public testimonies; we have now at last, (after other means of supplication, remonstrance, protestation, and sufferings,) for the preservation of ourselves and our religion from utter ruin and destruction, according to the commendable practice of these kingdoms in former times, and the example of GOD'S people in other nations, after mature deliberation, resolved and determined to enter into a mutual and solemn League and Covenant, wherein we all subscribe, and each one of us for himself, with our hands lifted up to the most High GOD, do swear,

I. THAT we shall sincerely, really, and constantly, through the grace of GOD, endeavour, in our several places and callings, the preservation of the reformed religion in the Church of Scotland, in doctrine, worship, discipline, and government, against our common enemies; the reformation of religion in the kingdoms of England and Ireland, in doctrine, worship, discipline, and government, according to the word of GOD, and the example of the best reformed Churches; and shall endeavour to bring the Churches of God in the three kingdoms to the nearest conjunction and uniformity in religion, confession of faith, form of church-government, directory for worship and catechising; that we, and our posterity after us, may, as brethren, live in faith and love, and the Lord may delight to dwell in the midst of us.

II. That we shall in like manner, without respect of persons, endeavour the extirpation of Popery, Prelacy, (that is, church-government by Archbishops, Bishops, their Chancellors, and Commissaries, Deans, Deans and Chapters, Archdeacons, and all other ecclesiastical Officers depending on that hierarchy,) superstition, heresy, schism, profaneness, and whatsoever shall be found to be contrary to sound doctrine and the power of godliness, lest we partake in other men's sins, and thereby be in danger to receive of their plagues; and that the Lord may be one, and his name one, in the three kingdoms.

III. We shall, with the same sincerity, reality, and constancy, in our several vocations, endeavour, with our estates and lives, mutually to preserve the rights and privileges of the Parliaments, and the liberties of the kingdoms; and to preserve and defend the King's Majesty's person and authority, in the preservation and defence of the true religion, and liberties of the kingdoms; that the world may bear witness with our consciences of our loyalty, and that we have no thoughts or intentions to diminish his Majesty's just power and greatness.

IV. We shall also, with all faithfulness, endeavour the discovery of all such as have been or shall be incendiaries, malignants, or evil instruments, by hindering the reformation of religion, dividing the king from his people, or one of the kingdoms from another, or making any faction or parties amongst the people, contrary to this League and Covenant; that they may be brought to publick trial, and receive condign punishment, as the degree of their offences shall require or deserve, or the supreme judicatories of both kingdoms respectively, or others having power from them for that effect, shall judge convenient.

V. And whereas the happiness of a blessed peace between these kingdoms, denied in former times to our progenitors, is, by the good providence of GOD, granted unto us, and hath been lately concluded and settled by both Parliaments; we shall each one of us, according to our place and interest, endeavour that they may remain conjoined in a firm peace and union to all posterity; and that justice may be done upon the wilful opposers thereof, in manner expressed in the precedent article.

VI. We shall also, according to our places and callings, in this common cause of religion, liberty, and peace of the kingdoms, assist and defend all those that enter into this League and Covenant, in the maintaining and pursuing thereof; and shall not suffer ourselves, directly or indirectly, by whatsoever combination, persuasion, or terror, to be divided and withdrawn from this blessed union and conjunction, whether to make defection to the contrary part, or to give ourselves to a detestable indifferency or neutrality in this cause which so much concerneth the glory of GOD, the good of the kingdom, and honour of the King; but shall, all the days of our lives, zealously and constantly continue therein against all opposition, and promote the same, according to our power, against all lets and impediments whatsoever; and, what we are not able ourselves to suppress or overcome, we shall reveal and make known, that it may be timely prevented or removed: All which we shall do as in the sight of God.

And, because these kingdoms are guilty of many sins and provocations against GOD, and his Son JESUS CHRIST, as is too manifest by our present distresses and dangers, the fruits thereof; we profess and declare, before GOD and the world, our unfeigned desire to be humbled for our own sins, and for the sins of these kingdoms: especially, that we have not as we ought valued the inestimable benefit of the gospel; that we have not laboured for the purity and power thereof; and that we have not endeavoured to receive CHRIST in our hearts, nor to walk worthy of him in our lives; which are the causes of other sins and transgressions so much abounding amongst us: and our true and unfeigned purpose, desire, and endeavour for ourselves, and all others under our power and charge, both in publick and in private, in all duties we owe to GOD and man, to amend our lives, and each one to go before another in the example of a real reformation; that the Lord may turn away his wrath and heavy indignation, and establish these churches and kingdoms in truth and peace. And this Covenant we make in the presence of ALMIGHTY GOD, the Searcher of all hearts, with a true intention to perform the same, as we shall answer at that great day, when the secrets of all hearts shall be disclosed; most humbly beseeching the LORD to strengthen us by his HOLY SPIRIT for this end, and to bless our desires and proceedings with such success, as may be deliverance and safety to his people, and encouragement to other Christian Churches, groaning under, or in danger of, the yoke of antichristian tyranny, to join in the same or like association and covenant, to the glory of GOD, the enlargement of the kingdom of JESUS CHRIST, and the peace and tranquillity of Christian kingdoms and commonwealths.

A SOLEMN ACKNOWLEDGMENT

OF

PUBLICK SINS AND BREACHES OF THE COVENANT;

AND

A SOLEMN ENGAGEMENT TO ALL THE DUTIES CONTAINED THEREIN;

NAMELY, THOSE WHICH DO IN A MORE SPECIAL WAY RELATE UNTO THE DANGERS OF THESE TIMES:

TOGETHER WITH

THE ACT OF THE COMMISSION OF THE GENERAL ASSEMBLY 1648, AND ACT OF PARLIAMENT 1649, FOR RENEWING THE LEAGUE AND COVENANT.

The Act of the Commission of the General Assembly for renewing the Solemn League and Covenant

Edinburgh, October 6, 1648.

THE Commission of the General Assembly considering, that a great part of this land have involved themselves in many and gross breaches of the Solemn League and Covenant; and that the hands of many are grown slack in following and pursuing the duties contained therein; and that many, who not being come to sufficient age when it was first sworn and subscribed, have not hitherto been received into the same; do, upon these, and other grave and important considerations, appoint and ordain the Solemn League and Covenant to be renewed throughout all the congregations of this kingdom. And, because it is a duty of great weight and consequence, ministers, after the sight hereof, would be careful to take pains, in their doctrine and otherwise, that their people may be made sensible of these things, wherein they have broken the Covenant, and be prepared for the renewing thereof with suitable affections and dispositions. And, that these things may be the better performed, we have thought it necessary to condescend upon a Solemn Acknowledgment of Publick Sins and Breaches of the Covenant, and a Solemn Engagement to all the Duties contained therein, namely, those which do in a more special way relate unto the dangers of these times: And this Solemn Acknowledgment and Engagement, sent herewith, shall be made use of, and the League and Covenant shall be renewed in such manner as follows: *First,* There shall be an intimation of a solemn publick humiliation and fast the second Sabbath of December, to be kept upon the next Thursday, and the Lord's day thereafter; at which intimation, the League and Covenant, and the Public Acknowledgment of Sins and Engagements unto Duties, are to be publickly read by the minister, in the audience of all the people; and they are to be exhorted to get copies thereof, that they may be made acquainted therewith; and the humiliation and fast is to be kept the next Thursday thereafter, in reference to the breaches of the Covenant, contained in the solemn public acknowledgment, as the causes thereof; and the next Lord's day thereafter, which is also to be spent in publick humiliation and fasting, immediately after the sermon, which is to be applied to the business of that day, the Publick Acknowledgment and Engagement is again to be publickly read; and thereafter prayer is to be made, containing the confession of the breaches mentioned therein, and begging mercy for these sins, and strength of God for renewing the Covenant in sincerity and truth; after which prayer the Solemn League and Covenant is to be read by the minister, and then to be sworn by him and all the people, who are to engage themselves for performance of all the duties contained therein; namely, these which are mentioned in the Publick Acknowledgment and Engagement, and are opposite unto the sins therein confessed: and the action is to be closed with prayer to God, that his people may be enabled, in the power of his strength, to do their duty, according to their oath, now renewed in so solemn a way. It is also hereby provided, That all those who renew the League and Covenant, shall again subscribe the same; and that none be admitted to the renewing or subscribing thereof, who are excluded by the other act and direction sent herewith
A. KER.

The Act of the Committee of Estates of Parliament for renewing the Solemn League and Covenant.

EDINBURGH, October 14, 1648.

THE Committee of Estates being very sensible of the grievous backslidings of this land, in the manifold breaches of the Solemn League and Covenant, made and sworn to the most high God; do therefore unanimously and heartily approve the seasonable and pious resolution of the Commission of the General Assembly for a solemn Acknowledgment of Publick Sins and Provocations, especially the breaches of the Covenant, and a solemn engagement to a more conscionable performance of the duties therein contained, and for renewing the Solemn League and Covenant; and do require and ordain, That the Directions of the said Commission of Assembly, in their act of the 6th of this month, for a publick Acknowledgment of Sins, and Engagement to Duties, be carefully followed; that the fast and humiliation, appointed by them, be religiously observed; and that the Solemn League and Covenant be sincerely and cordially renewed and subscribed, in the manner they have prescribed in their said act.

Extractum, MR THO. HENDERSON.

A SOLEMN ACKNOWLEDGMENT

OF

PUBLICK SINS, AND BREACHES OF THE COVENANT;

AND

A SOLEMN ENGAGEMENT TO ALL THE DUTIES CONTAINED THEREIN, NAMELY THOSE WHICH DO IN A MORE SPECIAL WAY RELATE UNTO THE DANGERS OF THESE TIMES.

WE Noblemen, Barons, Gentlemen, Burgesses, Ministers of the Gospel, and Commons of all sorts within this kingdom, by the good hand of God upon us, taking into serious consideration the many sad afflictions and deep distresses wherewith we have been exercised for a long time past; and that the land, after it hath been sore wasted with the sword and the pestilence, and threatened with famine; and that shame and contempt hath been poured out from the Lord against many thousands of our nation, who did in a sinful way make war upon the kingdom of England, contrary to the testimony of his servants, and desires of his people; and that the remnants of that army, returning to this land, have spoiled and oppressed many of our brethren; and that the malignant party is still numerous, and, retaining their former principles, wait for an opportunity to raise a new and dangerous war, not only unto the rending of the bowels of this kingdom, but unto the dividing us from England, and overturning of the work of God in all the three kingdoms; and considering also, that a cloud of calamities doth still hang over our heads, and threaten us with sad things to come, we cannot but look upon these things as from the Lord, who is righteous in all his ways, feeding us with the bread of tears, and making us to drink the waters of afflictions, until we be taught to know how evil and bitter a thing it is to depart away from him, by breaking the Oath and Covenant which we have made with him; and that we may be humbled before him, by confessing our sin, and forsaking the evil of our way.

Therefore being pressed with so great necessities and straits, and warranted by the word of God, and having the example of God's people of old, who in the time of their troubles, and when they were to seek delivery, and a right way for themselves, that the Lord might be with them to prosper them, did humble themselves before him, and make a free and particular confession of the sins of their princes, their rulers, their captains, their priests, and their people; and did engage themselves to do no more so, but to reform their ways, and be stedfast in this covenant; and remembering the practice of our predecessors in the year 1596, wherein the General Assembly, and all the kirk-judicatories, with the concurrence of many of the nobility, gentry, and burgesses, did, with many tears, acknowledge before God the breach of the National Covenant, and engaged themselves to a reformation; even as our predecessors and theirs had before done, in the General Assembly and Convention of Estates, in the year 1567; and perceiving that this duty, when gone about out of conscience and in sincerity, hath always been attended with a reviving out of troubles, and with a blessing and success from Heaven; we do humbly and sincerely, as in his sight, who is the Searcher of hearts, acknowledge the many sins and great transgressions of the land: we have done wickedly, our kings, our princes, our nobles, our judges, our officers, our teachers, and our people. Albeit the Lord hath long and clearly spoken unto us, we have not hearkened to his voice; albeit he hath followed us with tender mercies, we have not been allured to wait upon him, and walk in his way; and though he hath stricken us, yet we have not grieved; nay, though he hath consumed us, we have refused to receive correction: we have not remembered to render unto the Lord according to his goodness, and according to our own vows and promises, but have gone away backward by a continued course of backsliding, and have broken all the articles of that Solemn League and Covenant, which we swore before God, angels, and men.

Albeit there be in the land many of all ranks, who be for a testimony unto the truth, and for a name of joy and praise unto the Lord, by living godly, studying to keep their garments pure, and being stedfast in the covenant and cause of God; yet we have reason to acknowledge, that most of us have not endeavoured with that reality, sincerity, and constancy that did become us, to preserve the work of reformation in the kirk of Scotland: many have satisfied themselves with the purity of the ordinances, neglecting the power thereof; yea, some have turned aside to crooked ways, destructive to both. The profane, loose, and insolent carriage of many in our armies, who went to the assistance of our brethren in England, and the tamperings and unstraight dealing of some of our Commissioners, and others of our nation, in London, the Isle of Wight, and other places of that kingdom, have proved great lets to the work of reformation and settling of kirk-government there, whereby error and schism in that land have been increased, and sectaries hardened in their way. We have been so far from endeavouring the extirpation of profaneness, and what is contrary to the power of godliness, that profanity hath been much winked at, and profane persons much countenanced, and many times employed, until iniquity and ungodliness hath gone over the face of the land as a flood; nay, sufficient care hath not been had to separate betwixt the precious and the vile, by debarring from the sacrament all ignorant and scandalous persons, according to the ordinances of this kirk.

Neither have the privileges of the Parliaments and liberties of the subject been duly tendered; but some amongst ourselves have laboured to put into the hands of our King an arbitrary and unlimited power, destructive to both; and many of us have been accessory of late to those means and ways, whereby the freedom and privileges of Parliaments have been encroached upon, and the subjects oppressed in their consciences, persons, and estates; neither hath it been our care to avoid these things which might harden the King in his evil way; but, upon the contrary, he hath not only been permitted, but many of us have been instrumental to make him exercise his power, in many things tending to the prejudice of religion, and of the Covenant, and of the peace and safety of these kingdoms; which is so far from the right way of preserving his Majesty's person and authority, that it cannot but provoke the Lord against him, unto the hazard of both; nay, under a pretence of relieving and doing for the King, whilst he refuses to do what was necessary for the house of God, some have ranversed and violated most of all the articles of the Covenant.

Our own conscience within, and God's judgments upon us without, do convince us of the manifold wilful renewed breaches of that article which concerneth the discovery and punishment of malignants, whose crimes have not only been connived at, but dispensed with and pardoned, and themselves received into intimate fellowship with ourselves, and intrusted with our counsels, admitted into our Parliaments, and put in places of power and authority, for managing the publick affairs of the kingdom; whereby, in God's justice, they got at last into their hands the whole power and strength of the kingdom, both in judicatories and armies; and did employ the same unto the enacting and prosecuting an unlawful engagement in war against the kingdom of England, notwithstanding of the dissent of many considerable members of Parliament, who had given constant proof of their integrity in the cause from the beginning; of many faithful testimonies, and free warnings of the servants of God; of the supplications of many synods, presbyteries, and shires; and of the declarations of the General Assembly and their Commissioners to the contrary: which engagement, as it hath been the cause of much sin, so also of much misery and calamity unto this land; and holds forth to us the grievousness of our sin, of complying with malignants in the greatness of our judgment, that we may be taught never to split again upon the same rock, upon which the Lord hath set so remarkable a beacon. And after all that is come to pass unto us because of this our trespass; and after that grace hath been shewed unto us from the Lord our God, by breaking these men's yoke from off our necks, and putting us again into a capacity to act for the good of religion, our own safety, and the peace and the safety of this kingdom, should we again break this commandment and covenant, by joining once more with the people of these abominations, and taking into our bosom those serpents, which had formerly stung us almost unto death; this, as it would argue great madness and folly upon our part, so, no doubt, if it be not avoided, will provoke the Lord against us, to consume us, until there be no remnant nor escaping in the land.

And albeit the peace and union betwixt the kingdoms be a great blessing of God unto both, and a bond which we are obliged to preserve unviolated, and to endeavour that justice may be done upon the opposers thereof; yet some in this land, who have come under the bond of the Covenant, have made it their great study how to dissolve this union; and few or no endeavours have been used by any of us for punishing of such.

We have suffered many of our brethren, in several parts of the land, to be oppressed by the common enemy, without compassion or relief. There hath been great murmuring and repining, because of expence of means, and pains in doing of our duty. Many, by persuasion or terror, have suffered themselves to be divided and withdrawn, to make defection to the contrary part: many have turned off to a detestable indifferency and neutrality in this cause, which so much concerneth the glory of God, and the good of these kingdoms; nay, many have made it their study to walk so, as they might comply with all times, and all the revolutions thereof. It hath not been our care to countenance, encourage, intrust, and employ such only, as from their hearts did affect and mind God's work; but the hearts of such many times have been discouraged, and their hands weakened, their sufferings neglected, and themselves slighted; and many who were once open enemies, and always secret underminers, countenanced and employed: nay, even those who had been looked upon as incendiaries, and upon whom the Lord has set marks of desperate malignancy, falsehood, and deceit, were brought in, as fit to manage publick affairs: many have been the lets and impediments that have been cast in the way, to retard and obstruct the Lord's work; and some have kept secret, what of themselves they were not able to suppress and overcome.

Besides these, and many other breaches of the articles of the Covenant in the matter thereof, which it concerneth every one of us to search out and acknowledge before the

Lord, as we would wish his wrath to be turned away from us; so have many of us failed exceedingly in the manner of our following and pursuing the duties contained therein; not only seeking great things for ourselves, and mixing of our private interests and ends concerning ourselves, and friends, and followers, with those things which concern the publick good; but many times preferring such to the honour of God, and good of his cause, and retarding God's work, until we might carry along with us our own interests and designs. It hath been our way to trust in the means, and to rely upon the arm of flesh for success, albeit the Lord hath many times made us meet with disappointment therein, and stained the pride of all our glory, by blasting every carnal confidence unto us: we have followed for the most part the counsels of flesh and blood, and walked more by the rules of policy than piety, and have hearkened more unto men than unto God.

Albeit we made solemn publick profession before the world, of our unfeigned desires to be humbled before the Lord for our own sins, and the sins of these kingdoms, especially for our undervaluing of the inestimable benefit of the gospel, and that we have not laboured for the power thereof, and received Christ into our hearts, and walked worthy of him in our lives; and of our true and unfeigned purpose, desire, and endeavour, for ourselves, and all others under our power and charge, both in publick and private, in all the duties which we owe to God and man, to amend our lives, and each one to go before another in the example of a real reformation, that the Lord might turn away his wrath and heavy indignation, and establish these kirks and kingdoms in truth and peace; yet we have refused to be reformed, and have walked proudly and obstinately against the Lord, not valuing his gospel, nor submitting ourselves unto the obedience thereof; not seeking after Christ, not studying to honour him in the excellency of his person, nor employ him in the virtue of his offices; nor making conscience of publick ordinances, nor private nor secret duties; nor studying to edify one another in love. Ignorance of God, and of his Son Jesus Christ, prevails exceedingly in the land; the greatest part of masters of families, amongst Noblemen, Barons, Gentlemen, Burgesses, and Commons, neglect to seek God in their families, and to endeavour the reformation thereof; and albeit it hath been much pressed, yet few of our nobles and great ones, ever to this day, could be persuaded to perform family-duties themselves, and in their own persons; which makes so necessary and useful a duty to be misregarded by others of inferior rank; nay, many of the Nobility, Gentry, and Burrows, who should have been examples of godliness and sober walking unto others, have been ringleaders of excess and rioting. Albeit we be the Lord's people, engaged to him in a solemn way; yet to this day we have not made it our study, that judicatories and armies should consist of, and places of power and trust be filled with, men of a blameless and Christian conversation, and of known integrity, and approven fidelity, affection, and zeal, unto the cause of God; but not only those who have been neutral and indifferent, but disaffected and malignant, and others who have been profane and scandalous, have been intrusted: by which it hath come to pass, that judicatories have been the seats of injustice and iniquity; and many in our armies, by their miscarriages, have become our plague, unto the great prejudice of the cause of God, the great scandal of the gospel, and the great increase of looseness and profanity throughout all the land. It were impossible to reckon up all the abominations that are in the land; but the blaspheming of the name of God, swearing by the creatures, profanation of the Lord's day, uncleanness, drunkenness, excess and rioting, vanity of apparel, lying and deceit, railing and cursing, arbitrary and uncontrouled oppression, and grinding of the faces of the poor by landlords, and others in place and power, are become ordinary and common sins; and besides all these things, there be many other transgressions, whereof the lands wherein we live are guilty. All which we desire to acknowledge and to be humbled for, that the world may bear witness with us, that righteousness belongeth unto God, and shame and confusion of face unto us, as appears this day.

And because it is needful for those who find mercy, not only to confess, but also to forsake their sin; therefore, that the reality and sincerity of our repentance may appear, we do resolve and solemnly engage ourselves, before the Lord, carefully to avoid for the time to come all these offences, whereof we have now made solemn publick acknowledgment, and all the snares and tentations which tend thereunto; and to testify the integrity of our resolution herein, and that we may be the better enabled in the power of the Lord's strength to perform the same, we do again renew our Solemn League and Covenant; promising hereafter to make conscience of all the duties whereunto we are obliged, in all the heads and articles thereof, particularly of these that follow.

1. Because religion is of all things the most excellent and precious, the advancing and promoting the power thereof against all ungodliness and profanity, the securing and preserving the purity thereof against all error, heresy, and schism, and namely, Independency, Anabaptism, Antinomianism, Arminianism, and Socinianism, Familism, Libertinism, Scepticism, and Erastianism, and the carrying on the work of uniformity, shall be studied and endeavoured by us before all wordly interests, whether concerning the King, ourselves, or any other whatsomever. 2. Because many have of late laboured to supplant the liberties of the kirk, we shall maintain and defend the kirk of Scotland, in all her liberties and privileges, against all who shall oppose or undermine the same, or encroach thereupon, under any pretext whatsomever. 3. We shall vindicate and maintain the liberties of the subjects, in all those things which concern their consciences, persons, and estates. 4. We shall carefully maintain and defend the union betwixt the kingdoms, and avoid every thing that may weaken the same, or involve us in any mea-

sure of accession unto the guilt of those who have invaded the kingdom of England. 5. As we have been always loyal to our King, so we shall still endeavour to give unto God that which is God's, and to Cesar the things which are Cesar's. 6. We shall be so far from conniving at, complying with, or countenancing of, malignancy, injustice, iniquity, profanity, and impiety, that we shall not only avoid and discountenance those things, and cherish and encourage these persons who are zealous for the cause of God, and walk according to the gospel; but also shall take a more effectual course than heretofore, in our respective places and callings, for punishing and suppressing these evils; and faithfully endeavour, that the best and fittest remedies may be applied for taking away the causes thereof, and advancing the knowledge of God, and holiness and righteousness in the land. And therefore, in the last place, as we shall earnestly pray unto God, that he would give us *able men, fearing God, men of truth, and hating covetousness*, to judge and bear charge among his people; so we shall, according to our places and callings, endeavour that judicatories, and all places of power and trust, both in kirk and state, may consist of, and be filled with, such men as are of known good affection to the cause of God, and of a blameless and Christian conversation.

And, because there be many, who heretofore have not made conscience of the oath of God, but some through fear, others by persuasion, and upon base ends and human interests, have entered thereinto, who have afterwards discovered themselves to have dealt deceitfully with the Lord, in swearing falsely by his name; therefore we, who do now renew our Covenant, in reference to these duties, and all other duties contained therein, do, in the sight of him who is the Searcher of hearts, solemnly profess, that it is not upon any politick advantage, or private interest or by-end, or because of any terror or persuasion from men, or hypocritically and deceitfully, that we do again take upon us the oath of God, but honestly and sincerely, and from the sense of our duty; and that therefore, denying ourselves, and our own things, and laying aside all self-interest and ends, we shall above all things seek the honour of God, the good of his cause, and the wealth of his people; and that forsaking the counsels of flesh and blood, and not leaning upon carnal confidences, we shall depend upon the Lord, walk by the rule of his word, and hearken to the voice of his servants. In all which, professing our own weakness, we do earnestly pray to God, who is the Father of mercies, through his Son Jesus Christ, to be merciful unto us, and to enable us, by the power of his might, that we may do our duty, unto the praise of his grace in the churches. *Amen*

THE DIRECTORY

FOR

THE PUBLICK WORSHIP OF GOD;

AGREED UPON BY THE ASSEMBLY OF DIVINES AT WESTMINSTER, WITH THE ASSISTANCE OF COMMISSIONERS FROM THE CHURCH OF SCOTLAND, AS A PART OF THE COVENANTED UNIFORMITY IN RELIGION BETWIXT THE CHURCHES OF CHRIST IN THE KINGDOMS OF SCOTLAND, ENGLAND, AND IRELAND:

WITH

AN ACT OF THE GENERAL ASSEMBLY AND ACT OF PARLIAMENT, BOTH IN ANNO 1645, APPROVING AND ESTABLISHING THE SAID DIRECTORY.

---

1 Cor. xiv. 40.—Let all things be done decently, and in order.
Ver. 26.—Let all things be done unto edifying.

CONTENTS.

The Preface.
Of the Assembling of the Congregation.
Of Publick Reading of the Holy Scriptures.
Of Publick Prayer before the Sermon.
Of Preaching of the Word.
Of Prayer after Sermon.
Of the Sacrament of Baptism.
Of the Sacrament of the Lord's Supper.
Of the Sanctification of the Lord's Day.
Of the Solemnization of Marriage.
Of the Visitation of the Sick.
Of the Burial of the Dead.
Of Publick Solemn Fasting.
Of the Observation of Days of Public Thanksgiving.
Of Singing of Psalms.
An Appendix touching Days and Places of Publick Worship.

CHARLES I. Parl. 3. Sess. 5
An ACT *of the* PARLIAMENT *of the* KINGDOM *of* SCOTLAND, *approving and establishing the* DIRECTORY *for Publick Worship.*

AT EDINBURGH, *February* 6, 1645.

THE Estates of Parliament now convened, in the second session of this first triennial Parliament, by virtue of the last act of the last Parliament holden by his Majesty and the Three Estates, in *anno* 1641; after the publick reading and serious consideration of the act under-written of the General Assembly, approving the following Directory for the publick worship of God in the three kingdoms, lately united by the Solemn League and Covenant, together with the ordinance of the Parliament of England establishing the said Directory, and the Directory itself; do heartily and cheerfully agree to the said Directory, according to the act of the General Assembly approving the same. Which act, together with the Directory itself, the Estates of Parliament do, without a contrary voice, ratify and approve in all the Heads and Articles thereof; and do interpone and add the authority of Parliament to the said act of the General Assembly. And do ordain the same to have the strength and force of a law and act of Parliament, and execution to pass thereupon, for observing the said Directory, according to the said act of the General Assembly in all points.

ALEX. GIBSON, *Cler. Registri.*

ASSEMBLY AT EDINBURGH, February 3, 1645. Sess. 10.
ACT *of the* GENERAL ASSEMBLY *of the* KIRK *of* SCOTLAND, *for the establishing and putting in Execution of the* DIRECTORY *for the Publick Worship of God.*

WHEREAS an happy unity, and uniformity in religion amongst the kirks of Christ, in these three kingdoms, united under one Sovereign, having been long and earnestly wished for by the godly and well-affected amongst us, was propounded as a main article of the large treaty, without which band and bulwark, no safe, well-grounded, and lasting peace could be expected; and afterward, with greater strength and maturity, revived in the Solemn League and Covenant of the three kingdoms; whereby they stand straitly obliged to endeavour the nearest uniformity in one form of Church-government, Directory of Worship, Confession of Faith, and Form of Catechising; which hath also before, and since our entering into that Covenant, been the matter of many supplications and remonstrances, and sending Commissioners to the King's Majesty; of declarations to the Honourable Houses of the Parliament of England, and of letters to the Reverend Assembly of Divines, and others of the ministry of the kirk of England; being also the end of our sending Commissioners, as was desired, from this kirk, with commission to treat of uniformity in the four particulars afore-mentioned, with such committees as should be appointed by both Houses of Parliament of England, and by the Assembly of Divines sitting at Westminster; and beside all this, it being, in point of conscience, the chief motive and end of our adventuring upon manifold and great hazards, for quenching the devouring flame of the present unnatural and bloody war in England, though to the weakening of this kingdom within itself, and the advantage of the enemy which have invaded it; accounting nothing too dear to us, so that this our joy be fulfilled. And now this great work being so far advanced, that a Directory for the Publick Worship of God in all the three kingdoms being agreed upon by the Honourable Houses of the Parliament of England, after consultation with the Divines of both kingdoms there assembled, and sent to us for our approbation, that, being also agreed upon by this kirk and kingdom of Scotland, it may be in the name of both kingdoms presented to the King, for his royal consent and ratification; the General Assembly, having most seriously considered, revised, and examined the Directory afore-mentioned, after several publick readings of it, after much deliberation, both publickly and in private committees, after full liberty given to all to object against it, and earnest invitations of all who have any scruples about it, to make known the same, that they might be satisfied; doth unanimously, and without a contrary voice, agree to and approve the following Directory, in all the heads thereof, together with the Preface set before it; and doth require, decern, and ordain, That, according to the plain tenor and meaning thereof, and the intent or the Preface, it be carefully and uniformly observed and practised by all the ministers and others within this kingdom whom it doth concern: which practice shall be begun upon intimation given to the several presbyteries from the Commissioners of this General Assembly, who shall also take special care for timeous printing of this Directory, that a printed copy of it be provided and kept for the use of every kirk in this kingdom; also that each presbytery have a printed copy thereof for their use, and take special notice of the observation or neglect thereof in every congregation within their bounds, and make known the same to the Provincial or General Assembly, as there shall be cause.

Provided always, That the clause in the Directory, of the administration of the Lord's Supper, which mentioneth the communicants sitting about the table, or at it, be not interpreted as if, in the judgment of this kirk, it were indifferent, and free for any of the communicants not to come to, and receive at the table; or as if we did approve the distributing of the elements by the minister to each communicant, and not by the communicants among themselves. It is also provided, That this shall be no prejudice to the order and practice of this kirk, in such particulars as are appointed by the books of discipline, and acts of General Assemblies, and are not otherwise ordered and appointed in the Directory.

Finally, The Assembly doth, with much joy and thankfulness, acknowledge the rich blessing and invaluable mercy of God, in bringing the so much wished for uniformity in religion to such a happy period, that these kingdoms, once at so great a distance in the form of worship, are now, by the blessing of God, brought to a nearer uniformity than any other reformed kirks; which is unto us the return of our prayers, and a lightening of our eyes, and reviving of our hearts in the midst of our many sorrows and sufferings; a taking away, in a great measure, the reproach of the people of God, to the stopping of the mouths of malignant and disaffected persons; and an opening unto us a door of hope, that God hath yet thoughts of peace towards us, and not of evil, to give us an expected end; in the expectation and confidence whereof we do rejoice; beseeching the Lord to preserve these kingdoms from heresies, schisms, offences, profaneness, and whatsoever is contrary to sound doctrine, and the power of godliness; and to continue with us, and the generations following, these his pure and purged ordinances, together with an increase of the power and life thereof, to the glory of his great name, the enlargement of the kingdom of his Son, the corroboration of peace and love between the kingdoms, the unity and comfort of all his people, and our edifying one another in love.

THE DIRECTORY

FOR

THE PUBLICK WORSHIP OF GOD.

THE PREFACE.

IN the beginning of the blessed Reformation, our wise and pious ancestors took care to set forth an order for redress of many things, which they then, by the word, discovered to be vain, erroneous, superstitious, and idolatrous, in the publick worship of God. This occasioned many godly and learned men to rejoice much in the Book of Common Prayer, at that time set forth; because the mass, and the rest of the Latin service being removed, the publick worship was celebrated in our own tongue: many of the common people also receive benefit by hearing the scriptures read in their own language, which formerly were unto them as a book that is sealed.

Howbeit, long and sad experience hath made it manifest, that the Liturgy used in the Church of England, (notwithstanding all the pains and religious intentions of the Compilers of it,) hath proved an offence, not only to many of the godly at home, but also to the reformed Churches abroad. For, not to speak of urging the reading of all the prayers, which very greatly increased the burden of it, the many unprofitable and burdensome ceremonies contained in it have occasioned much mischief, as well by disquieting the consciences of many godly ministers and people, who could not yield unto them, as by depriving them of the ordinances of God, which they might not enjoy without conforming or subscribing to those ceremonies. Sundry good Christians have been, by means thereof, kept from the Lord's table; and divers able and faithful ministers debarred from the exercise of their ministry, (to the endangering of many thousand souls, in a time of such scarcity of faithful pastors,) and spoiled of their livelihood, to the undoing of them and their families. Prelates, and their faction, have laboured to raise the estimation of it to such a height, as if there were no other worship, or way of worship of God, amongst us, but only the Service-book; to the great hinderance of the preaching of the word, and (in some places, especially of late,) to the justling of it out as unnecessary, or at best, as far inferior to the reading of common prayer; which was made no better than an idol by many ignorant and superstitious people, who, pleasing themselves in their presence at that service, and their lip-labour in bearing a part in it, have thereby hardened themselves in their ignorance and carelessness of saving knowledge and true piety.

In the meantime, Papists boasted that the book was a compliance with them in a great part of their service; and so were not a little confirmed in their superstition and idolatry, expecting rather our return to them, than endeavouring the reformation of themselves: in which expectation they were of late very much encouraged, when, upon the pretended warrantableness of imposing of the former ceremonies, new ones were daily obtruded upon the Church.

Add hereunto, (which was not foreseen, but since have come to pass,) that the Liturgy hath been a great means, as on the one hand to make and increase an idle and unedifying ministry, which contented itself with set forms made to their hands by others, without putting forth themselves to exercise the gift of prayer, with which our Lord Jesus Christ pleaseth to furnish all his servants whom he calls to that office: so, on the other side, it hath been (and ever would be, if continued,) a matter of endless strife and contention in the Church, and a snare both to many godly and faithful ministers, who have been persecuted and silenced upon that occasion, and to others of hopeful parts, many of which have been, and more still would be, diverted from all thoughts of the ministry to other studies; especially in these latter times, wherein God vouchsafeth to his people more and better means for the discovery of error and superstition, and for attaining of knowledge in the mysteries of godliness, and gifts in preaching and prayer.

Upon these, and many the like weighty considerations in reference to the whole book in general, and because of divers particulars contained in it; not from any love to novelty, or intention to disparage our first reformers, (of whom we are persuaded, that, were they now alive, they would join with us in this work, and whom we acknowledge as excellent instruments, raised by God, to begin the purging and building of his house, and desire they may be had of us and posterity in everlasting remembrance, with thankfulness and honour,) but that we may in some measure answer the gracious providence of

God, which at this time calleth upon us for further reformation, and may satisfy our own consciences, and answer the expectation of other reformed churches, and the desires of many of the godly among ourselves, and withal give some publick testimony of our endeavours for uniformity in divine worship, which we have promised in our Solemn League and Covenant; we have, after earnest and frequent calling upon the name of God, and after much consultation, not with flesh and blood, but with his holy word, resolved to lay aside the former Liturgy, with the many rites and ceremonies formerly used in the worship of God; and have agreed upon this following Directory for all the parts of publick worship, at ordinary and extraordinary times.

Wherein our care hath been to hold forth such things as are of divine institution in every ordinance; and other things we have endeavoured to set forth according to the rules of Christian prudence, agreeable to the general rules of the word of God; our meaning therein being only, that the general heads, the sense and scope of the prayers, and other parts of publick worship, being known to all, there may be a consent of all the churches in those things that contain the substance of the service and worship of God; and the ministers may be hereby directed, in their administrations, to keep like soundness in doctrine and prayer, and may, if need be, have some help and furniture, and yet so as they become not hereby slothful and negligent in stirring up the gifts of Christ in them; but that each one, by meditation, by taking heed to himself, and the flock of God committed to him, and by wise observing the ways of Divine Providence, may be careful to furnish his heart and tongue with further or other materials of prayer and exhortation, as shall be needful upon all occasions.

Of the Assembling of the Congregation, and their Behaviour in the Publick Worship of God.

WHEN the congregation is to meet for publick worship, the people (having before prepared their hearts thereunto) ought all to come and join therein; not absenting themselves from the publick ordinances through negligence, or upon pretence of private meetings.

Let all enter the assembly, not irreverently, but in a grave and seemly manner, taking their seats or places without adoration, or bowing themselves towards one place or other.

The congregation being assembled, the minister, after solemn calling on them to the worshipping of the great name of God, is to begin with prayer.

" In all reverence and humility acknowledging the incomprehensible greatness and
" majesty of the Lord, (in whose presence they do then in a special manner appear,) and
" their own vileness and unworthiness to approach so near him, with their utter inability
" of themselves to so great a work; and humbly beseeching him for pardon, assistance,
" and acceptance, in the whole service then to be performed; and for a blessing on that
" particular portion of his word then to be read: And all in the name and mediation of
" the Lord Jesus Christ."

The publick worship being begun, the people are wholly to attend upon it, forbearing to read any thing, except what the minister is then reading or citing; and abstaining much more from all private whisperings, conferences, salutations, or doing reverence to any person present, or coming in; as also from all gazing, sleeping, and other indecent behaviour, which may disturb the minister or people, or hinder themselves or others in the service of God.

If any, through necessity, be hindered from being present at the beginning, they ought not, when they come into the congregation, to betake themselves to their private devotions, but reverently to compose themselves to join with the assembly in that ordinance of God which is then in hand.

Of Publick Reading of the Holy Scriptures.

READING of the word in the congregation, being part of the publick worship of God, (wherein we acknowledge our dependence upon him, and subjection to him,) and one mean sanctified by him for the edifying of his people, is to be performed by the pastors and teachers.

Howbeit, such as intend the ministry, may occasionally both read the word, and exercise their gift in preaching in the congregation, if allowed by the presbytery thereunto.

All the canonical books of the Old and New Testament (but none of those which are commonly called *Apocrypha*) shall be publickly read in the vulgar tongue, out of the best allowed translation, distinctly, that all may hear and understand.

How large a portion shall be read at once, is left to the wisdom of the minister; but it is convenient, that ordinarily one chapter of each Testament be read at every meeting; and sometimes more, where the chapters be short, or the coherence of matter requireth it.

It is requisite that all the canonical books be read over in order, that the people may be better acquainted with the whole body of the scriptures; and ordinarily, where the reading in either Testament endeth on one Lord's day, it is to begin the next.

We commend also the more frequent reading of such scriptures as he that readeth shall think best for edification of his hearers, as the book of Psalms, and such like.

When the minister who readeth shall judge it necessary to expound any part of what is read, let it not be done until the whole chapter or psalm be ended; and regard is always to be had unto the time, that neither preaching, nor other ordinances be straitened, or rendered tedious. Which rule is to be observed in all other publick performances.

T

Beside publick reading of the holy scriptures, every person that can read, is to be exhorted to read the scriptures privately, (and all others that cannot read, if not disabled by age, or otherwise, are likewise to be exhorted to learn to read,) and to have a Bible.

Of Publick Prayer before the Sermon.

AFTER reading of the word, (and singing of the psalm,) the minister who is to preach, is to endeavour to get his own and his hearers' hearts to be rightly affected with their sins, that they may all mourn in sense thereof before the Lord, and hunger and thirst after the grace of God in Jesus Christ, by proceeding to a more full confession of sin, with shame and holy confusion of face, and to call upon the Lord to this effect:

"To acknowledge our great sinfulness, First, by reason of original sin, which (beside "the guilt that makes us liable to everlasting damnation) is the seed of all other sins, "hath depraved and poisoned all the faculties and powers of soul and body, doth defile "our best actions, and (were it not restrained, or our hearts renewed by grace,) would "break forth into innumerable transgressions, and greatest rebellions against the Lord "that ever were committed by the vilest of the sons of men; and next, by reason of "actual sins, our own sins, the sins of magistrates, of ministers, and of the whole nation, "unto which we are many ways accessory: which sins of ours receive many fearful "aggravations, we having broken all the commandments of the holy, just, and good law "of God, doing that which is forbidden, and leaving undone what is enjoined; and that "not only out of ignorance and infirmity, but also more presumptuously, against the "light of our minds, checks of our consciences, and motions of his own Holy Spirit to "the contrary, so that we have no cloak for our sins; yea, not only despising the riches "of God's goodness, forbearance, and long-suffering, but standing out against many "invitations and offers of grace in the gospel; not endeavouring, as we ought, to receive "Christ into our hearts by faith, or to walk worthy of him in our lives.

"To bewail our blindness of mind, hardness of heart, unbelief, impenitency, security, "lukewarmness, barrenness; our not endeavouring after mortification and newness of "life, nor after the exercise of godliness in the power thereof; and that the best of us "have not so stedfastly walked with God, kept our garments so unspotted, nor been so "zealous of his glory, and the good of others, as we ought: and to mourn over such other "sins as the congregation is particularly guilty of, notwithstanding the manifold and "great mercies of our God, the love of Christ, the light of the gospel, and reformation of "religion, our own purposes, promises, vows, solemn covenant, and other special "obligations, to the contrary.

"To acknowledge and confess, that, as we are convinced of our guilt, so, out of a deep "sense thereof, we judge ourselves unworthy of the smallest benefits, most worthy of "God's fiercest wrath, and of all the curses of the law, and heaviest judgments inflicted "upon the most rebellious sinners; and that he might most justly take his kingdom and "gospel from us, plague us with all sorts of spiritual and temporal judgments in this life, "and after cast us into utter darkness, in the lake that burneth with fire and brimstone, "where is weeping and gnashing of teeth for evermore.

"Notwithstanding all which, to draw near to the throne of grace, encouraging our- "selves with hope of a gracious answer of our prayers, in the riches and all-sufficiency "of that only one oblation, the satisfaction and intercession of the Lord Jesus Christ, at "the right hand of his Father and our Father; and in confidence of the exceeding great "and precious promises of mercy and grace in the new covenant, through the same "Mediator thereof, to deprecate the heavy wrath and curse of God, which we are not "able to avoid, or bear; and humbly and earnestly to supplicate for mercy, in the free "and full remission of all our sins, and that only for the bitter sufferings and precious "merits of that our only Saviour Jesus Christ.

"That the Lord would vouchsafe to shed abroad his love in our hearts by the Holy "Ghost; seal unto us, by the same Spirit of adoption, the full assurance of our pardon "and reconciliation; comfort all that mourn in Zion, speak peace to the wounded and "troubled spirit, and bind up the broken-hearted: and as for secure and presumptuous "sinners, that he would open their eyes, convince their consciences, and turn them from "darkness unto light, and from the power of Satan unto God, that they also may receive "forgiveness of sin, and an inheritance among them that are sanctified by faith in "Christ Jesus.

"With remission of sins through the blood of Christ, to pray for sanctification by his "Spirit; the mortification of sin dwelling in and many times tyrannizing over us; the "quickening of our dead spirits with the life of God in Christ; grace to fit and enable "us for all duties of conversation and callings towards God and men; strength against "temptations; the sanctified use of blessings and crosses; and perseverance in faith "and obedience unto the end.

"To pray for the propagation of the gospel and kingdom of Christ to all nations; for "the conversion of the Jews, the fulness of the Gentiles, the fall of Antichrist, and the "hastening of the second coming of our Lord; for the deliverance of the distressed "churches abroad from the tyranny of the antichristian faction, and from the cruel "oppressions and blasphemies of the Turk; for the blessing of God upon the reformed "churches, especially upon the churches and kingdoms of Scotland, England, and "Ireland, now more strictly and religiously united in the Solemn National League and "Covenant; and for our plantations in the remote parts of the world: more particularly

"for that church and kingdom whereof we are members, that therein God would estab-
"lish peace and truth, the purity of all his ordinances, and the power of godliness;
"prevent and remove heresy, schism, profaneness, superstition, security, and unfruit-
"fulness under the means of grace; heal all our rents and divisions, and preserve us
"from breach of our Solemn Covenant.

"To pray for all in authority, especially for the King's Majesty; that God would make
"him rich in blessings, both in his person and government; establish his throne in
"religion and righteousness, save him from evil counsel, and make him a blessed and
"glorious instrument for the conservation and propagation of the gospel, for the encour-
"agement and protection of them that do well, the terror of all that do evil, and the
"great good of the whole church, and of all his kingdoms; for the conversion of the
"Queen, the religious education of the Prince, and the rest of the royal seed; for the
"comforting of the afflicted Queen of Bohemia, sister to our Sovereign; and for the res-
"titution and establishment of the illustrious Prince Charles, Elector Palatine of the
"Rhine, to all his dominions and dignities; for a blessing upon the High Court of Par-
"liament, (when sitting in any of these kingdoms respectively,) the nobility, the subor-
"dinate judges and magistrates, the gentry, and all the commonality; for all pastors
"and teachers, that God would fill them with his Spirit, make them exemplarily holy,
"sober, just, peaceable, and gracious in their lives; sound, faithful, and powerful in
"their ministry; and follow all their labours with abundance of success and blessing;
"and give unto all his people pastors according to his own heart; for the universities,
"and all schools and religious seminaries of church and commonwealth, that they may
"flourish more and more in learning and piety; for the particular city or congregation,
"that God would pour out a blessing upon the ministry of the word, sacraments, and
"discipline, upon the civil government, and all the several families and persons therein;
"for mercy to the afflicted under any inward or outward distress; for seasonable weather,
"and fruitful seasons, as the time may require; for averting the judgments that we
"either feel or fear, or are liable unto, as famine, pestilence, the sword, and such like.

"And, with confidence of his mercy to his whole church, and the acceptance of our
"persons, through the merits and mediation of our High Priest, the Lord Jesus, to pro-
"fess that it is the desire of our souls to have fellowship with God in the reverend and
"conscionable use of his holy ordinances; and, to that purpose, to pray earnestly for his
"grace and effectual assistance to the sanctification of his holy sabbath, the Lord's day,
"in all the duties thereof, publick and private, both to ourselves, and to all other con-
"gregations of his people, according to the riches and excellency of the gospel, this day
"celebrated and enjoyed.

"And because we have been unprofitable hearers in times past, and now cannot of
"ourselves receive, as we should, the deep things of God, the mysteries of Jesus Christ,
"which require a spiritual discerning; to pray, that the Lord, who teacheth to profit,
"would graciously please to pour out the Spirit of grace, together with the outward
"means thereof, causing us to attain such a measure of the excellency of the knowledge
"of Christ Jesus our Lord, and, in him, of the things which belong to our peace, that
"we may account all things but as dross in comparison of him; and that we, tasting the
"first-fruits of the glory that is to be revealed, may long for a more full and perfect
"communion with him, that where he is, we may be also, and enjoy the fulness of those
"joys and pleasures which are at his right hand for evermore.

"More particularly, that God would in a special manner furnish his servant (now
"called to dispense the bread of life unto his household) with wisdom, fidelity, zeal, and
"utterance, that he may divide the word of God aright, to every one his portion, in
"evidence and demonstration of the Spirit and power; and that the Lord would circum-
"cise the ears and hearts of the hearers, to hear, love, and receive with meekness the
"ingrafted word, which is able to save their souls; make them as good ground to receive
"in the good seed of the word, and strengthen them against the temptations of Satan,
"the cares of the world, the hardness of their own hearts, and whatsoever else may
"hinder their profitable and saving hearing; that so Christ may be so formed in them,
"and live in them, that all their thoughts may be brought into captivity to the obedience
"of Christ, and their hearts established in every good word and work for ever."

We judge this to be a convenient order, in the ordinary public prayer; yet so, as the minister may defer (as in prudence he shall think meet) some part of these petitions till after his sermon, or offer up to God some of the thanksgivings hereafter appointed, in his prayer before his sermon.

Of the Preaching of the Word.

PREACHING of the word, being the power of God unto salvation, and one of the greatest and most excellent works belonging to the ministry of the gospel, should be so performed, that the workman need not be ashamed, but may save himself, and those that hear him.

It is presupposed, (according to the rules for ordination,) that the minister of Christ is in some good measure gifted for so weighty a service, by his skill in the original languages, and in such arts and sciences as are handmaids unto divinity; by his knowledge in the whole body of theology, but most of all in the holy scriptures, having his senses and heart exercised in them above the common sort of believers; and by the illumination of God's Spirit, and other gifts of edification, which (together with reading and studying of the word) he ought still to seek by prayer, and an humble heart, resolving to admit and receive any truth not yet attained, whenever God shall make it known unto him. All which he is to make use of, and improve, in his private preparations, before he deliver in public what he hath provided.

Ordinarily, the subject of his sermon is to be some text of scripture, holding forth some principle or head of religion, or suitable to some special occasion emergent; or he may go on in some chapter, psalm, or book of the holy scripture, as he shall see fit.

Let the introduction to his text be brief and perspicuous, drawn from the text itself, or context, or some parallel place, or general sentence of scripture.

If the text be long, (as in histories or parables it sometimes must be,) let him give a brief sum of it; if short, a paraphrase thereof, if need be: in both, looking diligently to the scope of the text, and pointing at the chief heads and grounds of doctrine which he is to raise from it.

In analysing and dividing his text, he is to regard more the order of matter than of words; and neither to burden the memory of the hearers in the beginning with too many members of division, nor to trouble their minds with obscure terms of art.

In raising doctrines from the text, his care ought to be, *First*, That the matter be the truth of God. *Secondly*, That it be a truth contained in or grounded on that text, that the hearers may discern how God teacheth it from thence. *Thirdly*, That he chiefly insist upon those doctrines which are principally intended, and make most for the edification of the hearers.

The doctrine is to be expressed in plain terms; or, if any thing in it need explication, it is to be opened, and the consequence also from the text cleared. The parallel places of scripture, confirming the doctrine, are rather to be plain and pertinent, than many, and (if need be) somewhat insisted upon, and applied to the purpose in hand.

The arguments or reasons are to be solid, and, as much as may be, convincing. The illustrations, of what kind soever, ought to be full of light, and such as may convey the truth into the hearer's heart with spiritual delight.

If any doubt obvious from scripture, reason, or prejudice of the hearers, seem to arise, it is very requisite to remove it, by reconciling the seeming differences, answering the reasons, and discovering and taking away the causes of prejudice and mistake. Otherwise it is not fit to detain the hearers with propounding or answering vain or wicked cavils, which, as they are endless, so the propounding and answering of them doth more hinder than promote edification.

He is not to rest in general doctrine, although never so much cleared and confirmed, but to bring it home to special use, by application to his hearers: which albeit it prove a work of great difficulty to himself, requiring much prudence, zeal, and meditation, and to the natural and corrupt man will be very unpleasant; yet he is to endeavour to perform it in such a manner, that his auditors may feel the word of God to be quick and powerful, and a discerner of the thoughts and intents of the heart; and that, if any unbeliever or ignorant person be present, he may have the secrets of his heart made manifest, and give glory to God.

In the use of instruction or information in the knowledge of some truth, which is a consequence from his doctrine, he may (when convenient) confirm it by a few firm arguments from the text in hand, and other places of scripture, or from the nature of that common place in divinity, whereof that truth is a branch.

In confutation of false doctrines, he is neither to raise an old heresy from the grave, nor to mention a blasphemous opinion unnecessarily: but, if the people be in danger of an error, he is to confute it soundly, and endeavour to satisfy their judgments and consciences against all objections.

In exhorting to duties, he is, as he seeth cause, to teach also the means that help to the performance of them.

In dehortation, reprehension, and publick admonition, (which require special wisdom,) let him, as there shall be cause, not only discover the nature and greatness of the sin, with the misery attending it, but also shew the danger his hearers are in to be overtaken and surprised by it, together with the remedies, and best way to avoid it.

In applying comfort, whether general against all temptations, or particular against some special troubles or terrors, he is carefully to answer such objections as a troubled heart and afflicted spirit may suggest to the contrary.

It is also sometimes requisite to give some notes of trial, (which is very profitable, especially when performed by able and experienced ministers, with circumspection and prudence, and the signs clearly grounded on the holy scripture,) whereby the hearers may be able to examine themselves whether they have attained those graces, and performed those duties, to which he exhorteth, or be guilty of the sin reprehended, and in danger of the judgments threatened, or are such to whom the consolations propounded do belong; that accordingly they may be quickened and excited to duty, humbled for their wants and sins, affected with their danger, and strengthened with comfort, as their condition, upon examination, shall require.

And, as he needeth not always to prosecute every doctrine which lies in his text, so is he wisely to make choice of such uses, as, by his residence and conversing with his flock, he findeth most needful and seasonable; and, amongst these, such as may most draw their souls to Christ, the fountain of light, holiness, and comfort.

This method is not prescribed as necessary for every man, or upon every text; but only recommended, as being found by experience to be very much blessed of God, and very helpful for the people's understandings and memories.

But the servant of Christ, whatever his method be, is to perform his whole ministry:

1. Painfully, not doing the work of the Lord negligently.

2. Plainly, that the meanest may understand; delivering the truth not in the enticing words of man's wisdom, but in demonstration of the Spirit and of power, lest the cross of Christ should be made of none effect; abstaining also from an unprofitable use of unknown tongues, strange phrases, and cadences of sounds and words; sparingly citing sentences of ecclesiastical or other human writers, ancient or modern, be they never so elegant.

3. Faithfully, looking at the honour of Christ, the conversion, edification, and salvation of the people, not at his own gain or glory; keeping nothing back which may promote those holy ends, giving to every one his own portion, and bearing indifferent respect unto all, without neglecting the meanest, or sparing the greatest, in their sins.

4. Wisely, framing all his doctrines, exhortations, and especially his reproofs, in such a manner as may be most likely to prevail; shewing all due respect to each man's person and place, and not mixing his own passion or bitterness.

5. Gravely, as becometh the word of God; shunning all such gesture, voice, and expressions, as may occasion the corruptions of men to despise him and his ministry.

6. With loving affection, that the people may see all coming from his godly zeal, and hearty desire to do them good. And,

7. As taught of God, and persuaded in his own heart, that all that he teacheth is the truth of Christ; and walking before his flock, as an example to them in it; earnestly, both in private and publick, recommending his labours to the blessing of God, and watchfully looking to himself, and the flock whereof the Lord hath made him overseer: So shall the doctrine of truth be preserved uncorrupt, many souls converted and built up, and himself receive manifold comforts of his labours even in this life, and afterward the crown of glory laid up for him in the world to come.

Where there are more ministers in a congregation than one, and they of different gifts, each may more especially apply himself to doctrine or exhortation, according to the gift wherein he most excelleth, and as they shall agree between themselves.

Of Prayer after Sermon.

THE sermon being ended, the minister is "To give thanks for the great love of God, "in sending his Son Jesus Christ unto us; for the communication of his Holy "Spirit; for the light and liberty of the glorious gospel, and the rich and heavenly bless- "ings revealed therein; as, namely, election, vocation, adoption, justification, sanctifi- "cation, and hope of glory; for the admirable goodness of God in freeing the land from "antichristian darkness and tyranny, and for all other national deliverances; for the re- "formation of religion; for the covenant; and for many temporal blessings.

"To pray for the continuance of the gospel, and all ordinances thereof, in their purity, "power, and liberty: to turn the chief and most useful heads of the sermon into some "few petitions; and to pray that it may abide in the heart, and bring forth fruit.

"To pray for preparation for death and judgment, and a watching for the coming of "our Lord Jesus Christ: to entreat of God the forgiveness of the iniquities of our holy "things, and the acceptation of our spiritual sacrifice, through the merit and mediation "of our great High Priest and Saviour the Lord Jesus Christ."

And because the prayer which Christ taught his disciples is not only a pattern of prayer, but itself a most comprehensive prayer, we recommend it also to be used in the prayers of the church.

And whereas, at the administration of the sacraments, the holding publick fasts and days of thanksgiving, and other special occasions, which may afford matter of special petitions and thanksgivings, it is requisite to express somewhat in our publick prayers, (as at this time it is our duty to pray for a blessing upon the Assembly of Divines, the armies by sea and land, for the defence of the King, Parliament, and Kingdom,) every minister is herein to apply himself in his prayer, before or after sermon, to those occasions: but, for the manner, he is left to his liberty, as God shall direct and enable him in piety and wisdom to discharge his duty.

The prayer ended, let a psalm be sung, if with conveniency it may be done. After which (unless some other ordinance of Christ, that concerneth the congregation at that time, be to follow,) let the minister dismiss the congregation with a solemn blessing.

Of the Administration of the Sacraments:

AND FIRST, OF BAPTISM.

BAPTISM, as it is not unnecessarily to be delayed, so it is not to be administered in any case by any private person, but by a minister of Christ, called to be the steward of the mysteries of God.

Nor is it to be administered in private places, or privately, but in the place of publick worship, and in the face of the congregation, where the people may most conveniently see and hear; and not in the places where fonts, in the time of Popery, were unfitly and superstitiously placed.

The child to be baptized, after notice given to the minister the day before, is to be pre sented by the father, or (in case of his necessary absence) by some Christian friend in his place, professing his earnest desire that the child may be baptized.

Before baptism, the minister is to use some words of instruction, touching the institution, nature, use, and ends of this sacrament, shewing,

"That it is instituted by our Lord Jesus Christ: That it is a seal of the covenant of
" grace, of our ingrafting into Christ, and of our union with him, of remission of sins, re-
" generation, adoption, and life eternal: That the water, in baptism, representeth and
" signifieth both the blood of Christ, which taketh away all guilt of sin, original and ac-
" tual; and the sanctifying virtue of the Spirit of Christ against the dominion of sin, and
" the corruption of our sinful nature: That baptizing, or sprinkling and washing with
" water, signifieth the cleansing from sin by the blood and for the merit of Christ, to-
" gether with the mortification of sin, and rising from sin to newness of life, by virtue of
" the death and resurrection of Christ: That the promise is made to believers and their
" seed; and that the seed and posterity of the faithful, born within the church, have, by
" their birth, interest in the covenant, and right to the seal of it, and to the outward pri-
" vileges of the church, under the gospel, no less than the children of Abraham in the
" time of the Old Testament; the covenant of grace, for substance, being the same; and
" the grace of God, and the consolation of believers, more plentiful than before: That the
" Son of God admitted little children into his presence, embracing and blessing them,
" saying, *For of such is the kingdom of God:* That children, by baptism, are solemnly
" received into the bosom of the visible church, distinguished from the world, and them
" that are without, and united with believers; and that all who are baptized in the name
" of Christ, do renounce, and by their baptism are bound to fight against the devil, the
" world, and the flesh: That they are Christians, and federally holy before baptism, and
" therefore are they baptized: That the inward grace and virtue of baptism is not tied to
" that very moment of time wherein it is administered; and that the fruit and power
" thereof reacheth to the whole course of our life; and that outward baptism is not so
" necessary, that, through the want thereof, the infant is in danger of damnation, or the
" parents guilty, if they do not contemn or neglect the ordinance of Christ, when and
" where it may be had."

In these or the like instructions, the minister is to use his own liberty and godly wisdom, as the ignorance or errors in the doctrine of baptism, and the edification of the people, shall require.

He is also to admonish all that are present,

"To look back to their baptism: to repent of their sins against their covenant with
" God; to stir up their faith; to improve and make right use of their baptism, and of the
" covenant sealed thereby betwixt God and their souls."

He is to exhort the parent,

"To consider the great mercy of God to him and his child; to bring up the child in
" the knowledge of the grounds of the Christian religion, and in the nurture and ad-
" monition of the Lord; and to let him know the danger of God's wrath to himself and
" child, if he be negligent: requiring his solemn promise for the performance of his
" duty."

This being done, prayer is also to be joined with the word of institution, for sanctifying the water to this spiritual use; and the minister is to pray to this or the like effect:

"That the Lord, who hath not left us as strangers without the covenant of promise,
" but called us to the privileges of his ordinances, would graciously vouchsafe to sanctify
" and bless his own ordinance of baptism at this time: That he would join the inward
" baptism of his Spirit with the outward baptism of water; make this baptism to the in-
" fant a seal of adoption, remission of sin, regeneration, and eternal life, and all other
" promises of the covenant of grace: That the child may be planted into the likeness of
" the death and resurrection of Christ; and that, the body of sin being destroyed in him,
" he may serve God in newness of life all his days."

Then the minister is to demand the name of the child; which being told him, he is to say, (calling the child by his name,)

I baptize thee in the name of the Father, and of the Son, and of the Holy Ghost.

As he pronounceth these words, he is to baptize the child with water: which, for the manner of doing of it, is not only lawful but sufficient, and most expedient to be, by pouring or sprinkling of the water on the face of the child, without adding any other ceremony.

This done, he is to give thanks and pray, to this or the like purpose:

"Acknowledging with all thankfulness, that the Lord is true and faithful in keeping
" covenant and mercy: That he is good and gracious, not only in that he numbereth us
" among his saints, but is pleased also to bestow upon our children this singular token
" and badge of his love in Christ: That, in his truth and special providence, he daily
" bringeth some into the bosom of his church, to be partakers of his inestimable benefits,
" purchased by the blood of his dear Son, for the continuance and increase of his church.

"And praying, That the Lord would still continue, and daily confirm more and more
" this his unspeakable favour: That he would receive the infant now baptized, and
" solemnly entered into the household of faith, into his fatherly tuition and defence, and
" remember him with the favour that he sheweth to his people; that, if he shall be taken
" out of this life in his infancy, the Lord, who is rich in mercy, would be pleased to re-
" ceive him up into glory; and if he live, and attain the years of discretion, that the

"Lord would so teach him by his word and Spirit, and make his baptism effectual to
" him, and so uphold him by his divine power and grace, that by faith he may prevail
" against the devil, the world, and the flesh, till in the end he obtain a full and final
" victory, and so be kept by the power of God through faith unto salvation, through
" Jesus Christ our Lord."

OF THE CELEBRATION OF THE COMMUNION, OR SACRAMENT OF THE LORD'S SUPPER.

THE communion, or supper of the Lord, is frequently to be celebrated; but how often, may be considered and determined by the ministers, and other church-governors of each congregation, as they shall find most convenient for the comfort and edification of the people committed to their charge. And, when it shall be administered, we judge it convenient to be done after the morning sermon.

The ignorant and the scandalous are not fit to receive the sacrament of the Lord's Supper.

Where this sacrament cannot with convenience be frequently administered, it is requisite that publick warning be given the sabbath-day before the administration thereof: and that either then, or on some day of that week, something concerning that ordinance, and the due preparation thereunto, and participation thereof, be taught; that, by the diligent use of all means sanctified of God to that end, both in publick and private, all may come better prepared to that heavenly feast.

When the day is come for administration, the minister, having ended his sermon and prayer, shall make a short exhortation:

" Expressing the inestimable benefit we have by this sacrament, together with the ends
" and use thereof: setting forth the great necessity of having our comforts and strength
" renewed thereby in this our pilgrimage and warfare: how necessary it is that we come
" unto it with knowledge, faith, repentance, love, and with hungering and thirsting souls
" after Christ and his benefits: how great the danger to eat and drink unworthily.

" Next, he is, in the name of Christ, on the one part, to warn all such as are ignorant,
" scandalous, profane, or that live in any sin or offence against their knowledge or con-
" science, that they presume not to come to that holy table; shewing them, that he that
" eateth and drinketh unworthily, eateth and drinketh judgment unto himself: and, on
" the other part, he is in an especial manner to invite and encourage all that labour
" under the sense of the burden of their sins, and fear of wrath, and desire to reach out
" unto a greater progress in grace than yet they can attain unto, to come to the Lord's
" table; assuring them, in the same name, of ease, refreshing, and strength to their weak
" and wearied souls."

After this exhortation, warning, and invitation, the table being before decently covered, and so conveniently placed, that the communicants may orderly sit about it, or at it, the minister is to begin the action with sanctifying and blessing the elements of bread and wine set before him, (the bread in comely and convenient vessels, so prepared, that, being broken by him, and given, it may be distributed amongst the communicants; the wine also in large cups,) having first, in a few words, shewed that those elements, otherwise common, are now set apart and sanctified to this holy use, by the word of institution and prayer.

Let the words of institution be read out of the Evangelists or out of the First Epistle of the Apostle Paul to the Corinthians, Chap. xi. 23. *I have received of the Lord,* &c. to the 27th Verse, which the minister may, when he seeth requisite, explain and apply.

Let the prayer, thanksgiving, or blessing of the bread and wine, be to this effect:
" With humble and hearty acknowledgment of the greatness of our misery, from which
" neither man nor angel was able to deliver us, and of our great unworthiness of the
" least of all God's mercies; to give thanks to God for all his benefits, and especially for
" that great benefit of our redemption, the love of God the Father, the sufferings and
" merits of the Lord Jesus Christ the Son of God, by which we are delivered; and for all
" means of grace, the word and sacraments; and for this sacrament in particular, by
" which Christ, and all his benefits, are applied and sealed up unto us, which, notwith-
" standing the denial of them unto others, are in great mercy continued unto us, after
" so much and long abuse of them all.

" To profess that there is no other name under heaven by which we can be saved, but
" the name of Jesus Christ, by whom alone we receive liberty and life, have access to
" the throne of grace, are admitted to eat and drink at his own table, and are sealed up
" by his Spirit to an assurance of happiness and everlasting life.

" Earnestly to pray to God, the Father of all mercies, and God of all consolation, to
" vouchsafe his gracious presence, and the effectual working of his Spirit in us; and so
" to sanctify these elements both of bread and wine, and to bless his own ordinance, that
" we may receive by faith the body and blood of Jesus Christ, crucified for us, and so to
" feed upon him, that he may be one with us, and we one with him; that he may live
" in us, and we in him, and to him who hath loved us, and given himself for us."

All which he is to endeavour to perform with suitable affections, answerable to such an holy action, and to stir up the like in the people.

The elements being now sanctified by the word and prayer, the minister, being at the table, is to take the bread in his hand, and say, in these expressions, (or other the like, used by Christ or his apostle upon this occasion:)

" According to the holy institution, command, and example of our blessed Saviour
" Jesus Christ, I take this bread, and, having given thanks, break it, and give it unto
" you; (there the minister, who is also himself to communicate, is to break the bread

" and give it to the communicants;) *Take ye, eat ye; this is the body of Christ which is*
" *broken for you; do this in remembrance of him.*"
In like manner the minister is to take the cup, and say, in these expressions, (or other the like, used by Christ or the apostle upon the same occasion:)
" According to the institution, command, and example of our Lord Jesus Christ, I take
" this cup, and give it unto you; (here he giveth it to the communicants;) *This cup is*
" *the new testament in the blood of Christ, which is shed for the remission of the sins of*
" *many: drink ye all of it.*"
After all have communicated, the minister may, in a few words, put them in mind,
" Of the grace of God in Jesus Christ, held forth in this sacrament; and exhort them
" to walk worthy of it."
The minister is to give solemn thanks to God,
" For his rich mercy, and invaluable goodness, vouchsafed to them in that sacrament;
" and to entreat for pardon for the defects of the whole service, and for the gracious as-
" sistance of his good Spirit, whereby they may be enabled to walk in the strength of
" that grace, as becometh those who have received so great pledges of salvation."
The collection for the poor is so to be ordered, that no part of the publick worship be thereby hindered.

Of the Sanctification of the Lord's day.

THE Lord's day ought to be so remembered before-hand, as that all worldly business of our ordinary callings may be so ordered, and so timely and seasonably laid aside, as they may not be impediments to the due sanctifying of the day when it comes.

The whole day is to be celebrated as holy to the Lord, both in publick and private, as being the Christian sabbath. To which end, it is requisite, that there be a holy cessation or resting all that day from all unnecessary labours; and an abstaining, not only from all sports and pastimes, but also from all worldly words and thoughts.

That the diet on that day be so ordered, as that neither servants be unnecessarily detained from the publick worship of God, nor any other person hindered from the sanctifying that day.

That there be private preparations of every person and family, by prayer for themselves, and for God's assistance of the minister, and for a blessing upon his ministry; and by such other holy exercises, as may further dispose them to a more comfortable communion with God in his public ordinances.

That all the people meet so timely for publick worship, that the whole congregation may be present at the beginning, and with one heart solemnly join together in all parts of the publick worship, and not depart till after the blessing.

That what time is vacant, between or after the solemn meetings of the congregation in publick, be spent in reading, meditation, repetition of sermons; especially by calling their families to an account of what they have heard, and catechising of them, holy conferences, prayer for a blessing upon the publick ordinances, singing of psalms, visiting the sick, relieving the poor, and such like duties of piety, charity, and mercy, accounting the sabbath a delight.

The Solemnization of Marriage.

ALTHOUGH marriage be no sacrament, nor peculiar to the church of God, but common to mankind, and of publick interest in every commonwealth; yet, because such as marry are to marry in the Lord, and have special need of instruction, direction, and exhortation, from the word of God, at their entering into such a new condition, and of the blessing of God upon them therein, we judge it expedient that marriage be solemnized by a lawful minister of the word, that he may accordingly counsel them, and pray for a blessing upon them.

Marriage is to be betwixt one man and one woman only; and they, such as are not within the degrees of consanguinity or affinity prohibited by the word of God; and the parties are to be of years of discretion, fit to make their own choice, or, upon good grounds, to give their mutual consent.

Before the solemnizing of marriage between any persons, their purpose of marriage shall be published by the minister three several sabbath-days, in the congregation, at the place or places of their most usual and constant abode, respectively. And of this publication the minister who is to join them in marriage shall have sufficient testimony, before he proceed to solemnize the marriage.

Before that publication of such their purpose, (if the parties be under age,) the consent of the parents, or others under whose power they are, (in case the parents be dead,) is to be made known to the church officers of that congregation, to be recorded.

The like is to be observed in the proceedings of all others, although of age, whose parents are living, for their first marriage.

And, in after marriages of either of those parties, they shall be exhorted not to contract marriage without first acquainting their parents with it, (if with conveniency it may be done,) endeavouring to obtain their consent.

Parents ought not to force their children to marry without their free consent, nor deny their own consent without just cause.

After the purpose or contract of marriage hath been thus published, the marriage is not to be long deferred. Therefore the minister, having had convenient warning, and nothing being objected to hinder it, is publickly to solemnize it in the place appointed by authority for publick worship, before a competent number of credible witnesses, at some convenient hour of the day, at any time of the year, except on a day of publick humiliation. And we advise that it be not on the Lord's day.

And because all relations are sanctified by the word and prayer, the minister is to pray for a blessing upon them, to this effect:

"Acknowledging our sins, whereby we have made ourselves less than the least of all " the mercies of God, and provoked him to embitter all our comforts ; earnestly, in the " name of Christ, to entreat the Lord (whose presence and favour is the happiness of " every condition, and sweetens every relation,) to be their portion, and to own and " accept them in Christ, who are now to be joined in the honourable estate of marriage, " the covenant of their God : and that, as he hath brought them together by his provi- " dence, he would sanctify them by his Spirit, giving them a new frame of heart fit for " their new estate ; enriching them with all graces whereby they may perform the duties, " enjoy the comforts, undergo the cares, and resist the temptations which accompany " that condition, as becometh Christians."

The prayer being ended, it is convenient that the minister do briefly declare unto them, out of the scripture,

"The institution, use, and ends of marriage, with the conjugal duties, which, in all " faithfulness, they are to perform each to other ; exhorting them to study the holy word " of God, that they may learn to live by faith, and to be content in the midst of all " marriage cares and troubles, sanctifying God's name, in a thankful, sober, and holy " use of all conjugal comforts ; praying much with and for one another ; watching over " and provoking each other to love and good works ; and to live together as the heirs of " the grace of life."

After solemn charging of the persons to be married, before the great God, who search- eth all hearts, and to whom they must give a strict account at the last day, that if either of them know any cause, by precontract or otherwise, why they may not lawfully proceed to marriage, that they now discover it ; the minister (if no impediment be acknowledged) shall cause first the man to take the woman by the right hand, saying these words :

I N. do take thee N. to be my married wife, and do, in the presence of God, and before this congregation, promise and covenant to be a loving and faithful husband unto thee, until God shall separate us by death.

Then the woman shall take the man by the right hand, and say these words :

I N. do take thee N. to be my married husband, and I do, in the presence of God, and before this congregation, promise and covenant to be a loving, faithful, and obedient wife unto thee, until God shall separate us by death.

Then, without any further ceremony, the minister shall, in the face of the congregation, pronounce them to be husband and wife, according to God's ordinance ; and so conclude the action with prayer to this effect :

"That the Lord would be pleased to accompany his own ordinance with his blessing, " beseeching him to enrich the persons now married, as with other pledges of his love, " so particularly with the comforts and fruits of marriage, to the praise of his abundant " mercy, in and through Christ Jesus."

A register is to be carefully kept, wherein the names of the parties so married, with the time of their marriage, are forthwith to be fairly recorded in a book provided for that purpose, for the perusal of all whom it may concern.

Concerning Visitation of the Sick.

IT is the duty of the minister not only to teach the people committed to his charge in pub- lick, but privately ; and particularly to admonish, exhort, reprove, and comfort them, upon all seasonable occasions, so far as his time, strength, and personal safety will permit.

He is to admonish them, in time of health, to prepare for death ; and, for that purpose, they are often to confer with their minister about the estate of their souls ; and, in times of sickness, to desire his advice and help, timely and seasonably, before their strength and understanding fail them.

Times of sickness and affliction are special opportunities put into his hand by God to minister a word in season to weary souls : because then the consciences of men are or should be more awakened to bethink themselves of their spiritual estate for eternity ; and Satan also takes advantage then to load them more with sore and heavy temptations : therefore the minister, being sent for, and repairing to the sick, is to apply himself, with all tenderness and love, to administer some spiritual good to his soul, to this effect.

He may, from the consideration of the present sickness, instruct him out of scripture, that diseases come not by chance, or by distempers of body only, but by the wise and orderly guidance of the good hand of God to every particular person smitten by them. And that, whether it be laid upon him out of displeasure for sin, for his correction and amendment, or for trial and exercise of his graces, or for other special and excellent ends, all his sufferings shall turn to his profit, and work together for his good, if he sincerely labour to make a sanctified use of God's visitation, neither despising his chastening, nor waxing weary of his correction.

If he suspect him of ignorance, he shall examine him in the principles of religion, especially touching repentance and faith ; and, as he seeth cause, instruct him in the nature, use, excellency, and necessity of those graces ; as also touching the covenant of grace ; and Christ the Son of God, the Mediator of it ; and concerning remission of sins by faith in him.

He shall exhort the sick person to examine himself, to search and try his former ways, and his estate towards God.

And if the sick person shall declare any scruple, doubt, or temptation that are upon him, instructions and resolutions shall be given to satisfy and settle him.

If it appear that he hath not a due sense of his sins, endeavours ought to be used to convince him of his sins, of the guilt and desert of them; of the filth and pollution which the soul contracts by them; and of the curse of the law, and wrath of God, due to them; that he may be truly affected with and humbled for them: and withal make known the danger of deferring repentance, and of neglecting salvation at any time offered; to awaken his conscience, and rouse him up out of a stupid and secure condition, to apprehend the justice and wrath of God, before whom none can stand, but he that, lost in himself, layeth hold upon Christ by faith.

If he hath endeavoured to walk in the ways of holiness, and to serve God in uprightness, although not without many failings and infirmities; or, if his spirit be broken with the sense of sin, or cast down through want of the sense of God's favour; then it will be fit to raise him up, by setting before him the freeness and fulness of God's grace, the sufficiency of righteousness in Christ, the gracious offers in the gospel, that all who repent, and believe with all their heart in God's mercy through Christ, renouncing their own righteousness, shall have life and salvation in him. It may be also useful to shew him, that death hath in it no spiritual evil to be feared by those that are in Christ, because sin, the sting of death, is taken away by Christ, who hath delivered all that are his from the bondage of the fear of death, triumphed over the grave, given us victory, is himself entered into glory to prepare a place for his people: so that neither life nor death shall be able to separate them from God's love in Christ, in whom such are sure, though now they must be laid in the dust, to obtain a joyful and glorious resurrection to eternal life.

Advice also may be given, as to beware of an ill-grounded persuasion on mercy, or on the goodness of his condition for heaven, so to disclaim all merit in himself, and to cast himself wholly upon God for mercy, in the sole merits and mediation of Jesus Christ, who hath engaged himself never to cast off them who in truth and sincerity come unto him. Care also must be taken, that the sick person be not cast down into despair, by such a severe representation of the wrath of God due to him for his sins, as is not mollified by a sensible propounding of Christ and his merit for a door of hope to every penitent believer.

When the sick person is best composed, may be least disturbed, and other necessary offices about him least hindered, the minister, if desired, shall pray with him, and for him, to this effect:

"Confessing and bewailing of sin original and actual; the miserable condition of all "by nature, as being children of wrath, and under the curse; acknowledging that all "diseases, sicknesses, death, and hell itself, are the proper issues and effects thereof; "imploring God's mercy for the sick person, through the blood of Christ; beseeching "that God would open his eyes, discover unto him his sins, cause him to see himself lost "in himself, make known to him the cause why God smiteth him, reveal Jesus Christ to "his soul for righteousness and life, give unto him his Holy Spirit, to create and "strengthen faith to lay hold upon Christ, to work in him comfortable evidences of his "love, to arm him against temptations, to take off his heart from the world, to sanctify "his present visitation, to furnish him with patience and strength to bear it, and to give "him perseverance in faith to the end.

"That, if God shall please to add to his days, he would vouchsafe to bless and sanctify "all means of his recovery; to remove the disease, renew his strength, and enable him to "walk worthy of God, by a faithful remembrance, and diligent observing of such vows and "promises of holiness and obedience, as men are apt to make in times of sickness, that "he may glorify God in the remaining part of his life.

"And, if God have determined to finish his days by the present visitation, he may find "such evidence of the pardon of all his sins, of his interest in Christ, and eternal life by "Christ, as may cause his inward man to be renewed, while his outward man decayeth; "that he may behold death without fear, cast himself wholly upon Christ without doubt-"ing, desire to be dissolved and to be with Christ, and so receive the end of his faith, "the salvation of his soul, through the only merits and intercession of the Lord Jesus "Christ, our alone Saviour and all-sufficient Redeemer."

The minister shall admonish him also (as there shall be cause) to set his house in order, thereby to prevent inconveniences; to take care for payment of his debts, and to make restitution or satisfaction where he hath done any wrong; to be reconciled to those with whom he hath been at variance, and fully to forgive all men their trespasses against him, as he expects forgiveness at the hand of God.

Lastly, The minister may improve the present occasion to exhort those about the sick person to consider their own mortality, to return to the Lord, and make peace with him; in health to prepare for sickness, death, and judgment; and all the days of their appointed time so to wait until their change come, that when Christ, who is our life, shall appear, they may appear with him in glory.

Concerning Burial of the Dead.

WHEN any person departeth this life, let the dead body, upon the day of burial, be decently attended from the house to the place appointed for publick burial, and there immediately interred, without any ceremony.

And because the custom of kneeling down, and praying by or towards the dead corpse, and other such usages, in the place where it lies before it be carried to burial, are superstitious; and for that praying, reading, and singing, both in going to and at the grave, have been grossly abused, are no way beneficial to the dead, and have proved many ways hurtful to the living; therefore let all such things be laid aside.

Howbeit, we judge it very convenient, that the Christian friends, which accompany the dead body to the place appointed for publick burial, do apply themselves to meditations and conferences suitable to the occasion; and that the minister, as upon other occasions, so at this time, if he be present, may put them in remembrance of their duty.

That this shall not extend to deny any civil respects or deferences at the burial, suitable to the rank and condition of the party deceased, while he was living.

Concerning Publick Solemn Fasting.

WHEN some great and notable judgments are either inflicted upon a people, or apparently imminent, or by some extraordinary provocations notoriously deserved; as also when some special blessing is to be sought and obtained, publick solemn fasting (which is to continue the whole day) is a duty that God expecteth from that nation or people.

A religious fast requires total abstinence, not only from all food, (unless bodily weakness do manifestly disable from holding out till the fast be ended, in which case somewhat may be taken, yet very sparingly, to support nature, when ready to faint,) but also from all worldly labour, discourses, and thoughts, and from all bodily delights, and such like, (although at other times lawful,) rich apparel, ornaments, and such like, during the fast; and much more from whatever is in the nature or use scandalous and offensive, as gaudish attire, lascivious habits and gestures, and other vanities of either sex; which we recommend to all ministers, in their places, diligently and zealously to reprove, as at other times, so especially at a fast, without respect of persons, as there shall be occasion.

Before the publick meeting, each family and person apart are privately to use all religious care to prepare their hearts to such a solemn work, and to be early at the congregation.

So large a portion of the day as conveniently may be, is to be spent in publick reading and preaching of the word, with singing of psalms, fit to quicken affections suitable to such a duty: but especially in prayer, to this or the like effect:

"Giving glory to the great Majesty of God, the Creator, Preserver, and supreme Ruler
" of all the world, the better to affect us thereby with an holy reverence and awe of him;
" acknowledging his manifold, great, and tender mercies, especially to the church and
" nation, the more effectually to soften and abase our hearts before him; humbly con-
" fessing of sins of all sorts, with their several aggravations; justifying God's righteous
" judgments, as being far less than our sins do deserve; yet humbly and earnestly im-
" ploring his mercy and grace for ourselves, the church and nation, for our king, and all
" in authority, and for all others for whom we are bound to pray, (according as the pre-
" sent exigent requireth,) with more special importunity and enlargement than at other
" times; applying by faith the promises and goodness of God for pardon, help, and deliver-
" ance from the evils felt, feared, or deserved; and for obtaining the blessings which we need
" and expect; together with a giving up of ourselves wholly and for ever unto the Lord."

In all these, the ministers, who are the mouths of the people unto God, ought so to speak from their hearts, upon serious and thorough premeditation of them, that both themselves and their people may be much affected, and even melted thereby, especially with sorrow for their sins; that it may be indeed a day of deep humiliation and afflicting of the soul.

Special choice is to be made of such scriptures to be read, and of such texts for preaching, as may best work the hearts of the hearers to the special business of the day, and most dispose them to humiliation and repentance: insisting most on those particulars which each minister's observation and experience tells him are most conducing to the edification and reformation of that congregation to which he preacheth.

Before the close of the publick duties, the minister is, in his own and the people's name, to engage his and their hearts to be the Lord's, with professed purpose and resolution to reform whatever is amiss among them, and more particularly such sins as they have been more remarkably guilty of; and to draw near unto God, and to walk more closely and faithfully with him in new obedience, than ever before.

He is also to admonish the people, with all importunity, that the work of that day doth not end with the publick duties of it, but that they are so to improve the remainder of the day, and of their whole life, in reinforcing upon themselves and their families in private all those godly affections and resolutions which they professed in publick, as that they may be settled in their hearts for ever, and themselves may more sensibly find that God hath smelt a sweet savour in Christ from their performances, and is pacified towards them, by answers of grace, in pardoning of sin, in removing of judgments, in averting or preventing of plagues, and in conferring of blessings, suitable to the conditions and prayers of his people, by Jesus Christ.

Besides solemn and general fasts enjoined by authority, we judge that, at other times, congregations may keep days of fasting, as divine providence shall administer unto them special occasion; and also that families may do the same, so it be not on days wherein the congregation to which they do belong is to meet for fasting, or other publick duties of worship.

Concerning the Observation of Days of Publick Thanksgiving.

WHEN any such day is to be kept, let notice be given of it, and of the occasion thereof, some convenient time before, that the people may the better prepare themselves thereunto.

The day being come, and the congregation (after private preparations) being assembled, the minister is to begin with a word of exhortation, to stir up the people to the duty for which they are met, and with a short prayer for God's assistance and blessing, (as at other conventions for publick worship,) according to the particular occasion of their meeting.

Let him then make some pithy narration of the deliverance obtained, or mercy received, or of whatever hath occasioned that assembling of the congregation, that all may better understand it, or be minded of it, and more affected with it.

And, because singing of psalms is of all other the most proper ordinance for expressing of joy and thanksgiving, let some pertinent psalm or psalms be sung for that purpose, before or after the reading of some portion of the word suitable to the present business.

Then let the minister, who is to preach, proceed to further exhortation and prayer before his sermon, with special reference to the present work: after which, let him preach upon some text of Scripture pertinent to the occasion.

The sermon ended, let him not only pray, as at other times after preaching is directed, with remembrance of the necessities of the Church, King, and State, (if before the sermon they were omitted,) but enlarge himself in due and solemn thanksgiving for former mercies and deliverances; but more especially for that which at the present calls them together to give thanks: with humble petition for the continuance and renewing of God's wonted mercies, as need shall be, and for sanctifying grace to make a right use thereof. And so, having sung another psalm, suitable to the mercy, let him dismiss the congregation with a blessing, that they may have some convenient time for their repast and refreshing.

But the minister (before their dismission) is solemnly to admonish them to beware of all excess and riot, tending to gluttony or drunkenness, and much more of these sins themselves, in their eating and refreshing; and to take care that their mirth and rejoicing be not carnal, but spiritual, which may make God's praise to be glorious, and themselves humble and sober; and that both their feeding and rejoicing may render them more cheerful and enlarged, further to celebrate his praises in the midst of the congregation, when they return unto it in the remaining part of that day.

When the congregation shall be again assembled, the like course in praying, reading, preaching, singing of psalms, and offering up of more praise and thanksgiving, that is before directed for the morning, is to be renewed and continued, so far as the time will give leave.

At one or both of the publick meetings that day, a collection is to be made for the poor, (and in the like manner upon the day of publick humiliation,) that their loins may bless us, and rejoice the more with us. And the people are to be exhorted, at the end of the latter meeting, to spend the residue of that day in holy duties, and testifications of Christian love and charity one towards another, and of rejoicing more and more in the Lord; as becometh those who make the joy of the Lord their strength.

Of Singing of Psalms.

IT is the duty of Christians to praise God publickly, by singing of psalms together in the congregation, and also privately in the family.

In singing of psalms, the voice is to be tunably and gravely ordered; but the chief care must be to sing with understanding, and with grace in the heart, making melody unto the Lord.

That the whole congregation may join herein, every one that can read is to have a psalm book; and all others, not disabled by age or otherwise, are to be exhorted to learn to read. But for the present, where many in the congregation cannot read, it is convenient that the minister, or some other fit person appointed by him and the other ruling officers, do read the psalm, line by line, before the singing thereof.

AN APPENDIX,

Touching Days and Places for Publick Worship.

THERE is no day commanded in scripture to be kept holy under the gospel but the Lord's day, which is the Christian Sabbath.

Festival days, vulgarly called *Holy-days*, having no warrant in the word of God, are not to be continued.

Nevertheless, it is lawful and necessary, upon special emergent occasions, to separate a day or days for publick fasting or thanksgiving, as the several eminent and extraordinary dispensations of God's providence shall administer cause and opportunity to his people.

As no place is capable of any holiness, under pretence of whatsoever dedication or consecration; so neither is it subject to such pollution by any superstition formerly used, and now laid aside, as may render it unlawful or inconvenient for Christians to meet together therein for the publick worship of God. And therefore we hold it requisite, that the places of publick assembling for worship among us should be continued and employed to that use.

THE FORM

OF

PRESBYTERIAL CHURCH-GOVERNMENT

AND OF

ORDINATION OF MINISTERS;

AGREED UPON BY THE ASSEMBLY OF DIVINES AT WESTMINSTER, WITH THE
ASSISTANCE OF COMMISSIONERS FROM THE CHURCH OF SCOTLAND,
AS A PART OF THE COVENANTED UNIFORMITY IN RELIGION
BETWIXT THE CHURCHES OF CHRIST IN THE KINGDOMS
OF SCOTLAND, ENGLAND, AND IRELAND:

WITH

AN ACT OF THE GENERAL ASSEMBLY, ANNO 1645, APPROVING
THE SAME.

EZEK. xliii. 11.—And if they be ashamed of all that they have done, shew them the form of the house, and the fashion thereof, and the goings out thereof, and the comings in thereof, and all the forms thereof,—and all the laws thereof: and write it in their sight, that they may keep the whole form thereof, and all the ordinances thereof, and do them.

CONTENTS.

The Preface.
Of the Church.
Of the Officers of the Church.
Pastors.
Other Church-governors.
Deacons.
Of particular Congregations.
Of the Officers of a particular Congregation.
Of the Ordinances in a particular Congregation.
Of Church-government, and the several sorts of Assemblies for the same.
Of the power in common of all these Assemblies.
Of Congregational Assemblies, that is, the Meeting of the ruling Officers of a particular Congregation, for the government thereof.
Of Classical Assemblies.
Of Synodical Assemblies.
Of Ordination of Ministers.
Touching the Doctrine of Ordination.
Touching the Power of Ordination.
Concerning the Doctrinal Part of the Ordination of Ministers.
The Directory for the Ordination of Ministers.

ASSEMBLY AT EDINBURGH, February 10, 1645. Sess. 16.

ACT *of the* GENERAL ASSEMBLY *of the* KIRK *of* SCOTLAND, *approving the Propositions concerning Kirk-government, and Ordination of Ministers.*

THE General Assembly being most desirous and solicitous, not only of the establishment and preservation of the Form of Kirk-government in this kingdom, according to the word of God, books of Discipline, acts of General Assemblies, and National Covenant, but also of an uniformity in Kirk-government betwixt these kingdoms, now more straitly and strongly united by the late Solemn League and Covenant; and considering, that as in former times there did, so hereafter there may arise, through the nearness of contagion, manifold mischiefs to this kirk from a corrupt form of government in the kirk of England: likeas the precious opportunity of bringing the kirks of Christ in all the three kingdoms to an uniformity in Kirk-government being the happiness of the present times above the former; which may also, by the blessing of God, prove an effectual mean, and a good foundation to prepare for a safe and well-grounded pacification, by removing the cause from which the present pressures and bloody wars did originally proceed: and now the Assembly having thrice read, and diligently examined, the propositions (hereunto annexed) concerning the officers, assemblies, and government of the kirk, and concerning the ordination of ministers, brought unto us, as the results of the long and learned debates of the Assembly of Divines sitting at Westminster, and of the treaty of uniformity with the Commissioners of this kirk there residing; after mature deliberation, and after timeous calling upon, and warning of all, who have any exceptions against the same, to make them known, that they might receive satisfaction; doth agree to and approve the propositions afore-mentioned, touching Kirk-government and Ordination; and doth hereby authorize the Commissioners of this Assembly, who are to meet at Edinburgh, to agree to and conclude in the name of this Assembly, an uniformity betwixt the kirks in both kingdoms, in the afore-mentioned particulars, so soon as the same shall be ratified, without any substantial alteration, by an ordinance of the honourable Houses of the Parliament of England; which ratification shall be timely intimate and made known by the Commissioners of this kirk residing at London. Provided always, That this act be no ways prejudicial to the further discussion and examination of that article which holds forth, That the doctor or teacher hath power of the administration of the sacraments, as well as the pastor; as also of the distinct rights and interests of presbyteries and people in the calling of ministers; but that it shall be free to debate and discuss these points, as God shall be pleased to give further light.

THE FORM

OF

PRESBYTERIAL CHURCH-GOVERNMENT.

THE PREFACE.

JESUS CHRIST, upon whose shoulders the government is, whose name is called Wonderful, Counsellor, The mighty God, The everlasting Father, The Prince of Peace;[a] of the increase of whose government and peace there shall be no end; who sits upon the throne of David, and upon his kingdom, to order it, and to establish it with judgment and justice, from henceforth, even for ever; having all power given unto him in heaven and in earth by the Father, who raised him from the dead, and set him at his own right hand, far above all principalities and power, and might, and dominion, and every name that is named, not only in this world, but also in that which is to come, and put all things under his feet, and gave him to be the head over all things to the church, which is his body, the fulness of him that filleth all in all: he being ascended up far above all heavens, that he might fill all things, received gifts for his church, and gave officers necessary for the edification of his church, and perfecting of his saints.[b]

[a] Isa. ix. 6, 7.
[b] Matt. xxviii. 18, 19, 20. Eph. i. 20, 21, 22, 23. Compared with Eph. iv. 8, 11, and Ps. lxviii. 18.

Of the Church.

THERE is one general church visible, held forth in the New Testament.[a]

The ministry, oracles, and ordinances of the New Testament, are given by Jesus Christ to the general church visible, for the gathering and perfecting of it in this life, until his second coming.[b]

Particular visible churches, members of the general church, are also held forth in the New Testament.[c] Particular churches in the primi-

[a] 1 Cor. xii. 12. For as the body is one, and hath many members, and all the members of that one body, being many, are one body; *so also is Christ.* Ver. 13. For by one Spirit are we all baptized into one body, whether we be Jews or Gentiles, whether we be bond or free; and have been *all made to drink into one Spirit.* Ver. 28. And God hath set some in the church, first, apostles; secondarily, prophets; thirdly, teachers; after that miracles; then gifts of healings, helps, governments, diversities of tongues. [Together with the rest of the Chapter.]

[b] 1 Cor. xii. 12. [See before.] Eph. iv. 4. There is one body, and one Spirit, even as ye are called in one hope of your calling; Ver. 5. One Lord, one faith, one baptism. Compared with Ver. 10. He that descended is the same also that ascended up far above all heavens, that he might fill all things. Ver. 11. And he gave some, apostles; and some, prophets; and some, evangelists; and some, pastors and teachers; Ver. 12. *For the perfecting of the saints, for the work of the ministry, for the edifying of the body of Christ:* Ver. 13. Till we all come *in the unity of the faith,* and of the knowledge of the Son of God, unto a perfect man, unto the measure of the stature of the fulness of Christ. Ver. 15. But, speaking the truth in love, may grow up into him in all things, which is the head, even Christ: Ver. 16. From whom the whole body fitly joined together and compacted by that which every joint supplieth, according to the effectual working in the measure of every part, maketh increase of the body, unto the edifying of itself in love.

[c] Gal. i. 21. Afterwards I came into the regions of Syria and Cilicia; Ver. 22. And was unknown by face unto *the churches of Judea* which were in Christ. Rev. i. 4. John to *the seven churches which are in Asia:* Grace be unto you, and peace, from him

tive times were made up of visible saints, *viz.* of such as, being of age, professed faith in Christ, and obedience unto Christ, according to the rules of faith and life taught by Christ and his apostles; and of their children.[d]

Of the Officers of the Church.

THE officers which Christ hath appointed for the edification of his church, and the perfecting of the saints, are, some extraordinary, as apostles, evangelists, and prophets, which are ceased.

Others ordinary and perpetual, as pastors, teachers, and other church-governors, and deacons.

Pastors.

THE pastor is an ordinary and perpetual officer in the church,[e] prophesying of the time of the gospel.[f]

First, it belongs to his office,

To pray for and with his flock, as the mouth of the people unto which is, and which was, and which is to come; and from the seven Spirits which are before his throne. Ver. 20. The mystery of the seven stars which thou sawest in my right hand, and the seven golden candlesticks. The seven stars are the angels of the seven churches; and the seven candlesticks which thou sawest are the seven churches. Rev. ii. 1. Unto the angel of *the church of Ephesus* write; These things saith he that holdeth the seven stars in his right hand, who walketh in the midst of the seven golden candlesticks.

[d] Acts ii. 38. Then Peter said unto them, Repent, and be baptized every one of you in the name of Jesus Christ for the remission of sins, and ye shall receive the gift of the Holy Ghost. Ver. 41. Then *they that gladly received his word* were baptized: and the same day there were added unto them about three thousand souls. Ver. 47. Praising God, and having favour with all the people. And the Lord added to the church daily *such as should be saved.* Compared with Acts v. 14. And believers were the more added to the Lord, multitudes both of men and women. 1 Cor. i. 2. Unto the church of God which is at Corinth, to them that are sanctified in Christ Jesus, called to be saints, with all that in every place call upon the name of Jesus Christ our Lord, both theirs and ours. Compared with 2 Cor. ix. 13. Whilst by the experiment of this ministration, they glorify God for *your professed subjection unto the gospel* of Christ, and for your liberal distribution unto them, and unto all men. Acts ii. 39. For the promise is unto you, and to your *children*, and to all that are afar off, even as many as the Lord our God shall call. 1 Cor. vii. 14. For the unbelieving husband is sanctified by the wife, and the unbelieving wife is sanctified by the husband: else were your *children* unclean; but now are they *holy.* Rom. xi. 16. For if the first-fruit be holy, the lump is also holy; and if the root be holy, so are the branches. Mark x. 14. But when Jesus saw it, he was much displeased, and said unto them, Suffer the *little children* to come unto me, and forbid them not: for of such is the kingdom of God. Compared with Matt. xix. 13. Then were there brought unto him *little children*, that he should put his hands on them, and pray: and the disciples rebuked them. Ver. 14. But Jesus said, Suffer *little children*, and forbid them not, to come unto me; for of such is the kingdom of heaven. Luke xviii. 15. And they brought unto him also *infants*, that he would touch them: but when his disciples saw it, they rebuked them. Ver. 16. But Jesus called them unto him, and said, Suffer *little children* to come unto me, and forbid them not: for of such is the kingdom of God.

[e] Jer. iii. 15. And I will give you *pastors* according to mine heart, which shall feed you with knowledge and understanding. Ver. 16. And it shall come to pass, when ye be multiplied and increased in the land, in those days, saith the Lord, they shall say no more, The ark of the covenant of the Lord; neither shall it come to mind, neither shall they remember it, neither shall they visit it, neither shall that be done any more. Ver. 17. At that time they shall call Jerusalem the throne of the Lord; and all the nations shall be gathered unto it, to the name of the Lord, to Jerusalem: neither shall they walk any more after the imagination of their evil heart.

[f] 1 Pet. v. 2. *Feed the flock of God* which is among you, taking the oversight thereof, not by constraint, but willingly; not for filthy lucre, but of a ready mind; Ver. 3. Neither as being lords over God's heritage, but being ensamples to the flock: Ver. 4. And when the chief Shepherd shall appear, ye shall receive a crown of glory that fadeth not away. Eph. iv. 11. And he gave some, apostles; and some, prophets; and some, evangelists; and some, *pastors and teachers;* Ver. 12. For the perfecting of the saints, for the work of the ministry, for the edifying of the body of Christ: Ver. 13. Till we all come in the unity of the faith, and of the knowledge of the Son of God, unto a perfect man, unto the measure of the stature of the fulness of Christ.

God,g Acts vi. 2, 3, 4, and xx. 36, where preaching and prayer are joined as several parts of the same office.h The office of the elder (that is, the pastor) is to pray for the sick, even in private, to which a blessing is especially promised; much more therefore ought he to perform this in the publick execution of his office, as a part thereof.i

To read the scriptures publickly; for the proof of which,

1. That the priests and Levites in the Jewish church were trusted with the publick reading of the word is proved.k

2. That the ministers of the gospel have as ample a charge and commission to dispense the word, as well as other ordinances, as the priests and Levites had under the law, proved, Isa. lxvi. 21. Matt. xxiii. 34. where our Saviour entitleth the officers of the New Testament, whom he will send forth, by the same names of the teachers of the Old.l

Which propositions prove, that therefore (the duty being of a moral nature) it followeth by just consequence, that the publick reading of the scriptures belongeth to the pastor's office.

To feed the flock, by preaching of the word, according to which he is to teach, convince, reprove, exhort, and comfort.m

To catechise, which is a plain laying down the first principles of the oracles of God,n or of the doctrine of Christ, and is a part of preaching.

To dispense other divine mysteries.o

g Acts vi. 2. Then the twelve called the multitude of the disciples unto them, and said, *It is not reason that we should leave the word of God*, and serve tables. Ver. 3. Wherefore, brethren, look ye out among you seven men of honest report, full of the Holy Ghost and wisdom, whom we may appoint over this business. Ver. 4. But we will give ourselves continually to prayer, and to *the ministry of the word*. Acts xx. 36. And when he had thus spoken, he kneeled down, and prayed with them all.

h James v. 14. Is any sick among you? let him call for the elders of the church; and *let them pray over him*, anointing him with oil in the name of the Lord: Ver. 15. And the prayer of faith shall save the sick, and the Lord shall raise him up; and if he have committed sins, they shall be forgiven him.

i 1 Cor. xiv. 15. What is it then? I will pray with the spirit, and *I will pray with the understanding also; I* will sing with the spirit, and I will sing with the understanding also. Ver. 16. Else, when thou shalt bless with the spirit, how shall he that occupieth the room of the unlearned say Amen at thy giving of thanks, seeing he understandeth not what thou sayest?

k Deut. xxxi. 9. And Moses wrote this law, and *delivered it unto the priests* the sons of Levi, which bare the ark of the covenant of the Lord, and unto all the elders of Israel. Ver. 10. And Moses commanded them, saying, At the end of every seven years, in the solemnity of the year of release, in the feast of tabernacles, Ver. 11. When all Israel is come to appear before the Lord thy God in the place which he shall choose, *thou shalt read this law before all Israel in their hearing.* Neh. viii. 1. And all the people gathered themselves together as one man into the street that was before the water-gate; and they spake unto Ezra the scribe to bring the book of the law of Moses, which the Lord had commanded to Israel. Ver. 2. And Ezra the priest brought the law before the congregation, both of men and women, and all that could hear with understanding, upon the first day of the seventh month. Ver. 3. And *he read therein*—Ver. 13. And on the second day were gathered together the chief of the fathers of all the people, the priests, and the Levites, unto Ezra the scribe, even to understand the words of the law.

l Isa. lxvi. 21. And I will also take of them for *priests*, and for Levites, saith the Lord. Matt. xxiii. 34. Wherefore, behold, I send unto you *prophets*, and wise men, and scribes; and some of them ye shall kill and crucify; and some of them shall ye scourge in your synagogues, and persecute them from city to city.

m 1 Tim. iii. 2. A bishop then must be blameless, the husband of one wife, vigilant, sober, of good behaviour, given to hospitality, *apt to teach*. 2 Tim. iii. 16. All scripture is given by inspiration of God, and is *profitable for doctrine*, for reproof, for correction, for instruction in righteousness; Ver. 17. That the man of God may be perfect, throughly furnished unto all good works. Tit. i. 9. Holding fast the faithful word as he hath been taught, that he may be *able* by sound doctrine both *to exhort* and *to convince* the gainsayers.

n Heb. v. 12. For when for the time ye ought to be teachers, *ye have need that one teach you again* which be the first principles of the oracles of God; and are become such as have need of milk, and not of strong meat.

o 1 Cor. iv. 1. Let a man so account of us as of the ministers of Christ, and *stewards of the mysteries of God*. Ver. 2. Moreover, it is required in stewards, that a man be found faithful.

To administer the sacraments.p

To bless the people from God, Numb. vi. 23, 24, 25, 26. Compared with Rev. xiv. 5, (where the same blessings, and persons from whom they come, are expressly mentioned,q) Isa. lxvi. 21, where, under the names of Priests and Levites to be continued under the gospel, are meant evangelical pastors, who therefore are by office to bless the people.r

To take care of the poor.s

And he hath also a ruling power over the flock as a pastor.t

p Matt. xxviii. 19. Go ye therefore, and teach all nations, *baptising* them in the name of the Father, and of the Son, and of the Holy Ghost; Ver. 20. Teaching them to observe all things whatsoever I have commanded you: and, lo, I am with you alway, even unto the end of the world. Amen. Mark xvi. 15. And he said unto them, Go ye into all the world, and preach the gospel to every creature. Ver. 16. He that believeth, and is baptized, shall be saved; but he that believeth not shall be damned. 1 Cor. xi. 23. For *I have received of the Lord that which also I delivered unto you*, That the Lord Jesus, the same night in which he was betrayed, took bread. Ver. 24. And, when he had given thanks, he brake it, and said, Take, eat; this is my body, which is broken for you: this do in remembrance of me. Ver. 25. After the same manner also he took the cup, when he had supped, saying, This cup is the new testament in my blood: this do ye, as oft as ye drink it, in remembrance of me. Compared with 1 Cor. x. 16. The cup of blessing which *we bless*, is it not the communion of the blood of Christ? The bread which *we break*, is it not the communion of the body of Christ?

q Num. vi. 23. Speak unto Aaron, and unto his sons, saying, On this wise *ye shall bless the children of Israel*, saying unto them, Ver. 24. *The Lord bless thee, and keep thee;* Ver. 25. The Lord make his face shine upon thee,—Ver. 26. The Lord lift up his countenance upon thee, and give thee peace. Compared with Rev. i. 4. John to the seven churches which are in Asia: *Grace be unto you, and peace, from him which is, and which was, and which is to come;* and from the seven Spirits which are before his throne; Ver. 5. And from Jesus Christ, who is the faithful Witness, and the first-begotten of the dead, and the Prince of the kings of the earth. Isa. lxvi. 21. And I will also take of them for priests, and for Levites, saith the Lord.

r Deut. x. 8. At that time the Lord separated the tribe of Levi, to bear the ark of the covenant of the Lord, to stand before the Lord to minister unto him, and to *bless in his name*, unto this day. 2 Cor. xiii. 14. *The grace of the Lord Jesus Christ, and the love of God, and the communion of the Holy Ghost, be with you all.* Amen. Eph. i. 2. *Grace be to you,* and peace, from God our Father, and from the Lord Jesus Christ.

s Acts xi. 30. *Which also they did,* and sent it to the elders by the hands of Barnabas and Saul. Acts iv. 34. Neither was there any among them that lacked: for as many as were possessors of lands or houses sold them, and brought the prices of the things that were sold, Ver. 35. And laid them down at the apostles' feet: and *distribution was made unto every man according as he had need.* Ver. 36. And Joses, who by the apostles was surnamed Barnabas, (which is, being interpreted, The son of consolation,) a Levite, and of the country of Cyprus, Ver. 37. Having land, sold it, and brought the money, and laid it at the apostles' feet. Acts vi. 2. Then the twelve called the multitude of the disciples unto them, and said, It is not reason that we should leave the word of God, and serve tables. Ver. 3. Wherefore, brethren, look ye out among you seven men of honest report, full of the Holy Ghost and wisdom, whom we may appoint over this business. Ver. 4. But we will give ourselves continually to prayer, and to the ministry of the word. 1 Cor. xvi. 1. Now *concerning the collection for the saints, as I have given order to the churches of Galatia,* even so do ye. Ver. 2. Upon the first day of the week let every one of you lay by him in store, as God hath prospered him, that there be no gatherings when I come. Ver. 3. And when I come, whomsoever ye shall approve by your letters, them *will I send to bring your liberality* unto Jerusalem. Ver. 4. And if it be meet that I go also, they shall go with me. Gal. ii. 9. And when James, Cephas, and John, who seemed to be pillars, perceived the grace that was given unto me, they gave to me and Barnabas the right hands of fellowship; that we should go unto the heathen, and they unto the circumcision. Ver. 10. Only they would that *we should remember the poor;* the same which I also was forward to do.

t 1 Tim. v. 17. Let the elders that *rule* well be counted worthy of double honour, especially they who labour in the word and doctrine. Acts xx. 17. And from Miletus he sent to Ephesus, and called the elders of the church. Ver. 28. Take heed therefore unto yourselves, and to all *the flock, over the which the Holy Ghost hath made you overseers*, to feed the church of God, which he hath purchased with his own blood. 1 Thess. v. 12. And we beseech you, brethren, to know them which labour among you, and *are over you* in the Lord, and admonish you. Heb. xiii. 7. Remember them which have *the rule over you,* who have spoken unto you the word of God; whose faith follow, considering the end of their conversation. Ver. 17. Obey them that have *the rule over you,* and submit yourselves:

Teacher or Doctor.

THE scripture doth hold out the name and title of teacher, as well as of the pastor.ᵛ

Who is also a minister of the word, as well as the pastor, and hath power of administration of the sacraments.

The Lord having given different gifts, and divers exercises according to these gifts, in the ministry of the word;ʷ though these different gifts may meet in, and accordingly be exercised by, one and the same minister;ˣ yet, where be several ministers in the same congregation, they may be designed to several employments, according to the different gifts in which each of them doth most excel.ʸ And he that doth more excel in exposition of scripture, in teaching sound doctrine, and in convincing gainsayers, than he doth in application, and is accordingly employed therein, may be called a teacher, or doctor, (the places alleged by the notation of the word do prove the proposition.) Nevertheless, where is but one minister in a particular congregation, he is to perform, as far as he is able, the whole work of the ministry.ᶻ

A teacher, or doctor, is of most excellent use in schools and universities; as of old in the schools of the prophets, and at Jerusalem, where Gamaliel and others taught as doctors.

Other Church-Governors.

AS there were in the Jewish church elders of the people joined with the priests and Levites in the government of the church;ᵃ so for they watch for your souls, as they that must give account; that they may do it with joy, and not with grief: for that is unprofitable for you.

ᵛ 1 Cor. xii. 28. And God hath set some in the church, first, apostles; secondarily, prophets; thirdly, *teachers;* after that miracles; then gifts of healings, helps, governments, diversities of tongues. Eph. iv. 11. And he gave some, apostles; and some, prophets; and some, evangelists; and some, pastors and teachers.

ʷ Rom. xii. 6. Having then *gifts, differing* according to the grace that is given to us, whether prophecy, let us prophesy according to the proportion of faith; Ver. 7. Or ministry, let us wait on our ministering; or he that teacheth, on teaching; Ver. 8. Or he that exhorteth, on exhortation: he that giveth, let him do it with simplicity; he that ruleth, with diligence; he that sheweth mercy, with cheerfulness. 1 Cor. xii. 1. Now concerning spiritual gifts, brethren, I would not have you ignorant. Ver. 4. Now there are *diversities of gifts,* but the same Spirit. Ver. 5. And there are *differences of administrations,* but the same Lord. Ver. 6. And there are diversities of operations, but it is the same God which worketh all in all. Ver. 7. But the manifestation of the Spirit is given to every man to profit withal.

ˣ 1 Cor. xiv. 3. But he that *prophesieth* speaketh unto men, to edification, and exhortation, and comfort. 2 Tim. iv. 2. *Preach* the word; be instant in season, out of season; *reprove, rebuke, exhort,* with all long-suffering and doctrine. Tit. i. 9. Holding fast the faithful word as he hath been taught, that he may be able by sound doctrine both to *exhort* and to *convince* the gainsayers.

ʸ [See in letter w immediately preceding.] 1 Pet. iv. 10. *As every man hath received the gift,* even so minister the same one to another, as good stewards of the manifold grace of God. Ver. 11. If any man *speak,* let him speak as the oracles of God; if any man *minister,* let him do it as of the ability which God giveth; that God in all things may be glorified through Jesus Christ: to whom be praise and dominion for ever and ever. Amen.

ᶻ 2 Tim. iv. 2. *Preach* the word; be instant in season, out of season; *reprove, rebuke, exhort,* with all long-suffering and doctrine. Tit. i. 9. Holding fast the faithful word as he hath been taught, that he may be able by sound doctrine both to *exhort* and to *convince* the gainsayers. 1 Tim. vi. 2. And they that have believing masters, let them not despise them, because they are brethren; but rather do them service, because they are faithful and beloved, partakers of the benefit. These things *teach* and *exhort.*

ᵃ 2 Chron. xix. 8. Moreover, in Jerusalem did Jehoshaphat set *of the Levites, and of the priests, and of the chief of the fathers of Israel,* for the judgment of the Lord, and for controversies, when they returned to Jerusalem. Ver. 9. And he charged them, saying, Thus shall ye do in the fear of the Lord, faithfully, and with a perfect heart. Ver. 10. And what cause soever shall come to you of your brethren that dwell in their

Christ, who hath instituted government, and governors ecclesiastical in the church, hath furnished some in his church, beside the ministers of the word, with gifts for government, and with commission to execute the same when called thereunto, who are to join with the minister in the government of the church.[b] Which officers reformed churches commonly call Elders.

Deacons.

THE scripture doth hold out deacons as distinct officers in the church.[c]

Whose office is perpetual.[d] To whose office it belongs not to preach the word, or administer the sacraments, but to take special care in distributing to the necessities of the poor.[e]

Of Particular Congregations.

IT is lawful and expedient that there be fixed congregations, that is, a certain company of Christians to meet in one assembly ordinarily for publick worship. When believers multiply to such a number, that they cannot conveniently meet in one place, it is lawful and expedient that they should be divided into distinct and fixed congregations, for the better administration of such ordinances as belong unto them, and the discharge of mutual duties.[f]

The ordinary way of dividing Christians into distinct congregations, and most expedient for edification, is by the respective bounds of their dwellings.

First, Because they who dwell together, being bound to all kind of moral duties one to another, have the better opportunity thereby to discharge them; which moral tie is perpetual; for Christ came not to destroy the law, but to fulfil it.[g]

---

cities, between blood and blood, between law and commandment, statutes and judgments, ye shall even warn them that they trespass not against the Lord, and so wrath come upon you, and upon your brethren: this do, and ye shall not trespass.

[b] Rom. xii. 7. Or ministry, let us wait on our ministering; or he that teacheth, on teaching; Ver. 8. Or he that exhorteth, on exhortation: he that giveth, let him do it with simplicity; *he that ruleth*, with diligence; he that sheweth mercy, with cheerfulness. 1 Cor. xii. 28. And God hath set some in the church, first, apostles; secondarily, *prophets;* thirdly, *teachers;* after that miracles; then gifts of healings, *helps*, *governments*, diversities of tongues.

[c] Phil. i. 1. Paul and Timotheus, the servants of Jesus Christ, to all the saints in Christ Jesus which are at Philippi, with the bishops and *deacons*. 1 Tim. iii. 8. Likewise must the *deacons* be grave, not double tongued, not given to much wine, not greedy of filthy lucre.

[d] 1 Tim. iii. 8. Likewise must the *deacons* be grave, not double tongued, not given to much wine, not greedy of filthy lucre. [See in the Bible to Ver. 13.] Acts vi. 1. And in those days, when the number of the disciples was multiplied, there arose a murmuring of the Grecians against the Hebrews, because their widows were neglected in the daily ministration. Ver. 2. Then the twelve called the multitude of the disciples unto them, and said, It is not reason that we should leave the word of God, and serve tables. Ver. 3. Wherefore, brethren, look ye out among you seven men of honest report, full of the Holy Ghost and wisdom, whom we may appoint over this business. Ver. 4. But we will give ourselves continually to prayer, and to the ministry of the word.

[e] Acts vi. 1–4. [See before in letter d.]

[f] 1 Cor. xiv. 26. *Let all things be done unto edifying.* Ver. 33. For God is not the author of confusion, but of peace, as in all churches of the saints. Ver. 40. *Let all things be done decently*, and in order.

[g] Deut. xv. 7. If there be among you a poor man of one of thy brethren within any of thy gates, in thy land which the Lord thy God giveth thee, *thou shalt not harden thine heart, nor shut thine hand from thy poor brother.* Ver. 11. For the poor shall never cease out of the land: therefore I command thee, saying, Thou shalt open thine hand wide unto thy brother, to thy poor, and to thy needy, in thy land. Matt. xxii. 39. And the second is like unto it, *Thou shalt love thy neighbour as thyself.* Matt. v. 17. Think not that I am come to destroy the law or the prophets: I am not come to destroy, but to fulfil.

Secondly, The communion of saints must be so ordered, as may stand with the most convenient use of the ordinances, and discharge of moral duties, without respect of persons.[h]

Thirdly, The pastor and people must so nearly cohabit together, as that they may mutually perform their duties each to other with most conveniency.

In this company some must be set apart to bear office.

Of the Officers of a particular Congregation.

FOR officers in a single congregation, there ought to be one at the least, both to labour in the word and doctrine, and to rule.[i]

It is also requisite that there should be others to join in government.[k]

And likewise it is requisite that there be others to take special care for the relief of the poor.[l]

The number of each of which is to be proportioned according to the condition of the congregation.

These officers are to meet together at convenient and set times, for the well ordering of the affairs of that congregation, each according to his office.

It is most expedient that, in these meetings, one whose office is to labour in the word and doctrine, do moderate in their proceedings.[m]

Of the Ordinances in a particular Congregation.

THE ordinances in a single congregation are, prayer, thanksgiving, and singing of psalms,[n] the word read, (although there follow no immediate explication of what is read,) the word expounded and applied, catechising, the sacraments administered, collection made for the poor, dismissing the people with a blessing.

Of Church-Government, and the several sorts of Assemblies for the same.

CHRIST hath instituted a government, and governors ecclesiastical in the church: to that purpose, the apostles did immediately receive the keys from the hand of Jesus Christ, and did use and exercise them in all the churches of the world upon all occasions.

---

[h] 1 Cor. xiv. 26. *Let all things be done unto edifying.* Heb. x. 24. And *let us consider one another*, to provoke unto love, and to good works: Ver. 25. Not forsaking the assembling of ourselves together, as the manner of some is; but exhorting one another: and so much the more, as ye see the day approaching. James ii. 1. My brethren, have not the faith of our Lord Jesus Christ, the Lord of glory, with respect of persons. Ver. 2. For if there come unto your assembly a man with a gold ring, in goodly apparel, and there come in also a poor man in vile raiment, &c.

[i] Prov. xxix. 18. Where there is no vision, the people perish: but he that keepeth the law, happy is he. 1 Tim. v. 17. Let the elders that rule well be counted worthy of double honour, especially they who *labour in the word and doctrine*. Heb. xiii. 7. Remember them which have the rule over you, *who have spoken unto you the word of God;* whose faith follow, considering the end of their conversation.

[k] 1 Cor. xii. 28. And God hath set some in the church, first, apostles; secondarily, prophets; thirdly, teachers; after that miracles; then gifts of healings, helps, *governments*, diversities of tongues.

[l] Acts vi. 2. Then the twelve called the multitude of the disciples unto them, and said, It is not reason that we should leave the word of God, and serve tables. Ver. 3. Wherefore, brethren, look ye out among you seven men of honest report, full of the Holy Ghost and wisdom, *whom we may appoint over this business.*

[m] 1 Tim. v. 17. Let *the elders that rule well* be counted worthy of double honour, especially they who labour in the word and doctrine.

[n] 1 Tim. ii. 1. I exhort therefore, that, first of all, *supplications, prayers, intercessions,* and *giving of thanks*, be made for all men. 1 Cor. xiv. 15. What is it then? I will pray with the spirit, and I will pray with the understanding also; I will *sing with the spirit*, and I will sing with the

And Christ hath since continually furnished some in his church with gifts of government, and with commission to execute the same, when called thereunto.

It is lawful, and agreeable to the word of God, that the church be governed by several sorts of assemblies, which are congregational, classical, and synodical.

Of the power in common of all these Assemblies.

IT is lawful, and agreeable to the word of God, that the several assemblies before mentioned have power to convent, and call before them, any person within their several bounds, whom the ecclesiastical business which is before them doth concern.[o]

They have power to hear and determine such causes and differences as do orderly come before them.

It is lawful, and agreeable to the word of God, that all the said assemblies have some power to dispense church-censures.

Of Congregational Assemblies, that is, the Meeting of the ruling Officers of a particular Congregation, for the Government thereof.

THE ruling officers of a particular congregation have power, authoritatively, to call before them any member of the congregation, as they shall see just occasion.

To enquire into the knowledge and spiritual estate of the several members of the congregation.

To admonish and rebuke.

Which three branches are proved by Heb. xiii. 17; 1 Thess. v. 12, 13; Ezek. xxxiv. 4.[p]

Authoritative suspension from the Lord's table, of a person not yet cast out of the church, is agreeable to the scripture:

First, Because the ordinance itself must not be profaned.

Secondly, Because we are charged to withdraw from those that walk disorderly.

Thirdly, Because of the great sin and danger, both to him that comes unworthily, and also to the whole church.[q] And there was power

---

understanding also. Ver. 16. Else, when thou shalt bless with the spirit, how shall he that occupieth the room of the unlearned say Amen at thy giving of thanks, seeing he understandeth not what thou sayest?

o Matt. xviii. 15. Moreover, if thy brother shall trespass against thee, go and tell him his fault between thee and him alone: if he shall hear thee, thou hast gained thy brother. Ver. 16. But if he will not hear thee, then take with thee one or two more, that in the mouth of two or three witnesses every word may be established. Ver. 17. And if he shall neglect to hear them, *tell it unto the church:* but if he neglect to hear the church, let him be unto thee as an heathen man and a publican. Ver. 18. Verily I say unto you, Whatsoever ye shall bind on earth shall be bound in heaven; and whatsoever ye shall loose on earth shall be loosed in heaven. Ver. 19. Again I say unto you, That if two of you shall agree on earth as touching any thing that they shall ask, it shall be done for them of my Father which is in heaven. Ver. 20. For where two or three are gathered together in my name, there am I in the midst of them.

p Heb. xiii. 17. *Obey them that have the rule over you,* and submit yourselves: for they watch for your souls, as they that must give account; that they may do it with joy, and not with grief: for that is unprofitable for you. 1 Thess. v. 12. And we beseech you, brethren, to know them which labour among you, and are over you in the Lord, and admonish you; Ver. 13. And to esteem them very highly in love for their work's sake. And be at peace among yourselves. Ezek. xxxiv. 4. The diseased have ye not strengthened, neither have ye healed that which was sick, neither have ye bound up that which was broken, neither have ye brought again that which was driven away, neither have ye sought that which was lost; but with force and with cruelty have ye ruled them.

q Matt. vii. 6. Give not that which is holy unto the dogs, neither cast ye your pearls before swine, *lest they trample them under their feet, and turn again and rend you*

and authority, under the Old Testament, to keep unclean persons from holy things.ʳ

The like power and authority, by way of analogy, continues under the New Testament.

The ruling officers of a particular congregation have power authoritatively to suspend from the Lord's table a person not yet cast out of the church:

First, Because those who have authority to judge of, and admit, such as are fit to receive the sacrament, have authority to keep back such as shall be found unworthy.

Secondly, Because it is an ecclesiastical business of ordinary practice belonging to that congregation.

When congregations are divided and fixed, they need all mutual help one from another, both in regard of their intrinsical weaknesses and mutual dependence, as also in regard of enemies from without.

Of Classical Assemblies.

THE scripture doth hold out a presbytery in a church.ˢ

A presbytery consisteth of ministers of the word, and such other publick officers as are agreeable to and warranted by the word of God to be church-governors, to join with the ministers in the government of the church.ᵗ

The scripture doth hold forth, that many particular congregations may be under one presbyterial government.

This proposition is proved by instances:

1. *First,* Of the church of Jerusalem, which consisted of more congregations than one, and all these congregations were under one presbyterial government.

This appeareth thus:

First, The church of Jerusalem consisted of more congregations than one, as is manifest:

1*st,* By the multitude of believers mentioned, in divers [places], both

---

ʳ 2 Thess. iii. 6. Now we command you, brethren, in the name of our Lord Jesus Christ, that ye withdraw yourselves from every brother that walketh disorderly, and not after the tradition which he received of us. Ver. 14. And if any man obey not our word by this epistle, note that man, and have no company with him, that he may be ashamed. Ver. 15. Yet count him not as an enemy, but admonish him as a brother. 1 Cor. xi. 27. Wherefore, whosoever shall eat this bread, and drink this cup of the Lord, unworthily, shall be *guilty of the body and blood of the Lord.* [See on to the end of the chapter.] Compared with Jude, ver. 23. And others save with fear, pulling them out of the fire; hating even the garment spotted by the flesh. 1 Tim. v. 22. Lay hands suddenly on no man, *neither be partaker of other men's sins;* keep thyself pure.

ʳ Lev. xiii. 5. And the priest shall look on him the seventh day: and, behold, if the plague in his sight be at a stay, and the plague spread not in the skin; *then the priest shall shut him up seven days more.* Numb. ix. 7. And those men said unto him, We are defiled by the dead body of a man: *wherefore are we kept back,* that we may not offer an offering of the Lord in his appointed season among the children of Israel? 2 Chron. xxiii. 19. And *he set the porters* at the gates of the house of the Lord, *that none which was unclean in any thing should enter in.*

ˢ 1 Tim. iv. 14. Neglect not the gift that is in thee, which was given thee by prophecy, with the laying on of the hands of *the presbytery.* Acts xv. 2. When therefore Paul and Barnabas had no small dissension and disputation with them, they determined that Paul and Barnabas, and certain other of them, should go up to Jerusalem unto the apostles and elders about this question. Ver. 4. And when they were come to Jerusalem, they were received of the church, and of the apostles and elders, and they declared all things that God had done with them. Ver. 6. And *the apostles and elders came together for to consider of this matter.*

ᵗ Rom. xii. 7. Or *ministry,* let us wait on our ministering; or he that teacheth, on teaching; Ver. 8. Or he that exhorteth, on exhortation: he that giveth, let him do it with simplicity; *he that ruleth,* with diligence; he that sheweth mercy, with cheerfulness. 1 Cor. xii. 28. And God hath set some in the church, first, apostles; second-

before the dispersion of the believers there, by means of the persecution,[v] and also after the dispersion.[w]

2*dly*, By the many apostles and other preachers in the church of Jerusalem. And if there were but one congregation there, then each apostle preached but seldom;[x] which will not consist with Acts vi. 2.

3*dly*, The diversity of languages among the believers, mentioned both in the second and sixth chapters of the Acts, doth argue more congregations than one in that church.

Secondly, All those congregations were under one presbyterial government; because,

1*st*, They were one church.[y]

2*dly*, The elders of the church are mentioned.[z]

3*dly*, The apostles did the ordinary acts of presbyters, as presbyters in that kirk; which proveth a presbyterial church before the dispersion, Acts vi.

4*thly*, The several congregations in Jerusalem being one church, the elders of that church are mentioned as meeting together for acts of government;[a] which proves that those several congregations were under one presbyterial government.

arily, prophets; thirdly, teachers; after that miracles; then gifts of healings, helps, *governments*, diversities of tongues.

[v] Acts viii. 1. And Saul was consenting unto his death. And at that time there was a *great persecution* against the church which was at Jerusalem; and they were all scattered abroad throughout the regions of Judea and Samaria, except the apostles. Acts i. 15. And in those days Peter stood up in the midst of the disciples, and said, (the number of the names together were about *an hundred and twenty*.) Acts ii. 41. Then they that gladly received his word were baptised: and the same day there were added unto them about *three thousand souls*. Ver. 46. And they, continuing daily with one accord in the temple, and breaking bread from house to house, did eat their meat with gladness and singleness of heart, Ver. 47. Praising God, and having favour with all the people. And the Lord added to the church daily such as should be saved. Acts iv. 4. Howbeit many of them which heard the word believed; and the number of the men was about *five thousand*. Acts v. 14. And believers were the more added to the Lord, *multitudes both of men and women*. Acts vi. 1. And in those days, when *the number of the disciples was multiplied*, there arose a murmuring of the Grecians against the Hebrews, because their widows were neglected in the daily ministration. Ver. 7. And the word of God increased; and the number of the disciples multiplied in Jerusalem greatly: and *a great company of the priests* were obedient to the faith.

[w] Acts ix. 31. Then had the *churches* rest throughout *all Judea*, and *Galilee*, and *Samaria*, and were edified; and walking in the fear of the Lord, and in the comfort of the Holy Ghost, were *multiplied*. Acts xii. 24. But the word of God *grew and multiplied*. Acts xxi. 20. And when they heard it, they glorified the Lord, and said unto him, Thou seest, brother, how *many thousands* of Jews there are which believe; and they are all zealous of the law.

[x] Acts vi. 2. Then the twelve called the multitude of the disciples unto them, and said, *It is not reason that we should leave the word of God*, and serve tables.

[y] Acts viii. 1. And Saul was consenting unto his death. And at that time there was a great persecution against *the church which was at Jerusalem;* and they were all scattered abroad throughout the regions of Judea and Samaria, except the apostles. Acts ii. 47. Praising God, and having favour with all the people. And the Lord added to *the church* daily such as should be saved. Compared with Acts v. 11. And great fear came upon all the church, and upon as many as heard these things. Acts xii. 5. Peter therefore was kept in prison; but prayer was made without ceasing of *the church* unto God for him. Acts xv. 4. And when they were come to Jerusalem, they were received of *the church*, and of the apostles and elders, and they declared all things that God had done with them.

[z] Acts xi. 30. Which also they did, and sent it to *the elders* by the hands of Barnabas and Saul. Acts xv. 4. And when they were come to Jerusalem, they were received of the church, and of the apostles and *elders*, and they declared all things that God had done with them. Ver. 6. And the apostles and *elders* came together for to consider of this matter. Ver. 22. Then pleased it the apostles and *elders*, with the whole church, to send chosen men of their own company to Antioch with Paul and Barnabas; namely, Judas surnamed Barsabas, and Silas, chief men among the brethren. Acts xxi. 17. And when we were come to Jerusalem, the brethren received us gladly. Ver. 18. And the day following Paul went in with us unto James; and *all the elders* were present.

[a] Acts xi. 30. Which also they did, and sent it to the elders by the hands of Barnabas and Saul. Acts xv. 4. And when they

And whether these congregations were fixed or not fixed, in regard of officers or members, it is all one as to the truth of the proposition.

Nor doth there appear any material difference betwixt the several congregations in Jerusalem, and the many congregations now in the ordinary condition of the church, as to the point of fixedness required of officers or members.

Thirdly, Therefore the scripture doth hold forth, that many congregations may be under one presbyterial government.

II. *Secondly*, By the instance of the church of Ephesus; for,

First, That there were more congregations than one in the church of Ephesus, appears by Acts xx. 31,[b] where is mention of Paul's continuance at Ephesus in preaching for the space of three years; and Acts xix. 18, 19, 20, where the special effect of the word is mentioned;[c] and ver. 10 and 17 of the same chapter, where is a distinction of Jews and Greeks;[d] and 1 Cor. xvi. 8, 9, where is a reason of Paul's stay at Ephesus until Pentecost;[e] and ver. 19, where is mention of a particular church in the house of Aquila and Priscilla, then at Ephesus,[f] as appears, Acts xviii. 19, 24, 26.[g] All which laid together, doth prove that the multitudes of believers did make more congregations than one in the church of Ephesus.

Secondly, That there were many elders over these many congregations, as one flock, appeareth.[h]

Thirdly, That these many congregations were one church, and that they were under one presbyterial government, appeareth.[i]

---

were come to Jerusalem, they were received of the church, and of the apostles and elders, and they declared all things that God had done with them. Ver. 6. And *the apostles and elders came together for to consider of this matter*. Ver. 22. Then pleased it *the apostles and elders*, with the whole church, to send chosen men of their own company to Antioch with Paul and Barnabas; namely, Judas surnamed Barsabas, and Silas, chief men among the brethren. Acts xxi. 17. And when we were come to Jerusalem, the brethren received us gladly. Ver. 18. And the day following *Paul went in with us unto James; and all the elders were present.* [And so forward.]

b Acts xx. 31. Therefore watch, and remember, that, by *the space of three years,* I ceased not to warn every one night and day with tears.

c Acts xix. 18. And *many that believed* came, and confessed, and shewed their deeds. Ver. 19. *Many* of them also which used curious arts brought their books together, and burned them before all men: and they counted the price of them, and found it fifty thousand pieces of silver. Ver. 20. So *mightily grew the word of God and prevailed.*

d Acts xix. 10. And this continued by the space of two years; so that all they which dwelt in Asia heard the word of the Lord Jesus, *both Jews and Greeks.* Ver. 17. And this was known to *all the Jews and Greeks* also dwelling at Ephesus; and fear fell on them all, and the name of the Lord Jesus was magnified.

e 1 Cor. xvi. 8. But I will tarry at Ephesus until Pentecost. Ver. 9. For *a great door and effectual is opened unto me,* and there are many adversaries.

f 1 Cor. xvi. 19. The churches of Asia salute you. Aquila and Priscilla salute you much in the Lord, with *the church that is in their house.*

g Acts xviii. 19. And he came to *Ephesus,* and left them there: but he himself entered into the synagogue, and reasoned with the Jews. Ver. 24. And a certain Jew, named Apollos, born at Alexandria, an eloquent man, and mighty in the scriptures, came to *Ephesus.* Ver. 26. And he began to speak boldly in the synagogue: whom when Aquila and Priscilla had heard, they took him unto them, and expounded unto him the way of God more perfectly.

h Acts xx. 17. And from Miletus he sent to Ephesus, and called *the elders of the church.* Ver. 25. And now, behold, I know that ye all, among whom I have gone preaching the kingdom of God, shall see my face no more. Ver. 28. Take heed therefore unto yourselves, and to all the flock, over the which the Holy Ghost hath made you overseers, to feed the church of God, which he hath purchased with his own blood. Ver. 30. Also of your own selves shall men arise, speaking perverse things, to draw away disciples after them. Ver. 36. And when he had thus spoken, he kneeled down, and prayed with them all. Ver. 37. And they all wept sore, and fell on Paul's neck, and kissed him.

i Rev. ii. 1. Unto *the angel of the church of Ephesus* write; These things saith he that holdeth the seven stars in his right hand, who walketh in the midst of the seven golden candlesticks; Ver. 2. I know thy

Of Synodical Assemblies.

THE scripture doth hold out another sort of assemblies for the government of the church, beside classical and congregational, all which we call *Synodical*.[k]

Pastors and teachers, and other church-governors, (as also other fit persons, when it shall be deemed expedient,) are members of those assemblies which we call *Synodical*, where they have a lawful calling thereunto.

Synodical assemblies may lawfully be of several sorts, as provincial, national, and oecumenical.

It is lawful and agreeable to the word of God, that there be a subordination of congregational, classical, provincial, and national assemblies, for the government of the church.

Of Ordination of Ministers.

UNDER the head of Ordination of Ministers is to be considered, either the doctrine of ordination, or the power of it.

Touching the Doctrine of Ordination.

NO man ought to take upon him the office of a minister of the word without a lawful calling.[l]

Ordination is always to be continued in the church.[m]

Ordination is the solemn setting apart of a person to some publick church office.[n]

---

works, and thy labour, and thy patience, and how thou canst not bear them which are evil: and thou hast tried them which say they are apostles, and are not, and hast found them liars: Ver. 3. And hast borne, and hast patience, and for my name's sake hast laboured, and hast not fainted. Ver. 4. Nevertheless I have somewhat against thee, because thou hast left thy first love. Ver. 5. Remember therefore from whence thou art fallen, and repent, and do the first works; or else I will come unto thee quickly, and will remove thy candlestick out of his place, except thou repent. Ver. 6. But this thou hast, that thou hatest the deeds of the Nicolaitanes, which I also hate. Joined with Acts xx. 17, 28. [See in letter h.]

[k] Acts xv. 2. When therefore Paul and Barnabas had no small dissension and disputation with them, they determined that Paul and Barnabas, and certain other of them, should go up to Jerusalem unto the apostles and elders about this question. Ver. 6. And *the apostles and elders came together* for to consider of this matter. Ver. 22. Then pleased it *the apostles and elders, with the whole church*, to send chosen men of their own company to Antioch, with Paul and Barnabas; namely, Judas surnamed Barsabas, and Silas, chief men among the brethren: Ver. 23. And they wrote letters by them after this manner; *The apostles, and elders, and brethren*, send greeting unto the brethren which are of the Gentiles in Antioch, and Syria, and Cilicia.

[l] John iii. 27. John answered and said, A man can receive nothing, *except it be given him from heaven*. Rom. x. 14. How then shall they call on him in whom they have not believed? and how shall they believe in him of whom they have not heard? and how shall they hear without a preacher? Ver. 15. And *how shall they preach except they be sent?* as it is written, How beautiful are the feet of them that preach the gospel of peace, and bring glad tidings of good things! Jer. xiv. 14. Then the Lord said unto me, The prophets prophesy lies in my name: I sent them not, *neither have I commanded them*, neither spake unto them: they prophesy unto you a false vision and divination, and a thing of nought, and the deceit of their heart: Heb. v. 4. And no man taketh this honour unto himself, *but he that is called of God*, as was Aaron.

[m] Tit. i. 5. For this cause left I thee in Crete, that thou shouldest set in order the things that are wanting, and *ordain elders* in every city, as I had appointed thee. 1 Tim. v. 21. I charge thee before God, and the Lord Jesus Christ, and the elect angels, that thou observe these things, without preferring one before another, doing nothing by partiality. Ver. 22. *Lay hands suddenly on no man*, neither be partaker of other men's sins: keep thyself pure.

[n] Numb. viii. 10. And thou shalt bring the Levites before the Lord; and the children of Israel shall put their hands upon the Levites: Ver. 11. And Aaron shall offer the Levites before the Lord for an offering of the children of Israel, that they may execute the service of the Lord. Ver. 14. Thus *shalt thou separate the Levites* from among the children of Israel; and the Levites shall be mine. Ver. 19. And I have given the Levites as a gift to Aaron, and to his sons, from among the children of Israel, to do the

Every minister of the word is to be ordained by imposition of hands, and prayer, with fasting, by those preaching presbyters to whom it doth belong.º

It is agreeable to the word of God, and very expedient, that such as are to be ordained ministers, be designed to some particular church, or other ministerial charge.ᵖ

He that is to be ordained minister, must be duly qualified, both for life and ministerial abilities, according to the rules of the apostle.ᑫ

He is to be examined and approved by those by whom he is to be ordained.ʳ

No man is to be ordained a minister for a particular congregation, if they of that congregation can shew just cause of exception against him.ˢ

Touching the Power of Ordination.

ORDINATION is the act of a presbytery.ᵗ

The power of ordering the whole work of ordination is in the whole presbytery, which, when it is over more congregations than one, whether these congregations be fixed or not fixed, in regard of officers or members, it is indifferent as to the point of ordination.ᵛ

---

service of the children of Israel in the tabernacle of the congregation, and to make an atonement for the children of Israel; that there be no plague among the children of Israel, when the children of Israel come nigh unto the sanctuary. Ver. 22. And after that went the Levites in to do their service in the tabernacle of the congregation before Aaron, and before his sons: as the Lord had commanded Moses concerning the Levites, so did they unto them. Acts vi. 3. Wherefore, brethren, look ye out among you seven men of honest report, full of the Holy Ghost and wisdom, whom *we may appoint over this business.* Ver. 5. And the saying pleased the whole multitude: and they chose Stephen, a man full of faith and of the Holy Ghost, and Philip, and Prochorus, and Nicanor, and Timon, and Parmenas, and Nicolas a proselyte of Antioch; Ver. 6. Whom they set before the apostles: and when they had prayed, *they laid their hands on them.*

o 1 Tim. v. 22. *Lay hands* suddenly on no man, neither be partaker of other men's sins: keep thyself pure. Acts xiv. 23. And when they had ordained them elders in every church, and had *prayed* with *fasting*, they commended them to the Lord, on whom they believed. Acts xiii. 3. And when they had *fasted and prayed*, and *laid their hands on them,* they sent them away.

p Acts xiv. 23. [See before.] Tit. i. 5. *For this cause left I thee in Crete,* that thou shouldest set in order the things that are wanting, and ordain elders in every city, as I had appointed thee. Acts xx. 17. And from Miletus he sent to Ephesus, and called the elders of the church. Ver. 28. Take heed therefore unto yourselves, and to *all the flock, over the which the Holy Ghost hath made you overseers,* to feed the church of God, which he hath purchased with his own blood.

q 1 Tim. iii. 2. A bishop then must be *blameless, the husband of one wife, vigilant.*

sober, *of good behaviour, given to hospitality, apt to teach;* Ver. 3. *Not given to wine, no striker, not greedy of filthy lucre;* but *patient,* not a brawler, not covetous; Ver. 4. *One that ruleth well his own house,* having his children in subjection with all gravity; Ver. 5. (For if a man know not how to rule his own house, how shall he take care of the church of God?) Ver. 6. *Not a novice,* lest, being lifted up with pride, he fall into the condemnation of the devil. Tit. i. 5. For this cause left I thee in Crete, that thou shouldest set in order the things that are wanting, and ordain elders in every city, as I had appointed thee. Ver. 6. If any be *blameless, the husband of one wife, having faithful children, not accused of riot or unruly.* Ver. 7. For a bishop must be *blameless,* as the steward of God; *not self-willed, not soon angry, not given to wine, no striker, not given to filthy lucre;* Ver. 8. But *a lover of hospitality, a lover of good men, sober, just, holy, temperate;* Ver. 9. *Holding fast the faithful word* as he hath been taught, that he may be able by sound doctrine both to exhort and to convince the gainsayers.

r 1 Tim. iii. 7. Moreover, he must have a good report of them which are without; lest he fall into reproach and the snare of the devil. Ver. 10. *And let these also first be proved;* then let them use the office of a deacon, being found blameless. 1 Tim. v. 22. *Lay hands suddenly on no man,* neither be partaker of other men's sins: keep thyself pure.

s 1 Tim. iii. 2. A bishop then must be *blameless,* the husband of one wife, vigilant, sober, of good behaviour, given to hospitality, apt to teach. Tit. i. 7. For a bishop must be *blameless,* as the steward of God.

t 1 Tim. iv. 14. Neglect not the gift that is in thee, which was given thee by prophecy, with the laying on of the hands of the *presbytery.*

v 1 Tim. iv. 14. [See in letter t.]

It is very requisite, that no single congregation, that can conveniently associate, do assume to itself all and sole power in ordination:

1. Because there is no example in scripture that any single congregation, which might conveniently associate, did assume to itself all and sole power in ordination; neither is there any rule which may warrant such a practice.

2. Because there is in scripture example of an ordination in a presbytery over divers congregations; as in the church of Jerusalem, where were many congregations: these many congregations were under one presbytery, and this presbytery did ordain.

The preaching presbyters orderly associated, either in cities or neighbouring villages, are those to whom the imposition of hands doth appertain, for those congregations within their bounds respectively.

Concerning the Doctrinal Part of Ordination of Ministers.

1. NO man ought to take upon him the office of a minister of the word without a lawful calling.[w]

2. Ordination is always to be continued in the church.[x]

3. Ordination is the solemn setting apart of a person to some publick church office.[y]

4. Every minister of the word is to be ordained by imposition of hands, and prayer, with fasting, by these preaching presbyters to whom it doth belong.[z]

5. The power of ordering the whole work of ordination is in the whole presbytery, which, when it is over more congregations than one, whether those congregations be fixed or not fixed, in regard of officers or members, it is indifferent as to the point of ordination.[a]

6. It is agreeable to the word, and very expedient, that such as are to be ordained ministers be designed to some particular church, or other ministerial charge.[b]

7. He that is to be ordained minister, must be duly qualified, both for life and ministerial abilities, according to the rules of the apostle.[c]

8. He is to be examined and approved by those by whom he is to be ordained.[d]

9. No man is to be ordained a minister for a particular congregation, if they of that congregation can shew just cause of exception against him.[e]

10. Preaching presbyters orderly associated, either in cities or neighbouring villages, are those to whom the imposition of hands doth appertain, for those congregations within their bounds respectively.[f]

11. In extraordinary cases, something extraordinary may be done, until a settled order may be had, yet keeping as near as possibly may be to the rule.[g]

w See before in letter l.
x See before in letter m.
y See before in letter n.
z See before in letter o.
a See before in letter v.
b See before in letter p.
c See before in letter q.
d See before in letter r.
e See before in letter s.
f 1 Tim. iv. 14. Neglect not the gift that is in thee, which was given thee by prophecy, with the laying on of the hands of the *presbytery*.

g 2 Chron. xxix. 34. But the priests were too few, so that they could not flay all the burnt-offerings: wherefore *their brethren the Levites did help them*, till the work was ended, and until the other priests had sanctified themselves; for the Levites were more upright in heart to sanctify themselves than the priests. Ver. 35. And also the burnt-offerings were in abundance, with the fat of the peace-offerings, and the drink-offerings for every burnt-offering. So the service of the house of the Lord was set in order. Ver. 36. And Hezekiah rejoiced, and all the

12. There is at this time (as we humbly conceive) an extraordinary occasion for a way of ordination for the present supply of ministers.

The Directory for the Ordination of Ministers.

IT being manifest by the word of God, that no man ought to take upon him the office of a minister of the gospel, until he be lawfully called and ordained thereunto; and that the work of ordination is to be performed with all due care, wisdom, gravity, and solemnity, we humbly tender these directions, as requisite to be observed.

1. He that is to be ordained, being either nominated by the people, or otherwise commended to the presbytery, for any place, must address himself to the presbytery, and bring with him a testimonial of his taking the Covenant of the three kingdoms; of his diligence and proficiency in his studies; what degrees he had taken in the university, and what hath been the time of his abode there; and withal of his age, which is to be twenty-four years; but especially of his life and conversation.

2. Which being considered by the presbytery, they are to proceed to enquire touching the grace of God in him, and whether he be of such holiness of life as is requisite in a minister of the gospel; and to examine him touching his learning and sufficiency, and touching the evidences of his calling to the holy ministry; and, in particular, his fair and direct calling to that place.

The Rules for Examination are these:

" (1.) That the party examined be dealt withal in a brotherly way, with mildness of spirit, and with special respect to the gravity, modesty, and quality of every one.

" (2.) He shall be examined touching his skill in the original tongues, and his trial to be made by reading the Hebrew and Greek Testaments, and rendering some portion of some into Latin; and if he be defective in them, enquiry shall be made more strictly after his other learning, and whether he hath skill in logick and philosophy.

" (3.) What authors in divinity he hath read, and is best acquainted with; and trial shall be made in his knowledge of the grounds of religion, and of his ability to defend the orthodox doctrine contained in them against all unsound and erroneous opinions, especially those of the present age; of his skill in the sense and meaning of such places of scripture as shall be proposed unto him, in cases of conscience, and in the chronology of the scripture, and the ecclesiastical history.

" (4.) If he hath not before preached in publick with approbation of such as are able to judge, he shall, at a competent time assigned him, expound before the presbytery such a place of scripture as shall be given him.

---

people, that God had prepared the people: for the thing was done suddenly. 2 Chron. xxx. 2. For the king had taken counsel, and his princes, and all the congregation in Jerusalem, to keep the passover *in the second month.* Ver. 3. *For they could not keep it at that time, because the priests had not sanctified themselves sufficiently,* neither had the people gathered themselves together to Jerusalem. Ver. 4. And the thing pleased the king and all the congregation. Ver. 5. So they established a decree to make proclamation throughout all Israel, from Beersheba even to Dan, that they should come to keep the passover unto the Lord God of Israel at Jerusalem: for they had not done it of a long time in such sort as it was written.

"(5.) He shall also, within a competent time, frame a discourse in Latin upon such a common-place or controversy in divinity as shall be assigned to him, and exhibit to the presbytery such theses as express the sum thereof, and maintain a dispute upon them.

"(6.) He shall preach before the people,—the presbytery, or some of the ministers of the word appointed by them, being present.

"(7.) The proportion of his gifts in relation to the place unto which he is called shall be considered.

"(8.) Beside the trial of his gifts in preaching, he shall undergo an examination in the premises two several days, and more, if the presbytery shall judge it necessary.

"(9.) And as for him that hath formerly been ordained a minister, and is to be removed to another charge, he shall bring a testimonial of his ordination, and of his abilities and conversation, whereupon his fitness for that place shall be tried by his preaching there, and (if it shall be judged necessary) by a further examination of him."

3. In all which he being approved, he is to be sent to the church where he is to serve, there to preach three several days, and to converse with the people, that they may have trial of his gifts for their edification, and may have time and occasion to enquire into, and the better to know, his life and conversation.

4. In the last of these three days appointed for the trial of his gifts in preaching, there shall be sent from the presbytery to the congregation a publick intimation in writing, which shall be publickly read before the people, and after affixed to the church-door, to signify that such a day a competent number of the members of that congregation, nominated by themselves, shall appear before the presbytery, to give their consent and approbation to such a man to be their minister; or otherwise, to put in, with all Christian discretion and meekness, what exceptions they have against him. And if, upon the day appointed, there be no just exception against him, but the people give their consent, then the presbytery shall proceed to ordination.

5. Upon the day appointed for ordination, which is to be performed in that church where he that is to be ordained is to serve, a solemn fast shall be kept by the congregation, that they may the more earnestly join in prayer for a blessing upon the ordinances of Christ, and the labours of his servant for their good. The presbytery shall come to the place, or at least three or four ministers of the word shall be sent thither from the presbytery; of which one appointed by the presbytery shall preach to the people concerning the office and duty of ministers of Christ, and how the people ought to receive them for their work's sake.

6. After the sermon, the minister who hath preached shall, in the face of the congregation, demand of him who is now to be ordained, concerning his faith in Christ Jesus, and his persuasion of the truth of the reformed religion, according to the scriptures; his sincere intentions and ends in desiring to enter into this calling; his diligence in praying, reading, meditation, preaching, ministering the sacraments, discipline, and doing all ministerial duties towards his charge; his zeal and faithfulness in maintaining the truth of the gospel, and unity of the church, against error and schism; his care that himself and his

family may be unblameable, and examples to the flock; his willingness and humility, in meekness of spirit, to submit unto the admonitions of his brethren, and discipline of the church; and his resolution to continue in his duty against all trouble and persecution.

7. In all which having declared himself, professed his willingness, and promised his endeavours, by the help of God; the minister likewise shall demand of the people concerning their willingness to receive and acknowledge him as the minister of Christ; and to obey and submit unto him, as having rule over them in the Lord; and to maintain, encourage, and assist him in all the parts of his office.

8. Which being mutually promised by the people, the presbytery, or the ministers sent from them for ordination, shall solemnly set him apart to the office and work of the ministry, by laying their hands on him, which is to be accompanied with a short prayer or blessing, to this effect:

"Thankfully acknowledging the great mercy of God in sending
"Jesus Christ for the redemption of his people; and for his ascension
"to the right hand of God the Father, and thence pouring out his
"Spirit, and giving gifts to men, apostles, evangelists, prophets,
"pastors, and teachers; for the gathering and building up of his
"church; and for fitting and inclining this man to this great work:*
"to entreat him to fit him with his Holy Spirit, to give him (who in
"his name we thus set apart to this holy service) to fulfil the work
"of his ministry in all things, that he may both save himself, and
"his people committed to his charge."

9. This or the like form of prayer and blessing being ended, let the minister who preached briefly exhort him to consider of the greatness of his office and work, the danger of negligence both to himself and his people, the blessing which will accompany his faithfulness in this life, and that to come; and withal exhort the people to carry themselves to him, as to their minister in the Lord, according to their solemn promise made before. And so by prayer commending both him and his flock to the grace of God, after singing of a psalm, let the assembly be dismissed with a blessing.

10. If a minister be designed to a congregation, who hath been formerly ordained presbyter according to the form of ordination which hath been in the church of England, which we hold for substance to be valid, and not to be disclaimed by any who have received it; then, there being a cautious proceeding in matters of examination, let him be admitted without any new ordination.

11. And in case any person already ordained minister in Scotland, or in any other reformed church, be designed to another congregation in England, he is to bring from that church to the presbytery here, within which that congregation is, a sufficient testimonial of his ordination, of his life and conversation while he lived with them, and of the causes of his removal; and to undergo such a trial of his fitness and sufficiency, and to have the same course held with him in other particulars, as is set down in the rule immediately going before, touching examination and admission.

12. That records be carefully kept in the several presbyteries, of the names of the persons ordained, with their testimonials, the time

* Here let them impose hands on his head.

and place of their ordination, of the presbyters who did impose hands upon them, and of the charge to which they are appointed.

13. That no money or gift, of what kind soever, shall be received from the person to be ordained, or from any on his behalf, for ordination, or ought else belonging to it, by any of the presbytery, or any appertaining to any of them, upon what pretence soever.

Thus far of ordinary Rules, and course of Ordination, in the ordinary way; that which concerns the extraordinary way, requisite to be now practised, followeth.

1. In these present exigencies, while we cannot have any presbyteries formed up to their whole power and work, and that many ministers are to be ordained for the service of the armies and navy, and to many congregations where there is no minister at all; and where (by reason of the publick troubles) the people cannot either themselves enquire and find out one who may be a faithful minister for them, or have any with safety sent unto them, for such a solemn trial as was before mentioned in the ordinary rules; especially, when there can be no presbytery near unto them, to whom they may address themselves, or which may come or send to them a fit man to be ordained in that congregation, and for that people; and yet notwithstanding, it is requisite that ministers be ordained for them by some, who, being set apart themselves for the work of the ministry, have power to join in the setting apart others, who are found fit and worthy. In those cases, until, by God's blessing, the aforesaid difficulties may be in some good measure removed, let some godly ministers, in or about the city of London, be designed by publick authority, who, being associated, may ordain ministers for the city and the vicinity, keeping as near to the ordinary rules fore-mentioned as possibly they may; and let this association be for no other intent or purpose, but only for the work of ordination.

2. Let the like association be made by the same authority in great towns, and the neighbouring parishes in the several counties, which are at the present quiet and undisturbed, to do the like for the parts adjacent.

3. Let such as are chosen, or appointed for the service of the armies or navy, be ordained, as aforesaid, by the associated ministers of London, or some others in the country.

4. Let them do the like, when any man shall duly and lawfully be recommended to them for the ministry of any congregation, who cannot enjoy liberty to have a trial of his parts and abilities, and desire the help of such ministers so associated, for the better furnishing of them with such a person as by them shall be judged fit for the service of that church and people.

THE DIRECTORY FOR FAMILY-WORSHIP,

APPROVED BY THE GENERAL ASSEMBLY OF THE CHURCH OF SCOTLAND, FOR PIETY AND UNIFORMITY IN SECRET AND PRIVATE WORSHIP, AND MUTUAL EDIFICATION:

WITH

AN ACT OF THE GENERAL ASSEMBLY, ANNO 1647, FOR OBSERVING THE SAME.

ASSEMBLY AT EDINBURGH, August 24, 1647. Sess. 10.

Act for observing the Directions of the GENERAL ASSEMBLY *for secret and private Worship, and mutual edification; and censuring such as neglect Family-worship.*

THE General Assembly, after mature deliberation, doth approve the following Rules and Directions for cherishing piety, and preventing division and schism; and doth appoint ministers and ruling elders in each congregation to take special care that these Directions be observed and followed; as likewise, that presbyteries and provincial synods enquire and make trial whether the said Directions be duly observed in their bounds; and to reprove or censure (according to the quality of the offence), such as shall be found to be reprovable or censurable therein. And, to the end that these directions may not be rendered ineffectual and unprofitable among some, through the usual neglect of the very substance of the duty of Family-worship, the Assembly doth further require and appoint ministers and ruling elders to make diligent search and enquiry, in the congregations committed to their charge respectively, whether there be among them any family or families which use to neglect this necessary duty; and if any such family be found, the head of the family is to be first admonished privately to amend his fault; and, in case of his continuing therein, he is to be gravely and sadly reproved by the session; after which reproof, if he be found still to neglect Family-worship, let him be, for his obstinacy in such an offence, suspended and debarred from the Lord's supper, as being justly esteemed unworthy to communicate therein, till he amend.

DIRECTIONS OF THE GENERAL ASSEMBLY,

CONCERNING SECRET AND PRIVATE WORSHIP, AND MUTUAL EDIFICATION; FOR CHERISHING PIETY, FOR MAINTAINING UNITY, AND AVOIDING SCHISM AND DIVISION.

BESIDES the publick worship in congregations, mercifully established in this land in great purity, it is expedient and necessary that secret worship of each person alone, and private worship of families, be pressed and set up; that, with national reformation, the profession and power of godliness, both personal and domestick, be advanced.

I. And first, for secret worship, it is most necessary, that every one apart, and by themselves, be given to prayer and meditation, the unspeakable benefit whereof is best known to them who are most exercised therein; this being the mean whereby, in a special way, communion with God is entertained, and right preparation for all other duties obtained: and therefore it becometh not only pastors, within their several charges, to press persons of all sorts to perform this duty morning and evening, and at other occasions; but also it is incumbent to the head of every family to have a care, that both themselves, and all within their charge, be daily diligent herein.

II. The ordinary duties comprehended under the exercise of piety which should be in families, when they are convened to that effect, are these: First, Prayer and praises performed with a special reference, as well to the publick condition of the kirk of God and this kingdom, as to the present case of the family, and every member thereof. Next, Reading of the scriptures, with catechising in a plain way, that the understandings of the simpler may be the better enabled to profit under the publick ordinances, and they made more capable to understand the scriptures when they are read; together with godly conferences tending to the edification of all the members in the most holy faith: as also, admonition and rebuke, upon just reasons, from those who have authority in the family.

III. As the charge and office of interpreting the holy scriptures is a part of the ministerial calling, which none (however otherwise qualified) should take upon him in any place, but he that is duly called thereunto by God and his kirk; so in every family where there is any that can read, the holy scriptures should be read ordinarily to the family;

DIRECTIONS FOR FAMILY-WORSHIP.

and it is commendable, that thereafter they confer, and by way of conference make some good use of what hath been read and heard. As, for example, if any sin be reproved in the word read, use may be made thereof to make all the family circumspect and watchful against the same; or if any judgment be threatened, or mentioned to have been inflicted, in that portion of scripture which is read, use may be made to make all the family fear lest the same or a worse judgment befall them, unless they beware of the sin that procured it: and, finally, if any duty be required, or comfort held forth in a promise, use may be made to stir up themselves to employ Christ for strength to enable them for doing the commanded duty, and to apply the offered comfort. In all which the master of the family is to have the chief hand; and any member of the family may propone a question or doubt for resolution.

IV. The head of the family is to take care that none of the family withdraw himself from any part of family-worship: and, seeing the ordinary performance of all the parts of family-worship belongeth properly to the head of the family, the minister is to stir up such as are lazy, and train up such as are weak, to a fitness to these exercises; it being always free to persons of quality to entertain one approved by the presbytery for performing family-exercise. And in other families, where the head of the family is unfit, that another, constantly residing in the family, approved by the minister and session, may be employed in that service, wherein the minister and session are to be countable to the presbytery. And if a minister, by divine Providence, be brought to any family, it is requisite that at no time he convene a part of the family for worship, secluding the rest, except in singular cases especially concerning these parties, which (in Christian prudence) need not, or ought not, to be imparted to others.

V. Let no idler, who hath no particular calling, or vagrant person under pretence of a calling, be suffered to perform worship in families, to or for the same; seeing persons tainted with errors, or aiming at division, may be ready (after that manner) to creep into houses, and lead captive silly and unstable souls.

VI. At family-worship, a special care is to be had that each family keep by themselves; neither requiring, inviting, nor admitting persons from divers families, unless it be those who are lodged with them, or at meals, or otherwise with them upon some lawful occasion.

VII. Whatsoever have been the effects and fruits of meetings of persons of divers families in the times of corruption or trouble, (in which cases many things are commendable, which otherwise are not tolerable,) yet, when God hath blessed us with peace and purity of the gospel, such meetings of persons of divers families (except in cases mentioned in these Directions) are to be disapproved, as tending to the hinderance of the religious exercise of each family by itself, to the prejudice of the publick ministry, to the rending of the families of particular congregations, and (in progress of time) of the whole kirk. Besides many offences which may come thereby, to the hardening of the hearts of carnal men, and grief of the godly.

VIII. On the Lord's day, after every one of the family apart, and the whole family together, have sought the Lord (in whose hands the preparation of men's hearts are) to fit them for the publick worship, and to bless to them the publick ordinances, the master of the family ought to take care that all within his charge repair to the publick worship, that he and they may join with the rest of the congregation: and the publick worship being finished, after prayer, he should take an account what they have heard; and thereafter, to spend the rest of the time which they may spare in catechising, and in spiritual conferences upon the word of God: or else (going apart) they ought to apply themselves to reading, meditation, and secret prayer, that they may confirm and increase their communion with God: that so the profit which they found in the publick ordinances may be cherished and promoved, and they more edified unto eternal life.

IX. So many as can conceive prayer, ought to make use of that gift of God; albeit those who are rude and weaker may begin at a set form of prayer, but so as they be not sluggish in stirring up in themselves (according to their daily necessities) the spirit of prayer, which is given to all the children of God in some measure; to which effect, they ought to be more fervent and frequent in secret prayer to God, for enabling of their hearts to conceive, and their tongues to express, convenient desires to God for their family. And, in the meantime, for their greater encouragement, let these materials of prayer be meditated upon, and made use of, as followeth.

"Let them confess to God how unworthy they are to come in his presence, and how "unfit to worship his Majesty; and therefore earnestly ask of God the spirit of prayer.

"They are to confess their sins, and the sins of the family; accusing, judging, and "condemning themselves for them, till they bring their souls to some measure of true "humiliation.

"They are to pour out their souls to God, in the name of Christ, by the Spirit, for for-"giveness of sins; for grace to repent, to believe, and to live soberly, righteously, and "godly; and that they may serve God with joy and delight, walking before him.

"They are to give thanks to God for his many mercies to his people, and to them "selves, and especially for his love in Christ, and for the light of the gospel.

"They are to pray for such particular benefits, spiritual and temporal, as they stand "in need of for the time, (whether it be morning or evening,) as anent health or sick-"ness, prosperity or adversity.

"They ought to pray for the kirk of Christ in general, for all the reformed kirks and

T

"for this kirk in particular, and for all that suffer for the name of Christ; for all our superiors, the king's majesty, the queen, and their children; for the magistrates, ministers, and whole body of the congregation whereof they are members, as well for their neighbours absent in their lawful affairs, as for those that are at home.

"The prayer may be closed with an earnest desire that God may be glorified in the coming of the kingdom of his Son, and in doing of his will, and with assurance that themselves are accepted, and what they have asked according to his will shall be done."

X. These exercises ought to be performed in great sincerity, without delay, laying aside all exercises of worldly business or hinderances, notwithstanding the mockings of atheists and profane men; in respect of the great mercies of God to this land, and of his severe corrections wherewith lately he hath exercised us. And, to this effect, persons of eminency (and all elders of the kirk) not only ought to stir up themselves and families to diligence herein, but also to concur effectually, that in all other families, where they have power and charge, the said exercises be conscionably performed.

XI. Besides the ordinary duties in families, which are above mentioned, extraordinary duties, both of humiliation and thanksgiving, are to be carefully performed in families, when the Lord, by extraordinary occasions, (private or publick,) calleth for them.

XII. Seeing the word of God requireth that we should consider one another, to provoke unto love and good works; therefore, at all times, and specially in this time, wherein profanity abounds, and mockers, walking after their own lusts, think it strange that others run not with them to the same excess of riot; every member of this kirk ought to stir up themselves, and one another, to the duties of mutual edification, by instruction, admonition, rebuke; exhorting one another to manifest the grace of God in denying ungodliness and worldly lusts, and in living godly, soberly, and rightcously in this present world; by comforting the feeble-minded, and praying with or for one another. Which duties respectively are to be performed upon special occasions offered by Divine Providence; as, namely, when under any calamity, cross, or great difficulty, counsel or comfort is sought; or when an offender is to be reclaimed by private admonition, and if that be not effectual, by joining one or two more in the admonition, according to the rule of Christ, that in the mouth of two or three witnesses every word may be established.

XIII. And, because it is not given to every one to speak a word in season to a wearied or distressed conscience, it is expedient, that a person (in that case,) finding no ease, after the use of all ordinary means, private and publick, have their address to their own pastor, or some experienced Christian: but if the person troubled in conscience be of that condition, or of that sex, that discretion, modesty, or fear of scandal, requireth a godly, grave, and secret friend to be present with them in their said address, it is expedient that such a friend be present.

XIV. When persons of divers families are brought together by Divine Providence, being abroad upon their particular vocations, or any necessary occasions; as they would have the Lord their God with them whithersoever they go, they ought to walk with God, and not neglect the duties of prayer and thanksgiving, but take care that the same be performed by such as the company shall judge fittest. And that they likewise take heed that no corrupt communication proceed out of their mouths, but that which is good, to the use of edifying, that it may minister grace to the hearers.

The drift and scope of all these Directions is no other, but that, upon the one part, the power and practice of godliness, amongst all the ministers and members of this kirk, according to their several places and vocations, may be cherished and advanced, and all impiety and mocking of religious exercises suppressed: and, upon the other part, that, under the name and pretext of religious exercises, no such meetings or practices be allowed, as are apt to breed error, scandal, schism, contempt, or misregard of the publick ordinances and ministers, or neglect of the duties of particular callings, or such other evils as are the works, not of the Spirit, but of the flesh, and are contrary to truth and peace   A. KER.

A TABLE

OF

THE CHIEF MATTERS CONTAINED IN THE CONFESSION OF FAITH AND LARGER CATECHISM.

Con. signifies *the Confession of Faith.* The first number denotes the Chapter, the following figures denote the Paragraphs.
Cat. signifies *the Larger Catechism,* and the figures denote the numbers of the Questions.

A

ACCEPTANCE. The persons of believers are accepted as righteous in the sight of God only for the obedience and satisfaction of Christ, *con.* xi. 1. *cat.* 70. Which is imputed to them by God, and received by faith, *con.* xi. 1. *cat.* 70, 71, 72. How their good works are accepted in Christ, *con.* xvi. 6. Acceptance in prayer through Christ and his mediation, *cat.* 180.

Access. No access unto the presence of God without the Mediator Jesus Christ, *con.* xii. *cat.* 39, 55, 181. Who hath purchased for believers under the gospel a greater boldness of access to the throne of grace, than believers under the law did ordinarily partake of, *con.* xx. 1.

Actions. God orders and governs all the actions of his creatures by his most wise and holy providence, according to his infallible foreknowledge and immutable decree, *con.* v. 1. *cat.* 18. See *Providence.*

Actual sins proceed from the original corruption of nature, *con.* vi. 4. *cat.* 25. See *Sin.*

Admonition of the church, *con.* xxx. 4.

Adoption, the nature and privileges of it, *con.* xii. *cat.* 74.

Adultery, a just ground of divorce, *con.* xxiv. 5, 6.

Aggravations of sin, *cat.* 151.

Amen, the meaning of it, *cat.* 196.

Angels, God's decree concerning them, *con.* iii. 3, 4. *cat.* 13. How created, *cat.* 16. God's providence towards them, *cat.* 19. They are all employed at his pleasure in the administrations of his power, mercy, and justice, *ib.* Not to be worshipped, *con.* xxi. 2. *cat.* 105.

Antichrist, what, *con.* xxv. 6. The Pope is Antichrist, *ib.*

Antiquity, no pretence for using the devices of men in the worship of God, *cat.* 109.

Anxiety about the things of this life sinful, *cat.* 105, 136, 142.

Apocrypha, the, not being of divine inspiration, is of no authority in the church, *con.* i. 3.

Apparel, immodest, forbidden, *cat.* 139.

Ascension of Christ, *con.* viii. 4. *cat.* 53.

Assembly. See *Councils.*

Assemblies, publick, for the worship of God not to be carelessly or wilfully neglected, *con.* xxi. 6.

Assurance of grace and salvation attainable in this life, *con.* xviii. 1, 2. *cat.* 80. Without extraordinary revelation, *con.* xviii. 3. *cat.* 80. Upon what it is founded, *con.* iii. 8. xviii. 2. *cat.* 80. It is strengthened by good works, *con.* xvi. 2. Believers may want it, *con.* xviii. 3. *cat.* 80, 172. They may have it diminished and intermitted; and be deprived of comfort, and the light of God's countenance, *con.* xi. 5. xvii. 3. xviii. 4. *cat.* 81. But they are never utterly destitute of that seed of God, and life of faith and love, &c., out of which assurance may, by the Spirit, be in due time revived, *con.* xviii. 4. *cat.* 81. And by which, in the mean time, they are supported from utter despair, *ib.* It is the duty of all to endeavour after assurance, *con.* xviii. 3. And to pray for it, *cat.* 194. The fruits of it; it inclines not to looseness, *con.* xviii. 3.

Atheism, the denying or not having a God, *cat.* 105.

Attributes of God, *con.* ii. 1, 2. *cat.* 7, 8, 101.

B

BAPTISM, what, *con.* xxviii. 1, 2. *cat.* 165. To continue to the end of the world, *con.* xxviii. 1. *cat.* 176. But once to be administered to any person, *con.* xxviii. 7. *cat.* 177. By whom, *con.* xxvii. 4. xxviii. 2. *cat.* 176. To whom, *con.* xxviii. 4. *cat.* 166. Dipping not necessary in baptism: But it may be rightly administered by sprinkling, *con.* xxviii. 3. Baptism not necessary to salvation, yet it is a sin to neglect it, *con.* xxviii. 5. The efficacy of it, *con.* xxviii. 6. How to be improved, *cat.* 167. Wherein it agrees with the Lord's Supper, *cat.* 176. And wherein they differ, *cat.* 177.

Believers. See *Faith, Justification, Acceptance, Adoption, Sanctification, Union, Communion, Liberty, Works, Perseverance, Assurance.*

Benefits which the members of the invisible church enjoy by Christ, *cat.* 65. The benefits of Christ's mediation, *cat.* 57, 58.

Body, the, of Christ, how present in the sacrament, *con.* xxix. 7. *cat.* 170.

Body, the mystical, of Christ. True believers are members of Christ's mystical body, *con.* xxix. 1. *cat.* 168. Which is the whole number of the elect that have been, are, or shall be united to Christ as their head, *con.* xxv. 1. What that union is, *cat.* 66. See *Communion.*

Bodies, the, of the elect after death, and at the resurrection, *con.* xxxii. 2, 3. *cat.* 86, 87. Of the wicked, *ib.*

Books, lascivious, not to be read, *cat.* 139.

C

CALLING. See *Effectual Calling.* To have a lawful calling, and to be diligent in it, is a duty, *cat.* 141.

Celibacy, vows of, unlawful, *con.* xxii. 7. *cat.* 139.

Censures of the church, what, *con.* xxx. 2, 4. Their use, *con.* xxx. 3. Who are to be proceeded against by the censures of the church, *con.* xx. 4. xxix. 8. xxx. 2. They are to be managed according to the nature of the crime, and the demerit of the person,

con. xxx. iv. Penitent sinners are to be absolved from censures, con. xxx. 2.
Censuring. Rash, harsh, and partial censuring sinful, cat. 145.
Ceremonial law. See *Law*.
Charity towards our neighbour, wherein it consists, cat. 135, 141, 144, 147. What contrary to it, cat. 136, 142, 145, 148. Giving and lending freely according to our ability and the necessities of others, is a duty, con. xxvi. 2. cat. 141.
Charms unlawful, cat. 113.
Chastity, cat. 138.
Children that die in infancy, how saved, con. x. 3. The children of such as profess the true religion are members of the visible church, con. xxv. 2. cat. 62. And are to be baptized, con. xxviii. 4. cat. 166.
Christ, why so called, cat. 42. Is the only Mediator between God and man, con. viii. 1. cat. 36. Who being very God, of one substance, and equal with the Father, con. viii. 2. cat. 11, 36. In the fulness of time became man, con. viii. 2. cat. 36, 37. The necessity of his being God and man, cat. 38, 39, 40. He was ordained by God from eternity to be Mediator, con. viii. 1. He was sanctified and anointed with the Holy Spirit to execute the office of Mediator, con. viii. 3. cat. 42. To which he was called by the Father, con. viii. 3. And willingly undertook and discharged it, con. iv. 8. By his perfect obedience and sacrifice of himself, he purchased reconciliation and eternal life for all the elect, con. viii. 5. cat. 38. To whom, in all ages, the benefits of his mediation are effectually applied, con. viii. 6, 8. Christ's offices of prophet, priest, king, cat. 43, 44, 45. See *Acceptance, Access, Body of Christ, Church, Death of Christ, Exaltation, Expiation, Humiliation, Imputation, Intercession, Judge, Merit, Messiah, Name of Christ, Personal Union, Propitiation, Reconciliation, Redemption, Resurrection, Righteousness, Sacrifice, Salvation, Satisfaction, Surety.*
Christian liberty. See *Liberty*.
Church, the, is the object of God's special providence, con. v. 7. cat. 63. Christ the only head of it, con. viii. 1. xxv. 6. The catholick church invisible, what, con. xxv. 1. cat. 64. Given to Christ from all eternity, con. viii. 1. The benefits which the members of it enjoy by Christ, cat. 65, 66, 69, 82, 83, 86, 90. The catholick church visible, what, con. xxv. 2. cat. 62. Out of it no ordinary possibility of salvation, con. xxv. 2. Its privileges, con. xxv. 3. cat. 63. Particular churches more or less pure, con. xxv. 4. The purest subject to mixture and error, con. xxv. 5. There shall always be a church on earth to worship God according to his will, *ib*.
Church-censures. See *Censures*.
Church-government appointed by the Lord Jesus in the hand of church-officers, distinct from the civil magistrate, con. xxx. 1. cat. 45, 108. But they are not exempted from obedience to the magistrate, con. xxiii. 4. They have the power of the keys committed to them, con. xxx. 2. What that power is, and its use, con. xxx. 2, 3, 4. They are not to be opposed in the lawful exercise of their powers upon pretence of Christian liberty, con. xx. 4. See *Councils*. There are some circumstances concerning church-government, which are to be ordered by the light of nature and Christian prudence, according to the general rules of the word, con. i. 6.
Circumcision, one of the ordinances by which the covenant of grace was administered unto the law, con. vii. 5. cat. 34.
Civil magistrate, or civil powers. See *Magistrate*.
Commandments, the Ten, are the sum of the moral law, con. xix. 2. cat. 98. They are a perfect rule of righteousness, con. xix. 2. Rules for understanding them, cat. 99. The preface explained, cat. 101. The first Commandment, cat. 103–106. The second, cat. 107–110. The third, cat. 111–114. The fourth, cat. 115–121. The fifth, cat. 123–133. The sixth, cat. 134–136. The seventh, cat. 137–139. The eighth, cat. 140–142. The ninth, cat. 143–145. The tenth, cat. 146–148. The sum of the first four commandments, which contain our duty to God, cat. 102. The sum of the other six, which contain our duty to man, cat. 122. No man is able to keep the commandments of God perfectly, cat. 149.
Communion, the. See *The Lord's Supper*.
Communion of Saints, wherein it consists, con. xxvi. 1, 2. The enjoyment of it is one of the privileges of the visible church, cat. 63. In the Lord's supper communicants testify their mutual love and fellowship each with other, cat. 168. That sacrament being a bond and pledge of believers' communion with Christ, and with each other, as members of his mystical body, con. xxix. 1. The communion of saints doth not infringe a man's property in his goods and possessions, con. xxvi. 3.
Communion which the elect have with Christ, con. xxvi. 1. In this life, cat. 69, 83. Immediately after death, cat. 86. At the resurrection and day of judgment, cat. 87, 90. It is a consequence of their union with him, con. xxvi. 1. It doth not make them partakers of his Godhead, nor equal with him, con. xxvi. 3. It is confirmed in the Lord's supper, cat. 168.
Company, unchaste, not to be kept, cat. 139. Nor corrupt communications to be used or listened to, *ib*.
Condition. Perfect, personal, and perpetual obedience, the condition of the covenant of works, con. vii. 2. xix. 1. cat. 20. God requires faith as the condition to interest sinners in the Mediator of the covenant of grace, cat. 32.
Confession of sin always to be made in private to God, con. xv. 6. And is to be joined with prayer, cat. 178. When to be made to men, con. xv. 6. Upon confession the offending brother is to be received in love, *ib*.
Conscience. See *Liberty of Conscience*. Peace of conscience a fruit of the sense of God's love, con. xviii. 1, 3. cat. 83. Believers may fall into sins which wound the conscience, con. xvii. 3. xviii. 4. The wicked are punished with horror of conscience, cat. 28, 83.
Contentment. Submission to God is our duty, cat. 104. Discontent at his dispensations is sinful, cat. 105. A full contentment

with our condition is our duty, *cat.* 147. Discontentment with our own estate a sin, *cat.* 148.

Controversies. It belongs to synods and councils ministerially to determine controversies of faith, and cases of conscience, *con.* xxxi. 3. The Spirit speaking in the scriptures is the supreme judge of all controversies in religion, *con.* i. 10. The original text of the scriptures is that to which the church is finally to appeal, *con.* i. 8.

Conversation, our, ought to be in holiness and righteousness, answerable to an holy profession, *cat.* 112, 167.

Corruption of nature, what, *con.* vi. 2, 4. *cat.* 25. A consequence of the fall of man, *ib.* Actual sin a fruit of it, *con.* vi. 4. *cat.* 25. How it is propagated, *con.* vi. 3. *cat.* 26. It doth remain during this life in the regenerate, and all its motions are truly sin, *con.* vi. 5. xiii. 2. *cat.* 78. But it is pardoned and mortified through Christ, *con.* vi. 5.

Covenant. No enjoying of God but by way of covenant, *con.* vii. 1.

Covenant of works, what, and with whom made, *con.* iv. 2. vii. 2. xix. 1. *cat.* 20, 22. Perfect, personal, and perpetual obedience, the condition of it, *con.* vii. 2. xix. 1. *cat.* 20. It is called a law, and a command, *con.* iv. 2. and a law given as a covenant, *con.* xix. 1. and a covenant of life, of which the tree of life was a pledge, *cat.* 20.

Covenant of grace, what, *con.* vii. 3. *cat.* 30, 32. It was made with Christ as the second Adam, and with all the elect in him, as his seed, *cat.* 31. In it God requireth of sinners faith in Christ, that they may be justified and saved, *con.* vii. 3. *cat.* 71. Faith being required as the condition to interest them in Christ, *cat.* 32. Who is the Mediator of this covenant, *con.* viii. 1. *cat.* 36. Why it is called a testament, *con.* vii. 4. It was differently administered in the time of the law, and in the time of the gospel, *con.* vii. 5. *cat.* 33. How it was administered under the law, *con.* vii. 5. *cat.* 34. How under the gospel, *con.* vii. 6 *cat.* 35.

Councils or Synods ought to be, *c n.* xxxi. 1. They may be called by the civil magistrate, *con.* xxiii. 3. xxxi. 2. When ministers may meet without the call of the civil magistrate, *con.* xxxi. 2. What power councils have, *c. n.* xxxi. 3. What submission due to their decrees, *ib.* Not infallible since the apostles' time, *con.* xxxi. 4. But their determinations are to be tried by the scriptures, *con.* i. 10. How far they may meddle in civil affairs, *con.* xxxi. 5.

Creation of the world, *con.* iv. 1. *cat.* 15. Of man, *con.* iv. 2. *cat.* 17. Of angels, *cat.* 16.

Creatures. Dominion over the creatures given to man, *con.* iv. 2. *cat.* 17. They are cursed for our sakes since the fall, *cat.* 28. Religious worship to be given to no creature, *con.* xxi. 2. *cat.* 105.

Curiosity. Bold and curious searching into God's secrets discharged, *cat.* 105. Curious prying into God's decrees forbidden, *cat.* 113. Curious or unprofitable questions are to be avoided, *ib.*

Curse, the, and wrath of God, man liable to it, both by original and actual sin, *con.* vi. 6. *cat.* 27. How it may be escaped, *con.* vii. 3. *cat.* 153

Cursing sinful, *cat.* 113.

D

Dancing. Lascivious dancing forbidden, *cat.* 139.

Dead not to be prayed for, *con.* xxi. 4. *cat.* 183.

Death, being the wages of sin, *con.* vi. 6. *cat.* 28, 84. It is appointed for all men, *cat.* 84. How it is an advantage to the righteous, *cat.* 85. The state of believers immediately after death, *con.* xxxii. 1. *cat.* 86. of the wicked, *ib.*

Death, the, of Christ, *con.* viii. 4. *cat.* 49. In it he saw no corruption, *con.* viii. 4. *cat.* 52. The divine nature having sustained the human from sinking under the power of death, *cat.* 38. By his obedience and death, he made a proper, real, and full satisfaction to the justice of the Father, *con.* xi. 3. *cat.* 71. Through the virtue of his death and resurrection, believers are sanctified, *con.* xiii. 1. Believers have fellowship with Christ in his death, *con.* xxvi. 1. And from his death and resurrection they draw strength for the mortifying of sin, and quickening of grace, *cat.* 167. The Lord's supper is a memorial of his death, *con.* xxix. 1. *cat.* 168. And in that sacrament worthy communicants meditate affectionately on his death and sufferings, *cat.* 174. And receive and feed upon all the benefits of his death, *con.* xxix. 7.

Decalogue, the. See *Commandments.*

Decrees, the, of God, the nature, end, extent, and properties of them, *con.* iii. 1, 2. *cat.* 12. The decree of predestination, *con.* iii. 3, 4. Of election and reprobation, *con.* iii. 5, 6, 7. *cat.* 13. How God executeth his decrees, *cat.* 14. How the doctrine of decrees is to be handled, and what use to be made of them, *con.* iii. 8. Curious prying into God's decrees forbidden, *cat.* 113.

Desertion. Wilful desertion unlawful, *cat.* 139. Such as cannot be remedied by the church or civil magistrate, is cause sufficient of dissolving the bond of marriage, *con.* xxiv. 6.

Despair sinful, *cat.* 105. Believers always supported from utter despair, *con.* xviii. 4. *cat.* 81.

Devil, all compacts and consulting with him sinful, *cat.* 105.

Diligence in our calling a duty, *cat.* 141.

Dipping in baptism not necessary, *con.* xxviii. 3.

Discontent at the dispensations of God's providence sinful, *cat.* 105, 113. Discontentment with our own estate sinful, *cat.* 148.

Divorce, lawful in case of adultery after marriage, or of such wilful desertion as cannot be remedied, *con.* xxiv. 5, 6. A publick and orderly course of proceeding is to be observed in it, *con.* xxiv. 6.

Dominion. See *Sovereignty, Creatures, Sin.*

Doubting of being in Christ, may consist with a true interest in him, *con.* xvii. 3. xviii. 4. *cat.* 81, 172. And therefore should not hindor from partaking of the Lord's supper, *cat.* 172.

Drunkenness forbidden, *cat.* 139.

Duty to God by the light of nature, *con.* xxi. 1. Duties required in the first commandment, *cat.* 104. In the second, *cat.* 108. In the third, *cat.* 112. In the fourth, *cat.* 116. Duties of inferiors to their superiors, *con.*

xxiii. 4. *cat.* 127. What is required of superiors, *con.* xxiii. 2. *cat.* 129. Duties of equals, *cat.* 131. Duties of the sixth commandment, *cat.* 135. Of the seventh, *cat.* 138. Of the eighth, *cat.* 141. Of the ninth, *cat.* 144. Of the tenth, *cat.* 147.

E

ECCLESIASTICAL powers not to be opposed upon pretence of Christian liberty, *con.* xx. 4. Ecclesiastical persons not exempted from obedience to the civil magistrate, *con.* xxiii. 4.
Effectual calling, what, *con.* x. 1. *cat.* 67. It is of God's free grace, not from any thing foreseen in man, *con.* x. 2. *cat.* 67. All the elect, and they only, are effectually called, *con.* x. 1, 4. *cat.* 68. The elect united to Christ in their effectual calling, *cat.* 66.
Election, out of God's mere free grace, *con.* iii. 5. *cat.* 13. From all eternity in Christ, *ib.* Election not only to eternal life and glory, but also to the means thereof, *con.* iii. 6. *cat.* 13. All the elect, and they only, are effectually called and saved, *con.* iii. 6. x. 1, 4. *cat.* 68. Though others may be outwardly called by the word, and have some common operations of the Spirit, *ib.* Elect infants, and other elect persons who are incapable of being called by the word, how saved, *con.* x. 3. What use to be made of the doctrine of election, *con.* iv. 8. And how men may be assured of their eternal election, *ib.* See *Assurance.*
Envy sinful, *cat.* 128, 136, 142, 145, 146.
Equals, their duties and sins, *cat.* 131, 132.
Equivocation. Speaking the truth in doubtful and equivocal expressions, to the prejudice of truth or justice, sinful, *cat.* 145.
Eucharist. See *Lord's Supper.*
Exaltation of Christ, *con.* viii. 4 *cat.* 51. In his resurrection, *cat.* 52. In his ascension, *cat.* 53. In his sitting at the right hand of God, *cat.* 54. In his coming to judge the world, *cat.* 56.
Self-examination, *cat.* 171.
Excommunication, *con.* xxx. 2, 3, 4.
Expiation. Sin cannot be expiated but by the blood of Christ, *cat.* 152.

F

FAITH, what, *con.* xiv. 2. *cat.* 72. God requireth nothing of sinners that they may be justified, but faith in Christ, *con.* xi. 1. *cat.* 71. Which he requireth as the condition to interest them in the Mediator of the covenant of grace, *cat.* 32. It justifies a sinner in the sight of God only as it is an instrument by which he receiveth Christ and his righteousness, *con.* xi. 2. *cat.* 73. Faith is the gift of God, *con.* xi. 1. *cat.* 71. It being the work of the Spirit, *con.* xiv. 1. *cat.* 59, 72. It is ordinarily wrought by the ministry of the word, *con.* xiv. 1. Increased and strengthened by the word, sacraments, and prayer *ib.* Often weakened, but always gets the victory *con.* xiv. 3. Growing up in many to a full assurance, *con.* xiv. 3. *cat.* 80. Good works the fruit and evidence of true faith, *con.* xvi. 2. *cat.* 52. Which is never alone, but always accompanied with all other saving graces, and is no dead faith, but worketh by love, *con.* xi. 2. *cat.* 73.
Fall of man, the nature and effects of it, *con.* vi. *cat.* 21, 23, 25, 27, 28, 29. Why permitted,

con. vi. 1. How all mankind concerned in it, *con.* vi. 3. *cat.* 22.
Falling away. See *Perseverance.*
Family worship daily, required of God, *con.* xxi. 6.
Fasting. Religious fasting a duty, *cat.* 108. Solemn fasting a part of religious worship, *con.* xxi. 5.
Fellowship. See *Communion.*
Foreknowledge. All things come to pass infallibly according to the foreknowledge of God, *con.* v. 2.
Forgiveness. See *Pardon.*
Fornication committed after contract of marriage, a just ground of dissolving the contract, *con.* xxiv. 5.
Fortune. To ascribe any thing to fortune is sinful, *cat.* 105.
Free-will. See *Will.*
Frugality a duty, *cat.* 141.

G

GAMING. Wasteful gaming forbidden, *cat.* 142
Glory. The communion in glory with Christ, which believers enjoy in this life, *con.* xviii. 1, 2, 3, *cat.* 83. Immediately after death, *con.* xxxii. 1. *cat.* 86. At the resurrection and day of judgment, *con.* xxxii. 3. xxxiii. 2. *cat.* 87, 90.
Glory, the, of God the end of his decrees, *con.* iii. 3. *cat.* 12. The glory of his grace the end of election, *con.* iii. 5. *cat.* 13. The glory of his justice the end of the decree of reprobation, *con.* iii. 7. *cat.* 13. The glory of his eternal power, wisdom, and goodness, the end of the creation, *con.* iv. 1. The manifestation of the glory of his wisdom, power, justice, goodness, and mercy, is the end of all God's works of providence, *con.* v. 1. *cat.* 18. The end of God's appointing the last judgment is the manifestation of the glory of his mercy and justice, *con.* xxxii. 10. To glorify God is the chief end of man, *cat.* 1. God is glorified by good works, *con.* xvi. 2.
Gluttony a sin, *cat.* 139.
God. The light of nature sheweth that there is a God, *con.* xxi. 1. *cat.* 2. What it declares concerning him, and of our duty to him, *con.* i. 1. xxi. 1. It is not sufficient to give that knowledge of God, and of his will, which is necessary unto salvation, *con.* i. 1. *cat.* 2. The attributes or perfections of God, *con.* ii. 1, 2. *cat.* 7, 101. There is but one only God, *con.* ii. 1. *cat.* 8. There are three persons in the Godhead, distinguished by personal properties, *con.* ii. 3. *cat.* 9, 10. The co-equality of the persons proved, *cat.* 11. To him is due from all his creatures, whatsoever worship, service, or obedience, he is pleased to require, *con.* ii. 2. Our duty to God, *cat.* 104, 108, 112, 116. What contrary to it, *cat.* 105, 109, 113, 119. Religious worship is to be given to God the Father, Son, and Holy Ghost, and to him alone; and that only in the mediation of Christ, *con.* xxi. 2. *cat.* 179, 181. God is to be worshipped in that way only which he hath instituted in the scriptures, *con.* xxi. 1. *cat.* 109. To glorify God, and fully to enjoy him for ever, is the chief end of man, *cat.* 1.
Good works. See *Works.*
Gospel. How the covenant of grace is administered under the gospel, *con.* vii. 6. *cat.*

85. Without the gospel no salvation, *con.* x. 4. *cat.* 60. In it Christ doth not dissolve but strengthen the obligation to the obedience of the moral law, *con.* xix. 5. Believers under the gospel have a greater boldness of access to the throne of grace, than believers under the law did ordinarily partake of, *con.* xx. 1.

Government. See *Church, Magistrate.*

Grace, the, of God. Election is of God's mere free grace, *con.* iii. 5. *cat.* 13. How the grace of God is manifested in the second covenant, *con.* vii. 3. *cat.* 32. Effectual calling is of God's free and special grace, *con.* x. 2. *cat.* 67. Justification is only of free grace, *con.* xi. 3. *cat.* 70, 71. Adoption is an act of free grace, *con.* xii. *cat.* 74. The communion in grace which believers have with Christ, *cat.* 69. All saving graces are the work of the Spirit, *con.* xiii. xiv. xv. *cat.* 32, 72, 75, 76, 77. And do always accompany faith, *con.* xi. 2. *cat.* 73. Perseverance in grace, *con.* xvii. *cat.* 79. Increase in grace, *con.* xiii. 1, 3. *cat.* 75, 77. Assurance of grace, *con.* xviii. *cat.* 80, 81.

H

HARDEN. Why and how sinners are hardened, *con.* v. 6. Believers may have their hearts hardened, *con.* xvii. 3.

Head. The elect are inseparably united to Christ as their head, *con.* xxv. 1. xxvi. 1. *cat.* 64, 66. He is the only head of the church, *con.* xxv. 6.

Hearing. What is required of those that hear the word preached, *con.* xxi. 5. *cat.* 160.

Heaven, the state of the blessed, *con.* xxxii. 1. xxxiii. 2. *cat.* 86, 90.

Hell, the state of the damned, *con.* xxxii. 1. xxxiii. 2. *cat.* 29, 86, 89. The meaning of these words in the Creed, *He descended into hell, cat.* 50.

Hereticks to be rejected, *cat.* 105.

Holiness. God is most holy in all his counsels, works, and commands, *con.* ii. 2. Man was created holy after the image of God, *con.* iv. 2. *cat.* 17. But by the fall he became wholly defiled, *con.* vi. 2. Believers are, by the sanctifying Spirit of Christ, quickened and strengthened to the practice of holiness, *con.* xiii. 1, 3. *cat.* 75. And are made perfectly holy in heaven, *con.* xxxii. 1. *cat.* 86, 90. See *Sanctification.*

Holy Ghost, the, equal with the Father, *con.* ii. 3. *cat.* 11. He is promised to the elect in the covenant of grace, *con.* vii. 3. *cat.* 32. By him they are united to Christ, *con.* xxvi. 1. For by him the redemption purchased by Christ is applied to them, *con.* viii. 8. xi. 4. *cat.* 58, 59. By him they are effectually called, *con.* x. 1. *cat.* 67. And have faith wrought in their hearts, *con.* xiv. 1. *cat.* 59, 72. He is given to them in adoption, *con.* xii. *cat.* 74. And applying the death and resurrection of Christ to them, by his powerful operation, they are sanctified, *con.* xiii. 1. *cat.* 75. Having repentance wrought, and all other saving graces infused into their hearts, *con.* xiii. 1. *cat.* 32, 75, 76, 77. Through the continual supply of strength from him, believers grow in grace, *con.* xiii. 3. *cat.* 75. The outward means are by him made effectual to the elect for salvation, *con.* vii. 5, 6. xxv. 3. *cat.* 155, 161. Prayer is to be made by his help, *con.* xxi. 3. *cat.* 182. Ability to do good works is from him, *con.* xvi. 3. Assurance of faith is attained by his witnessing with our spirits that we are the children of God, *con.* xviii. 2. *cat.* 80. By his abiding within believers, they are secured from falling totally away from the state of grace, and are kept by the power of God through faith unto salvation, *con.* xvii. 2. *cat.* 79.

Hope of glory, *con.* xviii. 1. *cat.* 83. The hope of hypocrites, *con.* xviii. 1.

Humiliation of Christ, *con.* viii. 2, 4. *cat.* 46. In his conception and birth, *cat.* 47. In his life, *cat.* 48. In his death, *cat.* 49. After death, *cat.* 50.

Hypocrisy. Making profession of religion in hypocrisy, or for sinister ends, sinful, *cat.* 113. The hypocrite's hope, *con.* xviii. 1.

Hypostatical. See *Personal.*

I

IDLENESS unlawful, *cat.* 139, 142. Idolatry, all the kinds of it forbidden, *cat.* 105, 109. All monuments of idolatry ought to be removed, *cat.* 108.

Ignorant, not to be admitted to the Lord's table, *con.* xxix. 8. *cat.* 173.

Image. Man made after the image of God, in knowledge, righteousness, and holiness, *con.* iv. 2. *cat.* 17. This image is renewed by sanctification, *cat.* 75. And fully perfected in heaven, *con.* xxxii. 1. *cat.* 86, 90.

Image-worship of all kinds discharged, *cat.* 109.

Imputation. The guilt of Adam's first sin is imputed to all his posterity, *con.* vi. 3. The obedience and satisfaction of Christ is imputed to believers, *con.* xi. 1. *cat.* 70. His righteousness is imputed to them, *cat.* 71, 77.

Incarnation of Christ, *con.* viii. 2. *cat.* 37, 39.

Incest discharged, *cat.* 139. Incestuous marriages, which are within the degrees of consanguinity or affinity forbidden in the scriptures, can never be made lawful, *con.* xxiv. 4.

Inclosures and depopulations, unjust, forbidden, *cat.* 142.

Increase of grace is from a continual supply of strength from the sanctifying Spirit of Christ, *con.* xiii. 1, 3. *cat.* 75, 77.

Infants, how saved, *con.* x. 3. Infants of one or both believing parents are to be baptized, *con.* xxviii. 4. *cat.* 166.

Ingrossing commodities to enhance their price, unlawful, *cat.* 142.

Innocency. The state of man in innocency, *con.* iv. 2. *cat.* 17, 20.

Inspiration. The books of the Old and New Testament are given by inspiration of God, *con.* i. 2. But the Apocrypha is not of divine inspiration, *con.* i. 3.

Intercession. How Christ makes intercession, *cat.* 55. It is a part of his priestly office, *cat.* 44. He makes intercession, that the redemption which he hath purchased may be applied to all believers, *con.* viii. 8. *cat.* 55. And their perseverance depends upon his continual intercession for them, *con.* xvii. 2. *cat.* 79.

J

Jests. Perverting the scripture to profane jests, sinful, *cat.* 113.

Jesus, why so called, *cat.* 41. See *Christ.*

Joy in the Holy Ghost, the fruit of assurance, *con.* xviii. 1, 2. *cat.* 83. Believers, by fall ing into some sins, may grieve the Spirit, and be deprived of some measure of their comfort, *con.* xvii. 3. xviii. 4.

Judge. Christ the judge of the world, *con.* viii. 1, 4. xxxiii. 1. How he shall come at the last day, *cat.* 56.

Judgments, the, of God upon sinners in this world, *con.* v. 6. *cat.* 28, 83. How believers may bring temporal judgments on themselves, *con.* xvii. 3. God is just and terrible in his judgments, *con.* ii. 1.

Judgment, the last, what, *con.* xxxiii. 1. Appointed for angels and men, *con.* viii. 4. xxxiii. 1. *cat.* 88. The end of its appointment is the manifestation of God's mercy and justice, *con.* xxxiii. 2. Christ shall be the judge, *con.* viii. 4. xxxiii. 1. How he shall come to judge the world, *cat.* 56. Why he would have us certainly persuaded of it, *con.* xxxiii. 3. Why the time of it is concealed, *con.* xxxiii. 3. *cat.* 88. The judgment of the righteous, *con.* xxxiii. 2. *cat.* 90. The judgment of the wicked, *con.* xxxiii. 2. *cat.* 89.

Judicial law. See *Law*.

Justice, the, of God fully satisfied by Christ's obedience and death, *con.* viii. 5. xi. 3. *cat.* 38, 71. It is manifested in the works of providence, *con.* v. 1. In the justification of sinners, *con.* xi. 3. In the last judgment, *con.* xxxiii. 2.

Justice in contracts and commerce between man and man, *cat.* 141, 142.

Justification, what, *con.* xi. 1. *cat.* 70. All the elect, and they only, are justified, *con.* iii. 6. Whom God did from all eternity decree to justify, *con.* xi. 4. But they are not justified till the Holy Spirit doth in due time actually apply Christ unto them, *ib.* How justification is of God's free grace, *con.* xi. 3. *cat.* 71. Faith is necessarily required for justification, *cat.* 71. But it justifies a sinner only as it is an instrument by which he receiveth Christ and his righteousness, *con.* xi. 1, 2. *cat.* 73. The exact justice, and rich grace of God, are both glorified in the justification of sinners, *con.* xi. 3. Justification the same under the Old Testament as under the New, *con.* xi. 6. It is inseparably joined with sanctification, *cat.* 77. How they differ, *ib.* Those that are justified are perfectly freed in this life from the revenging wrath of God, that they never fall into condemnation, *con.* xvii. 1. *cat.* 77, 79. But corruption remaining in them, *con.* vi. 5. xiii. 2. *cat.* 78. They fall into many sins, *con.* xvii. 3. *cat.* 78. Which God continues to forgive, upon their humbling themselves, confessing their sins, begging pardon, and renewing their faith and repentance, *con.* xi. 5.

K

KEYS. The power of the keys, what, *con.* xxx. 2. Committed to church-officers, *ib.* The civil magistrate may not assume this power, *con.* xxiii. 3.

King. Christ the King of his church, *con.* xxx. 1. How he executeth the office of a king, *cat.* 45. What meant by the coming of his kingdom, *cat.* 191.

Knowledge. God's knowledge is infinite, infallible, and independent upon the creature, *con.* ii. 2. The knowledge which may be had of God and of our duty to him by the light of nature, *con.* i. 1. xxi. 1. *cat.* 1. The scriptures are only sufficient to give that knowledge of God and of his will which is necessary unto salvation, *ib.*

L

LABOUR is to be moderately used, *cat.* 135, 136.

Land-marks not to be removed, *cat.* 142.

Law. The Ceremonial Law, what, *con.* xix. 3. It is abrogated now under the New Testament, *con.* xix. 3. xx. 1. How the covenant of grace was administered under the law, *con.* vii. 5. viii. 6. *cat.* 34.

Law, the Judicial, expired with the state of the Jews, *con.* xix. 4. And obliges no further than the general equity of it requires, *ib.*

Law, the Moral, what, *cat.* 93. Given to Adam with a power to fulfil it, *con.* iv. 2. xix. 1. *cat.* 92. The ten commandments the sum of it, *con.* xix. 2 *cat.* 98. Though believers are not under it as a covenant, *con.* xix. 6. And are not able perfectly to keep it, *cat.* 149. Yet it continues to be a perfect rule of righteousness, *con.* xix. 2. Binding all, as well justified persons as others, *con.* xix. 5. Christ, in the gospel, having not abolished, but much strengthened the obligation to the obedience of it, *ib.* And although no man since the fall can, by the moral law, attain to righteousness and life, *con.* xix. 6. *cat.* 94. Which Christ alone hath purchased for the elect by his perfect obedience, *con.* viii. 5. Yet it is of great use to all, *con.* xix. 6. *cat.* 95. The use of it to the regenerate, *con.* xix. 6. *cat.* 97. The use of it to the unregenerate, *cat.* 96. Not contrary to the grace of the gospel, but doth sweetly comply with it, *con.* xix. 7. The Spirit of Christ subduing and enabling the will of man unto a free and cheerful obedience to the will of God, *con.* xix. 7. *cat.* 32.

Law-suits, unnecessary, to be avoided, *cat.* 141, 142.

Liberty. Christian liberty, what, *con.* xx. 1. Wherein it is enlarged under the gospel, *ib.* The end of Christian liberty, *con.* xx. 3. Liberty to sin inconsistent with it, *ib.* It is not intended to destroy ecclesiastical or civil powers, but to support and preserve them, *con.* xx. 4. Neither are men thereby allowed to publish opinions, or maintain practices, that are contrary to the light of nature, or to the known principles of Christianity, or such as are destructive of the peace and order of the church, *ib.*

Liberty of conscience, what it is, and what repugnant to it, *con.* xx. 2. Making men the lords of our faith and conscience unlawful, *con.* xx. 2. *cat.* 105.

Life. Eternal life purchased by Christ's perfect obedience to the law, *con.* viii. 5. The tree of life was a pledge of the covenant of works, *cat.* 20. The life of any not to be taken away except in case of public justice, lawful war, or necessary defence, *cat.* 136.

Light of nature, what may be known of God and of our duty to him by it, *con.* i. 1. xxi. 1. *cat.* 2. It is not sufficient to make us wise unto salvation, *con.* i. 1. x. 4. xxi. 1. *cat.* 2, 60. It is of the law of nature that a due portion of time be set apart for the worship of God, *con.* xxi. 7.

Looks, wanton, sinful, *cat.* 139.

Lord's Prayer. See *Prayer*.

Lord's Supper. The institution, nature, and ends of it, *con.* xxix. 1. *cat.* 168. Christ not offered up to his Father, nor any real sacrifice for sin made in it, *con.* xxix. 2. The mass abominably injurious to Christ's one only sacrifice, *ib.* The outward elements in this sacrament are not to be adored, *con.* xxix. 4. They still remain truly bread and wine, *con.* xxix. 5. The doctrine of transubstantiation is repugnant not only to the scripture, but even to common sense, and has been and is the cause of gross idolatries, *con.* xxix. 6. How Christ hath appointed bread and wine to be given and received in the sacrament, *con.* xxix. 3. *cat.* 169. It is only to be administered by a minister of the word lawfully ordained, *con.* xxvii. 4. *cat.* 176. It is not to be received by any one alone, *con.* xxix. 4. It is to be received in both kinds, *ib.* What relation the elements in this sacrament have to Christ crucified, *con.* xxix. 5. How Christ is present there, *con.* xxix. 7. *cat.* 170. How believers feed on him therein, *ib.* What preparation is required for receiving it, *cat.* 171. Doubting may consist with an interest in Christ, *con.* xvii. 3. xviii. 4. *cat.* 81. And therefore should not hinder from partaking of the Lord's supper, *cat.* 172. But the ignorant and scandalous are not to be admitted, *con.* xxix. 8. *cat.* 173. What duties required in the time of receiving, *cat.* 174. What duties after receiving, *cat.* 175. Frequent attendance on it a duty, *cat.* 175, 177. The agreement and difference between the Lord's supper and baptism, *cat.* 176, 177.

Lots, *cat.* 112, 113.

Love. Election is of God's free love, *con.* iii. 5. *cat.* 13. Which is unchangeable, *con.* xvii. 2. *cat.* 79. And therefore true believers can neither totally nor finally fall away from the state of grace, *ib.* The sense of God's love is attainable in this life, *cat.* 83. See *Assurance.* Love to God is a duty, *cat.* 104. Which the light of nature sheweth, *con.* xxi. 1. To love the Lord our God with all our heart, &c. is the sum of our duty to him, *cat.* 102. Love to God is necessary to the right performance of the duty of prayer, *con.* xxi. 3. *cat.* 185. Love to God and the brethren is necessary to right communicating, *cat.* 168, 171, 174. True believers are never utterly destitute of the love of Christ and the brethren, *con.* xviii. 4. Wherein love towards our neighbour consists, *cat.* 135, 141, 144, 147. What contrary to it, *cat.* 136, 142, 145, 148. It is the sum of our duty to man, *cat.* 122.

Lying sinful, *cat.* 145.

M

MAGISTRATES appointed by God, *con.* xxiii. 1. For what end, *ib.* Lawful for Christians to accept the office of a magistrate, *con.* xxiii. 2. The duty of the civil magistrate, *con.* xxiii. 2. *cat.* 129. *con.* xx. 4. *Read the scriptures letter* v. The sins of the magistrate, *cat.* 130, 145. He may wage war upon just and necessary occasions, *con.* xxiii. 2. His power in church affairs stated, *con.* xxiii. 3. The duty of the people towards their magistrates, *con.* xxiii. 4. *cat.* 127. Their sins against them, *cat.* 128. Ecclesiastical persons not exempted from obedience to the civil magistrate, *con.* xxiii. 4. The Pope hath no power or jurisdiction over magistrates, or their people, *ib.* The magistrate is not to be opposed in the lawful exercise of his power, upon pretence of Christian liberty, *con.* xx. 4. Infidelity or difference in religion doth not make void the magistrate's just and legal authority, *con.* xxiii. 4.

Man, how created, *con.* iv. 2. *cat.* 17. His state before the fall, *con.* iv. 2. *cat.* 17, 20 His fall, and the effects of it, *con.* vi. *cat* 21, 22, 23, 25, 26, 27, 28, 29. His state by the covenant of grace, *con.* vii. 3–6. *cat.* 30–35. Man's chief end, *cat.* 1.

Man-stealing discharged, *cat.* 142.

Marriage, the end of it, *con.* xxiv. 2. *cat.* 20. Between more than one man and one woman at a time unlawful, *con.* xxiv. 1. *cat.* 139. Lawful for all sorts of people who are capable to give their consent, *con.* xxiv. 3. And who are without the degrees of consanguinity or affinity forbidden in the scriptures, *con.* xxiv. 4. But marriages within those degrees can never be made lawful, *ib.* Protestants should not marry with infidels, Papists, or other idolaters, *con.* xxiv. 3. Nor such as are godly with those that are notoriously wicked, *ib.* A contract of marriage may be dissolved for adultery or fornication committed after the contract, *con.* xxiv. 5. The bond of marriage can only be dissolved for adultery after marriage, and such wilful desertion as cannot be remedied, *con.* xxiv. 5, 6. Undue delay of marriage, prohibiting of lawful, and dispensing with unlawful marriages, are sinful, *cat.* 139. Vows of perpetual single life are sinful snares in which no Christian may entangle himself, *con.* xxii. 7. *cat.* 139. Those who have not the gift of continency ought to marry, *cat.* 138. The duties of married persons, *cat.* 139, 141.

Mass, the, abominably injurious to Christ's one only sacrifice, *con.* xxix. 2.

Means. God in his ordinary providence maketh use of means; yet is free to work without, above, and against them at his pleasure, *con.* v. 3. The outward and ordinary means of salvation under the law, *con.* vii. 5. *cat.* 34. Under the gospel, *con.* vii. 6. *cat.* 35, 154. The diligent use of them is required in order to escape the wrath of God, *cat.* 153. How they are made effectual, *con.* xxv. 3. *cat.* 155, 161, 182. Trusting in means sinful, *cat.* 105. Unlawful means not to be used, *ib.*

Measures, false, unlawful, *cat.* 142.

Meat to be moderately used, *cat.* 135, 136.

Mediator. See *Christ.*

Mercy, the, of God, *con.* ii. 1. *cat.* 7. It is manifested in his works of providence, *con.* v. 1. It is of God's free love and mercy that the elect are delivered from sin and misery, and brought to an estate of salvation by the second covenant, *cat.* 30. God is merciful to penitent sinners in Christ, *con.* xv. 2. *cat.* 76. For whose sake mercy is to be prayed for, *cat.* 180. Works of mercy are to be done, even on the Lord's day, *con.* xxi. 8. *cat.* 117.

Merit. No merit in good works for pardon of sin or eternal life; and why, *con.* xvi

5. Nor can we merit the outward blessings of this life, *cat.* 193. But we are to trust in the merits of Christ, *cat.* 174. Who appearing in the merit of his obedience and sacrifice, maketh intercession for his people, *cat.* 55.

Messiah. The elect under the Old Testament believed in the promised Messiah, by whom they had full remission of sins, and eternal salvation, *con.* vii. 5. viii. 6. *cat.* 34.

Ministry, the, given by Christ to the visible church, *con.* xxv. 3. The maintenance thereof a duty, *cat.* 108. A minister of the gospel is one sufficiently gifted, and also duly approved and lawfully called and ordained to that office, *con.* xxvii. 4. xxviii. 2. *cat.* 158. By such only the word is to be read publickly and preached, and the sacraments dispensed, *con.* xxvii. 4. xxviii. 2. *cat.* 156, 158, 159, 169.

Moral Law. See *Law.*

Mortification. The regenerate have the corruption of nature mortified through Christ, *con.* vi. 5. And the several lusts of the body of sin, *con.* xiii. 1. Believers draw strength from the death and resurrection of Christ for the mortifying of sin, *cat.* 167.

N

Name, the, of Christ. That prayer be accepted, it is to be made in the name of Christ, *con.* xxi. 3. *cat.* 178. What it is to pray in the name of Christ, *cat.* 180. Why prayer is to be made in his name, *cat.* 181.

Name, the, of God is only that by which men ought to swear, and therein it is to be used with all holy fear and reverence, *con.* xxii. 2. How the name of God ought to be used, and how it is profaned, *cat.* 112, 113, 114, 190.

Nature. See *Corruption, Original Sin, Light of Nature.*

Natures, the two, of Christ. See *Christ, Incarnation, Personal Union.*

New Testament, the, in Greek is that to which the church is finally to appeal in controversies of religion, *con.* i. 8. The administration of the covenant of grace under the gospel is called the New Testament, *con.* vii. 6.

Neighbour. See *Charity, Love.*

Niggardliness sinful, *cat.* 142.

O

Oath, an, what it is, *con.* xxii. 1. It is a part of religious worship, *ib.* The name of God is that by which men ought only to swear, *con.* xxii. 2. *cat.* 108. Vain or rash swearing by his name is to be abhorred, *con.* xxii. 2. *cat.* 113. Yet, in matters of weight and moment, an oath is warrantable under the New Testament, *con.* xxii. 2. A lawful oath, imposed by lawful authority, ought to be taken, *ib.* It is a sin to refuse it, *con.* xxii. 3. A man must swear nothing but what he is fully persuaded is truth; neither may he bind himself by oath to any thing but what he believes to be just and good, and what he is able to perform, *ib.* An oath is to be taken in the plain and common sense of the words; and, in things not sinful, it binds to performance, though to a man's own hurt, or made to hereticks, *con.* xxii. 4. *cat.* 113. But it cannot oblige to sin, *ib.*

Obedience is due to God in whatsoever he is pleased to command, *con.* ii. 2. *cat.* 104. Christ hath performed perfect obedience to the law for us in our nature, *con.* viii. 4. *cat.* 38, 39, 48, 97. And by it purchased an everlasting inheritance in the kingdom of heaven for the elect, *con.* viii. 5. *cat.* 38. His obedience is imputed to believers, *con.* xi. 1. *cat.* 70. He hath not abolished, but much strengthened the obligation to the obedience of the moral law, *con.* xix. 5. Good works done in obedience to God's commands are the fruits and evidences of a true faith, *con.* xvi. 2. *cat.* 32. How the sincere though imperfect obedience of believers is accepted and rewarded, *con.* xvi. 6. Obedience is due to the lawful commands of a magistrate, *con.* xxiii. 4. *cat.* 127, 128.

Offices of Christ, of Mediator. See *Mediator.* His prophetical office, *cat.* 43; priestly, *cat.* 44; and kingly, *cat.* 45.

Old Testament, the, in Hebrew is that to which the church is finally to appeal in controversies of religion, *con.* i. 8. The administration of the covenant of grace under the law is called the Old Testament, *con.* vii. 5.

Ordinances, the, of God given by Christ to the visible church, *con.* xxv. 3. The ordinances under the law, *con.* vii. 5. *cat.* 34. Those under the gospel, *con.* vii. 6. *cat.* 35. Which are fewer, and administered with more simplicity, and less outward glory; yet in them grace and salvation are held forth in more fulness, evidence, and efficacy, *ib.* All God's ordinances, especially the word, sacraments, and prayer, are the outward and ordinary means of salvation, *cat.* 154. How they are made effectual, *con.* xxv. 3. *cat.* 155, 161, 182. The neglect, contempt, or opposing them sinful, *cat.* 109.

Original corruption. See *Corruption.*

Original sin. See *Sin.*

P

Papists. Protestants should not marry with Papists, *con.* xxiv. 3.

Pardon. See *Sin.*

Passions to be restrained, *cat.* 135, 136.

Passover, one of the types and ordinances by which the covenant of grace was administered under the law, *con.* vii. 5. *cat.* 34.

Patience. Patient bearing of the hand of God a duty, *cat.* 135. Patient bearing and forgiving of injuries a duty, *ib.*

Peace of Conscience. See *Conscience.*

Pedo-baptism. See *Infants.*

Perseverance of saints. They whom God hath accepted in Christ can never totally or finally fall away from the estate of grace, *con.* xvii. 1. *cat.* 77, 79. Upon what their perseverance depends, *con.* xvii. 2. *cat.* 79. How far they may fall, *con.* vi. 5. xi. 5. xiii. 2. xvii. 3. xviii. 4. *cat.* 78. They are always kept from utter despair, *con.* xviii. 4. *cat.* 81. How they are recovered. *con.* xi. 5. xiii. 3.

Persons in the Godhead, three, distinguished by personal properties, *con.* ii. 3. *cat.* 9, 10. The equality of the Persons proved, *cat.* 11. The personal union of the two natures in Christ, *con.* viii. 2. *cat.* 36, 37. By reason of this union, the proper works of each nature are accepted of God, and relied on by believers as the work of the whole Person. *con.* viii. 7. *cat.* 40.

Physick to be used moderately, *cat.* 135.
Pictures, lascivious, discharged, *cat.* 139.
Polygamy unlawful, *con.* xxiv. 1. *cat.* 139.
Pope, the, has no power or jurisdiction over civil magistrates, or their people, *con.* xxiii. 4. He is in no sense head of the church, but is Antichrist, *con.* xxv. 6.
Powers ecclesiastical or civil, not to be opposed upon pretence of Christian liberty, *con.* xx. 4. Power of the keys. See *Keys.*
Praises to be joined with prayer, *cat.* 196.
Praise, the, of any good we either are, have, or can do, not to be ascribed to fortune, ourselves, or any other creature, *cat.* 105.
Prayer, what, *cat.* 178. The duty of all men, *con.* xxi. 3. To be made to God only, and why, *con.* xxi. 2. *cat.* 179. That it may be accepted, it is to be made in the name of Christ, by the help of the Spirit, *con.* xxi. 3. *cat.* 178. What it is to pray in the name of Christ, *cat.* 180. Why prayer is to be made in his name, *cat.* 181. How the Spirit helps to pray. *cat.* 182. How prayer is to be made, *con.* xxi. 3. *cat.* 185. For what and for whom we are to pray, *con.* xxi. 4. *cat.* 183, 184. Prayer not to be made for the dead, nor for those of whom it may be known that they have sinned the sin unto death, *ib.* Prayer, now under the gospel, is not made more acceptable by any place in which it is performed, nor towards which it is directed, *con.* xxi. 6. The rule of prayer, *cat.* 186.
Lord's prayer, the, how to be used, *cat.* 187. *It is explained in the Catechism from Question* 188, *to the end.*
Preaching of the word a part of the ordinary worship of God, *con.* xxi. 5. One of the ordinances in which the covenant of grace is administered under the New Testament, *con.* vii. 6. *cat.* 35. None are to preach the word but ministers of the gospel, *cat.* 158. How they are to preach, *cat.* 159. How the preaching of the word is made effectual to salvation, *cat.* 155.
Predestination, *con.* iii. 3, 4. *cat.* 13. The doctrine of predestination, how to be handled and used, *con.* iii. 8.
Preparation required to the hearing of the word, *cat.* 160. What preparation requisite to the sabbath, *cat.* 117. What to the Lord's supper, *cat.* 171.
Prescience. See *Foreknowledge.*
Priestly office of Christ, *cat.* 44.
Private worship in families daily a duty, *con.* xxi. 6. *cat.* 156.
Privileges of the invisible church, and of the visible. See *Church.*
Prodigality a sin, *cat.* 142.
Profession, the, of the gospel is adorned by good works, *con.* xvi. 2. And ought to be attended with a conversation in holiness and righteousness, *cat.* 112, 167.
Property in goods, &c. not infringed by the communion of saints, *con.* xxvi. 3.
Prophecies. The covenant of grace administered by prophecies under the law, *con.* vii. 5. *cat.* 34.
Prophetical office, the, of Christ, how executed, *cat.* 43.
Propitiation. Christ's one only sacrifice the alone propitiation for all the sins of the elect, *con.* xxix. 2.

Protestants should not marry with Papists, *con.* xxiv. 3.
Providence, *con.* v. 1. *cat.* 18. Events are ordered according to the nature of second causes, *con.* iii. 1. v. 2. God in his ordinary providence maketh use of means, yet is free to work without, above, and against them at his pleasure, *con.* v. 3. How providence is exercised about sin, *con.* v. 4. See *Sin.* The actual influence of the Holy Spirit is required to do good works, *con.* xvi. 3. God's providence towards angels, *cat.* 19. Toward man when created, *cat.* 20. Is in a special manner over his church, *con.* v. 7. *cat.* 43, 45, 63.
Publick worship not to be neglected, *con.* xxi. 6.
Punishment. See *Sin.*
Purgatory, the scripture acknowledgeth no such place, *con.* xxxii. 1.

Q

QUARRELLING at God's decrees and providences sinful, *cat.* 113.
Quarrelling and provoking words sinful, *cat.* 136.
Questions that are curious or unprofitable are to be avoided, *cat.* 113.

R

READING the scriptures a part of religious worship, *con.* xxi. 5. How made effectual to salvation, *cat.* 155. The duty of all to read them apart by themselves, and with their families, *con.* i. 8. *cat.* 156. How to be read, *con.* xxi. 5. *cat.* 157.
Rebellion a sin, *cat.* 128.
Reconciliation with God purchased by Christ's sacrifice of himself, *con.* viii. 5. *cat.* 44.
Recreations to be moderately used, *cat.* 135, 136. But not on the Lord's day, *con.* xxi. 8. *cat.* 119.
Redemption, how purchased by Christ, *con.* viii. 5. *cat.* 38, 39, 40. For all the elect, and them only, *con.* iii. 6. To whom it is certainly applied, *con.* viii. 8. *cat.* 59. Although it was not actually wrought by Christ till after his incarnation; yet the virtue, efficacy, and benefits of it were communicated to the elect in all ages successively from the beginning of the world, *con.* viii. 6. How it is applied to them, *con.* viii. *cat.* 58, 59.
Regeneration. See *Effectual Calling.*
Regenerate, the, are all freely justified, *con.* xi. 1. See *Justification.* And sanctified, *con.* xiii. 1. See *Sanctification.* The corruption of nature remains in them, and all the motions of it are sin, *con.* vi. 5. But it is pardoned and mortified through Christ, *ib.* The use of the moral law to them, *con.* xix. 6. *cat.* 97.
Repentance, what, *con.* xv. 2. *cat.* 75. Although it be no satisfaction for sin, nor cause of pardon, yet no pardon without it, *con.* xv. 3. *cat.* 153. Nor condemnation where it is, *con.* xv. 4, 6. It is every man's duty to endeavour to repent particularly of his particular sins, *con.* xv. 5. The doctrine of repentance to be preached by every minister, as well as that of faith in Christ, *con.* xv. 1. To be declared to those that are offended, *con.* xv. 6.
Resurrection of Christ, *con.* viii. 4. *cat.* 52. The effect of his own power, *cat.* 52. It is

a proof of his being the Son of God, and of his satisfaction to divine justice, &c. *ib.* It is an assurance to believers of their resurrection, *ib.* They have fellowship with him in his resurrection, *con.* xxvi. 1. He rose again for their justification, *con.* xi. 4. *cat.* 52. And through the virtue of his death and resurrection they are sanctified, *con.* xiii. 1. *cat.* 75. They draw strength there for the mortifying of sin, and quickening of grace, *cat.* 52, 167.

Resurrection, the, of the dead, of the just and unjust, *con.* xxxii. 2, 3. *cat.* 87.

Revelation. The divers ways of God's revealing his will, *con.* i. 1.

Righteousness. Man was created righteous after the image of God, *con.* iv. 2. *cat.* 17. But by sin he fell from that original righteousness, *con* vi. 2. *cat.* 25. And since the fall no man can attain to righteousness by the moral law, *cat.* 94. Nor by having righteousness infused into them, *con.* xi. 1. *cat.* 70. But those whom God effectually calleth, he accepteth and accounteth as righteous, by imputing the obedience and satisfaction of Christ to them, they receiving and resting on him and his righteousness by faith, *ib.* See *Faith, Imputation, Justification.* Why the righteous are not delivered from death, *cat.* 85. Their state immediately after death, *con.* xxxii. 1. *cat.* 86. At the resurrection and day of judgment, *con.* xxxii. 3. xxxiii. 2. *cat.* 87, 90.

S

SABBATH. By the law of nature, a due proportion of time ought to be set apart for the worship of God, *con.* xxi. 7. God hath in his word, by a positive and perpetual commandment, binding all men in all ages, appointed one day in seven for a sabbath, to be kept holy to himself, *con.* xxi. 7. *cat.* 20, 116. The day observed under the Old and New Testament dispensations, *con.* xxi. 7. *cat.* 116. How the Sabbath is to be sanctified, *con.* xxi. 8. *cat.* 117. How it is profaned, *cat.* 119. Why we are commanded to remember it, *cat.* 121. It is a memorial of our creation and redemption, which contains a short abridgment of religion, *ib.* What are the reasons annexed to the fourth commandment, the more to enforce it, *cat.* 120. Why the charge of keeping the sabbath is directed to governors of families, and other superiors, *cat.* 118.

Sacrament, a. The institution, nature, and ends of it, *con.* xxvii. 1. *cat.* 162. Its parts, *con.* xxvii. 2. *cat.* 163. Only two sacraments instituted by Christ, *con.* xxvii. 4. *cat.* 164. Which are only to be dispensed by ministers of the word lawfully ordained, *con.* xxvii. 4. How made effectual to salvation, *con.* xxvii. 3. *cat.* 161. The sacraments of the Old Testament were the same for substance with those of the New, *con.* xxvii. 5. Wherein the sacraments of baptism and of the Lord's Supper agree, *cat.* 176. Wherein they differ, *cat.* 177.

Sacrifice. The covenant of grace was administered under the law by sacrifices, *con.* vii. 5. viii. 6. *cat.* 34. Which signified Christ to come, *ib.* Who hath fully satisfied the justice of his Father, in his once offering himself a sacrifice without spot to God, *con.* viii. 5. *cat.* 44. There is no real sacrifice made for sin in the Lord's supper, *con.* xxix. 2. That sacrament being instituted for the perpetual remembrance of Christ's one only sacrifice in his death, *con.* xxix. 1. *cat.* 168. To which the mass is most abominably injurious, *con.* xxix. 2.

Saints. See *Believers, Communion.* Not to be worshipped, *con.* xxi. 2. *cat.* 105.

Salvation, not to be attained by men who do not profess the Christian religion, be they never so diligent to live up to the light of nature, or the law of that religion which they profess, *con.* x. 4. *cat.* 60. There being no salvation but in Christ alone, *ib.* Who hath purchased it by his perfect obedience and sacrifice of himself, *con.* viii. 5. *cat.* 83. For all the elect, and them only, *con.* iii. 6. To whom the outward means are made effectual for their salvation by the Spirit, *con.* vii. 5, 6. xxv. 3. *cat.* 154, 155, 161, 182. Who worketh in their hearts faith in Jesus Christ, *con.* xiv, 1. *cat.* 72. Which is necessarily required of them for their justification and salvation, *con.* vii. 3. xi. 1. *cat.* 32, 71. The Spirit also worketh repentance, and infuseth all other saving graces, *con.* xiii. 1. *cat.* 32, 75, 76, 77. Which accompany faith, *con.* xi. 2. *cat.* 73. Likewise enables them unto all obedience and the practice of holiness, which is the way that God hath appointed them to salvation, *con.* xiii. 1. *cat.* 32. Elect infants dying in infancy are regenerated and saved by Christ through the Spirit, &c. *con.* x. 3.

Sanctification, what, *con.* xiii. 1. *cat.* 75. Inseparably joined with justification, *cat.* 77. Wherein they differ, *ib.* It is throughout in the whole man, *con.* xiii. 2. *cat.* 75. But in this life it is not perfect in any, *con.* xiii. 2. *cat.* 77. Whence this imperfection proceeds, *con.* xiii. 2. *cat.* 78. Through the continued supply of strength from the sanctifying Spirit of Christ, the saints grow in grace, perfecting holiness in the fear of God, *con.* xiii. 3. At death they are made perfect in holiness, *con.* xxxii. 1. *cat.* 86. And at the day of judgment they shall be fully and for ever freed from all sin, *cat.* 90.

Satisfaction. Repentance is no satisfaction for sin, *con.* xv. 3. nor good works, and why, *con.* xvi. 5. Neither we nor any other creature can make the least satisfaction for sin, *cat.* 194. Christ alone hath made a proper, real, and full satisfaction to the justice of his Father by his obedience and sufferings, *con.* viii. 5. xi. 5. *cat.* 38, 71. Which satisfaction is imputed to believers, *con.* xi. 1. *cat.* 70.

Scandalous, not to be admitted to the Lord's table, *con.* xxix. 8. *cat.* 173.

Scoffing and scorning sinful, *cat.* 113, 145.

Scripture, the, why necessary, *con.* i. 1. What books to be owned for scripture, *con.* i. 2, 3. *cat.* 3. How proved to be the word of God, *con.* i. 5. *cat.* 4. Upon what authority the scripture ought to be believed and obeyed, *con.* i. 4. The sufficiency and perfection of the scripture, *con.* i. 6. *cat.* 2, 5. Its perspicuity, *con.* i. 7. The infallible rule of interpreting scripture is the scripture itself, *con.* i. 9. The scripture is the only rule of faith and practice, *con.* i. 2.

vii. 3, 5. and of worship, *con*. xxi. 1. *cat.* 108, 109. The Spirit speaking in the scriptures is the supreme judge of all controversies on religion, *con.* i. 10. The original text of the scriptures is that to which the church is finally to appeal, *con.* i. 8. But they are to be translated into vulgar languages, *con.* i. 8. *cat.* 156. Because all sorts of people have an interest in them, and are commanded to read them, *ib.* How they are to be read, *cat.* 157. The illumination of the Spirit necessary for the saving understanding of the scriptures, *con.* i. 6. *cat.* 157. How the reading of the word is made effectual to salvation, *cat.* 155. Misinterpreting, misapplying, or any way perverting the word, or any part of it, sinful, *cat.* 113.

Sin, what, *cat.* 24. Original sin, what, *cat.* 25. The sin of our first parents, *con.* vi. 1. *cat.* 21. By it they fell from their original righteousness, and communion with God, and had their natures wholly corrupted, *con.* vi. 2. *cat.* 25, 27. The guilt of this sin is imputed, and the corruption of nature conveyed to all their posterity, *con.* vi. 3. *cat.* 22, 26. Who are thereby bound over to the wrath of God, and curse of the law, *con.* vi. 6. *cat.* 27, 194. From the original corruption of nature, all actual sins proceed, *con.* vi. 4. *cat.* 25. Which are not all equally heinous, *cat.* 150. The aggravations of sin, *cat.* 151. The demerit of every sin, *con.* vi. 6. *cat.* 152. Punishments of sin in this world, *con.* v. 5, 6. xvii. 3. xviii. 4. *cat.* 28, 83. In the world to come, *con.* xxxii. 1. xxxiii. 2. *cat.* 29, 86, 89. Sin is pardoned for Christ's sake alone, *con.* xi. 1. xv. 3. *cat.* 70. See *Justification, Sanctification.* Every man bound to pray for pardon of sin, *con.* xv. 6. God continues to pardon the sins of those that are justified, *con.* xi. 5. How pardon of sin is to be prayed for, *cat.* 194. The sin unto death, *con.* xxi. 4. *cat.* 183. Believers have the dominion of the whole body of sin destroyed, and the lusts thereof more and more weakened and mortified, *con.* vi. 5. xiii. 1. *cat.* 75. See *Mortification, Sanctification.* How providence is exercised about sin, *con.* v. 4. Why God permitted the sin of our first parents, *con.* vi. 1. Why he leaves his children to fall into sin, *con.* v. 5. Why and how sinners are hardened, *con.* v. 6. *cat.* 68.

Sins against the first commandment, *cat.* 105. Against the second, *cat.* 109. Against the third, *cat.* 113. Against the fourth, *cat.* 119. Sins of inferiors, *cat.* 128. Sins of superiors, *cat.* 130. Sins of equals, *cat.* 132. Sins against the sixth commandment, *cat.* 136. Against the seventh, *cat.* 139. Against the eighth, *cat.* 142. Against the ninth, *cat.* 145. Against the tenth, *cat.* 148.

Sincerity. Believers love Christ in sincerity, *con.* xviii. 1. They are never utterly destitute of sincerity of heart, *con.* xviii. 4. Ministers ought to preach sincerely, *cat.* 159. We are to pray with sincerity, *cat.* 185. God is pleased to accept and reward the good works of believers which are sincere, *con.* xvi. 6.

Singing of psalms a part of religious worship, *con.* xxi. 5.

Slandering sinful, *cat.* 145.
Songs that are lascivious forbidden, *cat.* 139.
Soul, the, of man is immortal, *con.* iv. 2. *cat.* 17. The state of souls when separate from their bodies, *con.* xxxii. 1. *cat.* 86.
Sovereignty. God hath most sovereign dominion over his creatures, *con.* ii. 2. The light of nature sheweth that God hath lordship and sovereignty over all, *con.* xxi. 1. Eternal sovereignty to be ascribed to God alone, *cat.* 196. To pray with due apprehensions of his sovereign power, *cat.* 185, 189.
Spirit. See *Holy Ghost.*
Stage-plays forbidden, *cat.* 139.
Stews, not to be tolerated, *cat.* 139.
Supererogation impossible, *con.* xvi. 4.
Superiors, why stiled *fathers* and *mothers*, *cat.* 125. How to be honoured, *con.* xxiii. 4. *cat.* 127. Their duty, *con.* xxiii. 1, 2, 3 *cat.* 129. Their sins, *cat.* 130. See *Magistracy.*
Superstition. God may not be worshipped according to the imaginations and devices of men, *con.* xxi. 1. Religious worship not instituted by God himself, is not to be used or approved, *cat.* 109. All superstitious devices, &c. sinful, *cat.* 109, 113.
Supper. See *Lord's Supper.*
Surety. Christ the surety for believers, *cat.* 71. Thoroughly furnished to execute that office, *con.* viii. 3. And God accepteth satisfaction from him, *cat.* 71.
Suretiship, that is not necessary, is to be avoided, *cat.* 141.
Suspension from the Lord's table, *con.* xxx. 4.
Swearing. See *Oaths.* Vain or rash swearing by the name of God, or to swear at all by any other thing, is to be abhorred. *con.* xxii. 2.
Synods. See *Councils.*

T

TALE-BEARING, *cat.* 145.
Temptation. Why God leaves his children to manifold temptations, *con.* v. 5. The wicked given up to the temptations of the world, *con.* v. 6. Temptations to sin are to be avoided and resisted, *cat.* 99. § 6, 135, 138. How temptation is to be prayed against, *cat.* 195.
Testament. The books of the Old and New Testament are the word of God, *con.* i. 2. *cat.* 3. And the only rule of faith and obedience, *ib.* See *Scripture.*
Testament. Why the covenant of grace is called a Testament, *con.* vii. 4. As it was administered under the law, it is called the Old Testament, *con.* vii. 5. And as administered under the gospel, it is called the New Testament, *con.* vii. 6.
Thanksgiving to be joined with prayer, *con.* xxi. 3. *cat.* 108, 178. It is to be made in the name Christ, *con.* xxi. 3. Solemn thanksgiving a part of religious worship, *con.* xxi. 5.
Toleration. A false religion not to be tolerated, *cat.* 109.
Tradition, no pretence for using superstitious devices in the worship of God, *cat.* 109. No traditions of men to be added to the Scripture, *con.* i. 6.
Transubstantiation is repugnant not only to scripture, but to common sense and reason, *con.* xxix. 6. And is the cause of

manifold superstitions, yea, of gross idolatries, *ib.*
The tree of life was a pledge of the covenant of works, *cat.* 20.
The Trinity. See *God, Persons.*
Truth between man and man, how preserved and promoted, *cat.* 144. What things are contrary to it, *cat.* 145.

U, V

UNION of the elect with Christ, *con.* xxv. 1. xxvi. 1. *cat.* 66. It is inseparable, *cat.* 79. Believers are united to one another in love, *con.* xxvi. 1.
Union of the two natures in Christ. See *Personal Union.*
Unregenerate, the use of the moral law to them, *cat.* 96. Their best works cannot please God, and why, *con.* xvi. 7. But their neglect to do what God commands is more sinful, *ib.*
Vocation. See *Calling.*
Vow, a part of religious worship, *con.* xxi. 5. What it is, and how to be made, *con.* xxii. 5, 6. To be made to God alone, *con.* xxv. 6. *cat.* 108. What vows are unlawful, *con.* xxii. 7. Violating of lawful vows, and fulfilling of unlawful, is sinful, *cat.* 113.
Usury unlawful, *cat.* 142.

W

WAR may be waged by Christians under the New Testament, *con.* xxiii. 2.
Wicked, the. Their condition in this life, *cat.* 83; immediately after death, *con.* xxxii. 1. *cat.* 86; in and after judgment, *con.* xxxiii. 2. *cat.* 89.
Will. The counsel of God's will is most wise and holy, *con.* iii. 1. *cat.* 12. It is unsearchable, *con.* iii. 7. *cat.* 13. It is free and immutable, *con.* v. 1. *cat.* 14; and most righteous, *con.* ii. 1. How the will of God is to be done and submitted to, *cat.* 192. The will of God, revealed in the scriptures, is the only rule of faith, worship, and practice. See *Scripture.* Christ revealeth to his church, by his Spirit and word, the whole will of God in all things concerning their edification and salvation, *cat.* 43.
Free-Will. The will of man is neither forced, nor by any absolute necessity of nature determined, to do good or evil, *con.* iii. 1. ix. 1. Man in his state of innocency had freedom and power to will and do good, *con.* iv. 2. ix. 2. *cat.* 17. By his fall he lost all ability of will to any spiritual good accompanying salvation, *con.* vi. 2, 4. ix. 3. *cat.* 25, 192. The will is renewed in conversion, *con.* ix. 4. x. 1. *cat.* 67. It is made perfectly and immutably free to do good alone in the state of glory only, *con.* ix. 5.
Word. See *Scripture, Reading, Preaching, Hearing.*
Worldly-mindedness sinful, *cat.* 105, 142.
Works. What are good works, and what not, *con.* xvi. 1. The fruits and evidences of a true and lively faith, *con.* xvi. 2. Their uses and ends, *ib.* Ability to do good works is wholly from the Spirit of Christ, *con.* xvi. 3. The actual influence of the Spirit is required for their performance, *ib.* This no plea for negligence, *ib.* Supererogation impossible, *con.* xvi. 4. We cannot by our best works merit pardon of sin or eternal life, and why, *con.* xvi. 5. Yet the good works of believers are accepted by God in Christ, and rewarded, *con.* xvi. 6. The works of unregenerate men cannot please God, and why, *con.* xvi. 7. But to neglect to do what God commands is more sinful, *ib.* All persons shall, in the day of judgment, receive according to what they have done in the body, whether good or evil, *con.* xxxiii. 1.
Worship. To God is due from his creatures, *con.* ii. 2. The light of nature sheweth that God is to be worshipped, *con.* xxi. 1. But the acceptable way of worshipping God is instituted by himself in the scriptures, *ib.* He may not be worshipped according to the imaginations and devices of men, *con.* xxi. 1. *cat.* 109. False worship is to be opposed, *cat.* 108. As also any worship not instituted by God himself, *cat.* 109. But there are some circumstances concerning the worship of God which are to be ordered by the light of nature and Christian prudence, according to the general rules of the word, *con.* i. 6. Religious worship is to be given to God the Father, Son, and Holy Ghost, and to him alone; and that only in the mediation of Christ, *con.* xxi. 2. *cat.* 179, 181. The parts of religious worship, *con.* xxi. 3, 5. Religious worship not tied to any place, but God is to be worshipped every where in spirit and truth, as in private families daily, and in secret, each one by himself; so more solemnly in the publick assemblies, which are not to be neglected, *con.* xxi. 6.
Wrath. See *Curse.*

Z

ZEAL for God, a duty, *cat.* 104.
Zeal, corrupt, blind, and indiscreet, sinful, *cat.* 105.

THE END.

www.ingramcontent.com/pod-product-compliance
Lightning Source LLC
Chambersburg PA
CBHW021152230426
43667CB00006B/356